PATTERN RECOGNITION IN PRACTICE II

To the memory of K.S. Fu (1930-1985)

PATTERN RECOGNITION IN PRACTICE II

Proceedings of an International Workshop
held in Amsterdam, June 19-21, 1985

edited by

Edzard S. GELSEMA
Department of Medical Informatics
Free University, Amsterdam

and

Laveen N. KANAL
Department of Computer Science
University of Maryland, College Park, Md.

1986

NORTH-HOLLAND
AMSTERDAM • NEW YORK • OXFORD

ISBN: 0 444 87877 7

Publishers:

ELSEVIER SCIENCE PUBLISHERS B.V.
P.O. Box 1991
1000 BZ Amsterdam
The Netherlands

Sole distributors for the U.S.A. and Canada:

ELSEVIER SCIENCE PUBLISHING COMPANY, INC.
52 Vanderbilt Avenue
New York, N.Y. 10017
U.S.A.

Library of Congress Cataloging-in-Publication Data
Main entry under title:

Pattern recognition in practice II.

Includes bibliographies and indexes.
1. Pattern perception--Congresses. 2. Image processing--Congresses. 3. Depth perception--Congresses. I. Gelsema, Edzard S., 1937- II. Kanal, Laveen N.
Q327.P378 1986 006.4 85-25247
ISBN 0-444-87877-7 (U.S.)

PRINTED IN THE NETHERLANDS

PREFACE

This book contains most of the papers presented at the conference "Pattern Recognition in Practice II" held in Amsterdam on June 19-21, 1985. This conference was organized to bring together scientists doing research in pattern recognition methodology and those interested in specific practical applications. Many of the participants are deeply involved in both technical development and one or more specific applications.

This book is organized in two parts. Part I deals with image processing. It is divided in four sections, containing 32 papers. Part II, called pattern recognition has three sections, two of which contain 11 papers covering a number of topics in feature extraction, clustering, mapping and population classification. The third section presents two papers on topics of interest both in pattern recognition and in artificial intelligence.

Section I contains papers dealing with various methodological aspects of image processing.
The first four papers consider some aspects of filtering problems.
The paper by Young et al. (p. 5) describes techniques to determine, from the image statistics, the parameters, e.g. neighbourhood size, of Minkowski filters applied to binary images. The robustness of the techniques is evaluated.
Biemond in his paper (p. 17) describes the similar problem of how to derive a Kalman filter for image restoration by identifying the degradation the image has suffered. The results of this identification procedure are illustrated by subsequently applying the derived Kalman filter to images with different amounts of noise.
The contribution by Bosman et al. (p. 31) describes two algorithms for robust enhancement of images: The lateral inhibition algorithm (LIA), inspired by a natural vision model and the constant volume response summation (CVRS) algorithm. The properties of both algorithms are evaluated and compared with each other.
The paper by Good (p. 47) illustrates computer experiments, simulating the growth of snow crystals in the free atmosphere and in the snow pack, by applying local transformations with differing neighbourhoods and 0-1 transition rules. A striking similarity of the configurations obtained with hexagonal plates, dendritic snow crystals and structural elements of depth hoar is shown.
Förstner et al. (p. 57) give an overview of methods of photogrammetry. The integration of image matching techniques into photogrammetric standard methods is shown to be advantageous for high-precision surface measurements in e.g. industrial objects and cartography.
Another aspect of precision of measurements in images is described in the paper by Dorst et al. (p. 73). These authors compare six methods of estimating the length of digitized straight line segments from their chain code. Also, aspects of computational complexity are considered and recommendations for or against the use of the various methods are given.
Haralick (p. 81) describes the implementation of edge and ridge detectors, based upon his cubic facet model.
A method of edge detection in noisy images based on dynamic programming is described and evaluated in the paper by Gerbrands et al. (p. 91). Results are

illustrated by applying the algorithm to cardiac scintigraphic images. Quantitative evaluation is performed using two synthetic images in the presence of varying amounts of noise. The performance is shown to compare favourably with that of various parallel edge detection schemes.
Saint-Jean et al. (p. 101) explain their pretopological texture model in some detail and show how this, when linked to a hierarchical classification method may be of use in the analysis of cytological data.
The use of contextual information in image processing by computing (in linear time) the joint likelihood of pixel labels and neighbouring image values, assuming a Markov mesh model is considered in the paper by Devijver (p. 113). Examples of image smoothing and segmentation are given to illustrate the technique and to validate the underlying assumptions.
The paper by Hertzberger et al. (p. 125) considers the properties of a virtual image understanding multiprocessor machine based on fifth-generation computer concepts.
Toussaint in his paper (p. 135) reviews various problems in computational geometry and presents solutions that are either computationally less complex or otherwise simpler than solutions published so far. The concept of "rotating calipers" is shown to lead to these surprising simplifications of the algorithms.

Section II contains 6 papers dealing with knowledge based or model driven image understanding systems.
Nagy et al. (p. 149) describe a system in which documents are represented as a tree structure of nested rectangular blocks. The problem of labeling the blocks using a knowledge base is considered in view of its complexity. The proposed solution has potential applications in document archival, transmission and retrieval.
Interpretation of industrial scenes using knowledge represented in either a procedural or in a declarative form is the subject of the paper by Stein et al. (p. 161). Advantages and disadvantages of both approaches are discussed. It is concluded that a combination of both forms of representation offers a promising solution in this class of image interpretation problems.
Hofman et al. (p. 173) describe a system for the interpretation of sequences of heart scintigrams, based on expert knowledge represented as an associative network. All modules of their system are described; the module containing the knowledge representation in considerable detail.
The dynamic modeling procedure (DMP) proposed by Tan et al. (p. 185) integrates the properties of an unknown shape into a set of basic shapes, thus creating a set of "suitable models". Global and local properties are used at different levels of the procedure. Results are illustrated using numeric characters from different typewriters.
The paper by Persoon (p. 199) describes hierarchical correlation techniques which with VLSI implementation are no longer prohibitive. The hardware realizations are described and illustrated on examples of industrial object location.
Another model based system is described by Dhome et al. (p. 211). Methods based on a generalization of the Hough-transform are used to accumulate hypotheses on the values of the parameters representing local patterns composing the objects in a scene. An application to scenes of overlapping objects is given.

Section III contains 6 papers treating 3-D reconstruction methods.
The first of these, by Shapiro et al. (p. 221) describes techniques to estimate the shape of three-dimensional surfaces from topographic labeling of images. Primitives such as peaks, pits, valleys, etc. appear to obey a set of rules that may be used to infer the shape of the surfaces of three-dimensional objects. Analytical and experimental results are presented, using various conic surfaces as test objects.
Determination of object pose under two imaging environments is the subject of the paper by Stockman (p. 233). Matching of evidence obtained from the image with model features leads to a candidate pose, which may then be verified by top-down checking or bottom-up clustering of all candidates. It is concluded that global image analysis is neither necessary nor desirable in the environments assumed, and

furthermore that it is relatively easy to use multiple views for pose determination.
The paper by Bolle et al. (p. 243) discusses techniques for the combination of partial information for object position estimation. By modeling an object by a small number of patches of planes, spheres and cylinders, the correspondence between sensed and model primitives constitutes the pieces of information which are then integrated using a probabilistic framework. This framework is applicable not only to position estimation, but may also be applied to entirely different problems that can be decomposed into subproblems.
The paper by Kaminuma et al. (p. 255) describes a system for three-dimensional reconstruction applied to sequences of microscopic images in biomedicine. Embryogenesis of nematodes is used as an example to illustrate the capabilities of the system.
The analysis of serial sections in histology, described in the paper by Abmayr et al. (p. 267) is another example where 3-D reconstruction is applied. Reconstruction of mouse brains from serial sections and the subsequent display of the result, using various display methods is reported to open new possibilities in histopathological work.
Three-dimensional reconstruction from projections is the subject of the paper by Harauz et al. (p. 279). The complicating circumstance is that the angular relationship between the various projections is unknown in the application of macromolecular structure determination. Correspondence analysis can be used to determine a set of eigenimages, which may then be clustered into classes, reflecting the angular relationships.

Section IV contains 8 application oriented papers.
The first paper in this sequence, by Van Heel (p. 291), describes a procedure to obtain the characteristic views from a set of images of macromolecules. Techniques of alignment, averaging and correspondence analysis are outlined and are shown to constitute a powerful sorting technique. The purpose of this eigenimage decomposition is the 3-D reconstruction of the macromolecule. This is described in the paper by Harauz et al. in Section III (page 279).
The paper by Mann et al. (p. 301) is concerned with the analysis of images generated by two-dimensional gel electrophoresis in order to localize, identify and quantify proteins. Also, methods to compare protein spots in different gel images are described. Possible future use of an expert system to guide the analysis is indicated.
Jordan et al. (p. 313) describe a study of intracellular movement of macrophages. Their procedure combines manual entry of aligned image sequences with computerized 3-D reconstruction and graphical display to appreciate the lysosome movement. In addition, quantitative analysis based on nearest neighbour techniques is discussed. Finally, the use of a model of lysosome movement is reported to have helped in understanding the mechanism of lysosome movement.
The paper by Harms et al. (p. 323) focuses on the use of colour in the segmentation of tissue sections. The authors have extended their methods proven in blood smear analysis to be applicable in histological preparations. Their method is reported to be robust against the usual variations in color and general quality found in routine laboratory preparations.
Artery detection in cine-angiograms is the subject of the contribution by Van Ommeren et al. (p. 331). They describe a minimum cost path algorithm to detect the coronary tree. The method is shown to be also applicable to retinal angiograms in order to study the quality of the retinal vessels. In a limited study the arteries could be traced without any human intervention.
An overview of industrial pattern recognition is given in the paper by Suetens et al. (p. 345). All components of a visual inspection system are discussed. Also, hardware realizations of specific functions such as, amongst others, run length encoding, edge detection and texture analysis, are outlined.
Groen et al. (p. 363) report on a method for the analysis of schematic diagrams. Global topology is first established, followed by probabilistic graph matching to classify the components. Cellular logic operations are reported to be a fast tool for the global analysis of electronical circuit diagrams and the classification is

stated to be robust against different designers and drawing types.
The paper by Parikh (p. 373) discusses the integration of low level information and geological expertise in order to detect geological fracture patterns. The integration process is guided by a knowledge base and applied to Landsat imagery. The system is designed to be implemented on the Massively Parallel Processor (MPP).

Section V is a collection of papers treating various aspects of statistical pattern recognition.
The paper by Morgera (p. 389) examines feature selection algorithms for use in VLSI implementation. The partial eigensystem decomposition is shown to have an intrinsic parallel structure if the input covariance matrix is centrosymmetric. When implemented as linear arrays of processing elements, computational complexity is O(N), where N is the problem dimensionality, as compared to O(N**2) in the sequentional approach.
The paper by Wu et al. (p. 401) considers the problem of object detection, regardless of orientation. The method of circular harmonic function expansion is used to generate rotation-invariant data. From these, features to be used in classification are selected, using the Foley-Sammon transform. Two examples supplement the mathematical exposition.
Diday et al. in their paper (p. 411) present the pyramidal representation as an extension of hierarchical clustering. Pyramids are reported to contain more information, are closer to the initial data and lead to overlapping classes rather than to partitions. The definition of pyramids, their graphical representation and their construction are outlined.
Clustering large data sets is the title of the paper by Kaufman et al. (p. 425). A clustering program of complexity O(N), in computation time as well as storage requirements (N being the number of objects) is described. Sets of tens of thousands of objects are reported to have been processed by the program, implemented on a CDC Cyber 170/750.
The paper by Pedrycz (page 439) deals with fuzzy sets as a formalism to be used in pattern recognition. Algorithms for classification and clustering, operating on linguistic object descriptions are derived. Three numerical studies conclude the paper.
Talmon in his paper (p. 449) presents a partitioning algorithm based on entropy reduction. This non-parametric technique, when applied to a general multiclass problem, results in a binary decision tree. At each branch point in the tree, an optimal feature and a corresponding optimal threshold is generated by maximizing the reduction in uncertainty of the object class-membership. In some of the examples it is shown that the algorithm performs well in cases which are totally unsuited for a parametric (Fisher linear discriminant) approach.
Sjöström (p. 461) presents a projection method based on partial least squares. Contrary to principle component mapping, this technique takes object class membership of the objects in the training set into account in the design of the projection transformation. The algorithm is illustrated on an example derived from molecular biology.
An application of pattern recognition in nuclear reactor monitoring is described in the paper by Dubuisson et al. (p. 471). Initially, only one state of the reactor (the normal state) is known and pattern vectors can only be classified as belonging to this class, or they are rejected. The use of a clustering algorithm on the rejected vectors is shown to lead to the detection of other states. Also, states evolving from one class to another may be detected, using a potential function approach.
The paper by Bietti et al. (p. 481) describes some applications of the interactive system for pattern analysis ISPAHAN. Applications in archaeology as well as in physics are outlined.

Section VI contains two papers on the problem of population classification, which has recently attracted much interest in automated cytology.
Smeulders (p. 497) describes a non-parametric technique to classify a population on the basis of observations on its members. He introduces the "population

function" which must be estimated from a learning set. Testprocedures to be applied in sequential classification are discussed.
The paper by Burger et al. (p. 509) considers the use of binary decision tree classifiers in the classification of specimens in cytology. When linear discriminant analysis is used, results are often degraded by the matrix pooling operation. An interesting comparison is made between the performance of decision trees constructed by pooling of classes (POC) and of trees constructed by selection of classes (SOC). Experimental results demonstrate the adverse effect of class pooling.

Section VII contains two papers on topics of interest in pattern recognition and in artificial intelligence.
Berenstein et al. (p. 523) present a survey of consensus and evidence theory and discuss potential research directions for combining consensus and evidence theory techniques.
The contribution by Chandrasekaran (p. 547) takes the reader through a progression of approaches to classification. Classification has been a major concern in pattern recognition and it is an important task performed by expert systems. Combining the opinions of experts is a problem of broad interest and considerable difficulty.

The collection of papers in this book indicates the continuing development of pattern recognition and image processing methodology and the strong need for such methodology in many fields of application. It also reflects the fact that techniques originally developed in artificial intelligence may be successfully incorporated in pattern recognition systems.

Amsterdam , Edzard S. Gelsema
College Park, Laveen N. Kanal

ACKNOWLEDGEMENTS

We wish to thank the following Organizations, Foundations and Companies for their financial support of the conference:

The Royal Dutch Academy of Sciences

Organization for Applied Physical Research TNO

US National Science Foundation

The Free University, Amsterdam

Philips International B.V.

KONTRON Bildanalyse GmbH

Shell Nederland B.V.

Oce-van der Grinten N.V.

Elettronica San Giorgio-Elsag

We also want to thank a number of individuals for their active help and support in the preparatory phase of the conference.
First of all, Mr. C.E. Queiros carried out his duties as a member of the Organizing Committee, including the less than interesting ones, with energy and enthousiasm. The success of the conference from the organizational point of view is for a large part due to his efforts.
As always, Professor J.H. van Bemmel was a willing source of advice and encouragement.
The stimulating discussions with Professor E. Backer regarding the organization of the conference are gratefully acknowledged. Also, his help as a member of the Program Committee, as well as the help received from Professor I.T. Young have contributed to a high-standard scientific content of the conference.
We wish to thank Dr. Warren Thompson, director of the National Science Foundation US-Netherlands program, for his assistance.
During the conference, much work was done by the two scientific secretaries J.A. Kors and J. van der Lei, under the skillful direction of Dr. J.L. Talmon. All discussions were transcribed in readable form and corrected by the discussants within hours after the closing session. Also, the editing of the discussions into the form in which they appear in this book is largely due to the efforts of Dr. Talmon. His help is gratefully acknowledged.
The secretariat of the conference was in the expert hands of Mrs. Ciska Kessler. She took a heavy burden off the shoulders of the conference organisers.
Mr. H.C. den Harink supervised the operation of the technical equipment.

The work behind the screens, in the editorial office of the two secretaries: Mrs. Mirella van Velzen and Mrs. Yolande Willemse is also gratefully acknowledged.
Finally, the speakers, authors of the contributions and the discussants determine for a large part the the scientific contents of a conference. It is mainly due to their contributions that this conference was a success. Many participants reported that they appreciated this format of a small conference, with many opportunities to discuss the problems and the possibilities of pattern recognition in practice.

The editors.

CONTENTS

SECTION IV APPLICATIONS

PART II PATTERN RECOGNITION

SECTION V FEATURE EXTRACTION, CLASSIFICATION, MAPPING

PART I

IMAGE PROCESSING

SECTION I

IMAGE PROCESSING TECHNIQUES

PATTERN RECOGNITION IN PRACTICE II
E.S. Gelsema and L.N. Kanal (Editors)

Choosing Filter Parameters for Non-Linear Image Filtering

Ian T. Young, Guus L. Beckers, Leo Dorst, Annelies Boerman
Department of Applied Physics
Delft University of Technology
Delft, The Netherlands

The use of non-linear image filters requires knowledge of the image statistics so that filter parameters can be appropriately chosen. We have developed efficient techniques for measuring the distribution of relevant image statistics for the case of filters based upon mathematical morphology, the Minkowski filters. These statistics can then be used to choose appropriate values for filter parameters. Further, we have evaluated the performance of the measuring techniques in the presence of image noise to determine their robustness.

Introduction

The development, implementation, and use of non-linear image filtering techniques have been one of the major innovations in image processing in the past decade. Filters such as the median filter (Huang, 1981), "rolling ball" filters (Sternberg, 1980), edge-preserving smoothers (Kuwahara, 1976), and Minkowski filters (Serra, 1982) have all proved their effectiveness in a wide variety of applications. Just as in linear filtering, each of these filters has associated with it one or more filter parameters. In the case of the median filter this might be the size of the filter and the shape of its two-dimensional domain. A problem of critical importance is, therefore, how are these parameters to be chosen?

In the absence of an encompassing theory for a given type of non-linear filter, it is often difficult to choose the appropriate parameters for a given application. This is equally true, of course, for linear filters. If we wish to choose the cutoff frequency of a low-pass filter for use in the processing of, say, seismic data, then, while various physical theories might yield a hypothesis of where that frequency may be, it is almost always necessary to make a series of measurements on actual seismic signals to determine precisely where the signal spectrum "rolls-off" into the noise spectrum. From these data the appropriate choice of the parameters of the filters can be made.

In the research we report here we have looked at the problem of choosing the neighborhood size - and to a certain extent shape - for the class of Minkowski filters applied to binary images. There are numerous examples in the literature of using the erosion filter in combination with the operation propagation (or reconstruction) to eliminate small objects, that is, objects with a "width" less than a certain amount. The question in the use of this technique then becomes, how many erosions should be used on a given class of images to separate "big" objects from "small" objects? Once again there might exist a theory predicting the size distribution(s) in the desired class of images but more than likely a series of empirical measurements will be used either to test the theory or to "fine-tune" the estimate of the parameters provided by the theory.

In both cases we must attempt to deduce the appropriate filter parameters by estimating the distribution of sizes of binary objects within an image. Fortunately, the erosion filter itself may be used to estimate this distribution.

Estimating the Size Distribution: The Erosion Filter

We assume for the moment that an erosion of size 1, **E(1)**, means one-pass of an algorithm that peels-off all 8-connected border points of a binary object. Through a series of erosions alternated with propagations,[1] we can then determine the number of binary objects **N** that vanish after **S** erosions, that is **N(S)**. Equivalently we can determine the area **A(S)** associated with the vanished objects. The precise mechanism for implementing this measurement is not of interest at this point. Suffice it to say that, if this direct measurement is to be implemented, then there exist both software techniques (Young, 1982), (Groen, 1984) and hardware techniques such as those directly implemented in the Leitz-TAS system (1980).

If we begin with a grey-level image rather a binary image, then this technique can be applied to estimate the size distribution for each possible threshold level. If simple grey-level thresholding is to be used to convert a grey-level image into a binary image, then the information contained in **A(T,S)** - the area of objects that have vanished after **S** erosions on an image thresholded with level **T** - may be used to simultaneously estimate an appropriate erosion filter size as well as an appropriate choice of grey-level threshold. Such a result is illustrated in Figure 1 below. We see that for an image composed of one large object (an interphase nucleus) and a collection of small objects there exists a clear multi-modal distribution of sizes over a broad range of thresholds.

In figure 2 we see that for a distribution of gold particles in a glass substrate the size distribution is not so clearly multi-modal but that the choice of a threshold for separating objects (collectively) from background is still straight-forward.

It is interesting to see how this distribution changes when noise is added to the image. By adding an image composed of 256^2 samples of Gaussian noise (μ=0.0, σ=5.0), we can look at the effect of noise on the distribution and the separability of various components within the distribution. In Figure 3 we see the distribution **A(T,S)** of the chromosome image corrupted by the additive, Gaussian noise.

The basic character of the distribution is essentially unchanged. At higher values of the threshold (where more bright points are included as part of the putative binary "object" points) a third, distinct population generated by noise points can be seen at

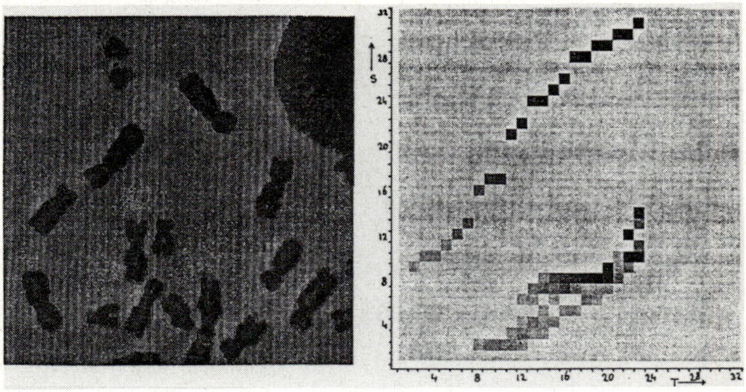

Figure 1: (a) Image of a human metaphase spread. The image is 256 x 256 with 256 grey-levels. For this example only a 5-bit, 32 level, version was analyzed. (b) Two-dimensional distribution of A(T,S). For a given size, S, and threshold, T, the area A(.,.) is shown. The darker the square the greater the area.

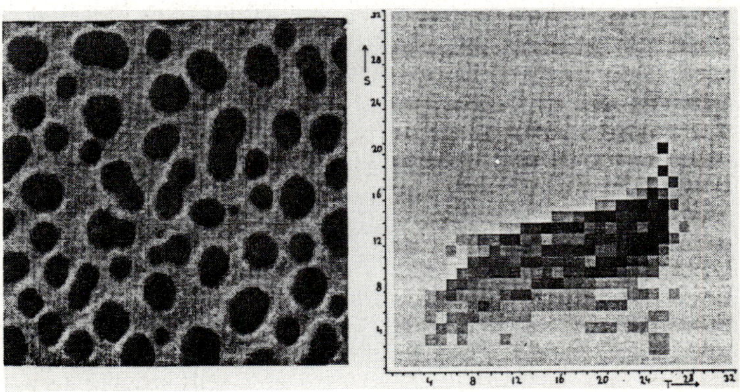

Figure 2: (a) Electron microscope image of gold particles in glass. Once again only a 5-bit, 32 level, image is analyzed. (b) Two-dimensional distribution of A(T,S). For a given size, S, and threshold, T, the area A(.,.) is shown. The darker the square the greater the area.

the small size levels.

While it is a simple matter to continue with this approach to estimate the influence of noise on the size distributions, the issue of computational complexity soon becomes important. Unless a special approach is used, the calculation of **N(T,S)** or **A(T,S)** for a specific threshold value $T=T_\theta$ involves at least two passes through an N x N image for each value of **S**. Because the maximum value of **S** is not

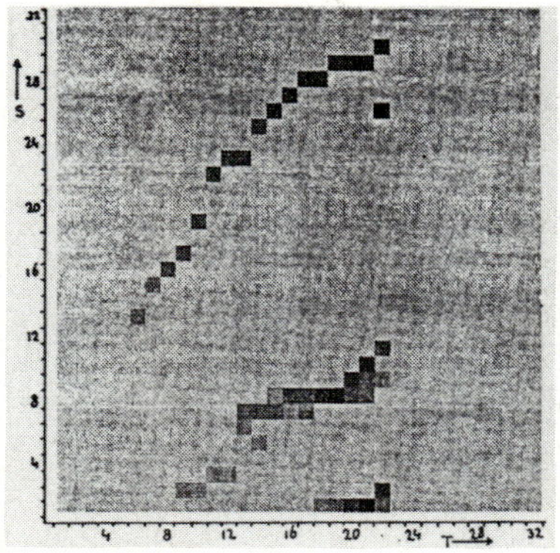

Figure 3: Two-dimensional distribution of **A**(T,S) for the chromosome image corrupted by noise. The signal to noise ratio of this image is 6:1.

known beforehand, this means that in general S_{max} = N/2 passes may be necessary. Thus the total number of passes necessary to compute **N(T_θ,S)** will be proportional to N. To reduce this complexity we turn to another method for computing the effect of successive erosions.

Estimating the Size Distribution: The Distance Transform

Several authors have pointed out that the transformation of a binary image into a grey-level image based upon a distance measure yields a coding of the boundaries of a binary object after successive erosions (Spider, 1983), (Borgefors, 1984). Starting from the binary image shown in Figure 4a we see that after a distance transform based upon the 8-connected definition of a neighborhood, the "grey-value" image of Figure 4b results.

To avoid confusion between original grey-value images and those obtained by a distance transform on a binary image, we shall term the latter "distance-value" images. It is clear from Figure 4b that all object points with a distance-value greater than two are points in the original binary object that would survive two passes of an 8-connected erosion. Thus erosion may be accomplished by thresholding of this grey level image. We can now use this technique to compute either the number of objects that vanish for a given **S** or their area.

```
* * * * * * * *          * * * * * * * *
* * ● ● ● * * *          * * 1 1 1 * * *
* ● ● ● ● ● * *          * 1 1 2 1 1 * *
* ● ● ● ● ● * *          * 1 2 2 2 1 * *
* ● ● ● ● ● * *          * 1 2 3 2 1 * *
* ● ● ● ● ● ● *          * 1 2 2 2 1 1 *
* ● ● ● ● ● * *          * 1 1 1 1 1 * *
* * * * * * * *          * * * * * * * *

      (a)                      (b)
```

Figure 4: (a) Binary image (b) Distance transform of the binary image. The number (grey-value) indicates the 8-connected distance to the background.

The distance transform itself may be accomplished in two passes through the binary image, a forward pass and a backward pass (see Borgefors, 1984). After the transformation step, one pass through the image reveals the maximum value in the new distance-value image. This maximum value is S_{max}. We can now determine the binary image corresponding to $S=S_0$ erosions by using threshold S_0 on the new distance-value image. To determine the size distribution it is <u>not</u> necessary, however, to cycle through all the size levels $0 \le S \le S_{max}$. In one pass through the distance-value image the maximum value of the distance within each object can be found (Veillon, 1980). The set of these maximum values, one per object in the original binary image, <u>is</u> the desired size distribution **N(S)**. Thus the number of passes through the binary image required to produce the size distribution is three instead of proportional to **N**.

Definition of Distance

The calculation of distance within the binary objects is a complex problem. There are a number of possible definitions of distance that can be used the most common being the 8-connected (illustrated above) and the 4-connected. What we seek is a definition of distance that recognizes that we are seeking the distribution of sizes of objects in the continuous spatial (analog) domain while what we have available to us is information in the spatially quantized (digital) domain. In the analog domain, of course, the concept of constant distance yields a circle and the associated distance measure is the Euclidean metric. In the digital domain we can only attempt to approximate circles through our choice of distance measure. Of the many approaches that have been studied one of the most promising techniques for approximating circular distance measures is the use of the chamfer measure (Borgefors, 1984). This family of distance mesaures permits approximation of the Euclidean metric by the use of rational approximations to $\sqrt{2}$. These distance measures (including an algorithm for calculating the chamfer distances in a forward and backward pass through an image) are given in the Borgefors paper. Further, the speed of the algorithm for the chamfer(**r**,**q**) distance is independent of the parameters **r** and **q**. The chamfer(2,3) measure therefore tries to approximate $\sqrt{2} \approx 1.414...$ by 3/2=1.5, the chamfer(3,4) by 4/3=1.333..., and the chamfer(5,7) by the excellent approximation 7/5=1.40.

In Figure 5 we see the result of applying various chamfer measures to families of circles, ellipses, and rectangles. In each case a binary image composed of a number of objects (5 circles, 9 ellipses, 16 rectangles) is transformed into a distance-value image by one of the chamfer metrics. The difference between the objects (e.g. ellipses) within a given binary image is the angle of orientation; all objects within a given family have the same (analog) size. For the circles, which are obviously rotation-invariant, all the measures yield a unique value. Due to the nature of the chamfer measure there is a scaling difference between these differing chamfers but the measure itself yields a single size independent of chamfer and rotation.

For the family of ellipses and the family of rectangles the story is somewhat different. The effect of the distance measure is seen clearly in the width of the size distributions. The 8-connected distance, chamfer(1,1), yields a strongly skewed size distribution for what should be a single peak. This is due to the strong anisotropy of this distance measure compared to the Euclidean measure. The 4-connected distance, chamfer(1,2), is also very skewed. The chamfer(2,3), chamfer(3,4), and chamfer(5,7) show progressive improvement towards the desired

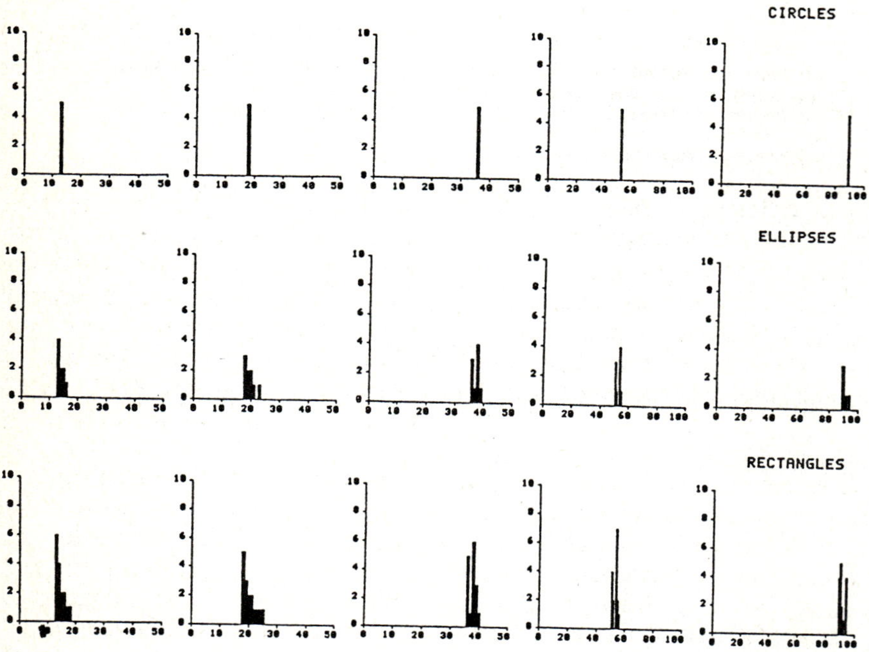

Figure 5: Size distributions computed according to various chamfer measures on families of tilted circles, ellipses, and rectangles. **Column 1**: Chamfer(1,1) the 8-connected distance; **Column 2**: Chamfer(1,2) the 4-connected distance; **Column 3**: Chamfer(2,3); **Column 4**: Chamfer(3,4); **Column 5**: Chamfer(5,7).

single peak. What we begin to see is that the use of chamfer(5,7) yields a significant improvement in the accuracy of the estimate of the size distribution **N(S)**. This result is even more obvious when we rescale all the histograms to a normalized value of 1.0. That is, since we know the size of the largest circle that can fit within each rectangle (or circle or ellipse) and we know the scaling effect associated with each chamfer measure, we can normalize and correct the horizontal (size) axis accordingly. The question of choosing the correct scale factor is non-trivial but the value is computable (Dorst and Smeulders, 1985). In Figure 6 we see this result for the family of rectangles. As we use chamfers associated with better and better parametric, rational approximations to $\sqrt{2}$, our size estimate becomes more precise <u>and</u> more accurate.

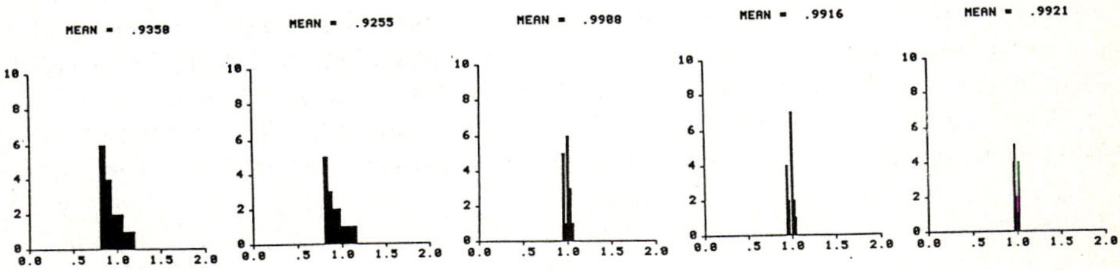

Figure 6: Normalized and corrected size distributions computed according to various chamfer measures on the family of tilted rectangles. **Column 1**: Chamfer(1,1) the 8-connected distance; **Column 2**: Chamfer(1,2) the 4-connected distance; **Column 3**: Chamfer(2,3); **Column 4**: Chamfer(3,4); **Column 5**: Chamfer(5,7).

A further indication of the power in this technique is given in Figure 7. These data represent the size distribution of 64 circles. Sixteen different diameters D were used with values D = 1,3,5,7,...,31 pixels. There were four circles per size group. The chamfer(1,1) measure, shown in Figure 7, shows an inability to distinguish between all 16 groups in the size distribution histogram **N(S)**. While the other four chamfer measures all show the capacity to separate the different classes, the chamfer(5,7) exhibits the greatest ability to distinguish between classes.

Effects of Noise

An important test of this procedure is how it behaves on noisy binary images. To evaluate this question we looked at the result of processing the original binary image of 64 rectangles through a binary symmetric channel (BSC). In a BSC the probability that the binary value of a pixel is unchanged is 1-**p**; the probability that a 0->1 or 1->0 is **p**. The rectangles are all the same size and are oriented at a fixed angle. In Figure 8 we see the effect of the various noise strengths on the measurement of the size distribution. As **p** goes from 0.0 to 0.10 the peak in the distribution shifts to the left (smaller sizes). In addition, a population appears at a size corresponding to a one-pixel diameter. At high **p** values this noise population increases to slightly larger diameters. Not until a noise level of **p**=0.30 does the

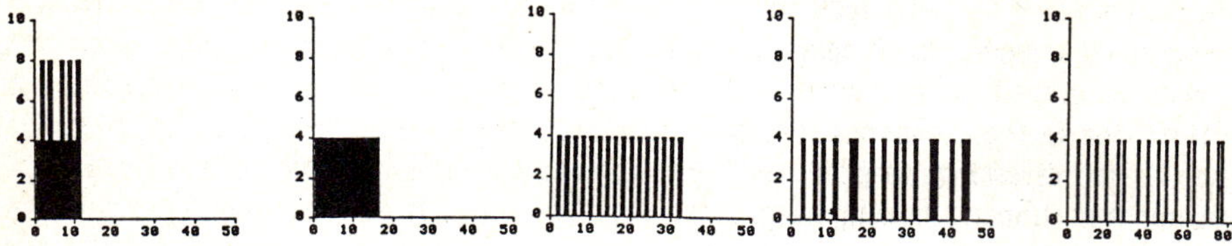

Figure 7: Size distribution of 64 circles of 16 different size classes, 4 per class. **Column 1**: Chamfer(1,1); **Column 2**: Chamfer(1,2); **Column 3**: Chamfer(2,3); **Column 4**: Chamfer(3,4); **Column 5**: Chamfer(5,7). Note the "high-resolution" sizing obtained by the last.

size distribution disappear into the noise distribution. While it is still possible to choose an erosion size on the basis of the size distribution to separate the binary rectangles from the noise, the ability to estimate the actual size of the rectangles would be compromised.

This problem can be overcome by first preprocessing the noisy binary image. Without knowing the size of holes generated by the noise within the rectangles, it is possible to fill these holes. The series of binary filtering operations - complement, propagation from the image edge into the image background, complement - will fill the holes within the rectangles. Measurement of the size distribution on this filtered image yields the distributions shown in Figure 9. The dramatic improvement shows that with this simple preprocessing step the size distribution can yield accurate estimates of the object sizes at a noise level of p=0.10. At p=0.30 two populations, pseudo-objects generated by noise and rectangles, are still separable.

Summary and Conclusions

We have shown that use of the size distribution **N(S)** (or **A(S)**) provides a robust technique for choosing filter parameters for non-linear filtering techniques based upon erosion. The presence of noise in an image (in the binary image case up to 30%!) does not prevent population discrimination. Further, in the binary case the distribution can be estimated in an efficient manner.

In the binary case the choice of the distance measure which, in a sense, infers a form for a quasi-circular structuring element, has little influence on the speed of the algorithm but an important influence on precision, accuracy, and sensitivity of the derived size distributions. The chamfer(5,7) measure yields the best results. Together with the binary pre-processing step for hole-filling extremely accurate measurements of size distributions (accurate to within 3%) can be achieved at even very high noise levels.

In future work we will look in greater detail to the extension of these ideas to grey-level images. By an appropriate choice of distance measure we hope to use the ideas developed here for grey-level dilation and erosion. In particular we are interested in the prospects for noise reduction in grey level images by a process of non-linear filtering adapted to the size distributions (of the signal and noise) rather than linear filtering adapted to their Fourier spectral distributions.

References:

[1] Huang T.S., **Two-Dimensional Digital Signal Processing II: Transforms and Median Filters,** Springer-Verlag, Berlin (1981).

[2] Sternberg S.R., Language and architecture for parallel image processing, in **Pattern Recognition in Practice,** North Holland Press, Amsterdam (1980) 35-44.

[3] Kuwahara M., Hachimura K., Eiho S., and Kinoshita M., Processing of RI-angiocardiographic images, in **Digital Processing of Biomedical Images,** K. Preston and M. Onoe, Ed's., Plenum Press, New York, (1976) 187-203.

[4] Serra J., **Image Analysis and Mathematical Morphology,** Academic Press, London, 1982.

[5] Young I.T., Peverini R.L., Verbeek P.W., and Van Otterloo P.J., A new implementation for the binary and Minkowski operators, **Computer Graphics and Image Processing,** Vol. 17:3 (1981) 189-210.

[6] Groen F.C.A. and Foster N.J., A fast algorithm for Cellular Logic operations on sequential machines, **Pattern Recognition Letters,** Vol. 5:2, (1984) 333-338.

[7] **Leitz Tasic Reference Manual,** Leitz Corporation, Wetzlar, Germany.

[8] DIST Subroutine, **Spider Users' Manual,** Joint Systems Development Corporation, Tokyo, (1983) III:121-III:124.

[9] Borgefors G., Distance transformations in arbitrary dimensions, **Computer Vision, Graphics, and Image Processing,** Vol. 27, (1984) 321-345.

[10] Veillon F., One pass computation of morphological and geometrical properties of objects in digital pictures, **Signal Processing,** Vol. 1, (1979) 175-189.

[11] Dorst L. and Smeulders A., Length estimators compared, **Pattern Recognition in Practice II,** North Holland Press, Amsterdam (1985).

[1]Propagation is a dyadic binary operation that permits the reconstruction of those objects in a mask image where one or more binary image points exist in a seed image.

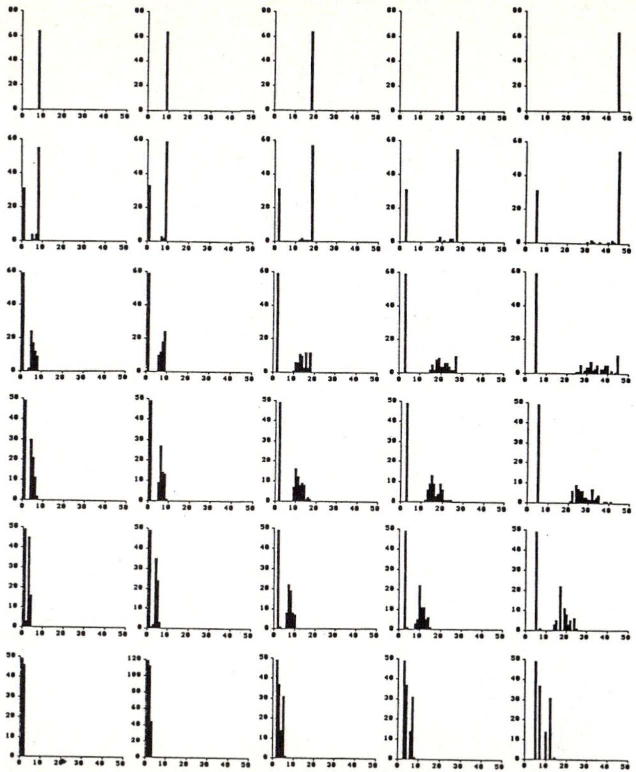

Figure 8. Size distribution of 64 rectangles in a noisy image. The columns represent the same chamfer distances used in the previous figures. The rows represent different noise levels (p) for a BSC. **Row 1**: p=0.0; **Row 2**: p=0.003; **Row 3**: p=0.01; **Row 4**: p=0.03; **Row 5**: p=0.10; **Row 6**: p=0.30

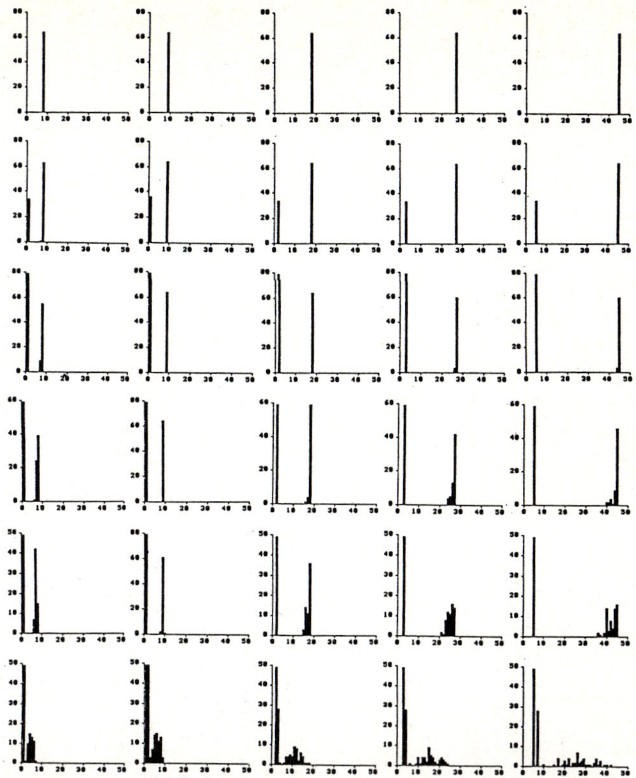

Figure 9. Size distribution of 64 rectangles in a noisy image after preprocessing to eliminate holes in the objects. The columns represent the previously used chamfer distances. The rows represent different noise levels (p) for a BSC. **Row 1**: p=0.0; **Row 2**: p=0.003; **Row 3**: p=0.01; **Row 4**: p=0.03; **Row 5**: p=0.10; **Row 6**: p=0.30

DISCUSSION

Smeulders:

You don't get anything for nothing. The Borgefors metric transposes your binary image into a grey level image. So the longer the distances you are going to measure, the earlier you run out of the number of bits you have available to store these distances.

Young:

That is true. When you make this distance measure, using the Borgefors technique you replace distances like 1 or 2 or 3 by multiples of 5 and 7. That means that you need three times as many bits as you would have needed had you just used a simple distance measure. "Everybody" is using a Motorola 68000. So everyone has 32 bits available. You just lost 3 bits.

I would like to point out, by the way, that once you have labelled the things in the distance transform you need maximally one more pass to find out the size distribution. What you now have is a gray level image and for each object you just pick the maximal brightness. That maximum brightness is exactly the maximal distance. I even think I can combine that with the second pass of the distance transform. So you don't need a very expensive processor. A Motorola 68000 will do.

Choudry:

I would like to add a comment. Chamfering is really an interesting concept in robot assembly. There is a recent article by Requicha of the University of Rochester in Robotics Research with a very detailed description of what chamfering means.

PATTERN RECOGNITION IN PRACTICE II
E.S. Gelsema and L.N. Kanal (Editors)

IMAGE RESTORATION AS AN IDENTIFICATION AND FILTERING PROBLEM

Jan Biemond

Department of Electrical Engineering
Delft University of Technology, Delft, The Netherlands

In this paper a fast parallel Kalman filter scheme is derived for the nearly optimal restoration of images degraded in a deterministic way by blur and in a stochastic way by additive noise. Since the Kalman filter requires the image model parameters as well as the blur parameters to be known, a priori, the parallel Kalman filter structure is extended with an on-line identification procedure. It is shown that the identification problem can be specified as a parallel set of one-dimensional autoregressive moving average (ARMA) identification problems in the Fourier domain. Several identification and restoration results are given as examples.

1. INTRODUCTION

Images are produced to provide useful information about some phenomenon of interest. Unfortunately, since physical imaging systems are imperfect, a recorded image invariably represents a degraded version of an original image or scene. For example, in aerial photography and remote sensing, the images can be degraded by atmospheric turbulence, optical aberrations, and relative motion between the camera and the scene. Medical images are typically of low resolution and low contrast and electron micrographs are degraded by the spherical aberration of the electron lens. The common problem confronting researchers in these fields is that of restoring the image data to improve quality. The problem is complicated by the random noise that is inevitably mixed with the data.

The first step towards the restoration of a degraded image is to be able to identify the kind of degradation the image has suffered. A model of the system that causes the degradation could be obtained analytically from the physical nature of the problem. In most real life situations, however, one can hardly have enough a priori information to determine the point-spread function (PSF) of the blurring system analytically. At best, the PSF can be parameterized from the knowledge about the source of degradation. For example, it is very common to model the blur due to one-dimensional object motion with a uniform PSF, in this case the problem reduces to the determination of the extent of the PSF in the spatial domain, or to the determination of the distance between zero crossings of the transfer function of the blur in the frequency domain. In previous work on blur identification the attention was focussed on both spectral and cepstral techniques for determining the location of these zeros [1,2]. These techniques, however, have a number of shortcomings [3]. First, there are always false sidelobes in the spectrum due to the truncation at the boundary of the image, which are not distinguishable from the sidelobes due to the zeros. Second, the range of the zeros to be identified is restricted to the unit bi-circle, the counterpart of the unit circle in two dimensions, since the Fourier transform is the z-transform, evaluated on the unit bi-circle. A Gaussian PSF, for example, which has no zeros on the unit bi-circle, could not be identified with the above techniques.

Here, we develop a spatial domain blur identification method. If we assume that the undistorted image can be reasonably well modelled by an AR model of low order, then the problem of blur identification becomes one of an ARMA identification problem, where the image model coefficients form the AR part and the blur parameters form the MA part [3,4]. Moreover, these MA parameters represent the zeros of the observed image spectrum, which are not necessarily on the distinguished boundary of the unit bi-circle.

The utility of Kalman filtering for image restoration has been demonstrated in the literature [5,6]. Kalman filters, however, require the image model parameters as well as the blur parameters to be known, a priori. Our identification algorithm will thus provide estimates of the image and blur parameters. The Kalman filter we propose here operates recursively on a line-by-line basis. By using a suitable decorrelating row transformation the actual filter consists of a parallel bank of N low-order one-dimensional Kalman filters, which process the data in the column direction in the transform domain. In this way reducing the number of computations from an order of $O(N^4)$ to that of $O(N^2 \log N)$ for an NxN image. The importancy of choosing correct boundary values for this parallel filter scheme will be discussed. Further, we will show that identification and filtering can be combined and that we are able to handle slowly varying image statistics and space-variant blurs in a line-by-line update fashion.

This paper is organized as follows. First, in Section 2, a matrix-vector formulation is given of the image generating process. By using circulant matrix approximations, in Section 3 this matrix-vector formulation of the noisy blurred image is decomposed into a set of decoupled subsystems in the Fourier domain suitable for the derivation of a parallel bank of Kalman filters. In Section 4, we specify the blur identification as a parallel set of one-dimensional (1-D) ARMA identification problems in the Fourier domain. Finally, in Section 5 several identification and restoration results will be given, both for simulated blurs and photographically blurred images.

2. IMAGE REPRESENTATION

It is assumed that the image can be represented by a zero-mean homogeneous discrete NxN random field. The image can then be modeled by the semicausal type of model

$$x(i,j) = \sum_{p,q \in \mathcal{W}} a(p,q)\,x(i-p,j-q) + u(i,j) \tag{1}$$

where

$$\mathcal{W} = \{p,q: 0 \le p \le p_2, -q_1 \le q \le q_2 \wedge (p,q) \ne (0,0)\}$$

and $u(i,j)$ is the noise input term for which the autocovariance function $r_u(k,\ell)$ is given by

$$r_u(k,\ell) = E[u(i,j)u(i+k,j+\ell)] = \begin{cases} \beta^2 & (k,\ell)=(0,0) \\ -\beta^2 a(0,\ell) & (0,\ell) \in \mathcal{W} \\ 0 & \text{elsewhere} \end{cases}$$

a function which describes a white-noise process in the "i" variable and a colored-noise process with nearest-neighbor support in the "j" variable [7].

If the imaging system is linear and spatially invariant and we assume the noise to be an additive process at the output of the system and the point-spread function to extend over a small number of points, then the observed or recorded image can be modelled by the following 2-D convolution summation

$$y(i,j) = \sum_{k=-k_1}^{k_2} \sum_{\ell=-\ell_1}^{\ell_2} g(k,\ell)x(i-k,j-\ell)+w(i,j) \tag{2}$$

where w(i,j) is a zero-mean white-noise process uncorrelated with the data and where $g(k,\ell)$ is the finite duration impulse response or point-spread function (PSF) of the blur.

Let us consider a vector-scan process, in which we process an entire line of data at a time. By defining the vectors $\mathbf{x}(i)$, $\mathbf{y}(i)$, $\mathbf{v}(i)$ and $\mathbf{w}(i)$, where for example $\mathbf{x}(i) = [x(i,1),x(i,2),...,x(i,N)]^t$, then (1) and (2) can be written as (for the moment we set the boundary conditions equal to zero):

$$\mathbf{A}_0\, \mathbf{x}(i) = - \sum_{p=1}^{p_2} \mathbf{A}_p\, \mathbf{x}(i-p) + \mathbf{u}(i) \tag{3}$$

$$\mathbf{y}(i) = \sum_{k=-k_1}^{k_2} \mathbf{G}_k\, \mathbf{x}(i-k) + \mathbf{w}(i), \qquad i=1,2,...,N, \tag{4}$$

with

$$\mathbf{A}_p = \begin{bmatrix} -a(p,0) & \cdots & -a(p,-q_1) & & \mathbf{O} \\ \vdots & \ddots & & \ddots & \\ -a(p,q_2) & & \ddots & & -a(p,-q_1) \\ & \ddots & & \ddots & \vdots \\ \mathbf{O} & & -a(p,q_2) & \cdots & -a(p,0) \end{bmatrix},$$

$$\mathbf{G}_k = \begin{bmatrix} g(k,0) & \cdots & g(k,-\ell_1) & & \mathbf{O} \\ \vdots & \ddots & & \ddots & \\ g(k,\ell_2) & & \ddots & & g(k,-\ell_1) \\ & \ddots & & \ddots & \vdots \\ \mathbf{O} & & g(k,\ell_2) & \cdots & g(k,0) \end{bmatrix}.$$

Note that both model and blur matrices have a band-Toeplitz structure. The input proces $\mathbf{u}(i)$ has the following autocovariance matrix

$$\Sigma_u(k) = E[\mathbf{u}(i)\mathbf{u}^t(i+k)] = \beta^2\, \mathbf{A}_0\, \delta(k). \tag{5}$$

3. MODEL DECOMPOSITION AND FILTER DESIGN

By approximating the band-Toeplitz matrices in (3), (4) and (5) by circulant matrices [6], we can make use of the nice property that an NxN circulant matrix $\mathbf{Q}^c$ can be diagonalized by

$$\Lambda_Q = \Phi^{-1} \mathbf{Q}^c \Phi, \tag{6}$$

where Λ_Q is an NxN diagonal matrix whose elements $\lambda_Q(j)$ are the eigenvalues of $\mathbf{Q}^c$ and where Φ is an NxN unitary (Fourier) matrix of eigenvectors of $\mathbf{Q}^c$.

By defining the transformed vectors $\bar{\mathbf{x}}(i)$, $\bar{\mathbf{y}}(i)$, $\bar{\mathbf{v}}(i)$ and $\bar{\mathbf{w}}(i)$, where for example

$\bar{\mathbf{x}}(i) = \Phi^{-1}\mathbf{x}(i)$ is the DFT of $\mathbf{x}(i)$

and by premultiplying (3) and (4) with Φ^{-1} we obtain the decoupled set of equations:

$$\lambda_{A_0}(j)\bar{x}(i,j) = -\sum_{p=1}^{p_2} \lambda_{A_p}(j)\ \bar{x}(i-p,j) + \bar{u}(i,j) \tag{7}$$

$$\bar{y}(i,j) = \sum_{k=-k_1}^{k_2} \lambda_{G_k}(j)\ \bar{x}(i-k,j) + \bar{w}(i,j), \qquad i,j=1,2,\ldots,N. \tag{8}$$

Thus, the 1-D matrix-vector description of the noisy blurred image (3), (4) has been decomposed into N uncorrelated equations (7), (8).

To derive a parallel set of N low-order vector Kalman filters both (7) and (8) must be written in matrix-vector notation to obtain N first-order vector dynamical models. We define a p_2x1 state vector $\bar{\mathbf{s}}(i,j)$ as

$$\bar{\mathbf{s}}(i,j) = [\bar{x}(i,j), \bar{x}(i-1,j), \ldots, \bar{x}(i-p_2+1,j)]^t \tag{9}$$

and a Kx1 vector $\bar{\mathbf{z}}(i,j)$, where $K=k_1+k_2+1$, as

$$\bar{\mathbf{z}}(i,j) = [\bar{x}(i+k_1,j), \ldots, \bar{x}(i,j), \ldots, \bar{x}(i-k_2,j)]^t. \tag{10}$$

Because we work with low-order image models, we assume that the dimension of the state-vector $\bar{\mathbf{s}}(i,j)$ in (9) is less than or equal to the dimension of $\bar{\mathbf{z}}(i,j)$, i.e. $p_2 \le K$. In that case the following dynamical model is used:

$$\bar{\mathbf{z}}(i,j) = \bar{\mathbf{A}}(j)\bar{\mathbf{z}}(i-1,j) + \bar{\mathbf{b}}(j)\ \bar{u}(i,j) \tag{11}$$

$$\bar{y}(i,j) = \bar{\mathbf{g}}^t(j)\bar{\mathbf{z}}(i,j) + \bar{w}(i,j). \tag{12}$$

Given the dynamical model of (11) and (12), the jth Kalman filter for obtaining the best linear MSE estimate $\bar{\mathbf{z}}(i,j)$ in terms of $\bar{y}(i,j)$ can be obtained. This results in the following filter equation in the Fourier domain

$$\hat{\bar{\mathbf{z}}}(i,j) = \bar{\mathbf{A}}(j)\hat{\bar{\mathbf{z}}}(i-1,j) + \bar{\mathbf{f}}(i,j)\ [\bar{y}(i,j) - \bar{\mathbf{g}}^t(j)\bar{\mathbf{A}}(j)\hat{\bar{\mathbf{z}}}(i-1,j)] \tag{13}$$

where $\bar{\mathbf{f}}(i,j)$ is the filter gain vector. In our experiments we have obtained $\hat{\bar{x}}(i,j)$ by setting

$$\hat{\bar{x}}(i,j) = [0\ .\ .\ .\ 0\ 1]\ \hat{\bar{\mathbf{z}}}(i+k_2,j), \tag{14}$$

which is the k_2-lag smoothed estimate of $\bar{x}(i,j)$. Once $\hat{\bar{x}}(i,j)$ is known for all i,j the spatial domain estimates $\hat{x}(i,j)$ are given by

$$\hat{x}(i) = \Phi\,\hat{\bar{x}}(i). \tag{15}$$

The resulting efficient filter scheme using the fast fourier transform (FFT) is illustrated in Fig. 1.

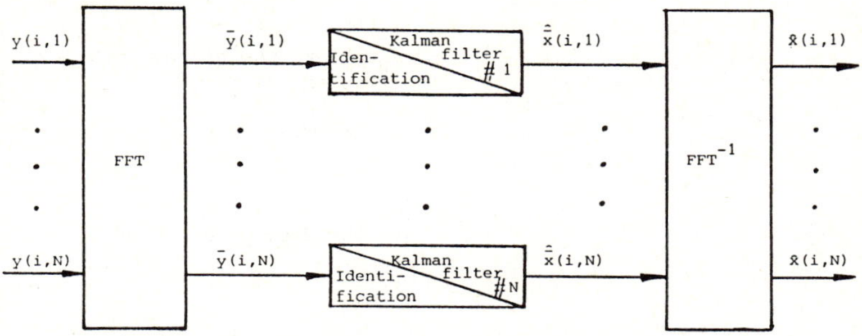

Fig. 1. Parallel identification and filter scheme.

The circulant matrix approximation means that instead of thinking of an image as a flat array, one can think of it as a cylinder so that the horizontal distance matters only modulo N. This results in implicit periodic boundary values for the 1-D DFT based horizontal processing. If there is a difference between right and left side edge values of the noisy blurred image, then frequency components will be introduced which were not originally present (leakage).

Leakage components which occur near the zeros of the transfer function of the blur (motion, defocussing) will be greatly amplified by the deconvolution action of the Kalman filter, particularly in the case of a large SNR.

One way of reducing the leakage components is by using a window technique. The final filter result will then be sharp and almost ringing free in the center part of the image but will have an unacceptable loss in contrast near the boundaries.

A more judicious way to improve the transient response is to extend the Nx1 image vectors y(i) with N_e pixels and to interpolate linearly between the gray values at N and $N+N_e+1$ (modulo $N+N_e$) of the right and left side boundary [8].

If we use in our interpolation scheme besides the two gray values also the two directional coefficients at N and $N+N_e+1$ (4 degrees of freedom), a better fit can be obtained between left and right side edge values by using a third-order polynomial MSE fitting procedure. Note, that by using the symmetry properties of the Fourier transform for real input data [9], we can reduce the number of Kalman filters (channels) in Fig. 1 to $\frac{N}{2}+1$, without affecting the quality of the final filter result. If we accept a small distortion an even larger reduction in the number of channels can be obtained [9], [10]. The performance of this hybrid filter scheme has been demonstrated in [6]. In [6], however, we assume the image model and blur parameters to be known, a priori. In the next section we will show that it is possible to estimate these parameters from the observed image itself.

4. BLUR IDENTIFICATION

In this section we try to extend the parallel filtering scheme with an on-line identification procedure. Due to the diagonalization our 1-D vector state-space description of the image generating process has been transformed into a set of decoupled equations in the Fourier domain. By omitting the minus sign in (7) and by assuming that the eigenvalues $\lambda_{A_0}(j)$ are each unequal to zero, and by transforming the noncausal blur in (8) into a causal blur by delaying the observations over k_1, we obtain the following set of equations in the Fourier domain:

$$\bar{x}(i,j) = \sum_{p=1}^{p_2} \frac{\lambda_{A_p}(j)}{\lambda_{A_0}(j)} \bar{x}(i-p,j) + \frac{1}{\lambda_{A_0}(j)} \bar{u}(i,j) \tag{16}$$

$$\bar{y}(i,j) = \sum_{k=0}^{k_0} \lambda_{G_k}(j) \bar{x}(i-k,j) + \bar{w}(i,j), \tag{17}$$

where $k_0 = k_1 + k_2$.

By eliminating $\bar{x}(i,j)$ from (16) and (17), we obtain the following input-output form:

$$\bar{y}(i,j) = \sum_{p=1}^{p_2} \frac{\lambda_{A_p}(j)}{\lambda_{A_0}(j)} \bar{y}(i-p,j) + \sum_{k=0}^{k_0} \frac{\lambda_{G_k}(j)}{\lambda_{A_0}(j)} \bar{u}(i-k,j)$$

$$+ \bar{w}(i,j) - \sum_{p=1}^{p_2} \frac{\lambda_{A_p}(j)}{\lambda_{A_0}(j)} \bar{w}(i-p,j), \qquad i,j=1,2,\ldots,N. \tag{18}$$

If we assume for a moment that the effect of the observation noise on the parameter estimates is negligible, then (18) reduces to

$$\bar{y}(i,j) = \sum_{p=1}^{p_2} \frac{\lambda_{A_p}(j)}{\lambda_{A_0}(j)} \bar{y}(i-p,j) + \sum_{k=0}^{k_0} \frac{\lambda_{G_k}(j)}{\lambda_{A_0}(j)} \bar{u}(i-k,j), \qquad i,j=1,2,\ldots,N. \tag{19}$$

Hence the parameter identification problem becomes one of an ARMA model identification problem. The estimation of the parameters of this parallel set of complex ARMA models for 2-D space-variant blurs using a recursive least-squares identification algorithm will be presented elsewhere. Here, we will show that for the case of linear motion blur and some reasonable assumptions about the underlying image model, the parallel identification procedure can be greatly simplified and that for this particular case there is no need to neglect the observation noise.

Parallel Identification of linear motion in the presence of noise

The quality of the restoration is related to the amount of a priori knowledge available about the image and the source of degradation. We assume that we have a prototype undistorted image available which can be reasonably well modelled by a separable exponentially decaying image autocovariance function

$$r_x(k,\ell) = \sigma_x^2 \rho_v^{|k|} \rho_h^{|\ell|}, \qquad 0 < \rho_v, \rho_h < 1, \tag{20}$$

where σ_x^2 is the image variance and ρ_v and ρ_h are the vertical and horizontal correlation coefficients, respectively; then the image can be exactly modelled by the semicausal model (1) with support $\mathcal{W} = \{0 \leq p \leq 1,\ -1 \leq q \leq 1 \text{ and } (p,q) \neq (0,0)\}$ [11]. Then, in the case of linear motion along the horizontal axis in the presence of noise (16) and (17) reduce to

$$\bar{x}(i,j) = \rho_v\, \bar{x}(i-1,j) + \frac{1}{\lambda_{A_0}(j)}\, \bar{u}(i,j) \tag{21}$$

$$\bar{y}(i,j) = \lambda_G(j)\, \bar{x}(i,j) + \bar{w}(i,j) \tag{22}$$

and the input-output equation (18) reduces to

$$\bar{y}(i,j) = \rho_v\, \bar{y}(i-1,j) + \frac{\lambda_G(j)}{\lambda_{A_0}(j)}\, \bar{u}(i,j) + \bar{w}(i,j) - \rho_v\, \bar{w}(i-1,j), \tag{23}$$

which is an AR(1) type of model with 2 different input terms. If we define

$$\bar{y}_v(i,j) = \bar{y}(i,j) - \rho_v\, \bar{y}(i-1,j) \tag{24}$$

then (23) can be rewritten as

$$\bar{y}_v(i,j) = \frac{\lambda_G(j)}{\lambda_{A_0}(j)}\, \bar{u}(i,j) + \bar{w}(i,j) - \rho_v\, \bar{w}(i-1,j). \tag{25}$$

Under the assumption of wide-sense stationarity of the observation noise $\bar{w}(i,j)$, we can write for the variance of $\bar{y}_v(i,j)$:

$$\text{Var}\{\bar{y}_v(i,j)\} = \left(\frac{\lambda_G(j)}{\lambda_{A_0}(j)}\right)\left(\frac{\lambda_G(j)}{\lambda_{A_0}(j)}\right)^{*} \text{Var}\{\bar{u}(i,j)\} + (1+\rho_v^2)\ \text{Var}\ \{\bar{w}(i,j)\}, \tag{26}$$

in which * denotes complex conjugate. Rewriting (26) yields for $\lambda_G(j)$:

$$|\lambda_G(j)|^2 = \frac{\lambda_{A_0}(j)^2}{\text{Var}\{\bar{u}(i,j)\}} \quad [\text{Var}\{\bar{y}_v(i,j)\} - (1+\rho_v^2)\ \text{Var}\{\bar{w}(i,j)\}]. \tag{27}$$

The eigenvalues $\lambda_{A_0}(j)$ in (27) are the eigenvalues of the circulant version of a tridiagonal matrix and can be approximated by the following nonnegative function [11]:

$$\lambda_{A_0}(j) = 1 + 2\alpha \cos \frac{j\pi}{N+1} \tag{28}$$

where $\alpha = \dfrac{\rho_h}{1+\rho_h}$. Further, due to the energy-preserving property of the unitary transform we can substitute

$$\text{Var}\{\bar{w}(i,j)\} = \sigma_w^2,\quad \text{Var}\{\bar{u}(i,j)\} = \sigma_x^2 \cdot \lambda_{A_0}(j) \cdot \frac{(1-\rho_v^2)(1-\rho_h^2)}{1+\rho_h^2},$$

while the variance of $\bar{y}_v(i,j)$ for every channel j can be estimated from the available samples $\bar{y}(i,j)$. Note that due to the real data structure only half of the number of channels $(\frac{N}{2} + 1)$ need to be computed.

5. EXPERIMENTS

A 256x256 test image of the "cameraman", each pixel quantized in 8 bits, is artificially degraded with linear motion blur in horizontal direction by means of the following discrete PSF

$$g(\ell) = \frac{1}{\ell_2+1}, \qquad \ell=0,1,\ldots,\ell_2 \qquad (29)$$
$$= 0 \qquad \text{elsewhere}$$

and with additive noise with different signal-to-noise ratios (SNR). In Fig. 2 $\ell_2=9$ and SNR= 40 dB. The transfer function $G(\omega)$ of the motion blur is given by

$$G(\omega) = \sum_{\ell=0}^{\ell_2} \frac{1}{\ell_2+1} e^{-j\omega\ell}$$

$$= \frac{1}{\ell_2+1} e^{-j\left(\frac{\ell_2}{2}\right)\omega} \frac{\sin\left(\omega \frac{\ell_2+1}{2}\right)}{\sin\left(\frac{\omega}{2}\right)} \qquad (30)$$

which describes a discrete sinc function with zero crossings at frequencies $\omega = \frac{2\pi}{\ell_2+1} \cdot k$. Thus, in the interval $\omega \in [0,\pi]$, the sinc function has 5 zerocrossings for $\ell_2=9$.
The complex eigenvalue function $\lambda_G(j)$, $j=1,2,\ldots,N$ of the circulant matrix $\mathbf{G}^c$ can be efficiently obtained by computing the DFT of the cyclic sequence describing the circulant matrix and corresponds with the transfer function $G(\omega)$, for $\omega = \frac{2\pi}{N} \cdot j-1$.

Fig. 2. Cameraman
$\ell_2=9$, SNR=40 dB

Fig. 4. Filter result

In fig. 3 the identification results of Fig. 2 are given. In Fig. 3a we have estimated $|\lambda_G(j)|$ over 50 rows and in Fig. 3b over 10 rows. In both cases the correct sinc function $|\lambda_G(j)|$ with 5 zerocrossings ($\ell_2=9$) was fitted to the data using a MSE fit criterion. The filter result using the identified parameter values is given in Fig. 4.

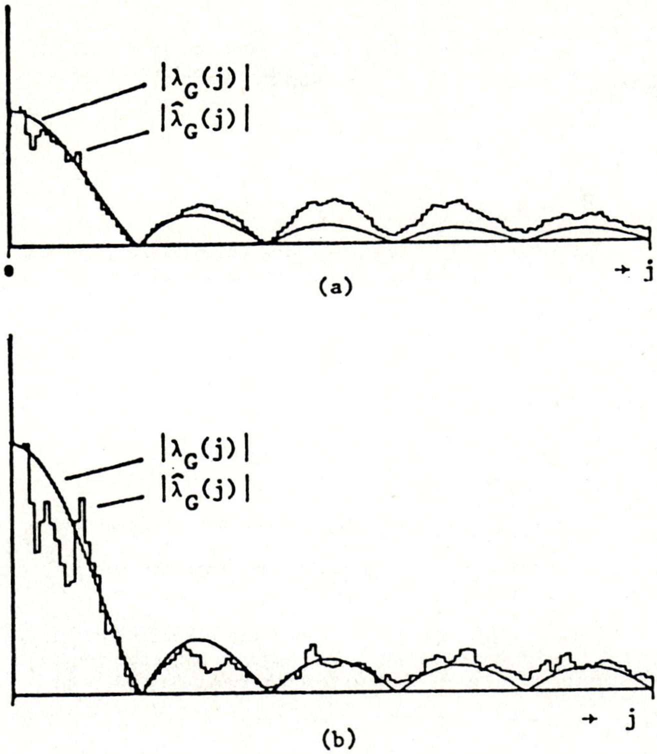

Fig. 3. Motion blur identification, ℓ_2=9, SNR = 40 dB
a) Estimate $|\hat{\lambda}_G(j)|$ over 50 rows of Fig. 2
b) Estimate over 10 rows.

The experiment was repeated for SNR=30 dB. Again a correct fit was found. If there is more noise in the image, for example SNR = 20 dB, then the zeros at higher frequencies are masked by the noise, Also in this case a correct fit can be found by using a weighted MSE fit criterion, where the lower frequencies are weighted more severely than the higher frequencies. See Fig. 5.

Finally, we present some identification-restoration results on a true photographically blurred image. In Fig. 6 a 320x470 image of a locally blurred train image is shown, each pixel quantized in 8 bits.
The identification result is given in Fig. 7, which means an estimated motion of the train over ℓ_2 = 7 pixels. The signal-to-noise ratio is estimated as SNR = 23 dB. The restoration result is shown in Fig. 8.

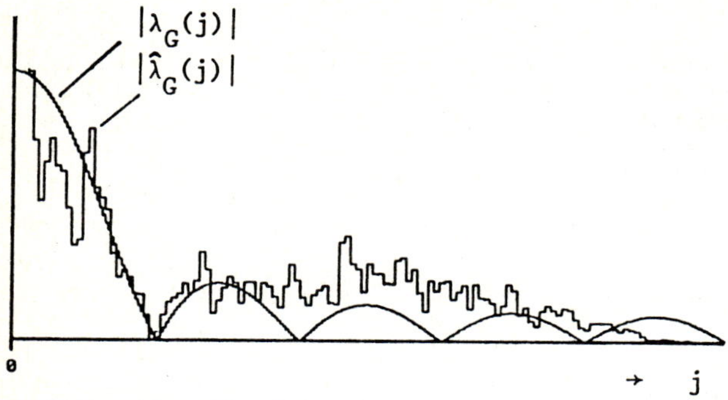

Fig. 5. Motion blur identification, ℓ_2=9, SNR = 20 dB.
Estimate over 10 lines, weighted MSE fit criterion.

Fig. 6. Train image
ℓ_2=7, SNR = 23 dB

Fig. 8. Filter result

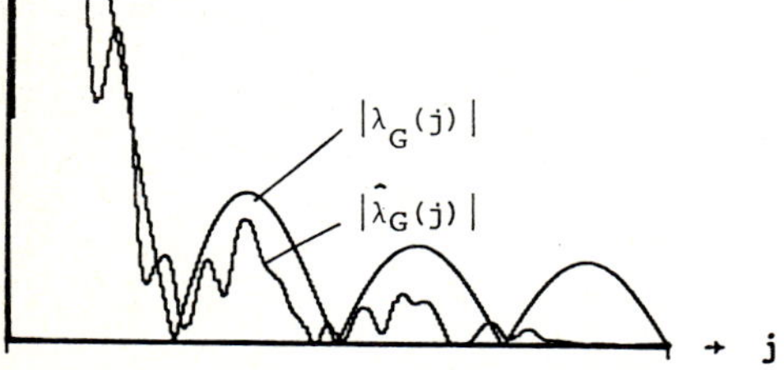

Fig. 7. Local Motion blur identification, ℓ_2=7, SNR = 23 dB. Estimate over 20 lines.

6. DISCUSSION

A simple and fast parallel identification and restoration algorithm was described for noisy motion-blurred image data. From the experiments in the previous section we observe that the correct motion blur parameters could be estimated from only a few image lines. In this way the identification restoration procedure can be made adaptive in order to track slowly varying image statistics and space-variant motion blurs in a line-by-line update version. Of special interest and subject of current investigation is the ARMA identification problem for 2-D noncausal blurs.

REFERENCES

[1] M. Cannon, "Blind Deconvolution of Spatially Invariant Image Blurs with Phase", IEEE Trans. on ASSP, Vol. ASSP-24, pp. 58-63, Feb. 1976.

[2] H.C. Andrews, B.R. Hunt, Digital Image Restoration, Englewood Cliffs, New Jersey, Prentice Hall, Inc. 1977.

[3] A.M. Tekalp, H. Kaufman, J.W. Woods, "Identification of Image and Blur Parameters for the Restoration of Noncausal Blurs", Proc. 1985 IEEE Int. Conf. on ASSP, Tampa, Florida, March 1985, pp. 656-659.

[4] J. Biemond, F.G. van der Putten,"Image Restoration using a Parallel Identification and Filtering Procedure", Proc. 1985 IEEE Int. Conf. on ASSP, Tampa, Florida, March 1985, pp. 660-664.

[5] J.W. Woods, and V.K. Ingle, "Kalman Filtering in Two Dimensions - Further Results", IEEE Trans. on ASSP, Vol. 29, pp. 188-197, April 1981.

[6] J. Biemond, J. Rieske, J.J. Gerbrands, "A Fast Kalman Filter for Images Degraded by Both Blur and Noise", IEEE Trans. on ASSP, vol. 31, pp. 1248-1256, Oct. 1983.

[7] A.K. Jain, "Advances in Mathematical Models for Image Processing", Proc. IEEE, vol. 69, May 1981, pp. 502-528.

[8] J.W. Woods, J. Biemond, A.M. Tekalp, "Boundary Value Problem in Image Restoration", 1985 IEEE Int. Conf. on Acoustics, Speech and Signal Processing, Tampa, Florida, March 1985, pp. 692-695.

[9] F.G. van der Putten, "Image Restoration using a Parallel Identification and Filtering Procedure", M.Sc. Thesis (in Dutch), Delft Univ. of Technology, The Netherlands, 1984.

[10] T. Katayama, "Restoration of Images Degraded by Motion Blur and Noise", IEEE Trans. on Automatic Control, Vol. AC-27, No. 5, Oct. 1982, pp. 1024-1033.

[11] A.K. Jain, "A Semicausal Model for Recursive Filtering of Two-Dimensional Images", IEEE Trans. Comput., Vol. C-26, April 1977, pp. 343-350.

DISCUSSION

Stark:

If you only handle a single line in your Kalman filter how do you handle the vertical correlations? Or do you mean by single line a whole bunch of lines?

Biemond:

I take one observed image line at a time but I stack a number of lines. For example, if you have a defocusing blur extending over nine image lines then you have at least to stack those nine image lines. In the parallel structure the parallel Kalman filter bank is then of the ninth order. So all those filters are not scalar filters but of the ninth order depending on the vertical extension of the blur.

If you have a motion blur in horizontal direction then, due to the decorrelating transform you arrive at scalar Kalman filters yielding a very fast filter procedure.

Stark:

So basically you are taking a two-dimensional field and convert it into a one-dimensional vector so that you can work with matrices instead of with a kind of four-dimensional objects.

Biemond:

Exactly.

Foerstner:

Do you assume that you have shift invariance in one line?

Biemond:

Yes, I assume shift invariance along one line but not in the vertical direction.

Foerstner:

How large is the region of support? Do you have to specify it in advance or is it estimated by the procedure?

Biemond:

In the ARMA identification procedure there is no need to know anything about the support region. A criterion is used to define elements belonging to the support region.

Foerstner:

Do you do any estimation of the noise variance?

Biemond:

Yes, for example in the train image we used a local area and made a noise estimate.

Foerstner:

How do you do that?

Biemond:

We assume that within a particular area of the original unblurred image there is no variance at all.

Choudry:

There are regions in your image which are motion blurred and some which are not. If you try to correct for motion blur in your whole image you introduce blurring in the regions which were

originally not blurred.
Do you go back then and try to compensate with the original image? You can do that for example by segmenting your image and say here I only estimate the noise and there I am going to correct for motion blur.

Biemond:
In our example we used human interaction.You can consider this problem as a detection problem in which you detect all kinds of different point spread functions but that needs future research.

PATTERN RECOGNITION IN PRACTICE II
E.S. Gelsema and L.N. Kanal (Editors)
Elsevier Science Publishers B.V. (North-Holland), 1986

TWO NON-LINEAR IMAGE ENHANCEMENT ALGORITMS

D. Bosman, H. Boterenbrood, H. van Huijstee

Twente University of Technology
Department of Electrical Engineering
pob 217, 7500 AE Enschede

1. INTRODUCTION

Computer vision applied to quality inspection jobs and to spatial control of real objects requires robust image acquisition and processing. Robust in the sense that the error rate of processed results is sufficiently low. In many industrial applications, the adjective should be replaced by "extremely". The generation of error pixels already starts at the earliest stage of image formation and acquisition; subsequent processing steps must not attach undue weights to them. Also these processing steps must not introduce extra noise. In our group we are concerned with robustness of acquisition and, among others, we look into the possibilities of robust enhancement by non-linear algoritms.

Functionally, one would require of the image acquisition and the preprocessing algoritms that:

1.1 The algoritm should compress large area, uniform gray levels without adversely affecting local area contrast signal to noise ratio (SNR).

1.2 If performing edge enhancement, the transfer (describing) function should, after initial gain increase, again be small at the Nyquist frequency;

1.3 The total operations should preserve pel SNR.

Such desired characteristics bring our research outside the scope of algoritms based on linear theory because, although (1.1) and (1.2) not necesssarily imply non-linearity, (1.3) does.

2. ALTERNATIVE METHODS OF ENHANCEMENT

2.1 The information to be processed is assumed to reside in the contrast of the image, not in its mean level. Moreover, the interest is focussed on high gray level gradients $dg/d\{\sqrt{(x^2+y^2)}\}$. To make optimum use of the limited dynamic range of computation, in relation to the already marginal contrast signal to noise ratio SNR(C) of the input image, processing algoritms should in the early stage emphasize desired and attenuate unwanted frequency components in the image. Conventional algoritms for this purpose are linear high-pass filters. Effective, efficient high pass filters are based on the use of point spread functions (psf) possessing many sidelobes and which require good to perfect matching to the characteristics of the gradients to be emphasized. When this condition is violated, ringing effects may occur, resulting in many displaced responses parallel to edges and lines. Therefore, emphasis usually is restricted. Ideally, one would want non-negative psfs (in linear theory associated with low pass filters) or well behaved psfs possessing at the most one sidelobe: in linear filters these obtain only limited enhancement. For stronger enhancement action using "forgiving" psf shapes, one has to take recourse to non-linear filters wherein both the volume and the shape of the psf may vary, dependent on local average image intensity or even on pel magnitude. One advantage of such realisations is, in our experience, that the non-linear neighbourhood operators are less sensitive to parameter tolerances of the psf than their linear counterparts - at the expense of considerably more computation time.

There are many more filter configuration options in non-linear than in linear theory. Furthermore it is very difficult to obtain insight into their operation: already the convolution operation with a space invariant psf is difficult enough to visualise. One good teacher of non-linear options is mother nature, but she employs other computing "hardware" than digital computers; thus enhancement algoritms gleaned from biological species cannot be expected to have a computer friendly structure. We chose to model an enhancement algoritm [1] after a natural vison example known as lateral inhibition [2,3]. Once this phenomenological model would demonstrate satisfactory results, a functional model producing similar results but with a computer friendly structure would be designed. During the course of development we came across another functional model [4] which is both computer friendly and produces good results. Both algoritms are briefly described and their processing results compared.

2.2 To build the phenomenological model of lateral inhibition, we found inspiration in the natural process as found in the arthropod "limulus" or horseshoe crab. In vision literature, the model of lateral inhibition most often is linear, the interaction between neighbouring channels occurs by superposition of properly weighted signals. The channel consists of a light-to-pulse frequency converter (LFC), inhibitory action substracts pulses (or pulse frequency) from the output of the LFC. In our model we also use the LFC but its gain factor is affected by the occurrence of pulses in neighbouring channels, by decreasing the content of the light exposure memory in the LFC. The number of pulses counted during a given integration time is the measure of the average accumulated exposure. In practice the performance of this realisation of the lateral inhibition algoritm (LIA) suffers from this modulation method, as additional noise is introduced when the integration time is too short. LIA as we implemented it [1] is a non-linear neighbourhood operator with multiplicative lateral interaction between pels.

In figure 1, either the input E(i) or the output O(i) of the channel i associated with pel (i), lowers the gain G(i,n) of neighbouring channels (i,n) by way of an interaction factor K(n). The index n denotes the distance measured in cell diameters between channels (i) and (i,n). The result is written as either (2.1) or (2.2) or a combination of both:

$$\frac{O(i,o)}{E(i,o)} = \frac{G(i,o)}{1 + \sum_{n>o} K(n).E(i,n)} \quad \text{(forward interaction), or} \tag{2.1}$$

$$\frac{O(i,o)}{E(i,o)} = \frac{G(i,o)}{1 + \sum_{n>o} K(n).O(i,n)} \quad \text{(recurrent interaction)} \tag{2.2}$$

wherein E(i,0) and O(i,0) denote the illumination, respectively the output signal, of the (central) channel(i,o) inhibited by its neighbours. In both cases the factor K(n) is a function of n but otherwise conveniently assumed to be invariant. We have shown that configuration 1.b. models LIA as discussed in section 3, where as confiquration 1.a produces results similar to the CVRS algoritm described in section 4.

2.3 In contrast to the modulation of channel gains, which changes both the shape and the volume of the psf dependent on image data, Cornsweet and Yellot [4] devised a functional model based on summation of psf's constrained to have constant shape and constant volume independent of stimulation magnitude: the Constant Volume Response Summation (CVRS) algoritm. The height of the (circularly symmetric) non-negative psf is proportional to pel i intensity E(i), the base area A(i) is inversely proportional to E(i): E(i). A(i) = 1. Denote the resulting psf:

$$S[E(x,y)\{(x-p)^2 + (y-q)^2\}] \tag{2.3}$$

which describes the contribution of irradiance E(x,y) (at the input of the sensor located at (x,y)), to the output O(p,q) of the channel associated with pel (p,q). Then

$$O(p,q) = \iint_{-\infty}^{+\infty} E(x,y)\ S[E(x,y)\ \{(x-p)^2+(y-q)^2\}\ dxdy \tag{2.4}$$

For any uniform field with E(x,y) = E, the response equals 1 independent of location. Proof: substitute $x' = (x-p).\sqrt{E}$ and $y' = (y-q).\sqrt{E}$; it follows that $dxdy = E^{-1}\ dx'\ .dy'$ so that the integral reduces to describe the volume of the psf itself, which equals 1.
(With this type of psf the catch of photons, as described by the product E(i).A(i) is constant. Then, at photon-limited light levels, the SNR also is constant, assuming Poisson distribution for the photon catch. This property is important in vision research).

3. LATERAL INHIBITION ALGORITM; FLOW DIAGRAM.

In natural vision, the individual receptors convert catches of photons into electrical pulses, producing output frequencies which, if lateral inhibition were not active, only are a function of the received amount of photons at the receptor. The lateral inhibition introduces a local spatial input light distribution dependence, for instance as described by (2,1) and (2,2). As the gain of a channel is heavier affected by a strongly illuminated neighbour than by a weakly ditto, the response to a pulse or edge shows relatively deeper troughs than peaks (asymmetrical overshoot); see figure 2. LIA does not normalize the response to uniform fields to a given constant level, but it does compress the input average level range at higher illumination levels. For a uniform field equation (2.2) then becomes:

$$\frac{O(i,0)}{E(i,o)} = \lim_{E\to\infty} \frac{G(i,c)}{1 + \Sigma\ K(n).O(i,n)} \to \frac{G(i,o)}{\Sigma\ K(n).O(i,n)} \text{ or } \frac{\{G(i,o)\}^2}{E(i)} = G(i) \tag{3.1}$$

It is tempting to linearise equation (2.2), which implies the condition that Σ K(n).0(i,n) < 1 as suggested in e.g. (2). However, it can be shown that for good enhancement operation and also from the point of view of just noticeable difference (JND) for small patches, this condition is not sufficiently met; therefore we proceeded with the non-linear model.

3.2 Returning to the actual implementation of LIA, figure 3 gives an electronic model of two channels of this algorithm. The inhibition action is postulated to take place in the (analogue) part of the light - to - frequency - conventer (LFC) mechanism of the modulator; instead of proportional freguency subtraction, each output pulse decreases the charge of a buffer in a neighbouring receptor. This buffer accumulates the photon catch of its own receptor, loses some of this amount due to inhibition. We also postulate that this loss is proportional to the charge accumulated just before inhibition, the electronic analogon of the buffer is a capacitor C_1 (which is charged by a current source, the current being proportional to the logaritm of light intensity) and partially discharged through a resistor (R_1 or R_2) which is switched into the circuit during a fixed amount of time τ, which is equal for all channels. The voltage build - up across C is linear with time when uninhibited, and hence is a measure of exposure E.t, see figure 4a. The LFC is composed of this input circuit, the comparator H with threshold voltage Vth, and the one - shot OS which produces the timing pulse of width τ. OS fires when Vc_1> Vth; the output pulse discharges completely the exposure buffer (capacitor C_1) belonging to its own channel, while discharging the buffers of neighbouring circuits only fractionally; the discharge slopes being determined by the products R_1 C_1, R_2 C_1, etc. For the sake of clarity only 4 of the 36 inhibitor leaks normally required are shown in the circuit diagram of figure 3.

If pulses arriving at a channel from neighbouring circuits add up to a higher inhibitor frequency (figure 4b) than the channel's own firing frequency, the charge build - up across its buffer is severely hampered. In figure 4b the case is depicted that Vc_1 almost reaches the threshold level Vth without exceeding it: the channel cannot fire even though there is sufficient exposure. This situation happens at the dark side of an edge or gradient; vice versa at the light side the channels become under - inhibited by the lack of firing neighbours at the dark side (mach band). However, an inhibited channel is optimally ready to fire if the situation changes such that one or more inhibiting pulse frequencies decreasy only slightly!

The equation (2,2) can be derived from this model as follows. Let the pulse repetition period of channel i be Ti, its buffer C_1 (i) is inhibited m times during this period (compare fiqure 4b). The combined voltage drop due to m partial discharges of the buffer C_1,(i) is denoted by Δ V. The total charge to be accumulated over C_1(i) thus equals Q(i)/C_1(i) = Vth + ΔV. The charging rate of C_1(i) is given by the illumination E. Thus, the time Ti between full discharges is proportional to:

(3.2) $$Ti = (Vth + \Delta V)/E$$

The voltage drop ΔV is determined by the combined action of the neighbours involved:

- the number of active inhibiting neighbours,
- the firing frequencies of individual neighbours, and
- the associated weight factors $K^1(n)$, which depend on the relative distance n (sensor diameters)

Then $\Delta V = \sum K^1(n).O/i,n)$
so that O(i,o), the output frequency of the channel under consideration becomes

$$(3.3) \quad O\,(i,o) = Ti^{-1} = \frac{E(i,o)}{Vth + \sum K^1(n).O(i,n)} = \frac{G(i,o).E(i,o)}{1 + \sum K(n).O(i,n)}$$

In figure 5 the flow diagram of the algoritm according to the model of figure 3 is given.

4. RESPONSES OF THE CVRS ALGORITM; FLOW DIAGRAM.

Apart from the properties under 2.3, Yellot [4] describes a number of interesting responses. The result of multiplying the input image by a constant factor c yields

$$(4.1) \quad O\,[cE(x,y)]\,(p,q) = O\,[E(\frac{x}{\sqrt{c}},\frac{y}{\sqrt{c}})]\,(p\sqrt{c},q\sqrt{c})$$

The consequences of this equation are that the result of processing the lighter image is the same as first expanding the input image spatially by a factor $\sqrt{c}$ in both directions x and y, then carry out the summation operation (2.4) and afterward shrinking back the so obtained result, again by a factor $\sqrt{c}$, to the original size. The responses become more spatially concentrated and steeper at higher irradiation levels. This is also true for edge response, where irradiation steps of D on a background of E occur, see figure 6, where D/E = 10 and the response is shown for E = 0.1; E = 1.0; E = 10; E = 100. It must be noted that this response in linear theory suggests a psf with one negative sidelobe, whereas the psf used here is a (non-negative) Gaussian function. Moreover, as predictable, the response has a band-pass quality which is strongly dependent on the magnitude of the background.

Other properties: since the response to any uniform field is constant, simple thresholding for binarisation is very effective. Using a fixed threshold level slightly larger than the uniform field response, one can calculate [4] the threshold sensitities for large area contrast and for contrast of small discs with area A. It turns out that Weber's law: $\Delta L/L$ is constant and Ricco's law: $\Delta L.A$ is constant both are modelled. In figure 7 the flow diagram of CVRS is given.

5. RESPONSES TO ACTUAL PICTURES; COMPARISON.

In figure 8, the original (input) image (64x64) and three LIA responses at different background levels are given; in figure 9 the same for CVRS but with one extra processing action: histogram equalisation. The latter action is necessary to make the processed images comparable, since LIA has not the constant response to uniform fields like CVRS, at least not for dark input areas. Therefore the CVRS images were stretched to have histograms similar to those processed by LIA.

Both LIA and CVRS have structures which allow a high degree of parallellism in their implementation. The software as developed for both on a serial machine (CADMUS 9112) performs as yet too slow to be useful in practice for e.g. computer vision. However, its realisation in dedicated hardware is quite possible; also implementation on parallel machines. We tried the latter, implementing LIA on CLIP IV at the dept. of physics and astronomy of prof. Duff, University College. The calculation time for a 96x96 image was 110ms for 250 iterations.

6. CONCLUSION.

Both the algoritms LIA and CVRS show advantages as a preprocessor in computer vision; as yet their implemention on a von Neumann machine is impractical due to very long computation times. The inherent parallellism opportunities in the algoritms should be made good use of in dedicated or parallel processor structures. The algoritms operate similarly, except that

- CVRS has perfect compression properties, LIA not
- a second harmonic generated at high spatial frequencies occurs in both but in opposite phase.

The authors acknowledge the cooperation of Pat Griffin, M.sc and of Anneke van Essen.

7. references.

1. Bosman, D, 1983, A non - linear technique for contour enhancement. In Fortschritte durch digitale Mesz -und Automatisierungstechnik, Interkama Kongresz, Dusseldorf.

2. Cornsweet, T.N. 1970, Visual Perception, Academic Press, New York.

3. Ratliff, F 1974, Studies on excitation and inhibition in the retina. Chapman and Hall, London.

4. Cornsweet, T.N. Yellot, J.I. 1984, Mach bands without inhibition: intensity dependent positive pointspread models of early visual processing. ARVO meeting.

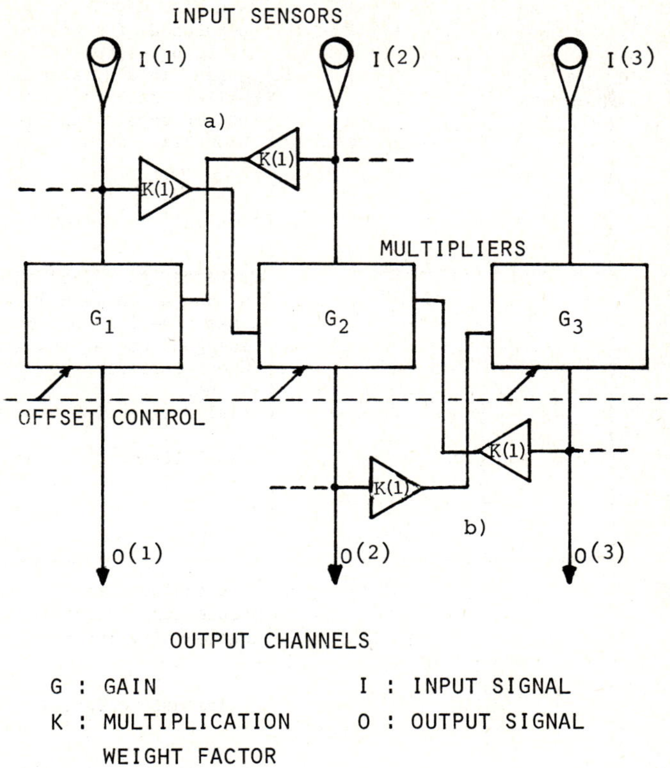

Figure 1
Multiplicative control of channel gains (inhibition).
K: interaction constant.

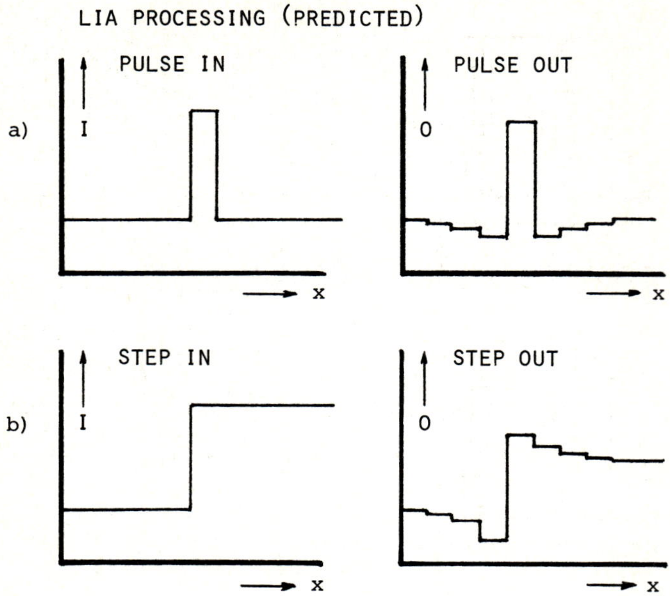

Figure 2

Pulse and edge response of LIA.

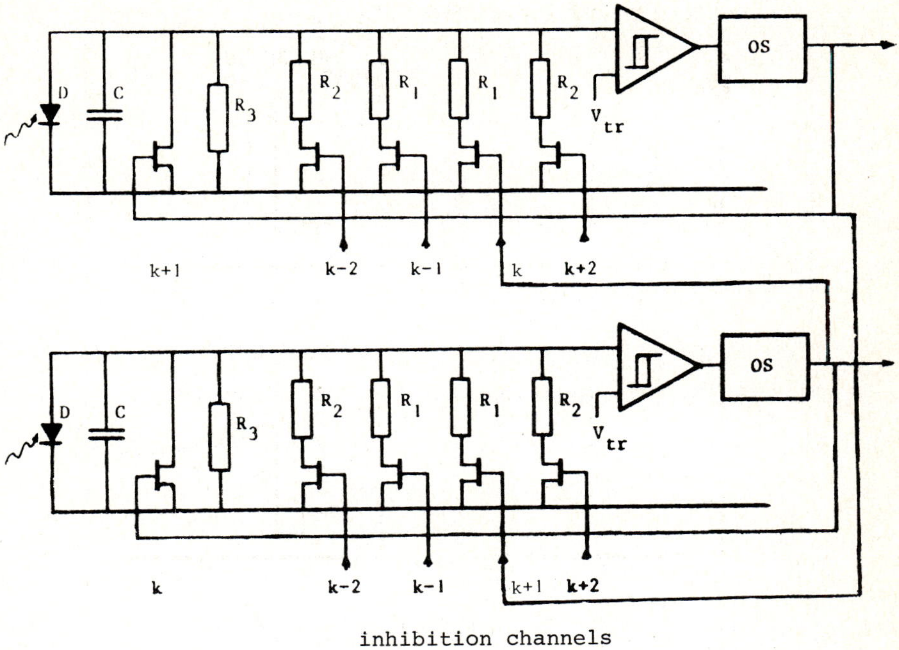

Figure 3
Electronic model of lateral inhibition; identical circuits with interconnecting lines.

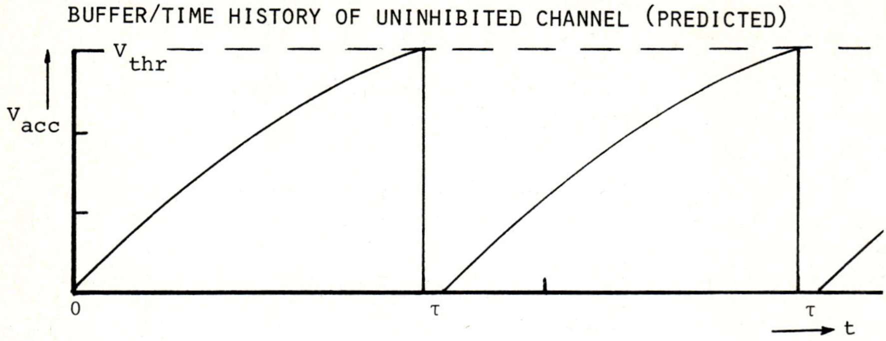

a) Voltage across sensor capacitor C_1, no inhibition.

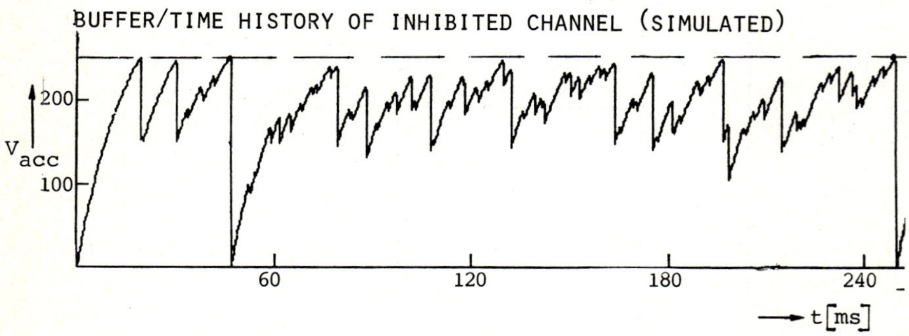

b) Voltage across sensor capacitor C_1, periodic decharging at moments t_1, t_2, t_3, t_4.

Figure 4

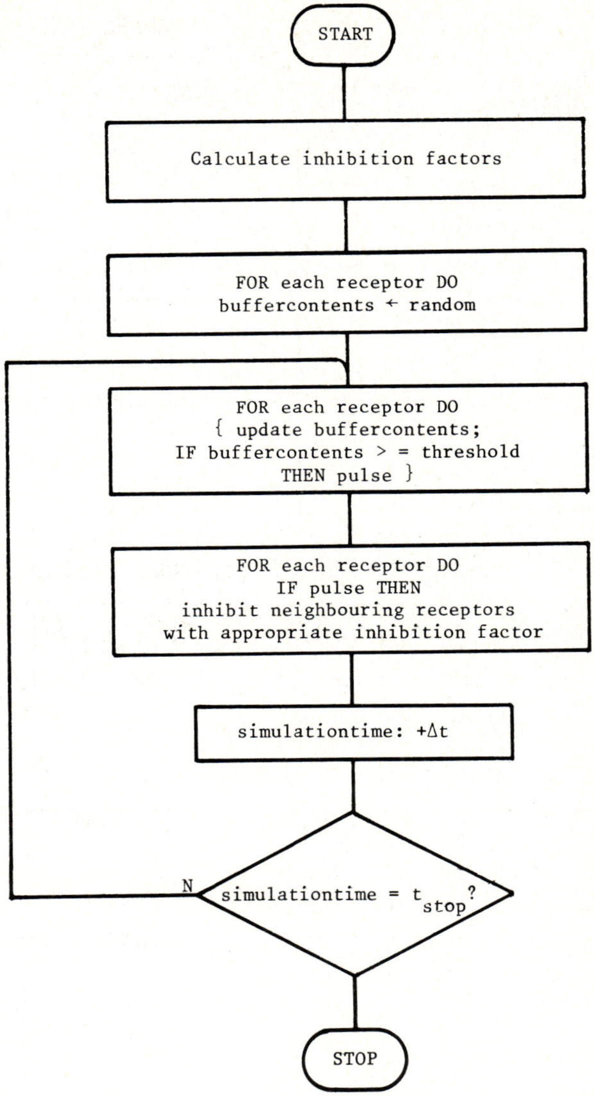

Figure 5
Flow diagram of LIA.

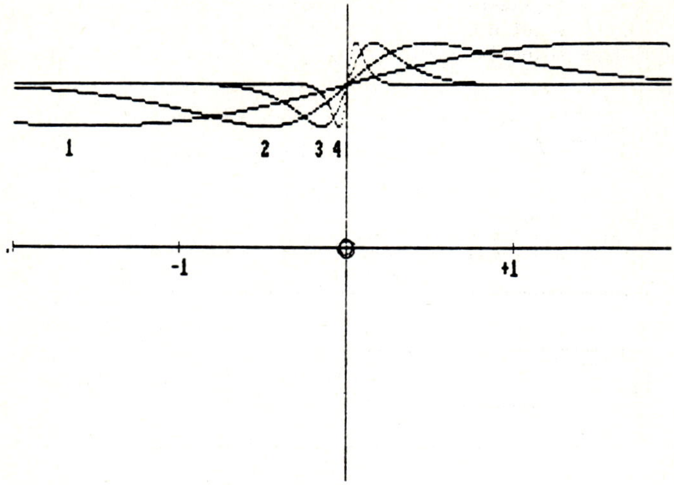

Figure 6
Response to one-dimensional step from E to E+D;
D/E = 10, E(1) = 0.1; E(2) = 1.0; E(3) = 10;
E(4) = 100.

I = intensity
N = total number of input pixels
I(n)= intensity of pixel n

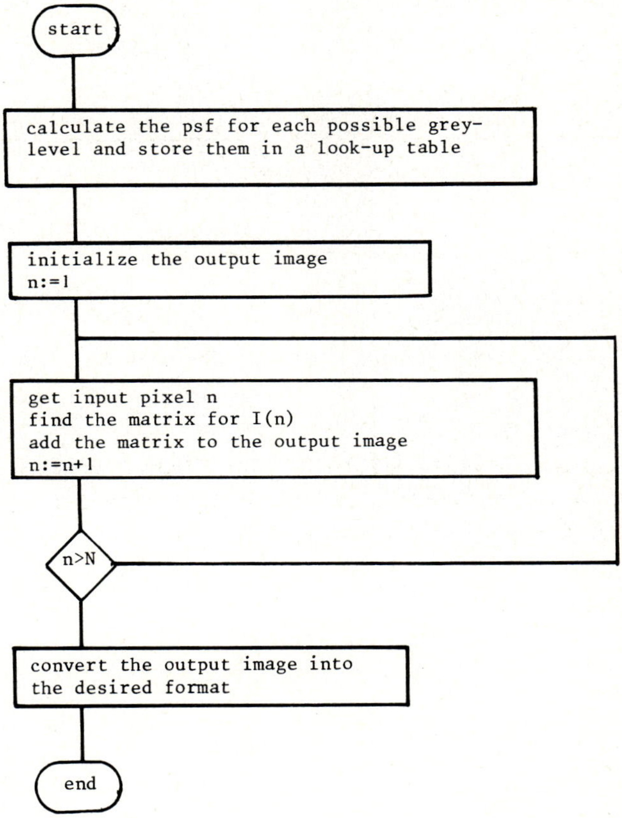

Figure 7
Flow diagram of CVRS.

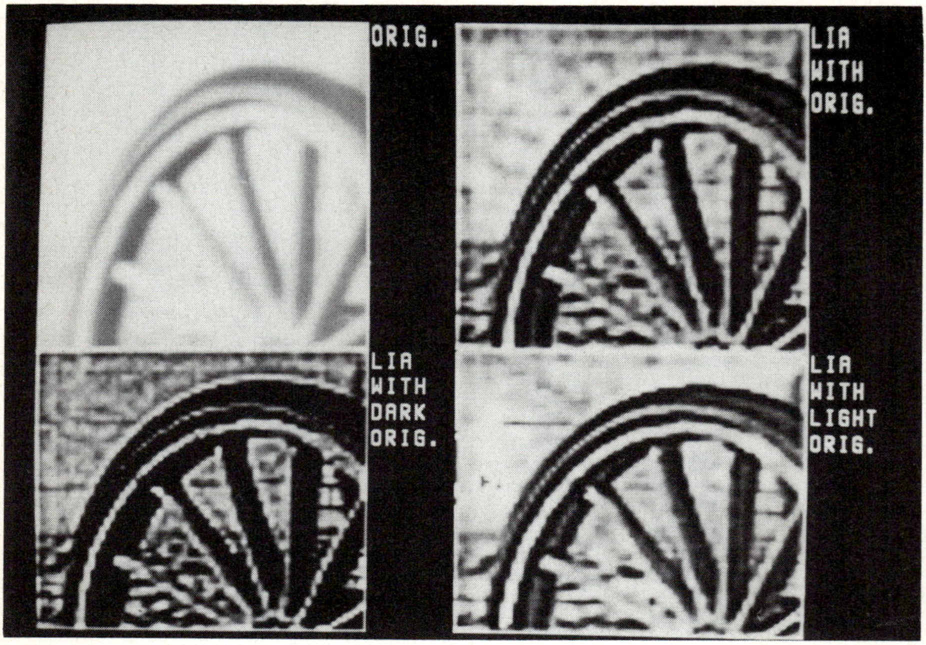

Figure 8
LIA responses to real image.

Figure 9
CVRS responses to real image after histogram equalisation.

DISCUSSION

Verbeek:

It is a nice model you made. I think for practical purposes there is a simple emulation possible. Firstly, the constant volume implies that the zero frequency result is the same and if you think of doing or adding a Laplace filtering then you don't change the results. By adding a Laplacian to a Gaussian you change your bandfilter and get something like your Gaussians. So in practice you could simply do a broad Gaussian filtering and partly compensate that by an intensity weighted Gaussian. In addition, you can simply do this by multiplying the Laplacian image by the intensity.

Bosman:

Yes, but then you are also introducing a nonlinearity by the intensity dependent part.

Verbeek:

That is right. We all know that linear filtering doesn't work.

Bosman:

I agree, it is especially this particular feature that the CVRS, when linearized, becomes lower cutoff at lower luminence which makes the procedure so special. If you use this particular recipe for the point-spread function control, you can adapt it to any type of image formation mechanism. Either it is photon limited and you have the root of N law or it is constant variance noise and you have the N law, etc. You can make this algorithm exactly compensate for the type of noise you have. And that is, I think, not possible in the way you suggested.

Verbeek:

You are right, but it is perhaps cheaper to do it my way.

PATTERN RECOGNITION IN PRACTICE II
E.S. Gelsema and L.N. Kanal (Editors)
Elsevier Science Publishers B.V. (North-Holland), 1986

LOCAL TRANSFORMATIONS TO SIMULATE CRYSTAL GROWTH

Walter Good

Swiss Federal Institute for Snow and Avalanche Research
Weissfluhjoch-Davos
Switzerland

Local transformations in the sense of cellular automata have either a geometrical or computational meaning or may be interpreted in a physical sense. One example of a cellular automaton is given to illustrate the formalism. Further transformations are used to simulate crystal growth. The obtained two-dimensional patterns have some similarity with hexagonal plates and dendritic snow crystals grown in the free atmosphere. In a next step geometrical elements of facetted crystal growth are obtained.

INTRODUCTION

In the free atmosphere the growth of natural snow crystals initiates from nuclei at temperatures between freezing point ($0^{\circ}C$) and the temperature of homogeneous nucleation (-40°). Temperature and supersaturation are the dominant parameters controlling the growth conditions and are responsible for the wealth of shapes occuring in nature. Nakaya [1] gives a range of temperatures between -10 and $-20^{\circ}C$ and a supersaturation of 1.1 to 1.3 for hexagonal plates and dendritic snow crystals. When the temperature is changed, the growing crystals react immediately. The rate of growth is related to the amount of water vapour. According to Hallett [2] the crystallographic surface properties and the release of latent heat control the growth process.

When deposited on the ground the individual snow crystals build the snowpack. It undergoes changes like settlement due to gravity or melt-freeze cycles due to radiation and heat. Changes of the shape of crystals or complexes of crystals occur also at conditions below the freezing point due to the flow of water vapour (metamorphism) [3], [4].

The formation of complex crystals in the atmosphere and in the snow cover are examples of self-organization and of non-equilibrium processes (Langer, 1980 [5]). Efforts have been made to model these phenomena and lately the word 'snowflake' appeared in non-glaciological literature very often. This aspect is not treated in this paper, it is, however, documented by the references [6], [7], [8], and [9].

On the other hand a number of workers have dealt with self-organizing phenomena, cellular automata, self-reproduction, self-similarity and fractals [10], [11]. These procedures are highly impressive for the purpose of representing scale-independent self-similarity and therefore, for simulating growth processes. It is not always easy, however, to gain clarity on the "physical" interpretation of the formalisms [12], [13].

The techniques of this second group are very similar, or, sometimes identical to operations used in image analysis and enhancement and in pattern recognition. The scope of this paper is to use these techniques and to show their potential for simulating complex growth processes.

LOCAL TRANSFORMATIONS IN IMAGE ANALYSIS

Local transformations involving different nearest neighbours are commonplace in image processing. They are used for image filtering and enhancement, for pattern recognition and for stereological operations, like erosion, dilation, and skeletoning (Serra, [14]). Widely used neighbourhoods are the v. Neumann-, pseudohexagonal-, hexagonal- and Moore-coordinate frames with 4, 6, 6 and 8 nearest neighbour points. Normally two states of a point (white/black or void/solid) are permitted and the inner point takes one or the other value according to the state of its nearest neighbours.

In pattern recognition, for instance, the inner and outer part of a homogenous area can be specified and a border separating both sets may be traced (figure 6). Once the confined area is known to the system in the sense of pattern recognition, this information may be used for a geometrical parametrization of the homogenous areas [15]. Table 2 gives a few parameters.

CELLULAR AUTOMATA FORMALISM

In a general way the operations of image processing belong to the group of cellular automata operations, a name that acknowledges v. Neumann's [16] basic work in trying to formalize selfreproducing systems. Perhaps the most legendary cellular automaton is at the base of Conway's "Game of Life" that simulates the growing and the dying of a fictive cell culture [17]. From a less folkloristic point of view, basic work in cellular automata was pioneered, collected and edited by Farmer, Toffoli, and Wolfram in the proceedings of the Los Alamos workshop, 1983 [18].

Cellular automata may be interpreted from a geometrical, computational or a physical point of view. Margolus [19] and Vichniac [20] stress the physical point in the proceedings mentioned above.

Cellular automata are defined via transition rules relating the state of a point P(m) at time step t+1 to the state of itself and of the neighbour points P(m,m-1,...,m+1,...) at the previous time step t. The simple disjunction (exclusive or, XOR) for three neighbours:

$$P(m)|_{t+1} = P(m-1)|_t \veebar P(m)|_t \veebar P(m+1)|_t$$

is a one-dimensional, computational and geometrical example.

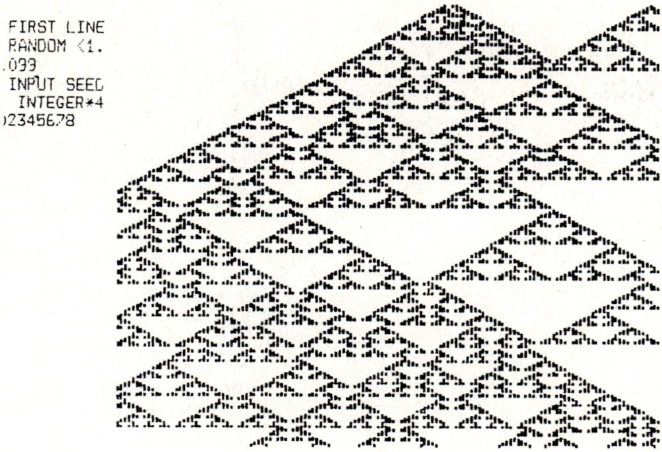

Figure 1. Cellular automaton according to a logical disjunction (XOR) as a linear three-neighbour model

In the explicit notation of Wolfram [13] it writes:

111	110	101	100	011	010	001	000	t
0	0	0	1	0	1	1	0	t+1

and corresponds to rule $2^1 + 2^2 + 2^4 = 22$.

The first line in figure 1, i.e. time step t=1, consists of 4 black dots at randomly selected positions. Each line represents a next time step. The resulting pattern is a good example of self-organization using a rigorously deterministic recipe without any probabilistic assumptions (except for the starting line). The vertical direction from top to bottom being a time axis, the pictorial representation of this XOR function has nothing to do with crystal growth.

CRYSTAL GROWTH

"Snow crystals"

In the next step we introduce a two-dimensional point lattice in which we choose different nearest neighbourhoods. For m the column and n the line indices the transition rules 0 $\rightarrow$ 1 are analogous to the linear example above:

v. Neumann: $$P(n,m)|_{t+1} = P(n-1,m)|_t \veebar P(n,m-1)|_t \veebar P(n,m+1)|_t \veebar P(n+1,m)|_t$$

Figure 2. Natural snow crystals intercepted in the free atmosphere.

pseudo-
hexagonal: $P(n,m)|_{t+1} = P(n-1,m-1)|_{t} \vee P(n-1,m+1)|_{t} \vee P(n,m-2)|_{t} \vee P(n,m+2)|_{t} \vee P(n+1,m-1)|_{t} \vee P(n+1,m+1)|_{t}$

Moore: $P(n,m)|_{t+1} = P(n-1,m-1)|_{t} \vee P(n-1,m)|_{t} \vee P(n-1,m+1)|_{t} \vee P(n,m-1)|_{t} \vee P(n,m+1)|_{t} \vee P(n+1,m-1)|_{t} \vee P(n+1,m)|_{t} \vee P(n+1,m+1)|_{t}$

The results are two-dimensional point arrays. They are to be found in figure 3 together with the respective coordinate frames. The hexagonal shapes show similarities with snow crystals (figure 2) with elements of hexagonal plates and dendritic growth as demonstrated in figure 4. Different time steps are illustrated. A new variety of shapes may be obtained for each imperfection introduced into the "crystal" lattice. In the idealized growth process according to this simple formalism, the probability of a point being added (molecule deposited) is the same at the tip or at the base of a growing dendrite. This is the reason why after a number of growth cycles the resulting shapes are basal plates. From there on new excrecences start at the six corners.

Figure 3. Two-dimensional cellular automata (XOR) in their respective coordinate frames. From left: v.Neumann, Moore, pseudohexagonal, and hexagonal coordinate frame

This oversimplified algorithm is not able to produce "real snow crystals". More complicated selection rules for the cellular automata and physical assumptions in the sense of diffusion-limited aggregation [9], [11] have to be introduced. It is fascinating, however, to see the result of a growth process that takes into account only local selection criteria and local symmetries.

"Snow Metamorphism"

In the snowpack the physical growth conditions are different from the free atmosphere. Depth hoar for instance is built in the dry (subzero) snowpack due to a strong temperature gradient [3], [4] (fig. 5).

We try to simulate a constant temperature gradient producing a vapour pressure difference and a flow of water molecules from the left side to the right side of the samples (pictures). To keep the system in thermal equilibrium, for each molecule deposited on the - left side, one molecule evaporates from the lattice at the right side of the crystal. As in crystal growth, we assume a scale-independent self-similarity [11]. Physically speaking, equivalence is assumed, in the sense of time averages, for the processes involved on the micro- and mesoscale.

Figure 4. Different building steps of "snow crystals" generated by a cellular automaton using a logical disjunction

The starting point of this computer experiment is a number of randomly oriented equilateral triangles of equal size. The variability to be obtained is larger compared to circles. Replacing the simple XOR expression by a few of the 2×2^6 - transition possibilities (table 1) in a hexagonal coordinate frame, the resulting shapes show structural elements of depth hoar (figures 5, 6). Angles of 120° between facets and crystallographic stages build up while the initial forms disappear and the structures grow to the left. The shift to the left may be seen in table 2, where the "particle" in the upper left corner is listed. The unbalance of evaporation and deposition corresponds to a ratio of 0.83.

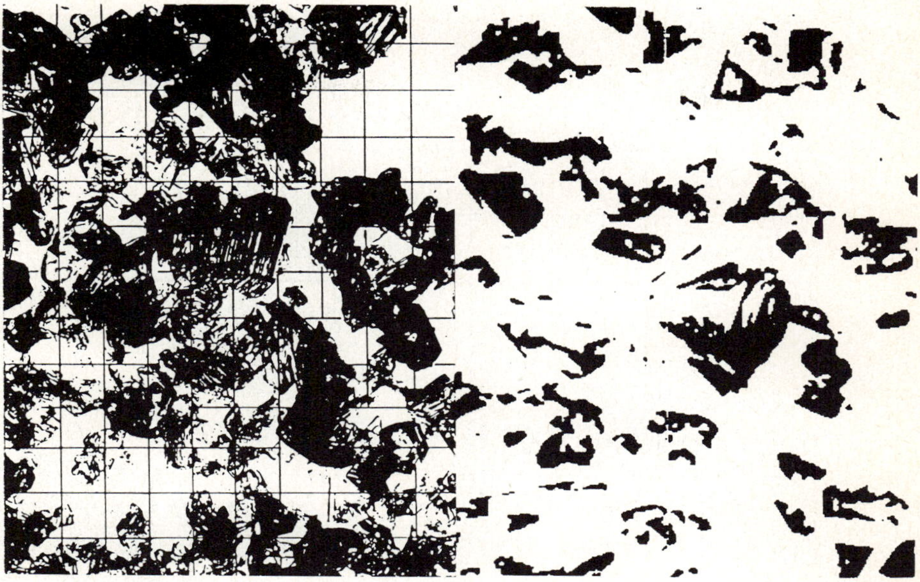

Figure 5. Natural depth hoar on a 2-mm grid (a), thin section in depth hoar (b) (linear extension 512 pixels = 10 mm)

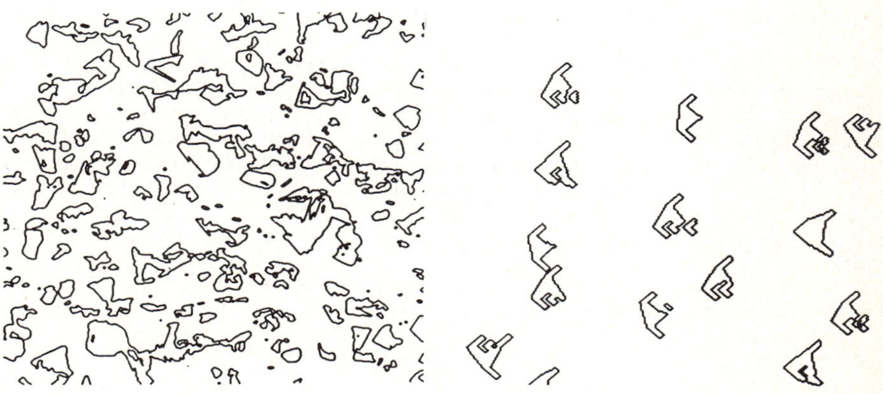

Figure 6. Pattern recognition of depth hoar (a) and building elements (b) (see table 2)

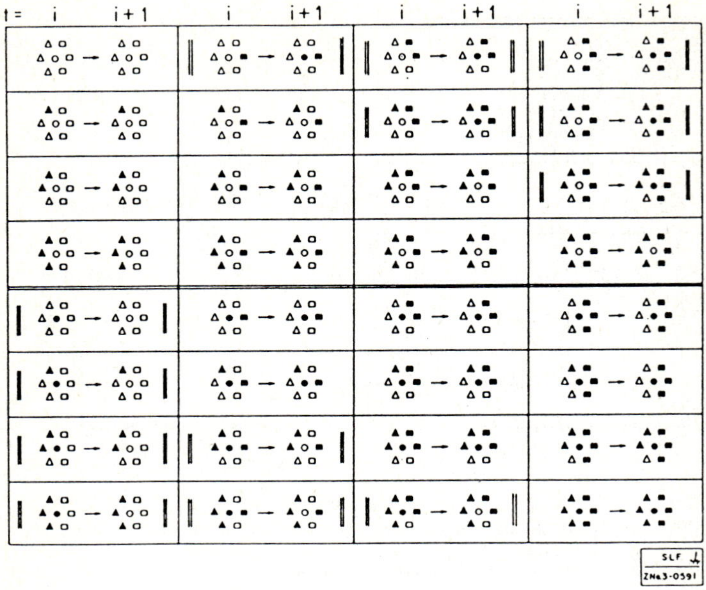

Table 1. Table of simple transitions void/solid and solid/void in a hexagonal coordinate frame. Sites where changes occur are emphasized with double bars

PARAMETRIZATION OF SHAPES

The transformation for finding homogenous inner points using a v. Neumann coordinate frame works with a logical AND - operation. The figure 6 shows the border points (first outer, inhomogeneous points). The delimited area is evaluated yielding a number of pattern recognition parameters [21]. Table 2 compares the different stages the triangles go through and the natural depth hoar crystals of figure 5.

CONCLUSION

Physical reality is far from the simple world of two-dimensional local transformations as outlined here. The concept of reducing interactions to the smallest elementary cells containing the nearest neighbours only, however, is fascinating and is complementary to the view of nature as seen through the optics of linear (and non-linear) differential equations. Cellular automata algorithms give a discrete and different approach of modelling and of "understanding" self-organizing, non-equilibrium phenomena.

Parameter / Sample	X	Y	N	Σc_i	$\bar{c}$	σ_c	$\measuredangle(X_1,X)$	r_-/r_+
	Center of gravity of upper left "particle"		Number	Border length			Orientation	concave/ convex
natural depth hoar (red. to D = 0.051)			21	1852	90.7	116.7	97.0	0.305
Triangles step t = 0	93.5	54.1	25	1534	60.6	2.6	70.7	0.258
Triangles step t = 3	87.2	53.4	27	2075	75.8	19.4	87.1	0.271
Triangles step t = 6	80.1	53.2	37	2879	82.4	38.3	87.6	0.194

Table 2. Pattern recognition parameters. Note the shift of the center of mass and the reorientation of the first particle in the upper left corner

REFERENCES:

[1] Nakaya, U., Snow Crystals: Natural and Artifical (Harvard Univ. Press, Harvard, 1954)

[2] Hallett, J., How Snow Crystals Grow, American Scientist, 72 6 (1984) pp. 582-589

[3] de Quervain, M.R., On Metamorphism and Hardening of Snow under Constant Pressure and Temperature Gradient, IAHS-AIHS publ. 46 (1958) pp. 225-239

[4] Colbeck, S.C., Theory of Metamorphism of Dry Snow, J. of Geophys.Res. 88 C9 (1983) pp. 5472-5482

[5] Langer, J.S., Instabilities and pattern formation in crystal growth, Rev. of Mod. Phys. 52 1 (1980) pp. 1-28

[6] Brower R.C., Kessler D.A., Koplik, J., Levine, H., Geometrical models of interface evolution, Phys. Rev. A 29 3 (1984) pp. 1335-1342

[7] Ben-Jacob, E., Goldenfeld, N., Langer, J.S., Schön, G., Boundary-layer model of pattern formation in solidification, Phys. Rev. A 29 1 (1984) pp. 330-340

[8] Kessler, D.A., Koplik, J., Levine, H., Numerical simulation of two-dimensional snowflake growth, Phys. Rev. A 30 5 (1984) pp. 2820-2823

[9] Vicsek, T., Pattern Formation in Diffusion-Limited Aggregation, Phys. Rev. Let. 53 24 (1984) pp. 2281-2282

[10] Mandelbrot, B.B., The Fractal Geometry of Nature (Freeman and Company, New York, 1983)

[11] Sander, L.M., Theory of Fractal Growth Processes, in: Family F., Landau, D.P. (eds.), Kinetics of Aggregation and Gelation (North-Holland, Amsterdam, 1984)

[12] Schulmann, L.S., Seiden, P.E., Statistical Mechanics of a Dynamical System Based on Conway's Game of Life, J. of Stat. Phys. 19 (1978) pp. 293-314

[13] Wolfram, S., Statistical mechanics of cellular automata, Rev. of Mod. Phys. 55 3 (1983) pp. 601-644

[14] Serra, J., Image Analysis and Mathematical Morphology (Academic Press, London, New York, 1982)

[15] Crettol, R., Good, W., MSTER - Ein Programm zur Bestimmung von strukturellen Parametern mittels Computer-kompatiblen Abbildungen von Schneedünnschnitten, Int. Report 536 Swiss Federal Institute for Snow and Avalanche Research, Weissfluhjoch-Davos (1974)

[16] v.Neumann, J., Theory of Self-Reproducing Automata, in: Burks, A.W. (ed.) (Univ. of Ill. Press, Urbana, 1966)

[17] Hayes, B., Computer recreations: The Cellular Automaton Offers a Model of the World and a Model unto Itself, Sci.Am. 250 3 (1984) pp. 10-16

[18] Farmer, D., Toffoli, T. Wolfram, S. (eds.), Cellular Automata, Proceedings of an Interdisciplinary Workshop, Los Alamos, New Mexico, March 7-11, 1983: Physica D 10D (1984)

[19] Margolus, N., Physics-Like Models of Computation, in [18] : pp. 81-95

[20] Vichniac, G.Y., Simulating Physics with Cellular Automata, in [18] : pp. 96-116

[21] Good, W., Structural Investigation of Snow, a Comparision of Different Parameter Sets, in: Gelsema, E.S., Kanal, L.N. (eds.), Pattern Recognition in Practice (North-Holland, Amsterdam, 1980)

PATTERN RECOGNITION IN PRACTICE II
E.S. Gelsema and L.N. Kanal (Editors)
Elsevier Science Publishers B.V. (North-Holland), 1986

PHOTOGRAMMETRIC STANDARD METHODS AND DIGITAL IMAGE MATCHING TECHNIQUES FOR HIGH PRECISION SURFACE MEASUREMENTS

Wolfgang Förstner and Alfred Pertl

Institute for Photogrammetry
University of Stuttgart

Photogrammetry is a flexible 3D-measuring technique based on images of the object. Its relative precision, ranging from 1:30 000 to 1:300 000, is due to the high quality of the hardware and the simultaneous treatment of all geometric information in a joint least squares estimation. The interactive measuring process allows a stepwise integration of algorithms from pattern recognition to support or replace manual tasks. A new image matching procedure has been developed and implemented on an analytical measuring device for high precision surface measurements. The paper discusses the methodology of analytical photogrammetry, the theoretical accuracy of stereopsy and the features of the image matching system.

0. INTRODUCTION

The paper describes a development of integrating digital image matching techniques into photogrammetric hard- and software for semiautomatic measurements of points and surfaces in industry and cartography.

Photogrammetry is a versatile tool for recovering 3D-information from images of an object. It has its main application in topographic mapping. But it is used to advantage also in close range applications such as in industry, medicine, biology, architecture, archaeology or even microscopy (Karara 1979, Atkinson 1980). This is due to several specific features, e. g. the short time for storing the information, the photos being an excellent document or the ability to remeasure even if the object has changed or is not available anymore.

The analysis or interpretation of the images is performed by an operator. This concerns the selection of points, line following operations and the classification of objects. The interpretation is heavily supported by the use of overlapping images, which the visual system can easily fuse to form a virtual small scale model. Standard photogrammetric instruments therefore directly provide 3D-information in object space, which often simultaneously is projected on a plane and mapped onto a plotter.

On the other hand the precision of this process is high enough that photogrammetry is an alternative measuring technique, e.g. for the densification of geodetic networks (Förstner 1985) or deformation monitoring (Fraser 1984). The relative precision ranges from 1:30 000 for single image pairs to 1:300 000 for large image mosaics (>100 images, say). This precision is due to 1) the quality of the photographic films, 2) the stability and inherent precision of the camera and the measuring devices and 3) the refinement of the mathematical, especially the geometric, model of the whole measuring process. This forms the basis for a simultaneous least squares estimation of the camera stations and the object points. The economy of the method especially relies on the ability of the human operator a) to control the measuring procedure and b) to fuse the content of image pairs stereoscopically and on the availability of powerful computer programs for solving the estimation problem.

Early attempts to replace the photographic film by digital images and the human stereopsy by digital image correlation, though successful for differential rectification of image pairs, only reached limited accuracy (cf. Förstner 1984). Theoretical studies, however, showed that the precision inherent in the images is not really exploited by most of the systems but would allow accuracies which are at least as good as human stereopsy. Recently, based on a simple model, the dependence of the precision (standard deviation) on different system parameters such as the patch size, the texture of the object, the signal to noise ratio, the preprocessing of the degree of distortion has been investigated. The results can be used for increasing the adaptility and for providing selfdiagnosis of an image matching algorithm. They also show that a robust and reliable method for finding corresponding points is indispensable in order to obtain good approximate values not only for the parallaxes but also for the relative geometric distortion between the images.

A new image matching procedure has been developed which is based on these studies. A photogrammetric standard measuring device (Zeiss Planicomp C 100) has been complemented with two video solid state cameras which scan a small (5×5 mm^2) patch of the photographic images. The numerical solution first selects corresponding points in the two patches using a robust estimation procedure and then matches the selected points by a geometric linear transformation using a least squares fit.

The first section of the paper discusses the methodology of analytical (in contrast to analog) photogrammetry, which only partly can be extracted from photogrammetric textbooks. Section 2 deals with the theoretical accuracy of stereoscopy. Some results with the image matching procedure are provided in section 3.

1. METHODOLOGY OF ANALYTICAL PHOTOGRAMMETRY

The geometric model of photogrammetry is that of the pin-hole camera. It is assumed that the ray from the object point, through the projection centre yielding the image point is a straight line. The image, analog (photo) or digital (video), preserves the geometry of the bundle of rays during exposition. Thus <u>angles</u> are measured. If the camera is calibrated and its orientation in space is <u>known</u> or can be reconstructed, <u>directions</u> can be derived. In order to determine <u>3D-positions</u> some <u>a priori information on the object (shape, size, distance, type of surface, geometry of structured light</u> etc.) and/or one or more <u>additional images</u> from a position being different with respect to the object <u>have to be available</u>.

In this context a moving camera observing a stable object and a moving object observed by a fixed camera are obviously equivalent; the only difference may be the coordinate system which is best suited to describe the relative movement. The analysis of a vehicle passing a video camera thus may use the same mathematical model for reconstruction as the analysis of a strip of aerial photos for mapping purposes. Moreover, also the case of observing several moving objects with one, two ore more cameras is included in the general model of aerial triangulation, where the number, orientation and mutual coverage of the images is arbitrary and additional information (constraints, observations) in object space or about the orientation of the cameras may be available.

The next subsections provide the basic principles of deriving 3D-coordinates from multiple images, some information on quality control, the principles of the measuring process and general results on the accuracy which can be achieved with classical methods.

1.1 Cameras and Calibration

The aim of the calibration is the reconstruction of the geometry of the bundle of rays up to adegree which is sufficient for a specific task. It therefore depends on the geometric properties of the camera and the required precision. Main calibration parameters are the focal length or principle distance $c=\overline{PS}$ (cf. fig. 1) and the position of the principal point P, where PS stands orthogonal on the image plane. The coordinates of the principal point are normally given in the image coordinate system (x, y), which is defined by the (also calibrated) fiducial marks (F_i) or a reseau grid, which both form a connection between the camera body and the film during exposure. In addition also the local deviations of the bundle from the ideal perspective model, due to lens distortion and film unflatness have to be considered. Depending on the stability of these parameters one basically distinguishes two types of cameras: metric cameras are fabricated with an accuracy of about $\pm$ 20 μm, whereas in non-metric cameras and amateur cameras the deviations from the perspective model may vary up to 1 mm or more (cf. Atkinson 1980, Brown 1971). The use of metric cameras and of proper calibration ($\pm$ 2-5 μm) is indispensable for high precision application.

Fig. 1
Geometric model used in photogrammetry

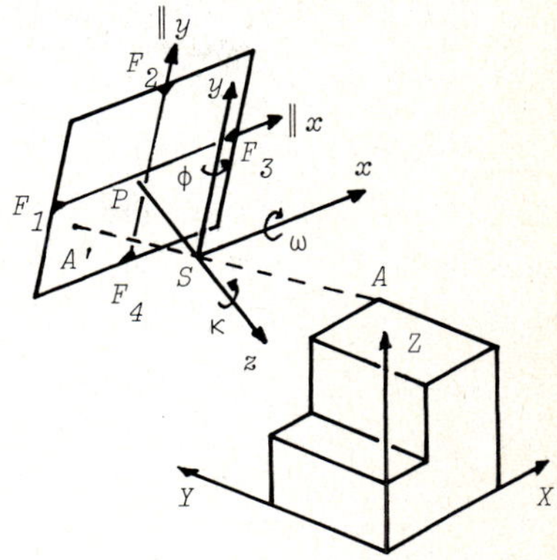

1.2 Geometric Relations

1.2.1 Relative Orientation of Multiple Images

We now assume that the coordinates x_{ij} and y_{ij} of several object points A_{ij} ($i=1,\ldots,n_i$) which may change position from exposure to exposure j ($j=1,\ldots,n_j$) are measured in n_j images. The orientation of each image is given by the position (X_{oj}, Y_{oj}, Z_{oj}) of its projection centre referring to the object space coordinate system (X, Y, Z) and by the rotation matrix $R_j(\omega_j,\phi_j,\kappa_j)$ transferring the object space coordinates system into the camera system (x,y,z) and depending on 3 rotational angles ω, ϕ and κ. The geometric model then reads as

$$\begin{pmatrix} x_{ij} - x_{Pj} \\ y_{ij} - y_{Pj} \\ - c_j \end{pmatrix} = \lambda_{ij} R_{ij}(\omega_j, \phi_j, \kappa_j) \begin{pmatrix} X_{ij} - X_{oj} \\ Y_{ij} - Y_{oj} \\ Z_{ij} - Z_{oj} \end{pmatrix} \quad \begin{matrix} i=1,\ldots,n_i \\ j=1,\ldots,n_j \end{matrix} \tag{1}$$

reflecting the collinearity of the object point (X_{ij}, Y_{ij}, Z_{ij}), the projection centre and the image point. The individual scale parameter λ_{ij} can be eliminated yielding the classical form of the collinearity equations:

$$\begin{aligned} x_{ij} &= x_{Pj} - c_j \frac{r_{11}(X_{ij}-X_{oj}) + r_{12}(Y_{ij}-Y_{oj}) + r_{13}(Z_{ij}-Z_{oj})}{r_{31}(X_{ij}-X_{oj}) + r_{32}(Y_{ij}-Y_{oj}) + r_{33}(Z_{ij}-Z_{oj})} \\ y_{ij} &= y_{Pj} - c_j \frac{r_{21}(X_{ij}-X_{oj}) + r_{22}(Y_{ij}-Y_{oj}) + r_{23}(Z_{ij}-Z_{oj})}{r_{31}(X_{ij}-X_{oj}) + r_{32}(Y_{ij}-Y_{oj}) + r_{33}(Z_{ij}-Z_{oj})} \end{aligned} \tag{2}$$

As there are only two observed values for 3 unknown coordinates and in addition unknown orientation parameters per image (position, rotation, possibly calibration parameters), one needs constraints to be able to solve for the unknowns.

In photogrammetry the position of the object is assumed to be stable during flight mission: $(X_{ij},Y_{ij},Z_{ij}) \equiv (X_i,Y_i,Z_i)$. Multiple exposures from different positions then enable to reconstruct the form of the point field. Image sequences can be handled similar. Eqs.(2) are the same, if the coordinate system (X,Y,Z) is connected to the moving object. For a fixed camera, only 6 orientation parameters are unknown, which is compensated by adding constraints $(X_{ij},Y_{ij},Z_{ij})' = R_{j,j-1}(X_{ij-1},Y_{ij-1},Z_{ij-1})'$ reflecting the form invariance of the moving object and the rotation matrices being unknown.

1.2.2 Absolute Orientation of Multiple Images

Eqs. (2) only provide information in the relative position between objects and camera stations. Specifically no information is available about position, orientation and scale of the point field. Only angular information is used. Additional observations or constraints to define the absolute orientation or at least the scale can be:

- coordinates of points in object space
- position and/or orientation of the camera during exposure
- distances in object space, if only the form of the object or the relative movement is required. In this case some arbitrary but convenient values can be given to a set of 6 coordinates or other unknowns.

1.3 Simultaneous Solution for the Unknown Parameters

The nonlinear relations between the observed values and the unknown parameters can be linearized and be brought into the form of a linear Gauß-Markov-Model (cf. Mikhail 1976), possibly with (linear) constraints between the unknowns, which will not be discussed further. The observations, collected in the (nx1)-vector l are treated as realizations of stochastical variables $\underline{l}$. Their expected value $E(\underline{l})$ linearily depends on the unknowns, collected in the (ux1)-vector x

$$E(\underline{l}) = A\,x \qquad \text{or} \qquad \underline{l} = A\,\underline{\hat{x}} + \underline{\hat{\varepsilon}} \tag{3}$$

where the (nxu)-matrix A contains the partial derivatives of eq. (2) with respect to the unknowns and of other relations between the observations and the unknowns. $\underline{\hat{x}}$ and $\underline{\hat{\varepsilon}}$ are estimates for the unknowns and the residuals. The precision of the observations is collected in the dispersion- or covariance matrix

$$D(\underline{l}) = C = \sigma_o^2\, W^{-1} \tag{4}$$

which can be derived from variances $\sigma_i^2 = C_{ii}$ and possibly covariances or from weights $w_i = W_{ii}$ of the measurements. σ_o^2 is an unknown variance factor.

Eqs. (3) and (4) can be solved for the unknowns from the normal equations

$$A'\,W\,A\,\underline{\hat{x}} = A'\,W\,\underline{l} \tag{5}$$

The solution has several optimum properties: It is the general least squares solution, the best linear unbiased estimator and the Maximum-Likelihood estimator in case the observations are assumed to be normally distributed. The statistical interpretation of the solution is preferred, as it allows the evaluation of the estimation process (cf. Koch 1980, McGillem/Svedlov 1976, 1977). The covariance matrix of the estimate $\underline{\hat{x}}$ is given by

$$C_{xx} = \sigma_o^2\ (A'\,W\,A)^{-1} \tag{6}$$

where the variance factor can be replaced by its estimate (using eq. (3))

$$\underline{\hat{\sigma}}_o^2 = \underline{\hat{\varepsilon}}'\,W\,\underline{\hat{\varepsilon}}\,/\,r\,, \qquad r = n - u \tag{7}$$

in which $r = n - u$ is the redundancy of the system.

1.4 Discussion

1.4.1 Special cases

The approach is general enough to cover large fields of application. On the other hand it allows specializations which are of practical value:

a.) <u>Spatial resection:</u> Form and size of an object are given by several points. Relative position and orientation of the object can be derived from one image. This requires at least 3 points if the camera is calibrated, 4 points, if only the focal length is known (cf. example in sect. 1.7).

b.) <u>Relative and absolute orientation of a stereopair:</u> The determination of the 12 parameters for the two camera stations can be split into the relative orientation of the two images (5 parameters) leading to a <u>model</u> of the object and subsequent absolute orientation based on object coordinates (7 parameters including scale). The first step needs 5 common points in the images, the second 3 points. This two step procedure is very common in photogrammetry as most measurements are performed in the stereo model.

c.) <u>Strip formation:</u> An image sequence where adjacent images have enough points in common, forms a strip and can be simultaneously oriented using the above procedure. In photogrammetry nonadjacent images usually have no points in common. This leads to a weak geometry and requires enough control points in object space. Also additional observations of the camera orientation parameters can be used, such as statoscope data or measurements from inertial systems or the global positioning system (Ackermann 1984). On the other hand the smoothness of the sensor- and/or object-path may be achieved by assuming a simple 2nd-order Markov-Model, specifically the curvature of the path to be a white noise process (Ebner 1976, cf. also Grimson 1981). Additional observations may then have the form

$$\underline{c} = \underline{\hat{x}}_{j-1} - 2\underline{\hat{x}}_j + \underline{\hat{x}}_{j+1} + \underline{\hat{\varepsilon}}_j \qquad \sigma_c^2 \tag{8}$$

where $\hat{x}_j$ are orientation parameters of subsequent images. The value of the curvature is assumed to be zero and to have variance σ_c^2. Eq. (8) can be integrated into eq. (3) and allows an estimation of the path of a single or of even several objects observed from a moving camera.

1.4.2 Numerical Considerations

The direct solution of the system has several attractive numerical features:

a.) Approximate values have only to be known up to about 30 % in position or 20° in orientation. 3 iterations are sufficient to achieve convergence, if the geometry is not too weak.

b.) The normal equations eq. (5) can be set up directly, without first forming the A-matrix, provided the observations are assumed to be uncorrelated.

c.) In photogrammetry a direct solution according to Gauß or Cholesky is prefered as the computing time is predictable in contrast to iterative (e.g. conjugate gradient) methods. This is due to the varying condition of the normal equation matrix. Main reason for a direct solution, however, is the availability of the covariance matrix of the unknowns and the residuals, which are needed for subsequent statistical tests.

d.) Recursive estimation of the parameters is possible, and leads to the classical formulas of the Kalman-Filter, which are used for real time applications (cf. Gelb 1974, Mikhail 1976).

e.) Additional parameters can be introduced to compensate for unknown systematic effects. This type of selfcalibration has proven to significantly improve the results (Ackermann 1980).

f.) The normal equation matrices in general are sparse Proper ordering of the unknowns leads to banded, or banded bordered systems. Special solution algorithms exploiting this property may be used (band-, profile- or sparsetechniques; cf. George 1973, Schek et. al. 1976, Steidler 1980).

g.) As a consequence also very large systems with several hundred or even thousand images can be handled (cf. Brown 1974, Klein 1980). There also exist quite a number of programs which are developed for close range applications with emphasis on allowing all kinds of constraints and observations (e.g. Kager/Kraus 1976, Brown 1982, Kruck 1983, Fuchs/Leberl 1984, Müller/Stephani 1984, Wester-Ebbinghaus 1984).

h.) The computing time per image and iteration in a large mosaic is in the order of 5 seconds on a VAX 11/780, depending on the structure of the mosaic and the degree of optimization. For strips, however, it is about a factor 20 to 100 faster.

1.5 Quality Control

Quality control in large systems is indispensable especially if high precision is required and one has to guarantee for the result. The following quality measures are standard in geodesy and photogrammetry. They concern the design of the experiment and the adequateness of the mathematical model.

The design of the experiment only depends on the matrices A and C in eqs. (3) and (4). Their coefficients do not depend on the actual observations. Thus the criteria for evaluating the design can be used for planning. There are three aspects to be considered:

1. The precision of the result is represented by the covariance matrix eq. (6) of the parameters, possibly only a subset is needed. The standard deviations σ_x measure the determinability of the parameters. If a required precision of the result can be described by a covariance matrix H_{xx}, the deviation of the actual covarinace matrix from H_{xx} can be evaluated using the eigenvalues of $C_{xx} H_{xx}^{-1}$, which should be near to one (cf. Bouloucos et al. 1984).
2. The controllability of the observations with respect to blunders is represented by the contribution r_i, the redundancy number, of each observation l_i to the total redundancy r of the system.The redundancy numbers should be of the same order. Small values (<0.1, say) indicate, that errors in the observations do not really show in the residuals, thus may not be detected by a statistical test (cf. Förstner 1985c).
3. The sensitivity of the result can be described by the effect of errors in the mathematical model which are not detectable by a statistical test. Such errors can be of systematic nature (e.g. unproper calibration, refraction) of blunders (e.g. due to incorrect correspondencies). For each type one can derive an upper bound $\bar{\delta}\cdot\sigma_x$ for the effect on the parameters (cf. Förstner 1980). The factors $\bar{\delta}$ should be smaller than 3 or 4, but may easily reach values of 10 or more, which indicates a high sensitivity of the design with respect to model errors due to improper planning of the experiment.

The adequateness of the mathematical model can be checked by statistical tests:

1. The global test of $\hat{\sigma}_o^2$ versus the a priori value indicates whether model errors have to be expected. If the variance factor σ_0^2 is not known and no model errors are present, $\hat{\sigma}_o^2 P^{-1}$ gives a reliable estimate for the precision of the observations. If the weight ratio between individual groups of observations is not known, individual estimates can be used to improve the dispersion matrix (cf. Förstner 1985b).This procedure can also be applied to estimate the variance of the smoothness constraints eq. (8).
2. The test of individual observations using standardized residuals $\hat{\varepsilon}_i/\sigma(\hat{\varepsilon}_i)$ is very effective to detect blunders . If the controllability of the observations is sufficient, robust methods are very useful too (Huber 1981, cf. Klein/Förstner 1984).
3. The effect of individual observations onto the result can be used to prove or disprove the quality of the actual result. It gives a clear indication whether it is worthwile to eliminate erroneous observations in case the standardized residuals do not.

The above mentioned quality criteria provide a sort of self control of the system which may be used to guide subsequent steps .

1.6 Measuring Process

The previous sections refer to all kind of 3D-point determination procedures using images, and are nearly independent of the actual measuring process. The main components of photogrammetric analytical measuring device are shown in fig. 2. The viewer presents two image patches (about 2 by 2 cm^2) to the operator. After relative orientation of the two images, which is only done numerically, not physically, the operator can control the positions of the two image carriers using hand wheels (X,Y) and a foot disk (Z) working in the virtual model of the object. The perspective transformations eq. (2) and the movements of the image carriers (x_1,y_1,x_2,y_2) are performed

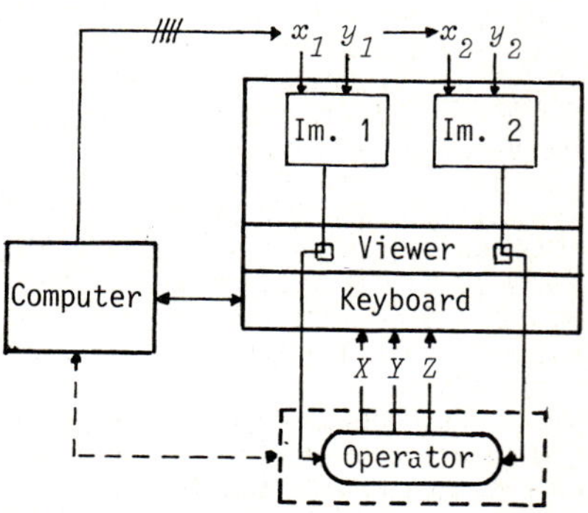

Fig. 2 Main components of an analytical measuring device (dashed: extensions for automatic measuring process)
(cf. Schwidefsky/Ackermann 1976)

in real time (30-50 Hz) guaranteeing no vertical parallaxes in the whole model area. Selection of special programs, point numbering etc. is done using the keyboard or a terminal (not shown). The advantages of this kind of instrument are manifold (cf. Konecny/Lehmann 1984):

a. All kind of imagery can be handled(metric or non-metric, cameras with fish-eye objectives, line scanner imagery etc.). This is due to the capability to compensate for any systematic errors in real time.
b. The precision is only limited by the film, the control of the image carriers and the mathematical model.
c. Parts of the measuring process can be automated, e.g. orientation of images, determination of approximate values for point positions, guiding the recording of surface measurements etc.
d. The difficult tasks, especially the interpretation of the image content, are left to the operator, allowing a smooth interaction.

Obviously the separation of tasks c) and d) is not fixed and developments in image processing, pattern recognition and artificial intelligence will support or replace the actions of the operator, provided the instrument is supplied with adequate digital cameras. The concept of the analytical measuring device is flexible enough to be able to integrate these developments in an evolutionary way. One example is given in section 3.

1.7 Quality of Photogrammetric Results

The quality of photogrammetrically determined 3D-coordinates and orientations mainly depend on the following parameters:

1. Photogrammetric measuring precision: Using metric cameras, stable films and adequate measuring devices the overall precision of the image coordinates range between 10 µm and about 2 µm standard deviation (The internal precision is in the order of 1 µm). Assuming a format of 23 cm x 23 cm (aerial images) this corresponds to a relative precision between 5 and about $1 \cdot 10^{-5}$. 10 µm can easily be reached, whereas for achieving 2 µm it is necessary to apply additional calibration (e.g. selfcalibration, cf. Klein 1980). For non-metric cameras the calibration is decisive.
2. Image scale: The precision of the image coordinates is practically independent of the image scale. Thus the precision in object space essentially is proportional to the distance, unless the relative movement between object and camera leads to image blur.
3. Control point accuracy: The variance of the control points has to be added. This is a good approximation for all points in the area between the control points and even holds for very large image mosaics which might be necessary to cover large objects. Then relative accuracies better than 10^{-5} can be reached (cf. Brown 1974, Förstner 1985a) Extrapolation outside the area of the control points should be avoided.
4. Viewing angle: The precision of position and distance decreases with the distance of the object from the camera, if the viewing angle is constant. If the base between two cameras is kept constant the standard deviations even increase with the square of the distance.
5. Overlap: Multiple overlap of course results in a higher precision. But what is more important it is necessary to achieve a higher controllability. Three rays are necessary to get full control. If a localization of individual gross errors is required , 4 or more rays per image point are necessary (cf. Förstner 1985c). For camera or object orientation one should at least use 5 points per image. In all cases groups of 2 or more points lead to high reliable results.

Example : The general dependencies of the quality criteria on the different parameters can be observed in the following simple example. The position (X,Y,Z) and the orientation angles (ω,ϕ,κ) of an object can be derived from a single image (spatial resection), if the relative position of some (5) points on the object and the orientation of the camera in space are known. The main parameters are the measuring accuracy (e.g. half a pixel, $\sigma_x=\sigma_y=10\ \mu m$, say), the focal length $(c=0.15\ m)$, the distance to the object $(d=3\ m)$ and the side of the square formed by the points $(2e=1\ m)$. Assuming the image and the object plane to be parallel, the general expressions for the standard deviations derived by analytical inversion of the normal equation matrix are:

$$\sigma_X=\sigma_Y=\frac{1}{\sqrt{5}}\, d\, \frac{\sigma_o}{c},\quad \sigma_Z=\frac{1}{\sqrt{8}}\, \frac{d}{e}\, d\, \frac{\sigma_o}{c},$$

$$\sigma_\omega=\sigma_\phi=\frac{1}{2}\left(\frac{d}{e}\right)^2 \frac{\sigma_o}{c},\quad \sigma_\kappa=\frac{1}{\sqrt{8}}\, \frac{d}{e}\, \frac{\sigma_o}{c}$$

Fig.3 Resection for orientation of an object

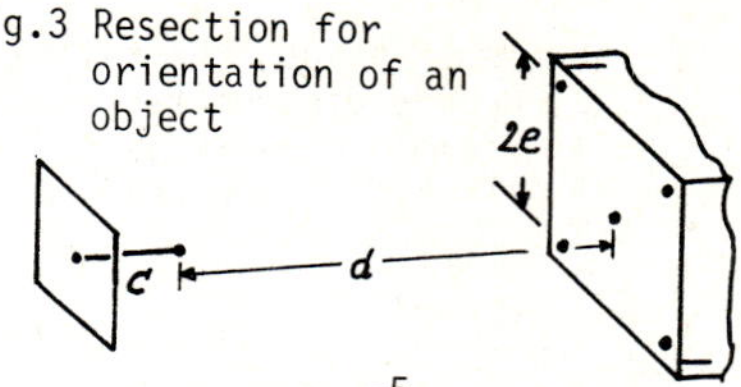

($e/d = \tan\alpha, \alpha$ = viewing angle; σ_o/c = relative precision = $7 \cdot 10^{-5}$). In our special case we obtain $\sigma_X = \sigma_Y = 0.2$ mm, $\sigma_Z = 0.8$ mm, $\sigma_\omega = \sigma_\phi = 0.14°$, $\sigma_\kappa = 0.016°$. The redundancy is nearly evenly distributed over the 10 observations yielding redundancy numbers of about 0.4. The influence of nondetectable blunders onto the orientation parameters is less than 6 times their standard deviation, which is quite satisfactory. ■

Summarizing, this section tried to sketch the specific features of analytical photogrammetry, quality control and operator guidance being the most important ones. Further automation of the procedure has either to be based on methods, whose theoretical base is suited to be integrated onto the existing concept or has to start from a conceptionally different point of view, but then has to prove that it yields qualitativly comparable results. In analytical photogrammetry there are three problems which might be automated: interpretation or image analysis, control of the procedure and stereopsy. The last seems to be the only one which under not too narrow restrictions can be expected to be economically realizable in the next future. There are quite some attempts to understand how human stereopsy works. However, classical digital image correlation is theoretically founded best and promises to yield results of comparable precision to human parallax measurements. Its features are discussed now.

2. QUALITY OF DIGITAL CORRELATION

2.1 Overview

Correlation techniques are widely used for relative and absolute measurements in time or space signals. Examples are electronic distance measurements based on the determination of phase differences, measurements of time delays in radio atronomy (very long base line interferometry), spectrum analysis in radar problems or speech analysis or parallax measurements in stereo vision systems. For more than 10 years automatic correlation techniques have been applied also in photogrammetry and remote sensing for the derivation of heights in stereo models for subsequent orthophoto projections or for registration and rectification of satellite images using ground control points. Hobrough in 1959 made the beginning with the instrumentation of parallax measurement for "Automatic Stereo Plotting". Since that time quite some systems have been developed. The applications mainly aim at high performance rates rather than at high precision (cf. Förstner 1984). Helava (1976) was the first to discuss the different aspects of digital correlation when it is realized in photogrammetric instruments, starting with an image model and using it for the evaluation of different parameters such as the pull-in range, the spot size and the optimum frequency, the effect of quantization etc. The theoretical studies of the quality of digital correlation have been collected by Förstner (1984) and tried to be discussed on common basis. The equivalence of the matched filters and the least squares fit mimimizing the grey value differences can be taken to advantage as all quality measures from statistics, which we discussed in section 1, are applicable here too. The following subsections want to sketch the main results.

2.2 The model of Digital Correlation

Let the reference image, the template, be given as a greylevel function $g(x_i,y_i)$ at n discrete points. The observed signal $\underline{g}_1(x_i,y_i)$ is obtained from g by shifting the template by $(\tilde{x},\tilde{y})$ and adding (white) noise $\underline{\varepsilon}(x_i,y_i)$. The discrete two-dimensional model then reads as:

$$\underline{g}_1(x_i,\, y_i) = g(x_i - \tilde{x},\, y_i - \tilde{y}) + \underline{\varepsilon}(x_i,\, y_i)\ ,\quad i = 1,\, \ldots,\, n \tag{9}$$

The equation holds for all n pixels, which in principle need not form a grid.

The idea is to linearize eq. (9) and solve the linearized problem using least squares techniques (cf. Limb/ Murphy 1975, Burckhardt/Moll 1978, Wild 1979, Meyers and Frank 1979, Thurgood/Mikhail 1982). Hence since nearly 10 years this method has been applied for image sequence analysis (Cafforio/Rocca 1976, Schalkoff/ McVey 1978, Fennema/Thompson 1979, Dinse et al. 1981, Huang 1981) and recently for target location and point transfer in photogrammetry and remote sensing (Ackermann/Pertl 1982, Förstner 1982, Mikhail 1983).

Starting from approximate values x_o and y_o and setting $\underline{\Delta g}_i=\underline{\Delta g}(x_i,y_i)=\underline{g}_1(x_i,y_i)-g(x_i-x_o,y_i-y_o)$ the unknown differences $\hat{\underline{x}}$ and $\hat{\underline{y}}$ (assuming $x_o=y_o=0$) for the moment) can be estimated from the n observation equations:

$$\underline{\Delta g}_i = g_{x,i}\,\hat{\underline{x}} + g_{y,i}\,\hat{\underline{y}} + \hat{\underline{\varepsilon}}_i, \tag{10}$$

where $g_x=\partial g/\partial x$ and $g_y=\partial g/\partial y$ are taken at the approximate values. The overdetermined equation system eq. (10) leads to the normal equations

$$\begin{pmatrix} \Sigma g_x^2 & \Sigma g_x\, g_y \\ \Sigma g_x\, g_y & \Sigma g_y^2 \end{pmatrix} \begin{pmatrix} \hat{\underline{x}} \\ \hat{\underline{y}} \end{pmatrix} = \begin{pmatrix} \Sigma g_x\, \underline{\Delta g} \\ \Sigma g_y\, \underline{\Delta g} \end{pmatrix} \tag{11}$$

The covariance matrix of the shifts for general σ_o^2 is

$$D\begin{pmatrix} \hat{\underline{x}} \\ \hat{\underline{y}} \end{pmatrix} = \begin{pmatrix} \sigma_x^2 & \sigma_{xy} \\ \sigma_{xy} & \sigma_y^2 \end{pmatrix} = \frac{\sigma_o^2}{n} \begin{pmatrix} \sigma^2_{g_x} & \sigma_{g_x g_y} \\ \sigma_{g_x g_y} & \sigma_y^2 \end{pmatrix}^{-1} \tag{12}$$

2.3 The Theoretical Precision of Digital Correlation

The precision of digital correlation is determined by three parameters

- the image noise variance σ_o^2
- the number of pixels n and
- the variances $\sigma(g_x)$ and $\sigma(g_y)$ and the covariances of the gradient images in x and y direction. This is a specification of the edge buisiness in an image which proves to be decisive for the precision of digital correlation.

If the image is isotropic, i. e. the covariance of the gradients is zero, we obtain the variances for $\hat{\underline{x}}$ and $\hat{\underline{y}}$ seperately, e.g. (cf. Förstner 1982):

$$\sigma_x^2 = \frac{1}{n}\,\frac{\sigma_o^2}{\sigma_{g_x}^2} = \frac{1}{n}\,\frac{\sigma_o^2}{-R_{xx,g}(o)} = \frac{1}{n}\,\frac{1}{SNR^2}\,\frac{1}{(2\pi b_x)^2} = \frac{1}{n}\,\frac{1}{SNR^2}\,\frac{\sigma_g^2}{\sigma_{g_x}^2} \tag{13}$$

with the signal to noise ratio $SNR=\sigma_g/\sigma_o$ and the effective bandwidth $b_x=\sigma(g_x)/(2\pi\sigma_g)$ in x-direction (cf. McGillem/Svedlow 1976, Ryan et al. 1980). Svedlov et al. (1976) have given the continuous form of eq.(13) ommiting the number of pixels and assuming the template and the noise to follow the same type of autocorrelationfunction. Eq.(13) also is the Cramer-Rao bound giving a lower bound for the variance when using an arbitrary filter (cf. Ryan et al. 1980, Meyers/ Frank 1980). Moreover the variance of the gradient is identical to the curvature of the autocorrelation function due to the moment theorem (cf. Papoulis 1965, Ryan et al. 1980).

The results of computer simulations by Huang and Hsu (1981) are in full agreement with these theoretical considerations.

2.4 Discussion

The differential approach (cf. Huang 1981) allows several extensions which are of practical and theoretical value.

1. The model eq. (9) can be extended by additional parameters to compensate for geometric and radiometric distortions. Linear transformations seem to be sufficient representing local perspective distortion while assuming the surface to be smooth and differences in brightness and contrast (cf. Pertl 1984) and leading to 8 unknown parameters which have to be estimated.
2. If the true template is not known, the correlation also can be performed with one of the images playing the role of the template. But then the gradients g_x and g_y have to be estimated, i.e. restored from the images, e.g. using a Wiener filter or any other low pass filter. In general this is an approximate solution, which, however, in most cases is satisfactory.
3. The effect of linear filters onto the precision can be studied if some assumptions on the power spectrum of the template are made. For aerial imagery one can show that using the gradient image (g_x say, for estimating $\tilde{x}$) leads to results with a standard deviation which is a factor 1.6 higher (cf. the experimental results by Anuta 1970).
4. Preprocessing the images with a median filter also leads to worse results! This seems to contradict theoretical investigations by Yang and Huang (1981) and Geiselmann (1983), but can be explained by the unstability of the median filtered signal near edges.
5. There exists an optimal pixel size, if the number of pixels and the signal to noise ratio is kept fixed. It depends on the reference distance d of the autocorrelation function. Assuming $R(x) \sim exp(-|x|/d)$ the optimum is $\Delta x(opt)=0.7\ d$. For good aerial imagery with $d = 40$ µm this is 30 µm (cf. Förstner 1982, 1984).

The next two items demonstrate the drawbacks and limitations of image correlation techniques.

6. The presence of geometric distortions, i.e. deviations from the assumed model, results in an optimal patchsize, as small patches do not contain enough pixels and large patches cannot be matched well because of the distortion. For a scale-difference c one obtains $s(opt)=2.5\ d/|c|$ (for d cf. 5.). For good aerial imagery and 50 % scale difference the optimum patch size is $s(opt)$x$s(opt)$ with $s(opt)=0.2\ mm$, i. e. about 7x7 pixels of optimum size (cf. Svedlow et al.1976).
7. The least squares estimation has to be iterated, as the model is highly nonlinear. The rate of convergence is cubic, which is due to the symmetry of the autocorrelation function (cf. Burckhardt/Moll 1978). The radius of convergence, however, is rather small. For a greylevel function which is ideal band limeted ($f<f_o$), the approximate values x_o must be better than 0.5 pixels (!) ($\Delta x = 1/(2f_o)$). Burckhardt and Moll showed that the knowledge of the curvature of the autocorrelation function can be used to increase the pull-in-range to 1.5 pixels. But even this larger value, being about 50 µm in an aerial image, is unacceptable in photogrammetry. Moreover, the small radius of convergence with respect to other, especially geometric parameters, such as the scale-difference or the rotation, requires automatic procedures for the determination of approximate values. This may be achieved by algorithms for finding corresponding points in image pairs (cf. Barnard/Thompson 1980, Dreschler 1981, Stockman et al. 1982, Zimmermann/Kories 1984). For the rectification of satellite imagery a new algorithm has been developed (cf. Paderes et al. 1984), which can also be used for smooth surfaces in close range applications.

3. RESULTS OF HIGH PRECISION POINT AND SURFACE MEASUREMENTS

Three examples using an analytical measuring device extended by two CCD-cameras want to show the applicability of the concepts of the previous sections. First the accuracy of the new correspondenc algorithm is demonstrated. The second example compares the precision of crosscorrelation and human stereopsy. This algorithm has been applied to surface measurements of an industrial workpiece.

3.1 Extension of the Zeiss Planicomp C 100 Measuring Device

The analytical measuring device Planicomp C 100 by Zeiss has been complemented by two CCD-cameras C-1035 M by Hamamatsu (cf. Gülch 1984). They scan an area of about 5 mm x 5 mm with a pixel size of 20 μm in the image, and thus provide the computer with two small image patches with 240 X 240 pixels (cf. fig. 2). Proper calibration allows to switch between manual and digital stereo fusion in a way that both can support each other. The operator controls the position of the two patches together with the measuring mark.

3.2 Accuracy of Approximate Values Using the New Correspondence Algorithm

The new correspondence algorithm (cf. Paderes et al. 1984), as all algorithms of this type (cf. Stockman et al. 1982), consists of three steps:

1. Using an interest operator one first selects distinct points in both images. In this case those points are selected, which promise to give the highest precision with crosscorrelation compared with the surrounding points and at the same time possess an error ellipse, which is near to a circle. Both criteria can easily be derived from the elements of the normal equation matrix in eq. (11). The interest operator is similar to the one by Moravec.
2. The similarity of the selected points in the two images is used to get a first list of candidates for corresponding points. The similarity here is measured by the trace of the estimated covariance matrix eq. (12) of crosscorrelation with $\hat{\underline{\sigma}}^2$ estimated from the two areas around the points and assuming $\hat{\underline{x}}=\hat{\underline{y}}=0$. Compared with the similarity measure by Barnard and Thompson (1980) also the difference in brightness and contrast of the images is taken into account.
3. The final selection of the corresponding point pairs is based on some consistency constraint. In this step a new approach is used. The parallaxes of the corresponding points are assumed to be the result of a general linear geometric transformation with 6 parameters. The parallaxes of <u>all</u> candidate pairs are used to solve for the parameters using a robust estimation procedure. Specifically, after each iteration the weights w_i of the observations (parallaxes) are adapted to the residuals. Thus the wrong correspondencies are weighted down according to a weight function $w(\hat{\underline{\epsilon}})$. For a large class of weight functions convergence of this procedure is guaranteed under general conditions (cf. Huber 1981).

The whole procedure needs about 2 seconds computing time on a VAX 11/780 for two images with 128x128 pixels. Geometric distortions up to about 20° can be handled.

This algorithm is used to obtain approximate values for the parallaxes <u>and</u> for the local geometric transformation parameters, which are required for subsequent high precision correlation. The accuracy of the approximate values for the parallaxes has been estimated using a relative orientation of two aerial images. 12 image patches, 6 pairs at the standard positions in a rectangular stereo model (in the middle of the two sides and in the corners) have been selected in both images by an operator. The original digital data have been reduced to get two image patches of 120 x 120 pixels with a pixel side of 4o μm. Except for one case, in all patch pairs corresponding points (4 to 47) have been found. A subset of these has been extracted, using only the first few points in each patch. The relative orientation with a redundancy of $r = 27$ yielded an estimated vertical parallax of 50 μm. After elimination of 5 wrong correspondencies the estimated parallax reduced to 16 μm, the maximum parallax being 42 μm. This accuracy is fully sufficient.

3.3 Empirical Precision of Crosscorrelation

The same method for evaluating the accuracy of the measuring process has been used to check the theoretical precision of crosscorrelation. Table 1 shows the standard deviations of the image coordinates derived from the parallaxes after relative orientation for natural and targeted points. The same points have been

Table 1 Standard deviations of image coordinates derived from relative orientation (Pertl 1984)

measurement	points natural	targeted
digital	2.7 µm	2.6 µm
manual	3.1 µm	2.2 µm

measured by an operator and by digital correlation. The table shows clearly that there is no significant difference between the measuring processes on one hand, and on the type of points on the other hand. As the theoretical precision in these cases was in the order of 1 - 1.5 µm, the values essentially reflect the overall precision of the hardware and the mathematical model and not the pure parallax measuring process.

3.4 Semiautomatic Determination of Surfaces

The correlation algorithm has been integrated into a semiautomatic procedure to measure surface profiles.The profiles are defined by the two end points A' and B' and the stepsize in one image. The first few (4) points have to be fused manually. The position and the parameters of the geometric transformation of the 5. point in the other photo is predicted. The cameras are moved accordingly. For the correlation algorithm only small patches of 12x12 and 18x18 pixels are scanned. The fusion of both points leads to new coordinates of the 5. point in the second image and to new transformation parameters. The process is repeated until the end of the profile and the next profile can be defined. If the correlation fails, the operator can decide how to proceed. The whole procedure is preliminary as far as the automation and the adaption is concerned. The following example wants to show the feasibility of an high precision surface measurement procedure.

Fig. 4 mm-contour lines of an industrial workpiece, 2491 points, image scale 1 : 20, focal length 100 mm, distance to object 2 m

a. manual measurements

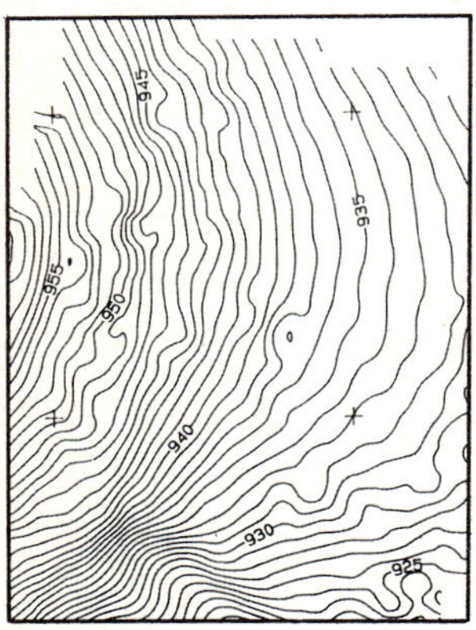

b. automatic measurements

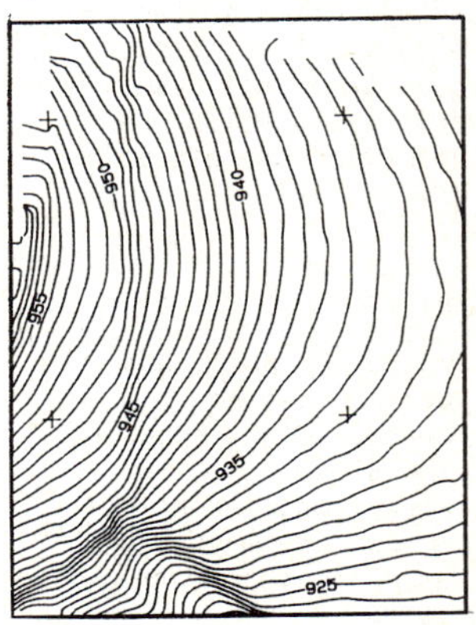

An industrial workpiece with a smooth surface has been selected. Its surface has been prepared to allow stereoscopic measurements. The two images were taken with a terrestrial metric camera, focal length c = 100 mm. The distance to the object was 2 m, the distance between the cameras 0.84 m. A small area of 1 cm^2 in the image has been chosen for this test. 35 profiles with about 75 points have been measured manually and with the semiautomatic procedure. Due to reflections not all points could be fused automatically, also several points showed an accuracy which is not satisfactory. The mm-contour lines of both measurements are given in Fig. 4. They are based on 2491 points. Fig. 5. shows the histogramm of the differences between the two surfaces. There is a systematic difference of 0.17 mm, the quadratic mean difference is $\hat{\bar{\sigma}}^2$= 0.5 mm. Though not quite in accordance with the theoretically expected value, being σ^2=0.3 mm, the result is quite satisfying. The manual measuring process obviously contains a smoothing property, which leads to a clearer impression of the surface.

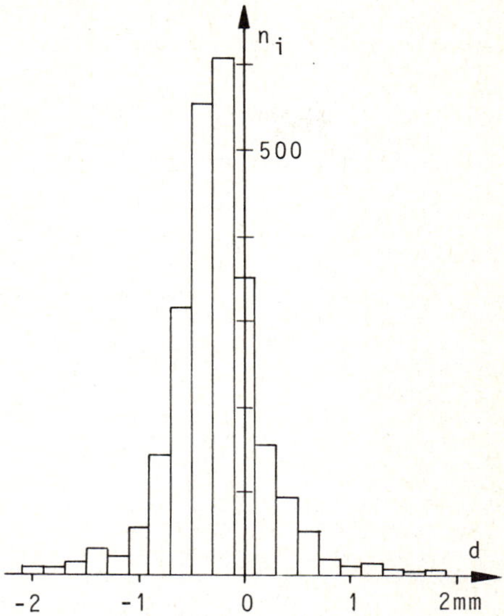

Fig. 5 Histogram of differences between manual and automatic measurement of a surface, scale 1:20

4. CONCLUSIONS

The paper wanted to describe an approach to integrate methods from digital image processing and pattern recognition into photogrammetric measuring procedures. The aim was to motivate the quality requirements, especially concerning the precision and the reliability, the new procedures have to meet. This can be seen in contrast to fully automated systems where the overall performance is of main interest. The photogrammetric measuring expert, the human operator, only accepts support if the quality of the result is not degraded. Therefore a specific task has been selected for automation, being aware that the solutions of the tasks following in the automation process will require effort which is orders of magnitude larger.

REFERENCES

Abbreviations:

CGIP	Computer Graphics and Image Processing
DGK	Deutsche Geodätische Kommission
IAP	International Archives for Photogrammetry
IEEE COM	Transactions on Communications
IEEE GE	IEEE Transactions on Geoscience Electronics
IEEE PAMI	IEEE Transactions on Pattern Analysis and Machine Intelligence
IPS	Schriftenreihe des Instiuts für Photogrammetrie Stuttgart
PhEng	Photogrammetric Engineering and Remote Sensing

Ackermann F. (1980): Blockadjustment with additional parameters, IAP Vol. 23-B3, Hamburg 1980, pp. 1-10

Ackermann F. (1984): Utilization of Navigation Data for Aerial Triangulation, IAP Vol. 25-A3a, Rio de Janeiro 1984, pp. 1-9

Ackermann F., Pertl A. (1983): Zuordnung kleiner Bildflächen durch digitale Korrelation zur Verknüpfung verschiedener oder verschiedenartiger Bilder im Anwendungsbereich Photogrammetrie und Fernerkundung, DFG-Abschlußbericht, Stuttgart 1983

Akey M.L., Mitchell R. (1984): Detection and sub-pixel location of Objects in digitized aerial images, 7th Conference on Pattern Recognition, Montreal 1984

Anauta P.E. (1970): Spatial Registration of multispectral digital imgery using Fast Fourier Transformation techniques, IEEE Vol. GE-8, 1970, pp. 353-368

Atkinson K.B. (1980 ed.): Developments in Close Range Photogrammetry - 1, Appl. Science Publ., London, 1980

Barnard S.T., Thompson W.W. (1980): Disparity Analysis of Images, IEEE Vol. PAMI-2, 1980, pp. 333-340

Bouloucos T., Karadaidis., Molenaar M. (1984): A substitute matrix for photogrammetrically determined point fields, IAP Vol. 25-A3a, Rio de Janeiro, 1984, pp. 59-69

Brown D.C. (1971): Close-range camera calibration, PhEng 1971

Brown D.C. (1974): Evolution, Application and Potential of the bundle method of photogrammetric Triangulation, Symp. of ISP-Comm. III, Stuttgart 1974

Brown D. C. (1982): STARS, a turnkey system for close range photogrammetry, IAP Vol. 24-V, York, England, 1982

Burckhardt H., Moll H. (1979): A modified Newton-Raphson search for the model-adaptive identification of delays, 5th IFAC-Symp. on Identification and System Parameter Estimation, Darmstadt 1979, pp.1279-1286

Cafforio C., Rocca F. (1979): Tracking moving objects in television images, Signal Processing 1

Dinse Th., Enkelmann W., Nagel H.H.(1981): Untersuchungen von Verschiebungsvektorfeldern in Bildfolgen, Inf. Fachberichte 49, Heidelberg 1981, pp. 59-75

Dreschler L. (1981): Ermittlung markanter Punkte auf Bildern bewegter Objekte und Berechnung einer 3D-Beschreibung auf dieser Grundlage, Diss. Fachbereich Informatik, Univ. Hamburg 1981

Düppe R.D. (1984): Kombinierte Ausgleichung in der Photogrammetrie: Programmkonzeption und Beispiele, IAP Vol. 25-A3a, Rio de Janeiro, 1984

Ebner H. (1976): A mathematical model for digital rectification of remote sensing data, IAP Vol. 21-III, Helsinki 1976

Fennema C.L., Thompson W.B. (1979): Velocity determination in Scenes containing several moving objects, CGIP Vol. 9, 1979, pp. 301-315

Förstner W. (1980): Evaluation of block-adjustment results, IAP Vol. 23-B3, Hamburg 1980, pp. 236-245

Förstner W. (1982): On the geometric precision of digital correlation, IAP Vol. 24-III, Helsinki 1982, pp. 176-189

Förstner W. (1984): Quality assessment of object location and point transfer using digital image correlation techniques, IAP Vol. 25-A3a, Rio de Janeiro, 1984

Förstner W.(1985a): High Precision Photogrammetric point determination, to appear in Allg. Verm. Nachr., Intern. Suppl., 1985

Förstner W. (1985b): Determination of the additive noise variance in observed autoregressive processes using variance component estimation techniques, to appear in Statistics & Decisions 1985

Förstner W. (1985c): The reliability of block triangulation, to appear in PhEng 1985

Fraser C.S., Gründig L. (1984): The analysis of photogrammetric deformation measurements on Turtle Mountain, Pres. paper to Eng. Surv. Conf., FIG, Comm. 6, Washington D.C., 1984

Fraser C.L. (1984): Multiple exposure in non-metric camera applications, IAP Vol. 25-A5, Rio de Janeiro 1984

Fuchs H., Leberl F. (1984): Universal analytical plotter software for photographs with perspective geometry (CRISP), ASP-ACSM Conv., Washington D.C.,1984

Geiselmann Ch. (1983): Theoretische Untersuchungen zu Genauigkeitssteigerung der Digitalen Bildkorrelation durch Medianfilterung, Selbst. Arb. am Inst. f. Photogr. Stuttgart, 1983

Gelb A. (1974): Applied Optimal Estimation, MIT-Press, 1974

George A. (1973): Nested Dissection of a regular finite element mesh, SIAM, J. Numer. Anal., 1973, pp. 345-363

Grimson W.E.L. (1981): From Images to Surfaces, MIT-Press, 1981

Gülch E. (1984): Geometric calibration of two CCD-cameras used for digital image correlation on the Planicomp C 100, IAP Vol. 25-B3, Rio de Janeiro, 1984

Helava U.V. (1976): Digital correlation in photogrammetric instruments, IAP Vol. 23-III, Helsinki, 1976

Hobrough G.L. (1959): Automatic stereo plotting, PhEng 25-5, 1959, pp. 763-769

Huang T.S.(1981, ed.): Image sequence analysis, Springer NY, 1981

Huber P.J. (1981): Robust Statistics, New York 1981

Kager H., Kraus K. (1976): Gemeinsame Ausgleichung photogrammetrischer, geodätischer und fiktiver Beobachtungen, IAP Vol. 23-B5, Helsinki 1976

Karara H.M. (1979, ed.): Handbook of non-topographic photogrammetry, Am. Soc. of Photogr., Falls Church, 1979

Klein H. (1980): New Results of bundle block adjustment with additional parameters, IPS, Heft 6, 1980

Klein H., Förstner W. (1984): Realization of automatic error detection in the block adjustment program PAT-M43 using robust estimators, IAP Vol. 25-A3a, Rio de Janeiro, 1984

Koch K.-R. (1980): Parameterschätzung und Hypothesentests in linearen Modellen, Dümmler, 1980

Konecny G., Lehmann G. (1984): Photogrammetrie, deGruyter, Berlin 1984

Kruck E. (1983): Lösung großer Gleichungssysteme für photogrammetrische Blockausgleichungen mit erweitertem funktionalen Modell, Diss. Fachb. Verm.-Wesen, Univ. Hannover 1983

Limb J. O., Murphy J.A. (1975): Measuring the speed of moving objects from television signals, IEEE Vol. COM-23, 1975, pp. 474-478

McGillem C.D., Svedlow M. (1976). Image registration error variance as a measure of overlay quality, IEEE Vol. GE-14, 1976, pp. 44-49

McGillem C.D., Svedlow M. (1977): Optimum filter for minimizing of registration error variance, IEEE Vol. GE-15, 1977, pp. 257-259

Meyers M.H., Frank L.E. (1980): Joint carrier phase and symbol timing recovery for PAM systems, IEEE Vol. COM-28, 1980, pp. 1121-1129

Mikhail E.M. (1976): Observations and least squares, IEP, NY 1976

Mikhail E.M. (1983): Photogrammetric target location to sup-pixel accuracy in digital images, IPS Heft 9, 1984

Müller F., Stephani M. (1984): Effiziente Berücksichtigung geometrischer Beobachtungen und Objektinformationen in der Bündelblockausgleichung, IAP Vol. 25-A5, Rio de Janeiro, 1984

Paderes F.C., Mikhail E.M., Förstner W. (1984): Rectification of single and multiple frames of satellite scanner imagery using points and edges as control, NASA-Symp. on Mathem. Pattern Recognition and Image Analysis, Houston 1984

Papoulis A. (1965): Probability, Random Variables and Stochastic Processes, McGraw Hills, 1965

Pertl A. (1984): Digital image Correlation with the analytical plotter Planicomp C 100, IAP Vol. 25-A3b, Rio de Janeiro 1984

Ryan T.W., Gray R.T, Hunt B.R. (1980): Prediction of correlation errors in stereopair images, Opt. Eng., 19/1980

Schalkhoff R.J., McVey E.S. (1979): Algorithms development for real time automatic video tracking systems, Proc. 3rd Int. Computer Software and Application Conf., Chicago, 1979, pp. 504-511

Schek H.J., Schauer U., Steidler F. (1976): The adjustment of large geodetic networks by sparse matrix techniques, TR 76-07-004, IBM Scientific Centre Heidelberg, 1976

Schwidefsky K., Ackermann F. (1976): Photogrammetrie, Teubner, 1976

Steidler F. (1980): Darstellung und Vergleich von Lösungsstrategien für große schwach besetzte Normalgleichungssysteme in der Geodäsie und in der Photogrammetrie, DGK C 261, München 1980

*Stockman G.C., Kopstein S., Bennett S. (1982):*Matching images to models for image registration and object location via clustering, IEEE Vol. PAMI-4, 1982, pp. 229-241

Svedlow M., McGillem C., Anauta P. (1976): Analytical and experimental design and analysis of an optimal processor for image registration, LARS, Inf. Note 090776, Purdue Univ., West Lafayette, 1976

*Thurgood J.D., Mikhail E.M. (1982):*Subpixel mensuration of photogrammetric targets in digital images, School of Civil Eng, Purdue, CH-PH-82-2

Wester-Ebbinghaus W. (1984): Ein allgemein formuliertes Konzept zur Bildtriangulation mit gemeinsamer Ausgleichung photogrammetrischer und geodätischer Beobachtungen, IAP Vol. 25-A3b, Rio de Janeiro 1984

Wild E. (1979): Internal reports, Inst. für Photogr., Stuttgart 1979

Yang G.J., Huang T.S. (1981): The effect of median filtering on edge location estimation, CGIP Vol. 15, 1981, pp. 224-245

Zimmermann G., Kories R. (1984): Eine Familie von Bildmerkmalen für die Bewegungsbestimmung in Bildfolgen, Inf. Fachberichte 87, Springer 1984

DISCUSSION

Ledley:

Do you actually make the stereo correlation with the computer?

Foerstner:

Yes, we do. It is an HP 1000 computer and up to now, because it is a serial one, it takes about 5 to 8 seconds per point, but if one would use special hardware this of course would go down significantly. The correspondance algorithm takes 10 seconds on the same computer for a window of 60 by 60 pixels.

Persoon:

When you found the candidate points in one picture how do you find the corresponding matching points in the other one?

Foerstner:

We first select points in both images seperately and we assume that the shift is at maximum one third of the size of the window because otherwise you do not have enough overlap. The second step is to look for similar points under these restrictions. The similarity is based on the correlation coefficient of the two surrounding greylevel functions. Of course you get a lot of correspondencies which might be correct so you have for instance 100 or 120 possible candidate pairs. Afterwards we say all these parallaxes should result from an affine transformation.
We then use a robust estimator to obtain these parameters.

Persoon:

Which correlation method do you use and how large is the window?

Foerstner:

The correlation coefficient uses just a 5x5 or 7x7 window. We do not shift anything in this algorithm, we just select the points and look whether the window around this point is similar to the other window and from that we get an initial weight for this correspondance.

PATTERN RECOGNITION IN PRACTICE II
E.S. Gelsema and L.N. Kanal (Editors)
Elsevier Science Publishers B.V. (North-Holland), 1986

LENGTH ESTIMATORS COMPARED

Leo Dorst
Pattern Recognition Group
Department of Applied Physics
Delft University of Technology
Lorentzweg 1
2628 CJ DELFT
The Netherlands

Arnold W.M. Smeulders
Pathologisch Instituut
De Boelelaan 1117
1007 MB AMSTERDAM
The Netherlands

Six methods to measure the length corresponding to a chaincode string are compared with respect to accuracy and algorithmic complexity. The comparison is performed for straight chaincode strings, for which the optimal method of length measurement is known. A sub-optimal method, the so-called 'corner-count method' seems to be the best to use in practice. It has an accuracy ranging from 3% for a sampling density of 5 points per unit length to .6% for infinite sampling density.

INTRODUCTION

Measuring geometrical properties of objects in digitized images has been important since the start of image processing. Area, contour length, and orientation are often parameters of interest, be it in industrial inspection, robot vision, biomedical research, or remote sensing. But not for all geometrical parameters is there an obviously best way in which they should be measured from the digital image. For length measurement, for instance, many methods have been proposed [1]-[7]. In this paper, we will compare these methods, both in terms of accuracy and in terms of algorithmic complexity. The comparison will be performed for the measurement of the length of a straight contour. For this situation the optimal solution is known [3], and thus the different methods can be gauged in an absolute sense.

LENGTH MEASUREMENT METHODS

Since more than 15 years people have tackled the problem of measuring the length of a digitized straight boundary. The methods that will be compared in this paper are now presented in chronological order.

In the dawn of image processing for measurement purposes, Freeman [4] proposed the chain code scheme to encode contours in a convenient way (fig. 1). This scheme is still in use today. Note that there are even codes (horizontal and vertical) and odd codes (diagonal). A length can be attributed to a chain coded contour by the formula

$$\ell_F = 1.n_e + \sqrt{2}\, n_o = 1.0\, n_e + 1.414\, n_o \qquad (1)$$

where n_e is the number of even codes in the chaincode of the contour, and n_o the number of odd codes. If this length estimate is used to measure the distance to a fixed grid point it can be compared to the Euclidean distance. In fig 2a the points of equal ℓ_F-distance to a point (the 'ℓ_F-circle') are drawn together with a Euclidean circle. It is seen that the ℓ_F distance is always smaller than or equal to the Euclidean distance. The ℓ_F-distance thus does not yield an unbiased estimate of the length of a straight line: it is consistently too small.

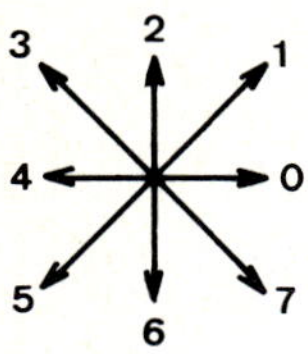

figure 1. Freeman's chaincode scheme

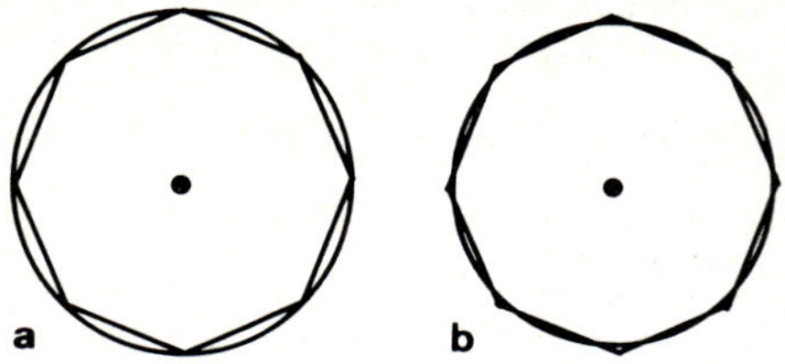

figure 2. A Euclidean circle compared to an ℓ_F-circle (a) and a ℓ_P-circle.

Formula (1) has the advantage of being easy to compute, and a number of authors concentrated on estimators of the form:

$$\ell = an_e + bn_o \ . \tag{2}$$

Groen and Verbeek [5] remarked that the ℓ_F formula does not take into account that the a-priori probabilities of odd and even codes in the string of a straight line are unequal. For an ensemble of lines that is uniformly distributed in the polar parameters r and ϕ [3], they found that the coefficients a = 1.059 and b = 1.183 in (2) yield a length estimate which is unbiased per chaincode. This leads to an estimator

$$\ell_G = 1.059\ n_e + 1.183\ n_o \tag{3}$$

These coefficients are the expected length of an even and odd chaincode, respectively.
Proffitt and Rosen [6] had also noticed that the ℓ_F-estimator is biased, and performed a calculation similar to Groen and Verbeek. They also calculated the expected length of an even and an odd chaincode in infinitely long strings and obtained a = .948 and b = 1.340. The resulting estimator thus is

$$\ell_P = .948\ n_o + 1.340\ n_e . \tag{4}$$

(In [6] the coefficients were originally calculated for 4-connective chain codes; in [7] they were calculated by the same method for 8-connectivity. This results in (4)). The difference with (3) is that Proffitt and Rosen considered the a-priori probabilities of the even and odd codes in infinitely long lines, whereas Groen and Verbeek calculated the a-priori probabilities considering 1 column of the grid.
Note that (4) can be rewritten as

$$\ell_P = .948\ (1.0n_e + 1.414\ n_o) = .948\ \ell_F \tag{5}$$

which is a rescaling of the Freeman estimator, to render it unbiased in the limit of infinitely long lines (fig. 2b).

In [6] the authors also tried to improve the accuracy by introducing an extra parameter in the estimator. In this extended version

$$\ell = a\ n_e + b\ n_o + c\ n_c, \tag{6}$$

the parameter n_c is a parameter called 'corner count', which is the number of transitions odd/even and even/odd in the chaincode string. They performed the calculation for 4-connectivity. A similar calculation was later done by Vossepoel & Smeulders in [7] for 8-connectivity and results in:

$$\ell_C = .980\ n_e + 1.406\ n_o - .091\ n_c \tag{7}$$

The use of n_o and n_e as parameters means that only begin- and endpoint of a line contribute to the length estimator. In [7] it was shown that the use of n_c effectively means that the points in the second and second last column also contribute, resulting in a considerable gain in accuracy.

Also in [7], Vossepoel and Smeulders noticed the difference between (3) and (4) and concluded that the coefficients in the estimators for the length of a discrete line should depend on the number of chaincodes in the string. They conjectured that optimal estimators could only result if each line was endowed with its own specific estimate. This requires a set of parameters characterizing an arbitrary chaincode string uniquely. They chose n_e, n_o and n_c, and thus arrived at estimators of the form

$$\ell_V = f(n_e, n_o, n_c) \tag{8}$$

The functions f are complicated and can be found in [7].

However, there is no one-to-one relationship between the triple of parameters (n_e, n_o, n_c) and a straight chaincode string : each string leads to a unique set of parameters, but the converse is not true. This implies that Vossepoel and Smeulders did not quite reach their own goal, and that their estimators could still be improved. This was done by Dorst and Smeulders [2]. In their paper they derived a set of 4 integer parameters (n,q,p,s) that characterizes an arbitrary straight string uniquely. In a future paper [3] these parameters are used to make length estimators that are optimal for the straight string under consideration. These estimators, which are of the form

$$\ell_D = g(n,q,p,s) \tag{9}$$

(where g is a known but complicated function specified in [3]) can be shown to be BLUE, i.e. Best (in the sense of minimal mean square error), Linear and Unbiased. For a straight string, no better estimate of the length can be found.

Recently, Borgefors [1] published a method to perform the distance transform on a binary image. She uses integer calculations and computes the so-called Chamfer distances:

$$\ell_B = an_e + bn_o \quad , \text{ a and b integer} \tag{10}$$

which afterwards is rescaled by a. The ratio b/a is an approximation of $\sqrt{2}$. We have not yet evaluated this estimator, but it is expected to behave like ℓ_F if the scale factor is taken to be a (as is proposed in [7]) and like ℓ_P if the scale factor is improved to remove the bias.

THE COMPARISON FOR STRAIGHT BOUNDARIES

Most of the methods presented in the previous section were derived originally for digitized straight lines, but are generally used for arbitrary chaincode strings. The comparison in this paper will be performed on digitized straight lines, for two reasons. The first is that it seems proper to use the estimators for the goal they were meant for. The second is that the optimal solution for straight lines is known (the BLUE estimators of [3]), so one can compare the estimators to the theoretically best possible. The major drawback of this choice is of course that the majority of objects of interest have no straight boundaries, and hence care should be taken in applying these results to arbitrary strings.

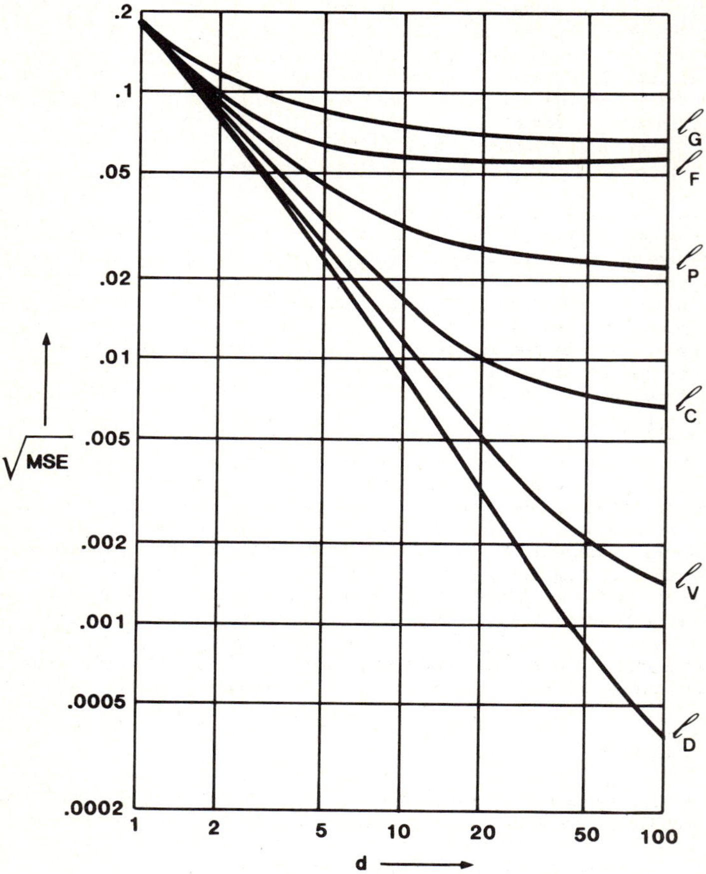

figure 3. A plot of the root MSE of the various length estimators as a function of the sampling density d.

The comparisons were done for the following situation. Consider a unit square grid with Cartesian coordinates x and y. An infinite line $y = \alpha x + e$ is digitized. Due to the symmetry of the grid one can assume $0 \leqslant e < 1$ and $0 \leqslant \alpha \leqslant 1$. The digitization method is an 8-connected chaincode, and leads to a straight string consisting of chain codes 0 and/or 1. Consider n codes of the infinitely long string, corresponding to n 'columns' (in the sense defined in [7]) of the grid. It is known how long the continuous line is between these columns, namely $\ell = n\sqrt{1+\alpha^2}$ .The estimated length of the string is calculated by one of the methods described and yields estimate ℓ_E. The square error $(\ell_E - \ell)^2$ is then averaged over all lines. Each line is weighted by its probability of occurrence, assuming a uniform distribution in the polar parameters r and ϕ [3].

This procedure need not be performed as a Monte-Carlo-simulation. Using the formulas for the domain of a chaincode string (a domain D_c of a string c is the set of all lines that could have generated c) given in [2], one can perform the calculation of the MSE exactly. The calculation was done for all estimators, and for various string lengths n=1,2,5,10,20,50,100. The root MSE was normalized per chaincode, to make it a dimensionless quantity.

RESULTS

Figure 3 shows the result of the evaluation for the different estimators. It is seen that for short strings all estimators behave similarly: the MSE is high, and approximately equal. For very long strings the estimators show remarkable differences: some MSE's reach limit values. The Freeman estimator, used universally, will never become more accurate than 6.6%. This is partially caused by its bias, but when this is removed (resulting in ℓ_P) the inaccuracy is still 2.6%. The corner count method is the best of the methods using a linear formula; it reaches 0.6% in the limit. The optimal estimator ℓ_D will never reach a constant limit value. From the figure it is empirically found that its limit is

$$\sqrt{MSE} = .3\ d^{-1.5} \tag{11}$$

where d is the sampling density, the number of columns per unit length. This is the best accuracy that can be achieved for length measurement.

It may be slightly unexpected that the linear methods do not become more accurate even at infinite sampling densities. The explanation is found from figure 2: these methods will always fit an octagon to a circle. Even if this is done optimally, as Proffitt and Rosen did with ℓ_P, there is still a residual error.

From the figure one can see what estimators are suited for straight lines according to their accuracy. In the next section we will discuss the algorithmic complexity.

COMPUTATIONAL ASPECTS

Usually one is interested in the length of an arbitrary curve rather than the length of a straight line. As far as we know, no estimators have been developed especially tailored even to specific curves such as circles or ellipses. Therefore, the best one can do at present is to apply the estimators for the length of a straight line to the chaincode strings of curves. It is not known yet how accurate these estimates are, but presumably the MSE of the estimators and their ranking are similar to the case of straight line length measurements. (Comparative measurements on the performance of the various estimators on circles are being performed. We hope to report on these experiments in the near future).

The application of the first three methods to arbitrary chaincode strings is straightforward: one just counts the number of odd and even codes in the chaincode string of the contour, and uses the estimation formula. The corner count method requires the evaluation of n_c, but this is also straight-forward. The formulas to be evaluated are linear, and this makes them very fast to compute.

The two methods ℓ_V and ℓ_D are much more complicated, and intimately connected to straight lines. If used for arbitrary curves they require a piece-wise-linear decomposition to be made (this can be done in O(N) time, if N is the number of codes in the contour), and the calculation of the parameters (n,m,k) or (n,q,p,s). This also requires O(N) time. Then the formulas (8) or (9) should be evaluated. These formulas contain logarithmic and exponential functions, requiring complicated floating-point arithmetic. A table containing the functions f and g will improve the speed of calculation.

CONCLUSIONS AND RECOMMENDATIONS

The conclusions that can be drawn certainly apply to the measurement of the length of a straight line. As mentioned before, work is being done to test the validity for arbitrary contours.

- The estimation ℓ_F and ℓ_G are out of date. With equal ease one can reach better results using ℓ_P, which is 2.5 times more accurate.
- Only in time-critical situations should one use ℓ_P. The corner count method ℓ_C is much more accurate (up to .6%) than ℓ_P, and hardly requires more computational effort.
- The sub-optimal estimator ℓ_V is outdated. With equal effort one can compute the optimal estimator ℓ_D.
- The optimal (BLUE) estimator ℓ_D is mainly of theoretical interest, since it comprises the best accuracy to be achieved in length measurement on digitized data. It's practical use is probably limited to situations where high accuracy is required, but (over-)sampling is expensive.

Summarizing, the corner count estimator (7), treated in [6] and [7] is the estimator to use in most practical situations. It is easy to compute, both for straight strings and for arbitrary contours. And it is reasonably accurate, ranging from 3% for strings of length 5 via 1.5% for length 10 to a limit accuracy of .6%.

ACKNOWLEDGEMENT
This research was partially supported by Stichting FOM, The Netherlands, under project DTN93.0329.

REFERENCES

[1] Borgefors, G., Distance Transformations in Arbitrary Dimensions, Computer Vision, Graphics, and Image Processing, 27, (1984) 321-345.

[2] Dorst, L. and Smeulders, A.W.M., Discrete Representation of Straight Lines, Pattern Analysis and Machine Intelligence, vol. PAMI-6, vol.4, (July 1984) 450-463.

[3] Dorst,L. and Smeulders, A.W.M., Best Linear Unbiased Estimators for Properties of Digitized Straight Lines, internal report, Delft University of Technology, Delft, The Netherlands (1985).
A short digest of this work can be found in :
Dorst, L. and Smeulders, A.W.M., The Estimation of Parameters of Digitized Straight Line Segments, Proceedings of the 6th International Conference on Pattern Recognition, Munich, Oct.19-22 (1982) 601-603.

[4] Freeman, H., Boundary Encoding and Processing, in Picture Processing and Psychopictorics (B.S. Lipkin and A. Rosenfeld, eds.), Academic Press, New York (1970) 241-266.

[5] Groen, F.C.A., and Verbeek, P.W., Freeman Code Probabilities of Object Boundary Quantized Contours, Computer Graphics and Image Processing, 7 (1978) 391-402.

[6] Proffitt, D., and Rosen, D., Metrication Errors and Coding Efficiency of Chain-encoding Schemes for the Representation of Lines and Edges, Computer Graphics and Image Processing, 10 (1979) 318-332.

[7] Vossepoel, A.M. and Smeulders, A.W.M., Vector Code Probability and Metrication Error in the Representation of Straight Lines of Finite Length, Computer Graphics and Image Processing, vol.20, (1982) 347-364.

DISCUSSION

Van Heel:
Have you ever tried to apply your method to real problems like fractional coast lines?

Smeulders:
No, you should keep in mind that our procedure is for straight lines and not for arbitrarily curved ones. Any other line than a straight one will give a biased result. One can in general not solve it in a model when you know nothing about your object. It is our experience that for reasonable sampling circumstances the approximation of a straight line is reasonable. Actually, only one or two percent of error is added.

Haralick:
What would happen if you did just a least squares fit to the points of the line and estimate the length from the coefficients of the estimated line?

Smeulders:
That is an alternative approach and you can also think of splines. Personally, I believe that filtering the contour with a differentiating filter in order to find the curvature and base your estimate on that curvature is one of the most accurate computational methods available.
Also spline functions give a very accurate result, even more accurate than the linear ones. For practical applications the filtering is the best approach since it removes noise. The BLUE method does not do that, at least not for the moment.

Young:
What is the computational complexity of the procedure?

Van Otterloo:
The complexity of the least square fit is proportional to the number of points you have in the data window.

Smeulders:
The BLUE estimator can only be used by tabulating the results for every possible combination. But when you look at the first 20 possible codes, then you already run out of computer memory.
We have also done Taylor series expansions to these BLUE estimators and by taking a first or second order approximation one has a next to optimal solution.

Choudry:
There are several problems here. Just a couple of minor points. First of all you started to say you did contour analysis. This method is strictly for line segments. There is no analytical way to deal with for example circles. Your procedure is based on the e-alpha plane and I do not see that there is an easy way to do that for more complex lines.

Smeulders:
I even think that it is impossible to parameterize a circle by a finite number of variables to make an estimation of the true length.

Stockman:

I just want to point out that around 1980 a paper appeared in Pattern Recognition dealing with a simulation study on arbitrarily shaped blobs. They coded the boundaries and used 5 different estimators. The errors were about 6% and none of the algorithms was better than the others.

PATTERN RECOGNITION IN PRACTICE II
E.S. Gelsema and L.N. Kanal (Editors)

CUBIC FACET MODEL EDGE DETECTOR AND RIDGE-VALLEY DETECTOR: IMPLEMENTATION DETAILS

Robert M. Haralick

Machine Vision International
325 E. Eisenhower Parkway
Ann Arbor, Michigan
U.S.A.

The cubic polynomial is analyzed and its translation invariant parameters are derived. These translation invariant parameters are scale and contrast and are related to the horizontal and vertical distance between relative extrema of the cubic. The implementation details of the facet model second directional derivative zero-crossing edge detector and facet model ridge and valley detector previously described by Haralick are then given in terms of these translation invariant parameters.

INTRODUCTION

In cubic facet model processing for edges and ridges and valleys, a bivariate cubic function is fit to the central neighborhood of each pixel. In a coordinate system whose origin is the center of the pixel, the fit produces the bivariate cubic function f which is an estimate of the underlying and unobserved function:

$$f(r,c) = k_1 + k_2 r + k_3 c + k_4 r^2 + k_5 rc + k_6 c^2 + k_7 r^3 + k_8 r^2 c + k_9 rc^2 + k_{10} c^3$$

Based on the estimated coefficients $k_1,\ldots,k_{10}$ a decision is made to label the pixel as edge or non-edge, or ridge or valley or non-ridge and valley. A pixel is labelled as an edge if the second directional derivative, taken in the direction of the gradient, has a negatively sloped zero crossing located near the center of the pixel. A pixel is labelled as a ridge or valley if the first directional image, taken in a direction which extremizes the second directional derivative, has a zero crossing located sufficiently near the center of the pixel.

The straightforward implementation of these definitions in terms of the fitting coefficients $k_1,\ldots,k_{10}$ can give rise to unnecessary artifacts. The purpose of this paper is to illustrate how to apply these definitions through the ''eyes'' of the fitted cubic. Section II discusses the edge detection case. Section III discusses the ridge valley detection case.

II THE FACET EDGE DETECTOR

By edge we mean a configuration of gray tone intensity values which on each side of the edge have relatively small variation in value and which across the edge have relatively large variation in value. An ideal edge of this kind is a step edge whose gray tone intensity values on each side of the edge take a different constant value.

The key idea in detecting edges is to look for relatively large contrasts in small distances. Change in value, or contrast, divided by change in location which causes the value change is the essence of what a first derivative is. A large contrast in a small distance means a large enough first derivative. The natural one to choose would be the one which has largest first derivative. If the first derivative is to be a relative maximum, then the second derivative must be zero and the third derivative must be negative if the edge is crossed from the lower value to the high value gray tone region.

In the second directional derivative zero crossing edge detector (Haralick, 1984), a bivariate cubic function is fit to the central neighborhood of pixel. The fit produces the estimated bivariate cubic function f:

$$f(r,c) = k_1 + k_2 r + k_3 c + k_4 r^2 + k_5 rc + k_6 c^2 + k_7 r^3 + k_8 r^2 c + k_9 rc^2 + k_{10} c^3 \quad (1)$$

Based on the estimated coefficients $k_1,\ldots,k_{10}$ a decision is made to label the pixel as edge or non-edge. A pixel is labelled as edge if the second directional derivative, taken in the direction of the gradient, has a negatively sloped zero crossing located near the center of the pixel.

The simplest way to think about directional derivatives is to cut the surface f(r,c) with a plane which is oriented in the desired direction and which is orthogonal to the row-column plane. By convention, we take the angle to be measured clockwise from the column axis. We define the desired direction to be the gradient direction at the center of the given pixel. Hence, the gradient angle θ, satisfies

$$\begin{aligned} \sin\theta &= k_2/(k_2^2 + k_3^2)^{.5} \\ \cos\theta &= k_3/(k_2^2 + k_3^2)^{.5} \end{aligned} \quad (2)$$

The angle θ is well defined providing that $k_2^2 + k_3^2 > 0$.

To cut the surface f(r,c) with a plane in the direction θ we just require that $r = p \sin\theta$ and $c = p \cos\theta$ where p is the independent variable. This requirement produces the cubic curve $f_\theta(p)$.

$$\begin{aligned} f_\theta(p) = {} & k_1 + (k_2\sin\theta + k_3\cos\theta)p + (k_4\sin^2\theta + k_5\sin\theta\cos\theta + k_6\cos^2\theta)p^2 \\ & + (k_7\sin^2\theta + k_8\sin^2\theta\cos\theta + k_9\sin\theta\cos\theta + k_{10}\cos^3\theta)p^3 \end{aligned}$$

Let

$$\begin{aligned} C_0 &= k_1 \quad (3) \\ C_1 &= k_2 \sin\theta + k_3 \cos\theta = (k_2^2 + k_3^2)^{.5} \\ C_2 &= k_4 \sin^2\theta + k_5 \sin\theta\cos\theta + k_6 \cos^2\theta \\ C_3 &= k_7 \sin^3\theta + k_8 \sin^2\theta\cos\theta + k_9 \sin\theta\cos^2\theta + k_{10}\cos^3\theta \end{aligned}$$

Then

$$f_\theta(p) = C_0 + C_1 p + C_2 p^2 + C_3 p^3 \quad (4)$$

from which it follows that the first, second and third directional derivatives are given by

$$\begin{aligned} f_\theta'(p) &= C_1 + 2C_2 p + 3C_3 p^2 \\ f_\theta''(p) &= 2C_2 + 6C_3 p \\ f_\theta'''(p) &= 6C_3 \end{aligned} \quad (5)$$

For a pixel to be labelled as an edge pixel, the second directional derivative must have a negatively sloped zero crossing sufficiently near the center of the pixel. In this case, with the origin taken as the center of the pixel, there must be a p sufficiently small in magnitude satisfying

$$f_\theta''(p) = 0 \quad \text{(this is the zero requirement)}$$

$$\text{and} \quad f_\theta'''(p) < 0 \quad \text{(this is the negative slope requirement).}$$

For $f_\theta'''(p) < 0$ we must determine that $C_3 < 0$. If $C_3 < 0$, then $C_3 \neq 0$ and a p having the value $-C_2/3C_3$ exists which makes $f_\theta''(p) = 0$. If $|C_2/3C_3| < p_0$, where we take p_0 to be somewhat less than a pixel length, we can label the pixel as an edge. In essence, this is the procedure given by Haralick (1984).

If our ideal edge is the step edge, then we can refine the above detection criteria by insisting that the cubic polynomial $f_\theta(p)$ have coefficients which make f_θ a suitable polynomial approximation of the step edge. Now a step edge does not change in its essence if it is translated to the left or right or if it has a constant added to its height. Since the cubic polynomial is representing the step edge, we must determine what it is about the cubic polynomial which is its fundamental essence after an ordinate and abscissa translation.

To do this, we translate the cubic polynomial so that its inflection point is at the origin. Calling the new polynomial g, we have

$$\begin{aligned} g_\theta(p) &= f_\theta(p - C_2/3C_3) - (C_0 + 2C_2^3/27C_3^2 - C_1C_2/3C_3) \\ &= ((3C_1C_3 - C_2^2)/3C_3)p + C_3p^3 \end{aligned} \tag{6}$$

In our case since $C_1 = (k_2^2 + k_3^2)^{.5}$ we know $C_1 > 0$. If a pixel is to be an edge the second derivative zero crossing slope must be negative. Hence, for edge pixel candidates $C_2 < 0$. This makes $-3C_1C_3 + C_2^2 > 0$ which means that $g_\theta(p)$ has relative extrema. The parameters of the cubic which are invariant under translation relate to these relative extrema. The parameters are the distance between the relative extrema in the abscissa direction and in the ordinate direction.

We develop these invariants directly from the polynomial equation for $g_\theta(p)$. First we factor out the term

$$\frac{(C_2^2 - 3C_1C_3)^{1.5}}{3^{1.5}\,C_3^2}$$

This produces

$$\begin{aligned} g_\theta(p) = {} & [(C_2^2 - 3C_1C_3)^{1.5}/3^{1.5}C_3^2][-3^{.5}C_3/(C_2^2 - 3C_1C_3)^{.5})p \\ & + (3^{1.5}C_3^3/(C_2^2 - 3C_1C_3)^{1.5}p^3] \end{aligned}$$

For candidate edge pixels, $C_3 < 0$. This permits a rewrite to

$$\begin{aligned} g_\theta(p) = {} & [C_2^2 - 3C_1C_3)^{1.5}/3^{1.5}C_3^2] \quad [(3C_3^2/C_2^2 - 3C_1C_3))]^{.5}p \\ & - (3C_3^2/(C_2^2 - 3C_1C_3))^{1.5}p^3 \end{aligned}$$

Let the contrast by C and the scale be S. They are defined by

$$C = \frac{(c_2^2 - 3c_1c_3)^{1.5}}{3^{1.5}c_3^2}$$

$$S = \frac{(3c_3^2)^{.5}}{(c_2^2 - 3c_1c_3)^{.5}} \tag{7}$$

Finally, we have

$$g_\theta(p) = C(Sp - S^3p^3)$$

In this form it is relatively easy to determine the character of the cubic. Differentiating,

$$g_\theta{}'(p) = C(S - 3S^3p^2)$$
$$g_\theta{}''(p) = 6CS^3p \tag{8}$$

The locations of the relative extrema only depend on S. They are located at $\pm 1/(3^{.5}S)$. The height difference between relative extrema depends only on the contrast. Their heights are $\pm 2C/(3^{1.5})$. Other characteristics of the cubic depend on both C and S. For example, the magnitude of the curvature at the extreme is $2(3^{.5})CS^2$ and the derivative at the inflection point is CS.

Of interest to us is the relationship between an ideal perfect step edge and the representation it has in the least squares approximating cubic whose essential parameters are contrast C and scale S. We take an ideal step edge centered in an odd neighborhood size N to have (N−1)/2 pixels with value −1, a center pixel with value 0, and (N−1)/2 pixels with value +1. Using neighborhood sizes of from 5 to 23 we find the following values for contrast C and scale S of the least squares approximating cubic.

Neighborhood Size N	Contrast C	Scale S
5	3.0867	.37796
7	3.1357	.26069
9	3.1566	.20000
11	3.1673	.16253
13	3.1734	.13699
15	3.1773	.11844
17	3.1799	.10434
19	3.1817	.09325
21	3.1830	.08430
23	3.1841	.076924

The average contrast of the approximating cubic is 3.16257. The scale S(N) appears to be inversely related to N; S(N) = S/N. The value of S minimizing the relative error

$$\left(\frac{S(N) - S/N}{S(N)}\right)$$

is 1.793157.

These two relationships

$$C = 3.16257$$

$$S = 1.793157/N$$

for ideal step edges having a contrast of 2 can help provide additional criteria for edge selection. For example the contrast across an arbitrary step edge can be estimated by

$$\text{Edge Contrast} = \frac{2C}{3.16257} \tag{9}$$

If the edge contrast is too small, then the pixel is rejected as an edge pixel. We have found that in many kinds of images, too small means smaller than 5 percent of the image's true dynamic range. Interestingly enough, edge contrast C depends on the three coefficients C_1, C_2, C_3 of the representing cubic. First derivative magnitude at the origin, a value used by many edge gradient magnitude detection techniques, only depends on the coefficient C_1. First derivative magnitude at the inflection point is precisely CS, a value which mixes both scale and edge contrast together.

The scale of the edge can be defined by

$$\text{Edge Scale} = \frac{SN}{1.793157} \tag{10}$$

Ideal step edges, regardless of their contrast, will produce least squares approximating cubic polynomials whose Edge Scale is very close to unity. Values of Edge Scale larger than one have the relative extrema of the representing cubic closer together than expected for an ideal step edge. Values of Edge Scale smaller than one have the relative extrema of the representing cubic further away from each other than expected for an ideal step edge. Values of Edge Scale which are significantly different from unity may be indicative of a cubic representing a data value pattern very much different from a step edge. Candidate edge pixels with an edge scale very different from unity can be rejected as edge pixels.

The determination of how far from unity is different enough requires an understanding of what sorts of non-edge situations yield cubics with a high enough contrast and with an inflection point close enough to the neighborhood center. We have found that such non-edge situations occur when a step like jump occurs at the last point in the neighborhood. For example, suppose all the observed values are the same except the value at an endpoint. If N is the neighborhood size then the inflection point of the approximating cubic will occur at $\pm(N + 3)/14$, the plus sign corresponding to a different left endpoint and the minus sign corresponding to a different right endpoint. Hence, for neighborhood sizes of N = 5, 7, 9, or 11 the inflection point occurs within a distance of 1 from the center point of the neighborhood. So providing the contrast is high enough, the situation would be classified as an edge if scale were ignored. For neighborhood sizes of N = 5, 7, 9, 11, and 13, however, the scale of the approximating cubic is 1.98, 1.81, 1.74, 1.71, and 1.68, respectively. This suggests that scales larger than 1 are significally more different from unity scale than corresponding scales smaller than 1. We have found that in many images restricting edge scale to be between .4 and 1.1 works well.

III THE FACET RIDGE VALLEY OPERATOR

In the facet ridge valley detector (Haralick, 1983), a bivariate cubic function is fit to the central neighborhood of a pixel. The fit produces the estimated bivariate function f:

$$f(r,c) = k_1 + k_2r + k_3c + k_4r^2 + k_5rc + k_6c^2 + k_7r^3 + k_8r^2c + k_9rc^2 + k_{10}c^3$$

Based on the estimated coefficients $k_1,\ldots,k_{10}$ a decision is made to label the pixel as ridge of valley. A pixel is labelled as a ridge or valley if the first directional derviative, taken in a direction which extremizes the second directional derivative, has a zero crossing located sufficiently near the center of the pixel.

To determine a direction θ extremizing the second directional derivative, we proceed as before and cut the surface f(r,c) with a plane in the direction θ. Letting $r = p \sin \theta$ and $c = p \cos \theta$, we obtain the cubic curve $f_\theta(p)$ defined by equation 4. Using the definition for C_0, C_1, C_2, and C_3 from equation 3 and equation 4 expressing $f_\theta(p)$ a cubic polynomial having coefficients C_0, C_1, C_2, and C_3, we readily obtain that the second directional derivative in direction θ evaluated at the origin is given by

$$f_\theta''(0) = 2C_2 = (\sin \theta \ \cos \theta) \begin{pmatrix} 2k_4 & k_5 \\ k_5 & 2k_6 \end{pmatrix} \begin{pmatrix} \sin \theta \\ \cos \theta \end{pmatrix} \qquad (11)$$

The directions extremizing $f_\theta''(0)$ are precisely the two orthogonal directions determined by the eigenvectors of

$$H = \begin{pmatrix} 2k_4 & k_5 \\ k_5 & 2k_6 \end{pmatrix} \qquad (12)$$

which, in fact, is the Hessian of f, the matrix of the second partial derivatives of f. The eigenvalues of H are given by

$$\lambda = k_4 + k_6 \pm \sqrt{(k_6 - k_4)^2 + k_5^2} \qquad (13)$$

Each eigenvector (x,y)' of H must satisfy

$$2k_4x + k_5y = [(k_4 + k_6) \pm \sqrt{(k_6 - k_4)^2 + k_5^2}\,]x \qquad (14)$$

Either $k_5 = 0$ or not. If $k_5 = 0$, then the eigenvectors of H are

$$\begin{pmatrix} 0 \\ 1 \end{pmatrix} \quad \text{and} \quad \begin{pmatrix} 1 \\ 0 \end{pmatrix}$$

If $k_5 \neq 0$, then equation 14 can be solved for y producing

$$y = \left(\frac{k_6 - k_4}{k_5}\right) + \left[\sqrt{\left(\frac{k_6 - k_4}{k_5}\right)^2 + 1}\right] x \tag{15}$$

The most numerically stable way of determining the eigenvectors is then to define

$$T = \text{Sign}\left(\frac{k_6 - k_4}{k_5}\right)\left[\left|\frac{k_6 - k_4}{k_5}\right| + \sqrt{\left(\frac{k_6 - k_4}{k_5}\right)^2 + 1}\right] \tag{16}$$

from which we obtain for eigenvectors

$$\frac{1}{\sqrt{1 + T^2}}\begin{pmatrix}1\\ T\end{pmatrix} \qquad \frac{1}{\sqrt{1 + T^2}}\begin{pmatrix}-T\\ 1\end{pmatrix} \tag{17}$$

The extremizing directions θ_1 and θ_2 are given by

$$\sin\theta_1 = \frac{1}{\sqrt{1 + T^2}} \qquad \sin\theta_2 = \frac{-T}{\sqrt{1 + T^2}}$$
$$\cos\theta_1 = \frac{T}{\sqrt{1 + T^2}} \qquad \cos\theta_2 = \frac{1}{\sqrt{1 + T^2}} \tag{18}$$

Having determined an extremizing direction, the cubic $f_\theta(p)$ must be analyzed to determine where its extrema are. The extrema are located at the zero crossings of $f'_\theta(p)$. If there is a value of p^* sufficiently close to 0 which makes

$$f'_\theta(p^*) = C_1 + 2C_2p^* + 2C_3p^{*2} = 0$$

and for which $f''_\theta(p^*) = 2C_2 + 6C_3p^{*2} \neq 0$, then the central pixel of the fitting neighborhood can be classified as a peak or pit in direction θ. It is a peak in direction θ if $f''_\theta(p^*) < 0$ and a pit in direction θ if $f''_\theta(p^*) > 0$. The central pixel is classified as a ridge if in one of the extremizing directions it is a dominant peak and in the other extremizing direction it is neither a peak or pit or if it is a peak or pit it is a relatively weak one. It is classified as a valley if in one of the extremizing directions it is a dominant pit and in the other extremizing direction it is neither a peak or a pit or if it is a peak or a pit it is a relatively weak one. Relative strength of pit or peak can be measured by the ratio of $\min\{|f_1''|, |f_2''|\}$ to $\max\{|f_1''|, |f_2''|\}$. When this ratio is close to 0 one extrema dominates the other.

To determine a value of p^*, if any, which makes $f_\theta(p^*) = C_1 + 2C_2p^* + C_3p^{*2} = 0$, there are three cases to consider. If $C_3 = 0$ and $C_2 = 0$, then $f_\theta'' = 0$ and there are no extrema. If $C_3 = 0$ and $C_2 \neq 0$, f_θ is quadratic and has one extrema located at $p^* = -C_1/2C_2$. If $C_3 \neq 0$, f_θ is cubic and has extrema only if

$C_2^2 - 3C_1C_3 > 0$. If it has extrema, the most numerically stable way of computing their location is by

$$p^*_{large} = \text{Sign}\ (C_2)(|C_2| + \quad C_2^2 - 3C_1C_3\ ] \tag{19}$$

$$p^{*small} = \frac{C_1}{3C^3 p^*_{large}} \tag{20}$$

The extrema closest to origin is located at p^*_{small}. If $|p^*_{small}|$ < radius, then a peak or pit in direction θ can be declared for the pixel.

However, there are some complications to this basic procedure. The first complications revolve around the fact that the fitted f_θ is, in general, a cubic. The cubics of interest have extrema. Such a fitted cubic arising from data which is as simple as piecewise constant with one jump have relative extrema even though the data does not. This is an artifact of using a cubic fit. It may or may not be significant; that is, they may or may not correspond to extrema in the data. To illustrate, consider a one-dimensional data pattern which is a constant with a jump change at one end. We analyze it in terms of the fitted cubic dynamic range, the relative depth of its extrema, and its inflection point.

The dynamic range of the cubic segment is defined by

$$\text{range} = \max_p f_\theta(p) - \min_p f_\theta(p)$$

The relative depth is defined as follows. Suppose the extrema is a relative minimum. Let a represent the left end point of the interval, b represent the right end point of the interval, i represent the location of the inflection point and v represent the location of the relative minimum. If the relative minimum occurs to the left of the relative maximum, the depth of the minimum is defined by

$$\text{depth} = \min\ \{f_\theta(a),\ f_\theta(i)\} - f_\theta(v)$$

If the relative minimum occurs to the right of the relative maximum, the depth of the minimum is defined by

$$\text{depth} = \min\ \{f_\theta(b),\ f_\theta(i)\} - f_\theta(v)$$

The relative depth of the minimum is then defined by

$$\text{relative depth} = \text{depth/range}$$

Data	Position of Extrema Closest to Origin	Position of Inflection Point	Relative Depth
00009	.241	-.571	.0408
0000009	.533	-.714	.0610
000000009	.811	-.857	.0731
000000099	-.755	-2.14	.0205
00000000099	.0237	-1.75	.0338
0000000000099	.519	-1.71	.0474

In each of these cases the cubic fitted to the data ''rings'' around the large constant region where the data is zero. One extrema of this ringing is close to the origin. This extrema is an artifact. Notice that in each of these cases, the inflection point is not too far from the origin indicating a relatively high frequency ringing. Also for all these cases, the relative depth, which measures the significance of the ringing, is close to zero.

Compare this situation to the case where the data clearly has an extrema near the origin as in the following one-dimensional patterns.

Data	Position of Extrema Closest to Origin	Position of Inflection Point	Relative Depth
01300	-.527	1.00	.279
0013000	-.569	2.14	.419
000130000	-.589	3.67	.604
00001300000	-.600	5.57	.821
0000013000000	-.607	7.86	.849
01900	-.235	2.71	.803
0019000	-.243	5.57	.874
000190000	-.246	9.38	.906
00001900000	-.247	14.14	.925
0000019000000	-.248	19.85	.937

Notice that in these cases the inflection points tend to be much further away from the extrema indicating the ''ringing'' behavior has a lower frequency. Also the relative depth tends to be much larger in the case of a true extrema.

What all this means is that in using f_θ to evaluate derivatives, we must understand and interpret the data through the ''eyes'' of a cubic polynomial. Not all extrema of the cubic are significant. A cubic extrema is significant in the sense that it reflects an extrema in the fitted data only if it passes the following tests

(1) |position of extrema from origin| < radius threshold

(2) |position of inflection from origin| > distance

(3) |distance between roots| > 1.756* Size of Interval

(4) relative depth > .2

(5) $|f_\theta''(p^*)|$ > curvature threshold

Test (1) guarantees that the extrema is close enough to the origin. Tests (2) and (3) guarantee that the ''ringing'' behavior has a long enough period, test (3) taking into account that for true extrema, the period increases with the size of the fitting interval. Test (4) guarantees that the relative extrema have a significant enough height compared to the dynamic range of the fitted cubic segment. Test (5) guarantees that the curvature at the extrema is sufficiently high.

REFERENCES

[1] Haralick, R.M., ''Ridges and Valleys on Digital Images'', Computer Vision, Graphics, and Image Processing, Vol. 22, (1983), pp. 28-38.

[2] Haralick, R.M., ''Digital Step Edges from Zero Crossing of Second Directional Derivatives'', IEEE Transactions on on Pattern Analysis and Machine Intelligence, Vol. PAMI-5, No. 1, January 1984, p. 58-68.

DISCUSSION:

Smeulders:
Is it necessary that the cubic spline goes right through the pixel point?

Haralick:
Yes, the estimation is done for each neighbourhood independently. These neighbourhoods are highly overlapping and the places where the grey values originated from are the centers of the pixels.

Smeulders:
Is that not in conflict with your initial assumption that you are considering noisy digitized images. Could you not take a looser sort of fit, for instance the least squares fit?

Haralick:
Well, the fit is a least squares fit. If you do not want to assume that the points come on a regular grid you increase the computations by a tremendous amount.

Choudry:
Can't you use something different from cubics.

Haralick:
The reason for the cubic model is that it is of just one higher degree of complexity than absolutely necessary to solve the problem. That extra degree actually gave me a specific location in the pixel which was not necessarily the center of the pixel. Suppose you use a higher order model. Then, in the case of the edge, instead of trying to solve a linear equation you are going to ask me to solve a quadratic equation. The complexity goes up. And if you ask me to change the basis into a spline basis or a discrete cosine basis, then again to compute the zero crossings is computationally more complex.

PATTERN RECOGNITION IN PRACTICE II
E.S. Gelsema and L.N. Kanal (Editors)

QUANTITATIVE EVALUATION OF EDGE DETECTION BY DYNAMIC PROGRAMMING

J.J. Gerbrands, E. Backer and W.A.G. van der Hoeven

Department of Electrical Engineering
Delft University of Technology
P.O. Box 5031, 2600 GA Delft, The Netherlands

A method is described for the detection of edges in noisy images, which is based on a dynamic programming optimal path algorithm. The performance has been evaluated with ROC analysis and Pratt's Figure of Merit for edge detectors. The dynamic programming method shows much better performance than the best parallel schemes for low values of SNR, but requires the definition of a region of interest.

INTRODUCTION

In a broad sense, digital image analysis deals with the extraction of information from two-dimensional pictorial data by using digital techniques. One of the crucial issues in digital image analysis is the problem of image segmentation. The goal of image segmentation is to partition the two-dimensional image domain into regions which are homogeneous according to some predefined criteria. The segmentation results forms the basis for all subsequent measurements, classification and, eventually, interpretation.

The large variety of image segmentation methods may be grouped into certain families depending on specific properties: parallel vs. sequential methods, and the region approach vs. the edge approach. In this paper we will discuss a sequential method of edge detection [1], which uses dynamic programming to detect the optimal edge in a specific region of interest. We confine ourselves to monochrome images containing regions with different mean grayvalues, separated by transitions with an intermediate grayvalue which are at least one pixel wide. In the image processing literature edges of this type are usually referred to as 'ramp edges'.

THE METHOD

An edge detection scheme is called sequential if the result at a specific pixel is influenced by the results at previously examined points. In general, sequential methods require

- the selection of an initial point
- a mechanism to nominate candidate pixels
- an acceptance criterion
- a termination criterion.

The dynamic programming approach described here is based on early results by Montanari [2] and Martelli [3]. The basic idea is to assign cost coefficients to all image points and to use state-space search techniques to find a minimal cost path from the initial point to a goal. Usually, the cost coefficients are based on the first and/or second discrete difference functions of the brightness function, as approximations of the gradient or the Laplacian. An edge is defined as the concatenation of individual pixels and the cost of an edge as the sum of the cost coefficients of the constituting pixels.

In order to apply our method to arbitrary edges in arbitrary directions, the image data in a selected region of interest are resampled into a rectangular matrix. From this transformed matrix the matrix of cost coefficients is obtained. Dynamic programming is used to find the optimal path from the bottom to the top of this cost matrix. Any point on the bottom row can serve as initial point and any point on the top row as goal. A path is defined as a sequence of 8-adjacent points, with exactly one point per row of the cost matrix. So each point has (at most) three candidate predecessors on the previous row.

Dynamic programming as used here is a breadth-first search technique. It should be noted that the cost function is not used to guide the search, but to select the terminal point of the best path once they have all been evaluated. The optimal path is then traced back to the initial point. To obtain true global optimality one has to vary over all possible starting points. In order to reduce the combinatorics of the problem it is attractive to define rather narrow regions of interest.

THE ALGORITHM

Let $C(r(h),h)$ denote the nxm matrix of cost coefficients of candidate edge pixels. On every row h of the cost matrix we want to select one single edge pixel $R(h)$. The selected points should form a connected path:

$$|R(h+1) - R(h)| \leq 1 \qquad \text{for} \qquad 1 \leq h \leq n-1. \tag{1}$$

The minimal cost path is then defined as the path $R(1),\ldots,R(n)$ for which the cumulative costs $F(R(1),\ldots,R(n))$ are minimal:

$$F(R(1),\ldots,R(n)) = F_{min} = \underset{r(1),\ldots,r(n)}{\text{MIN}} \sum_{h=1}^{n} C(r(h),h). \tag{2}$$

The minimization procedure is greatly simplified, if a convenient starting point $R(1)$ can be selected on the first row. If this is the case, the minimal cost path can be found serially. Let us denote the cumulative cost of the minimal cost path from $(R(1),1)$ to $(r(h),h)$ by $Q(r(h),h)$. Then the following formulas hold:

$$Q(r(1),1) = C(R(1),1) \qquad \text{for} \qquad r(1) = R(1) \tag{3}$$

$$\qquad = \infty \qquad \text{for} \qquad r(1) \neq R(1)$$

$$Q(r(h),h) = C(r(h),h) + \text{MIN}\,\{Q(r(h-1),h-1)\} \quad \text{for } 2 \leq h \leq n \tag{4}$$

where the minimum is selected from the 8-adjacent predecessors on row (h-1). Finally,

$$F_{min} = \underset{r}{\text{MIN}}\,\{Q(r(n),n)\}. \tag{5}$$

If the values of $r(h)$ corresponding with the selected minima in Eq. (4) are stored in a matrix of pointers $M(r(h),h)$, the minimal cost path can be traced back from the endpoint $R(n)$ found in Eq. (5).

This can be clarified for a simple 4x4 cost matrix. Let us select $(R(1),1) = (2,1)$ to be the starting position on the bottom row.

C(r(h),h)	Q(r(h),h)	M(r(h),h)
1 2 1 2	5 6 4 5	2 2 4 4
3 2 3 1	6 4 5 3	2 3 3 3
3 2 1 3	4 3 2 ∞	2 2 2 -
2 1 2 3	∞ 1 ∞ ∞	- - - -

It is clear that $F_{min} = Q(3,4) = 4$ and $R(4) = 3$ is the position of the end point on the top row. The optimal path can now be traced back easily from the matrix M(r(h),h):

$$R(3) = M(R(4),4) = 4$$
$$R(2) = M(R(3),3) = 3$$
$$R(1) = M(R(2),2) = 2.$$

Obviously, the detected path is conditionally optimal with respect to the chosen starting point. To obtain global optimality one has to vary over all possible starting points.

EXAMPLE

We originally developed this method for the detection of the left ventricular contour in cardiac scintigrams. The region of interest is defined by two concentric circles around an automatically detected midpoint. The image data in this region are resampled into polar coordinates. The cost coefficients are computed as the inverse of a convex combination of the first and second derivative. See Fig. 1. Due to its succes, the method is now used on a routine basis for various medical applications at the Thoraxcenter in Rotterdam [4,5].

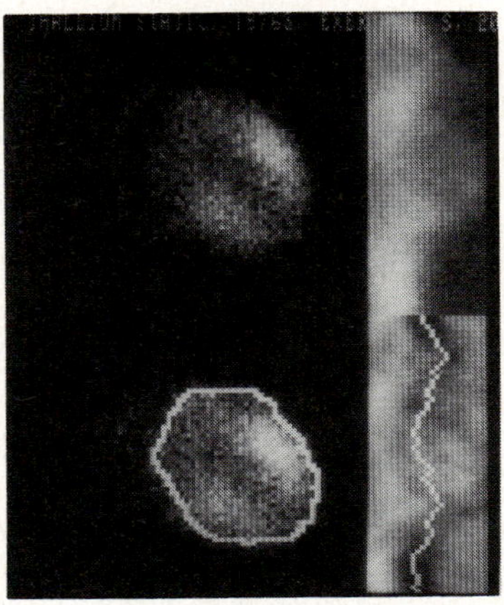

Fig. 1. Top left: Thallium scintigram; Top right: transformed image (rescaled); Bottom right: cost matrix and optimal path; Bottom left: detected contour superimposed.

EVALUATION

The quantitative evaluation of parallel edge detectors of the enhancement/threshold type has been carried out by Abdou and Pratt [6]. For the purpose of the analysis a continuous idealized luminance edge is defined as a planar ramp discontinuity. The ideal edge can be described by its position, orientation angle, base amplitude, contrast and width. Digital test images are generated by simulating the discretization process. The digital images are corrupted by additive noise. Edge detection schemes can then be evaluated on the basis of comparison of the probabilities of correct and false edge point detection (ROC-analysis) and a figure of merit. The figure of merit takes the distance between a detected point and the ideal edge into account:

$$F = \frac{1}{\mathrm{MAX}\,\{I_I, I_A\}} \sum_{i=1}^{I_A} \frac{1}{1 + \beta\, d^2(i)}$$

where I_I and I_A are the number of ideal and actual edge points, d(i) is the pixel miss distance and β is a scaling constant.

In an experimental study we have applied the evaluation technique used by Abdou and Pratt to the dynamic programming method described above. In order to facilitate comparison with the results obtained by Abdou and Pratt for parallel edge detectors, we use the same type of test images.

The digital test images contain a region with brightness level b and a region with brightness level (b+h), separated by a one pixel wide transition region with brightness level (b+h/2). This corresponds with the steepest edge that can occur in a correctly sampled real image. The first test image is of size (64x64) and contains one vertical edge in column 32. The second image is of size (128x128) and contains one diagonal edge from the top left to the bottom right. The evaluation, however, is restricted to a window defined by the corners [1,64], [64,128], [128,64] and [64,1], containing again 64 edge points. The lay-out of the test images is illustrated in Fig. 2.

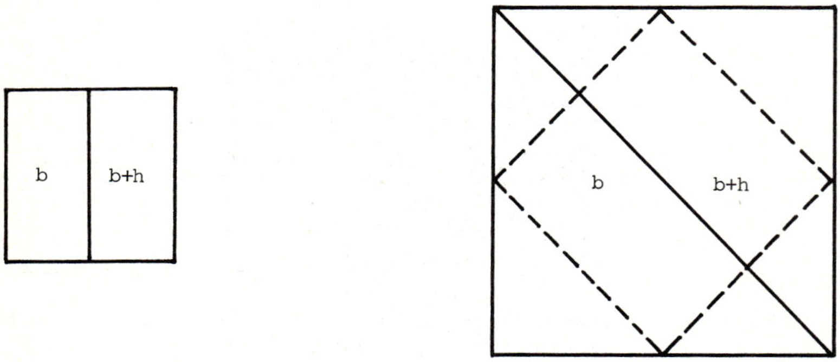

Fig. 2.a. Vertical edge. b. Diagonal edge and evaluation window.

The images are distorted by adding zero-mean uncorrelated signal-independent Gaussian noise with variance σ^2. The signal-to-noise ratio SNR is defined as

$$\mathrm{SNR} = \frac{h^2}{\sigma^2}$$

where h is the brightness contrast across the edge.

The dynamic programming method requires the definition of a region of interest (ROI). In practical applications this can often be achieved by some automated procedure [4,5]. In our experiments we indicated the region of interest interactively by entering two points of the straight midline of a rectangular ROI.

The image is resampled along 64 scanlines perpendicular to the midline of the ROI. The sample distance on a scanline and the distance between consecutive scanlines are equal to the grid constant of the image. In our experiments the number of samples on each scanline was set to 25 yielding a (64x25) transformed matrix. In the resampling process, we experimented with three types of interpolation: zero-order or nearest pixel resampling, unweighed averaging of the nearest four pixel values and distance-weighed linear interpolation of the nearest four pixels.

In our medical applications [4,5,7] it proved to be attractive to compute the cost coefficients C(i,j) by taking the first and second-order discrete differences along the rows of the transformed matrix. The cost coefficients are then defined as the inverse of a convex combination of the magnitudes of the first-order difference g'(i,j) and the second-order difference g"(i,j):

$$C(i,j) = M - \alpha|g'(i,j)| - (1-\alpha)|g''(i,j)|$$

where M is some large positive constant. We have experimented with various discrete difference filters:

[-2 -1 0 1 2]
[-1 -2 0 2 1]
[-1 -3 0 3 1]
[-1 0 1]

and with various values for the coefficient α.

The optimal path algorithm is applied to the (64x17) central part of the (64x25) cost matrix. The boundary strips are ignored because they contain no reliable values due to the discrete convolution with the discrete difference filters. The detected path is transformed back to the original image domain by using nearest pixel position assignment. The optimal path algorithm yields a connected path in the cost matrix, but this does not guarantee connectivity in the image. The edge may be closed by linear interpolation.

The final result is then evaluated quantitatively by computing the probability of correct detection P_d, the probability of false detection P_f and Pratt's figure of merit F, as defined above.

EXPERIMENTS

It will be quite obvious that the number of experimental variables is too large to allow for an exhaustive experiment over all possible combinations of discrete difference filter, weighing coefficient α and interpolation method. In practice, one has to settle for a reasonable number of experiments, yielding a possibly suboptimal selection of possibilities.

Filters and coefficient α

Experiments were performed for the vertical edge image, nearest pixel resampling and one noise realization only, with SNR-values of 1,5,10,20,50 and 100 to select the best discrete difference filter and the best value for the weighing coefficient α in the convex sum of the first and second order discrete differences. In the first series the region of interest was alligned perfectly with the actual edge. Based on the values of the figure of merit F and the detection and false detection probabilities P_d and P_f, the filters [-1 0 1] and [-2 -1 0 1 2] were discarded. In the second series we introduced an angle between the midline of the ROI and the vertical edge. Angles between 4 and 14 degrees were investigated. For SNR=1 and 5 different noise realizations the two remaining filters were compared. Based on these results, the filter [-1 -3 0 3 1] was discarded. For all further experiments the filter [-1 -2 0 2 1] was used, with a weighing coefficient α equal to

1.0, i.e. the cost coefficients are computed from the first derivative only.

Interpolation

The second issue to be discussed here is the choice of the interpolation method in the resampling procedure. All experiments were performed with the filter [-1 -2 0 1 2] and $\alpha = 1.0$. In the first series only one noise realization was used with values for SNR of 1,5,10,20,50 and 100. Both the vertical edge and the diagonal test images were used and the offset in the ROI-definition was varied between 0 and 14 degrees.

In the second series only SNR=1 was considered, but 5 different noise realizations were used. As an example, we give the average values for the figure of merit F and the correct and false detection probabilities P_d and P_f for the three interpolation schemes. The angle between the midline of the ROI and the actual vertical edge in this experiment was 7.1 degrees.

	F	P_d	P_f
no interpolation	0.70	0.24	0.01
first-order without distance weighing	0.75	0.22	0.01
first-order with distance weighing	0.75	0.26	0.01

From these experiments it is concluded that first-order interpolation with or without distance weighing shows better performance than nearest neighbor resampling for low values of SNR. The difference between both weighing methods is neglectable.

The obvious advantage of computational speed of the unweighed averaging leads to our conclusion that first-order interpolation by computing the average value of the nearest four neighbors is the method of choice to be used in the resampling process.

COMPARISON WITH PARALLEL METHODS

On the basis of the probabilities of correct and false detection P_d and P_f, and the values of the figure of merit F, our method of edge detection by dynamic programming can be compared with the performance of parallel edge detection schemes as published by Abdou and Pratt [6]. The results are shown in Figs. 3 and 4 for the vertical edge image and in Figs. 5 and 6 for the test image with the diagonal edge. We conclude that the dynamic programming method shows much better performance than the best parallel schemes for low values of the signal-to-noise ratio.

REFERENCES

[1] Davis, L.S., A survey of edge detection techniques, Comp. Graph. Image Proc. 4 (1975) 248-270.

[2] Montanari, U., On the optimal detection of curves in noisy pictures, Comm. ACM 14 (1971) 335-345.

[3] Martelli, A., Edge detection using heuristic search methods, Comp. Graph. Image Proc. 1 (1972) 169-182.

[4] Reiber, J.H.C., Lie, S.P., Simoons, M.L., Hoek, C., Gerbrands, J.J., Wijns, W. Bakker, W.H., Kooij, P.P.M., Clinical validation of fully automated computation of ejection fraction from gated equilibrium bloodpool scintigrams, Journ. Nucl. Med. 24 (1983) 1099-1107.

[5] Reiber, J.H.C., Kooijman, C.J., Slager, C.J., Gerbrands, J.J., Schuurbiers, J.C.H., den Boer, A., Wijns, W., Serruys, P.W., Hugenholtz, P.G., Coronary artery dimensions from cineangiograms-methodology and validation of a computer-assisted analysis procedure, IEEE Trans. Medical Imag. 3 (1984) 131-141.

[6] Abdou, I.E. and Pratt, W.K., Quantitative design and evaluation of enhancement/thresholding edge detectors, Proc. IEEE 67 (1979) 753-763.

[7] Gerbrands, J.J., Hoek, C., Reiber, J.H.C., Lie, S.P., Simoons, M.L., Automated left ventricular boundary extraction from technetium-99 m gated blood pool scintigrams with fixed or moving regions of interest. Proceedings IEEE 2nd Int. Conf. Visual Psychophysics and Medical Imaging (1981) 155-159.

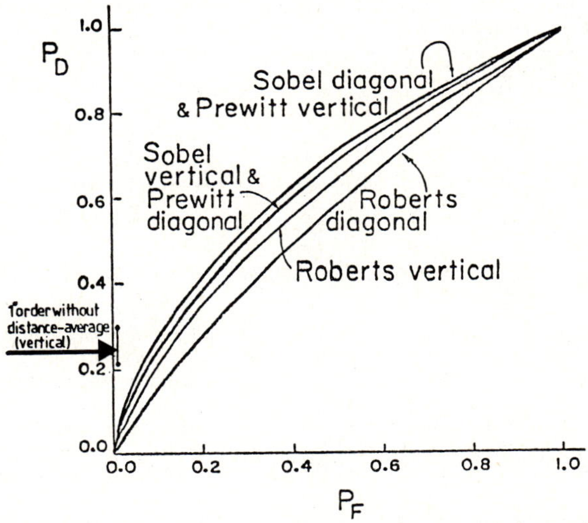

Fig. 3. Range of P_D vs. P_F for 5 noise realizations, SNR=1, vertical edge, 1st order interpolation

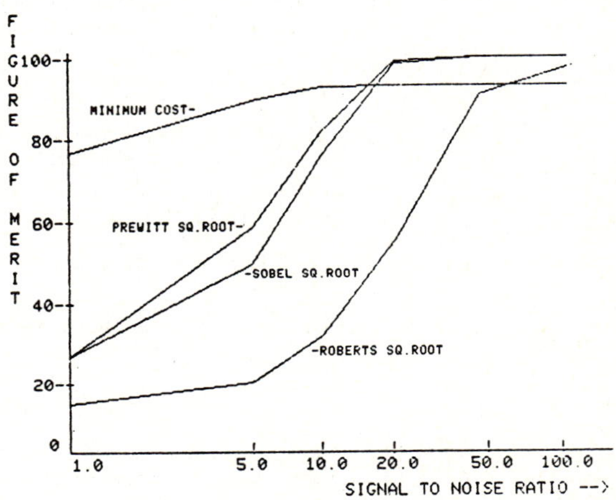

Fig. 4. Figure of Merit for various values of SNR, vertical edge, 1st order interpolation

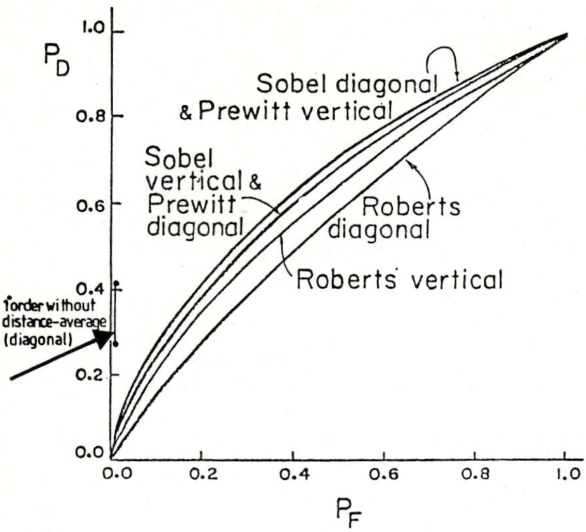

Fig. 5. Range of P_D vs. P_F for 5 noise realizations, SNR = 1, diagonal edge, 1st order interpolation

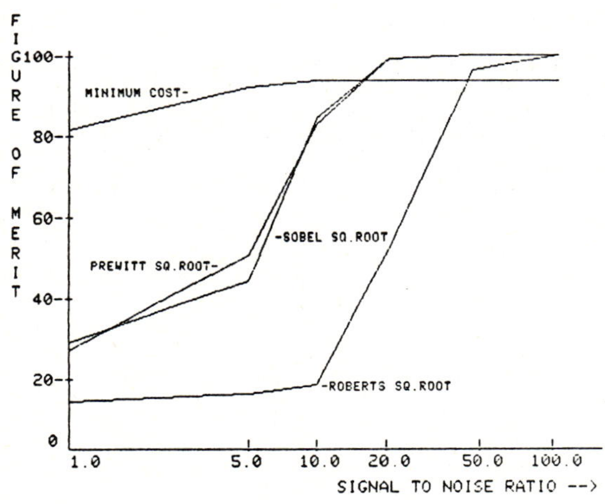

Fig. 6. Figure of Merit for various values of SNR, diagonal edge, 1st order interpolation.

DISCUSSION

Aus:

How does the processing time for your method compare with that for other methods?

Gerbrands:

It is difficult to make general statements concerning the processing time for this method since it depends on the implementation. We did evaluation studies on a VICOM digital image processor and on this system the Sobol-square-root operator can be performed within a few video frames. On that system, the resampling in our method requires already a substantial amount of time, since there is no floating point hardware available. It takes up to seven seconds to do only a 64*25 resampling of a region of interest.
For the implementation on a Gamma-11 system or a PDP-11/44 in the clinical setting in Rotterdam the processing time needed for this method is neglectible as compared to the total time required for the clinical study.
Obviously the method is computationally more complex than other methods but it yields better results. This is not surprising since we are using more a priori knowledge.

Van Bemmel:

The noise you added in your test images is uncorrelated. This is not true in your medical images. How can you compare results?

Gerbrands:

You are right. We did add uncorrelated Gaussian noise to our test images while in the medical images the noise has a Poisson distribution. I agree that the results on the noise test are not valid for the medical images. However, for the medical applications the whole procedure has been clinically evaluated. The clinicians are pleased with the results obtained with the system.

PATTERN RECOGNITION IN PRACTICE II
E.S. Gelsema and L.N. Kanal (Editors)

A PRETOPOLOGICAL TEXTURE MODEL, A MULTIPARAMETRIC IMAGE MODEL AND A HIERARCHICAL CLASSIFICATION METHOD FOR THE ANALYSIS OF DIGITIZED IMAGES

Patrick Saint-Jean (1,2), Victoria von Hagen (1,3), Ger Koper (1), Johan S. Ploem (1)

1 - Department of Cytochemistry and Histochemistry, Sylvius Laboratories, State University of Leiden, The Netherlands
2 - 83 Avenue d'Italie, 75Ø13 Paris, France.
3 - Institut National de la Sante et de la Recherche Medicale, Paris, France.

This paper presents a two stage approach for automated image processing. The first is a texture analysis based on a pretopological texture model which generates the parameters of the object images. The parameters in turn are used to form a multiparametric image in the display memory of the computer and this constitutes a visual data base. Each object is represented by a line of parameter "pixels". The grey level or color of each pixel corresponds to the value of the parameter. The second step is an automatic, multiparametric, hierarchical classification which uses image processing to classify the lines (objects) of the multiparametric image. This method has been applied to the analysis of a cytological data set from a Prototype Image Analyser (Leitz) using a PDP 11/44 (DEC) computer and a RAMTECK display device.

INTRODUCTION

Much attention has been given during the last ten years to the analysis of texture in digitized images (Serra J. 1982, Haralick R. 1973, Preston K. 198Ø , Castleman K. R. 1979, Ploem J. S. 1982), and applications to cytology in particular, have proved promising.

We propose here a texture model designed to address the problem of quantifying the properties of complex textures, i.e. those which have mutually embedded grey level structures. If this complexity can be expressed in terms of the interrelationship between the elements of all the grey level structures, then it is possible to obtain a meaningful quantitative measurement of local and global complex texture. This approach generates 255 meaningful parameters (high order multiparameters).

We will present a two step method of classifying digitized images. The first is a texture analysis based on a pretopological texture model which generates the parameters of the object image. These parameters in turn are used to form a multiparametric image of the texture parameters of the object images in the display memory of the computer and this constitutes a visual data base. The second step is an automatic, multiparametric, hierarchical classification which uses image processing to classify the lines of the multiparametric image.

Pretopological models were first introduced (Frechet 1924) for continuous sets. In 1971 we began the study of the properties of particular discrete mathematical sets, defining what we call pretopological spaces (Saint-Jean P. 1972). We have shown that these spaces can be used in image processing to define and measure texture spaces (Saint-Jean P. 1977,von Hagen et al 1981). Here texture is understood to be an organisation of more or less complex motifs. We will only briefly summarize those results which are needed here to present the model.

THE MATHEMATICAL MODEL

DEFINITION OF PRETOPOLOGICAL SPACES

Let $X = \emptyset$. For each $x \in X$ let $V(x)$ be a family of parts of X. Let V be a part of X and a member of $V(x)$. Then $V(x)$ defines a pretopology iff $V(x)$ satisfies the following axioms : 1. $V(x) \neq \emptyset$ and for $x \in X$ we have: $V \in V(x) \Longrightarrow x \in V$. 2. All finite intersections of any two members of $V(x)$ belong to $V(x)$: $V1$ and $V2 \in V(x) \Longrightarrow (V1 \cap V2) \in V(x)$. 3. All parts of X that contain a member of $V(x)$ belong to $V(x)$: 4. For $V \in V(x)$, $\exists y \neq x$ with $y \in V' \in V(x)$ such that $V \notin V(y)$.

Then $V \in V(x)$ is called a pre-neighborhood of x and $V(x)$ a pre-neighborhood system of a point of $x \in X$. The set X together with the family $V(x)$ is called a PRETOPOLOGICAL SPACE $P \equiv (X,V(x))$.

DEFINITION OF A PRETOPOLOGICAL TEXTURE SPACE

Let R be a binary relation in a set X. Then a point y is or is not in relation with x according to this relation. A fundamental property of R is the transitivity (y is related to x and z is related to y implies that z is related to x) or the intransitivity (for x,y,z being three different points of X, y is related to x and z is related to y does not necessarily imply that z is related to x). We have shown (Saint-Jean P. et al 1982) that the transitive and reflexive properties of R are equivalent and can define a topology on X, and that the intransitive and reflexive properties of R are equivalent and can define a pretopology on X. Thus we can state that (X,R) = (X,V(x)) is a PRETOPOLOGICAL SPACE. The relation R resulting from the composition of relations R1 and R2 (y is related to x according to the relation R1, and z is related to y according to the relation R2 implies that z is related to x according to the relation R = R2 R1) have the property of being transitive iff relations R1 and R2 are transitive, and are intransitive iff one of the relations R1 or R2 is intransitive.

Then a pretopological space (X,R), where R is the result of a composition of binary relations when one is intransitive, is a PRETOPOLOGICAL TEXTURE SPACE. See Fig.1 for the relationship between binary relations, topology and pretopology.

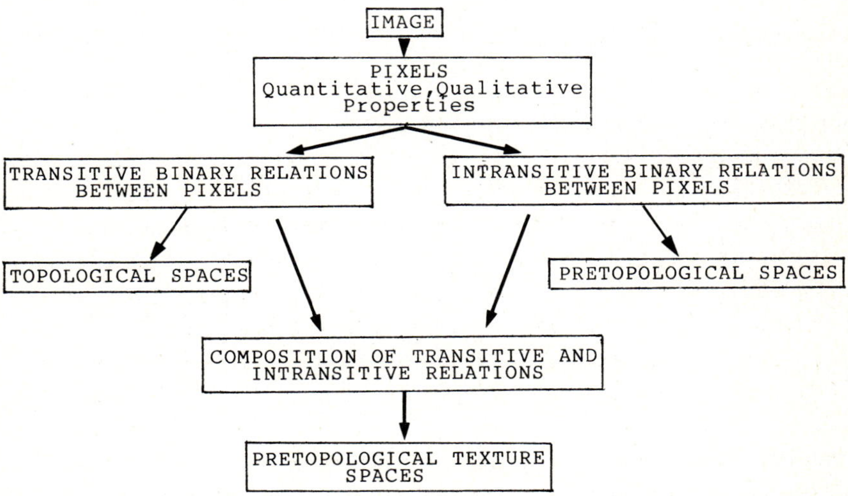

Fig.1 THE RELATIONSHIP BETWEEN BINARY RELATIONS AND PRETOPOLOGY

The pretopological texture spaces are defined on the set of digitized images as follows : for each space we count the elements belonging to particular sets of each grey level or color set. This gives the whole set of grey levels (histogram),the interior, and the adherence sets. In pretopological spaces these particular sets can be defined as they are in topology. See Fig. 2.

Fig.2 RESUME OF THE PRETOPOLOGICAL MODEL

COMMENTS	MATHEMATICAL STRUCTURE
1. VIDEO IMAGE: AMPLITUDE VARIATION WITH TIME	1. SPACE CONTINUUM: function $S(t)$
2. DIGITIZED VIDEO IMAGE. SUCCESSION OF NUMERIC VALUES IN MEMORY.	2. DISCRETE SPACE: a set X of elements representing image points : $X = \{x(i),\ \text{for } i=1 \text{ to } p.\}$
3. BASIC MEASUREMENTS -REFERENCE POINTS DIMENTIONAL SPACE. -QUALITATIVE PROPERTIES ex.GREY LEVELS	3. A SET OF PARAMETERS: PARAMETERS $I(s)$ SPACIO-TEMPORAL REFERENCES, $I(q)$ IMAGE PROPERTIES $I = \{I(s), I(q)\}$. A SET OF PARAMETRIC INDICES: $J = \{1,\ldots,s,\ldots,q,\ldots,n\}$
4. AN ELEMENTARY FORM WITH ITS SET OF PROPERTIES	4. AN ELEMENT $x(i)$ WITH ITS PARAMETERS $x(i) = \{x(i,j) \text{ for } j \in J\}$
5. CHOICE OF SPECIFIC PROPERTIES.ex.GREY LEVELS,SPATIAL WINDOW.	5. A SET $I' = \{I'(s) \subset I(s),\ I'(q) \subset I(q)\}$
6. DUAL RELATIONS BETWEEN ELEMENTARY FORMS ACCORDING TO EACH SPECIFIC PROPERTY.	6. BINARY RELATIONS $R(j)$ BETWEEN ELEMENTS $x(i)$ ACCORDING TO PARAMETERS $j \in J$.
7. REGROUPING OF ELEMENTARY PROPERTIES.	7. $S(s,k)$ AND $Q(q,l)$ ARE SUBSETS OF THE ELEMENTS $x(i)$, RELATED BY PARAMETERS k,l ACCORDING TO RELATIONS $R(s)$ AND $R(q)$.
8. DECOMPOSITION OF THE IMAGE OF DISTRIBUTION RELATIVE	8. $S(s) = S(s,k)$ IS THE SET OF LOCALLY DISTRIBUTED ELEMENTS. $Q(q) = \{Q(q,l)\}$ IS THE SET OF GLOBALLY DISTRIBUTED ELEMENTS.
9. REGROUPING OF ELEMENTARY FORMS HAVING PROPERTIES DISTRIBUTED LOCALLY AND GLOBALLY AS TEXTURE ELEMENTS.	9. TEXTURE ELEMENTS: $W(s,k,q,l) = (S(s,k) \cap Q(q,l))$
10. REGROUPING OF TEXTURE ELEMENTS HAVING THE PROPERTIES s AND q.	10. $Wsq(k,l) = \{W(s,k,q,l)\ \forall k, \forall l\}$ s and q given.
11. DEFINITION OF AN ELEMENTARY TEXTURE DESCRIPTOR.	11. $W(I'(s),I'(q),k,l) = [\bigcap_s (S(s,k) \cap Q(q,l))]q \ldots$ $\ldots [\bigcap_q (S(s,k) \cap Q(q,l))]s$
12. DEFINITION OF A COMPLEX TEXTURE.	12. $W(I'(s),I'(q)) = \ldots$ $\ldots \{W(I'(s),I'(q),k,l)\}$
13. PROXIMITY OF 2 ELEMENTARY TEXTURE DESCRIPTORS.	13. $d(W(I(s),I(q),i,j), \ldots$ $\ldots W(I(s),I(q),k,l))$
14. A THEORY SERVING AS A BASIS FOR THE MODEL: PRETOPOLOGY	14. $B(W(I'(s),I'(q),i,j),\rho)$ A SPHERE WITH RADIUS $\rho = 1$. A SYSTEM OF PRE-NEIGHBORHOODS $V(W(I'(s),I'(q),i,j)) =$ $\ldots V\ \{W(I'(s),I'(q))$, SUCH THAT $V \supset B(W(I'(s),I'(q),i,j),1)\}$ FOR WHICH THE 4 PRETOP. AXIOMS HOLD AND DEFINE PRETOPOLOGY. $(W(I'(s),I'(q)),P)$ IS A PRETOPOLOGICAL TEXTURE SPACE.

15. DESCRIPTION OF A TEXTURE BY 3 PRETOPOLOGICAL MEASUREMENTS :
HISTOGRAM
AGGREGATION ....>
DISPERSION ....>

15. CARD(Ai): CARDINAL OF THE SET
R INT(Ai):INTERIOR RATIO
R ADH(Ai):ADHERENCE RATIO
WHERE
INT (Ai)= $\{$x(i) ϵ X SUCH THAT
W(I'(s),I'(q))ϵV(W(I'(s),I'(q),i,j)
and W(I'(s),I'(q)) $\subset$ A(i)$\}$
ADH (Ai)= $\{$x(i) ϵ X SUCH THAT
W(I'(s),I'(q)) ϵ V(W(I'(s),I'(q),i,j))
and W(I'(s),I'(q))$\cap$ A(i) = Ø$\}$

16. EVALUATION OF A COMPLEX TEXTURE BY THE POSITION OF THE TRIPLETS IN THE DESCRIPTIVE PRETOPOLOGICAL SPACE.

16.
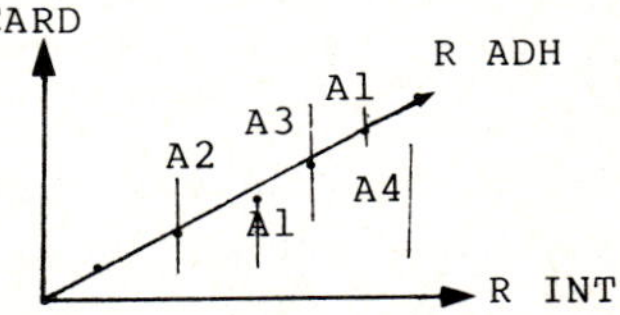

17. CHOICE OF PRETOPOLOGICAL TEXTURE SPACES TO GRADUATE THE COMPLEXITY OF THE TEXTURE (ANALYSIS LEVEL).

17. PRETOPOLOGICAL FILTER. BASE OF A PRETOPOLOGICAL FILTER.
FINEST FILTER=ULTRA FILTER.
BASES OF ULTRAFILTER.

COMPARISON OF BASES=SCALE OF ANALYSIS FROM MICROANALYSIS TO MACROANALYSIS.

18. EVOLUTION OF COMPLEX TEXTURES THROUGH THE SCALE OF ANALYSIS LEVELS.

18.
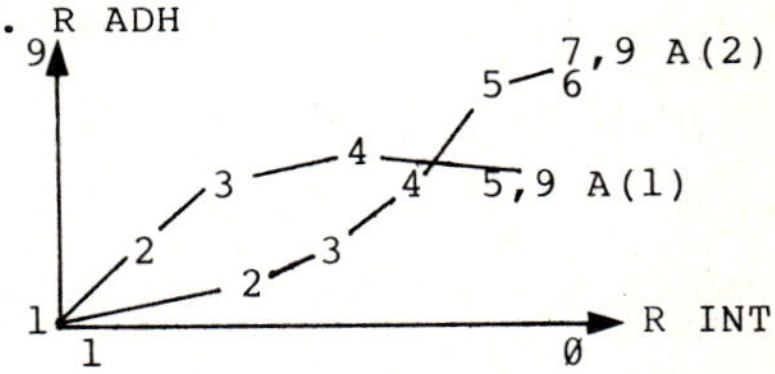

For this analysis we have defined 8 pretopological spaces by the relationship between two pixels of X ,where y R2 x, means " y belongs to a non directional window of s pixels with x as the central point" 2<s<8. We note that for s=1 the interior and adherence sets are the histogram. Thus, with the relation y R1 x meaning " the pixel y is isodense with the central point x ", we obtain 8 pretopological texture spaces with 3 independent parameters for each of them (cardinal of the set, of the interior and the adherence). The cardinals of the interior and the adherence are divided by the cardinals of each set to obtain the ratios of the interiors and adherences for each isodense set. Their corresponding ratios measure the aggregation and dispersion of the elements of each grey level set. In concrete terms these parameters give the coarseness or fineness of the complex texture. When 15 significant grey levels are used, 255 texture parameters are generated for 8 pretopological texture spaces (15+15*8+15*8)

Figure 3 shows the interpretation of the evolution of complex textures through the scale of analysis levels represented by the choice of the 8 pretopological texture spaces. With this representation it is easy to see that different grey level sets having the same cardinality could have different interior or adherence ratios depending on the texture.

This interpretation is given for a texture composed of isodense areas of the same size which are included in a 3*3 window having a size equal or superior to j in a pretopological texture space Pj. In real images the areas are not identical and we therefore analyse isodense sets composed of these different areas.

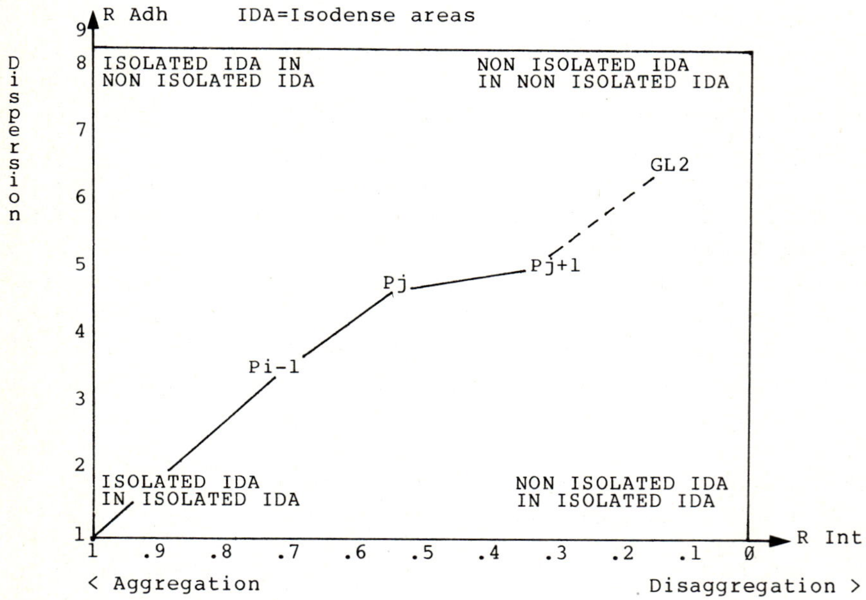

Figure 3: Evolution of complex textures through scale of analysis levels represented by choice of 8 pretop. texture spaces

THE CLASSIFICATION MODEL

To classify images with many parameters the usual statistical procedures are not cost effective. The multiparametric hierarchical classification method has been designed to handle such data bases.

The MULTIPARAMETRIC IMAGE (MPI) has been defined as follows : Each line represents an object in the order of acquisition. Each column represents a parameter of the pretopological texture. Each point of the parametric image has a grey level or color value proportional to the value of the parameter. Thus, using an appropriate digital screen image processor (i.e. LEYTAS or Ramtek), 255 parameters and 255 object images can be analysed and classified simultaneously. The MPI is analysed by a hierarchical classifier which is described as follows : The n lines and the m columns of the MPI are stored in an image memory, M1, which can be visualized on the display. The first line of the M1 image is copied n times in a second image memory, M2. The subtraction of the two images M1 and M2, line by line, gives the difference between the current line and the others for each parameter. The results remain in M2. The content of M2 is multiplied by itself point by point squaring the differences. The sum of all values for each line, $Dij = (Pi-Pj)$, $i=1,n$ and $j=1,m$ for each line is then stored in the 256th column of M2. The line in M1, which has the minimum value in the 256th column of M2, is exchanged with the line next to the current line and its position is noted in a table. The next line in M1 then becomes the new current line and so on...

When this process is completed, we have an MPI in which each line is hierarchically classified with the preceding line which is at a minimum distance from it. But at this stage the current line has only been compared with the succeeding lines and the preceding line, but not with the other preceding lines. Thus the classification is not optimum and has to be iterated. All the lines of M1 are shifted down by one line and the last line is moved to the first position in M1. The process is repeated until it converges to an oscillating classification in which the last line of one of the preceding classifications is obtained again. In an oscillation, several MPIs are obtained which represent the whole structure of the hierarchical classification, the last of which is the optimum classification.

The same algorithm can be used on the transposed multiparametric image to classify the parameters which eliminate the correlated parameters if desired. The alternative use of object images and parameter classification gives an optimal classification of the object image set. The degrees of liberty for the multiparametric model are : choice of object images and parameters and choice of limits for normalization (Histogram, R Int, R Adh). These choices allow us to adapt the model to the data base and to choose different methods according to the needs of the analysis.

METHODS

A diagram of automated cytological image processing is shown in Fig. 4. Hierarchical structure is built by hierarchically classifying the elements of the population and grouping elements having a minimum difference in subgraphs where branched points are elements with the smallest difference.

The elements which are nearest to each other are eliminated and an optimal MPI is obtained. Classification is reiterated until an MPI is obtained in which elements with a large difference are separated. This generates connected subgraphs. At the top elements have small differences; at the bottom the differences are largest. The branches are cut by the selection of a difference threshold thus generating subgroups.

We set two tasks for cell population analysis : cell image sorting and the morphological description of a cell population and its subpopulations according to correlated and independent parameters.

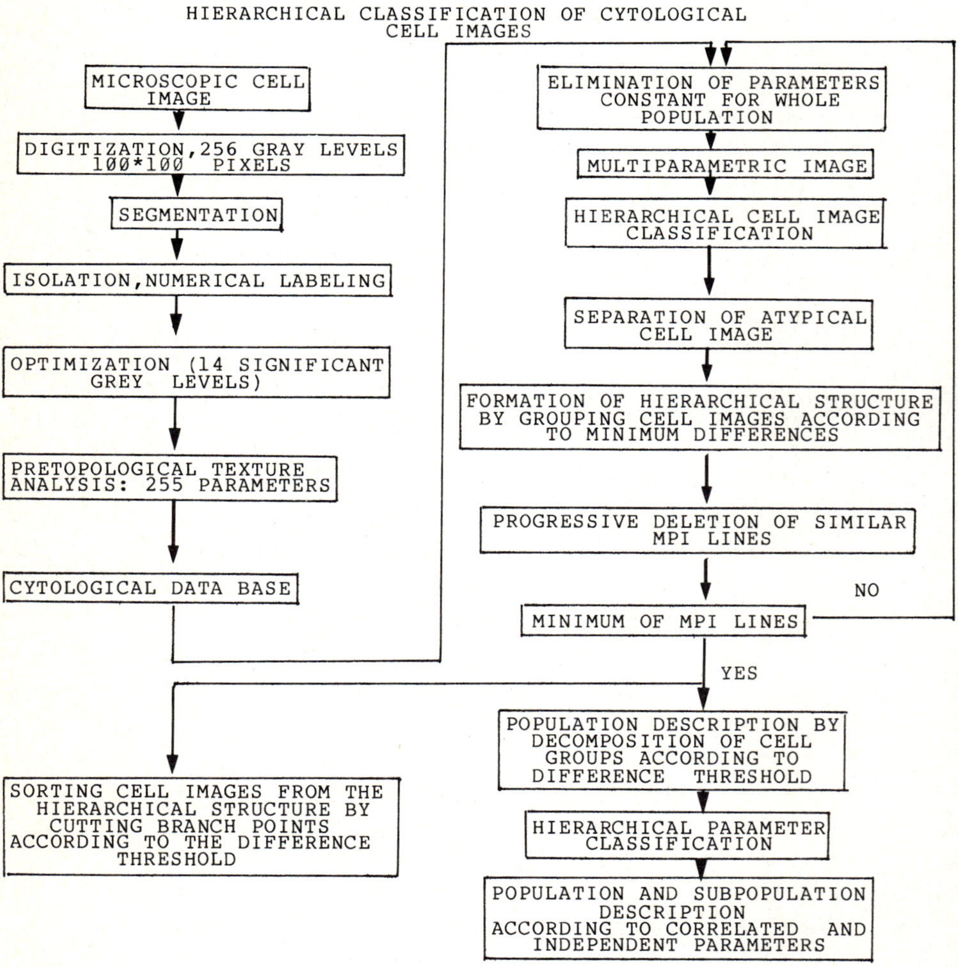

Figure 4.

These tasks require different methods (Fig. 5). Known cell populations are analysed in order to obtain a set of descriptions for groups of elements (Fig. 5a). When unknown cell populations are analysed, the same method can be used to separate hypothetical sub groups and describe them (Fig. 5b). In this case visual analysis is necessary to identify these subgroups. For automated recognition, this method first processes the known cells (and artifacts) to select typical members of each subgroup which are called specific markers.

The training sets thus obtained are mixed with an unknown population. The analysis of the mixed population gives subgroups containing the unknown elements and the markers. Pattern recognition by labeling unknown subgroups by the specific markers should then be straightforward (Fig. 5c). The limit of each subgroup is obtained by segmenting the graph starting from the markers and cutting the branches which represent a given difference threshold.

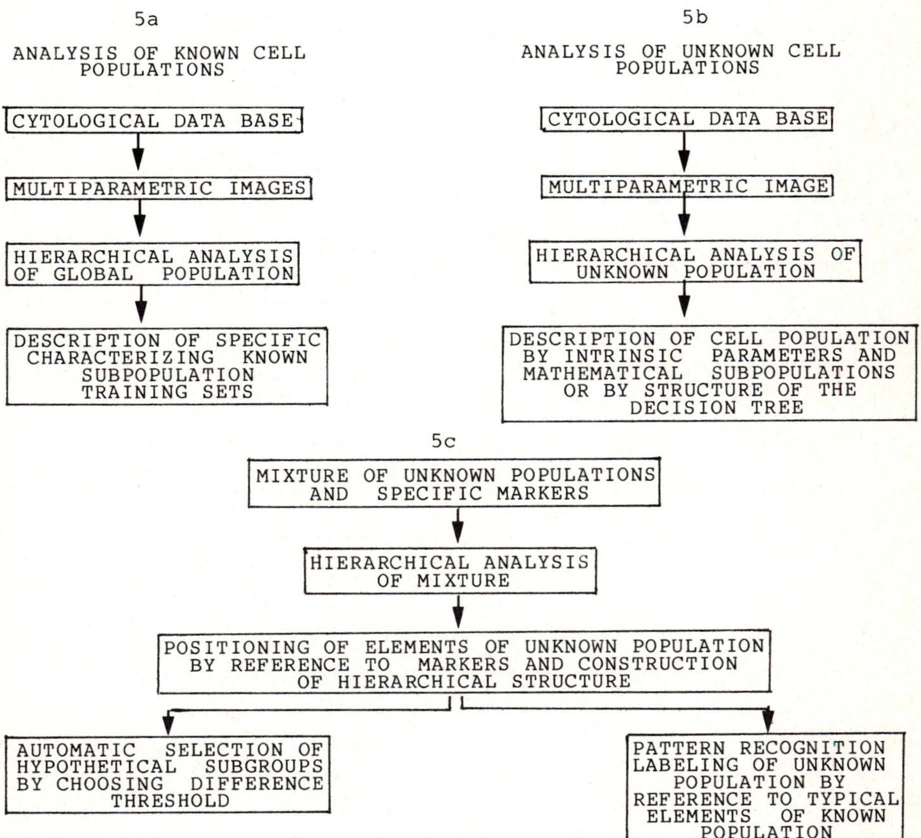

FIGURE 5

The image classifier then generates subgroups through the use of a threshold which sets the maximum allowable difference tolerated for subset membership. This threshold can be made to vary according to the hetereogeneity of the whole set and/or of each subgroup, either interactively or automatically. This procedure also calculates the stability of each subset during the successive classfication iterations thus giving the operator criteria for allowing cut-set separation.

Both of the methods described here have been designed to evolve as the operator gains experience and insight into the results of the classification of his data set. This is achieved through the large number of options available: e.g. the selection or deselection of coarse or fine textures at various grey levels, choice of the various classification thresholds, etc.

DISCUSSION

The pretopological texture model has been run on a Multi 20 computer (Intertechnique France) in assembler at the Protection Department of the Centre d'Energie Atomique (C.E.A.,France), on a Texture Analyser System (T.A.S. Leitz) and a PDP 11/34 (DEC) at the Quantitative Microscopy Laboratory of Bobigny (France), and on the Prototype Image Analyser from Leitz, computer-coupled with PDP 11/44 (DEC) and a Ramtek (Ramtek Corp.) display device at the Department of Histochemistry and Cytochemistry, Sylvius Laboratoria (The Netherlands). The hierarchical MPI classification was run at the latter two laboratories. At this point in our research with the two models about 5000 object images of different types have been analysed and we are in a position to address the following questions:

1 - Why are a large number of parameters useful to identify object images? It is true that many types of images can be recognised by using only a few parameters under defined experimental conditions. But some types of images cannot be described with so few parameters. We now have the possibility of using up to 255 parameters (and 511, 1023 or 2047 on the new image processing computers).
When some parameters correlate for a population, they can be eliminated. But when parameters are deleted, the implicit assumption is that they have the same value for all elements of the population, which is not often the case. Loss of discriminatory parameters through loosely defined correlation thresholds can lead to a serious loss of precision in classification procedures.

2- Why do we feel that image processing is the best solution for high order multiparametric analysis? First, their use causes problems that cannot be cost effectively resolved by classical methods; they require big central memories and long running times which is not practicable on mini or micro computers. Second,image display devices now exist that have image memories which permit us to do two things: to store and process large data sets and to display the differences due to object dissimilarity, acquisition conditions and variation in the preparation of the material. This in turn makes it possible for the operator to visually assess the classification as it proceeds and intervene interactively when necessary. The classified MPI looks very different from the unclassified MPI and subgroups or homogeneity can be readily distinguished by the observer. Image contrast can be can be set by the operator thus defining one of the levels of the analysis. The visual images representing population data sets are precious tools for the researcher.

The modularity of the hierarchical classification model permits us to set up several methods with the same tools. That is why these models are well adapted to image processing computers. In LEYTAS or Ramtek the processor is external (PRETEX program) and the image is accessed through an interface. For greater speed and interactivity this image processing can be simulated by computer in standard memory by processing the data base as a matrix (Apolo, MIAS), or directly by a specialized processor for image memory (Cytix-Vicom of Digital Research , Pericolor of SEP Numelec France).

We have chosen to analyse image data sets, but these models can also be used on other types of data sets by transforming data into an MPI. Texture analysis can be used as a method of classifying object images by dividing the image into a two dimensional space. Because topological texture MPIs have been defined according to explicit relations, each point of the MPI can be interpreted in language. This means image processing with MPI and a language interpreter can be used to resolve artificial intelligence problems (expert systems) by mixing language and vision as in robotics applictions. Thus these models are general and flexible and can be applied to a wide variety of problems.

REFERENCES

CASTLEMAN K.R. (1979) : Digital Images Processing Series. Prentice Hall, Signal Processing Series. Alan V. OPPENHEIM, ed.

FRECHET (1924) : Les espaces abstraits. Congres International des mathematiciens, VII pp 399-412, Toronto.

HARALICK R., SHANMUGAM K., DINSTEIN I. (1973) : Texture features of image classification. IEEE Transaction on Systems, Man and Cybernetics, vol. SMC-3 N 6, November.

PLOEM J.S., Van DRIEL KULLER A. (1982): Automated analysis of Papanicolaou stained cervical specimens using a television-based analysis system (LEYTAS). Biomedical Images and Computers. Proceedings edited by SKLANSKY J., Springer Verlag pp 11-25.

PRESTON K. (1980) : Automation of the analysis of cell images. Anal. Quant. Cytol., 2 (1), pp 1-14.

SAINT-JEAN P. (1972) : Notion de Topologie Generale: Report at Ecole Superieure d'Informatique Electronique Automatique Paris, France

SAINT-JEAN P. (1977) : Work report, DPr, SRP, CEN-FAR,Commissariat a l'Energie Atomique, France.

SAINT-JEAN P., Von HAGEN V., BISCONTE J.C. (1982) : Un modele pretopologique pour l'analyse d'images. Un exemple applique a l'analyse de texture en imagerie biomedicale. Proc. Congress " Analyse et Traitement des Images Biomedicales ", Tours,France.

SAINT-JEAN P., Von HAGEN V., BISCONTE J.C. (1983) : A Multiparameter image processing technique for classification and cluster formation. Proceeding 39. Fourth International Conference on Automation of Diagnostic Cytology. Montreal, CANADA. Analytical and Quantitative Cytology, volume 55, September N 3 ISSN0190-0471.

SERRA J. (1982), editor : Image Analysis and Mathematical Morphology Academic Press , New York

VON HAGEN V., SAINT-JEAN P., VAN DRIEL-KULKER A., LE GO R. (1983) A texture analysis model for the classification of video images of B and T cells and the formation of subcatagories. Anal. Quant. Cytol. vol 5: 4, pp 291-301

PATTERN RECOGNITION IN PRACTICE II
E.S. Gelsema and L.N. Kanal (Editors)

PROBABILISTIC LABELING IN A HIDDEN SECOND ORDER MARKOV MESH

Pierre A. Devijver

Philips Research Laboratory
Avenue E. Van Becelaere 2, Box 8
B–1170 Brussels, BELGIUM

Abstract: In this paper, we address the pixel labeling problem under the assumption that contextual information in the picture is encoded in the transition probabilities of a second order Markov mesh random field. We show that the exponential complexity of the problem can be overcome by the virtue of a truly innocuous assumption that leads to a virtually optimal solution expressed in terms of a non-linear recurrence relation. We derive linear-time algorithms for computing the joint likelihood of the pixel label and past and present (and some look-ahead) image measurements. The smoothing and segmentation of coarsely quantized pictures are taken as example-problems to validate our assumption and demonstrate the effectiveness of the technique proposed.

1. Introduction

We outline hereafter a new approach to the use of context in image processing, under the assumptions that contextual information is encoded in the transition probabilities of a second order, Markov mesh random field [2] [10], and the image is observed in memoryless noise. The problem is approached here from the viewpoint of the theory of compound decisions [7] which was used with varying degrees of success for the purposes of detection, estimation, smoothing, segmentation, texture classification, data compression, etc.

The problem is formulated as one of computing the joint likelihood of the labels—at some arbitrary pixel location—and past, present (and look-ahead) image measurements, where the words "past", "present" (and "look-ahead") are given a precise interpretation that depends on the order of the assumed Markov mesh model. In the case of causal Markov fields which is of interest here, the problem complexity is exponential in the number of image pixels and has been overcome only at the cost of rather restrictive simplifying assumptions (see Section 1.3). Iterative solutions, based on the Gibbs distribution, are available for non-causal Markov fields but the work effort required remains prohibitive [5] [8].

In this paper, we concentrate on the simplest possible Markov mesh model, *viz.*, a second order model. We outline a fairly natural generalization of well established 1-D approaches in which the exponential complexity barrier was broken by the virtue of simple linear recurrence relations [1] [3] [13]. We show that a truly innocuous assumption is all that is needed to obtain a virtually optimal solution expressed in terms of non-linear recurrence relations. In Section 2, we discuss real-time labeling and the look-ahead mode of decision and we exhibit linear-time solutions in both cases. In Section 3, the smoothing and segmentation of coarsely quantized pictures are taken as example-problems to validate our assumption and demonstrate the effectiveness of the technique proposed. In the remainder of this section, we concentrate on theoretical perequisites.

1.1. The Markov field image model

Let $V_{M,N} = \{(i,j) : 1 \le i \le M, 1 \le j \le N\}$ denote the finite, $M \times N$ integer lattice. Equivalently, let (a,b) designate the pixel at the intersection of row a and column b in a digitized $M \times N$ image. Associated with every pixel (a,b) are a label $\lambda_{a,b}$ and a feature vector—or image measurements vector—$x_{a,b}$. Accordingly, we use $V^{(\lambda)}_{M,N}$ and $V^{(x)}_{M,N}$ to denote $M \times N$ arrays of labels and feature vectors respectively. We regard $V^{(\lambda)}_{M,N}$ as a sample realization of a homogeneous, second order Markov mesh random field, [2], [10]:

Definition 1: A second order Markov mesh random field is defined by the property

$$P[\lambda_{a,b}|\lambda_{i,j} : (i,j) \in V_{a-1,N} \cup V_{M,b-1}] = P[\lambda_{a,b}|\lambda_{a-1,b}; \lambda_{a,b-1}], \qquad \forall (a,b) \in V_{M,N} \tag{1}$$

with the boundary conditions

$$\begin{aligned} P[\lambda_{a,b}|\lambda_{a-1,b}; \lambda_{a,b-1}] &= P[\lambda_{1,1}] && \text{if } a = b = 1, \\ &= P[\lambda_{1,b}|\lambda_{1,b-1}] && \text{if } b > a = 1, \\ &= P[\lambda_{a,1}|\lambda_{a-1,1}] && \text{if } a > b = 1. \end{aligned} \tag{2}$$

Moreover, let Λ be the finite set of possible pixel labels, and $q, r, s \in \Lambda$. Then the Markov mesh is homogeneous if $P[\lambda_{a,b} = q|\lambda_{a-1,b} = r; \lambda_{a,b-1} = s] = P_{q|r,s}$, uniformly in (a,b). □

The causality of the Markov mesh model is well apparent in Eq.(1). In fact, Eq.(1) would be sufficent to define a periodic random field on a toroidal, integer lattice, *viz.*, a rather peculiar image model. From an image modeling viewpoint, the assumption that there exist boundary conditions—an initial distribution for the upper left pixel, and Markov chain structures along the first row and first column—is therefore more natural. As noted in [6], these image models may be readily simulated and constitute as surprisingly rich subclass of Markov random fields. We use the notation $P[\lambda_{1,b} = q|\lambda_{1,b-1} = s] = P_{q|\square,s}$, and $P[\lambda_{a,1} = q|\lambda_{a-1,1} = r] = P_{q|r,\square}$ in order to distinguish between the transition probabilities along the first row and first column respectively.

Theorem 1: [2], [10] For any $(a,b) \in V_{M,N}$, $P\left[V^{(\lambda)}_{a,b}\right] = \prod_{i=1}^{a} \prod_{j=1}^{b} P[\lambda_{i,j}|\lambda_{i-1,j}; \lambda_{i,j-1}]$. □

Theorem 2: [2], [10] For any $(a,b) \in V_{M,N}$

$$P[\lambda_{a,b} \mid \lambda_{i,j} : (i,j) \in V_{M,N} - \{(a,b)\}] = P\left[\lambda_{a,b} \;\middle|\; \begin{matrix} \cdots & \lambda_{a-1,b} & \lambda_{a-1,b+1} \\ \lambda_{a,b-1} & & \lambda_{a,b+1} \\ \lambda_{a+1,b-1} & \lambda_{a+1,b} & \cdots \end{matrix}\right],$$

with obvious simplifications along the first and last rows and columns. □

Theorem 3: Let $R_a \doteq \{(i,j) \in V_{M,N} : i = a\}$, $C_b \doteq \{(i,j) \in V_{M,N} : j = b\}$, *viz.*, the ath row and bth column of $V_{M,N}$. Then, under appropriate initial conditions, the rows $R^{(\lambda)}_a$'s, $a = 1, \cdots, M$, and columns $C^{(\lambda)}_b$'s, $b = 1, \cdots, N$, of a second order, homogeneous Markov mesh random field form multidimensonal vector Markov chains respectively. □

The property expressed by Theorem 3 was taken advantage of in [6] under a third order Markov mesh assumption. However, it is not clear how to determine the joint distribution for the elements of $R^{(\lambda)}_a$ or $C^{(\lambda)}_b$, from the assumptions specified in Definition 1. A simpler situation occurs in the following theorem.

Theorem 4: Let $D_{a+b} \doteq \{(i,j) \in V_{M,N} : i + j = a + b\}$, *viz.*, the (sub)-diagonals of $V_{M,N}$. Then, under appropriate initial conditions, the (sub)-diagonals $D^{(\lambda)}_{a+b}$'s, $a + b = 1, \cdots, M + N$, of a second order Markov mesh random field form a multidimensional vector Markov chain. Moreover, given $D^{(\lambda)}_{a+b-1}$, the elements of $D^{(\lambda)}_{a+b}$ are statistically independent in the sense that

$$\begin{aligned} P[\lambda_{i,j} : (i,j) \in D_{a,b}|\lambda_{k,l} : (k,l) \in D_{a+b-1}] &= \textstyle\prod_{(i,j) \in D_{a+b}} P[\lambda_{i,j}|\lambda_{k,l} : (k,l) \in D_{a+b-1}] \\ &= \textstyle\prod_{(i,j) \in D_{a+b}} P[\lambda_{i,j}|\lambda_{i-1,j}; \lambda_{i,j-1}] \quad \square \end{aligned} \tag{3}$$

1.2. The noise model

We shall make the assumption that the original, noise-free image is corrupted by conditionally independent noise. Specifically, suppose that the set Λ of possible pixel labels serves as an index set for the probability distributions $p_\lambda(x)$, in other words, that the distribution of $x_{i,j}$ is $p_q(x_{i,j})$ when it is known that $\lambda_{i,j} = q$. Readily, the state-conditional—or memoryless—assumption implies that

$$P\left[V_{a,b}^{(x)}|V_{a,b}^{(\lambda)}\right] = \prod_{i=1}^{a}\prod_{j=1}^{b} p_{\lambda_{i,j}}\left(x_{i,j}\right). \tag{4}$$

1.3. Statement of the problem

In what follows, we shall assume that both the underlying Markov and noise models are known to us and our problem will be that of recovering the array of labels $V_{M,N}^{(\lambda)}$, corresponding to a given array of image measurements $V_{M,N}^{(x)}$ (or part thereof). Our criterion will be that of minimizing the error probability per pixel labeling.

The first problem that will be addressed will be that of estimating the current label $\lambda_{a,b}$ given the "past and present image measurements in $V_{a,b}$". For obvious reasons, we call this the real-time problem. A standard decision theoretic argument permits to show that minimum probability of error is achieved by the rule

$$\hat{\lambda}_{a,b} = q \text{ if } q = \text{argmax}_r \left\{P\left[\lambda_{a,b} = r; V_{a,b}^{(x)}\right]\right\}. \tag{5}$$

The look-ahead mode of decision is defined by straightforward analogy with its 1-D equivalent [13]. Let $V_{\overline{a,b}} \doteq \{(i,j) \in V_{a,b} - \{(a,b)\}\}$, *viz.*, the rectangular array $V_{a,b}$ with the lower left pixel removed. Then, in accordance with Theorem 2, minimum probability of error under the look-ahead mode is achieved by the rule

$$\hat{\lambda}_{a,b} = q \text{ if } q = \text{argmax}_r \left\{P\left[\lambda_{a,b} = r; V_{\overline{a+1,b+1}}^{(x)}\right]\right\}. \tag{6}$$

A brief examination of the joint likelihood in Eq.(5) reveals the source of all our ills:

$$\begin{aligned} P\left[\lambda_{a,b}; V_{a,b}^{(x)}\right] &= \sum_{\lambda \in V_{\overline{a,b}}^{(\lambda)}} P\left[V_{\overline{a,b}}^{(\lambda)}; \lambda_{a,b}; V_{a,b}^{(x)}\right] = \sum_{\lambda \in V_{\overline{a,b}}^{(\lambda)}} P\left[V_{a,b}^{(\lambda)}\right] P\left[V_{a,b}^{(x)}|V_{a,b}^{(\lambda)}\right] \\ &= \sum_{\lambda \in V_{\overline{a,b}}^{(\lambda)}} \prod_{i=1}^{a}\prod_{j=1}^{b} P\left[\lambda_{i,j}|\lambda_{i-1,j}; \lambda_{i,j-1}\right] p_{\lambda_{i,j}}\left(x_{i,j}\right), \end{aligned} \tag{7}$$

where the summation runs over all possible label assignments in $V_{\overline{a,b}}^{(\lambda)}$. If labels can assume σ different values, this sum has $\sigma^{a \times b - 1}$ terms. Hence, the intrinsic complexity of processing a $M \times N$ image is exponential in $M \times N$.

A number of simplifying assumptions have been proposed to break the exponential complexity barrier. For instance, in [9], it was assumed that the spatial dependence imposed by the transition probabilities could be factored into the product of the dependences along each of the principal axes; in [11], [12], [14] it was not attempted to maximize the likelihood of all the data in $V_{a,b}$, but rather the likelihood of data in small regions around (a, b); in [6], the computation was done over relatively narrow strips in which—by Theorem 3—vectors of labels form a 1-D vector Markov chain. It will be seen that the derivation hereafter is based on a more natural, and truly harmless simplifying assumption.

2. Linear Time Recurrences

2.1. The real-time recurrence

In this section, we concentrate on the problem of computing the joint likelihood required by Eq. (5). To simplify the notation, let us pose $\mathcal{F}_{a,b}(q) \doteq P\left[\lambda_{a,b} = q; V^{(x)}_{\overline{a,b}}\right]$ for $1 \leq a \leq M$, and $1 \leq b \leq N$, and $\mathcal{G}_{a,b}(r,s) \doteq P\left[\lambda_{a-1,b} = r; \lambda_{a,b-1} = s; V^{(x)}_{\overline{a,b}}\right]$ for $2 \leq a \leq M$ and $2 \leq b \leq M$, and where the labels are as shown in Figure 1. Readily, $\mathcal{F}$ and $\mathcal{G}$ are related according as

$$\mathcal{F}_{a,b}(q) = \sum_{r,s} \mathcal{G}_{a,b}(r,s) P_{q|r,s}\, p_q(x_{a,b}). \tag{8}$$

Likewise, let $\mathcal{H}_{a,b}(t,u,v) \doteq P\left[\lambda_{a-2,b} = t; \lambda_{a-1,b-1} = u; \lambda_{a,b-2} = v; V^{(x)}_{\overline{\overline{a,b}}}\right]$ for $2 < a \leq M$, and $2 < b \leq N$, and where $V_{\overline{\overline{a,b}}} \doteq \{(i,j) \in V_{\overline{a,b}} - \{(a-1,b),(a,b-1)\}\}$. By straightforward conditional probability calculations, we get

$$\mathcal{G}_{a,b}(r,s) = \sum_{t,u,v} \mathcal{H}_{a,b}(t,u,v) P_{r|t,u} P_{s|u,v}\, p_r(x_{a-1,b})\, p_s(x_{a,b-1}). \tag{9}$$

We are now in a position to state the key assumption which leads to the linearization of the complexity of computing $\mathcal{F}_{a,b}(q)$. Stated quite informally, it says that the value v of $\lambda_{a,b-2}$ and the x's in $R_{a,b-2}$—refer to Figure 1—are independent of the value t of $\lambda_{a-2,b}$ and the x's in $C_{a-2,b}$ once the value u of $\lambda_{a-1,b-1}$ and the x's in $V_{a-1,b-1}$ are given. More precisely, we have the following result.

Lemma 5: If, for $2 < a \leq M$ and $2 < b \leq N$, $\mathcal{F}_{a-1,b-1}(u) > 0$ and it holds that

$$\begin{aligned} P\left[\lambda_{a-2,b}; \lambda_{a,b-2}; C^{(x)}_{a-2,b}; R^{(x)}_{a,b-2} | \lambda_{a-1,b-1}; V^{(x)}_{a-1,b-1}\right] &= P\left[\lambda_{a-2,b}; C^{(x)}_{a-2,b} | \lambda_{a-1,b-1}; V^{(x)}_{a-1,b-1}\right] \\ &\times P\left[\lambda_{a,b-2}; R^{(x)}_{a,b-2} | \lambda_{a-1,b-1}; V^{(x)}_{a-1,b-1}\right], \end{aligned}$$

then,

$$\mathcal{H}_{a,b}(t,u,v) = \frac{\mathcal{G}_{a-1,b}(t,u)\,\mathcal{G}_{a,b-1}(u,v)}{\mathcal{F}_{a-1,b-1}(u)}. \qquad \square \tag{10}$$

Proof: We use a simplified notation. Reference to Figure 1 should make it self-explanatory.

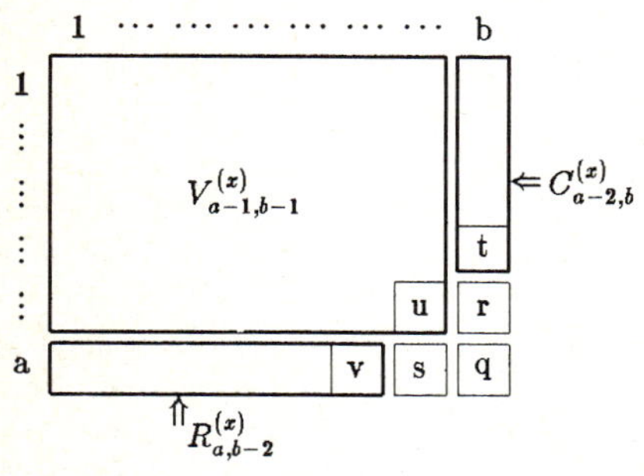

Figure 1. The basic assumption

$$\begin{aligned} \mathcal{H}_{a,b}(t,u,v) &= P\left[t; u; v; C^{(x)}_{a-2,b}; V^{(x)}_{a-1,b-1}; R^{(x)}_{a,b-2}\right] \\ &= P\left[t; u; C^{(x)}_{a-2,b}; V^{(x)}_{a-1,b-1}\right] \\ &\times P\left[v; R^{(x)}_{a,b-2} | t; u; C^{(x)}_{a-2,b}; V^{(x)}_{a-1,b-1}\right] \\ &= \mathcal{G}_{a-1,b}(t,u) P\left[v; R^{(x)}_{a,b-2} | u; V^{(x)}_{a-1,b-1}\right] \\ &= \frac{\mathcal{G}_{a-1,b}(t,u) P\left[u; v; V^{(x)}_{a-1,b-1}; R^{(x)}_{a,b-2}\right]}{\mathcal{F}_{a-1,b-1}(u)} \\ &= \frac{\mathcal{G}_{a-1,b}(t,u)\,\mathcal{G}_{a,b-1}(u,v)}{\mathcal{F}_{a-1,b-1}(u)}, \end{aligned}$$

as was to be shown. $\square$

At this stage, it should be clear that Eqs. (8), (9), and (10) form a well defined non-linear recurrence for computing $\mathcal{F}$, $\mathcal{G}$ and $\mathcal{H}$ in linear time. We collect these results in a single statement.

Theorem 6: Under the assumptions in Lemma 5, $\mathcal{F}_{a,b}(q)$, $\mathcal{G}_{a,b}(r,s)$, and $\mathcal{H}_{a,b}(t,u,v)$ can be computed inductively forward for $a = 3,\cdots,M$, and $b = 3,\cdots,M$ in time proportional to $MN\sigma^5$ by the recurrence (where boundary conditions are ignored)

$$\mathcal{F}_{a,b}(q) = \sum_{r,s} \mathcal{G}_{a,b}(r,s) P_{q|r,s}\, p_q(x_{a,b}), \tag{8}$$

$$\mathcal{G}_{a,b}(r,s) = \sum_{t,u,v} \mathcal{H}_{a,b}(t,u,v) P_{r|t,u} P_{s|u,v}\, p_r(x_{a-1,b})\, p_s(x_{a,b-1}), \tag{9}$$

$$\mathcal{H}_{a,b}(t,u,v) \doteq \frac{\mathcal{G}_{a-1,b}(t,u)\mathcal{G}_{a,b-1}(u,v)}{\mathcal{F}_{a-1,b-1}(u)}. \quad \square \tag{10}$$

There should be no need to comment that the $O(\sigma^5)$ complexity per pixel is due to Eq. (9). This complexity will be further reduced hereafter. Taking boundary conditions into account presents no real difficulty, as is shown in the following complete version of Theorem 6.

Theorem 6: (Complete version) **The FGH recurrence.** Under the assumption in Lemma 5, $\mathcal{F}_{a,b}(q) = P\left[\lambda_{a,b} = q; V_{a,b}^{(x)}\right]$ can be computed recursively forward for $a = 1,\cdots,M$ and $b = 1,\cdots,N$ in time proportional to $MN\sigma^5$ by the recurrence

$$\mathcal{F}_{a,b}(q) = \begin{cases} P_q\, p_q(x_{a,b}) & \text{for } a = b = 1, \\ \sum_s \mathcal{F}_{a,b-1}(s) P_{q|\square,s}\, p_q(x_{a,b}) & \text{for } b > a = 1, \\ \sum_r \mathcal{F}_{a-1,b}(r) P_{q|r,\square}\, p_q(x_{a,b}) & \text{for } a > b = 1, \\ \sum_{r,s} \mathcal{G}_{a,b}(r,s) P_{q|r,s}\, p_q(x_{a,b}) & \text{for } a,b \geq 2, \end{cases} \tag{11}$$

$$\mathcal{G}_{a,b}(r,s) = \begin{cases} \sum_u \mathcal{F}_{a-1,b-1}(u) P_{r|\square,u} P_{s|u,\square}\, p_r(x_{a-1,b})\, p_s(x_{a,b-1}) & \text{for } a = b = 2, \\ \sum_{u,v} \mathcal{G}_{a,b-1}(u,v) P_{r|\square,u} P_{s|u,v}\, p_r(x_{a-1,b})\, p_s(x_{a,b-1}) & \text{for } b > a = 2, \\ \sum_{t,u} \mathcal{G}_{a-1,b}(t,u) P_{r|t,u} P_{s|u,\square}\, p_r(x_{a-1,b})\, p_s(x_{a,b-1}) & \text{for } a > b = 2, \\ \sum_{t,u,v} \mathcal{H}_{a,b}(t,u,v) P_{r|t,u} P_{s|u,v}\, p_r(x_{a-1,b})\, p_s(x_{a,b-1}) & \text{for } a,b \geq 3, \end{cases} \tag{12}$$

$$\mathcal{H}_{a,b}(t,u,v) = \left\{ \frac{\mathcal{G}_{a-1,b}(t,u)\mathcal{G}_{a,b-1}(u,v)}{\mathcal{F}_{a-1,b-1}(u)} \right. \quad \text{for } a,b \geq 3, \tag{13}$$

and the definition that $\mathcal{H}_{a,b}(t,u,v) = 0$ if the right hand side of (13) is $\frac{0}{0}$. $\square$

Proof: The first cases of (11) and (12) are obvious. The second and third cases of (11) reproduce the one-dimensional recurrence of Baum [3] [4]. The second one is readily estabished as follows:

$$\begin{aligned} \mathcal{F}_{1,b}(q) &= P\left[\lambda_{1,b} = q; V_{1,b}^{(x)}\right] = \sum_s P\left[\lambda_{1,b} = q; \lambda_{1,b-1} = s; x_{1,b}; V_{1,b-1}^{(x)}\right] \\ &= \sum_s P\left[\lambda_{1,b-1} = s; V_{1,b-1}^{(x)}\right] P_{q|\square,s}\, p_q(x_{1,b}) = \sum_s \mathcal{F}_{1,b-1}(s) P_{q|\square,s}\, p_q(x_{1,b}). \end{aligned}$$

The third case of (11) as well as the second and third cases of (12) are proved in exactly the same way. The last cases of (11), (12) and (13) were proved above. Hence the proof of the theorem is completed.

2.2. The look-ahead recurrences

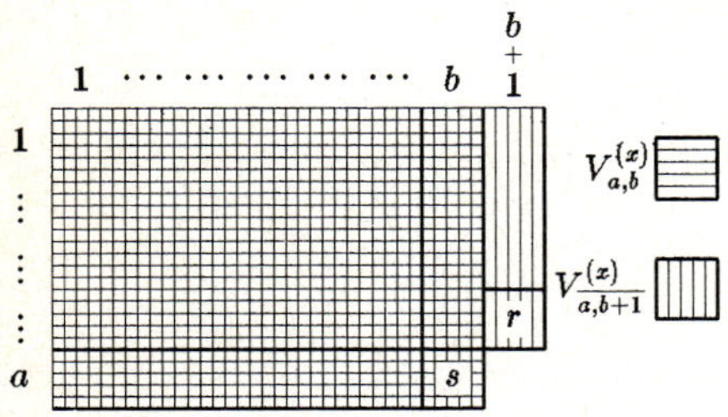

Figure 2. Look-ahead in real time

If the image is acquired in standard, raster-scan mode, it is plain that $V^{(x)}_{\overline{a,b+1}}$ is at hand at the time that the scan has reached pixel (a, b). We can take advantage of this observation to use the results in Theorem 6 in a way that enables us to exploit the information about $\lambda_{a,b}$ encoded in $C^{(x)}_{a-1,b}$ for $a = 2, \cdots, M$ and $b < N$. We shall do this by computing the probability $\mathcal{L}^h_{a,b}(s) = P\left[\lambda_{a,b}; V^{(x)}_{\overline{a,b+1}}\right]$ (where $\mathcal{L}^h$ stands as a mnemonic for horizontal look-ahead). The following theorem shows that this can be done at very little additional cost.

Theorem 7: Let $\mathcal{L}^h_{a,b}(s) = P\left[\lambda_{a,b} = s; V^{(x)}_{\overline{a,b+1}}\right]$ for $a \geq 2$ and $b < N$, where the labels are as shown in Figure 2. Then, $\mathcal{L}^h_{a,b}(s)$ can be computed inductively forward by the recurrence in Theorem 6 and the additional $O(\sigma^2)$ relationship: $\mathcal{L}^h_{a,b}(s) = \sum_r \mathcal{G}_{a,b+1}(r, s)$.

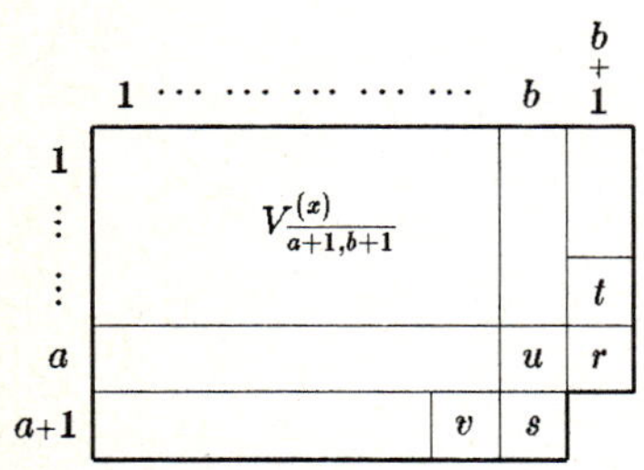

Figure 3. Look-ahead with time-lag

A similar argument would show that the labeling of (a, b) could be postponed until $V^{(x)}_{\overline{a+1,b+1}}$ has been acquired. (In raster scan mode, this obliges us to relinquish our real-time requirement.) The reader should have no difficulty to show that this goal is accomplished by letting $\mathcal{L}^{h,v}_{a,b}(u) = P\left[\lambda_{a,b} = u; V^{(x)}_{\overline{a+1,b+1}}\right]$, computing $\mathcal{H}_{a,b}(t, u, v)$ as in Theorem 6, and using the $O(\sigma^3)$ relationship $\mathcal{L}^{h,v}_{a,b}(u) = \sum_{t,v} \mathcal{H}_{a+1,b+1}(t, u, v)$. From Theorem 4 in Section 3.1, it is easy to conclude that, under the assumption in Lemma 5,

$$\mathcal{L}^{h,v}_{a,b}(u) \propto P\left[\lambda_{a,b}; \{x_{i,j} : i + j \leq a + b\}\right].$$

As discussed in Section 1.3, the appropriate look-ahead technique consists in postponing the decision on $\lambda_{a,b}$ until $V^{(x)}_{\overline{a+1,b+1}}$ has been acquired, and making decision according to Eq. 6. The solution to this problem is given in the following theorem.

Theorem 8: Let $\mathcal{L}_{a,b}(u) \doteq P\left[\lambda_{a,b} = u; V^{(x)}_{\overline{a+1,b+1}}\right]$ for $a < M$ and $b < N$, and where the labels are as shown in Figure 3. Then, $\mathcal{L}_{a,b}(u)$ can be computed inductively forward by the recurrence in Theorem 6 and the additional $O(\sigma^5)$ relationship

$$\mathcal{L}_{a,b}(u) = \sum_{t,v} \mathcal{H}_{a+1,b+1}(t, u, v) \sum_{r,s} P_{r|t,u} P_{s|u,v}\, p_r(x_{a,b+1})\, p_s(x_{a+1,b}) \qquad \square \tag{14}$$

So far, the complexity was of the order of $O(\sigma^5)$ operations per pixel. In the next section we shall briefly demonstrate that this complexity can still be lowered to $O(\sigma^3)$.

2.3. One further complexity reduction

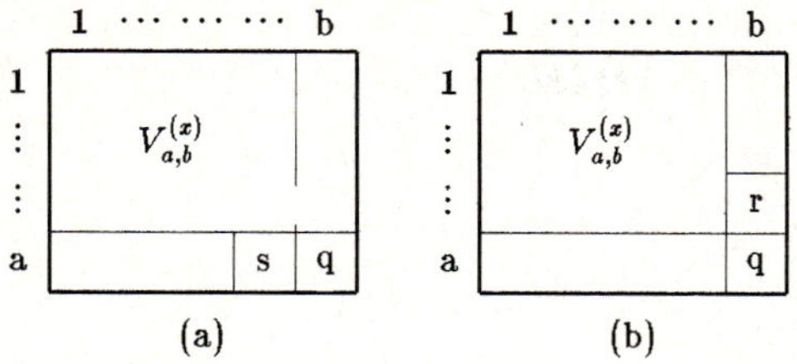

Figure 4. Definitions of $\mathcal{Y}$: (a), and $\mathcal{Z}$: (b).

Presently, our goal is to show that the computational complexity of the algorithms described above can be reduced to $\mathcal{O}(MN\sigma^3)$. A simple combinatorial argument indicates that, up to a proportionality factor, this complexity is minimal. All that will be needed are two more auxiliary definitions (see Figure 4) and repeated use of the distributivity property for the addition. Thus, we define:

$$\mathcal{Y}_{a,b}(q,s) \doteq P\left[\lambda_{a,b}=q;\lambda_{a,b-1}=s;V^{(x)}_{a,b}\right], \text{ and } \mathcal{Z}_{a,b}(q,r) \doteq P\left[\lambda_{a,b}=q;\lambda_{a-1,b}=r;V^{(x)}_{a,b}\right]. \quad (15)$$

Readily, $\mathcal{Y}$, $\mathcal{Z}$ and $\mathcal{F}$, $\mathcal{G}$ are related according as

$$\begin{aligned} \mathcal{Y}_{a,b}(q,s) &= \mathcal{F}_{a,b-1}(s)P_{q|\Box,s}\,p_q(x_{a,b}) && b>a=1, \\ &= \sum_r \mathcal{G}_{a,b}(r,s)P_{q|r,s}\,p_q(x_{a,b}) && a,b>1, \end{aligned} \quad (16)$$

$$\begin{aligned} \mathcal{Z}_{a,b}(q,r) &= \mathcal{F}_{a-1,b}(r)P_{q|r,\Box}\,p_q(x_{a,b}) && a>b=1, \\ &= \sum_s \mathcal{G}_{a,b}(r,s)P_{q|r,s}\,p_q(x_{a,b}) && a,b>1. \end{aligned} \quad (17)$$

Theorem 9: For $a,b>1$, and under the assumptions in Lemma 5, it holds that

$$\mathcal{G}_{a,b}(r,s) = \sum_u \frac{\mathcal{Y}_{a-1,b}(r,u)\mathcal{Z}_{a,b-1}(s,u)}{\mathcal{F}_{a-1,b-1}(u)}, \quad (18)$$

where the labels are as shown in Figure 1. □

Proof: By substituting $\mathcal{H}$ from (10) into (9), and invoking the distributivity property for the addition, we can write

$$\mathcal{G}_{a,b}(r,s) = \sum_u \frac{1}{\mathcal{F}_{a-1,b-1}(u)} \sum_t \mathcal{G}_{a-1,b}(t,u)P_{r|t,u}\,p_r(x_{a-1,b}) \sum_v \mathcal{G}_{a,b-1}(u,v)P_{s|u,v}\,p_s(x_{a,b-1}). \quad (19)$$

Two additional substitutions from the last cases in (16) and (17) into the right hand side of (19) yield the desired result. □

At this point, we shall leave it to the reader to verify that Eq. (20) together with (16)–(18) constitute a well formed recurrence for computing $\mathcal{F}_{a,b}(q)$ for $a=1,\cdots,M$, and $b=1,\cdots,N$. Moreover, the complexity of the recurrence is dominated by that of (18) which is obviously of the order $MN\sigma^3$.

$$\begin{aligned} \mathcal{F}_{a,b}(q) &= P_q\,p_q(x_{a,b}) && a=b=1, \\ &= \sum_s \mathcal{Y}_{a,b}(q,s) && b>1, \\ &= \sum_r \mathcal{Z}_{a,b}(q,r) && a>b=1. \end{aligned} \quad (20)$$

The case of the look-ahead mode can be handled in exactly the same way. By referring to Figure 3, substituting for $\mathcal{H}_{a+1,b+1}(t,u,v)$ in (14), and rearranging terms we get

$$\begin{aligned} \mathcal{L}_{a,b}(u) &= \sum_{t,v} \frac{\mathcal{G}_{a,b+1}(t,u)\mathcal{G}_{a+1,b}(u,v)}{\mathcal{F}_{a,b}(u)} \sum_{r,s} P_{r|t,u}P_{s|u,v}\,p_r(x_{a,b+1})\,p_s(x_{a+1,b}), \\ &= \frac{1}{\mathcal{F}_{a,b}(u)} \sum_{t,r} \mathcal{G}_{a,b+1}(t,u)P_{r|t,u}\,p_r(x_{a,b+1}) \sum_{v,s} \mathcal{G}_{a+1,b}(u,v)P_{s|u,v}\,p_s(x_{a+1,b}), \\ &= \sum_{r,s} \frac{\mathcal{Y}_{a,b+1}(r,u)\mathcal{Z}_{a+1,b}(s,u)}{\mathcal{F}_{a,b}(u)}. \end{aligned} \quad (21)$$

Hence, $\mathcal{L}_{a,b}(u)$ can also be computed with $\mathcal{O}(\sigma^3)$ effort per pixel.

2.4. The real-time algorithm

From the foregoing discussion, it appears that actual labeling algorithms can be obtained by a mere translation of the relevant formulas into computer programs. However, this naive implementation would fail for all but extremely small images because the joint likelihoods $\mathcal{F}_{a,b}(q)$, $\mathcal{G}_{a,b}(r,s)$, $\mathcal{Y}_{a,b}(q,s)$, and $\mathcal{Z}_{a,b}(q,r)$ become excessively small as a and b increase, thereby causing underflow in any existing computers. Fortunately, there is a simple way to remedy the situation: All that need be done is to translate joint likelihoods into a posteriori probabilities. As these sum to one, underflows may then occur only if some of the labels actually have a posteriori probability zero. Thus, we define $\tilde{\mathcal{F}}_{a,b}(q) = P\left[\lambda_{a,b} = q | V_{a,b}^{(x)}\right]$, and similarly for $\tilde{\mathcal{G}}_{a,b}(r,s)$, $\tilde{\mathcal{Y}}_{a,b}(q,s)$, and $\tilde{\mathcal{Z}}_{a,b}(q,r)$. Then, a numerically safe algorithm is given by the following theorem which incorporates the required normalization.

Theorem 10: The F-G-Y-Z algorithm.

$$\begin{aligned} \tilde{\mathcal{F}}_{a,b}(q) &= \frac{P_q\, p_q(x_{a,b})}{\sum_{q'} P_{q'}\, p_{q'}(x_{a,b})} && a=b=1, \\ &= \sum_s \tilde{\mathcal{Y}}_{a,b}(q,s) && b>1, \\ &= \sum_r \tilde{\mathcal{Z}}_{a,b}(q,r) && a>b=1. \end{aligned} \tag{22}$$

$$\tilde{\mathcal{Y}}_{a,b}(q,s) = \frac{\mathcal{Y}'_{a,b}(q,s)}{\sum_{q',s'} \mathcal{Y}'_{a,b}(q',s')} \qquad \tilde{\mathcal{Z}}_{a,b}(q,r) = \frac{\mathcal{Z}'_{a,b}(q,r)}{\sum_{q',r'} \mathcal{Z}'_{a,b}(q',r')}. \tag{23}$$

$$\begin{aligned} \mathcal{Y}'_{a,b}(q,s) &= \tilde{\mathcal{F}}_{a,b-1}(s) P_{q|\square,s}\, p_q(x_{a,b}) && b>a=1, \\ &= \sum_r \tilde{\mathcal{G}}_{a,b}(r,s) P_{q|r,s}\, p_q(x_{a,b}) && a,b>1. \end{aligned} \tag{24}$$

$$\begin{aligned} \mathcal{Z}'_{a,b}(q,r) &= \tilde{\mathcal{F}}_{a-1,b}(r) P_{q|r,\square}\, p_q(x_{a,b}) && a>b=1, \\ &= \sum_s \tilde{\mathcal{G}}_{a,b}(r,s) P_{q|r,s}\, p_q(x_{a,b}) && a,b>1. \end{aligned} \tag{25}$$

$$\tilde{\mathcal{G}}_{a,b}(r,s) = \sum_u \frac{\tilde{\mathcal{Y}}_{a-1,b}(r,u)\tilde{\mathcal{Z}}_{a,b-1}(s,u)}{\tilde{\mathcal{F}}_{a-1,b-1}(u)} \qquad a,b>1, \tag{26}$$

with the definition that $\tilde{\mathcal{G}}_{a,b}(r,s) = 0$ if the right hand side of (26) is $\frac{0}{0}$. □

From (23), it is seen that the normalization is achieved with $O(\sigma^2)$ effort per pixel. Thus the F-G-Y-Z algorithm processes an $M \times N$ image in time proportional to $O(MN\sigma^3)$. As for (26), Eq. (21) can be readily translated in terms of a posteriori probabilities, thereby leading to an additional $O(MN\sigma^3)$ effort in the (full) look-ahead mode.

3. Experimental Results

The various methods described above were implemented and extensive experimentation was performed with the aim of assessing the validity of the assumption underlying our derivations—*viz.*, the basic hypothesis in Lemma 5—and for comparison purposes with competing algorithms. Due to space limitation, these experiments will be described here in a rather cursory way. In the first place, we shall describe an application to picture smoothing. Our second application will be concerned with image segmentation.

3.1. An application to picture smoothing

In the picture smoothing experiments, we used simulated Markov mesh pictures in order to measure the effectiveness of the algorithms. (The simulation of pseudo-random Markov mesh pictures was performed in an obvious way.) While the use of simulated pictures may look rather artificial, it offers the advantage that experimental results cannot be affected by possible departure of experimental data from the assumed theoretical model. Two-state random fields were chosen in order to allow accurate visualization of the results as black and white pictures. White noise was added to the simulated Markov mesh pictures and the image so obtained served as input data to a number of smoothing algorithms.

For comparison purposes, two algorithms proposed by Kanefsky and Strintzis [11] were implemented. The first one is non-contextual in nature and was merely intended to provide an upper-bound to the probability of mislabeling. It uses the standard maximum likelihood decision rule $\hat{\lambda}_{a,b} = q$ if $q = \operatorname{argmax}_r p_r(x_{a,b})$. The second one exploits the Markovian dependence, but at the local level only, by maximizing the likelihood in small regions within the image. Specifically, it reads: $\hat{\lambda}_{a,b} = q$ if $q = \operatorname{argmax}_r [K_{a,b}(r)]$, where

$$K_{a,b}(q) = \sum_{r,s} P[r,s]\, p_r(x_{a-1,b})\, p_s(x_{a,b-1}) P_{q|r,s}\, p_q(x_{a,b}), \tag{27}$$

and where $P[r,s]$ is the probability of occurrence of the event $\{\lambda_{a-1,b} = r; \lambda_{a,b-1} = s\}$ over the entire image. In [11], as hereafter, this myopic procedure is called the "block constraint" method. In the present context, it provides a convenient reference as it appeared to be the best among the various approaches investigated in [11]. The remaining four algorithms are those discussed above, namely, the F-G-Y-Z algorithm in Theorem 10, the partial look-ahead techniques discussed in Section 2.2, and the full look-ahead algorithm specified by Theorem 8.

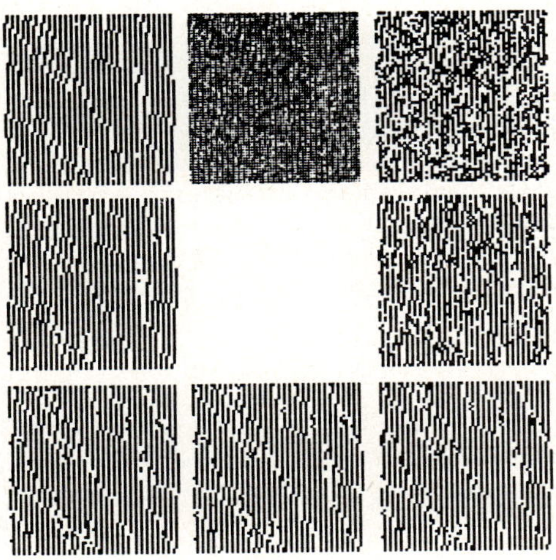

Figure 5. Illustration of the smoothing experiments. Starting from the upper left corner and proceeding clockwise: *i)* original, noise-free pseudo-random Markov mesh, *ii)* the same plus noise, *iii)* non-contextual smoothing, *iv)* "block constraint" smoothing, smoothing with *v)* the F-G-Y-Z algorithm, *vi)* horizontal look-ahead, *vii)* horizontal and vertical look-ahead, *viii)* full look-ahead.

One example of input data and smoothed images is illustrated by Figure 5. In this particular experiment, the signal to noise ratio (SNR) was 0.7, corresponding to a non-contextual error-rate of 0.21. At that SNR level, the underlying Markovian structure is completely overshadowed by the noise, and the block-constraint method is practically unable to recover that structure (in spite of an error-rate lowered to 0.11). The major step towards recovering the original image is clearly taken by the F-G-Y-Z algorithm (with an error-rate of 0.5). From there on, one can observe a gradual improvement corresponding to our successive extensions of the look-ahead range, and leading to an error-rate of 0.03 under the full look-ahead mode. Other experiments have shown that for higher SNR values, the improvement obtained with the full look-ahead mode over the block-constraint method may exceed one order of magnitude. It is felt that this reduction in error-rate which is corroborated by the visual evaluation of the smoothed images, provides ample empirical justification for the hypothesis—in Lemma 5—which underlies all of our theoretical developments.

3.2. An application to picture segmentation

Smoothing algorithms can be readily appied to solve the segmentation problem [6] [8] [9]: Readily, uniform (*e.g.*, black or white) regions are degenerate examples of Markov fields. The only perequisite is the need to estimate the transition probabilities in the noise-free picture. In the case of the artificial data illustrated by Figure 6, these probabilities were estimated prior to adding the noise to the original image (not shown).

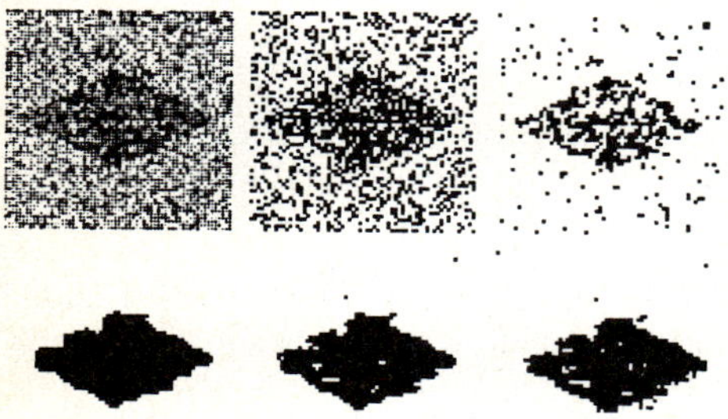

Figure 6. Illustration of the segmentation experiments. Starting from the upper left corner and proceeding clockwise: *i)* input image, *ii)* non-contextual segmentation, *iii)* "block constraint" segmentation, segmentation with *iv)* the F-G-Y-Z algorithm, and *v)* full look-ahead, *vi)* median filtered version of *v)*.

In the experiment illustrated by Figure 6, only four of the six smoothing algorithms were implemented. They were the non-contextual and block constraint methods, the F-G-Y-Z and full look-ahead algorithms. The result obtained with the latter was further improved by application of a 3×3 median filter. As evidenced by Figure 6, the last two algorithms produce fairly uniform regions (in spite of a fairly low SNR). The only remaining problem is that edges in the original image are treated in an anisotropic manner—as could be expected from a low order Markov mesh model. It is expected that this problem will be partly remedied by increasing the order of the model.

REFERENCES

[1] K. Abend, "Compound decision procedures for unknown distributions and for dependent states of nature," in *Pattern Recognition*, L.N. Kanal ed., Washington D.C.: Thompson Book Cy, 1968, pp. 207–249.

[2] K. Abend, T.J. Harley, and L.N. Kanal, "Classification of binary random patterns," *IEEE Trans. Inform. Theory*, IT–11, pp. 538–544, Oct. 1965.

[3] L.E. Baum, "An inequality and associated maximization technique in statistical estimation for probabilistic functions of Markov processes," *Inequalities*, **3**, pp. 1–8, 1972.

[4] L.E. Baum, T. Petrie, G. Soules, and N. Weiss, "A maximization technique occurring in the statistical analysis of probabilistic functions of Markov chains," *Ann. Math. Statist.*, **41**, pp. 164–171, 1972.

[5] G.R. Cross, and A.K. Jain, "Markov random field texture models," *IEEE Trans. Pattern Anal., Machine Intell.*, **PAMI-5**, pp. 25–39, Jan. 1983.

[6] H. Derin, H. Elliot, R. Cristi, and D. Geman, "Bayes smoothing algorithms for segmentation of binary images modeled by Markov random fields," *IEEE Trans. Pattern Anal., Machine Intel.*, **PAMI-6**, pp. 707–720, Nov. 1984.

[7] K.S. Fu, and T.S. Yu, *Statistical Pattern Classification Using Contextual Information*, Chichester: RSP (Wiley), 1980.

[8] S. Geman, and D. Geman, "Stochastic relaxation, Gibbs distributions, and the Bayesian restoration of images," *IEEE Trans. Pattern Anal., Machine Intel.*, **PAMI–6**, pp. 721–741, Nov. 1984.

[9] F.R. Hansen, and H. Elliott, "Image segmentation using simple Markov fields models," *Computer Graphics and Image Processing*, **20**, pp. 101–132, 1982.

[10] L.N. Kanal, "Markov mesh models," *Computer Graphics and Image Processing*, **12**, pp. 371–375, 1980 (also in *Image Modeling*, A. Rosenfeld Ed., New York: Academic Press, 1981, pp. 239–243).

[11] M. Kanefsky, and M.G. Strintzis, "A decision theory approach to picture smoothing," *IEEE Trans. Comput.*, C–27, pp. 32–36, Jan. 1978.

[12] M. Kanefsky, and C.-B. Fong, "Predictive source coding techniques using maximum likelihood prediction for compression of digital images," *IEEE Trans. Inform. Theory*, **IT–30**, pp. 722–727, Sept. 1984.

[13] J. Raviv, "Decision making in Markov chains applied to the problem of pattern recognition," *IEEE Trans. Inform. Theory*, IT–3, pp. 536–551, Oct. 1962.

[14] C.W. Therrien, "Linear filtering models for texture classification and segmentation," *Proc. 5th Internat. Conf. Pattern Recognition*, Miami, Fl. 1980, pp. 1132–1135.

PATTERN RECOGNITION IN PRACTICE II
E.S. Gelsema and L.N. Kanal (Editors)

Abstract Data Types and Multiprocessor Architecture for Image Understanding

L. O. Hertzberger and A. Choudry
Computer Science Department
University of Amsterdam, The Netherlands

Abstract

Image Understanding has become an important activity in the current attempt towards industrial automation. As contrasted to Image Processing, it has not been possible to execute Image Understanding in real-time as required in the industrial environment. Recent advances in software technology, such as Object Oriented Functional Language Programming with Abstract Data Types and Multiprocessor architecture for parallel execution are considered for Image Understanding.

Introduction

Traditionally, the bulk of Image Analysis activity has been devoted to such low level tasks as Image enhancement and restoration, feature extraction e. g. edge detection etc. The task of Image Understanding was largely left to a human interpreter. This was particularly so in those cases where the images tended to be rather ill-structured such as medical images. The technique used for these problems is almost entirely based on a bottom-up approach. At the bottom is the Image in the form of a set of pixels and, hopefully, a well-understood Image emerges at the top (Ballard, 1982). Guided by this, an immense amount of hardware/software has been developed (Rosenfeld, 1984). It is also known that the more demanding task of Image Understanding, as practiced by human beings, is more top-down than bottom-up (Marr, 1981). Besides this, the recent research activity in Robotic Sensory Control has brought forward the important role played by the real-time aspect of Image Understanding. Our goal in this study is to reexamine some of the existing techniques of Image Analysis and hardware/software development in the context of real-time Image Understanding and arrive at the design of a virtual Image Understanding machine.

Parallel to the advances in Image Processing and Image Understanding there have also been significant recent advances in computer hardware/software. Digital signal processing has undergone an astonishing change in the last 50 years since its beginning as classical signal processing before the Second World War (Allen, 1985). In particular, parallel processing for Image Processing, in one form or other, is a much researched area and numerous special purpose implementations have been realised, (Reeves, 1984). By and large the emphasis here is still on performing, in parallel, the Image Processing primitives i. e. point operations, convolutions etc. As for software, there are over 100 software packages developed for Image Processing, (Preston, 1984). Developments in allied fields are also finding interesting applications in Image Processing. Thus, Graphics, in the form of Solid Modelling including synthetic Shading, is being used in Pattern Recognition (Shapiro, 1985). Chamfer, a stock-in-trade of the assembly operation, has been analysed for geometric tolerancing (Requicha, 1983), and it has also found an interesting application in non-linear filtering of Images (Young, 1985). On the whole, the software structure for Image Processing clearly reflects the bottom-up approach mentioned above and thus lacks the facility of providing a high-level interface which a top-down approach might have furnished.

On the other hand the recent Japanese initiative to develop the Fifth Generation computer, (Hertzberger, 1984), is primarily based on a top-down approach. One of the characteristics of the Fifth Generation Computer project is to define high level primitives and implement them in firmware. This results in rather comp[ex micro code, however, using advanced VLSI components, it does not pose a serious problem. We would like to examine the question of Image Understanding in the context of the Fifth Generation Computer philosophy i. e. high level Image Understanding primitives implemented directly into advanced VLSI processors. We shall first review some of the salient features of Image Understanding and Fifth Generation Computer and then discuss the concept of a virtual Image Understanding machine along the lines of the Fifth Generation Computer project.

Image Understanding

Real-time Image Understanding has been the goal of several major research projects such as the DARPA-IU (Image Understanding) project, (Nudd, 1980). At the highest level, the Image Understanding problem has been historically divided into two steps, namely;

1. Functional Specification of Image Understanding primitives, and
2. Implementation of the above into dedicated hardware.

The first step refers to the identification of computationally simple image processing operations (algorithms) of general utility. The belief is, that complex Image Processing operations, as required in practice, can be constructed from these primitives. This issue has been the subject of much research traditionally performed on large scale general purpose computers. After nearly three decades of research and experimentation in Image Processing it is fair to say that there does exist a fairly well defined body of functions that can be called Image Processing primitives (Preston, 1983). Of course this does not imply that a widely accepted enumeration of primitives has been adopted by general consensous. This set of primitives is now supposed to include such operations as;

--2D-Convolutions, e.g. Laplacian, Smoothing
--Logical Filters, e.g. Erosion, Dilation, Skeletonization
--Data Operations, e.g. Thresholding, False Color, Gama Correction
--Gradient Operations, e.g. Edge Detection
--Statistical Operations, e.g. Histogram, Entropy

For such primitive operations algorithms are developed to maximise throughput and minimise memory requirements. For development work these algorithms are run on a general purpose computer where the execution time, i. e. the real-time aspect, ia not crucial. However, for exacting applications such as industrial adaptive control, target acquisition and identification, the real-time aspect is of paramount importance. For such purposes special hardware has to be developed as discussed below.

It is perhaps safe to say that Image Understanding, more than any other application, has spurred the development of special purpose computers. Starting from the ILLIAC; developed in the 50's to analyse binary images of bubble chamber tracks; to the Massively Parallel Processor (MPP) of NASA (Batcher, 1980), there has been a tremendous activity in developing Special Purpose Computers. This activity has generally followed the pattern of first developing a Special Purpose Computer for a given primitive operation and subsequently combining several of them into a larger Special Purpose Computer. In this sense, this activity could be called 'Primitive Algorithm Driven Special Purpose Computer Development'.. As a result the hardware implementations of the individual algorithms have tended to be simple, whereas the higher level programming and the user interface of the overall system becomes more complex..

From the above it is clear that both, the algorithms and their hardware implementations have been 'Primitive-Driven', i. e. bottom-up approach, resulting in system complexity at the user level and the lack of high level programming support. Further, it should also be noted here that such a set of primitives is not enough for true Image Understanding since it includes only the Image Processing part which helps in feature extraction. These features have to be combined together and 'Understood' as objects with the help of a Relational Analysis' (RA). The RA part of Image Understanding requires a sort of approach very different from that of Image Processing. Whereas a large amount of success has been achieved in Image Processing and a certain level of consensous has been reached, RA is still in a nascent stage and requires major effort before it can become widely usable. The possibilty of a causal connection, between the absence of a well developed RA and the traditional bottom-up approach, cannot be denied. In a parallel manner the problem of low-level machine computations and high-level intelligence has been addressed in the Fifth Generation Computer project in Japan. It is perhaps worthwhile to see if the Fifth Generation Computer approach could be employed for Image Understanding. To establish a frame of reference a brief discussion of some of the relevant points of the Fifth Generation Computer project is given below.

Fifth Generation Computer

One of the primary aims of the Fifth Generation machine is to provide the user with a high level functional programming environment. Loosely speaking, functional programming or task-level programming allows the user to merely specify the functions or tasks to be performed at a high level. All details of how to execute these tasks is, hopefully, taken care of by the system. This is in sharp contrast to the conventional imperative or procedural programming where not only what has to be done but also how it has to done, must be specified. As conventional software systems become large, as is the case in Image Understanding, side-effects such as type-mismatch, throughput bottlenecks etc., develop since the sheer magnitude of the details taxes the human capacity inordinately. This is partly due to the architecture of the conventional machines which is organised around simple and short micro-code. Typically the conventional computer is organised as follows;

-- High Level (Imperative) Language
-- Operating System
-- Machine Level
-- Simple Short Micro-Code, can be implemented easily in TTL.

The Fifth Generation approach is quite different from this and is more direct i. e.

-- High Level Functional Language

----- leading directly to ------

-- Complex, large Micro-Code which can be implemented only in VLSI form.

This allows an optimum use of the VLSI technology and as the latter advances, the Fifth Generation will benefit accordingly. The idea is that all user interface will be at a very high level and then using powerful modules such as the parallel inference machine, an optimum set of low level operations will be carried out. Logic programming plays a dominant role at this stage for tree-search, back-track etc. However, details of these operations are hidden from the user. For Image Understanding two major aspects of Fifth Generation are of especial interest, namely;

-- User interface through a high-level task oriented language
-- Top-Down analysis for Tree-Search, Back-track, Low-Level primitive operation assignment, hidden from the user.

It should however be emphsised that at the moment the role of Fifth Generation in Image Understanding has not been studied in any great detail. It would therefore be instructive to try to design a Virtual Image Understanding Machine which would offer the advantages of the Fifth Generation.

Virtual Image Understanding Machine

A Virtual Image Understanding Machine as envisaged here should be able to accept input in the form of functional programs and carry out the subsequent low-level operations without the help of the user. A similar situation exists for Digital Signal Processing in general where it is felt that a deep fundamental understanding of functional specification coupled to the semantics of programming environment is needed (Allen, 1985). In these deliberations two trends could be discerned, namely, that of Abstract Data Type (Liskov, 1979) and their application to digital signals (Kopec, 1985). The second concept is that of data flow architecture for highly parallel systems. An Abstract Data Type (ADT) is a data type defined exclusively by a set of operations. To each ADT a Cluster of operations is associated. The ADT along with its Cluster may be called an Object. Strongly typed languages such as ADA have been used for Object Oriented programming for Robotic Vision (Volz, 1984 and Buzzard, 1985).

Data Flow Architectures have been studied extensively for some time now for highly parallel systems. Specification of high level functional languages that can be compiled directly into fully parallel representation as data flow-graphs. Once compilation of the high-level functional specification to the maximally parallel data-flow representation has taken place, an interpreter maps the compiler output to the available computational resources. This is an important research activity in the current software technology and promises to yield a unified approach to high performance engines at very high high level.

In the Fifth Generation project the implementation of the system is preceeded by a simulation in an MIMD (Multiprocessor) environment as follows;

-- High-Level Programming
-- Simulation in MIMD
-- VLSI design
-- Custom Chip implementation

It should be noted that whereas low-level image processing has largely been implemented on special purpose processors which are almost always a variant of SIMD (Single Instruction Multiple Data Stream) structure, the high-level Image Understanding demands a true MIMD environment for efficient execution. This has an attractive analogy with the Fifth Generation and we plan to pursue it. A tentative scheme for a Virtual Image Understanding Machine realisation would thus be;

-- Identify Image Understanding abstract data types and objects
-- Specification of an Object Oriented Functional Language
-- Simulation of the Language execution in MIMD environment

A comprehensive MIMD testbed for such tasks is under development in our laboratory.

References

Allen, J 1985
Computer Architecture for Digital Signal Processing
Proc. IEEE 73 (May 1985) 852

Ballard, D and Brown, C. 1981
Computer Vision
Prentice Hall, Englewood Cliffs, N. J.

Batcher, K. E. 1980
Design of a Massively Parallel Processor
IEEE Trans. Comp. C-31 (1980) 836

Buzzard, G. D. and Mudge, T. N. 1985
Object-Based Computing and the Ada Programming Language
Computer, IEEE, March (1985) 11

Hertzberger, L. O. and van de Riet, R. P. 1984
Progress in the Fifth Generation Inference Architecture
FGCS (Future Generations Computer Systems), 1 (1984) 93
North-Holland, Amsterdam

Kopec, G. F. 1985
The Signal Representation Language SRL
IEEE Trans Acoust, Speech, Signal Procs.
(to be published 1985)

Liskov, L. and Zilles, S, 1979
Programming with Abstract Data Types
Proc. ACM, Sigplan Conf. on
Very high level languages
Sigplan Notices, (ACM) 9 (1979) 50

Marr, D, 1982
Vision
W. H. Freeman & Co., San Francisco. 1982

Nudd, G. R. 1980
Image Understanding Architectures
Proc. of the National Comp. Conf. 1980, 377-390

Preston, K. 1981
Comparison of Parallel Processing Machines; A proposal
Languages and Architecture for Image Processing
Eds. M. J. B. Duff and S. Levialdi
Academic Press, New York 1981

Preston, K. 1983
Progress in Image Processing Languages
Computing Structures for Image Processing
Ed. M. J. B. Duff
Academic Press, New York 1983

Reeves, A. P. 1984
Parallel Computer Architecture for Image Processing
Computer Vision, Graphics and Image Processing, 25 (1984) 68

Requicha, A. A. G. 1983
Toward a theory of Geometric Tolerancing
Int. J. of Robotic Research 2 (1983) 45
M I T Press 1983

Rosenfeld, A 1984
Survey: Picture Processing 1983
Computer Vision, Graphics and Image Processing, 26 (1984) 347

Shapiro, L. G. 1985
The use of Pattern Recognition to estimate three dimensional shape from topographic labelling of images
(Presented at this Conf.)
Proc. Pattern Recognition in Practice II, June 19-21 1985, Amsterdam.
North-Holland, 1985

Volz, R. A., Mudge, T. N. and Gal, D. A. 1984
Using ADA as a Programming Language for Robot-Based Manufacturing Cells
IEEE Trans. on Systems, Man and Cybernetics 14 (1984) 863

Young, I. T. 1985
Choosing filter parameters for non-linear image filtering
(Presented at this Conf.)
Proc. Pattern Recognition in Practice II, June 19-21 1985, Amsterdam.
North-Holland, 1985

PATTERN RECOGNITION IN PRACTICE II
E.S. Gelsema and L.N. Kanal (Editors)

NEW RESULTS IN COMPUTATIONAL GEOMETRY RELEVANT TO PATTERN RECOGNITION IN PRACTICE

Godfried T. Toussaint

School of Computer Science
McGill University
805 Sherbrooke Street West
Montreal, Quebec
Canada H3A 2K6

Finding convex hulls, intersecting convex polygons, and triangulating sets of points are computational geometric problems that occur frequently in pattern recognition. In this paper we present new results on these three problems. Let S be a set of n points in the plane specified by their cartesian coordinates. Almost all $O(n \log n)$ convex hull algorithms published to date contain explicit sorting and/or backtracking as steps towards their final goal. We show here that the "rotating calipers" can be used to obtain an extremely simple $O(n \log n)$ divide-and-conquer algorithm that neither sorts nor uses backtracking. For the triangulation problem, an $O(n^2 \log n)$ algorithm was recently proposed for computing the "onion" triangulation of a set S. We show here that the "rotating calipers" can be used in conjunction with a result of Chazelle to obtain $O(n \log n)$ algorithms for computing the "onion" and "spiral" triangulations of S. Finally, let P and Q be two convex polygons with m and n vertices, respectively, which are specified by their cartesian coordinates in order. A simple $O(m+n)$ algorithm is presented for computing the intersection of P and Q. Unlike previous algorithms the new algorithm consists of a two-step combination of two simple procedures for finding convex hulls and triangulations of polygons.

1. INTRODUCTION

Let $S = \{p_1, p_2, \ldots, p_n\}$ be a set of n points in the plane specified by their cartesian coordinates. We assume that the points are in *general position* in the sense that no three of them are colinear. The convex hull of S has proved to be a very useful structure in the pattern recognition literature [1]. Many algorithms of varying complexities exist for this problem. Several of these have a worst-case running time of $O(n \log n)$. Almost all these algorithms either use explicit sorting or backtracking, or both, as steps toward the final solution [1], [6], [7]. For example, the divide-and-conquer algorithm of Shamos [8] does not sort but uses backtracking as it merges the resulting possibly-overlapping convex polygons. Shamos' method merges the convex polygons into *star-shaped* polygons and then finds the convex hull of these using backtracking. A simpler approach is given in [6] where the convex polygons are merged into *monotone* polygons, after which the same backtracking step is used. On the other hand, the algorithm of Preparata and Hong [9] first sorts the points and then uses divide and conquer. Here, since the convex polygons to be merged do not overlap, backtracking can be avoided. In section 2 we present an extremely simple D&C algorithm for computing the convex hull of S without sorting or backtracking. The key idea is to use the *rotating calipers* [2].

Another structure which appears to be very useful in pattern recognition is a triangulation of S [1], [3]. A triangulation of S, denoted by T(S), is a graph G(S,E) with S as its nodes and edges E connecting the nodes such that as many triangles as possible are formed with the constraint that the edges of E intersect only at their endpoints in S. Triangulations occur frequently in cartographic data-bases where they are typically used for storing approximations of surfaces [10]. It is often of interest to obtain triangulations with certain special properties. Such triangulations include the Delaunay, "onion", and "spiral" triangulations [1], [3]. The problem of "onion peeling" a set S, consists of repeatedly computing the convex hull of the subset of S that remains in the interior of the previous convex hull computed. Figure 1 shows the OP(S), (onion peeling), of a set S. The *"onion" triangulation* of S, denoted by OT(S), is a triangulation graph G(S,E) such that OP(S) is a subgraph of G. Figure 2 illustrates an OT(S) for the set S of Fig. 1. A closely related structure to the onion peeling is the convex "spiral" of S, denoted by CS(S). Unlike the OP(S), the CS(S) is not unique. If S has H points on its convex hull then there are 2H clockwise and counter-clockwise convex spirals. If one thinks of attaching a string on a convex hull vertex of S, say h_i, and then wrapping it around S always ignoring the points of S already touching the string, then the convex spiral $CS(S,h_i)$ for S and h_i is obtained. A convex spiral for the set S of Fig. 1 is shown in Fig. 3. We assume here a clockwise traversal. The *"spiral" triangulation* of S, denoted by ST(S), is a triangulation graph G(S,E) such that a CS(S) is a subgraph of G. The spiral triangulation of S corresponding to the convex spiral of Fig. 3 is illustrated in Fig. 4. Given a convex spiral of S we can compute the onion peeling, and vice versa, in O(n) time [8].

Let $P = \{p_1, p_2, \ldots p_m\}$ and $Q = \{q_1, q_2, \ldots, q_n\}$ be two convex polygons whose vertices are specified by their cartesian coordinates in clockwise order. It is assumed that the polygons are in *standard* form, i.e., the vertices of each polygon are distinct and no three consecutive vertices are colinear [8]. Also let Q be completely contained in the interior of P.

Definition: An *annulus*, ANN(P,Q), is defined as the union of bd(P), bd(Q), and the region of the plane which is both interior to P *and* exterior to Q. Here bd denotes boundary. It is clear that the onion peeling of S produces a nested sequence of *annuli* together with either a point, line segment, or convex polygon at its "center". Thus one way of computing the onion triangulation is to first do the peeling and subsequently triangulate the *annuli*. This is precisely the method proposed by Wismath [3]. Wismath's algorithm repeatedly computes the convex hull with an O(n log n) convex hull algorithm. This requires a total of $O(n^2 \log n)$ steps for peeling. He also presents an $O(n^2)$ algorithm for triangulating an annulus ANN(P,Q), and thus the entire algorithm takes time $O(n^2 \log n)$.

It should be pointed out that the convex spiral of S can easily be computed in $O(n^2)$ time using a trivial modification of Jarvis' convex hull algorithm [1]. Furthermore, the interior of the spiral can be triangulated in linear time with a trivial modification of an algorithm for triangulating *spiral polygons* [1]. Since the onion peeling of S can be obtained in linear time, we see that both the *onion* and *spiral* triangulations of S can be computed in $O(n^2)$ time. In section 3 we present a very simple algorithm, based on the *rotating calipers* [2], for triangulating an *annulus* in linear time. Combining this result with the O(n log n) onion peeling algorithm of Chazelle [4] yields O(n log n) procedures for solving both of the above problems.

Let $P = \{p_1, p_2, \ldots, p_m\}$ and $Q = \{q_1, q_2, \ldots, q_n\}$ be two arbitrarily located convex polygons whose vertices are specified by their cartesian coordinates

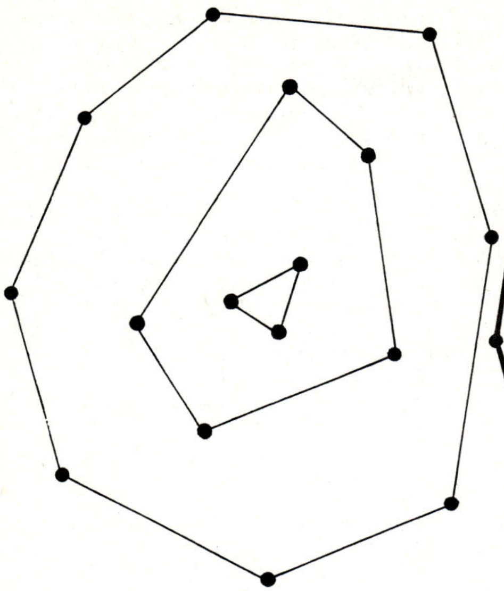

Figure 1: "Onion peeling" the set S.

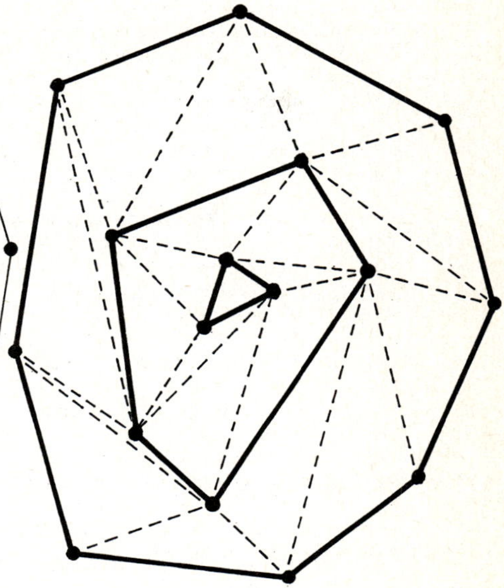

Figure 2: The "onion" triangulation of S.

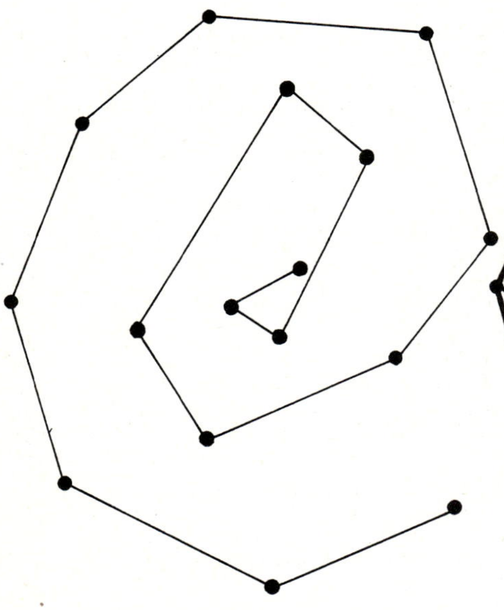

Figure 3: A "convex spiral" of S.

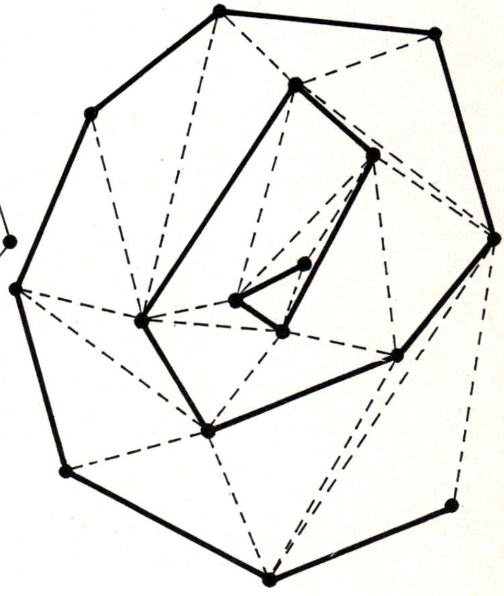

Figure 4: A "spiral" triangulation of S.

in clockwise order. It is assumed, as before, that the polygons are in *standard* form. Several linear time algorithms have recently been proposed for computing the intersection of P and Q, which is itself another convex polygon of at most m + n vertices [5], [8], [11], [12]. The algorithms in [8], [11]-[12] are relatively cumbersome to program due to the large number of cases that arise when intersecting the trapezoids that result with the "slab" method employed in [12]. The simplest and most elegant of the above algorithms is the one due to O'Rourke et al. [5].

In section 4, we present a new simple algorithm for constructing the intersection of P and Q in O(m + n) time in the worst case. Unlike the previous algorithms, the new algorithm is a combination of existing simple procedures for computing convex hulls and triangulations of polygons. Furthermore, the algorithm is conceptually transparently clear and affords an easy proof of correctness.

2. COMPUTING CONVEX HULLS WITH ROTATING CALIPERS

In order to obtain an O(n log n) divide-and-conquer algorithm without sorting, it is sufficient to demonstrate that two arbitrarily located (possibly intersecting) convex polygons can be merged in linear time. We now show that this can be done without backtracking using the rotating calipers.

Let $L(p_i)$ denote the directed line of support of polygon P at vertex p_i. The *direction* of $L(p_i)$ is such that no part of P lies to the *left* of $L(p_i)$. Also let p_{xmin} and q_{xmin} denote the vertices of P and Q, respectively, with smallest x coordinate and refer to Fig. 5. Given two lines of support $L(p_i)$ and $L(q_j)$ let $Left(p_i, q_j)$ denote the *leftmost* of the two and let r_{ij} denote the corresponding vertex.

Algorithm CHRCMERGE

Input: Two convex polygons $P = (p_1, p_2, \ldots, p_m)$ and $Q = (q_1, q_2, \ldots, q_n)$.

Output: The convex hull of $P \cup Q$, $H = (h_1, h_2, \ldots, h_\ell)$.

Begin

Step 1: Find p_{xmin} and q_{xmin} (call them p_1, q_1), construct $L(p_1)$ and $L(q_1)$, and compute $Left(p_1, q_1)$ and r_{11};

$h_1 \leftarrow r_{11}$.

Step 2: (rotate calipers in clockwise direction in parallel until they return to starting location)

Compute the angle between the upper half-line $L(p_1)$ and edge $\overline{p_1p_2}$. Similarly for $L(q_1)$ and edge $\overline{q_1q_2}$.

Advance to the vertex corresponding to smallest angle. Recompute Left( ) and r. Insert r in H if it is not already there.

End

It is easy to prove that this algorithm works correctly in linear time. The linearity is obvious because the algorithm advances one vertex of either P or Q at each step until both P and Q are completely scanned once and at each step the computations are done in constant time. The correctness follows from the fact that the Left ( ) operation ensures we only keep, and never miss, the "outermost" points. The details are left to the reader.

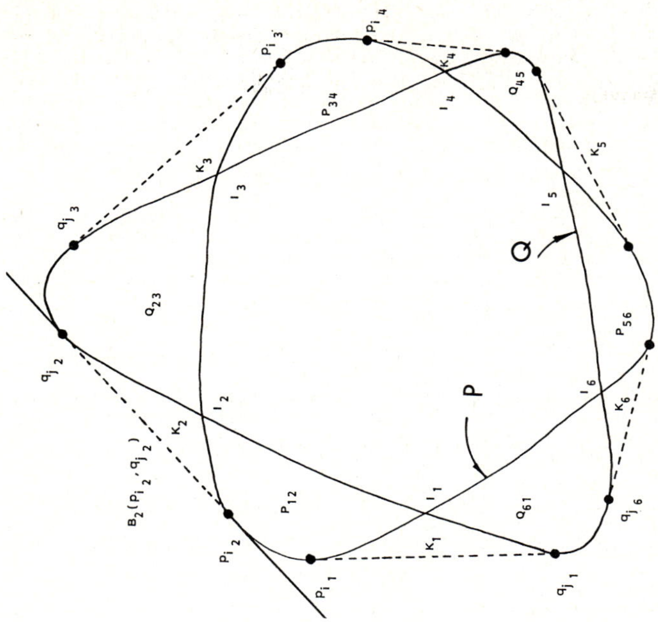

Figure 7

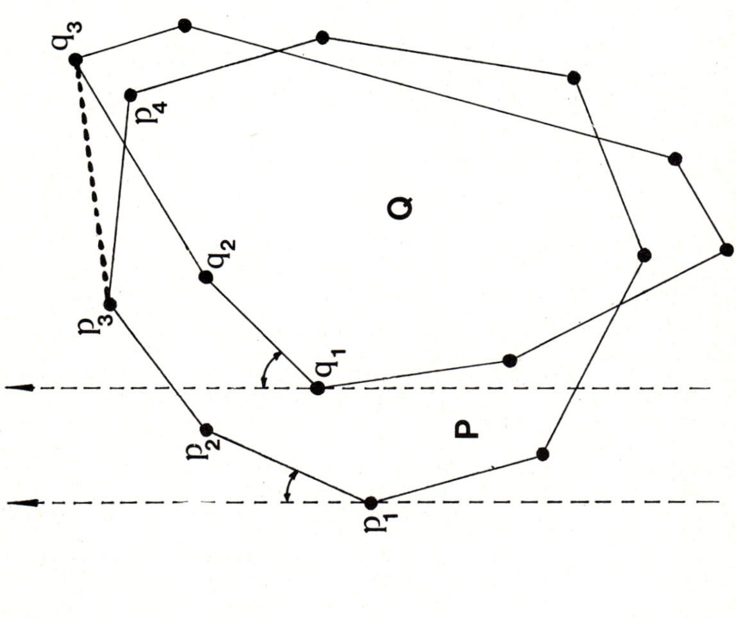

Figure 5: Finding the convex null of two convex polygons with the "rotating calipers."

3. TRIANGULATING AN ANNULUS IN LINEAR TIME WITH THE ROTATING CALIPERS

Let Q now be completely contained in P and refer to Fig. 6.

Algorithm TRIANNULUS

Input: An annulus ANN(P,Q) where $P = (p_1, p_2, \ldots, p_m)$ and $Q = (q_1, q_2, \ldots, q_n)$.
Output: A triangulation of ANN(P,Q), T.

Begin
Step 1: Insert P and Q into T.
Step 2: Find p_{xmin} and q_{xmin} (call them p_1, q_1) and insert edge $\overline{p_1 q_1}$ into T. We thus obtain a *spiral* polygon
$SP = (p_1, p_2, \ldots, p_m, p_1, q_1, q_n, q_{n-1}, \ldots, q_1, p_1)$.
Step 3: Repeat until polygon SP is scanned once.
Rotate calipers until a vertex is advanced on either P,Q, or both.
case 1: Insert edge $\overline{p_2 q_1}$ into T.
case 2: Insert edge $\overline{p_1 q_2}$ into T.
case 3: Insert edge $\overline{p_2 q_2}$ and either $\overline{p_1 q_2}$ or $\overline{p_2 q_1}$ into T.

End

The proof of linearity and correctness is also straightforward for this algorithm. The linearity arguments are as before. The correctness can be proved by induction. Initially we have the spiral polygon SP of n + m + 2 vertices. When the line segment (say $\overline{p_2 q_1}$) is added we cut off a triangle from SP and obtain a new spiral polygon without p_1, i.e., with one less vertex. The details are left to the reader.

4. INTERSECTING TWO CONVEX POLYGONS

4.1 Preliminary Results

In this section we present an informal description of the algorithm and some preliminary results. A more detailed description of the algorithm is included in section 4.2. We assume in this paper that the interiors of the polygons P and Q intersect. If this is not true there is no intersection polygon to construct and the intersection then is either a line segment, a point, or the empty set. In any case, determining whether the interiors of P and Q intersect can be easily performed in $O(\log(m + n))$ time [13], [14]. In order to simplify the description of the algorithm and to prevent the essential aspects from drowning in a sea of detail we further assume that no three vertices in $P \cup Q$ are colinear and all vertices in $P \cup Q$ are distinct. This implies that if P and Q intersect then so do their interiors. It also implies that if the boundaries of P and Q intersect the intersection points do not coincide with vertices of P or Q. Special case tests can be included for the "singularities" that arise when this assumption is not made and these are similar for all algorithms. A very clear exposition on these cases is given by O'Rourke et al. [5].

Consider then two polygons P and Q whose boundaries intersect and construct the convex hull of their union (Fig. 7). Let the boundaries of P and Q intersect at k intersection points $I_1, I_2, \ldots, I_k$ indexed in clockwise order. The boundaries of P, Q, and the convex hull of P and Q, $CH(P \cup Q)$, partition the plane into 2k + 1 bounded regions: the convex intersection region $(I_1, \ldots, I_2, \ldots, I_k, \ldots)$, k regions where P and Q lie outside P ∩ Q (P_{st} associated with I_s and I_t, and Q_{uv} associated with I_u and I_v) and k "pockets" $K_1, K_2, \ldots, K_k$ where a pocket K_v is associated with I_v and is in the region inside CH(P ∪ Q) but outside P ∪ Q. With each pocket K_v we associate a bridge which is an edge of CH(P ∪ Q). denoted by $B_v(p_{i_v}, q_{j_v})$, and which joins vertex p_{i_v} of P with vertex q_{j_v} of Q. The algorithm for computing P ∩ Q can now be described informally as the following three-step procedure: first construct the convex hull of P ∪ Q, then for each bridge B_i find its corresponding intersection point I_i, and finally "merge" the corresponding polygonal chains that connect adjacent intersection points.

The following lemma has been proved by Guibas et al. [15] using a powerful new framework involving convolutions (a special case of fiber products) of polygons.

Lemma 1: If P and Q intersect there exists a unique mutual one-to-one correspondence between the *bridges* of CH(P ∪ Q) and the *intersection points* of P ∩ Q.

We now define a restricted class of simple polygons and state some results concerning their triangulation. While we are not explicitly interested in triangulating these polygons these results are useful in understanding, and proving the correctness of, the algorithm. A polygonal chain $C(p_i, p_{i+1}, \ldots, p_j)$ is a portion of consecutive vertices and edges of a simple polygon. If all turns are *right* (convex angles) we have a *convex chain*. If all turns are *left* (reflex angles) we have a *concave chain*.

Definition: A *sail* polygon P_s is one that contains an edge $\overline{p_i p_{i+1}}$ called the *mast* of P and a vertex p_j called the *sail tip* of P such that p_j is connected to p_i and p_{i+1} by *concave chains* (Fig. 8).

Definition: Three consecutive vertices $p_i\ p_{i+1}\ p_{i+2}$ are said to form an *ear* of P at p_{i+1} if the diagonal joining p_i and p_{i+2} lies in P.

Definition: Two ears are *non-overlapping* if their interior regions are disjoint.

Meisters [16] proves the following "two-ears" theorem.

Lemma 2: Every polygon of n sides (n > 3) has at least two non-overlapping ears.

Lemma 3: The *tip* of a *sail* polygon is an *ear*.

Lemma 4: Either the *mast top* or the *mast bottom* of a *sail* polygon is an *ear*.

Lemma 4 allows us to triangulate P_s in O(n) time by "wrapping the sail around the mast" until only the sail tip remains. In other words, starting at the mast we cut off either the top ear or the bottom ear and proceed to the polygon remaining. The correctness of the algorithm follows from the induction hypothesis that, at each step, the polygon remaining is a *sail* polygon. The proof of this induction hypothesis is left as an exercise for the reader. The linearity follows from the fact that at each step which takes constant time P_s contains one less vertex.

For proofs of all these lemmas see [17].

4.2 The Algorithm

Before describing the complete algorithm we present PROCEDURE STEPDOWN which receives as input a bridge $B_k(p_i, p_j)$ of $CH(P \cup Q)$ and exits with the corresponding pair of edges that determine the intersection point I_k. Without loss of generality assume p_1 and q_1 form the bridge, Q is given in counter-clockwise order, and $\overline{p_s p_{s+1}} \cap \overline{q_t q_{t+1}}$ determines the intersection point I. A convenient data structure for P and Q here is a doubly-linked circular list so that we can scan in either direction and set up pointers between the vertices of P and those of Q. Procedure STEPDOWN finds the two vertices p_s and q_t that can then be used to compute I. The variables p_i and q_j are the "current" vertices under consideration and are a tentative solution. When the algorithm stops $p_i = p_s$ and $q_j = q_t$. The boolean variable "finished" indicates when p_s and q_t are reached by taking on the value "true" after an execution of the "repeat" loop.

```
PROCEDURE STEPDOWN

{initialization} i ← 1; j ← 1
      repeat
          finished ← true
          while (p_i p_i+1 q_j+1) left do
          begin
                j ← j+1
                finished ← false
          end
          while (q_j q_j+1 p_i+1) right do
          begin
                i ← i+1
                finished ← false
          end
      until finished
p_s ← p_i; q_t ← q_j
END STEPDOWN
```

Lemma 5: Procedure STEPDOWN correctly computes the intersection point corresponding to a bridge in O(n) time.

Proof: The proof follows essentially from the realization that STEPDOWN is an implementation of the "ear-cutting" triangulation algorithm for *sail* polygons given in the previous section. For the details the reader is referred to [17].

We now describe the algorithm for computing the intersection of two intersecting convex polygons P and Q. The portions of the boundaries of P and Q outside $P \cap Q$ will be referred to as *outer chains*, those portions inside $P \cup Q$ as *inner chains*.

ALGORITHM INTERCONPOL

Begin

Step 1: Find the convex hull of the union of P and Q, CH(P ∪ Q).

If CH(P ∪ Q) = P(or Q)
then Exit with Q(or P) as
the intersection; Else continue.

Step 2: For each *bridge* of CH(P ∪ Q) call procedure STEPDOWN to compute the intersection points of P ∩ Q.

Step 3: Merge the *inner chains* of P and Q determined by the intersection points found in step 2.

End

Theorem: Algorithm INTERCONPOL correctly computes the intersection polygon of two intersecting convex polygons P and Q in O(m + n) time.

Proof: The correctness of the algorithm follows from lemmas 1 and 5. Thus we turn to its complexity. Finding the convex hull of two intersecting convex polygons in step 1 can be done in O(m + n) time with the rotating calipers. If there are k *bridges* on CH(P ∪ Q) then STEPDOWN is called k times in step 2. Each call requires time linear in the number of vertices processed and the total number of these vertices is the sum total of the vertices on all the *outer chains* of P and Q. Thus step 2 runs in O(m + n) time. Finally, if we leave pointers from the intersection points to the *inner* and *outer* chains in both directions, as we find them in step 2, then the merge step of the inner chains in step 3 can be done in linear time by a mere traversal of the two lists for P and Q. Q.E.D.

REFERENCES

[1] Toussaint, G. T., Pattern recognition and geometrical complexity, Proc. Fifth Int. Joint Conf. Pattern Recognition, Miami (December 1980).

[2] Toussaint, G. T., Solving geometric problems with the rotating calipers, Proc. IEEE MELECON '83, Athens, Greece (May 1983).

[3] Wismath, S. K., Triangulations: an algorithmic study, Tech. Rept. 80-106, Dept. of Computer Science, Queen's Univ., Kingston, Canada (July 1980).

[4] Chazelle, B., Optimal algorithms for computing depths and layers, Tech. Rept. CS-83-13, Dept. of Computer Science, Brown Univ. (April 1983).

[5] O'Rourke, J., et al., A new linear algorithm for intersecting convex polygons, Comp. Graphics and Image Proc., vol. 19 (1982) 384-391.

[6] Toussaint, G. T., Computational geometric problems in pattern recognition, in: Pattern Recognition Theory and Applications, NATO Advanced Study Institute, J. Kittler (ed.), Oxford Univ. (1981) 73-91.

[7] Toussaint, G. T., A historical note on convex hull finding algorithms, Pattern Recognition Letters, vol. 3 (January 1985) 21-28.

[8] Shamos, M. I., Computational Geometry, Ph.D. thesis, Yale Univ. (1978).

[9] Preparata, F. P., and Hong, S., Convex hulls of finite sets in two and three dimensions, Comm. A.C.M., vol. 20 (1977) 87-93.

[10] De Floriani, L., Falcidieno, B., Nagy, G., and Pienovi, C., A hierarchical

structure for surface approximation, Comput. & Graphics, vol. 8, no. 2 (1984) 183-193.

[11] Shamos, M. I., Problems in Computational Geometry, Carnegie-Mellon Univ., (1977).

[12] Shamos, M. I., and Hoey, D., Geometric intersection problems, Proc. Seventeenth Annual IEEE Symposium on Foundations of Computer Science (October 1976) 208-215.

[13] Chazelle, B., Computational geometry and convexity, Ph.D. thesis, Carnegie-Mellon Univ. (July 1980).

[14] Chazelle, B., and Dobkin, D., Detection is easier than computation, Proc. Twelfth Annual ACM Symposium on Theory of Computing (April 1980) 146-153.

[15] Guibas, L., Ramshaw, L., and Stolfi, J., A kinetic framework for computational geometry, Tech. Rept., Xerox Park and Stanford Univ. (May 1983).

[16] Meisters, G. H., Polygons have ears, American Mathematical Monthly (June/July 1975) 648-651.

[17] Toussaint, G. T., A simple linear algorithm for intersecting convex polygons, Tech. Rept. 83.8 (June 1983) School of Computer Science, McGill Univ.

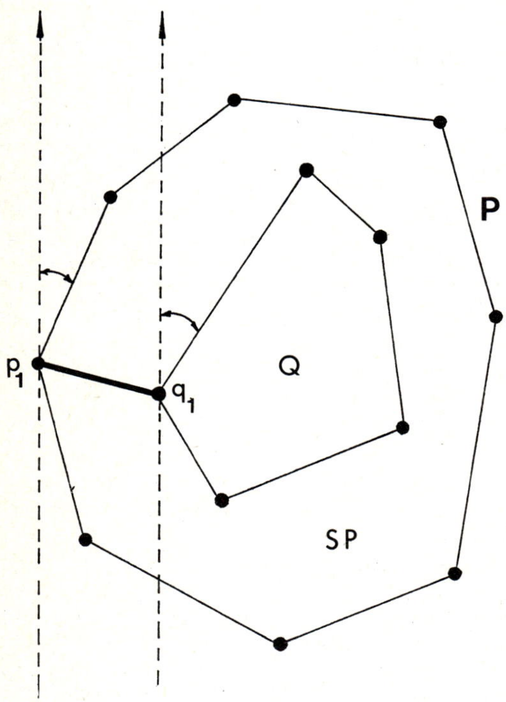

Figure 6: Triangulating an "annulus" with the "rotating calipers."

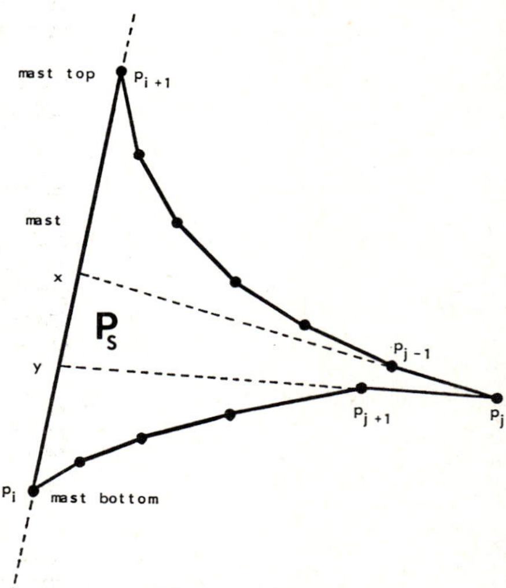

Figure 8

DISCUSSION

Van Heel:

What happens if the space to be segmented is three dimensional rather than a plane?

Toussaint:

We cannot rotate calipers in three dimensions. So basically this procedure is limited to two dimensions.

Van Heel:

Does tis mean that you limit your research to segmentation of two dimensional images?

Toussaint:

Yes, for the time-being, but we are also interested in these problems in three dimensions. But the presented algorithm cannot be extended to three dimensions. That is not to say that algorithms do not exist for these kind of problems in three dimensions. They do, but they are more complicated.

Aus:

You mentioned in the beginning of your presentation some books. Can you state them, so that they appear in the transcript?

Toussaint:

The first book published is called Computational Geometry published by JAI-press in 1984 edited by Franco Preparata.
The second one is a textbook by Kurt Melhorn published by Springer Verlag in 1984 also titled Computational Geometry. It is actually volume 3 of an algorithms and data structures series.
The third one that will come out in August is a textbook by F. Preparata and M. Shamos and is also called Computational Geometry.
The fourth one with the same name will come out in september. It is edited by myself and will be published by North-Holland.

Choudry:

In practice you want to have some sort of constrained triangulation. I will give an example. You have some set of contours of something on which you want to make a smooth surface in 3-D by triangulation. There, the crux is not so much finding some triangulation but finding a particular type of triangulation. If you want to add constraints to your algorithms, is there a general way in doing so or do you have to start from square one?

Toussaint:

That depends on the type of constraint. I assume that you want that certain line segments between certain specified points appear in the triangulation?

Choudry:

That is one of the constraints. Another is that you take the contours of a 3-D image and that you want to make a depth map of it and afterwards reconstruct the 3-D surface from the depth map. In this case you don't want just any arbitrary set of triangles filling that surface. You could put some constraints on, for example, the angle between two planes.

Toussaint:

When you give me as a constraint that certain line segments are to be present, then there is no problem. One way to cope with this problem is to compute a triangulation and then insert the line segments you want to have. For other constraints, like an angular constraint, the solution is more difficult. The Delauney triangulation can handle certain types of constraints similar to the angular ones, but the algorithms are more complicated.

Young:

You showed in the presentation of the parallel caliper algorithm the intersection of two polygons, both being convex and you suggested that the way to form those two polygons was just to take a random number of points, say 5 and make a polygon out of them. Then you take the next 5 points and proceed. What is not obvious to me is how to select these 5 points and how to draw the initial polygon without sorting the points. You said that you wanted to avoid sorting and backtracking. I agree, that once you have the initial polygons, you can use the parallel caliper algorithm but I fail to see how you can avoid sorting for the initial polygons.

Toussaint:

I do not care about sorting 5 points. This is not a time-consuming task since it can be done in constant time. It is, as a matter of fact, just initialization. But if you don't like sorting 5 points you can even start with 3 and begin with triangles. Then there is no sorting at all.

SECTION II

KNOWLEDGE BASED AND MODEL DRIVEN SYSTEMS

PATTERN RECOGNITION IN PRACTICE II
E.S. Gelsema and L.N. Kanal (Editors)

DOCUMENT ANALYSIS WITH AN EXPERT SYSTEM

George Nagy, Sharad C. Seth, Spotswood D. Stoddard

Department of Computer Science
University of Nebraska-Lincoln
Lincoln, Nebraska 68588
U. S. A.

With the decreasing cost of secondary storage it is becoming attractive to store optically scanned technical documents such as reports and articles in digital form as an array of pixels. The array may be compressed with techniques based on run-length coding. In many applications, it is desirable to access only a portion of the document, such as the title, author, abstract, or bibliography. With a knowledge base comprising layout and composition rules for specific classes of documents, these documents may be automatically subdivided into nested rectangles corresponding to meaningful blocks. The resulting structure is represented as a tree. An algorithm is proposed for assigning labels to the blocks according to their location, extent, and relative position with respect to other (possibly already labeled) blocks.

INTRODUCTION

In an earlier paper we proposed a hierarchical representation of a raster-scanned document, called the X-Y tree (Nagy 84). It was argued that because of its various desirable properties, this representation might be useful for automated document analysis in a wide range of applications which include document capture, archival, transmission, and retrieval. These applications do not require any character recognition; instead the spatial structure of a document serves to identify its component blocks. This paper focuses on the problem of labeling the blocks using a given rule base. We propose a run-length encoded data structure for the X-Y tree, define a scheme for the rule base, and establish a theoretical framework to identify the complexity of the labeling problem.

Several recent developments render experiments along the lines we suggest timely. The advent of public data networks has hastened the establishment of standards for digital facsimile, where the selection of the optimal data compression method for economical transmission depends on the accurate identification of the type of material being transmitted: algorithms that work well on text are different from those that work well on line drawings, or on half-tone photographs. Digital document archival using mass-storage devices is beginning to rival the cost-effectiveness of microfilm, particularly when the costs of indexing are taken into consideration.

An early attempt to extend standard optical character recognition (OCR) techniques to complex documents is described in (Nagy 68). A more comprehensive approach to document analysis, which "assists the user in encoding printed documents for computer processing" was reported by a team from IBM (Wong 1982). Other research pertinent to our objectives includes those aspects of optical character recognition which deal with the classification of isolated symbols, as reviewed in (Nagy 82), and the extensive literature on picture grammars (Narasimhan 64, Pfaltz 69) and scene analysis (Levine 81). We will take it for granted that suitable application programs, such as query systems, character recognition and image data compression algorithms are available for further processing and utilization of documents. We are, however, developing our own formalism for page representation because we believe that documents form a very special class of images for which data structures, grammars, and algorithms capable of dealing with completely arbitrary pictures would be inefficient.

DOCUMENT DECOMPOSITION

Here we consider only single-page documents. The page is scanned by an optical digitizer operating in a raster mode. Scan resolution is dictated by the number of samples required to represent the finest essential detail on the page: for a two-level (black-and-white) scanner, 400 lines per inch (62.5 micron spatial sampling interval) is considered adequate.

The structural elements of the page - columns, paragraphs, titles, figures, lines of text, printed symbols - are generally laid out in rectangular blocks. We conjecture that this type of "modular" layout is so common precisely because it can be specified relatively simply with both conventional and digital composition devices.

Because of its size, one cannot afford to store the pixel-level data (the original digitized page array) more than once. Some mechanism is therefore necessary to define and manipulate the location and extent of the meaningful constituents of a page. The data structure we use for this purpose is the X-Y tree. Each node in the X-Y tree corresponds to a rectangle. The successors of a node correspond either to a set of rectangles obtained by horizontal partitions (X-cuts) of the parent rectangle, or to a set of rectangles obtained by vertical partitions (Y-cuts). Horizontal and vertical subdivisions (X cut-sets and Y cut-sets) alternate strictly, level by level. The first subdivision may be arbitrarily set to either horizontal or vertical. The root of the X-Y tree is the rectangle corresponding to the entire page. The leaves constitute a tesselation (tiling) of the page. Some properties of the X-Y tree representation are shared by the series-parallel polar graph used for VLSI layout (Otten 83, Lauther 83), by the K-D tree (Bentley 74), and by the quad-tree (Samet 84).

To obtain the X-Y tree decomposition of a page as a set of nested rectangles, at each step of the recursive process of page decomposition we subdivide a rectangle into smaller rectangles by making cuts along a predetermined (horizontal or vertical) direction. The decision about where the cuts need to be placed is made by examining a certain number of pixel vectors (beyond the current one) that run across the width (or height) of the block being considered for further division. To determine the location of the cuts we currently use a local peak detector on the output of a linear filter which processes horizontal and vertical "profiles".

Within the X-Y tree, the nodes are labeled by a block-index B. The block index consists of a sequence of H's and V's separated by integers. Each H denotes a horizontal cut-set, and each V denotes a vertical cut-set. The integers give the number of cuts in each set, with "0" corresponding to a vacuous cut. An example of a block index B is:

1H3V2H4V0H2 (which might correspond to the array
xm=10, xM=50, ym=15, yM=25).

Each node in the X-Y tree corresponds to a rectangular block containing a particular configuration of pixels. It is very inefficient to store this information at each node of the X-Y tree since a nested block will be replicated as many times as its nesting level. Further, even if only one copy of the document is stored, it would be advantageous to use standard run-length encoding (RLE) schemes to achieve further compaction. A suitable representation is shown in Figure 1.

The RLE equivalent of a page is stored in a global structure (shown in the lower part of the figure) for both the horizontal and the vertical directions of scanning. For each row (column) the positions of B/W and W/B transitions are recorded in a variable length array. For each block, there is a header (shown at the top of the figure) that stores block-specific information pertaining to its position on the page and to its relatives (parent, siblings, and children) on the X-Y tree. In addition, the two pointer fields point to two arrays of records with as many elements as there are rows and columns in the block in question. Each record contains three fields related to the row or column: the pixel value of the first point (B or W), the number of transitions (B/W or W/B), and a pointer to the global structure indicating the transition element corresponding to the start of the block in this scan line.

The above representation, while storing the document image in a compressed form, still contains 100% redundancy since either the horizontal or the vertical scan by itself would be sufficient to recreate the original image exactly. However, with this duplication, it becomes much easier to create and update an X-Y tree, and to compute profiles to determine the location of further cuts. In order to verify this a program was written to process an X-Y tree represented as above. For the mockup page shown in Fig. 2, the program extracted and printed the block corresponding to each node in the X-Y tree without ever unpacking the run length codes. Only the top three levels are shown in the figure.

KNOWLEDGE BASE FOR LABEL ASSIGNMENT

Document components must not only be isolated but also labeled. Each application or document type (such as the title page of the Research Contributions section of the Comm. ACM) is characterized by a set of layout rules sufficient to identify components of interest. For instance, we might have rules of the following type:

line-of-characters:	sequence of adjacent character blocks of same height, separated by character-segmenting rule;
paragraph:	sequence of blocks of line-of-character of same length, separated by line-finding rule;
column:	sequence of paragraph blocks of same width, separated by paragraph-cutting rule;
photo:	large blocks with approximately equal frequency of "1" and "0" pixels;

```
BLOCK HEADER data structure (each block has one of these allocated)
=================================================
| block creation number    |   block label     |
--------------------------------------------------====================
| parent | left sibling | right sibling | left child |right child |
-------------------------------------------------------==============
| left column   |  right column   |  number of columns   |
-----------------------------------------------------------
| left row      |  right row      |  number of rows      |
------------------------------------------------------------=========
| horizontal lines' definitions | vertical lines' definitions |
=====================================================================
__________|                                |
|__________________________________________|
||
||
||  LINE HEADER data structure (each block has an array of these
||                  alocated with 'number of columns' elements)
||  =============================================================
||->| start color (B/W) | number of transitions | transitions |____
|   -------------------------------------------------------------   |
|   |       .           |          .          |      .      |->  |
|   |       .           |          .          |      .      |->  |
|   |       .           |          .          |      .      |->  |
|   =============================================================   |
|                                                                   |
|                                                                   |
|  LINE HEADER data structure (each block has an array of these    |
|                   allocated with 'number of rows' elements)       |
|  =============================================================    |
|->| start color (B/W) | number of transitions | transitions |_____|
   -------------------------------------------------------------   ||
   |       .           |          .          |      .      |->   ||
   |       .           |          .          |      .      |->   ||
   =============================================================   ||
                                                                   ||
                                              _____________________||
    TRANSITION data structure                |                      |
      (each block points at the element      |                      |
       which represents the start of the     |                      |
       line for THIS block)                  |                      |
  ^   ===================================V==========================|
  |   | transition 0  | transition 1  |   ...    | transition n1 ||
  | R ---------------------------------------------------===========|
G N 0 | transition 0  |     ...       | transition n2 |             |
  | W -----------------------------------------------------=========  |
L | S | transition 0  |          ...          | transition nN |     |
  V   =============================================================   |
O                                      ___________________________|
                                      |
B ^ C ==========================|====================
  | 0 | transition 0  |      ... |    | transition m1 |
A | L --------------------------V---------------------===========
  M U | transition 0  | transition 1 |    ...    | transition m2 |
L | M -----------------------------------------------------=========
  | N | transition 0  |          ...          | transition mM |
  V S ======================================================
```

Figure 1. Data Structure for X-Y Tree

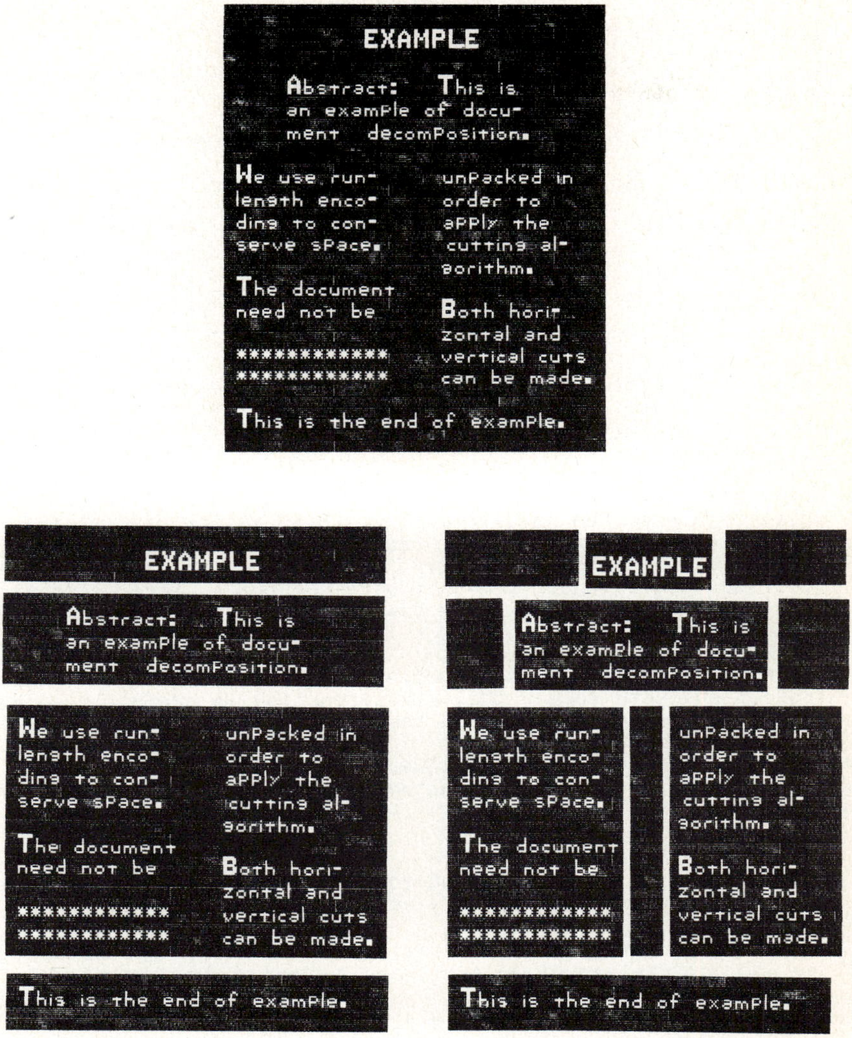

Fig. 2. Three levels of X-Y tree for a 240 x 200 pixel mockup page.

A formal structure for rules of this type is presented below in terms of the results of the decomposition rules discussed earlier.

A label is a semantic, application-dependent identifier which can be associated with a rectangular block. Examples of labels are:

L1 := title of article; L2 := authors; L3 := character.

Each rule itself is a boolean combination of one or more primitive predicates called "conditions". The rule can always be expressed in a sum-of-products or a product-of-sums of a set of conditions. Note that the disjunctive form allows a subset of the conditions to validate a rule, while the conjunctive form allows a subset of conditions to invalidate a rule. An example of a rule for L(3) is:

R3(B) = [C4(B) AND C7(B)] OR NOT C2(B).

A rule is instantiated for a particular block (B = H2V3) as follows:

R3(H2V3) = [C4(H2V3) AND C7(H2V3)] OR NOT C2(H2V3)

A condition C is a binary valued function (formula or program) evaluated for the block with index B on an X-Y tree. It represents the relationship of the particular block B to all or part of the tree. If C = 1, then we say that the condition applies to block B; if it is 0, then it does not apply. There may be an arbitrary number of prescribed conditions. Together with the rules, these conditions constitute the labeling knowledge base for a particular application or type of document.

Conditions may be classified according to the amount of information required to evaluate them. This classification is useful in setting priorities in the control program that assigns labels to blocks.

Simple conditions require for evaluation only the block index and spatial coordinates of the designated block. Examples are (K is an arbitrary parameter):

Is width of block B < K?
Is the level of B in the X-Y tree > K?
Is the cutting rule ultimately responsible for B of type K?

Complex conditions require, in addition to the above, the block indices and coordinates of an arbitrary number of related blocks.

Is the number of siblings of B > K?
Is the aspect ratio of the parent of B < K?
Is maximum width of any sibling of parent (i.e., "uncles") of B > K?

Dynamic conditions require, in addition to the above, the labels of related blocks. Such conditions can be evaluated only after partial labeling of the X-Y tree.

Is parent of B a "line of abstract"?
Is distance of B to "author" block < K?

One possibility for storing the information required for instantiating a condition is a frame structure with preassigned slots for each type of information (Nau 83).

LABELING RULES AND ALGORITHMS FOR LABEL ASSIGNMENT

A labeling is a function from the set of blocks to the set of all possible labels. Given a labeling, we can determine whether or not it is valid in terms of the rules introduced above: it is valid if and only if all the applicable rules evaluate to be true.

An important issue yet to be resolved is whether to "cut before labeling" or to "cut while labeling". In other words, the question is whether the conceptually attractive partioning of the whole task into cutting followed by labeling entails significant computational penalty in implementation. Note that "cutting while labeling" is analogous to the common practice of implementing lexical scanning and parsing as coroutines in compilers. Initially, however, we propose to study the two processes in sequence to better understand the fundamental issues involved in each. Thus in the following discussion we will assume that the page has been completely decomposed into its constituent blocks before the labeling process is invoked.

The _label_ of a block B is a symbol L currently assigned to B. L is drawn from the set of label symbols LABELS defined for the application. The special symbol NULL (unlabeled) is included in LABELS for every application and is initially assigned to every block by default.

Suppose a document has been cut into the XY tree containing m blocks with block indexes B1 ... Bm as described above. In this discussion, each Bj carries the information:

> (1) The position and extent of the block in the document (on the page), e.g., min/max X and Y coordinates, etc; the position in the XY tree of the block, as given by the block index itself in our notation; and information about the pixel content of the block. We can summarize this as the _syntax_ of the block.
>
> (2) The current label of the block, that is, an assignment to the block of one of the set of label symbols, possibly null (unlabeled). We can summarize this as the _semantics_ of the block.

A _labeling rule_ (l-rule) R[L] is a boolean function of a block index B which should be thought of as a functional procedure with B as an argument that performs a test to see if B can be labeled with the label L. R[L](B) returns TRUE if B satisfies the rule, and FALSE otherwise.

An l-rule R[L] is parameterized by a collection of (possibly zero) block indexes P1 ... Pk, which in general may depend upon the argument B (e.g., parent of B, children of B, etc.). That is to say, the assignment of a label to a block B may depend on blocks other than B itself. We write R[L](B; P1 ... Pk) to show the parameterization explicitly. The appearance of a block index, either as the independent variable B or as a parameter P1 ... Pk, stands for all the information that the block index represents.

We denote by LAB(B) the current label (semantics) of block B and by SYN(B) the syntax (document/tree position and pixel content) of B. In the discussion to follow, it will be necessary to consider the dependence of an l-rule R[L] on the syntax of a parameter block separately from its dependence on the semantics of the block. To show the distinction explicitly, we write

R[L](B; S(PS1) ... S(PSj) LAB(PL1) ... LAB(PLk))

where PS1 ... PSj and PL1 ... PLk are block indexes. The meaning of this is that R[L] depends on the syntax of the blocks PS1 ... PSj and on the semantics (labels) of the blocks PL1 ... PLk. The same block index may appear in both PS1 ... PSj and in PL1 ... PLk, meaning that R[L] depends on both the syntax and semantics of this block.

For a given application (type of document) we must define a set of l-rules that are used to assign labels to blocks. If the set of label symbols LABELS is a reasonable one for the application, then there must be an l-rule for each non-null L in LABELS, and we take this to be so. Each different value for L in LABELS requires a different l-rule, that is, R[L1] and R[L2] are different rules (different functional procedures) for L1≠L2. Let LRULES designate the set of all l-rules defined for the application.

A <u>labeling algorithm</u> is a terminating procedure which assigns labels to blocks. We say a labeling algrithm is <u>rule driven</u> if it assigns a label to a block if, and only if, the block satisfies a rule in the set of LRULES for the application. Thus, a rule-driven algorithm essentially consists of combinations of steps of the form

if(R[L](B) then L(B) := L

and computations to order the sequence of such steps.

A labeling algorithm is <u>complete</u> (with respect to an application) if it assigns a label to every block for every document in the application. If a complete, rule-driven algorithm exists for a set of rules LRULES, then we say LRULES is a complete set of rules. Finally, a set of rules is <u>consistent</u> if every complete, rule-driven algorithm defined on it produces the same labeling for each individual document in the application. Alternatively, we can think of LRULES as defining an application, namely, that class of documents for which LRULES is complete and consistent.

Supposing LRULES is complete and consistent for an application, then the following exhaustive algorithm is a complete, rule-driven algorithm for LRULES:

```
while there are unlabeled blocks in B1 ... Bm do
    for each unlabeled block B in B1 ... Bm do
        for each rule R[L] in LRULES do
            if(R[L](B) then
                LAB(B) := L
                exit inner do
            endif
        enddo
    enddo
enddo
```

Assuming that R[L](B) can be evaluated in constant time, this algorithm has worst case complexity m*m*n, where m is the number of blocks and n is the number of rules in LRULES.

<u>Conjecture</u>: Every complete consistent set of l-rules is equivalent to a set of static (i.e., non-dynamic) rules.

We might therefore attempt to form rule sets arranged in a hierarchical sequence of rule classes, as follows:

Class I0 (static rules): Rules which depend only on block syntax (do not check labels).

Class I1: Rules which depend only on labels assigned by I0 rules and block syntax.

.
.
.

Class In: Rules which depend only on labels assigned by I0, I1, ..., I(n-1) rules and block syntax.

If we can write a set of complete, consistent rules for an application in this form, then the following algorithm is a complete algorithm for these rules:

```
for k = 0 to n do
    for each unlabeled block B in B1 ... Bm do
        for each rule R[L] in Ik do
            if(R[L](B)) then
                L(B) := L
                exit inner do
            endif
        enddo
    enddo
enddo
```

This algorithm is of worst-case complexity m*n, as opposed to m*m*n above, and complexity m**n in the completely general case. An alternative family of search methods that we also propose to study experimentally are relaxation methods, as described in (Rosenfeld 76, Zucker 78). The exhaustive labeling algorithm has been implemented in Lisp but, as expected, it can conveniently process X-Y trees of only a few hundred nodes.

CONCLUSION

A prospectus has been presented for extending current document entry methods, which depend on optical character recognition and ad hoc line-finding and character-isolation methods or on interactive guidance, to more complex documents. It is argued that this application is not only timely and important in its own right, but that the proposed study represents an important area of information science research that draws on recent advances in image processing and artificial intelligence. While our application is challenging, it does not require the full power of general-purpose picture grammars, complex segmentation algorithms, texture analysis and structural pattern recognition that are necessary for interpreting arbitrary outdoor scenes, for biomedical images, and for computer vision. The task is well defined and of a reasonable level of difficulty: tangible results may be expected, but are not guaranteed.

To facilitate document analysis, we have defined two new tools, X-Y trees and formal block-labeling schemata. Our cutting rules are based on a relatively simple analysis of pixel patterns drawn from optical character recognition. We are combining a standard method of knowledge representation with a block structure derived from current document composition methods to assign labels, using heuristic search algorithms, to meaningful parts of a technical document. We will test the correctness of our data structure both directly, by comparing it to the specifications used to generate artificial sample documents, and indirectly, by implementing a simple information retrieval system for real raster-scanned documents.

REFERENCES

Aho, A.V. and J.D. Ullman, Principles of Compiler Design, Addison Wesley, Reading, MA, 1977.

Bentley, J.L., "Multidimensional binary search trees used for associative searching", Comm. ACM 18, 8, pp. 509-517, September 1975.

IBM Document Composition Facility and Document Library Facility, General Information, Program Product GH20-9158-2, File No. S370-34, Second Edition, 1979.

Lauther, U., "Cell Based VLSI Design System", Hardware and Software Concepts in VLSI, Van Nostrand and Reinhold (ed. G. Rabbat), pp. 481-493.

Levine, M.D. and S.I. Shaheen, "A modulare computer vision system for picture segmentation and interpretation", IEEE-PAMI 2, 5, pp. 540-556, September 1981.

Nagy, G., "A preliminary investigation of techniques for the automated reading of unformatted text", Comm, ACM 11, 7, pp. 480-487, July 1968.

Nagy, G., "Optical character recognition - theory and practice", Handbook of Statistics II, (L. Kanal and P.R. Krishnaiah, eds.), North Holland, Amsterdam, pp. 621-649.

Nagy, G., "Optical scanning digitizers", IEEE Computer 16, 5, pp. 13-25, May 1983.

Narasimhan, R., "Labeling schemata and syntactic description of pictures", Information and Control 7, pp. 151-179, June 1964.

Nau, D., "Expert Computer Systems", IEEE Computer 16, 2, pp. 63-85, February 1983.

Otten, R.M.J.M., "VLSI Layout", Hardware and Software Concepts in VLSI, Van Nostrand Reinhold, (ed. G. Rabbat), pp. 407-451, 1983.

Pfaltz, J.L. and A. Rosenfeld, "Web Grammars", Proc. 1st Int. Conf. Artificial Intelligence, Washington D.C., pp. 609-619, 1969.

Rosenfeld, A., R. Hummel, and S. Zucker, "Scene Labeling by Relaxation Operations", IEEE-SCM 6, p. 420, 1976.

Samet, H., "Region representation: quadtrees from boundary codes", Comm. ACM 23, 3, pp. 163-170, March 1980.

Wong, K.Y., R.G. Casey, and F.M. Wahl, "Document analysis system", IBM J. Res. and Dev. 26, 6, pp. 647-656, November 1982.

Zucker, S.W. et al., "Relaxation processes for scene labeling: convergence, speed and stability", IEEE-SCM, pp. 41-48, 1978.

DISCUSSION

Choudry:

Aren't you forced to do run-length coding of pixels if you have graphics with alpha-numeric text?

Nagy:

For graphics run-length coding is only one way to code. Some kind of compression is probably necessary and one solution might be to recognize whether it is a line drawing or a photograph-style drawing and then invoke the appropriate compression algorithm.

Choudry:

We are going through a sort of transition era. There is the Gutenberg era and the text processing era. If the Mac and PC prices plummet, all the documents will be generated by a certain code and so the document is already coded. Thus the life cycle of your program is up to 1990 roughly. Won't the text processing source codes solve all the problems that you have considered?

Nagy:

Well, two things about that. If we now think to solve this problem in five years that takes us up to 2005 since we always have underestimated the development time by a factor of three and that is good enough for me.

Secondly, there will be those people who still want to read the stuff we have written which is not in computer readable form.

PATTERN RECOGNITION IN PRACTICE II
E.S. Gelsema and L.N. Kanal (Editors)

INTERPRETATION OF INDUSTRIAL SCENES USING AUGMENTED TRANSITION NETWORKS AND PRODUCTION SYSTEMS: PROCEDURAL VS. DECLARATIVE MODELS

G. Stein, H. Tropf, I. Walter

Fraunofer-Institut für Informations- und Datenverarbeitung
Karlsruhe, F.R. of Germany

Both a procedural and a declarative approach to the interpretation of industrial scenes are described. The goal of this contribution is to report on our experience with both approaches and to point out our current ideas of how to combine them.

Each approach has been implemented and applied to contour primitives (lines, circles, corners). In the system based on the procedural approach, a single CAD-like description of each object defines a 3-D geometric model. An Augmented Transition Network (ATN) is used as a control structure for relating model elements to contour primitives. Results are given for the model-based 3-D location of randomly oriented parts in single images.

In the other implementation based on the declarative approach, the 2-D geometric models are defined as sets of productions. This system has no explicit problem-specific control structure. Results are given for the classification and 2-D location of workpieces with varying illumination as well as for the detection of surface flaws.

1. INTRODUCTION

There has been some discussion in which situations knowledge should be better represented in a procedural or in a declarative form. This discussion originated in the field of Artificial Intelligence; it is the old distinction between "knowing that" and "knowing how" (Winograd (1975)). In Barr/Davidson (1981) advantages and disadvantages of these approaches are discussed under the general aspect of knowledge representation. The discussion naturally came up also in model-based pattern analysis. Nagao (1984) describes a declarative approach for the detection of objects in aerial photographs and a procedural approach for face recognition. Havens/Mackworth (1983) stress that rather than using a uniform control structure in order to guide the search procedural knowledge specific to each model should be used.

In the following a procedural as well as a declarative approach to the interpretation of industrial scenes is described. We have realized the two systems in parallel. As a procedural model, we use an Augmented Transition Network (ATN for short; adopted from the natural language understanding domain (Woods (1970))). We describe a model for the 3-D location of polyhedral workpieces in single images. In the declarative approach, the geometric models are defined as sets of productions, each denoting a condition-action pair. There is no problem-specific control structure explicitly formulated.

2. DESCRIPTION OF THE TWO APPROACHES

In both approaches, contour primitives are extracted as a first step. This preprocessing step is performed without any knowledge about the structure of the objects to be recognized; only some knowledge about the grey value contour characteristics is involved in order to select the parameters for the extraction of contour primitives. The extraction of contour primitives is not a subject of our contribution. The contour primitives are given as a list to be handled by the subsequent procedure.

A general view that applies to both approaches is the notion of "analysis by synthesis": At each recognition step, partially instantiated object models - called partial prototypes - are created or further completed. This is done on the basis of partial prototypes that have been created in previous steps and of contour primitives. Some measure of similarity is associated with each partial prototype. It indicates how well the prototype matches the image data. Recognition consists of finding the prototype with maximum similarity.

2.1 THE AUGMENTED TRANSITION NETWORK APPROACH

2.1.1 SYSTEM DESCRIPTION

ATNs were developed and mainly used in the field of natural language understanding and speech recognition (Woods (1970)). The advantages of the ATN formalism, namely its perspicuity and generative power, can also be brought to bear in the field of patterns and models with more than one dimension (Breu/Mackworth (1980)). Here, we present the use of an ATN mechanism for the 3-D location of randomly oriented parts with known geometry. We give only a survey of the approach; it is described in detail in Tropf/Walter (1983) and Walter/Tropf (1983). An additional example for the use of ATNs in image analysis (classifying parts on a hanging conveyor with nearly 1000 possible classes) is described in Tropf et al. (1984).

The basic idea of the recognition of rigid parts is as follows: While following the path through the transition network from the initial state to the goal state, model elements are associated with contour primitives. Thus, the number of degrees of freedom of a 3-D object model is more and more constrained until the object is fixed in 3-D. The possible location of model elements in the 2-D image is calculated based on their tentative 3-D positions. After fixation, the rest is hypothesis verification by checking the contour primitives at clearly defined locations in the image plane. The ATN describes several alternatives of model-to-pattern association sequences (Walter/Tropf (1983)).

The following example demonstrates the method: Only points (e.g. corner points, center points of circles) are used as model elements; orthogonal projection is assumed; occlusion is neglected. The distance d between two model points P1 and P2 is known. So, after the fixation of the first point P1 in 3-D, the second point P2 to be fixed must lie on the surface of a sphere with center P1 and radius d - therefore, due to the assumption of orthogonal projection, the corresponding pattern point must lie within a circle with radius d. Having chosen such a point, we know (neglecting ambiguity) the axis P1-P2. The third point P3 (not lying on P1-P2) must lie on a circle around P1-P2 which in the projection is an ellipse. Having selected a contour primitive point close enough to the ellipse, the object is fixed. The remainder is verification.

2.1.2 RESULTS

We realized an ATN network for the point-to-point association example given above. Figure 1 shows an example result with a single 3-D workpiece.

When executing the recognition procedure using only the constraints of the geometric formulas, we obtained the following results for a typical example with 11 model elements and 15 contour primitives: If the three model elements to be used for the fixation were dictated by the user (approach a), about 1000 search nodes were created. When the fixation model points were not dictated by the user (approach b), the number of search nodes exceeded reasonable limitations. Since only approach b is sufficiently flexible to deal with a single 3-D model, we incorporated the following straightforward constraints in form of ATN tests:

1. The distance between the first two model elements chosen for fixation must not exceed some threshold.
2. Pattern primitives with nearly identical position must not be chosen for the fixation.
3. Pattern primitives associated with the second model element must have a distance from the first one between d and d*1/sqrt(2), where d is the distance between the first two model elements.

With these constraints, but otherwise unchanged conditions, the number of search nodes was reduced to about 50 and 1000 for approach a and b, respectively.

We have found that ATNs are a good tool for controlling the search. Speedup heuristics are easily introduced into an existing model in the form of ATN tests without sacrificing a clear system structure.

2.2 THE PRODUCTION SYSTEM APPROACH

2.2.1 SYSTEM DESCRIPTION

Figure 2 shows the components of the production system. For primitive extraction, contour points are detected. Consecutive contour points are connected to form short strokes (called contour strokes). The contour point detection is homogeneous on the image data and stroke finding is a simple local procedure so that the steps up to this point can be processed in parallel by special hardware. From these contour strokes the contour primitives are constructed (circular arcs and straight line segments). This process is still data driven.

The next step is a model driven construction of local shape elements, e.g. S-curves, concentrical circles, parallel lines with some predefined distance from each other. The models of these shape elements are given as production rules describing how the shape elements are decomposable into more and more simple constituents down to the contour primitives. The constituents comprise contour primitives, nonterminals, shape elements, and picture descriptions. The next step is the description of the workpiece as a whole, based on the local shape elements built up in the previous step. Here, exactly the same production system mechanism is used as before; only the set of production rules is changed.

Newly built constituents are stored into a database. All productions which are applicable to the constituent with the highest figure of merit are executed. The heuristic figure of meret attempts to measure completeness and quality of shape. If a production is not applicable and the constituent can be accepted as a final element (shape element or workpiece description) this constituent is regarded as system output and all the constituents it is composed of are eliminated from the database. Since these constituents are no longer available for building alternative constituents, there is no guarantee that the optimal interpretation (in terms of the measure of goodness) will be found. Introducing this elimination of constituents, however, turned out to be necessary in order to keep the computational effort within manageable limits. Note that the elimination is only done when a final element has been found; as long as nonterminals are treated, alternative interpretations remain open.

2.2.2 RESULTS

For the workpiece description, the following local shape elements are used (see Figure 3): Concentric 90-degree circular arc, U-shape with two circles, circles with 5 smaller circles around it in a pentagon arrangement. The workpiece is described in form of a triangle. Figure 3 shows an example of local shape elements and a workpiece description that have been extracted from a scene. Upper left shows the grey value image, upper right the contour primitives (lines and arcs with their radii), lower left the shape element and lower right the final representation of the workpiece. For modelling such workpieces, 20-40 production rules are necessary, more than two thirds of them being required for the shape elements. The number of rule applications is heavily dependent on a clever definition of the measure of goodness which until now must be determined heuristically. For the scenes shown, typically 350-500 rule applications are necessary (on the average at each step of the search, 4 elements are taken from the database and 3 rules can be applied to each of these elements).

In the surface flaw detection example of Figure 4, the following shape elements are used: A polygon formed by the midpoints of circular arcs with some additional local consistency conditions and a polygon made up of straight line segments and chords of arcs. Figure 4 shows shape elements that have been extracted as an indication of a surface flaw on a plate of porcelain. Upper left shows the grey value image, upper right the contour strokes, lower left the contour primitives (lines and arcs with their midpoints) and lower right the shape elements of the flaw (F) and the plate (T).

Although it is possible to find suitable production rules for such an application (and production systems are generally considered the right choice for "diffuse knowledge areas" (Barr/Davidson (1981)), defining the production rules for this application turned out to be crucial. This is mainly due to different types of surface flaws which require different illumination arrangements. The data driven analysis steps are heavily dependent on the lighting circumstances so that each illumination requires additional production rules.

With the growing number of production rules some typical problems arise:

1. **Consistency:**
   It becomes difficult for the designer to retain the overview whether the rules are consistent. The consistency of attribute values (e.g. the length of a chord) in the condition and action parts of the rules are much more difficult to maintain than the consistency of the symbolic labels of contour primitives and nonterminals.

2. **Completeness:**
   Nonterminals and their attribute values have to be defined properly in order to avoid premature termination of the construction process. Nonterminals demanded by productions to build constituents up in a higher position of the hierarchy must be producible by some rule. This is self-evident but it is not easy to guarantee with a growing number of attributes and rules.

3. DISCUSSION

The pros and cons of procedural and declarative methods with respect to the analysis of industrial scenes are summarized in Table 1.

3.1 SYSTEM DESIGN AND EFFICIENCY

Comfort of system design and efficiency are both important for industrial applications. The design of ATNs requests a relatively deep insight into how the mechanism works. Therefore an intelligent ATN model editor is a necessary tool.

The design of production systems is easy and quick as long as the number of rules is small (about 40 in our example). With a growing number of attributes and production rules, the specification of properties for contour primitives and nonterminals becomes tedious. Tools for controlling consistency and completeness of the rules are demanded for. In picture processing, the raw data are noisy and call for the automatic estimation of attribute tolerances. Since in the field of industrial part recognition the geometric primitives obey some general geometric rules, a model-guided learning of problem specific production rules from more general rules seems possible.

To speed up the search, problem specific heuristics must be used. We have found that ATNs provide a useful way to cope with the sometimes complicated structure of the search. New constraints are easily inserted into an existing model in the form of ATN tests. The request for hierarchy and procedural adequacy (Havens/Mackworth (1983)) is clearly complied with.

To speed up the search in production systems, situation dependent and well known procedural knowledge is difficult to incorporate. It requires detailed knowledge of the handling of data by the underlying analysis mechanism. A crucial point is the method of conflict resolution, i.e. the strategy of how to select a single rule under several possible choices (McDermott/Forgy (1978)). The usual irrevocable conflict resolution makes the solution dependent on the evaluation scheme.

3.2 COMBINATION OF BOTH APPROACHES

Procedural and declarative approaches should supplement each other. Production systems are well suited for "domains in which a process can be represented as a set of independent actions" (Barr/Davidson (1981)). In terms of our application examples, this means that there are, for example, subpatterns to be detected independently from each other in different image areas. This is the case for the model guided detection of shape elements which could arise anywhere in the picture. As far as the geometrical conditions under which an element should be found depends on some other elements found previously, a procedural approach is more appropriate in order to avoid unnecessary rule application attempts. In our examples, this can happen at different levels: within the detection of a single shape element and for describing a single workpiece as a whole.

What would be needed then is a framework that incorporates procedural as well as declarative components. Georgeff (1982) describes a controlled production system with a separately specified control structure of production invocation independent of the search strategy. Procedural and declarative languages are special cases of a controlled production system (Georgeff (1982)). A first idea is to choose an ATN mechanism that incorporates the invocation of production systems as an ATN action. Such a production system should be invoked at ATN arcs where the sequence of operations within this ATN action is of no concern; e.g. because there are many independent ways. It is not invoked before information needed in order to apply the production rules of this production system is available. Thus, unnecessary rule application trials are avoided. However, this model is still insufficient. This becomes clear by the following consideration: The detection of shape elements (anywhere in the image) may be triggered by the invocation of a production system. After the first few production rules have been applied, the rest of the detection of a somewhat complicated shape element, however, is best described as a sequential process. Thus, we need also a reverse formalism: Invocation of an ATN subnetwork as a special production rule. This is analogous to the introduction of complex procedural knowledge in the form of metarules (Davis/Buchanan (1977)).

In any case, both approaches as well as the outlined combinations of them require sophisticated tools for model design and for speed optimisation in order to be acceptable for real industrial applications.

4. REFERENCES

[1] Barr, A. and Davidson, J. (eds.),
Knowledge representation, in: Barr, A. and Feigenbaum, E.A. (eds.), The Handbook of Artificial Intelligence 1 (William Kaufmann, Los Altos, California, 1981), 141-222.

[2] Breu, H. and Mackworth, A.K.,
Push and pop on pictures; generalizing the Augmented Transition Network formalism to capture the structure and meaning of images, Proc. Canadian Soc. Computational Studies of Intelligence, 3rd Nat. Conf. (1980), Victoria, B.C., 179-187.

[3] Davis, R. and Buchanan, B.,
Production rules as a representation for a knowledge-based consultation programm, Artificial Intelligence 8 (1977) 15-45.

[4] Georgeff, M.P.,
Procedural control in production systems, Artificial Intelligence 18 (1982) 175-201.

[5] Havens, W. and Mackworth, A.,
Representing knowledge of the visual world, Computer 16, No. 10 (Oct. 1983) 90-96.

[6] McDermott, J. and Forgy, C.,
Production system conflict resolution strategies. In: Waterman, D.A. and Hayes-Roth, F. (eds.), Pattern-Directed Inference Systems (Academic Press, New York, 1978) 177-199.

[7] Nagao, M.,
Control strategies in pattern analysis, Pattern Recognition 17 (1984) 45-56.

[8] Tropf, H and Walter, I.,
An ATN model for 3-D recognition of solids in single images, Proc. 8th IJCAI (1983), Karlsruhe, 1094-1097.

[9] Tropf, H., Walter, I. and Kammerer, H.-P.,
Erweiterte Übergangsnetze als prozedurale Modelle im Bereich der Bildanalyse, in: Kropatsch, W. (ed.), Mustererkennung 1984, Informatik-Fachberichte 87 (Springer, Berlin, 1984) 290-296.

[10] Walter, I. and Tropf, H.,
3-D recognition of randomly oriented parts, Proc. RoViSeC3 (1983), Cambridge, Mass. 171-178.

[11] Winograd, T.,
Frame representations and the declarative/procedural controversy, in: Bobrow, D.G. and Collins, A. (eds.), Representation and Understanding: Studies in Cognitive Science (Academic Press, New York, 1975) 185-210.

[12] Woods, W.A.,
Transition network grammars for natural language analysis, CACM 13 (1970) 591-606.

<table>
<tr><td>Arguments to choose a procedural approach</td><td>Arguments to choose a declarative approach</td></tr>
<tr><td colspan="2">1. DATABASE
A-priori knowledge about the primitives to be processed</td></tr>
<tr><td>PROCEDURAL

Industrial scenes contain much more restrictions and regularities which are known a-priori than natural scenes.</td><td>DECLARATIVE

Easy adaptability to a-priori unknown tasks is demanded for. Industrial surrounding is noisy with unknown random process characterization.</td></tr>
<tr><td colspan="2">2. FOUNDATION OF KNOWLEDGE
Is the knowledge theoretically justified or a collection of empirical assertions?</td></tr>
<tr><td>PROCEDURAL

For workpiece recognition, general geometric rules and models of surface reflection can be used.</td><td>DECLARATIVE

For surface flaw detection, geometric relations are fuzzy. Surface reflection is strongly influenced by rust and dust.</td></tr>
<tr><td colspan="2">3. COURSE OF ANALYSIS
Interdependence of actions</td></tr>
<tr><td>PROCEDURAL

Preferable sequences of actions exist (example: At first construction of long strokes out of short strokes).</td><td>DECLARATIVE

Several similar short sequences of actions exist (example: Model of a symmetric object).</td></tr>
<tr><td colspan="2">4. INDEPENDENCE OF KNOWLEDGE AND COURSE OF ANALYSIS
Can the knowledge and its application be separated?</td></tr>
<tr><td>PROCEDURAL

Complex geometric forms must be sequentially constructed from simpler forms.</td><td>DECLARATIVE

Local connections and symmetric relations are independent from the order of rule application.</td></tr>
</table>

Table 1:
Criteria for the choice of procedural and declarative approaches with respect to industrial applications of image analysis.

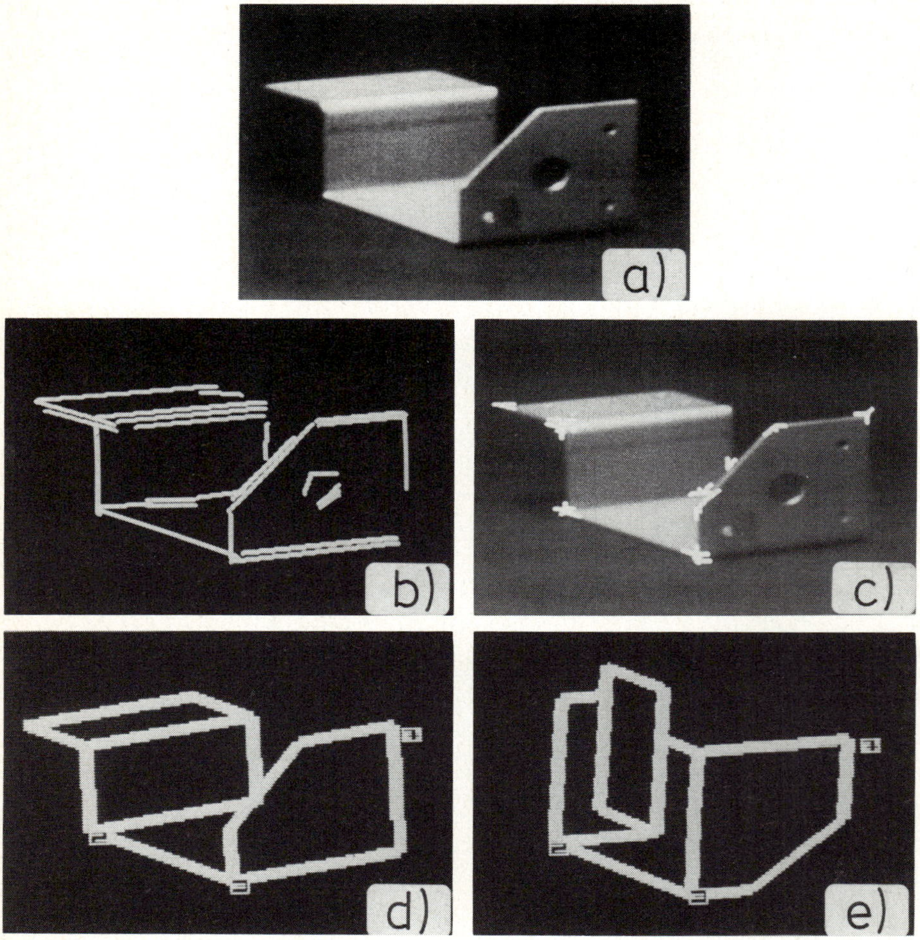

Figure 1:
An example for the 3-D location of a workpiece:
a) original image of the part
b) edge image
c) calculated corners using the edges
d,e) the two alternative object positions derived by the technique described in Section 2.1.2 for the same image-to-model matches of points marked 2,3 and 7.

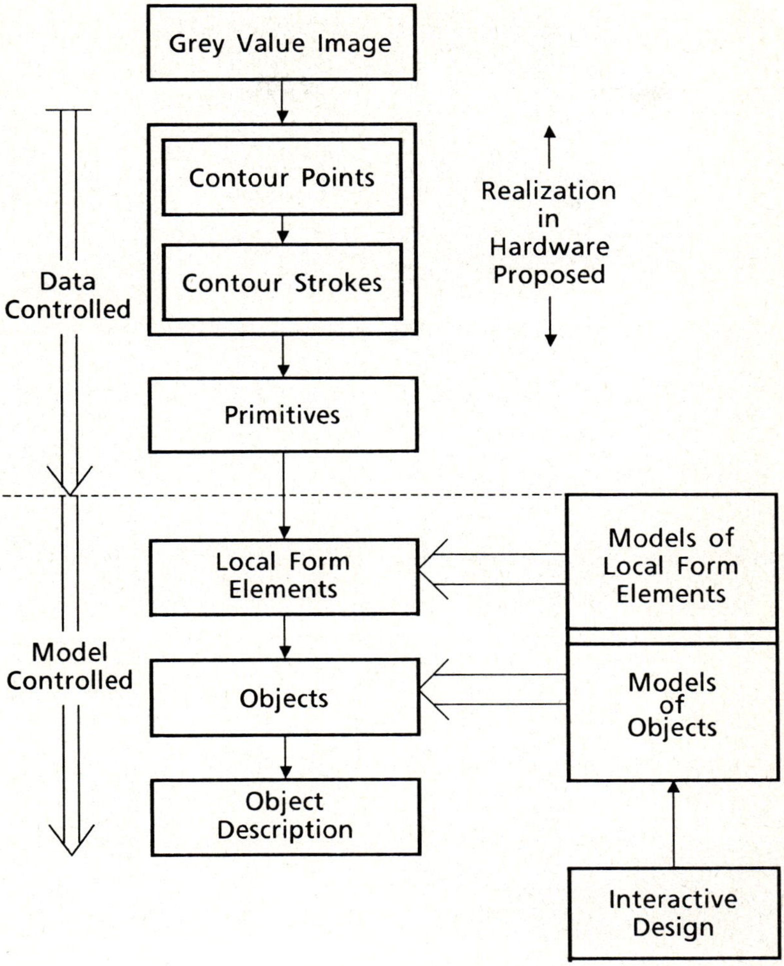

Figure 2:
Components of the declarative approach.

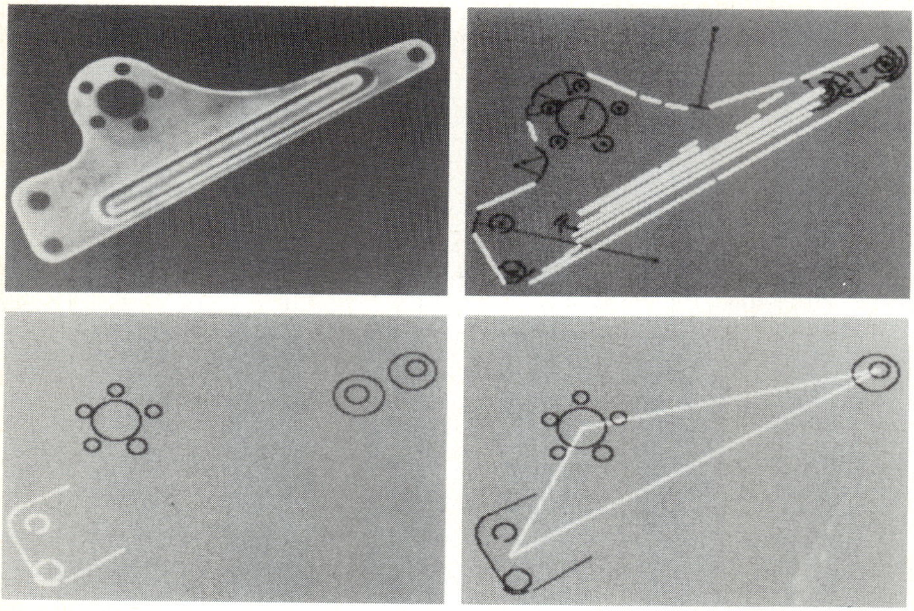

Figure 3:
Recognition of a workpiece (see chapt. 2.2.2).

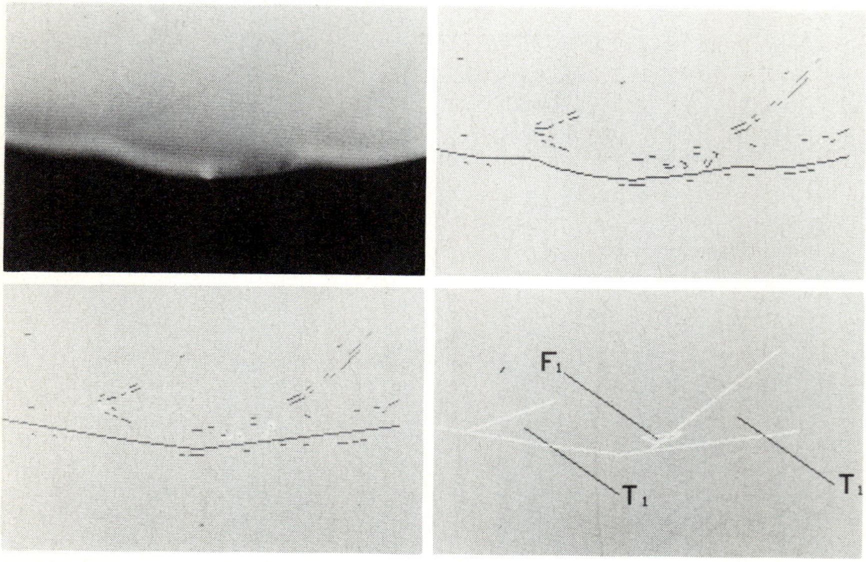

Figure 4:
Recognition of a surface flaw on a plate (see chapt. 2.2.2).

DISCUSSION

Smeulders:
How do you detect circular arcs?

Tropf:
We try to compose circular arcs out of the short strokes by means of a kind of synthesizing algorithm. We take one of those short strokes. Then we look for the next short stroke within a certain region. If we find it we assume that this could be a circular arc. Then we look for the next short stroke within the next region and so on. It turned out to be very dificult at the lowest level to compute the circular arcs because of quantization errors. Quite a large look-up-table had to be constructed to cope with the different possibilities. But at higher levels simple geometrical considerations were sufficient to find the arcs.

Mann:
In what language is your production-rule system written?

Tropf:
It is written in PASCAL. We did not use PROLOG because it is less flexible since the backtrack mechanism is fixed. We can, for example, define a figure of merit and use other tricks which are either impossible or at least very difficult to realize in PROLOG.

Suetens:
I have not completely understood how you implement your transition networks. Are you doing it in the form of procedures? Can you explain how they are used in the production system?

Tropf:
Let me go to the ATN example for part classification. There it is a data structure which is constructed using a menu-driven program. You are asked what is the name of the next node you want to take, you can select one node or you can add an arc etc. You can also edit the operations associated with the arcs in textual form. This text is interpreted during the analysis. The production system is basically a collection of procedures.

Persoon:
At this moment you use only corners as model elements for your 3-D recognition system. If you look at more complex shapes like circles or holes then you have to take into account the transformation into ellipses. These ellipses are different for different views in 2-D depending on the position of your object relative to the camera. To what extent do you have to take this knowledge of the shape variation into account in your analysis?

Tropf:
The problem you mentioned will be dealt with in a project we hope to start in October using more powerful features and multiple cameras. In that project we intend to use as primitives in the fixation phase the corners, lines and circular arcs but for the latter only the center point and a measure of the radius. It will be possible to make a synthesized image for the verification phase. This is a CAD-technique.

Richetin:

I don't understand how you can recognize a 3-D part using corner primitives when you do not use a recursive estimation of the position of the part during the fixation/verification procedure.

Tropf:

When I make an association between a pattern element and a model element I put a constraint on the position of the part in 3-D. This is only a trial. Much of those attempts are made to verify the position of the part and hopefully only one of them will be successful. It is not necessary to make highly sophisticated position estimates since the position of the camera with respect to the plane in which the objects are positioned is fixed. So we assume parallel projection. Since the distance is fixed the length of the edges is, within certain tolerances, a priori known.

Stockman:

In our work we are getting angle errors between 5 to 10 degrees. It seems that you do a lot better. Otherwise, Richetin has made a valid point. You have to fix your transformation as you accumulate more evidence.

Tropf:

I have shown that in certain circumstances the result is highly dependent on the accurate determination of the positions of the corners. When you have a lot of corners, there is a good chance that some of them will reasonably fit. The position of the corners, however, were very well determined because they are at the intersection of two long lines. The position of the long lines is rather accurate since we use a differentiating component perpendicular to the line and an integrating component along the line. This makes the estimate of the position of the line very accurate. When two lines are nearly perpendicular, then also the estimate of the corner position will be accurate.

PATTERN RECOGNITION IN PRACTICE II
E.S. Gelsema and L.N. Kanal (Editors)

MODEL BASED INTERPRETATION OF IMAGE SEQUENCES FROM THE HEART

I. Hofmann, H. Niemann, G. Sagerer
Lehrstuhl fuer Informatik 5 (Mustererkennung)
University of Erlangen-Nuernberg
Martensstr. 3

D - 8520 Erlangen (FRG)

1. Abstract

The following paper describes an expert system dealing with the automatic analysis of heart scintigrams. The aim of the system is to detect motional abnormalities of a part of the human heart, the left ventricle. In principle, there are five modules, each of which is fit for a special task. The routines doing image preprocessing up to contour extraction build one module METHODS. The knowledge needed for analyzing an image sequence is contained in the module MODEL. The model is represented by means of an associative network. The module INSTANCES organizes the results of an analysis in the same way as it is done in the module MODEL. A third module CONTROL controls an analysis of an image sequence based on the model creating instances of model concepts. The concern of the last module HUMAN INTERFACE is to provide some means for communications between user and system.

2. Introduction

Due to its noninvasive nature, nuclear imaging has become very important for the diagnosis of human heart diseases. We are concerned with heart scintigrams, i.e. image sequences (Fig. 1) showing the radiation emitted by the blood pool

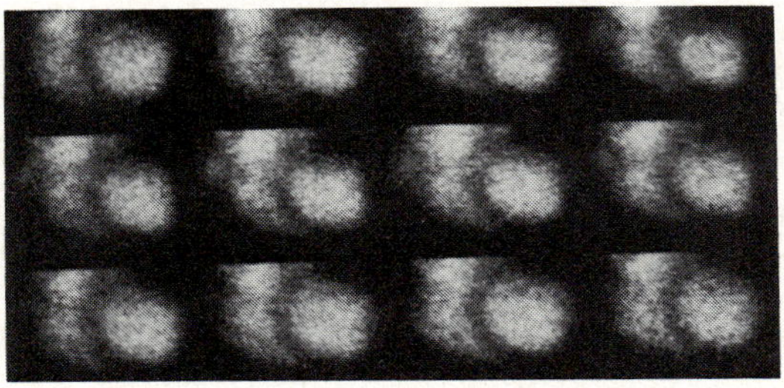

Fig. 1 Image sequence

after equal distribution of the radionuclide Tc-99m which has been injected into the vein of the patient. Observing the two-dimensional intensity distribution over a sequence of images representing one cycle of the human heart offers the possibility to visualize the cavities of the heart and to describe the motility of the heart by interpreting the changes in volume of those cavities. In order to get a representative cycle of the beating heart, there is the need of sufficient gamma particles per image. Therefore, the image sequences of about 500 cycles are synchronously added. The images are taken under a left anterior projection of 45 degrees. The main applications of gated blood pool studies are in diagnosis and periodical supervision after heart surgeries. Up to now interpretation of those image sequences (location and gravity of abnormalities of the heart, especially of the left ventricle) is usually performed via visual inspection. It is well-documented that the interpretation requires considerable experience from the observer and is very time-consuming.

At our institute, a prototype version of a system for the automatic analysis of scintigraphic image sequences has been completed. The objective is to assist the physician in diagnosis by providing both quantitative and qualitative information. In literature there are discussed qualitative [1] approaches concerning cardiac x-ray films and quantitative approaches (i.e. [2]) which are developped for gated cardiac blood pool studies. In our approach we combine artificial intelligence methods, especially methods of computer vision systems, with methods well-known in pattern recognition to design an expert system able to infer a medical description of the static and the dynamic behaviour of the human heart from pictorial data without any user interactions required.

3. System overview

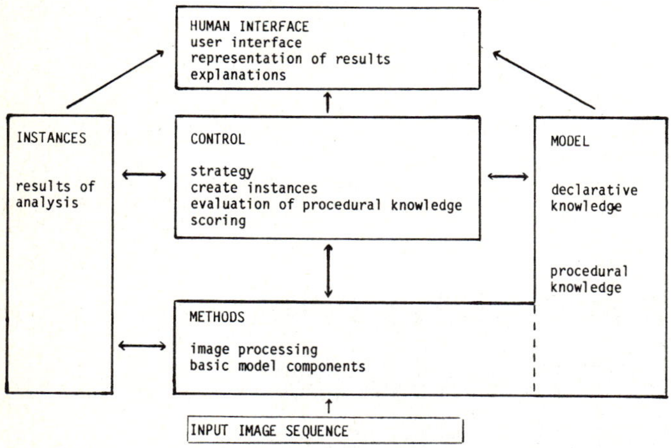

Fig. 2 System architecture

The principal architecture of the system (Fig. 2) is based on the concept proposed in [3]. The system consists of five major modules. Every module is concerned with a particular task which will be described in the following sections. The module METHODS contains routines doing image preprocessing. In order to perform this task external knowledge about the shape of the human heart is needed. Therefore a detailed description of this module is given in section `procedural knowledge`.

3.1 Module MODEL

As mentioned above, interpretation of a scintigraphic image sequence requires an experienced observer, that is a certain kind of knowledge to guide the analysis. Two kinds of knowledge are to be distinguished:

- declarative or static knowledge to describe objects, facts or medical terms

- procedural or dynamic knowledge to compute quantitative parameters.

3.1.1 **Declarative knowledge.** Knowledge representation is a major topic in research concerning artificial intelligence methods. There are known different representation schemes from literature, i.e. predicate logic [4], production systems [5], relational databases [6], frames [1, 7], or associative networks [4, 8, 9, 10].

In our approach associative networks had been chosen as representational formalism. Such networks are graphlike structures consisting of nodes named concepts to describe terms and objects, and edges to describe the relations between different nodes. A node may be interpreted as an abstract data structure, which consists of a name, some attributes and attribute constraints. The knowledge needed to describe the motional behaviour of the human heart consists of different types of objects like the left ventricle and its segments (see 3.1.2), motion, shape, and medical evidence, each of which is represented by a node or a class of nodes. The relations between them are restricted to three different types:

- \`necessary-part-of\` to introduce a hierarchy in the network. It is used to formulate terms like "if one wants to talk about the motional cycle, it is necessary to get information about the time parameter \`number of images per sequence\` and the object to be observed".

- \`semantic-part-of\` to describe a partitioning which result from the problem space, like "a heart consists of the semantic parts \`left ventricle\` and \`heart without left ventricle\`". Semantic parts might be dependent on the context of the concept belonging to the semantically higher level, i.e. a concept \`contraction\` is semantic part of the concept \`motion cycle\` and, additionally, dependent on the values concerning phases of contraction computed in concept \`motion cycle\`.

- \`specialization\` like "the concept for a regional motility interpretation has concepts as specializations which describe the regional motility of each region as a whole".

The principal structure of our model is given in Fig. 3. There are 8 levels of abstraction. The lowest level 0 provides the interface to the input image sequence and performs image processing like extracting contours of the special objects. The concept TIME REFERENCE determines time parameters like the number of images in a sequence, the concept SPACE REFERENCE for instance angles of the anatomical segments. Level 1 collects information about single images to form a complete sequence, level 2 examines the shape of the left ventricle and its segments. The two levels 3 and 4 describe the motional cycle of the heart in terms of contraction, expansion and stagnation, level 3 as a comparison of areas from image i to i+1, level 4 as phases covering several images succeeding one another. An anatomical interpretation of the heart cycle found at level 4 is given in level 5. There are used medical terms like systol or diastole. The last two levels give medical evidence, level 6 describes the regional motility, level 7 relates motion and shape to one global diagnosis.

A more detailed description of our model is given in [11].

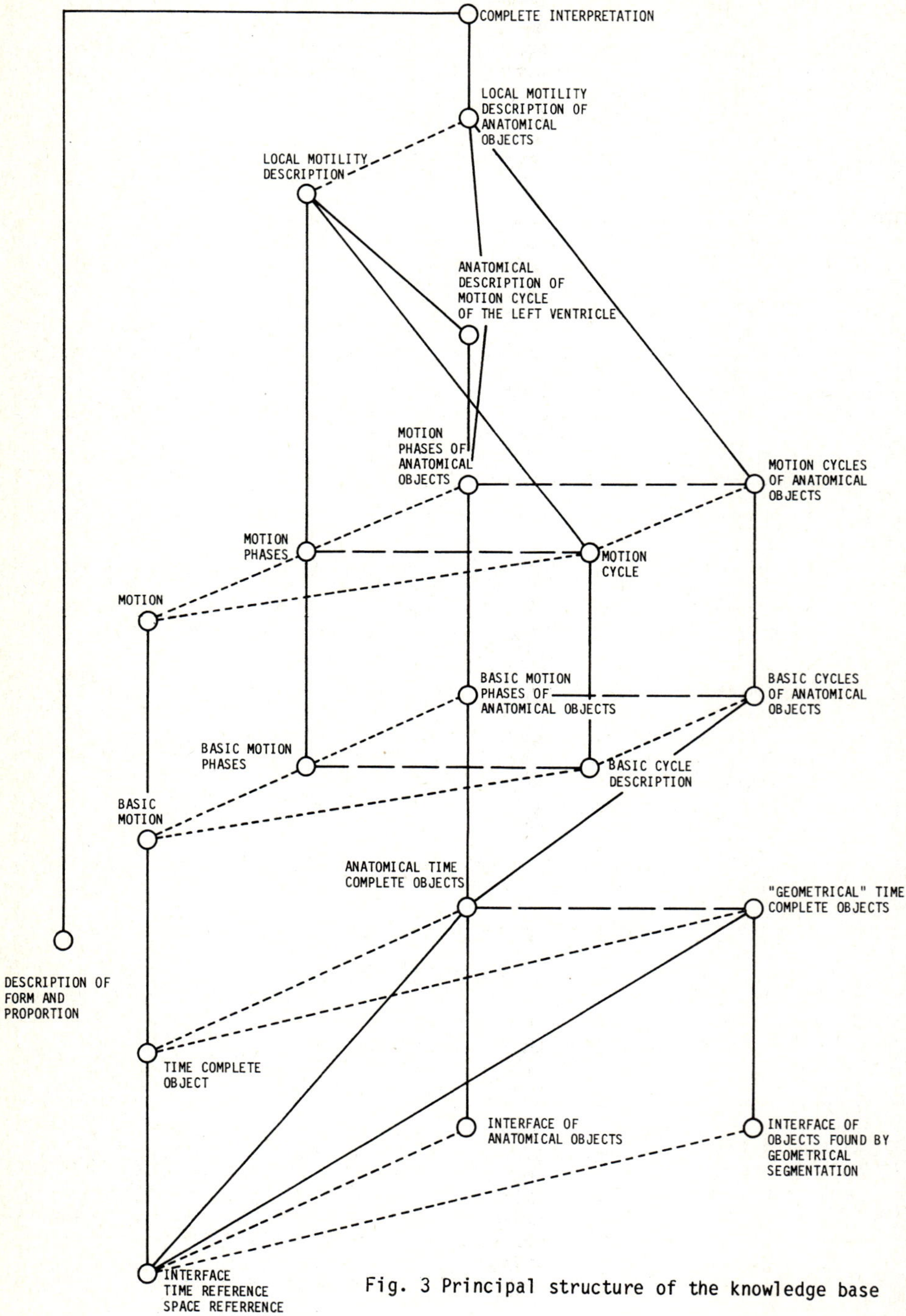

Fig. 3 Principal structure of the knowledge base

3.1.2 **Procedural knowledge.** Besides static knowledge, procedures are necessary to transform information contained in an image sequence to a medical description and to derive medical parameters. Those procedures are referred to by substructures called \`attributes\` or \`structures\`, which define functions of the type:

input data ⟶ [function] ⟶ output data

obeying the condition that input data are restricted to data computed in necessary or semantic parts of a concept. The following only describes functions associated with the type \`attribute\`, \`structure\`-functions are test functions with values of \`attributes\` and \`attributes\` of parts as arguments. Dependent on levels in the network different classes of routines can be distinguished:

- image processing: Attributes of level 0 (concept class INTERFACE) extract contours out of an image which are the basis of a motility interpretation.

A major shortcoming in nuclear imaging is the low count rate leading to noisy images. We are working on sequences consisting of $2<n<32$ images (12 images, in general) with a spatial resolution of 64x64 pixels and an intensity

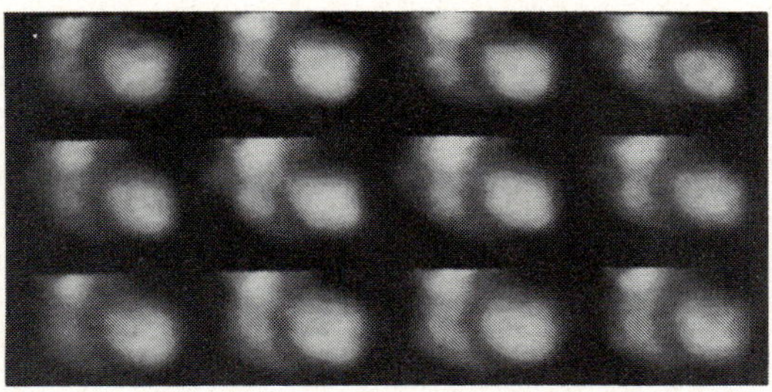

Fig. 4 Image sequence after median filtering

resolution of 8 bit. To facilitate further processing, first a median filtering is performed with window size of 7x7. Fig. 4 shows the sequence of Fig. 1 after filtering. The next steps aim at separating the heart from the background by thresholding and locating the septum for dividing the heart into left and right ventricle.

There are known from literature several approaches to the automatic detection of the left ventricular contour. A modification of a gradient operator used by [12] provided pleasant results. A polar coordinate transform uses the a-priori knowledge of the circular or elliptical shape of the left and right ventricle, respectively, in anterior projection. The center of the transform is a point inside the left ventricle, which is detected by means of a heuristic procedure. The application of a local edge detector and a contour following procedure based

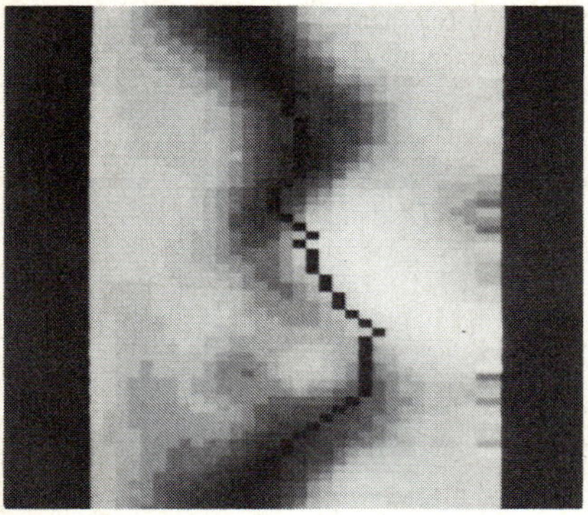

Fig. 5 Polar coordinate transform and application of a local edge detector

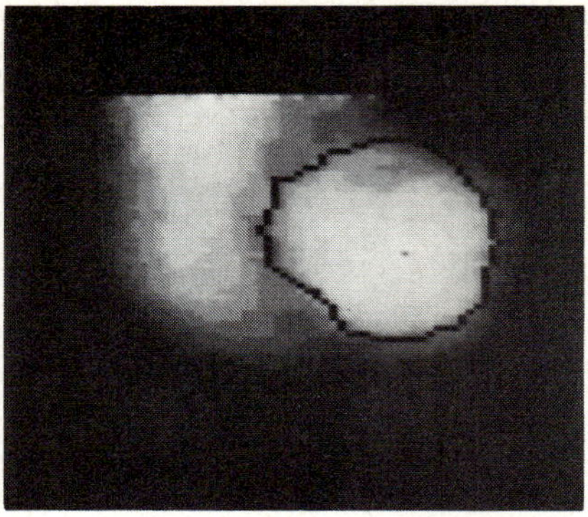

Fig. 6 Contour of the left ventricle after backtransform

on dynamic programming result in contours which show a correlation of $r = 0.93$ to contours manually outlined by physicians [13]. Fig. 5 and Fig. 6 trace the mentioned processing steps.

After contour extraction, a segmentation of the left ventricle is performed. Two methods supplement one another. One segmentation is given by fixed angles $2\pi/n$, another one is guided by medical criteria. The anatomical definition of those segments is given by a certain range of occurence and an expected direction of the left ventricular contour. The contours of a special anatomical segment are determined by using fuzzy membership functions [14, 15] which realize the conditions described above. The combination of both types of segmentation allows for testing effects of a weak motility of one segment on its neighbours and, therefore, is the basis of a regional and global motility interpretation.

- areas, angles, centers of gravity: Attributes of level 1 (concept class TIME COMPLETE OBJECTS) and 2 (concept class DESCRIPTION OF SHAPE) are straight forward and, therefore, not described in details here.

- motion cycles: The medical basis of a motility description is given by 9 prototypes of heart cycles, each of which represents a normal or abnormal behaviour of the left ventricle or its segments. Attributes of levels 3 and 4 perform the matching process between actual input data (changes in area) and expected prototypes. Syntactic pattern recognition offers a possibility to find the optimal fit with a dynamic programming procedure. Input data are a certainty matrix which assesses changes in area as contraction, expansion or stagnation. A detailed description of this approach is given in [16]. At level 5 (concept class ANATOMICAL DESCRIPTION OF A HEART CYCLE) motion phases are named by medical terms depending on start and end points during one cycle.

- medical evidence: The aim of our automatic system is to derive medical interpretations to be described by the facts which have to be fulfilled if a special heart disease occurs. The connections can be expressed by giving rules, which are the attributes of level 6 (concept class REGIONAL MOTILITY INTERPRETATION) and level 7 (concept class COMPLETE INTERPRETATION). Presently the system knows about 45 diagnostic interpretations of the type "there is weak motion of the left ventricle" including a rejection class. Each interpretation is inferred by applying a set of rules, about 120 as a whole. Each rule is assessed by using fuzzy membership functions. The advantage over a statistical approach is the possibility to formulate statements using terms "a few", or "weak" for instance without being forced to absolute decisions. The results are that there will be more possibilities of competing decisions depending on a certain context. This corresponds to medical routine to a certain extent, which allows for statements like "the left ventricle has weak motion" with certainty 0.8 and "the left ventricle is almost motionless" with certainty 0.4 not being contradictory.

Since those rules are embedded in the associative network, there is no need for an interpreter, but they are activated during an analysis process by the module CONTROL by calculating attributes.

At different levels of the network there is the possibility of alternative decisions resulting from the application of procedural knowledge. Based on the same input data, i.e. on the same instances at a lower level, competing instances of a concept at higher levels can be derived. This is necessary for overcoming noise and distortions caused by image processing. For example, a small increase of area from images succeeding one another might be interpreted as an expansion or a stagnation with a special certainty in dependence on a larger context. In either case there is the need for a special description of the resulting motion cycle, that is the need for creating two competing instances.

To assess the "goodness" of an instance, a set of special procedures `Certainty Functions` belongs to procedural knowledge. The calculation of these functions is based again on fuzzy membership functions using the the value of certainty of the parts of the actual concept (if there are any) and the certainty of some attributes and structures of this concept. These values are used for controlling analysis.

3.2 Module INSTANCES

While the module MODEL can be looked at as the long term memory independent of special input data, the module INSTANCES contains the results based on a special input image sequence. Created data structures are similar to those in the MODEL except for substituting links to procedures by actually computed values and the fact that there may be more than one instance attached to a concept in the MODEL. The optimal description of one image sequence consists of an associative network of instances, which is the basis for the module HUMAN INTERFACE.

3.3 Module CONTROL

This module controls the analysis of an image sequence based on the knowledge stored in the model. Analysis is started by giving a concept to be instantiated (goal concept) as input. Now, the tasks of this module are

- to evaluate declarative knowledge

- to declare a special data structure (`empty` instance) corresponding to an actual concept in the model

- to activate procedural knowledge and store actually computed values in the instance(s).

The instantiation rule for a concept A is given by

```
instantiate(A):
IF( instantiated(all necessary parts) AND
    instantiated(all semantic parts without those dependent on context) )
THEN create( empty instance )

IF( set SET(C) of concepts being dependent on context NOT EQUAL empty )
THEN
  activate computation of attributes of instance
  instantiate( SET(C) )
  activate computation of structures and CF of instance
ELSE activate computation of attributes, structures and CF of instance
```

This rule implies a top-down evaluation of the knowledge base.

Since there is the possibility to create competing instances, each of which is assessed, a search space results giving all possible paths to get an instance of the goal concept. The aim is to find the `optimal` path containing an instance of the goal concept having the highest possible value concerning the CF-function. An `optimal` algorithm would find this path without evaluating all possible instantiation rules. In our approach we have chosen a heuristic graph search procedure which is a modification of the well-known A^*-algorithm. It selects at each step of analysis only the best scoring instance for further computations. The protocol of analysis (the knowledge expanded together with all instances created up to this moment) is fixed in the SEARCH TREE. Competing instances are kept in different nodes of the tree. Now the algorithm chooses that leaf in the tree containing the optimal search state given by the highest certainty value. A more detailed description is also given in [11].

3.4 Module HUMAN INTERFACE

In medical routine at least a physician's letter is needed to describe the motional behaviour of the heart by giving the results of the automatic analysis. In order to control the reasoning of the system a system utility would be preferable showing intermediate results and offering the possibility to check the history of the analysis. Since all results obtained during an analysis are contained in the module INSTANCES and the protocol of the analysis is contained in the SEARCH TREE, it is possible to trace the path of decisions. A comfortable interface is under development allowing for displaying all of these values. The results are stored alphanumerically, so an independent graphic procedure has to transform them adequately. For instance, contours stored as chain code are superimposed to the original image sequence, the interpretation of volume curves by using medical terms (Fig. 7) or certainties for special diagnoses (Fig. 8) might be presented as graphics. Up to now, only the optimal search path can be traced. An automatic comparison of alternative instances is not possible, and there is no explanation facility.

4. Results

The whole system is implemented in RATFOR on a PDP11/34 under RSX11/M. Currently a new implementation on an UNIX-System of the PC class using the C programming language is under development.

A comparison of manually derived diagnoses by a physician and automatically derived interpretations by our system showed an agreement of 80%. There had been 20% rejection rate, that is the system could not give any interpretations. In some of the cases the system refined a diagnosis given by the physician, i.e. if the physician said "the left ventricle shows weak motion", the system even gave a regional interpretation locating the regions within the left ventricle showing

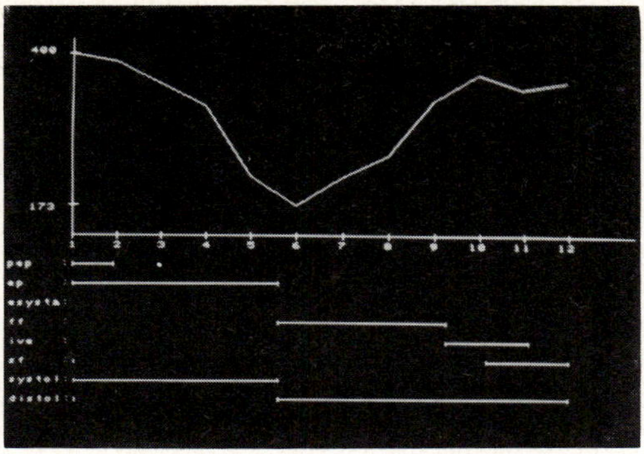

Fig. 7 Volume curve medically interpreted

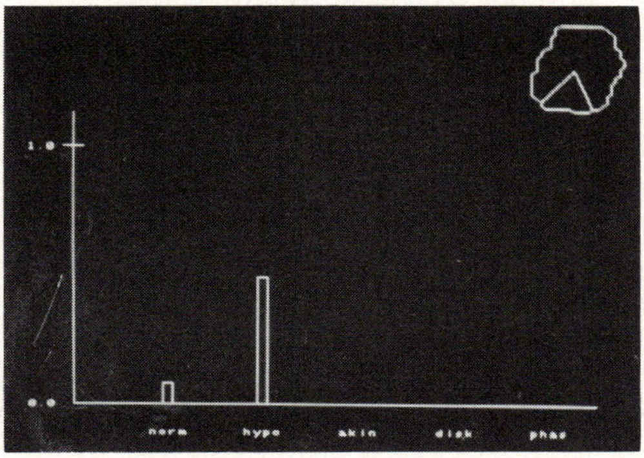

Fig. 8 Certainty for diagnosis of the inferioapical segment of the left ventricle

an abnormal behaviour.

Besides numerical results the system produces a short report in medical terms describing the motional behaviour, the shape of the left ventricle and documenting some medical parameters.

Acknowledgements

The research project described above was performed in cooperation with the Institute of Nuclear Medicine of the University of Erlangen, and supported by the Deutsche Forschungsgemeinschaft.

REFERENCES

[1] Tsotsos, J. K.: A Framework for Visual Motion Understanding, Technical Report, CSRG-114, June 1980

[2] Geffers, H. et al: Data Processing and Functional Imaging in Radionuclide Ventriculography, Proc. 5th Int. Conf. on Inform. Processing in Medical Imaging, 1978, pp. 322-331

[3] Niemann, H.: Pattern Analysis, Springer-Verlag, Berlin, 1981

[4] Ballard, D.; Brown, C.: Computer Vision, Prentice Hall, New York, 1982

[5] Winston, P. H.: Artificial Intelligence, Addison-Wesley, New York, 1977

[6] Date, C. J.: An Introduction to Database Systems, Reading, Massachussetts, 1981

[7] Winograd, T.: Frame Representation and the Declarative/Procedural Controversy, in: Proc. IJCAI, 1983, Tutorial on Artificial Intelligence

[8] Hanson, A. R.; Riseman, E. M. (eds): Computer Vision Systems, Academic Press, New York, 1978

[9] Findler, N. V. (ed): Associative Networks: Representation and Use of Knowledge by Computer, Academic Press, New York, 1979

[10] Mylopoulos, J.; Levesque, H.: An overview of knowledge representation, in: Brodie, M; Mylopoulos, J.; Schmidt, J. V. (eds): On conceptual modelling: perspectives from artificial intelligence, databases, and programming languages, Springer-Verlag, New York, 1983

[11] Sagerer, G.: Darstellung und Nutzung von Expertenwissen fuer ein Bildanalysesystem, Dissertation, Lehrstuhl fuer Informatik 5, Universitaet Erlangen-Nuernberg, in preparation to appear 1985

[12] Gerbramd, I. J.; Hoek, C.: Automated Left Ventricular Boundary Extraction from Technetium-99m Gated Blood Pool Scintigramm with Fixed or Moving Region of Interest, Proc. 2nd Int. Conf. on Visual Psychophysics and Medical Imaging, 1981, pp. 155-159

[13] Niemann, H., Bunke, H., Hofmann, I., Sagerer, G., Wolf, F., Feistel, H.: A Knowledge Based System for Analysis of Gated Blood Pool Studies. in: IEEE Transactions on Pattern Analysis and Machine Intelligence, vol. PAMI-7, no. 3, to appear May 1985

[14] Zadeh, L. A.: Fuzzy Sets, in: Information and Control 8, 1965, pp. 338-353

[15] Zadeh, L. A.: A theory of approximate reasoning, in: Hayes, J.; Mitchie, D.; Mikulich, L. I. (eds): Machine Intelligence, vol 9, 1979

[16] Bunke, H.; Grebner, K.; Sagerer, G.: Syntactic analysis of noisy input strings with an application to the analysis of heart-volume curves, Proc. 7th ICPR, 1984, pp. 1145-1147

DISCUSSION

Morgera:

I have a question with respect to the certainty factors. When you combine two of them, do you take the minimum of the two?

Sagerer:

This is not always the case. One can define at each node of the network its own function for the computation of the certainty. This function may contain both minimum and maximum operators as well as multiplications of certainty factors. One can select the function that seems most suitable for the task. As a matter of fact, the min/max operators in fuzzy logic are equivalent with the and/or operators in ordinary logic.

Morgera:

Can you define your certainty factors in such a way that they obey the rules of probability theory, that is to say that they add up to one?

Kanal:

In fuzzy logic, a different concept is used than in probability theory. One can consider the certainty factors as a possibility measure. If more than one outcome is possible to a high degree, then the sum of the possibility measures or certainty factors may well be greater than one.

PATTERN RECOGNITION IN PRACTICE II
E.S. Gelsema and L.N. Kanal (Editors)

SHAPE CLASSIFICATION BASED ON DYNAMIC MODELLING PROCEDURE

H.S. Tan, J.T.W. Damen

Dr. Neher Laboratories - P.T.T.
Leidschendam, The Netherlands

The proposed "Dynamic Modelling Procedure" creates models capable of coping with the varieties of shapes within a class. Application to numeric characters suggests that under certain conditions the DMP may be applicable for general shape classification purposes.

1. INTRODUCTION

In general, shapes can be classified by applying template and/or feature techniques. In many cases a number of templates and feature descriptions are required for each class, because of the varieties of patterns. The goodness of the classification depends on the suitability of the set of templates or feature descriptions. Problems arise when the range of varieties within a class is large, e.g. printed or written alpha numeric characters. In that case a simple procedure for selecting a number of suitable templates or feature descriptions is probably not sufficient.

Intuitively we feel that a shape can be classified if the basic shape is known. In this paper a procedure is proposed which creates a new template based on integration of a basic shape and an unknown pattern. The properties of the unknown pattern are integrated gradually into the basic shape. The proposed classification is based on a set of models (basic shapes) which are then modified into "suitable" models by the proposed "Dynamic Modelling Procedure" (DMP).

The proposed DMP is a multi-level process. Traditional shape analysis techniques can be applied at each level. A review of these techniques is given in [1].

2. DYNAMIC MODELLING PROCEDURE (DMP)

The integration process occurs gradually, starting with global properties and ending with local ones. In this paper a level-by-level integration process is proposed. The DMP is a top down creation procedure (fig. 1).

An essential feature of the proposed procedure is that the properties of the unknown pattern or object are described in the same way as the models. The properties can be given as a set of descriptions of relationships between the elements. The properties of the unknown object are integrated by influencing the elements of the models. The purpose of the influencing is to let the elements of the models obtain the properties of the elements of the object. The influences on the models can be manipulated so that the essential properties of the models are preserved, while other possible properties of the object are integrated. An element of a model may be influenced only by elements of an object which have similar essential properties. A labeling process is required to control the influencing process.

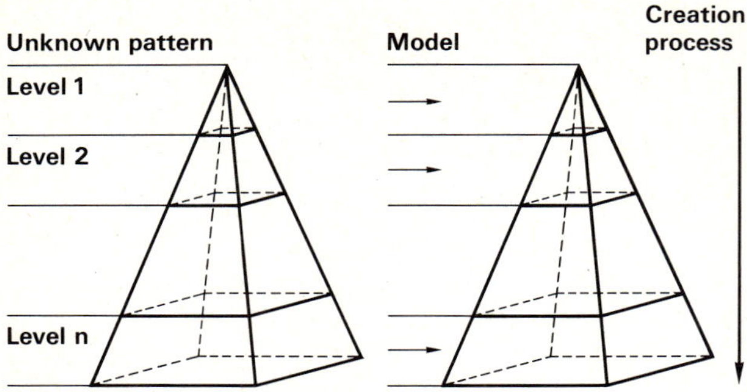

Figure 1: Proposed "Dynamic Modelling Procedure" (DMP).

Let M = { m(n), n=1,2, ..., N } an O = { o(k), k=1,2, ..., K-1 } be the representation of the model and the object. In general, K may be greater, equal to or less than N. Each model element m(n) is labeled either as an object element o(k) or as not belonging to O, denoted by o(K) (o(K) = Nil). Each model element m(n) has K possible labels (fig. 2). Labeling factor P, which is denoted as P = { p(m(1),o(1)), p(m(1),o(2)), ..., p(m(N),o(K)) }, can be normalized according to

$$\sum_{k=1}^{K} p(m(n),o(k)) = 1 \ ,$$

so that P can be thought of as the probability of labeling.

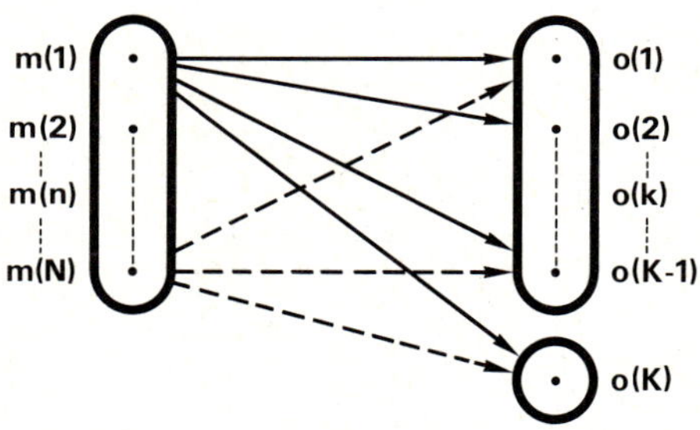

Figure 2: The labeling of m(n) to o(k) and o(K).

The properties of O are integrated into M to an extent proportional to the influence. Assuming that the elements of the models are known within each level, the Dynamic Modelling Procedure for a level processing can be described as follows:

1. Segmentation of unknown pattern into comparable elements of the model.
2. Determination of the influence.
3. Integration of these properties proportional to the influence.

A "suitable" model is created by integrating the whole set of properties of the unknown pattern into the model. The DMP can be carried out in many ways for various applications. The most suitable techniques can be chosen, depending on specific relevant properties of the shapes and their specific influence. In our experiments the DMP is applied to create the best shapes for recognition of alpha numeric characters.

3. DMP FOR SHAPE

Human perception may recognize shapes independently of their location, size, orientation and other variations. Contrary to flexible human recognition, traditional machine recognition is rigid, because the machine tries to match unknown objects with "static" references. As is known, static references cannot cope with variations of unknown objects. When variations within a class are large, it is necessary to have a large set of static references which can cope with the whole range of possible variations. These references are traditionally represented by a number of templates or feature descriptions. An optimum set of references of a class is usually chosen after careful study. New research may be required to include new classes in an existing recognition system.

The proposed DMP offers the possibility of creating "suitable" models dynamically, the models being able to cope with variations of unknown objects. The variations of an object are integrated in the basic shapes (references). Shape classification based on the proposed DMP has the following advantages:

1. A large set of models for one class is not required.
2. Simplified shapes can be used as models.
3. Existing systems can simply be extended by adding new classes.

Shapes approximated by straight line-segments will be used in our application as basic shapes (models). Figure 3 shows examples of an unknown pattern and superimposed basic shapes.

In our implementation we limit the hierarchy of a shape to two levels, which are represented by straight line-segments and pixels. A level-by-level integration process is applied. The DMP modifies the shapes of a set of models gradually into the essential shape of a digitized unknown pattern. The global properties of a shape can be modified by moving line-segments or moving the end-points (line level). At this level the global shape can be modified by changing the location, size, rotation and shape proportions. Shapes cannot always be represented by line-segments. However, the hierarchy with straight line-segments is preferred to other line forms (e.g. arcs or curves), because the model is simpler and the processing of line-segments is less complex.

The differences between the shape and the approximated shape are considered as local variations. Local variations can be integrated by moving the pixels (pixel level). The movements are restricted by a defined degree of freedom at the higher level of hierarchy. Straight line-segments can be moved as long as the relations within a shape are maintained. Pixels can be moved as long as the properties of the line they belong to are not distorted.

The realization of the DMP for described shapes requires techniques for different processing stages (fig. 4):

- Line level:
  1. Segmentation : Approximation of the shape of an unknown pattern by straight line-segments.
  2. Influencing : Line labeling from the model to the approximated line-segments.
  3. Integration : Line displacement (end-point displacement).

- Pixel level:
  1. Segmentation : Digitized patterns consist of grey pixels. No special segmentation process is required.
  2. Influencing : Pixel labeling from the processed models to the grey pixels of an unknown pattern.
  3. Integration : Pixel displacement.

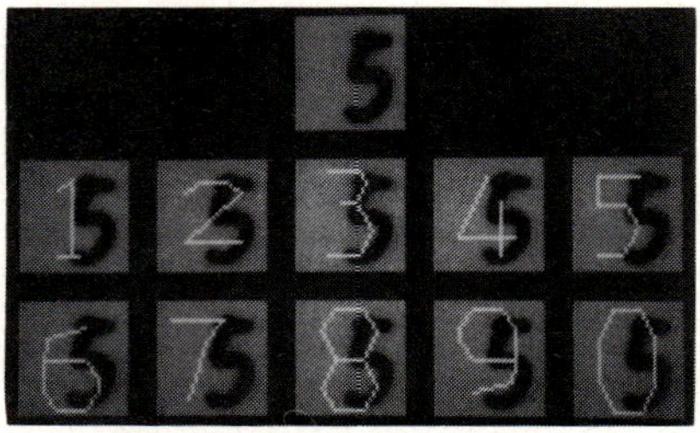

Figure 3: A digitized unknown pattern and examples of models.

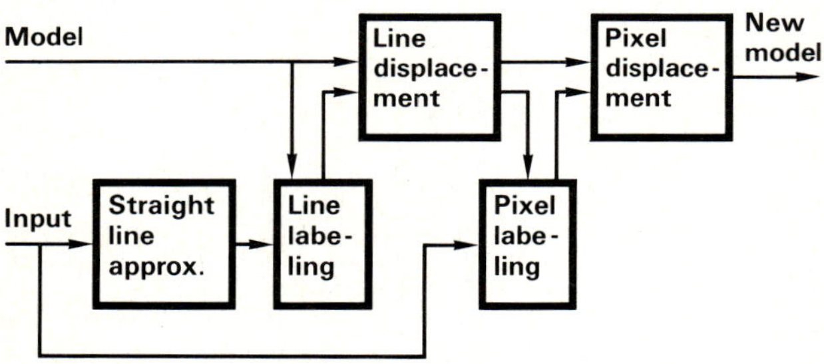

Figure 4: Proposed "Dynamic Modelling Procedure" for shape classification.

3.1 Structure description of line patterns

In our application, line patterns are used as basic shapes. Let $M^L = (m^L(1), m^L(2), \ldots m^L(N))$ be the representation of the models, where $m^L(n)$ are line-segments (n=1, 2, ...i, j, ..., N) and L is the index of line-level. The shape is described by 2x $\binom{N}{2}$ (N > 2) structure descriptions of all pairs of line-segments [4].

The descriptions of a pair of line-segments consist of a set of relational descriptions and a set of topological descriptions:

1. Relational descriptions (fig. 5a):
   - $r1(i,j) = \alpha_{ij} \pmod{\pi}$
   - $r2(i,j) = \alpha_{ji} \pmod{\pi}$

- $r3(i,j) = |l_i| \,/\, |z_{ij}|$
- $r4(i,j) = |l_j| \,/\, |z_{ij}|$

with:

z_{ij} : (virtual) line-segment connecting the middle points of l_i and l_j
α_{ij} : angle between z_{ij} and l_i
α_{ji} : angle between z_{ij} and l_j
$|z_{ij}|$: length of line-segment z_{ij}
$|l_i|$: length of line-segment l_i
$|l_j|$: length of line-segment l_j

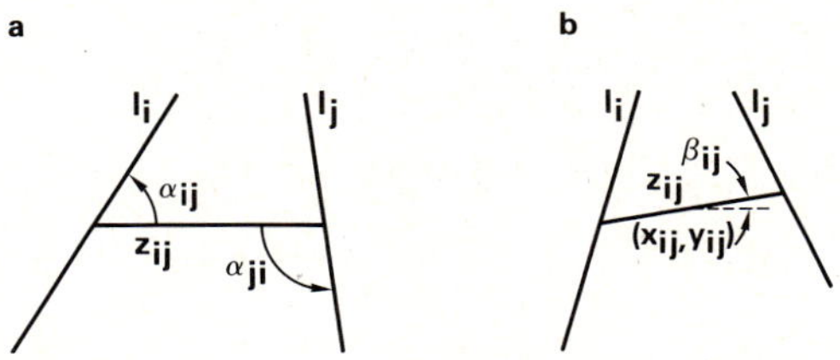

Figure 5: Parameters for a. relational description and b. topological description.

2. Topological description (fig 5b):
   - $t1(i,j) = (x_{ij},\, y_{ij})$ (location)
   - $t2(i,j) = \beta_{ij} \pmod{2\pi}$ (rotation)
   - $t3(i,j) = |z_{ij}|$ (size)

with:

(x_{ij}, y_{ij}): the position of the middle point of the connecting line-segment z_{ij}
β_{ij} : the angle between positive x-axis and z_{ij}
$|z_{ij}|$: the length of z_{ij}

3.2 DMP on line level

3.2.1 Straight line-segments approximation

A new technique [2] has been developed which approximates the essential shape of a grey scale image by straight line-segments. A discussion regarding the use of this technique instead of a published algorithm is given in [2]. Let $O^L = (o^L(1), \ldots, o^L(K-1))$ be the representation of the object at line level, where $o^L(k)$ are approximated line-segments, k=1,2, ..., K-1 (fig. 6).

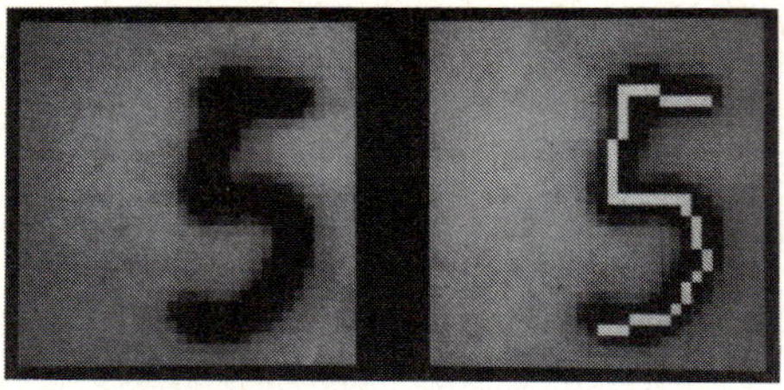

Figure 6: Straight line-segment approximations.

3.2.2. Line labeling

In the line labeling procedure, properties at the line level are used. Some properties are preserved, some are integrated into the models. Although properties t2(i,j), r1(i,j) and r2(i,j) are preserved, small deviations are allowed:

$$\hat{t2}(i,j) = t2(i,j) \pm \Delta t2(i,j) \quad (1)$$

$$\hat{r1}(i,j) = r1(i,j) \pm \Delta r1(i,j)$$

$$\hat{r2}(i,j) = r2(i,j) \pm \Delta r2(i,j)$$

The other properties (t1(i,j), t3(i,j), r3(i,j) and r4(i,j)) are integrated into the models, proportional to the requirements of the preserved properties. Labeling based on relationships between pairs of elements can be realized with a relaxation and labeling procedure. Probabilistic relaxation and labeling procedure [3] has been implemented in our case.

3.2.3 Line displacement

In our implementation line-segments are displaced by moving the end-points. The probabilistic relaxation and labeling procedure determines the influence from line to line. This influence is translated into influence from end-point to end-point. When rotation is limited to 90 degrees, 2 pairs of nearest end-points can be found by locating the middle points of both lines on the same position (fig. 7).

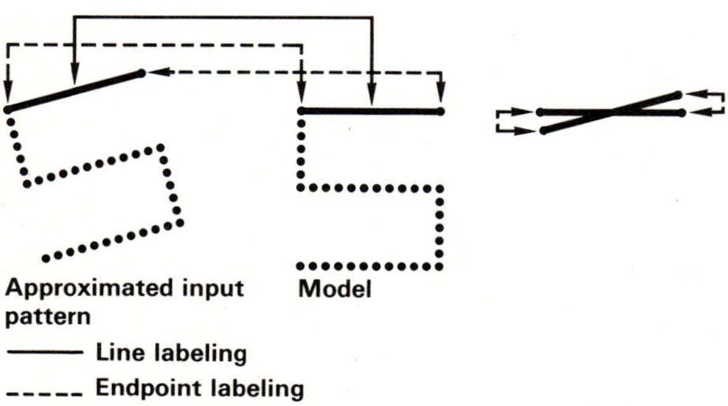

Figure 7: Finding end-point labeling from line labeling.

Let $p^L = (p^L(m^L(1),o^L(1)), \ldots, p^L(m^L(N),o^L(K))$ be the representation of the line labeling, $\overline{Em}(g)$ (g=1,2, ...,G) the end-points of a model and $\overline{Eo}(h)$ (h= 1,2, ..., H) the end-points of the approximated shape, then the translated labeling of the end-points $\overline{Em}(g)$ to $\overline{Eo}(h)$ will be denoted as

$$Pe(g,h) = p^L(m(n),o(k)) \tag{2}$$

with

$\overline{Em}(g)$: an end-point of line-segment m(n)

$\overline{Eo}(h)$: an end-point of line-segment o(k)

$\overline{E}$ is a vector with x and y coordinates. Pe(g,h) indicates a tendency that an end-point $\overline{Em}(g)$ can be moved towards $\overline{Eo}(k)$. The displacement $\overline{D}(g)$ is determined by plausible tendencies. Let us denote

$$W(g) = \sum_{h=1}^{H} Pe(g,h) \tag{3}$$

and

$$WTOT = \sum_{g=1}^{G} W(g), \tag{4}$$

then the displacement $\overline{D}(g)$ falls apart into 3 distinctive categories, which depend on 3 conditions:

1. End-point $\overline{Em}(g)$ is influenced.
   Condition I : W(g) > 0

2. End-point $\overline{Em}(g)$ is not influenced (unlabeled), while there is at least 1 end-point $\overline{Em}(g')$ ($g \neq g'$) with $W(g') > 0$.
   Condition II : W(g) = 0 and WTOT > 0.

3. None of the end-points $\overline{Em}(g)$ are influenced.
   Condition III: WTOT = 0

The displacement $\overline{D}(g)$ is defined as :

$$\overline{D}(g) = \begin{cases} \dfrac{\sum_{h=1}^{H} Pe(g,h) \cdot (\overline{Eo}(h) - \overline{Em}(g))}{W} & \text{for Condition I} \\ \overline{DFIT}(g) & \text{for Condition II} \\ 0 & \text{for Condition III} \end{cases} \tag{5}$$

with

$\overline{DFIT}(g)$: Approximated vector, based on application of the least square fit to all $\overline{D}(g")$ (g"=1,2, ...,G) with W(g") > 0.

The new positions of the end-points are

$$\overline{Em}(g)_{new} = \overline{Em}(g)_{old} + \overline{D}(g)$$

Figure 8 shows the result of the line displacement.

Figure 8: Result of the line displacement.

3.3 DMP at pixel level

Digitized patterns consist of grey pixels. Elements at pixel level are indicated by P. Let $\overline{O}^P = (o^P(1), o^P(2), \ldots, o^P(S))$ be the representation of the object and $\overline{M}^P = (m(1), m^P(2), \ldots, m^P(T))$ be the representation of the model, with

$o_x^P(s)$: x-position of the s-th element of $\overline{O}^P$

$o_y^P(s)$: y-position of the s-th element of $\overline{O}^P$

$o_g^P(s)$: grey value of the s-th element of $\overline{O}^P$

and

$m_x^P(t)$: x-position of the t-th element of $\overline{M}^P$

$m_y^P(t)$: y-position of the t-th element of $\overline{M}^P$

$m_g^P(t)$: chosen representative grey value of the t-th element of $\overline{M}^P$

At this stage the new model has already been modified, so that it globally matches the unknown pattern. The remaining differences are considered as local variations. The global position of the model is essential for creating suitable models and will be preserved. The labeling at pixel level is based on the "city block distance", which is defined as

$$CBD(t,s) = ADIFX(t,s) + ADIFY(t,s) + Wg \times ADIFG(t,s) \quad (6)$$

with

$$ADIFX(t,s) = m_x^P(t) - o_x^P(s)$$

$$ADIFY(t,s) = m_y^P(t) - o_y^P(s)$$

$$ADIFG(t,s) = m_g^P(t) - o_g^P(s)$$

Wg : scaling value

The labeling at pixel level is represented by

$$p^P(\bar{m}^P(t),\bar{o}^P(s)) = \begin{cases} 1 & \text{for pixels with } CBD(t,s) = \min\limits_{t'=1,2,\ldots,T} \{ CBD(t',s) \} \\ 0 & \text{for other pixels} \end{cases} \tag{7}$$

The displacement vector is defined as

$$\bar{D}(t) = \frac{\sum\limits_{s=1}^{S} p^P(\bar{m}^P(t),\bar{o}^P(s)) \times (\bar{o}^P(s) - \bar{m}^P(t))}{\sum\limits_{s=1}^{S} p^P(\bar{m}^P(t),\bar{o}^P(s))} \tag{8}$$

The displacement vectors are sometimes too noisy for our application. The "suitable" model is created with a smoothed displacement vector, which is defined as

$$\overline{DS}(t) = \frac{Ws1 \times \bar{D}(t-1) + Ws2 \times \bar{D}(t) + Ws3 \times \bar{D}(t+1)}{Ws1 + Ws2 + Ws3} \tag{9}$$

as long as m(t-1), m(t) and m(t+1) are elements of the same line segment.

Ws1, Ws2 and Ws3 are smoothing weight factors. The "suitable" model (fig. 9) is created by using this displacement:

$$\bar{m}(t) := \bar{m}(t) + \overline{DS}(t) \quad (t=1,2,\ldots,T) \tag{10}$$

3.4 Shape classification

The input pattern is classified as one of the reference shapes (models) with least difference. Differences are measured and used as match factors. In this paper two kinds of differences are distinguished:

1. Models which have more essential parts than the input pattern. Fig. 10a shows a created model of "6" superimposed on an input pattern "5". These particular parts of the model are characterized as "unlabeled" (see labeling on line-level).
2. Models which have less essential parts than the input pattern. Fig. 10b shows a created model of "0" superimposed on an input pattern "8". The difference is indicated as shaded area.

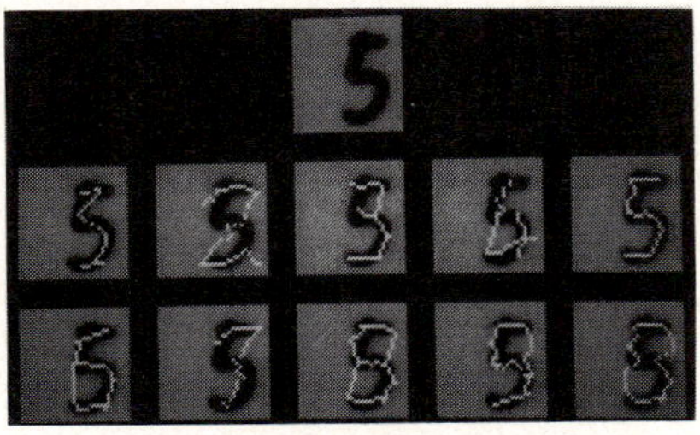

Figure 9: Created "suitable" models.

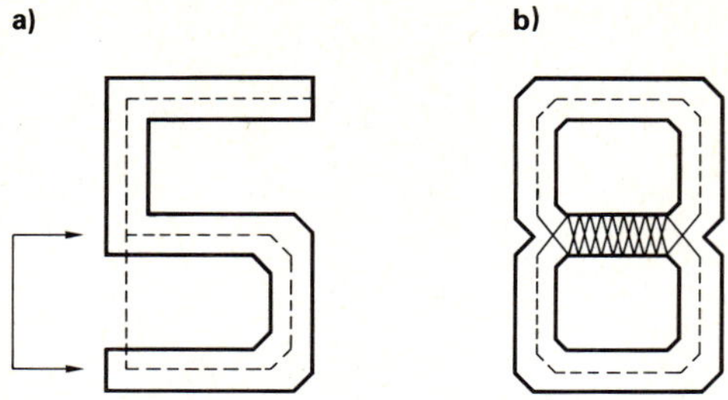

Figure 10: Superimposed created models on input patterns.

The "thickness" of the input pattern might give rise to complications in measuring the differences mentioned. Two algorithms which are less sensitive to the thickness have been developed. Let GMIN and GMAX be the representation of the minimum and maximum grey values of the input pattern, then

$$\text{CONTRAST} = \text{GMAX} - \text{GMIN} \tag{11}$$

Algorithm for measuring the differences of the first kind:

1. Initialization:
   Line number : n = 1 (N is the number of line-segments of the model).
   Difference factor : DIF1 = 0
   Threshold : THR1 = GMIN + a1 x CONTRAST
   a1 = 0.4 gives good results in our implementation.
2. If line n of the model is unlabeled (result of labeling at line level), proceed to step 6.
3. Compute the average grey value GAVR of those pixels of the input pattern which are "covered" by the line n.
4. $$\text{DIFL} = \begin{cases} \text{GAVR} / \text{THR1} & \text{for GAVR} > \text{THR1} \\ 0 & \text{for GAVR} \leq \text{THR1} \end{cases}$$
5. DIF1 := DIF1 + DIFL
6. n := n + 1
7. If n ≤ N, step 2.

Algorithm for measuring the differences of the second kind:

1. Initialization :
   Threshold : THR2 = GMIN + a2 x CONTRAST
   a2 = 0.4 gives good results in our implementation.
2. Select pixels with grey value ≤ THR2
3. Assign the selected pixels to the nearest elements of the model.
4. Make a histogram of the number of selected pixels assigned to each of the elements of the model.
5. Compute the σ^2 of the histogram.
6. Difference factor:
   $$\text{DIF2} = \begin{cases} 0 & \text{for } \sigma \lessgtr 1 \\ \sigma^2 & \text{for } \sigma > 1 \end{cases}$$

Finally, the match factor MF is defined as

$$\text{MF} = \text{DIF1} + \text{DIF2} \tag{12}$$

4. RESULTS AND DISCUSSION

The described shape classification algorithm has been applied on 100 numeric characters from 100 different typewriters. Theoretically we may expect good results without paying too much attention to the choice of the reference shapes. However, the shapes of the numeric characters are not always suitable for approximation by straight line-segments. In this experiment we have given more attention to the choice of the models of curved shapes. For example, the reference shape of the symbol "8" was represented by 15 line-segments. Table 1 gives the result of numeric characters classification using 11 models. Because an open "4" and a closed "4" have different structures, two models of "4" were used.

TEST SET		CLASSIFICATION RESULTS										
CLASS	N	0	1	2	3	4	5	6	7	8	9	?
0	100	100	.	.	.	.	.	.	.	.	.	.
1	100	.	98	.	1	.	.	.	.	.	.	1
2	100	.	.	100	.	.	.	.	.	.	.	.
3	100	.	.	.	97	.	1	.	1	.	.	1
4	100	.	.	.	.	99	.	.	.	.	.	1
5	100	.	.	.	.	.	98	2	.	.	.	.
6	100	.	.	.	.	.	3	96	.	.	1	.
7	100	.	.	.	.	.	.	.	100	.	.	.
8	100	.	.	.	.	.	.	4	.	96	.	.
9	100	.	.	.	1	.	1	.	.	1	97	.

TABLE 1. Results of numeric characters recognition.

The result of 981 correct classifications is promising. The proposed DMP appears to be a powerful procedure for coping with wide variation within a class. However, problems arise when two classes are discriminated by "small" deviations in the structure description. Experiments with alpha characters show that "K" and "X" cannot be distinguished because the differences between their structure descriptions are regarded as deviations. Further study into control of the "evolution" process is necessary.

The described classification algorithm appears to be applicable for all kinds of shapes under the following conditions:
1. The shape is suitable for approximation by straight line-segments.
2. The structure of every class should be different.

We feel that the classifcation based on the proposed DMP is close to the intuitive idea as regards the human recognition process. Further study will be necessary to find out whether the DMP is the right philosophy for further research into recognition systems.

Acknowledgement

The authors wish to thank R.J.N. Kalberg (Delft University of Technology) for his valuable contribution to this work. The support given by E. Backer, J.J. Gerbrands (Delft University of Technology) and S.P. Lie (Dr. Neher Laboratories) is gratefully acknowledged.

References

1. Pavlidis, T., "A Review of Algorithms for Shape Analysis", Computer Graphics and Image Processing 7 (1978) p. 243 -258.

2. Tan, H.S., Damen, J.T.W., "New Approach on Straight Line Approximation of Graphics Images", will be submitted for a publication.

3. Kalberg, R.J.N., "Classificatie m.b.v. Dynamic Elastic Matching", MSc. Thesis, Delft University of Technology, Dept. of Electrical Eng., The Netherlands (November 1983), in Dutch.

4. Damen, J.T.W., Tan, H.S., "Generalized Line Pattern Description", will be submitted for a publication.

5. Burr, D.J., "A Dynamic Model for Image Registration", Computer Graphics and Image Processing 15 (1981) p. 102 - 112,.

DISCUSSION

De Vogel:
Do you think that your method can be implemented in such a way that it could, for instance, be used in the post office where a very high throughput is required?

Tan:
We apply procedures, like the relaxation, which take a lot of computing time. On a VAX-750, the simulations take about 15 seconds per character. This is too slow for real time applications.

Van Bemmel:
You showed error rates of about 2%. What percentage of errors would be acceptable for reading say numbers of 6 digits? Are you going to put some effort in a direction to improve on the error rates?

Tan:
To give a figure on acceptable error rates is rather difficult. The producers of OCR equipment specify a recognition rate of 99% but that is under certain conditions like a restriction on the type of typewriter. What will be acceptable in real practice is difficult to assess. Sometimes we receive mail with adresses of very poor quality and then the recognition rate will be low.

Jansen:
I found some peculiar things in your results. For example, four '8's were classified as '6', but no '6' was misclassified as an '8'. Furthermore I noted that no misclassifications occurred for the highly similar looking '1's and '7's but that one '6' was classified as '9'. I found that rather strange. Can you explain these results.

Tan:
At the moment the results are based on the straight line approximation. For certain characters this is a poor approximation especially for the '8's. Some of the misclassifications will be due to this poor approximation by line segments.

Jansen:
Does this not imply that you should add curvature in your model?

Tan:
Possibly. But the straight lines are easier to apply.

Jansen:
That's right, but if the results are not good enough your method will never be used.

PATTERN RECOGNITION IN PRACTICE II
E.S. Gelsema and L.N. Kanal (Editors)

Hierarchical Correlation for Fast Industrial Object Location

E.Persoon
Philips Research Laboratories
Eindhoven , The Netherlands

Abstract

To obtain a powerful and flexible image recognition system, such a system must begin with analyzing the image in a data driven mode and when sufficient specific information is available, switch to a model driven mode. Typical analysis methods used in the data driven mode are edge detection and edge linking. In this mode usually one retains only the most reliable information. In the model driven mode, model guided search is used to detect less reliable image features. This paper deals with the data driven analysis part. It presents an hierarchical correlation scheme in which it is possible to detect on the fly (moving images) specific image features that can immediatly be used in a model driven mode. Such an hierarchical system can consist of several layers of processing. In a first layer of the hierarchy edges, lines and small holes are detected. The results of this first layer are fed into a second layer in which the following structures can be detected : parallel lines, end points of lines, corners and T-junctions, texture edges and curve segments. In the paper it will be shown that in some situations three to four layers of processing might be used. Correlation techniques are frequently thought to be inflexible and computationally expensive. However with current available computation power on VLSI, this is no problem anymore. Moreover correlation techniques have the advantage that they can cope effectively with missing elements in an image (which can be missing edge pixels in the first layer or missing edge segments in the second layer). Another advantage of the technique is that the required computation time in the data driven mode is independent of the image content which is important for industrial applications which have to be time bound. It will be shown how this technique has been implemented in hardware. Also examples will be given on how this has been used to process industrial images.

Introduction

Images of objects are frequently modelled in an hierarchical manner. At the lowest level, elements such as edges and texture measures are used. A next level can use elements such as edge segments and texture edges. In a third level,elements such as complete connected edges and texture regions may appear. The models used at those different levels consist typically of features (with their associated feature values) together with spatial relationships among them.

The concept of features must be interpreted in broad sense. Examples of features with their associated feature values (between brackets) are the following : pixels (gray value),edges(edge direction and strength),corners(curvature),line segments(segment end points) and regions(shape and area).

The spatial relationship is frequently expressed either as : a matrix arrangment, a chain code, a list consisting of features with their corresponding x,y coordinates or a list of features accompanied by attributes and relations between different features such as (on top of),(to the left of).
An hierarchical correlation scheme has the specific property that it models the

spatial relationship throughout the several layers as two-dimensional matrices. The features and their corresponding feature values are modelled as entries in these matrices. We will call such a matrix, filled with features and their corresponding values, a Model Matrix. Such a model matrix models in fact a feature at the next level of the hierarchy. Its purpose is to detect or recognize such a feature in image data. In image data, the feature never appears exactly as it is encoded in the model matrix. The main reasons why image data and model data are different are : rotation differences, size differences, noise, overlap or interference with other features present in the image. Especially, since different orientations and sizes must be recognized by the same model matrix, in general the size of the model matrices must be limited to 16 by 16 elements.
Such a modelling technique is frequently used at the first layer of a recognition process. Image enhancement and edge detection typically make use of two-dimensional filters. The values in the filter matrix are typically scalar variables defining the filter coefficients.
In this paper it will be shown how also good use can be made of such models at higher levels of the recognition process. There are several aspects one must take into account when choosing for one modelling technique versus another. Important aspects are modelling power and accuracy, required memory to store the models, required computation time to match the model with image data, hardware implementation and so on. There are several reasons why an hierarchical correlation method is attractive :

With such a method the output of one layer of processing has the same nature as its input, namely it is a matrix form. Since also the input image is a matrix, this method allows for an homogeneous processing structure in which inputs and outputs have the same nature. Thus it is necessary to study in depth only one processing layer in order to understand how all the other layers basically behave. Furthermore, it is possible to conceive and build one hardware architecture and this same architecture can be used in the several layers.
There is also a distinct advantage concerning processing time. When matching image models to image data, one must always match the two basic elements which are mentioned above :the feature values and their spatial relation. Since the spatial relationship is modelled in matrix form, the matching can be done by a correlation method.

A correlation method can be realized in hardware in the following way : by scanning the image in a line by line fashion and by buffering the last N lines in digital delay lines, a window can be realized of N*N pixels which moves accross the image pixel by pixel and line by line as the image is generated. If now, together with the window generating hardware, means are provided to compare each window element with a element of a model matrix and also when all comparisons can be added together, a very fast (real-time) means is available for correlating one model matrix with the input image at every image position.

If this way of basic hardware processing is used, we can see that correlation methods achieve a constant computation time regardless of image complexity. This is in contrast with other methods that store models in non-matrix models. Usually the required computation time increases with model complexity as well as with image complexity and in general also increases when the image quality decreases. Especially for an industrial environment it is important to achieve quasi constant computation times.

The structure of an Hierarchical Correlation System

In this section the general structure of a multilayered correlation system is described. We will use Figure 1 as the main aid to explain this structure.

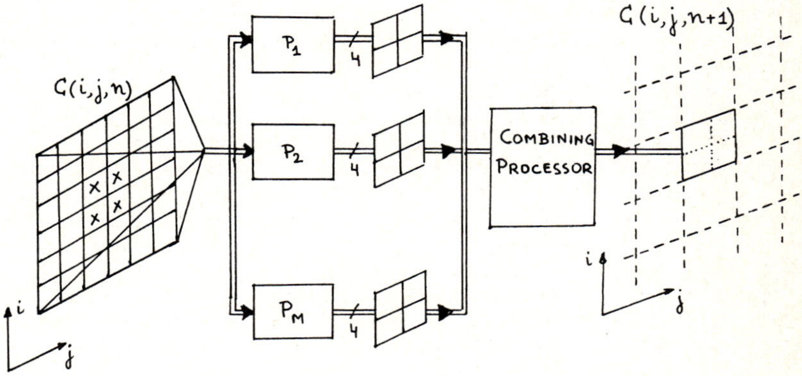

Figure 1
One layer of the hierarchical correlation system

Since the system consists of a set of identical layers, it is sufficient to specify one layer. One such a layer has inputs, processing elements and outputs. The inputs and outputs have the same structure and we will name them 'connection matrix'. Those will be denoted as C(i,j,n). The indices i and j are the row and column indices of the matrix. C(i,j,n) forms the inputs for layer n and is the output of layer (n-1). The input for the first layer (n=1) consists of a gray level image. Therefore the matrix elements of C(i,j,1) consist of scalars, denoting the image intensity at pixel position (i,j). This input layer is connected to several processing elements P1,..,PM. A processing element is used to 'recognize a feature' in the connection matrix C at every position (i,j). However to be able to recognize such a feature at a position (i,j), the processing element needs information inside a submatrix positioned around (i,j). In the example of Figure 1 we assume that the size of this matrix (receptive field) is 5 by 5 pixels.

In Figure 1 a (6 by 6) submatrix is shown instead of (5 by 5) and this will be explained next. As has been mentioned in the introduction, the size of the model matrices is limited to 16 by 16 elements. This means that if one wants to recognize complex objects consisting of several features one has to reduce the spatial resolution of the produced results. This means that a matrix element in C(i,j,n+1) corresponds to a larger area in the original image than a matrix element of C(i,j,n). In the example of Figure 1 a resolution reduction of a factor 2 has been used in order to get a clear presentation. This means that an element in C(i,j,n+1) corresponds to four elements in C(i,j,n). The processing elements have therefore to look at four (5 by 5) windows in order to produce the information to form C(i,j,n+1). In Figure 1 are shown now the processing functions of one layer of the hierarchy in order to produce one entry in the matrix C(i,j,n+1) given a resolution reduction of 2. Let us follow now in detail the information flow from C(i,j,n) to C(i,j,n+1). Let us write in the following processing elements as PE.

The information of a (6 by 6) window is applied at the inputs of all PE´s. For each of the 2 by 2 positions of a 5 by 5 window inside this 6 by 6 window, they produce matching information in the form of a real number. In general this real number is not bounded from below and from above. But in order to obtain a good recognition performance, it is good to limit this output from both sides. By clipping negative output values to the value zero, we eliminate weak responses of the PE. A value of zero means that the feature, modelled by the model matrix in the PE, has not been recognized. We can as well limit the maximum response of such a PE to say the value 1. The value 1 means that the feature has been recognized with very high certainty. After the PE´s we obtain therefore 4M signals. Those are fed into the ´combining processor´ to produce at its output C(i,j,n+1). If one wants to preserve all the information produced by the PE´s, we see that C(i,j,n+1) must contain 4M values. In practice, as we will see further, we want to reduce this information as much as possible. In the next section, we will discuss the combining processor and the PE´s in detail to obtain more insight into such a layered system. We will use in the following the abbreviation CP for Combining Processor.

Combining Processor (CP)

The function of the CP is to combine the results of the PE´s and to lower the spatial resolution of those results, with the restriction that essential information ,needed for the recognition, should not be thrown away at this stage and that its output is suited to be processed by the PE´s of the next layer.
We will start with defining the requirements for the output of the CP. Some of those can easily be seen when visualizing what happens when an horizontal line must be recognized by such a system. It is clear that, in order to limit the number of model matrices, only one model must be used to recognize also slightly rotated lines, slighlty curved lines or noisy lines. This means that at the input of layer n, we may expect the following patterns (we assume here for simplicity binary values):

```
     111111               11111              11  111
  11111          or    111     111     or   1  111  11
```

Figure 2

whereas the model, incorporated in the model matrix will be of the form

```
1111111111
```

Figure 3

In Figure 2 and 3, the matrix elements that are not shown, have a zero content. If we assume that the PE´s work on the basis of correlation methods, then it is clear that in the above situation the correlation results will not be so strong since model data and input data are different at several matrix positions. The CP can be designed such that this problem can be overcome. One solution is to make the receptive fields at its input (in Figure 1 they are 2 by 2 pixels) larger, for example 4 by 4 pixels so that the CP also ´sees something in its neigborhood´. The result which is obtained in this way is a thickening of the inputs for the next layer. The input patterns of Figure 1 then become typically

```
  111111              11111            11   111
1111111111    or    1111111111    or    1111111111
11111               111    111          1  111  11
```

Figure 4

We see now that in those patterns the shape of the model matrix of Figure 3 appears exactly and ,when some precautions are taken in the PE´s of the next layer, a strong correlation result can be obtained. Another method to obtain such a thickening effect is to keep the receptive fields as indicated in Figure 1 and to apply a pixel-grow operation after the subsampling, which is performed in the CP. It is this last technique that we have chosen in an hardware implementation of a CP because of its simplicity and flexibility.

So far we have seen how the CP can perform a required thickening operation. Some more things must however be taken into account. If no information reduction is performed, the output of the CP will contain 4M real numbers, as explained before. In general, this is too much information to be processed by the next layer. If we define S as the subsample ratio, then the size of nonoverlapping receptive fields for the CP is S*S (in case of Figure 1 S=2) and in case of overlapping receptive fields we obtain typically 4S*S. A first reduction operation is to reduce the S*S values to one value. This can be done by summing up the outputs of the corresponding PE inside the S*S area and thresholding the resulting sum. In this case we obtain one bit of information corresponding to each PE. This bit indicates whether enough response has ocurred inside this S*S field. We feel that the processing for this reduction should not be made more sophisticated (one could for instance consider to perform shape recognition inside this S*S window) than the summing operation which we propose since in general the subsample ratio S should not be chosen much larger than 2. With small subsample ratios, the shape information inside a 2*2 window will be very limited. Also small subsample ratios are preferred since otherwise too much information loss will occur in such a layer. Also, for the sake of simplicity, one should try to perform all required shape recognition in the PE´s and use the CP only for the resolution reduction operation.

In the hardware implementation we have chosen for a CP which processes the outputs of each PE separately. The total CP therefore consists of M CP-elements. A block diagram of one such a CP-element is shown in Figure 5(for the case S=2). Its input consists of S*S numbers and it produces one bit of information for each position in C(i,j,n+1). So the total CP produces M bits of information for each position in C(i,j,n+1).

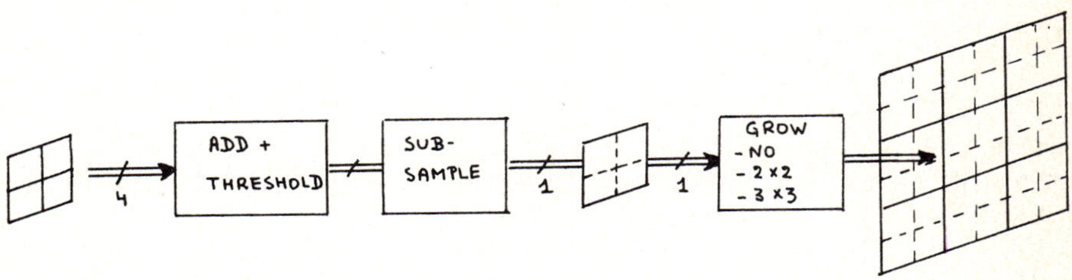

Block diagram of one CP-element
Figure 5

The first operation is to add and threshold all information inside the S*S window which is produced by the corresponding PE. The output of this operation is one bit. This information is subsampled to the resolution of the next layer. The grow operation now follows. Three modes are possible: a no-grow, a 2*2 grow and a 3*3 grow. For example the 2*2 grow operation happens as follows : if, at the resolution of the next layer, the output of the subsample operation is ´one´, then the three neighboring matrix elements are also made ´one´.
Figure 5 shows the structure of our hardware implementation. It is however possible to make this more general. For example, one can omit the threshold operation and work in the subsample and grow operations with real values instead of the binary values as shown here.
We have added another operation to the CP. As we have explained we have chosen a separate CP-element as shown in Figure 5 for each available PE. The extra operation we have implemented is to logically combine the M output bits of the several CP-elements. In this way one can still further reduce the amount of bits at the output of the CP. In the hardware implementation therefore we obtain a maximum of M bits for each entry of C(i,j,n+1) instead of the 4M real values which are possible in the general case[1].

The processing elements (PE)

In general, the PE´s receive 4M or less signals from the CP for each pixel position i,j [1]. The window on which they perform operations is shown to be 5*5 pixels in Figure 1, but can range from 3*3 to 16*16 pixels. The PE´s peform mostly the following operation (shown is the output of PE(k))

$$\text{output}(i,j,k) = \sum_{p,q} \text{OPER}\,(\,C(i+p,j+q,n)\,,\,\text{coef}(p,q,k)) - \text{Threshold}$$

(Formula 1)

The variables p and q will vary to cover the window on which the PE operates (in case of Figure 1 p and q take the values -2,-1,0,1,2). The operation OPER is either a multiplication of inputs and coefficients or the absolute value of the difference of inputs and coefficients or the squared difference of both inputs and coefficients. The threshold is used to eliminate small responses of the PE´s. Frequently one makes the output value of the PE zero in case it becomes negative. As has been mentioned before, it is good to limit the response of a PE between a minimum value (say zero) and a maximum value (say one). In fact then the true response of the PE is given in Formula 2

$$\text{outputPE}(i,j,k) = \text{LIMIT}\,(\,\text{output}(i,j,n)\,) \qquad (\text{ Formula 2 })$$

It is good to look at Figures 3 and 4 to discuss in detail the required performance of a PE. Suppose that coef(p,q,k) contain the information as shown in Figure 3. This means that coef(p,q,k) is zero everywhere except for one row which contain ones. The wish we have now is that the PE correctly recognizes the input patterns of for example Figure 4 but rejects input patterns which are basically different from the model in Figure 3. By ´correctly recognizes´ we mean that the output is large and by ´reject´ we mean that the output becomes zero. This requirement is not easily satisfied. It is known that, in case the multiply operation is chosen, one has to divide the SUM in formula 1 by the total energy in the input pattern C(i,j,n) otherwise the PE will always recognize high energy input signals regardless of their shape. However this energy normalization is often not sufficient. This can be seen as follows. Suppose the input C(i,j,n) consists of a pattern as in Figure 3 (exactly the model) but at one pixel position the value is not 1 but say 10(this is a noisy pixel). Due to the energy normalization, it is likely that the filter output will become negative or very small although the model is present in the input. Because of all this, but also because of the hardware realization, we have chosen for OPER to be the squared difference but also we have chosen for one-bit representations of both C(i,j,n) and coef(p,q,k). This combines well with the hardware implementation of the CP which also outputs one bit for each PE connected to its input. In that case, the squared differences operator reduces to an Exclusive Or operation. In order to get still better performance on the cases shown in Figures 3 and 4, we have added to the coef-matrix an extra bit (do care bit). The model used in case of Figure 3, becomes then :

```
0000000000
0000000000
----------
1111111111
----------
0000000000
0000000000
```

Figure 6

Where the symbol - appears, the corresponding values in C(i,j,n) are not taken into account when computing the SUM in Formula 1. With such a model, it is clear that an exact match can be obtained between the input data of Figure 4 and the model data of Figure 6.
In the hardware implementation we have chosen for PE´s that can process only one type of feature from the preceding layer (one bit values). It is however advantageous to have PE´s that can handle several features at the same time. However this means that also the model matrices become more complex since they also have to code the different features. To obtain a good extension of the matching operation of Formula 1 to this case is however not trivial.

The hardware realization of the PE consists actually of a 16 * 16 window in which coef(p,q,k) can be programmed as two bits per matrix element (one bit indicates the presence or absence of the feature in the model and the other bit indicates do or don´t care) [3]. It is also equipped with line buffers to build up on the fly a 16*16 window.
We have experienced that in some cases it is advantageous to split up a model matrix into several submatrices. Therefore several PE´s are needed to recognize one basic shape. In that case the output of the needed PE´s is logically ANDed in order to obtain the output. The model of Figure 6 is actually a good example of a shape which is preferably split up in different smaller shapes as we shall see next.

Application examples - what are the several layers used for

In industrial environments, the orientation of parts to be recognized is often well determined. Orientation uncertainty can frequently be kept into a range of plus or minus 10 degrees. In that case one model matrix is sufficient for each basic shape. Otherwise, if the orientation is arbitrary, several model matrices must be used for the different rotation angles. The same is valid for size changes of the object to be recognized. Size changes are mostly due to varying distances of the object to the camera. Except for some situations ,such as product identification at a distance, usually the size can be controlled. If this is however not the case, one is not forced to use other model matrices (as is the case for rotation uncertainty). What one has to do is to modify the subsample ratios at the different layers (in fact only necessary at the first layer). It is therefore important to have programmable subsample ratios available in an hardware system and not to work with a fixed subsample ratio of two as in the example shown in Figure 1.

We will discuss next a simple example but which often occurs in the same or a similar situation in industrial object location. Suppose we have an image in which appear two intersecting black lines on a white background. A possible image is shown in Figure 7-a. It shows a black horizontal line and a vertical line but with missing elements in it. Furthermore, the lines appear in a noisy environment. Also notice that at the cross section of the lines, there appears a black bloblike defect. We will assume that the image of Figure 7-a requires a matrix size of 30*30 pixels and that the vertical and horizontal lines are one pixel thick. The problem is to detect the position of the intersection of both lines. In order words the problem is how to progam an hierarchical system so that it gives at its output a match result at the intersection of both lines.

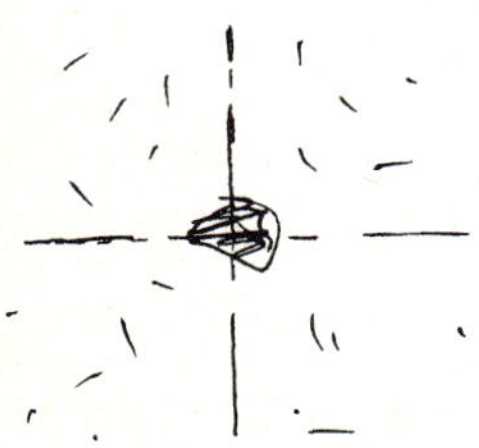

Figure 7-a

Figure 7-b

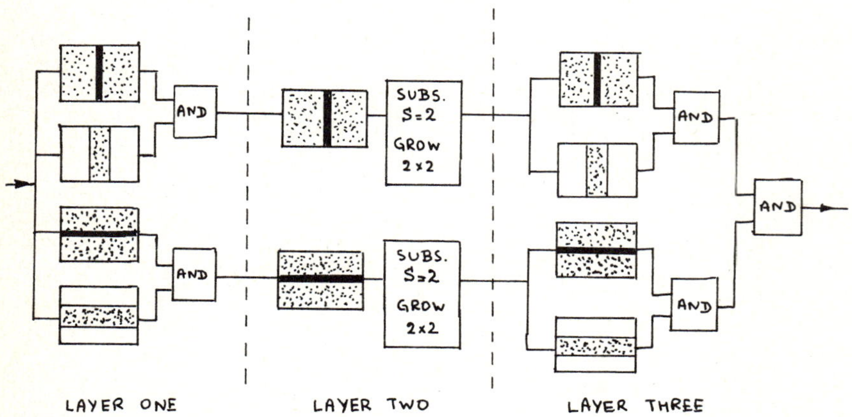

Figure 8

One should realize that it is not possible to reliably detect this intersection using a one-layer system. This is mainly because of the following facts : the size of the model matrices must not be larger than 16*16 elements, the black lines are only one pixel thick and they appear in a quite noisy environment. Therefore, the system will have to contain several layers. An overall diagram of one solution to solve this problem is shown in Figure 8.

In a first layer we program two PE´s to detect a black horizontal line. Two PE´s are used to be immune to white backgrounds. In one model matrix we program the value ´one´ at the same places as is indicated in Figure 6. The rest of the matrix entries are set to don´t care. In the next model matrix we program the value ´zero´ at the same places as where zero´s appear in Figure 6. The rest of the matrix entries are set to don´t care. Together the two model matrices form a model for a black line on a white background. Two PE´s are used for this and their outputs are ANDed together. Note that in Figure 8, dotted areas are used to indicate don´t care areas in the model matrices of the PE´s.
In a similar manner two PE´s are programmed to detect a vertical black line . So in total four PE´s are used in the first layer. Note that in the model matrices around 10 matrix positions are used along the direction of each line. This is to be immune to noise in the image. The result of this first layer is shown in Figure 7-b and consists of two binary matrices each one corresponding to one feature. Notice that noise in the image has been eliminated to a great extent but that due to the black blob at the intersection no output of the PE´s is available. This is also due to the large size (10 pixels along the direction of the lines) of the model matrices. Furthermore, a faulty recognition of an horizontal black line occurs at the bottom right due to the appearance of two small horizontal lines at the bottom right of Figure 7-a. In order to make the result of the first layer more suited for further processing at a lower resolution, we propose to use a second layer which operates at the same resolution as the first layer.
This second layer must ´ close the holes ´ which appear in the output of the first layer. To achieve this, we use two PE´s one for the horizontal and one for the vertical direction. It will be explained how the PE for the horizontal direction is programmed. It is filled with a model matrix as shown in Figure 6 but all zero´s replaced by don´t cares. Furthermore, whereas in the first layer a large threshold (see Formula 1) must be chosen, in this layer a small threshold is chosen. This has the effect of ´ lengthening ´ the recognitions which appear at the input in the horizontal direction. Also in this layer, we will reduce the resolution by a factor of 2, and apply a grow operation. The result of this operation can be summarized in Figure 7-c

Figure 7-c

Figure 7-d

In a third layer, we aim at recognizing the cross point, but effectively use now information of an area of 20 * 20 image points (since we have subsampled by a factor of two and since we will use model matrices in the third layer which contain 10 pixels along one dimension). We will need then two PE´s in the third layer, one for each direction and logically AND their outputs to obtain the recognition of the cross point of the two lines. The model matrix used for detecting the horizontal line can be the same as in Figure 6 and a rotated version of it, is used to detect the vertical line. But also in this layer, the models can be split up into two parts as has been done in the first layer(this is shown in Figure 8). The result of the last layer is shown in Figure 7-d. It will not consist of one single point, but of a small cluster of points.
This example shows how an hierarchical correlation system can be programmed. It shows how missing elements but also noise can be coped with at different resolutions of an image.

Conclusions

In this paper some results have been presented about an hierarchical correlation scheme and it is explained what choices have been made for a hardware implementation,which can process images on the fly. Extensions to the current solution are possible and also more theoretical analysis is needed for the different elements of such an hierarchical system. References to related material are listed in the reference list. They provide extra information concerning the working of hierarchical correlation systems. Also the aspect of learning the model matrices automatically is addressed in those papers.

References

[1]. K.Fukushima, Neocognitron: A Self-organizing Neural Network Model for a Mechanism of Pattern Recognition Unaffected by Shift in Position, Biological Cybernetics 36,pp. 193-202 (1980)

[2]. H. Marko," A biological approach to Pattern recognition", IEEE Trans on Systems, Man and Cybernetics, Vol. SMC-4, No.1,pp.34-39,1974

[3]. E. Persoon, " Learning algorithms applied to the processing of industrial images", in Pattern Recognition in Practice,E.S. Gelsema and L.Kanal (eds.), North-Holland Publishing Company, 1980,pp.87-97.

DISCUSSION

Haralick:

I did not understand the subsampling. It really looked to me as if you were doing a morphological dilation.

Persoon:

In a square window of so many by so many pixels you count the number of recognitions you got in there and you threshold this into a binary signal. And that performs the sub-sampling. It has nothing to do with dilation. It is in fact a low-pass filter with a square window and a sample and hold.

Gerbrands:

In the abstract you mentioned that you could also detect texture edges in real time. Could you comment on that?

Persoon:

The idea is that we do, in a first layer, the detection of the primitive forms which are typically direction dependent. Then we look upon this as an image in which primarily on one side of the texture edge many responses are seen and on the other side not. In this image you have the problem of detecting a black/white transition.

Foerstner:

What is the minimum cost of the system if you want to detect simple features?

Persoon:

This one is about $4000. But you have your results in real time.

Smeulders:

Could you, in general, describe classes of images which can't be detected in such a way?

Persoon:

If you want to look for edge-type details in an image I think it can go quite far. The only problem is that you need quite a few operators to do it: you need an operator in the first layer for black-white transitions but also for thin lines and little holes if you want to be complete. But if you take enough of them it may go quite far.

Smeulders:

Yes, but I was hoping to raise a general question. You have a sort of hierarchical structure and with that particular structure comes a class of images you can't detect. So I was trying to gain some insight.

Persoon:

You have to be careful. You have to distinguish between the data driven part and the model driven part. Data driven means the analysis of the images without any prior knowledge of the general models of what is in your scene. If you purely use the data driven part this at some time will brake down. For example 3-D models, perspective views and the notions of the position of an object in 3D cannot be handled. There is certainly more processing required after this correlation process. I hope that the results of this type of processing can ease quite a bit the burden of the model driven part in your recognition system.

PATTERN RECOGNITION IN PRACTICE II
E.S. Gelsema and L.N. Kanal (Editors)

MODEL-BASED RECOGNITION AND LOCATION OF LOCAL PATTERNS IN POLYGONAL CONTOURS VIA HYPOTHESIS ACCUMULATION

M. DHOME, M. RICHETIN, G. RIVES
Electronics Laboratory, UA 830 of the CNRS
University of Clermont II, BP 45
63170 AUBIERE -FRANCE-

For industrial scene analysis, structural pattern recognition is a necessary way when the objects can be partially viewed. Recognition and location of local patterns are then the first steps to achieve and for that a new method is proposed. It is based on the use of a model of the piecewise linear segmented contour of these local patterns, and on a hypothesis accumulation procedure analogous to the generalized Hough transform. This method is applied to scenes of overlapping industrial pieces with local patterns having quite different shapes.

INTRODUCTION

Scene analysis by recognition of the objects which are present in the field of a camera is an active domain of research because of the great number of potential applications in Robotics or in Automatic Inspection, and since the difficulties are numerous in the design of robust computer programs. Indeed it is necessary to handle automatically great variations in the scenes to be analyzed, concerning for example the lighting conditions, the scaling factor, the nature of the objects, their individual and relative positions.

This paper deals with scenes of partially observed pieces having a finite number of stable positions on a plane (fig. 1). For that type of scenes, two groups of recognition methods have emerged from the litterature in the recent past.

The first group comprises the prediction-verification ones [1,2,3]. The object models are relational structures of simple primitives which exist in the contour of the objects. These primitives are generally straight lines. When one of these primitives is found in the scene, a prediction is made on the position of a next one, according to the structure of the model. Then verification is done in the scene. The repeated and controlled application of this prediction-verification procedure leads to the recognition of objects even partially observed and to their accurate location.

The second group gathers the method derived from the Hough transform and more precisely from its generalization given by Ballard [4]. The local patterns which compose the objects have a parametric representation. The recognition procedure consists in making hypotheses on the values of these parameters, in accumulating the hypotheses in numerical arrays called accumulators, and at last in locating the local patterns by looking for maxima in the accumulators. When the local patterns are parts of the contour of the objects, an application of this procedure has been recently proposed for polygonal contours [5]. In order to reduce the number of hypotheses, and to get at the end of the procedure both the recognition and the complete location of the locals patterns, the parametric models have been completed as described in the next section.

REPRESENTATION OF A LOCAL PATTERN

The representation of a local pattern is a set of records called a S-table which is in some ways analogous to a R-table used by Ballard [4]. Each record is related to a straight segment Si of the pattern model. It contains 4 parameters which define this segment from a reference point G and a reference axis $\vec{0}$ (fig. 2), and a confidence index. The reference point G can be any point and has been chosen here as the gravity center of the contour of the local pattern.

These parameters are :
- the length Li of segment Si,
- the algebraic distance Di1 = $\vec{u}.\vec{j}$ from G to segment Si,
- the algebraic distance Di2 = $\vec{u}.\vec{i}$ from the projection of G on Si and the middle of segment Si,
- the orientation class Ci of segment Si,
- the confidence index NbCi of segment Si. This index is used to rubber the differences between the contour polygonal segmentation of the model and of the scene. It has a low value for long segments and a high one for short ones.

Pattern models can be obtained according either to a learning by showing which involves contour extraction [6] and contour polygonal segmentation [7], or to a learning by saying. Both have been implemented in the reported experiments, and appear in fig. 3 where the NbCi index is given for each segment Si.

RECOGNITION AND LOCATION OF A LOCAL PATTERN
Supposing at first that occurencies of this local pattern having the same orientation that the model one are researched, the basic idea of the procedure is to consider each segment S of the scene as a segment Si (or as a part of it) only if they have a similar orientation, ie if the orientation class C of segment S is comprised between (Ci-NbCi) and (Ci+NbCi). In that case all the possible discrete coverings of S by Si give different locations of reference point G, calculated with the ith record of the S-table. The values of these coverings are then added at these locations in an accumulator which has the size of an image.
Figure 4a gives an example of such an accumulation. In order to handle variations in the segmentations of the model and of the patterns in the scene, accumulations are made thick as shown in fig. 4b and 4c. From a computational point of view, the accumulation function is piecewise linear as indicated by fig. 5.

For the detection of the occurrencies of a pattern having an unknown orientation, it is then sufficient to rotate successively the model of a value corresponding to one class of orientation, and to activate at each time the accumulation procedure. But in order not to use a 3D-accumulator, and ad-hoc procedure has been designed. The corresponding algorithm is the following.

```
BEGIN
Init;Global Accumulator:=0;
FOR Orientation Index:=1 TO Number Model Orientation DO
  BEGIN
  Oriented Accumulator:=0;
  Rotation S-table;
  FOR Model Segment Index:=1 TO Number Model Segments DO
    BEGIN
    Partial Accumulator:=0;
    FOR Image Segment Index:=1 TO Number Image Segments DO
    IF Similar Orientation (Image Segment, Model Segment) THEN Accumulation;
    Add (Partial Accumulator, Oriented Accumulator);
    END;
  Save (Oriented Accumulator, Global Accumulator);
  END;
Find Maximums (Global Accumulator);
END.
```

In this algorithm, 4 2D-accumulators are used. The first one, the Partial Accumulator (PA) contains the accumulation values for a given orientation of the model, for a given segment Si of the model, and for all the hypotheses between Si and any segment S of the scene. The maximum value at any point of (PA) is forced to be no greater than the length of segment Si. (PA) is then added to an Oriented Accumulation (OA) which contains the accumulation results for a given orientation of the model.
Before another orientation is considered, (OA) is saved in a Global Accumulator (GA) so that the resulting value at each point of (GA) is the maximum of the previous value in (GA) and of the present value in (OA).

At last (GA) contains at each point :
- the maximum value of accumulations for all the possible orientations of the model, normalized between 0 and 255.
- the orientation of the model for which this maximum value has been obtained.

Locations of reference point G occurrencies are then obtained at the highest peaks of the global accumulator that can be found with well-suited algorithms [8]. Examples of peaks in local areas of (GA) are given in fig. 6.

It must be noted that this pattern recognition algorithm
(i) is highly parallel since accumulations for each orientation of the model can be made independently as well as for the accumulations for each segment Si of the model for a given orientation of it,
(ii) is not too complex since a hypothesis is made if and only if segments S and Si have a similar orientation,
(iii) does not require too much memory since only 4 arrays of the size of an image are needed (1 for (PA), 1 for (OA) and 2 for (GA)).

Figure 7 presents the detection results obtained with the scene of fig. 1. The pattern models have been drawn at the local maximums found in (GA), and with the orientation given also in (GA). In the experiments reported in this paper, orientation classes have a width of 3 degrees. Moreover the height of the peaks at the different locations for reference point G are indicated. These results show that the two local patterns have been correctly detected, that the detection is quite robust, and that the value of a local maximum in (GA) gives a quality index of the detection of a pattern.

SCENE ANALYSIS OF OVERLAPPING OBJECTS

As an application of the proposed method for the recognition and the location of local patterns, analysis of scenes of overlapping identical objects have been realized from the detection results.

Figures 8, 9 and 10 respectively give a scene to be described, show the various detection results of the two local patterns, and give the locations of the object model deduced from the locations of the local patterns. This last result has been obtained after the inspection of the superposition of the contours of the detected object models (tails or heads) and the occurrencies of the object in the scene. Indeed this step was necessary because of the great ambiguity in the detections of the curve extremity of the knife blades due to the symmetrical aspect of its contour [9].

An analysis of the superpositions of the objects and of the detected models exhibited in fig. 10, leads to table 1 which indicates the evaluated relative positions of the objects [9]. The computer vision of the scene deduced from this table is represented in fig. 11.

		under				
		1	2	3	4	5
	1		55%			17%
	2	20%		13%	8%	
on	3		48%		22%	33%
	4		48%	30%		19%
	5	60%		78%	76%	

Table 1. Evaluation of the superpositions of the objects.

CONCLUSION

The hypothesis accumulation approach extended to the recognition of patterns described by a polygonal contour proves to be very simple, and involves easy computations that can be mainly done with a parallel computer structure. It has also the advantage of taking into account noises in the polygonal segmentation. But one can think that it is a brute force method since hypotheses are made all over the image. Shape analysis of the contours in the scene would be useful to extract parts of contours which could be the local patterns to detect, and could be based, for example in the application presented in this paper, on geometrical concepts such as symmetry, parallelism or convexity. Moreover to recognize objects having multiple local patterns, after the detection of a first one, a prediction-verification procedure could be implemented to detect the other ones. It would greatly reduce the number of hypotheses since the processing task would be applied in smaller windows and for limited angular sectors of orientation of the models. These ideas are presently under study and the corresponding works under progress.

REFERENCES

[1] AYACHE N., FAUGERAS O.D., A New Method for the Recognition and the Positionning of 2D-Objects, Proc. of the 7th ICPR, Montréal, July 1984.

[2] LUX A., SOUVIGNIER V.,PVV-A Goal Oriented System for Industrial Vision, Proc. of the 8th IJCAI, Karlsruhe, August 1983.

[3] FAUGERAS O.D., New Steps toward a Flexible 3D-Vision System for Robotics, Proc. of the 7th ICPR, Montréal, July 1984.

[4] BALLARD D.H., BROWN C.M., Computer Vision, Prentice Hall, Englewood cliffs, 1982.

[5] RIVES G., DHOME M., LAPRESTE J.T., RICHETIN M., Detection of Patterns in Images from Piecewise Linear Contours, Pattern Recognition Letters, vol 3, n° 2, 99-104, 1985.

[6] DHOME M., RIVES G., LAPRESTE J.T., Adaptive Contour Detection for the Analysis of Industrial Scenes, Proc. of PROLAMAT 1985, Paris, June 1985.

[7] DHOME M., RIVES G., RICHETIN M., Sequential Piecewise Linear Segmentation of Binary Contours, Pattern Recognition Letters, vol 2, n° 2, 101-107, 1983.

[8] O'GORMAN L., SANDERSON A.C., The Converging Squares Algorithm : An efficient Method for Locating Peaks in Multidimensions, IEEE Trans. on PAMI, vol 6, n° 3, 280-287, 1984.

[9] DHOME M., Contours and Pattern Recognition for Scene Analysis in Robotics, Doctoral thesis (in French), n° D1-153, University of Clermont II, October 1984.

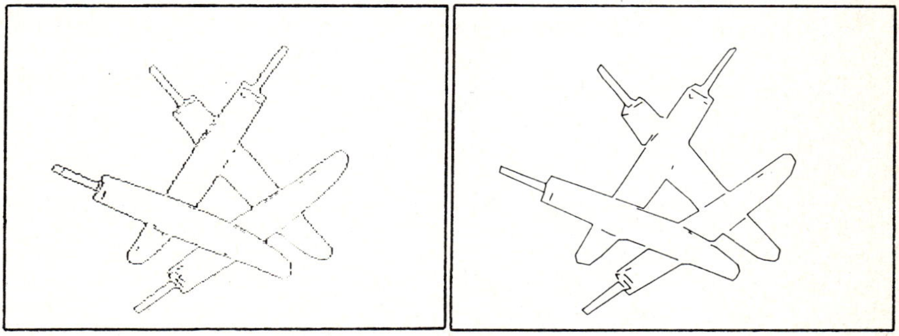

Figure 1. Example of a scene (binary and segmented contours).

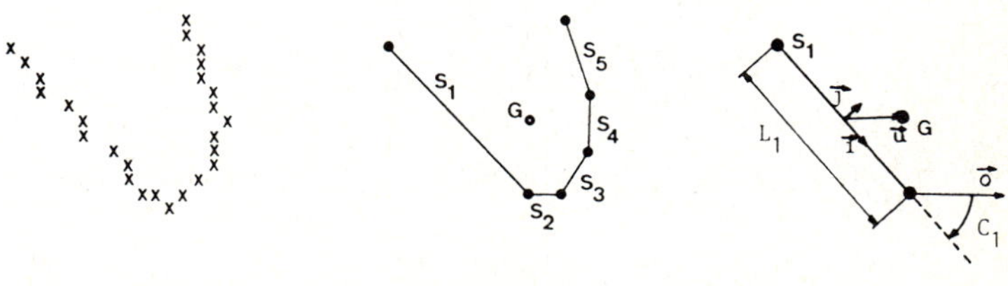

Figure 2. Representation of a local pattern.

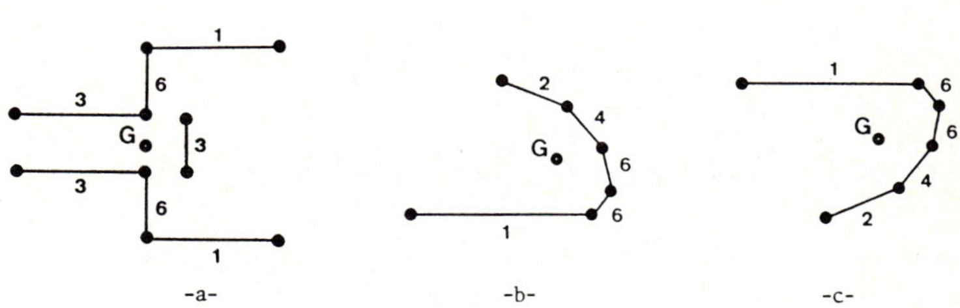

Figure 3. Models of local patterns
(a) hand-made model (b) segmented model (heads) (c) segmented model (tails)
The value of parameter NbCi is indicated for each segment.

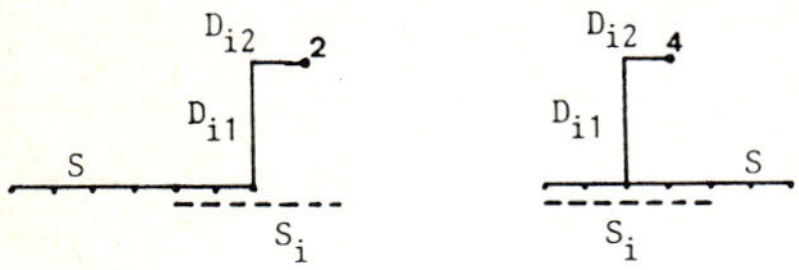

(a)

0 1 2 3 4 3 2 1 0

(b)

0 1 2 3 4 4 4 3 2 1 0
0 1 2 3 4 4 4 3 2 1 0
0 1 2 3 4 4 4 3 2 1 0

(c)

Figure 4. Accumulation principle

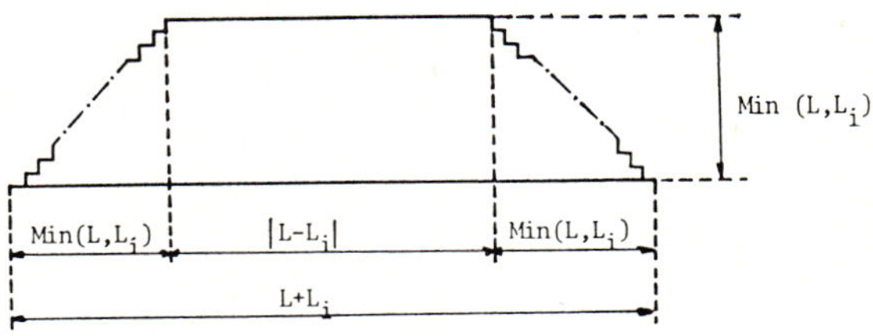

Figure 5. Accumulation function.

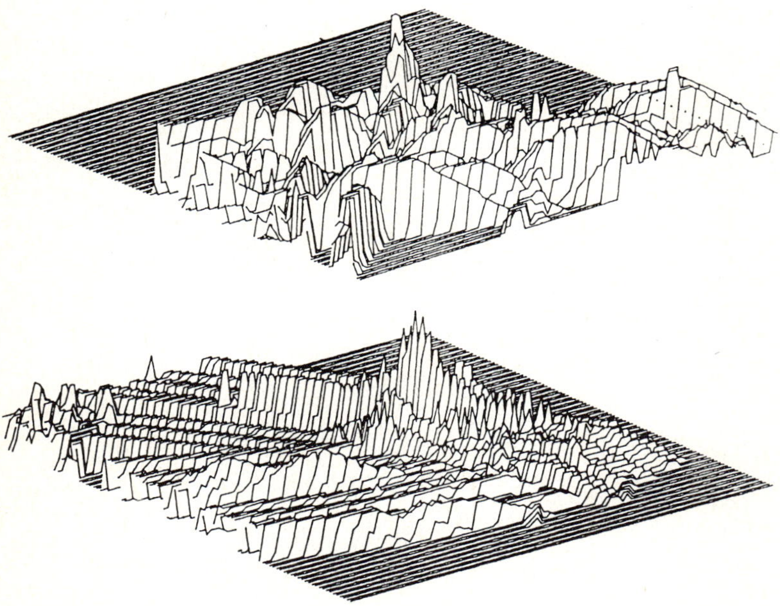

Figure 6. Examples of peaks in local areas of the global accumulator.

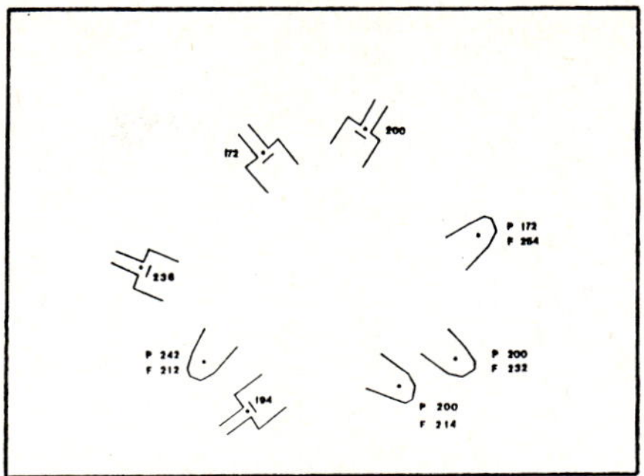

Figure 7. Detection results
(P for tails, F for heads).

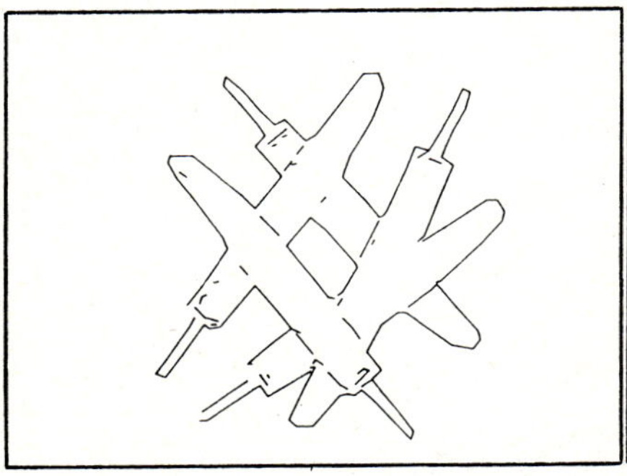

Figure 8. Analyzed scene.

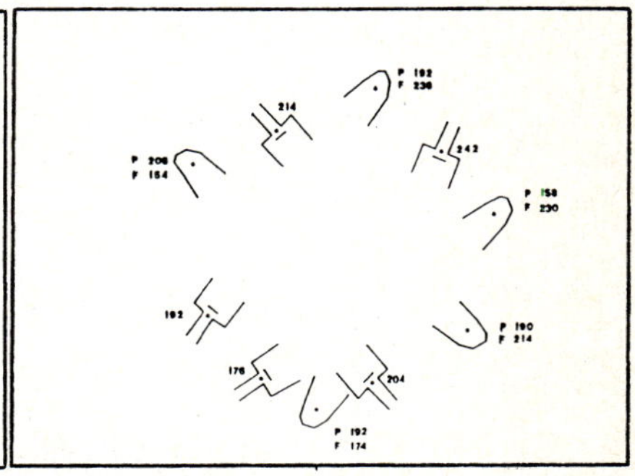

Figure 9. Detection results.

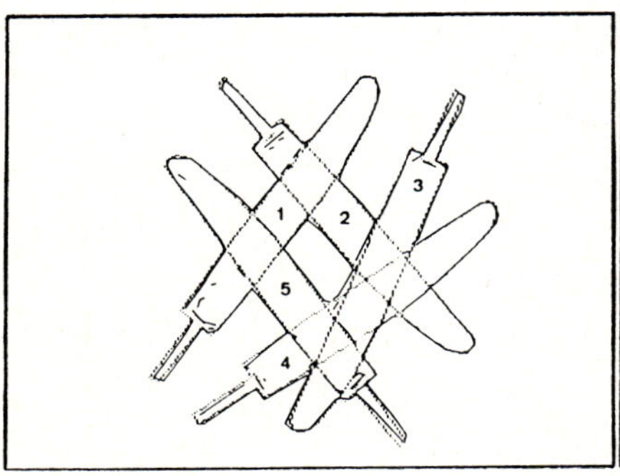

Figure 10. Locations of the object model (dotted lines) deduced from the analysis of the detection results.

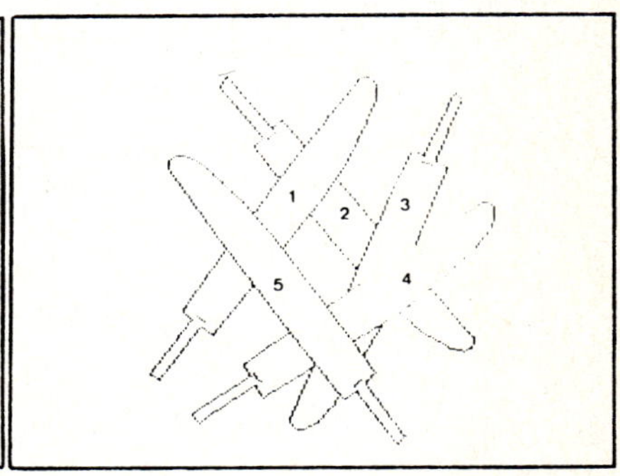

Figure 11. Computer vision of the scene.

DISCUSSION

Persoon:

I noticed that in forming your hypothesis on the direction of the models you use only the endpoints of the knife. Actually you base your analysis on this very limited amount of information. What is in between these two endpoints is not used for evidence accumulation. You only use it in the feedback phase. It is very dangerous to confuse your algorithm in this way because if you have two knives which are parallel or with only a little rotation, you may have great difficulties in deciding which endpoints belong together.

Richetin:

When you detect the local patterns and their center, the reference point of the local patterns have to be paired in order to identify the objects. The result will depend on the quality of the detection of the local patterns. We have tried this method on several scenes in which the local patterns were very well seen.

Persoon:

I have experimented a lot with this kind of images. The ones that were the most difficult were the scenes in which the endpoints of the objects were covered by other objects.

Richetin:

If you implement a prediction-verification procedure, you normally will not have a peak at the predicted position of the second pattern. This will give you a clue that the object was partially observed.

SECTION III

3-D RECONSTRUCTION

PATTERN RECOGNITION IN PRACTICE II
E.S. Gelsema and L.N. Kanal (Editors)

THE USE OF PATTERN RECOGNITION TO ESTIMATE THREE-DIMENSIONAL SHAPE FROM TOPOGRAPHIC LABELING OF IMAGES

Linda G. Shapiro
Machine Vision International
325 E. Eisenhower
Ann Arbor, MI 48104
USA

Ting-Chuen Pong
Department of Computer Science
University of Minnesota
Minneapolis, MN 55455
USA

Given a gray tone image of a three-dimensional object, a topographic labeling of the image indicates the peaks and pits, ridges and valleys, and flats and hillsides of the underlying, continuous, gray tone surface. The patterns of these topographic labels capture information about the original three-dimensional object in the scene and about the illumination. In order to determine if estimation of three-dimensional shape from a topographic labeling is feasible, we have both analytically and experimentally determined the topographic labelings for images of several three-dimensional surfaces with varied directions of illumination. From these labelings, we have determined the patterns that characterize these surfaces. In this paper, we describe the technique for obtaining the patterns and discuss how the patterns obtained may be used in a recognition system.

INTRODUCTION

Consider an image of a three-dimensional object illuminated by an arbitrary light source and viewed from an arbitrary position. Although ambiguities are possible, frequently the human viewer can estimate a) the three-dimensional shape of the object, b) the camera position, and c) the location of the light source. The original "shape-from-shading" techniques [2] solve systems of differential equations to derive three-dimensional shape from gray tone intensity variations and operate under a limiting set of restrictions. In additional to low level shading cues, we believe that the human viewer also recognizes patterns in the image that give cues leading to estimation of the shape of the object.

Extracting patterns from the original gray tone image is, in most nontrivial cases, an impossible task. In fact, it is for this reason that syntactic pattern recognition systems have had to first extract descriptions consisting of primitives, their properties, and their interrelationships from the image and then to parse these descriptions according to the rules of a grammar. Instead of trying to recognize patterns at the gray-tone intensity level, we propose to work at the topographic labeling level.

To obtain a topographic labeling, a gray tone image may be viewed as a three-dimensional surface whose height at each row-column position corresponds to the intensity value of the image at that position. While the image is a discrete matrix of values, the underlying surface is continuous. Each point of the surface may be labeled as part of a peak, pit, ridge, valley, saddle, hillside, or flat area. Hillsides can be further broken down into the subcategories inflection point, convex hill, concave hill, saddle hill, and slope. In [1], these categories are defined mathematically and the topographic classification of image pixels is described.

Our goal is to use patterns to estimate three-dimensional shape. The section entitled "Shape from Topographic Patterns" discusses results employing two methods for determining such topographic patterns from gray tone intensity images of simple surfaces. The following section describes an object surface classification scheme based on the topographic structures extracted from the image. In the remainder of this section, the imaging geometry and the illumination model to be used in our discussion are defined, and the topographic primal sketch is briefly summarized.

IMAGING GEOMETRY

The relationship between scene coordinates and image coordinates is illustrated in Figure 1. We assume that the camera lens is at the origin and that the z-axis is directed towards the image plane which is in front of the lens. The image plane is placed at a distance f, the focal length of the lens, in front of the origin so that the image is oriented in the same way as the scene. As seen from Figure 1, the following relations hold for perspective projection:

$$u = \frac{fx}{z} \quad \text{and} \quad v = \frac{fy}{z} .$$

In our discussion, the perspective projection is approximated by an orthographic projection. This approximation is good when the size of the objects being imaged is small compared to the viewing distance. In this case, appropriate coordinate systems can be chosen such that the following relations hold:

$$u = x \quad \text{and} \quad v = y .$$

ILLUMINATION MODEL

In the following discussion we will use a simple illumination model that assumes a distant point light source and a Lambertian reflectance model. A Lambertian surface scatters light equally in all directions. The brightness of a Lambertian surface illuminated by a distant point light source is given by: $I = I_0 N.L$ where I_0 is a constant depending on the surface albedo and the intensity of the light source, N is the unit surface normal vector, and L is the unit vector of the illumination direction.

The unit vector which points in the direction of the light source can be specified by the two angles shown in Figure 1. The first is the azimuth (θ) which is the angle between the x-axis and the projection of the vector onto the x-y plane, while the second is the angle of elevation (ϕ) of the light source. If we represent this unit vector by [a, b, c], then $a = \cos\theta \cos\phi$, $b = \sin\theta \cos\phi$, and $c = - \phi$. In our discussion, we will consider only positive values of ϕ. Therefore, c is always less than zero.

If the height of the object surface above the x-y plane is expressed as a function of x and y, $z = S(x,y)$, then the surface normal is given by the vector:

$$N = [S_z, S_y, -1]/(1 + S_z{}^2 + S_y{}^2)^{1/2}$$

where S_x and S_y denote first partials of S with respect to x and y, respectively. By carrying out the dot product, it follows that

$$I = I_0 \frac{aS_x + bS_y - c}{(1 + S_x{}^2 + S_y{}^2)^{1/2}} .$$

EXTRACTING TOPOGRAPHIC STRUCTURES

The topographic primal sketch can be used to represent the underlying intensity surface of a digital image. A complete mathematical treatment of the topographic primal sketch is given in [1]. We will summarize here the concepts necessary to understand the remainder of this paper. A digital image may be interpreted as a sampling and quantizing of a real-valued function f. While the image is a discrete matrix of values, the underlying surface is continuous. Since the underlying surface is continuous, we can work with such well-defined concepts as its gradient magnitude and its first and second directional derivatives.

The topographic labeling scheme is based on the estimation of the values of the gradients and the directional derivatives of the surface. In order to obtain these values, we need first to assume some kind of parametric form for the underlying function f. If we assume that the neighborhood around each pixel is suitably fit by the bivariate cubic:

$$f(x,y) = k_1 + k_2x + k_3y + k_4x^2 + k_5xy + k_6y^2 + k_7x^3 + k_8x^2y + k_9xy^2 + k_{10}y^3,$$

then the parameters k_1 through k_{10} can be estimated by a least squares fit to each pixel in the neighborhood. Once these parameters are estimated, the gradient vector (∇f) is given by $(\partial f/\partial x, \partial f/\partial y)$ and its magnitude ($||\nabla f||$) is

$$[(\partial f/\partial x)^2 + (\partial f/\partial y)^2]^{1/2}.$$

The first and second directional derivatives may be calculated by forming the Hessian matrix

$$H = \begin{bmatrix} \partial^2 f/\partial x^2 & \partial^2 f/\partial x\,\partial y \\ \partial^2 f/\partial x\,\partial y & \partial^2 f/\partial y^2 \end{bmatrix}.$$

The gradient magnitude and the directional derivatives obtained from the Hessian are used in determining the topographic labeling of the surface.

SHAPE FROM TOPOGRAPHIC PATTERNS

There are two possible methods for determining the pattern of topographic labels that will appear, given a particular three-dimensional shape category, a particular reflectance model, a particular light source, and a particular viewpoint. The first method is to work the problem analytically, obtaining exact equations for the illuminated surface. At each point the gradient, eigenvectors, and eigenvalues can be computed in order to determine precisely which sets of points have the various topographic labels. The second method is to work the problem experimentally, using software to generate digital images of illuminated three-dimensional surfaces, to fit these images with either polynomials, splines, or discrete cosines, and to assign topographic labels to each pixel. The first method has the advantage of exactness and the disadvantage of becoming extremely difficult for all but the simplest surfaces. The second method has the advantage of being applicable to a wide variety of surfaces and illuminating conditions and the disadvantage of yielding some inaccurate results due to possible errors in fitting the gray tone image. We have begun to experiment with both methods, starting with very simple surfaces, the Lambertian reflectance model, and point light sources. We have worked with four simple surfaces: (1) the top half of a cylinder, (2) the upper hemisphere of a sphere, (3) the top half of an ellipsoid, and (4) the upper half of a hyperboloid. Figures 2-5 illustrate the four three-dimensional surfaces.

METHOD 1: THE EXPERIMENTAL APPROACH

The process for topographic classification can be done in one pass through the image. At each pixel of the image, the following four steps, which are discussed in more detail in [1], need to be performed.

1. Calculate the least-squares fitting coefficients of a two-dimension cubic polynomial in an n x n neighborhood around the pixel.

2. Use the coefficients calculated in step 1 to find the gradient, the gradient magnitude, and the eigenvalues and eigenvectors of the Hessian at the center of the pixel's neighborhood.

3. Search in the direction of the eigenvectors calculated in step 2 for a zero-crossing of the first directional derivative within the pixel's area.

4. Recompute the gradient, gradient magnitude, and values of second directional derivative extrema at each zero crossing. Then classify the pixel based on these mathematical properties.

METHOD 2: THE ANALYTICAL APPROACH

Using the analytic approach, we have determined closed form solutions for the cylinder and sphere. Since the sphere is the more interesting of the two, we use it as our illustration of the analytic approach.

In the case of the sphere, the equation of a spherical surface with radius r is given by:

$$S(x,y) = d - (r^2 - x^2 - y^2)^{1/2} \quad \text{for } -r \le x \le r \quad \text{and } -r \le y \le r \tag{1}$$

Its intensity illuminated from direction [a,b,c] is given by:

$$I(x,y) = I_0 * [ax + by - c(r^2 - x^2 - y^2)^{1/2}]/r \tag{2}$$

After some simplifications, the first and second partials of I are found to be:

$$I_x = I_0[a + cx(r^2 - x^2 - y^2)^{-1/2}]/r,$$

$$I_y = I_0[b + cy(r^2 - x^2 - y^2)^{-1/2}]/r$$

$$I_{xx} = I_0 c(r^2 - y^2)(r^2 - x^2 - y^2)^{-3/2}/r,$$

$$I_{xy} = I_{yx} = I_0 cxy(r^2 - x^2 - y^2)^{-3/2}/r, \text{ and}$$

$$I_{yy} = I_0 c(r^2 - x^2)(r^2 - x^2 - y^2)^{-3/2}/r.$$

The gradient magnitude ($||\nabla I||$) is given by:

$$||\nabla I|| = (I_x^2 + I_y^2)^{1/2},$$

which is zero when

$$a(r^2 - x^2 - y^2)^{1/2} + cx = 0 \text{ and}$$

$$b(r^2 - x^2 - y^2)^{1/2} + cy = 0$$

are satisfied simultaneously. By squaring and invoking the constraint $a^2 + b^2 + c^2 = 0$ on the unit vector [a,b,c], the solution to the simultaneous equations is found to be:

$$x = ra \quad \text{and} \quad y = rb .$$

The Hessian for the intensity surface of the illuminated sphere is given by:

$$H = \frac{I_0 c}{r(r^2 - x^2 - y^2)} * \begin{bmatrix} r^2 - y^2 & xy \\ xy & r^2 - x^2 \end{bmatrix}.$$

Its eigenvalues are found to be:

$$X_1 = I_0 cr(r^2 - x^2 - y^2)^{-3/2} \text{ and}$$

$$X_2 = I_0 c(r^2 - x^2 - y^2)^{-1/2}/r.$$

Notice that both eigenvalues are always less than zero since c is always less than zero. The eigenvector corresponding to X_1 is given by:

$$w_1 - [x(x^2 + y^2)^{-1/2}, y(x^2 + y^2)^{-1/2}]$$

and the eigenvector corresponding to X_2 is given by:

$$w_2 - [-y(x^2 + y^2)^{-1/2}, x(x^2 + y^2)^{-1/2}].$$

The dot product of the gradient with w_1 is

$$\nabla I.w_1 = \frac{I_0}{r(x^2 + y^2)^{1/2}} [x a + \frac{cx}{(r^2 - x^2 - y^2)^{1/2}} + Y b + \frac{cy}{(r^2 - x^2 - y^2)^{1/2}}] \quad (3)$$

and the dot product of the gradient with w_2 is

$$\nabla I.w_2 = I_0(-ay + bx)(x^2 + y^2)^{-1/2}/r . \quad (4)$$

We determine the topographic labels by considering two cases.

CASE 1: ZERO GRADIENT MAGNITUDE

The gradient magnitude is equal to zero when $(x,y) = (ra, rb)$. Since both eigenvalues are less than zero on the illuminated sphere, it follows directly from Table 1 that a peak is located at $(x,y) = (ra, rb)$.

CASE 2: POSITIVE GRADIENT MAGNITUDE

In the case when the gradient magnitude is given to be positive, since both eigenvalues are known to be negative, it follows from [1] that there is a ridge at those locations where either $\nabla f.w_1 = 0$ or $\nabla f.x_2 = 0$ is satisfied. We obtain from Eq.(3) and Eq.(4) that

$$\nabla I.w_1 = 0 \text{ when } (ax + by)(r^2 - x^2 - y^2)^{1/2} + c(x^2 + y^2) = 0 \text{ and}$$

$$\nabla I.w_2 = 0 \text{ when } -ay + bx = 0.$$

[1] also says that hillsides appear at places where both $\nabla f.w_1$ and $\nabla f.w_2$ are non-zero.

OTHER CONIC SURFACES

We have also attempted to derive analytical results for the following conic surfaces:

(1) Ellipsoid:

$$S(x,y) = d - (l^2 - m^2x^2 - n^2y^2)^{1/2},$$

(2) Hyperboloid of one sheet:

$$S(x,y) = d - (l^2 - m^2x^2 - n^2y^2)^{1/2},$$

(3) Hyperboloid of two sheets:

$$S(x,y) = d - (m^2x^2 - n^2y^2 - l^2)^{1/2}, \text{ and}$$

(4) Paraboloid:

$$S(x,y) - d - (nx^2 + my^2).$$

Unfortunately, no simple closed form solution has been obtained for the first and second directional derivatives of these surfaces. Some of the analytical equations of these surfaces are given in [5]. Results of the topographic patterns on these surfaces are described in the section titled "Experimental Results." Results show that patterns also emerged for these surfaces.

CLASSIFICATION OF OBJECT SURFACES

We will propose here a scheme for partial classification of three-dimensional object surfaces. The basic goal of this classification scheme is to group together pixels which are likely to come from the same surface patch. We will limit our consideration to five types of object surfaces. They are planar, developable (one which may be unrolled onto a plane without distortion), spherical, elliptical, and hyperbolic surfaces.

Based on the above discussions, it is evident that topographic labels together with the signs and magnitudes of their second directional derivatives bear a strong relationship to the nature of the three-dimensional object surface in the scene. This evidence leads to the assumption that maximally connected sets of pixels having the same topographic label belong to the same surface patches. To extract these connected sets of topographic structures, the feature extraction process described in [5] is employed. The resulting structures of this feature extraction process are arcs, regions and topographic labels. The desired topographic structures are then determined by applying a connected components algorithm [3] to the topographic labels within each region segment.

The assembled topographic structures may be divided into three categories: (1) areal structures which consist of convex hillsides, concave hillsides, saddle hillsides, flat surfaces, and sloped surfaces; (2) arc structures which include edges, ridges, and valleys; and (3) point structures which include peaks, pits, and saddle points. In what follows, we suggest hypotheses that can be made about the three-dimensional objects based on the analytical results that we have derived and the results of the experiments that we have performed. We believe that three-dimensional object shape can be inferred by feeding this knowledge into a hypothesis based reasoning system such as [4].

AREAL STRUCTURES

FLAT

A flat is a simple surface with zero gradient and no curvature. That is, the gray level intensity is constant in a connected flat structure. Since the surface normal vectors within a planar surface are constant, we can be almost certain that pixels belonging to a connected flat structure come from the same planar surface. Although this may not hold for shadow areas, we can usually separate shadow areas by identifying flat structures with relatively low intensity averages.

HILLSIDES

We first hypothesize that a concave/convex hillside assembly is part of a spherical, elliptical or developable surface, and a saddle hillside assembly is part of a hyperbolic surface. Our first hypothesis is driven by the analytical and experimental results of the cylindrical, spherical, elliptical and hyperbolic surfaces that we have considered.

We further postulate that a concave/convex hillside assembly is part of a developable surface if it is adjacent to a straight and horizontal ridge. In particular, it is part of a cylindrical surface if it is concave and the second directional derivative of the hillside in the direction of the ridge is zero.

A hillside assembly can be considered as part of a spherical surface if it is concave and the radii of the approximating spheres within the hillside assembly are similar enough. We have not been able to derive a complete classification scheme for all the areal structures. Nonetheless, since the assembled regions are likely to come from the same surface patches, they are good starting regions for the shape-from-shading method described in [5].

LINE AND POINT STRUCTURES

While edges are considered to be good indications of surface discontinuities, peaks and ridges are found to be significant structures in the images of the conic surfaces that we have considered. The following observations are gathered from the topographic structures of the conic surface:

1. The ridge arcs obtained from the images of the sphere are found to be symmetrical around the peaks.

2. Ridges for the images of the ellipsoid and the hyperboloid are found to be symmetrical around the peaks only if the projection of the light vectors are parallel to one of the axes of these conic surfaces.

3. Straight ridge lines are found in the images of the cylinder. The gray tone intensities along the ridge lines are found to be constant.

4. While the ridges around the peaks found in the image of the ellipsoid curve away from the light sources, those of the hyperboloid curve towards the light sources.

5. The peaks located in the images of the conic surfaces correspond to locations where the surface normals are pointing towards the light sources.

A pictorial illustration of the above observations are given in Figure 6.

In this section, we have listed a set of criteria that can be used to infer shapes of three-dimensional objects. These criteria are supported by the experimental results to be described in the following section. We believe that an integrated knowledge based vision system can benefit by effectively using the knowledge about these topographic structures.

RESULTS

In the next three sections, we show the analytical and experimental results of the topographic patterns on the cylinder and sphere of Figures 2 and 3. Three illumination conditions are considered for each surface: (1) the light direction is (0,0,-1) which means directly above the center of the surface; (2) the light direction is $(0,\sqrt{3}/2,-1/2)$ which translates to azimuth 0 degrees and elevation 30 degrees; (3) the light direction is $(1/2,1/2,-1/\sqrt{2})$ which translates to azimuth 45 degrees and elevation 45 degrees.

ANALYTICAL RESULTS FOR THE CYLINDER

When the light direction is from azimuth 0 degrees, elevation 90 degrees, analytical results indicate a ridge parallel to the axis of the cylinder and running along the center of the top half as shown in Figure 7a. When the light direction is from azimuth 0 degrees and elevation 30 degrees, the ridge appears as in Figure 7b. When the light direction is from azimuth 45 degrees and elevation 45 degrees, the ridge appears as in Figure 7c. In all three cases, the remaining points of the cylinder are hillsides.

ANALYTICAL RESULTS FOR THE SPHERE

When the light source is directly above the center of the sphere, the gradient magnitude is zero at (0,0), therefore, a peak is located at the center of the sphere. The gradient magnitude is positive and the first directional derivative in the direction w_2 is zero at the remaining points of the sphere. It follows from our analytical results that ridges are located at these points. (This result is due to the analysis used in [1] and may not be intuitively obvious to all readers.)

When the light direction is $(0,\sqrt{3}/2,-1/2)$, a peak is found at $(0,\sqrt{3}r/2)$. At the remaining points,

$$\nabla I.w_1 = 0 \text{ when } (x^2 + y^2) = \sqrt{3}/2y(r^2 - x^2 - y^2)^{1/2} \quad \text{and}$$

$$\nabla I.w_2 = 0 \text{ when } x = 0.$$

Therefore, there are ridges when either one of the above two equations is satisfied and hillsides otherwise.

Similarly, a peak is found at (r/2,r/2) when the light direction is $(1/2,1/2,-1/\sqrt{2})$. Ridges can be located at places where either

$$\sqrt{2}(x^2 + y^2) = (x + y)(r^2 - x^2 - y^2)^{1/2} \quad \text{or}$$

$$x = y \quad \text{is satisfied.}$$

At the remaining points hillsides are the correct categories. Figure 8 shows the topographic labels for the illuminated spheres.

EXPERIMENTAL RESULTS

Experimentally, we are working in the GIPSY (General Image Processing System) environment. There currently exist GIPSY commands to construct three-dimensional surfaces, to produce images of these surfaces from various viewpoints and light directions, to fit these images with either cubic polynomials, splines, or discrete cosines, and to calculate the topographic labelings. Experimental results show very good correspondence with the analytical results, except for the sphere when the light direction is (0,0,-1). In this case, when points are labeled ridge and have neighboring points in a direction orthogonal to the gradient that are also labeled ridge, our software reclassifies these ridge continuums as hillsides.

Our results show that the most informative features found in the images of the cylinder and sphere are ridges and peaks. While the ridges found in the cylinder images are intuitive, the ellipse-like ridges found in the sphere images are unexpected. Although most ridge points found in the sphere images are weak ridges, experimental results show that these ridges are detectable. These ellipse-like ridges will be a definite clue to 3-dimensional surface identifications. Once the shape of the 3-dimensional surface is hypothesized as cylindrical or spherical, information such as the direction of the light source and the cylinder/sphere radius may also be estimated by examining the topographic labels.

RESULTS FOR THE OTHER CONIC SURFACES

Experiments have been performed on the ellipsoid and hyperboloid of Figures 4 and 5. Figures 9 and 10 illustrate the topographic labels that resulted from the analytical equations given [5]. Results show that the dominant structures in the images of the ellipsoid and hyperboloid are respectively concave and saddle hillsides. It was also found that only portions of the ridges that appear in Figures 9 and 10 were detected by the experimental method. Careful examinations showed that the ridges detected by the experimental method were dominant ridges which gave high curvatures (or eigenvalues), and the undetected ridges were weak ridges which gave very small curvatures. It was also observed that the intersection of the two ridge lines produced a peak.

SUMMARY

Both the analytical and experimental results so far indicate that there are definite patterns emerging that can help indicate the shape of the original three-dimensional surface and the direction of the light sources. For both methods, we anticipate a great deal more work. We would like to carry out the analytic approach for several more simple surfaces, perhaps using a symbol manipulator to help solve the equations. For the experimental methods, we need to work on getting results as close as possible to the analytic results. We will then perform a large series of experiments with various surfaces, combinations of surfaces forming objects, viewpoints, reflectance functions, and lighting conditions. Only then will we be able to complete the work of analyzing the patterns of topographic labls produced and predicting three-dimensional shape from these patterns.

BIBLIOGRAPHY

[1] Haralick, R.M., L.T. Watson and T.J. Laffey, "The Topographic Primal Sketch", The International Journal of Robotics Research, Vol. 2, No. 1, 1983, pp. 50-72.

[2] Horn, B.K.P., "Obtaining Shape from Shading Information", The Psychology of Computer Vision, P.H. Winston (ed.), McGraw-Hill, New York, 1975, pp. 115-155.

[3] Lumia, R., L.G. Shapiro and O. Zuniga, "A New Connected Components Algorithm for Virtual Memory Computers", Computer Vision, Graphics, and Image Processing, Vol. 22, No. 2, May 1983, pp. 287-300.

[4] Mulgaonkar, P.G., "Analyzing Perspective Line Drawings Using Hypothesis Based Reasoning", Virginia Polytechnic Institute and State University, Ph.D. Dissertation, Aug. 1984.

[5] Pong, T.C., "Determining Intrinsic Scene Characteristics from Images", Virginia Polytechnic Institute and State University, Ph.D. Dissertation, Aug. 1984.

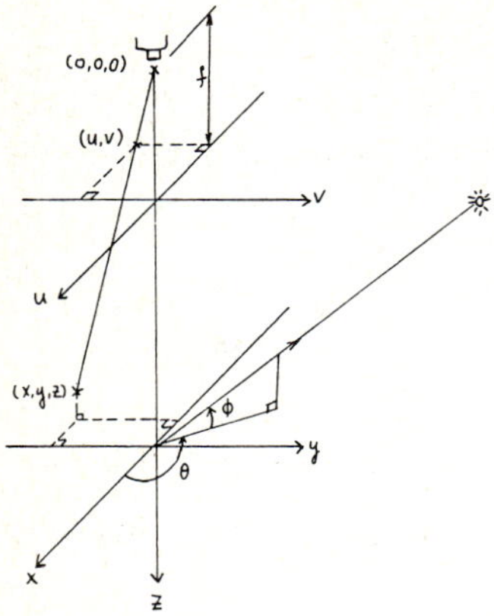

Figure 1: Relationship between scene coordinates and image coordinates.

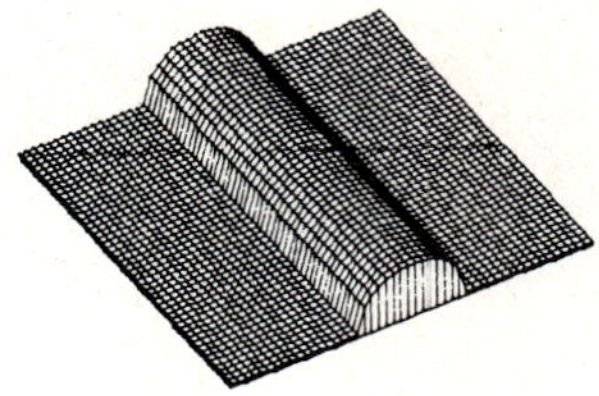

Figure 2: The cylindrical object used in our experiments.

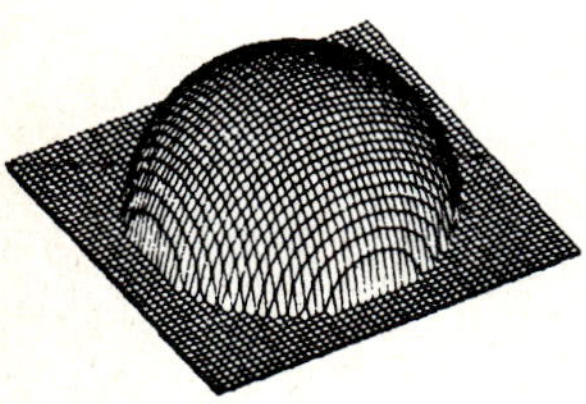

Figure 3: The spherical object used in our experiments.

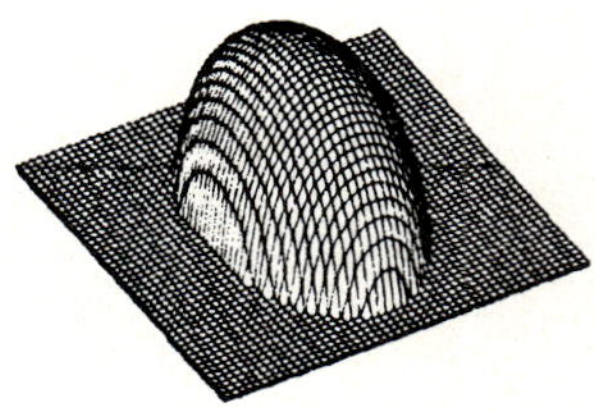

Figure 4: The ellipsoid used in our experiments.

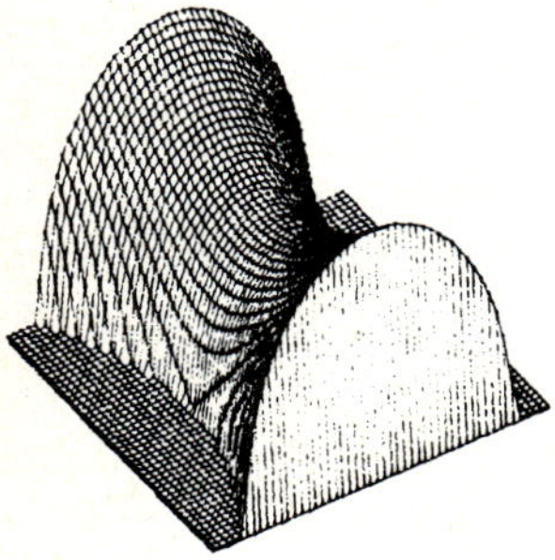

Figure 5: The hyperboloid used in our experiments.

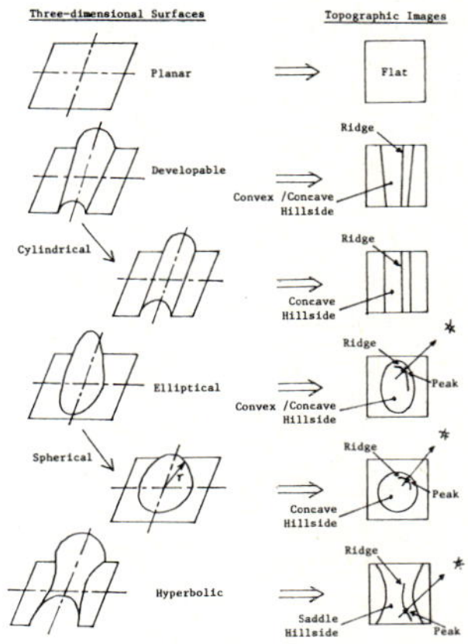

Figure 6: An illustration of the topographic patterns.

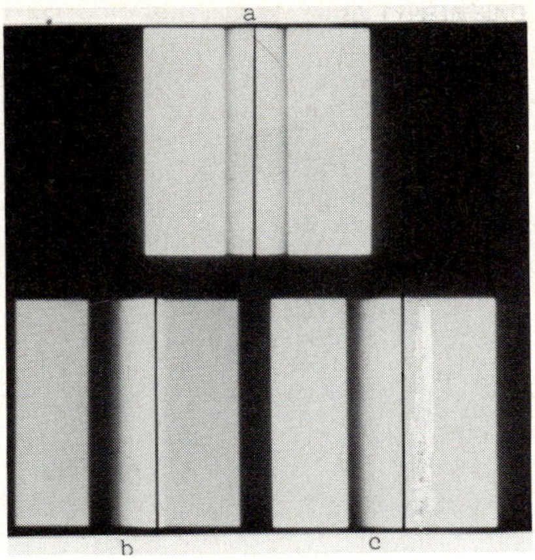

Figure 7: The analytically derived topographic labeling of the cylinder.

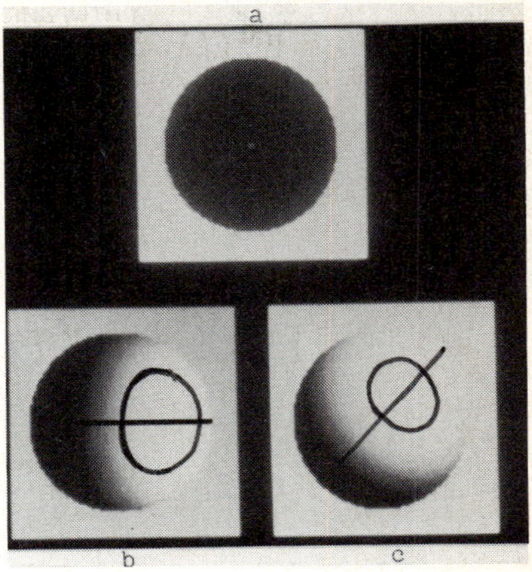

Figure 8: The analytically derived topographic labeling of the sphere.

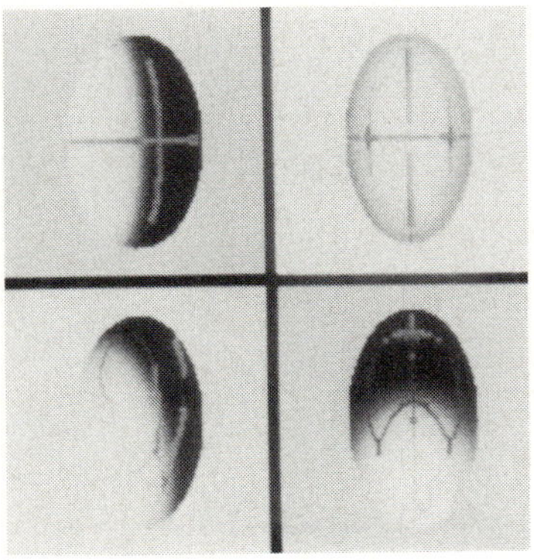

Figure 9: The analytically derived topographic labelings of the images of the ellipsoid.

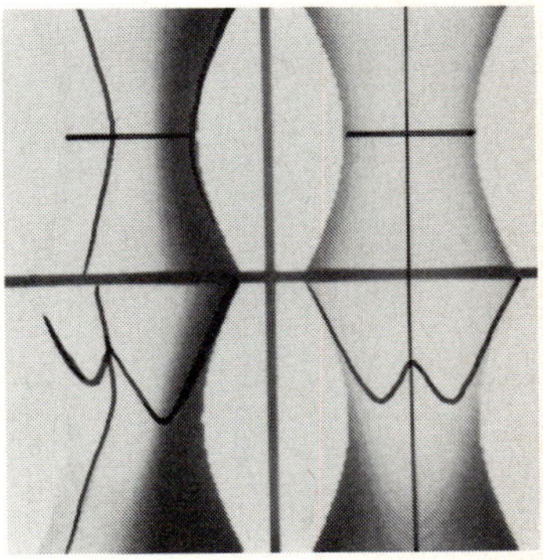

Figure 10: The analytically derived topographic labelings of the images of the hyperboloid.

PATTERN RECOGNITION IN PRACTICE II
E.S. Gelsema and L.N. Kanal (Editors)

THREE-DIMENSIONAL POSE COMPUTATIONS FROM MULTIPLE VIEWS

George C. Stockman

Department of Computer Science
Michigan State University
East Lansing, MI 48824 USA

The geometrical constraints of two imaging environments are specified. In each case it is shown how a candidate pose of the object can be determined from only a few matches between sensed features and model features. A candidate pose can then be verified by either hypothesize-and-test or by clustering of similar candidates. Results of simulations and experiments are given which demonstrate the strength of geometric constraints and the feasibility of clustering with multiple views.

INTRODUCTION

Recently there has been a great deal of interest and activity in the modeling and machine recognition of 3D industrial objects. For the current paper the domain of objects is limited to those which are rigid and opaque. For rigid objects, recognition and pose detection can be achieved by deducing a rigid transformation that matches features from a stored model to features observed by sensors. Four methods for sensing the structure of a 3D scene are as follows.

1) Only one camera is needed provided that it is calibrated to the global 3D space and that objects with known models will lie on a known support plane in a limited number of stable states. Research done under these assumptions include Roberts (1966), Chakravarti (1982), and Stockman (1984). Because of the limiting assumptions,the rigid transformation matching object and model is parameterized by only three parameters;--one rotational and two translational.

2) One camera and one projector can be used (active lighting) to sense 3D coordinates on the surfaces of objects. With several features having 3D coordinates, it is possible to acquire a known object freely placed in the global space. In this case the rigid matching transformation has three rotational and three translational parameters. A few of the many projects using this method are Hall (1982), Horaud (1984), and Faugeras (1983).

3) By correlating features from two camera images (stereo) it is possible to create a 3D depth map of the visible surfaces of a scene. Analysis of the depth information can then produce 3D features for use in matching to models. Representative projects include Kak (1983) and Grimson (1985).

4) Tactile sensors as well as visual sensors can be used to sense 3D space. Although currently slow, tactile sensors can deliver the approximate (x,y,z) location and normal direction N of points on the surface of an object. Description of such a sensor can be found in Bacsjy (1984) and use of tactile data for pose detection has been studied by Grimson and Lozano-Perez (1984).

In this paper some of the details of cases 1) and 2) above will be examined. Special attention will be given to the strength of purely geometric constraints in the model-data matching process.

The first ten years of computer vision research has shown that perfect 2D analysis of an image cannot be achieved due to noise, occlusion, non-ideal illumination, etc. Many scientists also believe that image analysis and understanding is impossible without a priori models. This second point has deep philosophical and psychological implications, which will not be discussed here. Instead, we go forward with the assumption that *observations are imperfect and that initial hypotheses about object identity and pose must be made with only partial information.* In the next section it is shown that in the highly constrained case 1 above,matching of only two point features from the model to two observed features is usually sufficient to compute a pose hypothesis. Section 3 then treats the more general case 2 environment, where the matching of two edge features is usually enough, and where other combinations of features can also be used. A pose computed from a (minimal) number of feature matches is called a *candidate pose* (CP). A candidate pose is only supported by a small amount of matching evidence so must be confirmed (or denied) on more global evidence.

In case 1) a CP consists of an object label, a stable state, and a 3 parameter transformation; in case 2) it consists of an object label and a 6 parameter transformation. There are at least two distinct methods for gathering global evidence in support of a candidate pose. First, using the given CP, model features could be transformed into the observed feature space and checked for a match; the more model features found, the higher our confidence in the CP. If the matching turns sour, an alternate CP can be tried, and there are a number of search strategies for controlling this. This is the well-known hypothesize-and-test paradigm. A second paradigm is that of clustering [Stockman 1982] or generalized Hough transform [Ballard 1981]. With this paradigm, many sets of minimal feature matches are used, each set yielding a single CP. The globally best pose is detected as the best cluster in the set of all CPs. Results using clustering are reported in Section 2 and the use of hypothesize-and-test and tree search is discussed in Section 3.

2. PASSIVE SENSING WITH A CAMERA AND SUPPORT PLANE

The environment assumed is shown is Figure 1. Object model M has pose (Θ,Tx,Ty) in the global space. The vision system detects feature points P1 and P2 in the image but cannot be certain which model points are actually being observed. The geometric constraints are that a) the block must be stable on the support plane, b) the first 3D point of the object must lie along the ray LP1, and c) the second 3D point of the object must lie along the ray LP2. From these geometrical considerations, it should be clear that certain poses of the block imaging J at P1 and B at P2 , or imaging B at P1 and J at P2 should be possible, while the pose imaging E at P1 and A at P2 should be impossible. The geometric constraints are nicely represented algebraically, and impossible object imaging situations correspond to a failure to get a solution to the algebraic equations.

Let R=(xm,ym,zm,1) be a model point in a body-centered coordinate system, Q=(xw,yw,zw,1) be the world point corresponding to R placed in the global 3D space, and let P=(tu,tv,t) be the image of Q. All points are in homogeneuos coordinates; (u,v) is the actual image point. In matrix form we have the following equations.

$$Q = R\ T \quad \text{(this is the instance, or pose, transformation)} \quad (1)$$

$$(xw,yw,zw,1) = (xm,ym,zm,1) \begin{bmatrix} \cos\theta & \sin\theta & 0 & 0 \\ -\sin\theta & \cos\theta & 0 & 0 \\ 0 & 0 & 1 & 0 \\ Tx & Ty & 0 & 1 \end{bmatrix}$$

$$P = Q\ A = (R\ T)\ A \quad \text{(perspective transformation)} \quad (2)$$

$$(tu,tv,t) = (xw,yw,zw,1) \begin{bmatrix} a_{11} & a_{12} & a_{13} \\ a_{21} & a_{22} & a_{23} \\ a_{31} & a_{32} & a_{33} \\ a_{41} & a_{42} & 1 \end{bmatrix}$$

$$u = \frac{xw \cdot a_{11} + yw \cdot a_{21} + zw \cdot a_{31} + a_{41}}{xw \cdot a_{13} + yw \cdot a_{23} + zw \cdot a_{33} + 1}$$

$$v = \frac{xw \cdot a_{12} + yw \cdot a_{22} + zw \cdot a_{32} + a_{42}}{xw \cdot a_{13} + yw \cdot a_{23} + zw \cdot a_{33} + 1}$$

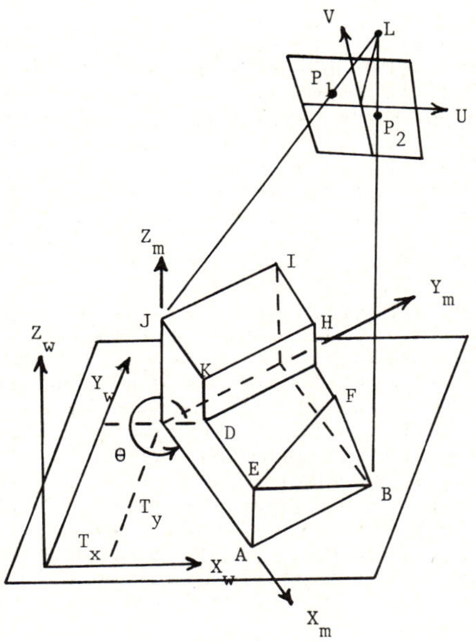

Fig. 1. Model block on a known support plane viewed by a camera.

The camera matrix A is gotten via calibration and is constant for a given view. Different cameras viewing the scene will have different but constant camera matrices. If it is known that model points R1 and R2 image at P1 and P2,then only the 3 pose parameters (θ,Tx,Ty) are unknown, yet there are 4 equations (two for each point) constraining their values. Thus, we should be able to solve for pose from the correspondences (R1,P1) and (R2,P2) and A, *when a solution exists.* As we shall show later, if the correspondences are arbitarily chosen, the chances of producing a mathematically feasible pose are small.

A. POSE SOLUTION

If the hypothesis is that a given model point R images at a given image point P then we can compute the location of the intermediate world point Q=(xw,yw,zw). First, by the stable state and support plane assumptions, we obtain the equation zw = zm. Second, from (2) there are two more equations and no new unknowns; and thus it is easy to solve for the three unknowns xw,yw,zw. This is often called *inverse perspective* because we are locating the ray of points (LPi in Figure 1) imaging at P. Of course, we are also intersecting that ray with the plane zw = zm. With a reasonable bench setup this solution always exists. If there are two correspondences (P1,R1) and (P2,R2) the computations of world points Q1 and Q2 can proceed independently; moreover, solutions should always exist, but may not satisfy joint constraints.

Given world points Q1 and Q2 assumed to correspond to model points R1 and R2, the object pose is now computed. This computation is likely to fail if the correspondences are incorrect. First of all, the 3D distances d(Q1,Q2) and d(R1,R2) should agree;--if they do not, then the correspondences are wrong. Also, if R1 and R2 differ only in the z coordinate, the rotation θ cannot be determined. Given that R1 and R2 are not vertically alligned and are the right distance apart, the object pose (θ,Tx,Ty) is computed with 2D algebra as follows.

$$\begin{aligned}
&\theta 1 = \text{the direction of the projection of R1R2 on x-y plane.}\\
&\theta 2 = \text{the direction of the projection of Q1Q2 on x-y plane.}\\
&\theta = \theta 2 - \theta 1\\
&Tx = Q1x - (R1x \cos\theta - R1y \sin\theta)\\
&Ty = Q1y - (R1x \sin\theta + R1y \cos\theta)
\end{aligned} \tag{3}$$

Errors in the pose will result from errors in the computation of of Q1 and Q2. From our experience, the location of P in the image plane could be off by one pixel radially and the root mean square error of the modeling by the calibrated camera matrix could yield another pixel. A 2-pixel error in locating the true P in 3D space will be multiplied by the standoff to yield an expected radial error of 3mm in locating Q on the plane zm = zw, when standoff is about one meter and the tilt of the camera is greater than 45 degrees downward. If the optical axis makes a glancing angle with the plane zw = zm, then the expected error grows very large. If radial errors of 3mm in Q1 and Q2 add in the worst manner, then in order to have θ computed within 3 degrees we need to have the projection of Q1Q2 be 10 cm or more.

B. VERIFICATION OF POSE CANDIDATES

If a pair of assumed correspondences (P1,R1) (P2,R2) yields a mathematically acceptable solution then a candidate pose CP = (θ,Tx,Ty) exists. Using the CP, any or all of the model feature points could be forward transformed through (1) and (2) to get a set of image points. A large number of methods exist for scoring the similarity of 2D sets of points,which could be used here to accept or reject the CP. This would be the hypothesize-and-test approach.

In an alternative approach, many or all feature pairings could be tried and the correct pose could be detected by clustering the many CPs. If there are N feature points in the image, a cluster of size N(N-1)/2 is possible if all feature pairings are tried. This method was studied by both simulation and actual laboratory tests. The primary reason for the study was to gain some insight into the strengths of purely geometric constraints. An o(K*K) clustering algorithm was used to cluster K CPs. For each of the K CPs the algorithm counts how many of the other CPs are close to it. The distance tolerance was set from the expected error,as described above,to be ($\pm 3^\circ$,$\pm$3mm,$\pm$3mm).

The results of some simulations are summarized in Table I. Two sets of 3D points were used as a model; the first was the block of Figure 1 and the second was a randomly generated set. For a few combinations of view and object pose, the model points were forward transformed using (1) and (2) to produce image points. Then all pairings of model and image points were tried and results of the pose computations studied. The models had 12 points each and all ((12*12)/2)*(12*12)=9504 possible pairings were tried. Only 3 to 15% of the pairings tried resulted in feasible pose parameters. In each case there was a substantial cluster of correct pose parameters representing 6 to 20% of the CPs in the cluster space.

Table I. Simulation results for clustering of candidate poses.

Object Type	Pose Parameters θ	Tx	Ty	Camera f	standoff	#/% CPs	Cluster Size
block	18	2	2	1	10	510/5%	61*
block	30	-2	3	25	1000	1450/15%	88
random	30	-0.4	-0.6	0.25	5.0	287/3%	62

* The predicted cluster size is (12*11)/2 = 66 less 5 for verticle pairs for which the computation fails = 61.

Three experiments were run in a real imaging environment. In addition, two views of each object were integrated in the following manner. For each camera, the CPs from feature point pairings were computed exactly as before. Since the two cameras were calibrated to the same global space, all resulting CPs could be merged in the same cluster space. This effectively allows an object to be viewed from several sides with merging of evidence and avoidance of the stereo correspondence problem. The three objects used were the block of Figure 1, a soft drink can, and a common box from a grocery store. Feature points used were either corners or easily distinguished markings. Image points were human selected from the monitor attached to the camera.

Some of the results of the lab experiments are given in Table II. The same pattern is shown as in the simulations. Typically the number of candidate poses was between 3% and 5% of all pairings tried. The use of two cameras appears to be essential to get enough feature points, especially for the coke can. Accuracy of the computed pose is well within the possible error predicted from analysis.

Table II. Results of clustering candidate poses from real data.

Object ---------- true pose	#points image 1 / 2	CPs # / %	Best Cluster Size	 θ	 Tx	 Ty
Block (12pts) (0deg,75mm,80mm)	6 / 10	415/5%	14	1	75	79
Coke Can (18pts) (250,102,240)	6 / 5	258/3%	4	257	104	140
Glad Box (21pts) (218,185,188)	10 / 6	939/4%	15	219	186	189

3. 6-PARAMETER POSE VIA ACTIVE SENSING WITH CAMERA AND PROJECTOR

In the previous section, the assumptions were more limiting than what is desirable for industrial applications. In this section, the use of active lighting is discussed for the purpose of obtaining more general 3D features for unconstrained pose detection, possibly in a jumble of objects. First of all,we need a general set of 3D features on which to base a pose hypothesis. Figure 2 illustrates a potential set:each feature in the set provides three kinds of information

a) type - such as the kind of edge, +, -, abstract,etc.
b) location - such as the 3D coordinates of a surface point, or the center of a circle.
c) direction - such as the direction of an edge or normal.

A 3D 6-parameter CP can be computed from a variety of combinations of sensed feature and model feature pairings. For example, the pose of a polyghedron may be determined by matching 3 faces of the object to 3 faces of the model [Grimson 84], or the pose of a circular cylinder may be obtained by matching the axes (or surfaces) of the cylinders and the planer ends [Bolles 84]. If object acquisition is to be done in a cluttered environment, a CP will have to be hypothesized from as small a set of features as possible. Moreover, it is likely that multiple views and interleaved acquisition of multiple objects will be needed.

Once a CP is computed, both hypothesize-and-test and clustering alternatives are available, as before, for verifying or denying it. The mathematics will only be slightly more complex than in Section 2 and the models are basically the same, so we should expect that the available geometric constraint will be just as great.

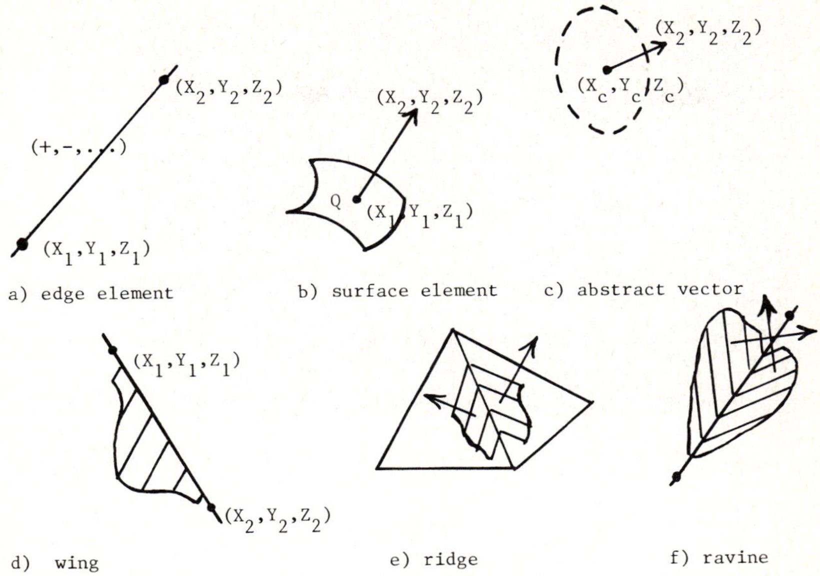

Fig. 2. Elementary 3D features for 6-parameter pose detection.

A. OBTAINING 3D FEATURES

With structured light, we illuminate points of the object surface with either a sheet or ray of light. Algebraically, this gives one or two more equations which the surface point (xw,yw,zw) must satisfy. A thorough treatment of this topic is given in [Hall,1982]. Figure 3 shows the view of a jumble illuminated with a grid. *If* the vision system knows that the point (xw,yw,zw) imaging at (u,v) is illuminated by projected grid intersect (r,c), then the following constraint holds in addition to the imaging constraint (2), where B is the matrix that models the projector in the same way that A models the camera.

$$(sr, sc, s) = (xw, yw, zw, 1) \begin{bmatrix} b_{11} & b_{12} & b_{13} \\ b_{21} & b_{22} & b_{23} \\ b_{31} & b_{32} & b_{33} \\ b_{41} & b_{42} & b_{43} \end{bmatrix} \qquad (3)$$

Grid coordinates r and/or c may be known by scanning a laser beam or sheet of light across the scene over time. Our approach has been to tackle the multiple-line image as in Figure 3 and to develop various methods for determining the grid coordinates (r,c). Those methods will be the subject of a future paper;--for this paper we assume that the grid coordinates, and hence the 3D surface points are available. It is important to emphasize in passing that once the 3D features are extracted from a camera/projector pair, the features from several such systems can be merged for matching because all coordinates are in the global 3D space.

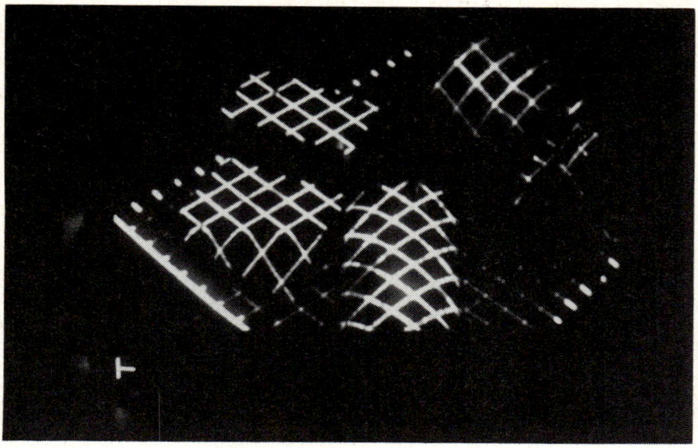

Fig. 3. View of jumble illuminated by projected light grid.

B. DEVELOPING 6-PARAMETER CANDIDATE POSES

A tree search method can be used to consider all possible pairings of observed features and model features of the same type [Grimson,84; Bolles,84]. Whenever two such pairings have been made, relational constraints can be checked. A global rigid transformation must preserve all distances and angles, so the distances and directions between the model features must be compatible with those of the corresponding observed features. An efficient means of checking these pairwise constraints can be found in [Grimson,83]. As before, most arbitrary pairings by feature type alone will fail these constraints. Survivors can be extended to triples and beyond. At some point there will be m pairs of matched features, each pair of which passes the distance and angle constraints. Usually m=2 or 3 is sufficient to compute an approximate 6-parameter CP. During verification on other features the CP can be made more accurate using least-squares techniques. In order to allow for features that are detected from other objects, or from artifacts, a NIL feature is added to the model, which will match any observed feature but provide no constraint.

We have run several experiments matching model features, such as in Figure 2., to observed features extracted from actively lit scenes, such as shown in Figure 3. A few results are illustrated in Table III. In this case the model has 19 edge elements as in Figure 2a. Observed edge elements are easy to get from the structured light setup; eight edge elements were observed in the case at hand, but only sets of four were used for matching. Eight different sets of four features were used to create Table III. Allowing for the match to NIL there are (19+1)**4 = 160,000 possible ways to correspond the 4 observed features to the model. As Table III shows, very few of the possiblilites tried will satisfy all pairwise distance and angle constraints, so even fewer will result in CPs. More CPs are possible as the tolerance on the constraints is relaxed. Errors in the data which are larger than the constraint tolerances will cause valid CPs to be missed, but larger tolerances will also increase the number of incorrect CPs. We are still working toward getting more accurate data, establishing appropriate tolerances on the constraints, and choosing the optimal number of features to match.

Table III. Number of correspondences surviving pairwise constraints out of a total of 160000 possible.

TOLERANCE		RUN #							
Dist.	Angle	1	2	3	4	5	6	7	8
10mm	5deg.	8	0	0	1	4	1	8	6
15mm	10deg.	8	6	7	23	4	2	9	52

4. DISCUSSION

Determination of object pose was considered under two general imaging environments. It was shown that the geometrical constraints available in the imaging environment are very powerful in reducing the possible interpretation of image features and the possibilities for object pose. Topological and type constraints can be added to what was used in the study to further enhance pose detection. Candidate poses, gotten from partial matching evidence, can be verified by either top-down checking or (bottom-up) clustering. In any case, it appears that global image analysis, usually a very difficult task with real imagery, is neither necessary nor desirable for the environments assumed in this paper. Another conclusion is that with the assumed environments and object models it is relatively easy to use multiple views. In both cases, objects can be profitably viewed from different sides. 2D analysis is used only for the detection of local features. By concentrating on 3D imaging geometry and models, the global analysis and matching becomes free from correspondence problems encountered in stereo viewing. We are continuing work on pose detection in jumbles of objects, and we are working toward the use of more general surface assumptions in our 3D feature extraction.

5. REFERENCES

Ballard, D. Generalizing the Hough transform to detect arbitrary shapes, *Pattern Recognition,* 13,2(1981)111-122.

Bajcsy, R. and Hager, G., Tactile Information Processing - the Bottom Up Approach, in *Proc. of 7th Int. Conf. on Pattern Recognition,* Montreal Canada (30July-2Aug, 1984)809-811.

Bolles,R. and Horaud,P., Configuration understanding in range data, *Proc. of the First Conf. on A.I. Applications,* Denver, CO (5-7 Dec 1984)

Chakravarti,I., The use of characteristic views as a basis for recognition of 3D objects, (PhD Dissertation) *IPL-TR-034,* Image Processing Lab. RPI, Troy, NY. (1982).

Faugeras,O. and Hebert, M. , A 3-D recognition and positioning algorithm using geometrical matching between primitive surfaces, *Proc. Int. Joint Conf. on Artificial Intelligence,* Karlsruhe, West Germany (8-12 Aug 1983)996-1002.

Grimson,W. and Lozano-Perez,T. , Model based recognition and localization from sparse range or tactile data, *Proc. Int. Conf. on Robotics,* Atlanta, Georgia (13-14 Mar 1984). Also see *M.I.T. Art. Intell. Memo #738* by the same authors (Aug 1983).

Grimson,W. Computational Experiments with a feature based stereo algorithm, *IEEE Transactions on PAMI* (Jan 1985)17-33.

Hall,E. , Tio, J. McPherson, C., and Sadjadi, F., Measuring curved surfaces for robot vision, *Computer* (Dec 1982).

Horaud,P. and Bolles,R., 3DPO's strategy for matching three-dimensional objects in range data, *Proc. Int. Conf. on Robotics,* Atlanta, GA (13-14 Mar 1984)78-85

Kak, A. , Depth Perception for Robots, *TR-EE-83-44* (Oct 1983) School of Electrical Engineering, Purdue Univ., West Lafayette, IN 47907

Roberts,L., Machine Perception of 3D Solids, in *Optical and Electro-optical Information Processing,* (Ed) J.Tippett et al, M.I.T. Press (1965).

Stockman,G., Kopstein, S., and Benett,S., Matching images to models for registration and object detection via clustering, *IEEE Trans. on PAMI-4,* (May 1982)229-241.

Stockman,G. and Esteva,J.C. , 3D Object pose via cluster space stereo, *TR#84-005,* Dept. of Computer Science, Michigan State Univ., E.Lansing, MI 48824 (Apr 1984).

Acknowledgement: This work was supported in part by Grant #MCS-83-04011 from the National Science Foundation.

DISCUSSION

Persoon:

If you work with those striped matrices and you project them you have problems in identifying which line in your image corresponds with which line in your matrix. Have you ever worked with the idea of having two matrices, a coarse one and a fine one and use two images?

Stockman:

That is one technique. In another technique, you scan with a laser and syncronize. Then you can differentiate in time. The people at the University of Maryland have been blocking out squares so they have totally illuminated squares in their images. That tells them which street and avenue they are looking at.

PATTERN RECOGNITION IN PRACTICE II
E.S. Gelsema and L.N. Kanal (Editors)

Optimal Statistical Techniques for Combining Pieces of Information Applied to 3-D Complex Object Position Estimation

Ruud M. Bolle
IBM - T.J. Watson Research Center
Yorktown Heights, NY 10598

David B. Cooper
Brown University, Division of Engineering
Providence, RI 02912

This paper uses techniques appropriate to the analysis of probability density functions for the large sample case. These techniques permit controlled decomposition of a large problem into small problems where maximum likelihood estimation or Bayesian estimation or recognition can be realized locally, and the results can be combined to arrive at globally optimum estimation or recognition or both.

To illustrate the results, a maximum likelihood approach to 3-D complex-object position estimation is presented. To this end, a simple 3-D modeling scheme for complex objects is proposed using primitive quadric surface patches. The object-position estimation is based on sets of range data points, each set associated with a primitive object patch. The work reported here appears to be the first to treat object positioning as a single large estimation problem.

1. Introduction

Computer vision involving the segmentation and labeling of complex scenes, the recognition of complex objects in scenes, or the estimation of the position of a complex object in the 3-D world requires the estimation of *a priori* partially unknown parameters. It is computationally infeasible to use all the data at once in estimating the unknown parameters and carrying out recognition. Rather, the problem must be decomposed into subproblems, where each subproblem is an estimation or an estimation and recognition that uses only a portion of the available data. This both reduces the amount of data and permits real-time operation by carrying out these subproblem computations in parallel. This approach raises the questions of what are appropriate sizes for the subproblems and how are the results obtained from each subproblem to be combined in order to achieve *roughly* globally optimal estimations and recognitions, i.e., final results that are essentially as accurate as if all the data were used at once to achieve the required estimations and recognitions.

As an example, we present a probabilistic approach to the 3-D object orientation and location (hereafter referred to as *position*) estimation problem that is computationally attractive and is close to optimal in accuracy. A significant percentage of manufactured parts can be perfectly represented or can be well approximated by a small number of patches of planes, cylinders, and spheres, (about 85 percent). Therefore, we model a complex object as composed of these primitive simple 3-D surfaces, and first estimate these separately in parallel. Our probabilistic framework is applied to optimally integrating the information obtained from these separate estimations. In order to carry out this integration, it is necessary that a correspondence be established between each primitive surface sensed in the data and a primitive surface in the stored model. We do not deal with this matching problem in this paper, but rather assume it is solved by employing techniques from artificial intelligence. The capability, provided by our algorithms, for optimal primitive surface shape recognition and parameter estimation based on a local data patch is of great value in simplifying the matching process.

1.1. Maximum Likelihood Position Estimation

The 3-D information upon which the estimate of the position of an object is based is range data, that is, collections of points in three-space near the object's surface patches. If a collection of range points denoted by $Y = \{\mathbf{r}_i\}$, with $\mathbf{r}_i = (x_i, y_i, z_i)^t$, constitutes measurements of points on the surface of the object, the goal is to estimate the position of the object in 3-D space that most likely corresponds to the range data Y. Hence, the likelihood $p(Y \mid \textit{object position})$ has to be maximized as a function of the object position. (This provides an optimal estimation of position, unlike procedures based on measuring many arbitrary features and combining feature information in *ad hoc* ways.) Ideally, the estimation should be achieved by computing the likelihood of the range data Y for all possible object positions in three-space and selecting that position for which the likelihood is maximal -- a seemingly horrendous computational task. In this paper, $p(Y \mid \textit{object position})$ is formulated in a way that makes approximate maximum likelihood estimation computationally feasible.

1.2. Related Work

A variety of approaches to model-based object position estimation and recognition using range data is found in the computer vision literature. Faugeras et al. [7] fit planar patches to range data. The position of the object is estimated by matching these patches with a list of planar patches in a stored model; this is achieved by least squares error techniques applied to a vector of geometric features. In [10] an object model is built in terms of properties of regions of range points and relations between the regions, in a learning stage. In the recognition stage, matching is achieved by a model and data driven search procedure. An object positioning scheme using edge information in range data can be found in [4]. The approach is based on sequentially finding significant features in the range data. In [1] an object position estimation technique is described where the object is modeled as a collection of planes, cylinders, and spheres. Using geometric techniques, information from each of the primitive quadrics is combined to arrive at an estimate of the position of the complex object. If the data is noisy, some of these approaches will be plagued by strange errors inherent to the least squares fitting techniques used (see [5]), and *none* is optimal from a statistical estimation point of view.

1.3. Organization of the Paper

In Sect. 2 the asymptotic techniques used in this paper are examined in detail and placed in perspective. Section 3 proposes a simple model for complex 3-D objects. Also in Sect. 3 a probabilistic model for the generation of range points measured on the primitive surfaces is discussed. In Sect. 4 an approximately maximum likelihood estimate of the position of an object in three-space is formulated using one of the asymptotic results from Sect. 2. Section 5 discusses the incorporation of 3-D edge information found in the range data.

2. On Some Asymptotic Forms For The Likelihood Of Large Data Sets

Let $p(\mathbf{g} \mid \alpha)$ be an arbitrary pdf such that the second partial derivatives with respect to the parameter vector α are continuous functions of α for almost all $\mathbf{g}$. Let $\mathbf{g}_1, \mathbf{g}_2, \ldots, \mathbf{g}_M$ be a sequence of M independent identically distributed (iid) random variables with common pdf as above and let Y be a vector having the $\mathbf{g}_m$ as its components. The joint pdf for the sequence is

$$\prod_{m=1}^{M} p(\mathbf{g}_m \mid \alpha). \tag{1}$$

Under mild restrictions [9,6], (1) is asymptotically Gaussian in α, i.e.,

$$\prod_{m=1}^{M} p(\mathbf{g}_m \mid \alpha) \approx \left[\prod_{m=1}^{M} p(\mathbf{g}_m \mid \hat{\alpha}_M)\right] \exp\{-(1/2)(\alpha - \hat{\alpha}_M)^t \Psi(Y,\hat{\alpha}_M)(\alpha - \hat{\alpha}_M)\} \tag{2}$$

where $\hat{\alpha}_M$ is the maximum likelihood estimate of the true α, based on Y, and $\Psi(Y,\hat{\alpha}_M)$ is a matrix with ijth element

$$-\frac{\partial^2}{\partial\alpha_j\,\partial\alpha_i} \log \prod_{m=1}^{M} p(\mathbf{g}_m \mid \alpha) \Big|_{\alpha = \hat{\alpha}_M}.$$

Furthermore, under minor restrictions, $\hat{\alpha}_M$ converges with probability 1 to the true α as $M \to \infty$, and $(1/M)\Psi(Y,\hat{\alpha}_M)$ converges with probability 1 to the so-called Fisher information matrix $E[(1/M)\Psi(Y,\alpha)]$. Thus the exponential function in (2) becomes an impulse function centered at $\hat{\alpha}_M$ and of area $(2\pi)^{d/2} | \Psi(Y,\hat{\alpha}_M) |^{-1/2}$ for M large, where d is the number of components in the vector α, ($|\cdot|$ denotes determinant). The elegance of (2) is that for any reasonably smooth *a priori* pdf $p(\alpha)$ for α,

$$\int \left[\prod_{m=1}^{M} p(\mathbf{g}_m \mid \alpha)\right] p(\alpha)\, d\alpha \approx (2\pi)^{d/2} | \Psi(Y,\hat{\alpha}_M) |^{-1/2} \left[\prod_{m=1}^{M} p(\mathbf{g}_m \mid \hat{\alpha}_M)\right] p(\hat{\alpha}_M). \tag{3}$$

Since $| \Psi(Y,\hat{\alpha}_M) |^{-1/2} = M^{-d/2} | (1/M)\Psi(Y,\hat{\alpha}_M) |^{-1/2}$, it is seen that as M goes to infinity, the logarithm of (3) converges to

$$\log \left[\prod_{m=1}^{M} p(\mathbf{g}_m \mid \hat{\alpha}_M)\right] - (d/2)\log(M). \tag{4}$$

Expressions (3) and (4) constitute discriminants for Bayesian recognition. See [2,3] for applications and for technical considerations in their use.

2.1. Extension to the Non-Identically Distributed Case

Now assume the $\mathbf{g}_m$ are independently distributed as $p(\mathbf{g}_m \mid \alpha, m)$. For example, the $\mathbf{g}_m$ may consist of a zero-mean additive noise plus a mean-value function parameterized by α and which is a function of m, such as a linear or quadric mean-value function. Subject to the appropriate conditions on the $p(\mathbf{g}_m \mid \alpha, m)$, the above results are extendible. To emphasize the distinction, $\Psi(Y,\hat{\alpha}_M)$ is now denoted as $\Psi_L(Y,\hat{\alpha}_M)$, since there exists some integer L such that $(1/M^L)\Psi_L(Y,\hat{\alpha}_M)$ converges with probability 1 to the matrix having ijth element

$$E[-(1/M^L)\frac{\partial^2}{\partial\alpha_j\,\partial\alpha_i} \log \prod_{m=1}^{M} p(\mathbf{g}_m \mid \alpha, m)]. \tag{5}$$

Hence, (4) becomes

$$\log \left[\prod_{m=1}^{M} p(\mathbf{g}_m \mid \hat{\alpha}_M, m) \right] - (L/2) \log (M). \tag{6}$$

A sufficient condition for this to be true is that the $\mathbf{g}_m$ are independent Gaussian random variables with equal variance and a mean-value function that is asymptotically polynomial in α; these conditions can be weakened significantly. The integer L is an increasing function of the degree of the polynomial.

The results of this section were used successfully in a Bayesian approach to shape-from-shading by Bolle and Cooper [2]. They can be used for Bayesian recognition of small or large patches of range data.

2.2. Multiple Blocks of Data, Each with Different Parameter Vector

We examine the joint pdf for the data in the blocks. Let the data set consist of K subsets. Let $\mathbf{g}_{km}$ be a data point (a vector) in the subset k, where m takes values $1,\ldots, M_k$. Let $p_k(\mathbf{g}_{km} \mid \boldsymbol{\alpha}_k)$, the pdf of $\mathbf{g}_{km}$, be parameterized by the parameter vector $\boldsymbol{\alpha}_k$. Assume the $\mathbf{g}_{km}$ in subset k, given $\boldsymbol{\alpha}_k$, are iid random vectors, but the results apply to the model of Sect. 2.1 as well. Let Y_k be a vector with components $\mathbf{g}_{km}$, $m = 1,\ldots, M_k$, and assume that $Y_1,\ldots, Y_K$ given $\boldsymbol{\alpha}_1,\ldots, \boldsymbol{\alpha}_K$ are independent random vectors. Denote by $\boldsymbol{\alpha}$ the vector $(\boldsymbol{\alpha}_1,\ldots, \boldsymbol{\alpha}_K)$ and by Y the entire data set. Then using (2)

$$\begin{aligned} p(Y \mid \boldsymbol{\alpha}) &= \prod_{k=1}^{K} p_k(Y_k \mid \boldsymbol{\alpha}_k) = \prod_{k=1}^{K} \left[\prod_{m=1}^{M_k} p_k(\mathbf{g}_{km} \mid \boldsymbol{\alpha}_k) \right] \\ &\approx \left[\prod_{k=1}^{K} p_k(Y_k \mid \hat{\boldsymbol{\alpha}}_k) \right] \exp \{ -(1/2) \sum_{k=1}^{K} (\boldsymbol{\alpha}_k - \hat{\boldsymbol{\alpha}}_k)^t \Psi_k(Y_k, \hat{\boldsymbol{\alpha}}_k)(\boldsymbol{\alpha}_k - \hat{\boldsymbol{\alpha}}_k) \}, \end{aligned} \tag{7}$$

with $\hat{\boldsymbol{\alpha}}_k$ the mle of $\boldsymbol{\alpha}_k$ based on the data Y_k.

Now suppose $\boldsymbol{\alpha}_k$ is a function $\mathbf{T}_k(\boldsymbol{\beta})$ of a parameter vector $\boldsymbol{\beta}$, that is,

$$p(Y \mid \alpha(\boldsymbol{\beta})) = \prod_{k=1}^{K} p_k(Y_k \mid \mathbf{T}_k(\boldsymbol{\beta})). \tag{8}$$

Then we can use

$$p(Y \mid \boldsymbol{\beta}) \approx \left[\prod_{k=1}^{K} p_k(Y_k \mid \hat{\boldsymbol{\alpha}}_k) \right] \exp \{ -(1/2) \sum_{k=1}^{K} [\mathbf{T}_k(\boldsymbol{\beta}) - \hat{\boldsymbol{\alpha}}_k]^t \Psi_k(Y_k, \hat{\boldsymbol{\alpha}}_k) [\mathbf{T}_k(\boldsymbol{\beta}) - \hat{\boldsymbol{\alpha}}_k] \}. \tag{9}$$

The $\hat{\boldsymbol{\alpha}}_k$ and the $\Psi_k(Y_k, \hat{\boldsymbol{\alpha}}_k)$ in the quadratic forms

$$(1/2) [\mathbf{T}_k(\boldsymbol{\beta}) - \hat{\boldsymbol{\alpha}}_k]^t \Psi_k(Y_k, \hat{\boldsymbol{\alpha}}_k) [\mathbf{T}_k(\boldsymbol{\beta}) - \hat{\boldsymbol{\alpha}}_k], \; k = 1,\ldots, K \tag{10}$$

can be computed in parallel -- $\hat{\boldsymbol{\alpha}}_k$ and $\Psi_k(Y_k, \hat{\boldsymbol{\alpha}}_k)$ depend only on the kth data set, Y_k. Once these are computed, the maximization of (9) with respect to $\boldsymbol{\beta}$ is simply minimization of the sum of quadratic forms in (10) with respect to $\boldsymbol{\beta}$. Note that the approximation in (9) will improve in general by adding to (10) the linear term $-[\nabla_{\boldsymbol{\alpha}_k} \log p_k(Y_k \mid \hat{\boldsymbol{\alpha}}_k)]^t [\mathbf{T}_k(\boldsymbol{\beta}) - \hat{\boldsymbol{\alpha}}_k]$ in the Taylor series expansion, ($\nabla_{\boldsymbol{\alpha}_k}$ denotes gradient with respect to $\boldsymbol{\alpha}_k$).

When there are constraints among the components of $\boldsymbol{\alpha}_k$, or more generally among the $\boldsymbol{\alpha}_k$, the approach of expanding $p(Y \mid \boldsymbol{\beta})$ in terms of $\boldsymbol{\alpha}$ and then dealing with the sum of quadratics in the $\mathbf{T}_k(\boldsymbol{\beta})$ in (9) is a powerful tool and was used by Bolle and Cooper in [2].

3. Modeling Complex Objects and 3-D Measurements

3.1. The Primitive Surfaces

First we determine how the geometric parameters of the surfaces may be specified and how these parameters change under the influence of scaling, rotation, and translation. Let rotation in 3-D Euclidean space be expressed by a 3×3 rotation matrix, satisfying $RR^t = R^tR = I$, that is, an orthogonal matrix $R(\phi,\theta,\xi)$ uniquely defining a rotation, with ϕ, θ, ξ the Euler angles [8].

3.1.1. Planar Surface

A 3-D planar surface is completely specified by a unit vector $\mathbf{v}$ in the direction of the normal to the plane and an arbitrary point $\mathbf{p}$ on the plane; the plane is given by the points $\mathbf{r}' = (x, y, z)^t$ that satisfy

$$\mathbf{v} \cdot (\mathbf{r}' - \mathbf{p}) = 0. \tag{11}$$

Rotating the plane can be achieved by replacing $\mathbf{r}'$ by $R^t\mathbf{r}$, resulting in

$$\mathbf{v} \cdot (R^t\mathbf{r} - \mathbf{p}) = R\mathbf{v} \cdot (\mathbf{r} - R\mathbf{p}) = 0. \tag{12}$$

Hence, the rotated plane is specified by the orientation vector $R\mathbf{v}$ and the location vector $R\mathbf{p}$. Translating the plane in the direction $\mathbf{t}$ is accomplished by replacing $\mathbf{r}'$ by $\mathbf{r} - \mathbf{t}$, yielding

$$\mathbf{v} \cdot (\mathbf{r} - \mathbf{t} - \mathbf{p}) = 0, \tag{13}$$

and the new location vector can be chosen as $\mathbf{p} + \mathbf{t}$. In this expression the translation $\mathbf{t}$ appears only in the inner product $\mathbf{v} \cdot \mathbf{t}$. Hence notice that given a translated plane only the translation of the plane from its original location in the direction of the normal $\mathbf{v}$ can be recovered.

3.1.2. Spherical Surface

A sphere with radius P and its center located at $\mathbf{p}$ has the quadric equation in $\mathbf{r}' = (x, y, z)^t$

$$(\mathbf{r}' - \mathbf{p}) \cdot (\mathbf{r}' - \mathbf{p}) = P^2. \tag{14}$$

It is seen that rotating this sphere around the origin by replacing $\mathbf{r}'$ by $R^t\mathbf{r}$ alters this expression to

$$(R^t\mathbf{r} - \mathbf{p}) \cdot (R^t\mathbf{r} - \mathbf{p}) = (\mathbf{r} - R\,\mathbf{p}) \cdot (\mathbf{r} - R\,\mathbf{p}) = P^2, \tag{15}$$

and the rotated sphere is specified by its rotated center $R\,\mathbf{p}$ and radius P. Translation of the sphere, performed by replacing $\mathbf{r}'$ by $\mathbf{r} - \mathbf{t}$ gives

$$(\mathbf{r} - \mathbf{t} - \mathbf{p}) \cdot (\mathbf{r} - \mathbf{t} - \mathbf{p}) = P^2, \tag{16}$$

which indicates that the translated sphere has center $\mathbf{p} + \mathbf{t}$. This shows that translation information can be recovered from a single sphere.

3.1.3. Cylindrical Surface

A cylinder with axis in the direction of the unit vector $\mathbf{v}$, a point $\mathbf{p}$ on its axis, and of radius P can be expressed as

$$(\mathbf{r}' - \mathbf{p})^t [I - \mathbf{v}\mathbf{v}^t] (\mathbf{r}' - \mathbf{p}) = P^2, \tag{17}$$

where I is the 3×3 identity matrix.

Replacing $\mathbf{r}'$ by $R^t\mathbf{r}$ to rotate the cylinder gives

$$(R^t\mathbf{r} - \mathbf{p})^t [I - \mathbf{v}\mathbf{v}^t] (R^t\mathbf{r} - \mathbf{p}) = (\mathbf{r} - R\,\mathbf{p})^t [I - R\,\mathbf{v}(R\,\mathbf{v})^t] (\mathbf{r} - R\,\mathbf{p}) = P^2, \tag{18}$$

hence the rotated cylinder has orientation vector $R\,\mathbf{v}$ and location vector $R\,\mathbf{p}$. Translation of the cylinder by replacing $\mathbf{r}'$ by $\mathbf{r} - \mathbf{t}$ in (17) gives

$$(\mathbf{r} - \mathbf{t} - \mathbf{p})^t [I - \mathbf{v}\mathbf{v}^t] (\mathbf{r} - \mathbf{t} - \mathbf{p}) = P^2, \tag{19}$$

so that for the new location vector, $\mathbf{p} + \mathbf{t}$ may be selected. To gain insight into this expression, the following identity is useful. If $\{\mathbf{e}_1,\mathbf{e}_2,\mathbf{e}_3\}$ is any orthonormal basis, then $\mathbf{e}_1\mathbf{e}_1^t + \mathbf{e}_2\mathbf{e}_2^t + \mathbf{e}_3\mathbf{e}_3^t \equiv \mathbf{I}$. Now with $\mathbf{v}$ the direction of the cylinder axis, let $\{\mathbf{v},\mathbf{v}_1,\mathbf{v}_2\}$ be an orthonormal basis. Then using this identity,

$$I - \mathbf{v}\mathbf{v}^t = \mathbf{v}_1\mathbf{v}_1^t + \mathbf{v}_2\mathbf{v}_2^t \tag{20}$$

with both $\mathbf{v}_1$ and $\mathbf{v}_2$ perpendicular to the cylinder axis. Substituting this in (19), the equation of the translated cylinder, yields

$$[\mathbf{v}_1 \cdot (\mathbf{r} - \mathbf{t} - \mathbf{p})]^2 + [\mathbf{v}_2 \cdot (\mathbf{r} - \mathbf{t} - \mathbf{p})]^2 = P^2. \tag{21}$$

The translation vector $\mathbf{t}$ appears only in the inner products $\mathbf{v}_1 \cdot \mathbf{t}$ and $\mathbf{v}_2 \cdot \mathbf{t}$. Hence, after translating the cylinder from its original location only the translation perpendicular to the cylinder axis can be recovered.

3.1.4. A Simple Geometric Model for 3-D Objects

In the model of a complex 3-D object each primitive quadric S is described in terms of a triplet $S = (\mathbf{v}, \mathbf{p}, P)$, where $\mathbf{v}$ is an orientation vector, $\mathbf{p}$ a location vector, and P a scalar indicating size. For a complex object composed of N_1 planes, N_2 cylinders, and N_3 spheres, the model surface-patches are denoted as follows:

(1) Planes: $S_{1i} = (\mathbf{v}_{1i}, \mathbf{p}_{1i}, 0)$, i = 1, 2,..., N_1. $\mathbf{v}_{1i}$ is the unit vector perpendicular to plane i, and $\mathbf{p}_{1i}$ is a point on this plane. The signed distance from plane i to the origin is $\mathbf{v}_{1i} \cdot \mathbf{p}_{1i}$.

(2) Cylinders: $S_{2i} = (\mathbf{v}_{2i}, \mathbf{p}_{2i}, P_{2i})$, i = 1, 2,..., N_2. For a particular cylinder i, $\mathbf{v}_{2i}$ is the unit vector in the direction of the axis, while $\mathbf{p}_{2i}$ is a point on the axis and P_{2i} is the radius.

(3) Spheres: $S_{3i} = (0, \mathbf{p}_{3i}, P_{3i})$, i = 1, 2,..., N_3. There is no orientation vector for sphere i, the location vector $\mathbf{p}_{3i}$ is the center point, and P_{3i} is the radius of the sphere.

3.1.5. Similarity Transformation of the Model

Given an arbitrary scale factor s, rotation matrix $R(\phi,\theta,\xi)$, and translation vector $\mathbf{t}$, it is possible to scale, rotate, and translate the model of a particular rigid object. A model, consisting of a collection of surfaces

$\{\{S_{ji}, i = 1, 2, ..., N_j\}, j = 1, 2, 3\}$, simply transforms into a new collection of surfaces $\{\{S'_{ji}, i = 1, 2, ..., N_j\}, j = 1, 2, 3\}$, with surface $S'_{ji} = (R\,\mathbf{v}_{ji}\,,\, sR\,\mathbf{p}_{ji} + \mathbf{t}\,,\, sP_{ji})$.

3.2. Modeling 3-D Measurements

In this section we describe an underlying probabilistic model that generates range points on the primitive 3-D quadrics under consideration. This probabilistic model is useful for two purposes: (1) it accounts for imprecisions in the 3-D measurements, and (2) it accounts for distortions from the ideal 3-D quadric primitive surfaces. The model used treats the noise component of the range data as perpendicular to the 3-D surface and independently, identically, normally distributed (normal iid). See [3] for a justification of this noise mechanism.

3.2.1. Planar Range Points

Consider a plane in three-space described by location vector $\mathbf{q}$ and orientation vector $\mathbf{w}$. Then the set of M range data points $Y = \{\mathbf{r}_m\}_{m=1}^{M}$ measured on this plane can be modeled as samples of random variables with the plane as mean-value function and perturbation vectors perpendicular to the plane. If we assume that the signed lengths of the noise vectors, $\mathbf{w} \cdot (\mathbf{r}_m - \mathbf{q})$, are a zero-mean Gaussian white noise field with standard deviation σ, the likelihood of the range data can be expressed as

$$p(Y \mid \mathbf{w}, \mathbf{q}) = \prod_{m=1}^{M} \frac{1}{\sigma\sqrt{2\pi}} \exp\{-\frac{1}{2\sigma^2}[\mathbf{w} \cdot (\mathbf{r}_m - \mathbf{q})]^2\} = (\sigma^2 2\pi)^{-M/2} \exp\{-\frac{1}{2\sigma^2}\mathbf{w}^t [\sum_{m=1}^{M} (\mathbf{r}_m - \mathbf{q})(\mathbf{r}_m - \mathbf{q})^t]\mathbf{w}\}. \quad \textbf{(22)}$$

It can be shown [3] that a maximum likelihood estimate (mle) of the location vector is (23). This estimate

$$\hat{\mathbf{q}} = \bar{\mathbf{r}} = \frac{1}{M}\sum_{m=1}^{M} \mathbf{r}_m . \quad (23)$$

is *not unique* -- any vector $\hat{\mathbf{q}}' = \hat{\mathbf{q}} + \mathbf{e}$ with $\hat{\mathbf{w}} \cdot \mathbf{e} = 0$ is a mle of location. The unit orientation mle vector $\hat{\mathbf{w}}$ is the eigenvector associated with the smallest eigenvalue of the scatter matrix $\sum_{m=1}^{M} (\mathbf{r}_m - \bar{\mathbf{r}})(\mathbf{r}_m - \bar{\mathbf{r}})^t$.

3.2.2. Spherical Range Points

Suppose the set of range points $Y = \{\mathbf{r}_m\}_{m=1}^{M}$ is measured from a spherical object patch with center $\mathbf{q}$ and radius Q. Using the same noise model as for the plane, for a particular $\mathbf{r}_m$ the quantity $(\|\mathbf{r}_m - \mathbf{q}\| - Q)$ is the signed length of the noise vector. Hence the likelihood of Y is

$$p(Y \mid \mathbf{q}, Q) = (\sigma^2 2\pi)^{-M/2} \exp\{-\frac{1}{2\sigma^2}\sum_{m=1}^{M} (\|\mathbf{r}_m - \mathbf{q}\| - Q)^2\}. \quad (24)$$

Mle's of the sphere parameters are more cumbersome to determine. The estimates $\hat{\mathbf{q}}$ and $\hat{Q}$ can be found by minimizing (25) with respect to $\mathbf{q}$ and Q.

$$\sum_{m=1}^{M} (\|\mathbf{r}_m - \mathbf{q}\| - Q)^2 \quad (25)$$

3.2.3. Cylindrical Range Points

For a cylinder, with $\mathbf{w}$ the direction of the axis, $\mathbf{q}$ a point on the axis, and Q the radius, the likelihood of a set of range points $Y = \{\mathbf{r}_m\}_{m=1}^{M}$ can be formulated also. The distance from a range point to the true cylinder axis has to be determined. This distance is given by [cf. (17)]

$$\sqrt{(\mathbf{r}_m - \mathbf{q})^t [I - \mathbf{w}\mathbf{w}^t] (\mathbf{r}_m - \mathbf{q})} = \|\mathbf{r}_m - \mathbf{q} - (\mathbf{r}_m - \mathbf{q}) \cdot \mathbf{w}\,\mathbf{w}\| . \quad (26)$$

Now the $(\|\mathbf{r}_m - \mathbf{q} - (\mathbf{r}_m - \mathbf{q}) \cdot \mathbf{w}\,\mathbf{w}\| - Q)$ are assumed to be zero-mean Gaussian and independent, yielding

$$p(Y \mid \mathbf{w}, \mathbf{q}, Q) = (\sigma^2 2\pi)^{-M/2} \exp\{-\frac{1}{2\sigma^2}\sum_{m=1}^{M} (\|\mathbf{r}_m - \mathbf{q} - (\mathbf{r}_m - \mathbf{q}) \cdot \mathbf{w}\,\mathbf{w}\| - Q)^2\}. \quad (27)$$

As with the plane, the mle's $\hat{\mathbf{w}}$, $\hat{\mathbf{q}}$, and $\hat{Q}$ of the cylinder parameters are not unique.

4. Object Position Estimation

Suppose the range data Y obtained from an object has been properly segmented into K subsets corresponding to actual planar, cylindrical, and spherical object patches. Hence $Y = \bigcup_{k=1}^{K} Y_k$ with

$Y_k = \{\mathbf{r}_{km}\}_{m=1}^{M_k}$. Assume the correspondence between the model surfaces S_{ji} and the subsets of range data is known, that is, a pairing (S_{ji}, Y_k), $k = 1,\ldots, K$ has been established.

4.1. Asymptotic Analysis

Let $\beta^t = (s, \phi, \theta, \xi, \mathbf{t}^t)$ denote a similarity transformation. The objective is to find the mle of β, i.e., the most likely transformation that maps the model surfaces onto the measured range data. Hence the likelihood

$$p(Y \mid \beta) = p(Y \mid s, \phi, \theta, \xi, \mathbf{t}) \tag{28}$$

has to be determined and maximized with respect to β. If we relabel the matched model surfaces with the labels of the corresponding range data sets, hence, S_k, $k = 1,\ldots, K$, then (28) can be written as

$$p(Y \mid \beta) = \prod_{k=1}^{K} p(Y_k \mid \beta) = \prod_{k=1}^{K} p\left(Y_k \mid \mathbf{T}_k(\beta)\right). \tag{29}$$

Here $\mathbf{T}_k(\beta)$ denotes the similarity transformation of a model surface, i.e., $\mathbf{T}_k(\beta) = [(R\,\mathbf{v}_k)^t, (sR\,\mathbf{p}_k + \mathbf{t})^t, sP_k]^t$. If β is the true similarity transformation, the transformed parameters are equal to the true geometric parameters of the sensed 3-D object surface-patch, denoted by $\alpha_k^t = (\mathbf{w}_k^t, \mathbf{q}_k^t, Q_k)$.

Now the likelihood (29) is of the form (8) which is approximately equal to (9)

$$p(Y \mid \beta) \approx \left[\prod_{k=1}^{K} p_k(Y_k \mid \hat{\alpha}_k)\right] \exp\{-(1/2) \sum_{k=1}^{K} [\mathbf{T}_k(\beta) - \hat{\alpha}_k]^t\, \Psi_k(Y_k, \hat{\alpha}_k)\, [\mathbf{T}_k(\beta) - \hat{\alpha}_k]\},$$

where $\hat{\alpha}_k = (\hat{\mathbf{w}}_k^t, \hat{\mathbf{q}}_k^t, \hat{Q}_k)$ is the mle of the geometric parameter vector of surface k. If there are no constraints among the elements of α_k, the first term is already maximized; replacing the α_k and $\hat{\alpha}_k$ by the geometric parameter vectors and maximizing $p(Y \mid \beta)$ with respect to β amounts to minimizing

$$\sum_{k=1}^{K} \begin{bmatrix} R\,\mathbf{v}_k - \hat{\mathbf{w}}_k \\ sR\,\mathbf{p}_k + \mathbf{t} - \hat{\mathbf{q}}_k \\ sP_k - \hat{Q}_k \end{bmatrix}^t \Psi(\hat{\mathbf{w}}_k, \hat{\mathbf{q}}_k, \hat{Q}_k) \begin{bmatrix} R\,\mathbf{v}_k - \hat{\mathbf{w}}_k \\ sR\,\mathbf{p}_k + \mathbf{t} - \hat{\mathbf{q}}_k \\ sP_k - \hat{Q}_k \end{bmatrix}. \tag{30}$$

Expression (30) is an important conceptual innovation. It specifies how the pieces of separately found information are to be combined to arrive at a global estimate of β, that is, not by determining the β that minimizes, e.g., $\sum_{k=1}^{K} \{\| R\,\mathbf{v}_k - \hat{\mathbf{w}}_k \|^2 + \| sR\,\mathbf{p}_k + \mathbf{t} - \hat{\mathbf{q}}_k \|^2 + (sP_k - \hat{Q}_k)^2\}$, but rather the β that minimizes (30).

In the next sections the different terms of the summation in (30) will be evaluated and interpreted.

4.2. Contribution of Planes to the Position Estimate

For the case that $Y_k = \{\mathbf{r}_{km}\}_{m=1}^{M_k}$ is planar range data with mle's of orientation and location vectors $\hat{\mathbf{w}}_k$ and $\hat{\mathbf{q}}_k = \bar{\mathbf{r}}_k$ [cf. (23)] respectively, the corresponding term in (30) is equal to (ignoring the multiplying factor $1/\sigma^2$)

$$(R\,\mathbf{v}_k - \hat{\mathbf{w}}_k)^t \left[\sum_{m=1}^{M} (\mathbf{r}_{km} - \hat{\mathbf{q}}_k)(\mathbf{r}_{km} - \hat{\mathbf{q}}_k)^t\right] (R\,\mathbf{v}_k - \hat{\mathbf{w}}_k) + M_k\, [(sR\,\mathbf{p}_k + \mathbf{t} - \hat{\mathbf{q}}_k) \cdot \hat{\mathbf{w}}_k]^2. \tag{31a}$$

However, since $\hat{\mathbf{w}}_k$ is constrained to be of length one, the likelihood of the range data [Eq. (22)] is not at a maximum and the linear term

$$\lambda\, (R\,\mathbf{v}_k - \hat{\mathbf{w}}_k)^t\, \hat{\mathbf{w}}_k \tag{31b}$$

has to be included in the expansion of (30). (Here λ is the minimum eigenvalue of the scatter matrix of the range data associated with eigenvector $\hat{\mathbf{w}}_k$.) Hence, (31) provides the appropriate weighting of the errors $R\,\mathbf{v}_k - \hat{\mathbf{w}}_k$ and $sR\,\mathbf{p}_k + \mathbf{t} - \hat{\mathbf{q}}_k$ for maximum likelihood position estimation.

Denoting the other eigenvalues of the scatter matrix by λ_1, λ_2, and the corresponding orthonormal eigenvectors by ν_1, ν_2, it is seen that

$$(R\,\mathbf{v}_k - \hat{\mathbf{w}}_k)^t \left[\sum_{m=1}^{M} (\mathbf{r}_{km} - \hat{\mathbf{q}}_k)(\mathbf{r}_{km} - \hat{\mathbf{q}}_k)^t\right] (R\,\mathbf{v}_k - \hat{\mathbf{w}}_k) = \lambda(R\,\mathbf{v}_k \cdot \hat{\mathbf{w}}_k - 1)^2 + \lambda_1(R\,\mathbf{v}_k \cdot \nu_1)^2 + \lambda_2(R\,\mathbf{v}_k \cdot \nu_2)^2.$$

Note first that the weighting increases linearly, on the average, with the number M_k of data points in the patch. Secondly, observe that errors in the direction ν_1 and ν_2 are weighted most heavily. Since range data points associated with a planar patch are apt to lie near the plane but will be distributed widely along the plane, λ_1 and λ_2 will be much larger than λ. If range data is measured on a rectangle, one of the eigenvalues will be larger ($\lambda_1 > \lambda_2$) and the error in the estimated normal will be smallest in the direction of the larger side of the true planar patch. This is illustrated in Fig. 1. The error in the second term of (31) is also weighted by the number M_k of data points used. More interesting, however, this term shows that only the component of error in the

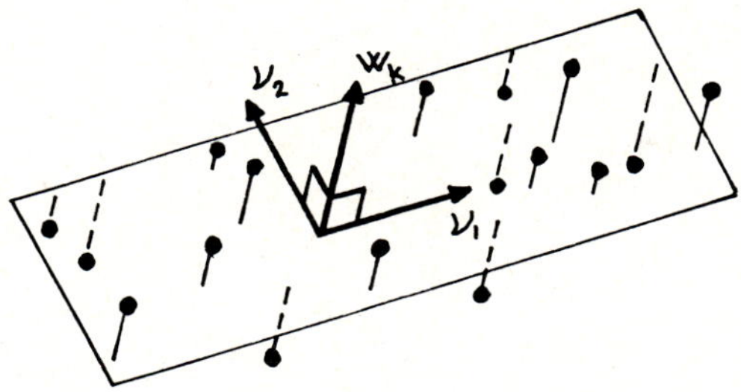

Figure 1: Range data on planar patch; the points are offset from the plane.

direction of $\hat{\mathbf{w}}_k$ is being considered since the error appears only in an inner product with $\hat{\mathbf{w}}_k$. That is, in (31) only the component of $sR\,\mathbf{p}_k + \mathbf{t}$ in the direction of $\hat{\mathbf{w}}_k$ is being considered, and other directions remain unaffected, reflecting the fact that translation of the plane in those other directions cannot be estimated.

4.3. Contribution of Spheres to the Position Estimate

Let $Y_k = \{\mathbf{r}_{km}\}_{m=1}^{M_k}$ be spherical range data in this section. Denote the mle of the geometric parameters, obtained by maximizing (24), by $\hat{\mathbf{q}}_k$ and $\hat{Q}_k$. The center is given by $\mathbf{q}_k = sR\,\mathbf{p}_k + \mathbf{t}$ and the radius by $Q_k = sP_k$. Then the contribution to (30) is given by

$$(sR\,\mathbf{p}_k + \mathbf{t} - \hat{\mathbf{q}}_k)^t \Big[\sum_{m=1}^{M} \Big(1 - \frac{\hat{Q}_k}{\| \mathbf{r}_{km} - \hat{\mathbf{q}}_k \|}\Big) I + \hat{Q}_k \frac{(\mathbf{r}_{km} - \hat{\mathbf{q}}_k)(\mathbf{r}_{km} - \hat{\mathbf{q}}_k)^t}{\| \mathbf{r}_{km} - \hat{\mathbf{q}}_k \|^3} \Big] (sR\,\mathbf{p}_k + \mathbf{t} - \hat{\mathbf{q}}_k)$$
$$+ M_k (sP_k - \hat{Q}_k)^2 + 2\,(sP_k - \hat{Q}_k) \Big[\sum_{m=1}^{M} (\mathbf{r}_{km} - \hat{\mathbf{q}}_k)^t / \| \mathbf{r}_{km} - \hat{\mathbf{q}}_k \| \Big] (sR\,\mathbf{p}_k + \mathbf{t} - \hat{\mathbf{q}}_k). \quad (32)$$

In interpreting the components of (32), we shall see that they can be positive or negative. However, since (32) is the negative of a quadric approximation to a function at its maximum, (32) will always be nonnegative. Consider the first line of (32). It can be shown that $\sum_{m=1}^{M} (1 - \hat{Q}_k / \| \mathbf{r}_{km} - \hat{\mathbf{q}}_k \|)$ is nonpositive, with equality iff $\| \mathbf{r}_{km} - \hat{\mathbf{q}}_k \| = \hat{Q}_k$ for all $m = 1,\ldots, M_k$ [3]. The sum is a decreasing function of the variance of $\| \mathbf{r}_{km} - \hat{\mathbf{q}}_k \|$. Hence, the larger this variance, the more unreliable the system considers $\hat{\mathbf{q}}_k$ and the less is the contribution of the error $sR\,\mathbf{p}_k + \mathbf{t} - \hat{\mathbf{q}}_k$ to (30). Consider the second term of the first line

$$\sum_{m=1}^{M} \frac{\hat{Q}_k}{\| \mathbf{r}_{km} - \hat{\mathbf{q}}_k \|} (sR\,\mathbf{p}_k + \mathbf{t} - \hat{\mathbf{q}}_k)^t \frac{(\mathbf{r}_{km} - \hat{\mathbf{q}}_k)}{\| \mathbf{r}_{km} - \hat{\mathbf{q}}_k \|} \frac{(\mathbf{r}_{km} - \hat{\mathbf{q}}_k)^t}{\| \mathbf{r}_{km} - \hat{\mathbf{q}}_k \|} (sR\,\mathbf{p}_k + \mathbf{t} - \hat{\mathbf{q}}_k). \quad (33)$$

Since $(\mathbf{r}_{km} - \hat{\mathbf{q}}_k)/ \| \mathbf{r}_{km} - \hat{\mathbf{q}}_k \|$ is a unit vector, a summand in (33) is $\hat{Q}_k / \| \mathbf{r}_{km} - \hat{\mathbf{q}}_k \|$ times the square of the component of the error $sR\,\mathbf{p}_k + \mathbf{t} - \hat{\mathbf{q}}_k$ in the direction of $\mathbf{r}_{km} - \mathbf{q}_k$. Now, if the $\mathbf{r}_{km}$ are distributed uniformly along the entire sphere, all components of the error vector are weighted equally. But if the data is present in only a small patch on the sphere surface as in Fig. 2, then the $\mathbf{r}_{km} - \hat{\mathbf{q}}_k$ point largely from the sphere center to the patch, and it is only the error component in this direction that contributes to (30). The error weighting is proportional to the number M_k of range data points on the sphere.

The contribution $M_k (sP_k - \hat{Q}_k)^2$ is self explanatory.

The cross term of (32),

$$2\,(sP_k - \hat{Q}_k) \Big[\sum_{m=1}^{M} (\mathbf{r}_{km} - \hat{\mathbf{q}}_k)^t / \| \mathbf{r}_{km} - \hat{\mathbf{q}}_k \| \Big] (sR\,\mathbf{p}_k + \mathbf{t} - \hat{\mathbf{q}}_k), \quad (34)$$

can be thought of as a measure of the consistency of the two errors $sP_k - \hat{Q}_k$ and $sR\,\mathbf{p}_k + \mathbf{t} - \hat{\mathbf{q}}_k$. To see this, assume that the data $\mathbf{r}_{km}$ constitutes a small patch so that the $\mathbf{r}_{km} - \hat{\mathbf{q}}_k$ all have roughly the same direction. Note that $[(\mathbf{r}_{km} - \hat{\mathbf{q}}_k)/ \| \mathbf{r}_{km} - \hat{\mathbf{q}}_k \|](sR\,\mathbf{p}_k + \mathbf{t} - \hat{\mathbf{q}}_k)$ is the component of the error $sR\,\mathbf{p}_k + \mathbf{t} - \hat{\mathbf{q}}_k$ in the

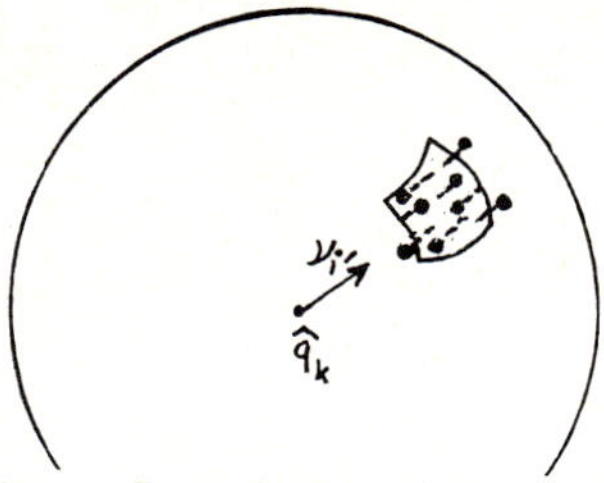

Figure 2: Range data on spherical patch.

direction of $\mathbf{r}_{km}$ from $\hat{\mathbf{q}}_k$. Hence, (34) is roughly the transformed sphere location error $sR\,\mathbf{p}_k + \mathbf{t} - \hat{\mathbf{q}}_k$ in the direction $\mathbf{r}_{km} - \hat{\mathbf{q}}_k$ multiplied by M_k times the error $sP_k - \hat{Q}_k$. If both errors are positive, the transformed model radius sP_k is larger than $\hat{Q}_k$ and the transformed location vector $sR\,\mathbf{p}_k + \mathbf{t}$ is closer to the data than is $\hat{\mathbf{q}}_k$. These are inconsistent errors, and estimates of the transformation parameters should try to reduce both these errors. Other combinations of the signs of these errors have similar effects.

4.4. Contribution of Cylinders to the Position Estimate

Modeling cylindrical range data results in a complex mechanism for weighting the various mle's of the geometric parameters of a cylinder; details can be found in [3].

4.5. Experimental Results

A number of experiments are performed on objects formed by planar patches, (31b) is not included in the position estimator. Insight can be gained by studying orientation and location estimation-performance based on artificially generated range data for a cube. A picture of the cube and the surfaces forming the cube are given in Fig. 3.

As a first example, the effect of the number of range points on the location estimate is examined. (The number of range points generated on the various planar patches for this experiment is listed in the last column of the table in Fig. 3.) In Fig. 4 the estimated position of the cube is given for the case of zero variance of the signed distance from the range points to the planes. When the range points exhibit a perpendicular variance with respect to the surfaces, the effect of the number of measured range points becomes apparent. Remember from Sect. 3.1.1 that a planar patch determines only the component of the object's translation in the direction of its normal. Hence the translation of the cube in the direction of the normals of the planes 1 and 4, $(1,0,0)^t$, is estimated least accurately. This is clearly reflected in the estimate of the translation of the cube in Fig. 4. The estimated Euler angles are more difficult to interpret. A rotation of an object by the Euler angles 180, 180, 180 amounts to no rotation.

The accuracy with which the normals to the planes, and hence the orientation of the cube, can be determined depends largely on the spread of the measured range points over the planar patches. This is shown in the

PLANE	Orientation vector	Location vector	Number of range points
1	$(1,0,0)^t$	$(10,0,0)^t$	10
2	$(0,1,0)^t$	$(0,10,0)^t$	100
3	$(0,0,1)^t$	$(0,0,10)^t$	1000
4	$(-1,0,0)^t$	$(-10,0,0)^t$	10
5	$(0,-1,0)^t$	$(0,-10,0)^t$	100
6	$(0,0,-1)^t$	$(0,0,-10)^t$	1000

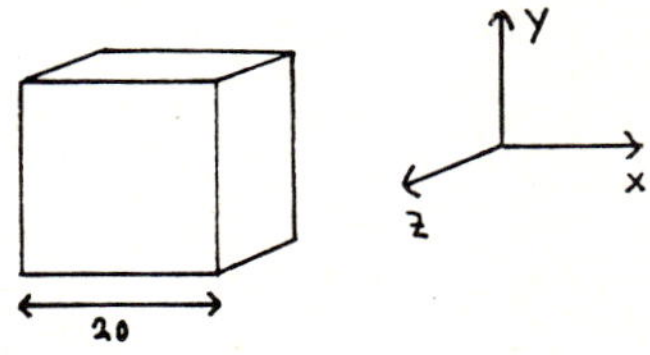

Figure 3: Planar surfaces forming a cube.

experiments listed in the table of Fig. 5. Here on each of the six surfaces forming the cube a hundred range points, with variance of the perpendicular distance $\sigma^2 = 1$, are generated. In the first experiment a cube of side 10 is chosen, while for the second experiment the side is selected to be 20. The range points are generated randomly over each of the planar patches. Notice the increased accuracy of the cube's orientation estimate and the similar accuracy of the location estimate for both experiments.

In Fig. 6 a more interesting object composed of planar patches is shown, an approximation to a telephone receiver. The visible planar surfaces are given in the table of Fig. 7. A number of experiments using generated range data of different perpendicular variance are performed. In contrast to the above experiments, however, the range data for a particular patch is *not* generated such that its expected center is the location vector of the planar surface. Instead, for each planar surface a square 4×4 patch, small compared with the surface, is used.

Experiments Cube	Scale fac. s	Euler angles ϕ, θ, ξ	Trans. vector $\mathbf{t}$	St. dev. σ
Given	1	0, 0, 0	$(10,20,30)^t$	0
Estimated	1.0	0.0, 0.0, 0.0	$(10.0,20.0,30.0)^t$	
Given	1	0, 0, 0	$(10,20,30)^t$	1
Estimated	0.993	187.24, 179.49, 177.67	$(9.33,20.08,29.98)^t$	

Figure 4: Location estimation results of the cube.

Experiments Cube	Scale fac. s	Euler angles ϕ, θ, ξ	Trans. vector $\mathbf{t}$	St. dev. σ
Given	1	20, 40, 60	$(0,0,0)^t$	1
Estimated	.9967	23.70, 40.10, 58.75	$(-.085,.088,.125)^t$	
Given	1	20, 40, 60	$(0,0,0)^t$	1
Estimated	0.9975	21.65, 40.05, 59.44	$(-.081,.082,.143)^t$	

Figure 5: Orientation estimation results of the cube.

The patch center is offset from the location vector listed in the model. All the offset vectors are chosen to be of 3.5 units length. Range data is generated at 50 locations randomly chosen in such a patch on each of the seven visible surfaces in Figure 6. Figure 8 lists the estimation results. The estimates are obtained from only 350

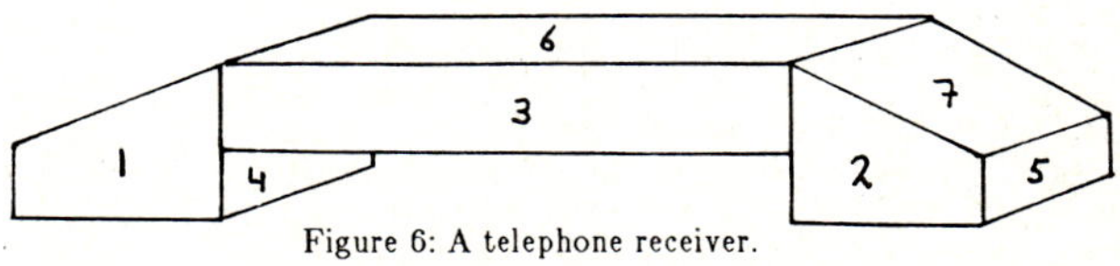

Figure 6: A telephone receiver.

PLANE	Orientation vector	Location vector
1	$(0,0,1)^t$	$(-32.5,0,5)^t$
2	$(0,0,1)^t$	$(32.5,0,5)^t$
3	$(0,0,1)^t$	$(0,2.5,5)^t$
4	$(1,0,0)^t$	$(-15,0,5)^t$
5	$(1,0,0)^t$	$(20,-2.5,0)^t$
6	$(0,1,0)^t$	$(0,5,0)^t$
7	$(1,1,0)^t$	$(32.5,2.5,0)^t$

Figure 7: Planar surfaces forming the telephone receiver.

Experiments Receiver	Scale fac. s	Euler angles ϕ, θ, ξ	Trans. vector $\mathbf{t}$	St. dev. σ
Given	1	10, 20, 30	$(40,50,60)^t$	1
Estimated	.9411	6.81, 20.12, 40.12	$(36.73,49.76,60.72)^t$	
Given	1	10, 20, 30	$(40,50,60)^t$	.5
Estimated	1.0105	11.05, 20.21, 28.61	$(39.41,50.11,60.04)^t$	
Given	1	10, 20, 30	$(40,50,60)^t$	.125
Estimated	1.0014	10.20, 20.06, 29.35	$(39.90,50.00,60.01)^t$	

Figure 8: Position estimation results of the telephone receiver.

range points; better estimation results are obtained when the the variance of the range noise is smaller. The system is able to integrate poor individual estimates for the various planar patches to arrive at considerably better overall complex object position estimates. When the standard deviation of the range noise is zero, perfect estimations are obtained.

5. Incorporating 3-D Edge Information

The approach taken in this paper lends itself to incorporate the contribution of 3-D edge information to the overall 3-D complex object position estimate. This is the case for detected line segments and circular arc segments in the range data, since, similarly to the quadric 3-D surfaces, these 3-D curves may be specified in terms of geometric parameters. Hence, in addition to the surfaces listed in Sect. 3.1.4, N_4 linear edges and N_5 circular edges may be specified in the object model, and they transform in the same way as the surface parameters:

(1) Lines: $C_{4i} = (\mathbf{v}_{4i}, \mathbf{p}_{4i}, 0)$, i = 1, 2,..., N_4. Here $\mathbf{v}_{4i}$ is a unit vector in the direction of line segment i and $\mathbf{p}_{4i}$ is a point on this line.

(2) Circles: $C_{5i} = (\mathbf{v}_{5i}, \mathbf{p}_{5i}, P_{5i})$, i = 1, 2,..., N_5. For a particular circular arc i, $\mathbf{v}_{5i}$ is the direction unit vector perpendicular to the circle, $\mathbf{p}_{5i}$ is its center point, and P_{5i} is its radius.

Now it is possible to formulate likelihood functions underlying the generation of boundary range points in three-space. A noise mechanism similar to that discussed in Sect. 3.2 can be employed, that is, the signed distance from detected edge data points to the 3-D curve may be modeled as a zero-mean iid Gaussian one-dimensional random sequence [3]. Asymptotic analysis naturally provides us with the appropriate weighting matrices for the various pieces of information -- even though these pieces of information are fundamentally different from the information about 3-D surfaces. An extensive treatment of considerations when incorporating edge information is given in [3].

6. Conclusions

(1) It is shown that for an important fairly general class of large data-set parameter estimation problems, roughly maximum likelihood or Bayesian estimates of global parameters can be computed by processing relatively small subsets of data individually and in parallel, and then combining the locally extracted information in a computationally simple way. The specific example treated is the estimation of the position of a complex object in three-space using range data. Roughly "optimal" combining of the locally derived estimates to obtain roughly "optimal" estimates of global parameters involves weighting with matrices the interaction of the locally derived pieces of information. These weighting matrices are derived and are shown to have great intuitive meaning in most cases. Bayesian primitive object recognition based on a local patch of data is possible (Sect. 2.0-2.1 and [2]).

(2) The approach described is capable of obtaining highly accurate global parameter estimates even if the local parameter estimates used in this approach are poor and contribute only partial information to the global parameters.

(3) It is not necessary that the local estimates be maximum likelihood. Other estimates, for example, more easily computed least squares estimates [5] may be employed. If these local estimates are biased, our basic approximation (9) can be modified to include an appropriate mean other than $\hat{\alpha}_M$. The appropriate mean arises automatically by including a linear term in the Taylor expansion used to obtain (9).

(4) With the framework presented in this paper, it is possible to combine both local 3-D surface parameter estimates and 3-D boundary parameter estimates to obtain the complex object position estimate.

(5) With the techniques described in Sect. 2, it is possible to decide what the appropriate size of the subproblems should be (i.e., the surface patch size for the object positioning problem).

(6) The weighting matrices appearing in the combining and weighting of pieces of information may suggest appropriate heuristics for combining locally derived information in nonprobabilistic estimation schemes.

(7) The techniques discussed in this paper apply not only to object position estimation, but also to other estimation problems that can be decomposed into subproblems. These can be both 2-D and 3-D problems, as well as estimation problems involving entirely different types of data and applications.

(8) Various important modeling and computational subtleties are discussed in [3]. For example, it seems that greatest estimation accuracy will roughly occur for $\mathbf{p}_k$ chosen to be the centroid of the associated surface patch, and for the stored reference model to have its centroid at the origin of the world coordinate system used.

Acknowledgement

This work was partially supported by Army Research Office Grant DAAG-29-81-K-0167, National Science Foundation Grant ECS-81-19676, and the IBM Corporation.

References

[1] R.M. Bolle, *Information Extraction About Complex Three-Dimensional Objects From Visual Data*, Brown University Ph. D. thesis, May 1984.

[2] R.M. Bolle and D.B. Cooper, "Bayesian Recognition of Local 3-D Shape by Approximating Image Intensity Functions with Quadric Polynomials," *IEEE Trans. on Pattern Analysis and Machine Intelligence*, Vol. 6, No. 5, July 1984, pp. 418-429.

[3] R.M. Bolle and D.B. Cooper, *On Optimally Combining Pieces of Information, with Application to Estimating 3-D Complex-Object Position from Range Data*, Brown University Technical Report #LEMS-8, February 1985, (under review for journal publication).

[4] R.C. Bolles, P. Horaud, and M.J. Hannah, "3DPO: A Three-Dimensional Part Orientation System," *Proc. of the 8th International Joint Conference on Artificial Intelligence*, IJCAI-83, August 1983, Karlsruhe, West Germany, pp. 1116-1120.

[5] B. Cernuschi-Frias, *Orientation and Location Parameter Estimation of Quadric Surfaces in 3-D Space from a Sequence of Images*, Brown University Ph. D. thesis, May 1984.

[6] D.B. Cooper, "When Should a Learning Machine Ask for Help?," *IEEE Trans. on Information Theory*, Vol. 12, No. 4, July 1974, pp. 455-471.

[7] O.D. Faugeras and M. Hebert, " A 3-D Recognition and Positioning Algorithm Using Geometrical Matching Between Primitive Surfaces," *Proc. of the 8th International Joint Conference on Artificial Intelligence*, IJCAI-83, August 1983, Karlsruhe, West Germany, pp. 996-1002.

[8] G.A. Korn and T.M. Korn, *Mathematical Handbook for Scientists and Engineers*, McGraw-Hill, New York, 1961.

[9] D.V. Lindley, " The Use of Prior Probability Distributions in Statistical Inference and Decisions," *Proc. Fourth Berkeley Symposium on Mathematical Statistics and Probability*, Vol. 12, July 1961, pp. 453-468.

[10] M. Oshima and Y. Shirai, "Object Recognition Using Three-Dimensional Information," *IEEE Trans. on Pattern Analysis and Machine Intelligence*, Vol. 3, No. 4, July 1983, pp. 353-361.

PATTERN RECOGNITION IN PRACTICE II
E.S. Gelsema and L.N. Kanal (Editors)
Elsevier Science Publishers B.V. (North-Holland), 1986

3D RECONSTRUCTION OF SPATIO-TEMPORAL SERIES OF OPTICAL PICTURES

Tsuguchika Kaminuma, Reiko Minamikawa and Isamu Suzuki

Tokyo Metropolitan Institute of Medical Science
Bunkyo-ku, Tokyo, 113
JAPAN

An interesting extension of present pattern recognition and image processing technologies is to apply them to spatio-temporal series of images. A project is ongoing to develop hardware and software to study three dimensional images in biomedicine. The primary goal is to support embryogenesis study of nematodes. The system has been developed on VAX 11/750 and PDP 11/70 . Currently two dimensional optical dissect images are analized interactively, and reconstructed into three dimensional cellular images.

INTRODUCTION

Technologies of pattern recognition and picture processing have been well developed. Various algorithms have successfully been applied to many practical problems. The performance to cost ratio of computers and image processing peripherals is greatly improved. However very few studies have been carried out for processing moving three dimensional objects. This paper reports state-of-the-art of our ongoing project on this topic.

Generally,pattern recognition or picture processing of three dimensional moving objects are very difficult. Therefore it is crucial to choose an appropriate problem domain, which is not too difficult yet has some practical value. We chose our problem as reconstruction of three dimensional images from series of two dimensional dissect images.

Reconstruction consists of two parts, image analysis and image synthesis. It is interesting to note that these two methodologies of picture processing have been developed rather independently. Image analysis has been considered as pattern recognition, and image syntesis as computer graphics. In our study these two methodologies have been used complementary.

COMPUTER HARDWARE

The system which will be described in the following pages is part of a larger system called MINERVA. The MINERVA system is an integrated biomedical research computing system developed by the authors at the TOKYO Metropolitan Institute of Medical Science (TIMS) since 1976.

MINERVA consists of such general program package as statistics, pattern recognition, interactive signal and image analysis, the so called molecular graphics, protein and nucleic acid structural data retrieval, communication. It also consists of a real time experiment support system called CERS. The CERS (C. elegans Research Support) system has designed for developmental biology research using a nematode , C. elegans.

Figure 1 shows the essential hardware organization of MINERVA. It consists of a VAX 11/750 and a PDP 11/70, two image displays, NAC and AED 512, and other peripherals. Since some features of the general system were described elsewhere[1,2] we shall only explain the additional hardwares.

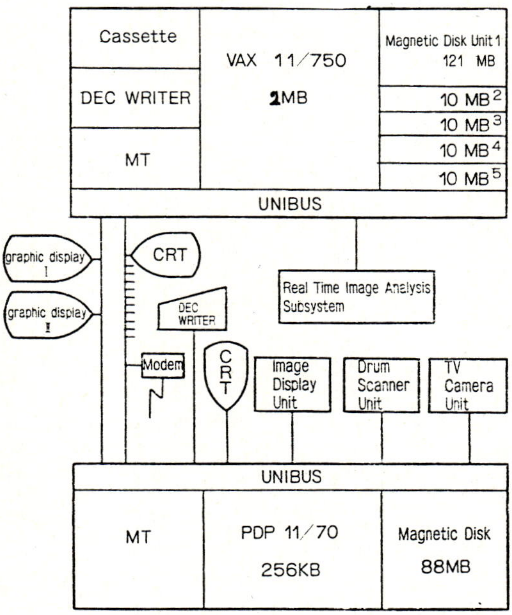

Figure 1

Hardware Organization of MINERVA

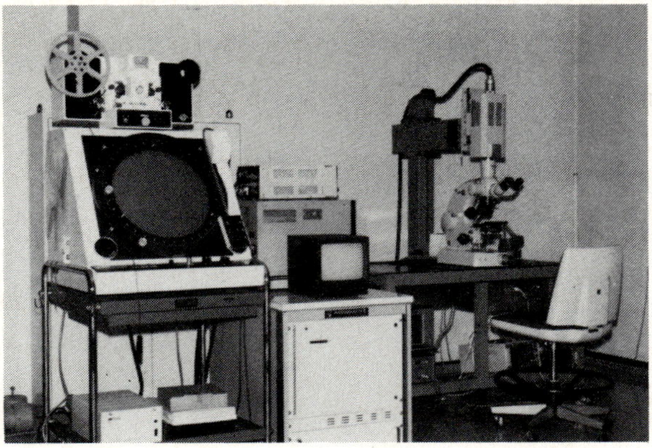

Figure 2
Normarski Microscope and Movie Film Digitizer

Figure 2 shows a computer-controlled microscope and a movie film digitizer. The film digitizer has a A/D conversion interface, which transmit one picture frame digital data to VAX storage disks by DMA mode within a second. The x, y, and z coordinates of the microscope stage are controlled by an interface unit of the VAX . The stage controller can communicate with the image input units, which is either 16mm movie camera shutter or the TV camera control unit. Thus stage control and image recording are synchronized by VAX program commands.

PICTURE MANAGEMENT SYSTEM

A picture management system called ALBUM was developed over the general system in order to handle large number of pictures efficiently. The ALBUM program manages a set of pictures, which have some attributes. These attributes may include extracted feature parameters, process history, or relation to other pictures . The ALBUM program has the data structure called ALBUM. ALBUM is an ordered set of Pages. A Page consists of a picture data and a description table. A description table consists of several columns (descriptions), and each column consists of vectors, character and symbol strings , and their countable combinations.

With ALBUM, one can easily create new elements by applying some operation (or a series of operations) to a picture. One can also apply some operation to a set of elements. The latter may be a series of pictures with respect to time or space. One can also create new relations among a set of pictures very easily. The ALBUM program thus enables flexible application of series of operations to (a series of) pictures.

Table 1 illustrates the command system of ALBUM. The ALBUM program has interface not only to other picture processing modules but also to statistical or pattern recognition packages. The ALBUM greatly improved flexibility and efficiency of our previous pattern analysis and picture processing system.

Table 1. ALBUM command

(1) Album data management command	A_SHOW	Printing the contents of album
	A_DIRECTORY	Listing the album directory
	A_CLMS	Reference/updating the description data
	A_Display	displaying picture data
(2) Display/Graphics command	A_ATOM	converting the structure data for graphics
(3) Application/User written command	A_INCEL	Interactive nucleus position editing
		Image processing modules
(4) Image aquisition command	A_XTVIN	data aquisiton program
(5) Image/Album system command	A_SYMBOL A_LOGICAL A_FILELIST A_CAMERA	System maintenance programs
(6) HELP	IMAGE	General help facility

IMAGE ANALYSIS AND DISPLAY PROGRAMS

Since the general purpose image analysis programs of our system are explained in the previous paper[1] , we only introduce an interactive cell image input program here. This program,called INCEL, enables the "scanner " to identify and register the nuclei positions of a cell shown on the (NAC) display screen.

Table 2 illustrates some display commands for this purpose. There are two basic display modes, the single static mode and the window dynamic mode. The latter displays dynamic images embedded in the window area of a single static picture.

Table 2. Display Command

PAGE	Set range of pages to be displayed
AOI	Set area of interest
DISPLAY	Display (one picture/continuously)
FOCUS	Dynamic display of AOI

Table 3 shows the commands that help the scanner to identify and store the nuclei positions.

Table 3. Analysis Command

LOAD	Load picture
NUCLEUS	Define nucleus position and name
POLAR	Define polar position
CONTOR	Define contour
RELOAD	Refer the picture and the nucleus the polar position and the contour
STATUS	Show status of analysis

In order to display cell nuclei, we use the molecular graphic program, which have been developed separately. Cells are more distorted than spherical shape atoms. Moreover cell division process is difficult to represent by a molecular image. Therefore molecular graphics is not identical to cellular graphics .

APPLICATION

PURPOSE

Our computer system has been developed in parallel with our developmental biological study of nematodes. We have used Caenorahabditis elegans (C. elegans) mainly,but also used Aphelenchoides composticola. We can observe these nematode from zygot to newly hatched larva under Nomarski optics. The whole embryogenesis takes 11 to 12 hours for C. elegans at 21℃. The embryonic development is approximately ten times slower for Aphelenchoides composticola. For the first falf period of embryonic development, there is no whole body (coordinated) movement. Thus we can record this process by either TV camera or movie camera attached to the microscope. In this period cells not only divide,but also migrate from one position to another. Biologically it is interesting to determine three dimensional cell (nucleus) positions in time. This data also allows us to elucidate positions and timing of cell divisions and to determine cell lineages.

J. Sulston et al succeeded in determining the entire cell lineage of C. elegans[3]. Their study completed a long research project, which had been carried out by a group of MRC Laboratory of Molecular Biology at Cambridge, and by a group of Max -Plank Institute group at Göttingen directed by late G. von Ehrenstein. The latter had used computer and video recorder for recording, analyzing, and displaying celluar imagesHowever their work was terminated before completing their final goal.

Our methodology are different from the formers in the following two points. First,we have used 16mm film which has better resolution than video recorder, though we are considering to use TV camera for real time image analysis in the next stage. Second, we are interested in developing "a general system" ,rather than an ad hoc system for C. elegans studies.

METHOD

Optical dissect images of nematodes eggs (zygots) are recorded as serial pictures on 16mm movie films. The eggs, whose width is approximatly 50μ are scanned up and down every minute. Forty shots are recorded one way, so that there produced 80 z-axis serial pictures at each minute.

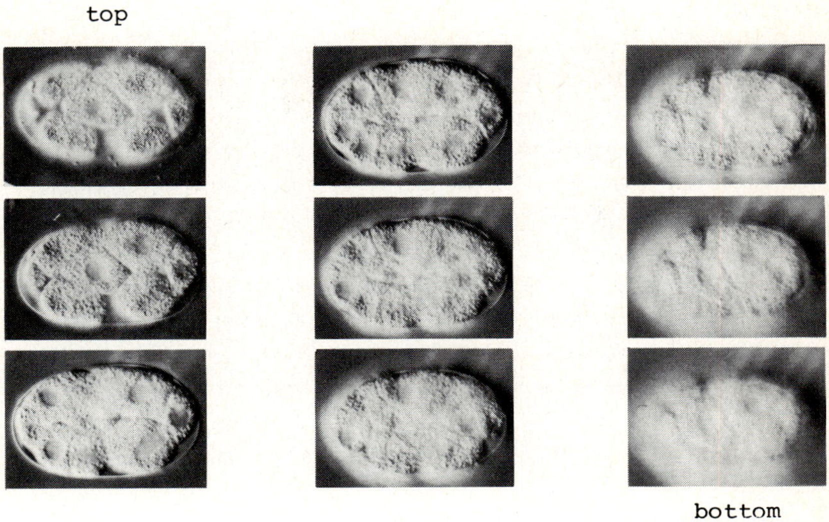

Figure 3
Series of Optical Disect Images

Figure 3 shows different sectional images of a 12-14 cell stage egg. When mounted on an agar plate, eggs can take only two opposite orientations. Moreover the mode of division is invariant. Therefore it is not so difficult to compare or even "match " images of different eggs.

Already up to 7 hours films are recorded for C. elegans and 32 hours recordings were tried for Aphelenchoides compositicola. These films are first examined on film digitizer screen. Each frame is digitized into a 512 x 480 8 bit matrix and stored in the PDP or VAX disks.

The program INCEL is used to identify nuclei positions interactively on the display by the scanner. At this operation such information as the identification of the frame, the scanner name are also stored in ALBUM file. Figure 4 shows this operation, in that the polar body of the egg is marked by x. The polar body is a good indicator which tells the anterior-posterior orientation of the egg. Three dimensional nuclei coordinates are determined from a series of two dimensional nuclei positions.

The dynamical display mode was used to help identifing vague nucleus images. Because of the limitation of DMA capacity, this display mode is only applicable to "window" area embedded in the entire display screen. Within this limited window area, images that belong to different z-axis are circularly displayed in repeated manner. So the resultant image is dynamic as if we are looking at moving object. See Figure 5. This mode of display greatly amplifies human image perception.

Figure 6 shows a display of reconstructed nuclei. It is a three dimensional view of aggregate of nuclear balls. It is possible to assign different colors to different types of nuclei. This help us to study developmental anatomy of the embryo. In Figure 6 two sister cells from same mother cells are paired by rods.

RESULT

A feasibility study of our method was carried out with J. Sulston, who stayed with us a few weeks in March 1984. The dynamical display mode is a product of our collaborative work. We shall briefly summarize tentative findings.

(1) With the current method we may identify all nuclei positions and cell lineage up to 200-300 cell stages.
(2) In order to refine analysis, the data input speed must be increased. For that picture input mechanism must be speeded up.
(3) In displaying aggregate of nuclei, we adapted our molecular graphic program. In the cellular representation not all balls nuclei are connected, and this representation gives very "plane" visual impression. Improvements are needed for displaying unconnected ball type objects stereographically.

CONCLUSION

A computer system which reconstructs three dimensional images from series of two dimensional optical dessect images was described. The system has been applied to embryogenesis study of nematodes. Optical images under Nomarski differential interference microscope were recorded as serial pictures either by 16mm movie camera or TV camera. Cell nuclei are identified interactively using image displays. Preliminary experiments suggest that our method is useful for the above application.

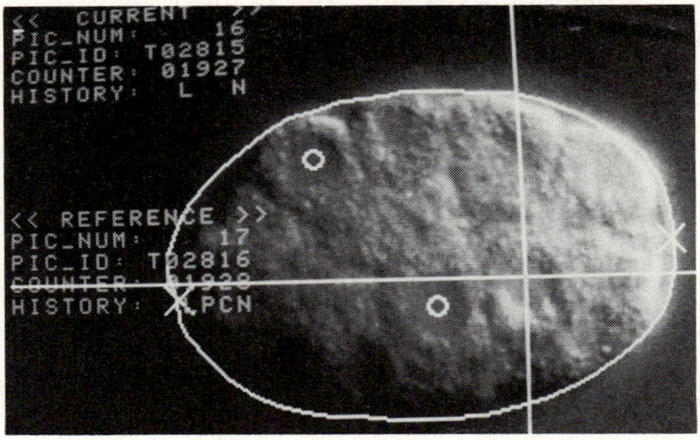

Figure 4
Interactive Nuclei Identification

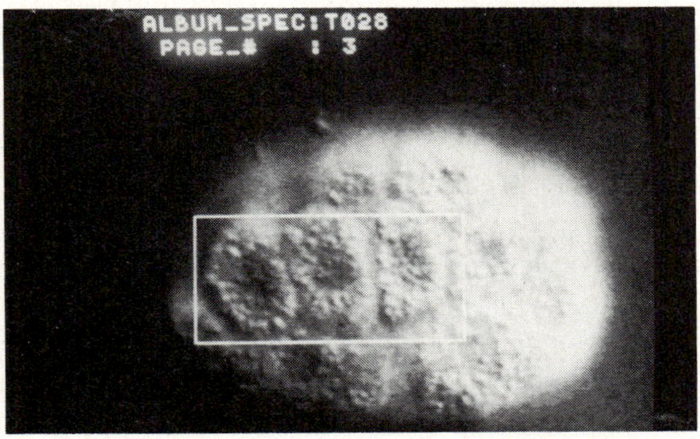

Figure 5
Dynamic Display Mode

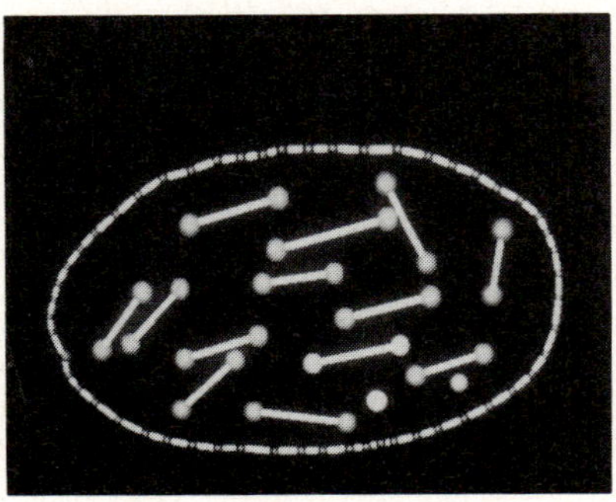

Figure 6
Reconstructed Nuclei Graphics

Two future goals are under consideration. One is to semi-automatize the nuclei identification process. Due to limitation of optical resolution full automatization of this process seems impossible. Another goal is to implement specialist of seeing into computer. Powerful human perception may partly be supported by "hypothesis-driven " judgemental process. The so called knowledge-based approach seems useful for this purpose.

Though the current system have specially be designed for developmental study of nematode, our system is of general character.

ACKNOWLEDGEMENT

The authors greatly thank to Drs. J. Miwa and Y.Tabuse (now at The Basic Research Lab. of NEC) and E. Hedgecock (now at Roshe Co.) who kindly gave us worms and trained us basic handling and observation of C.dlegans. They also thank to Dr. J. Sulston at MRC laboratory of Molecular Biology who explained us human expertise of visual perception, and who also gave useful suggestions to computerized embryogenesis. Our thanks are also to Mr. Masumoto, Msses. N.Kosaka and M.Fujita for their laboratory works.

REFERENCES

1. Kaminuma,T. and Suzuki,I., Experience with an interactive pattern analysis system for medical applications, (in Patter Recognition in Practice,Gelsema, E.S. and Kanal, L. N. eds.), North-Hollands Pub. Co., p.259, (1980)
2. Kaminuma, T. and Suzuki, I., Computer imaging as a creative tool for medical researchers, Proc. ISMIII' 82, IEEE Computer Society, p.542, (1982)
3. Sulston,J.E., et al, The embryonic cell lineage of the nematode Caenorhabditis elegans, Developmental Biology, vol.100, pp64-119, (1983)
4. Kimmel, C.B., Personal Communication

DISCUSSION

Ledley:
What is the magnification of the object-lens of the microscope?

Minamikawa:
The object-lens magnifies 100 *, the ocular 10 *. There is an additional magnification of 1.25 in the system so that the total magnification is 1250.

Mayall:
I think the most important question is "what is the numerical aperture of the objective", not the magnification. The depth of focus of the optical sections depends on the numerical aperture of the objective. This allows you to make the slices through the organism. I think I missed it, but what is the distance between each of the 40 sections you are looking at?

Minamikawa:
Each step is about one micron.

PATTERN RECOGNITION IN PRACTICE II
E.S. Gelsema and L.N. Kanal (Editors)
Elsevier Science Publishers B.V. (North-Holland), 1986

ANALYSIS OF HISTOLOGICAL SERIAL SECTIONS

W. Abmayr and U. Heinzmann

Gesellschaft für Strahlen- und Umweltforschung m.b.H,
München,
Institut für Strahlenschutz und
Abteilung fuer Nuklearbiologie,
8042 Neuherberg, Ingolstädter Landstrasse 1, FRG

Anatomical alterations in the brain ventricular system of NMRI mice following irradiation during late organogenesis (12 GT) were investigated using computerised 3D reconstruction of histological sections. The brains were fixed and embedded in paraffin, and serial sections were cut and stained. Sections were matched interactively, digitized using a TV camera and stored in a computer for 3D analysis. The whole brain area and different ventricular areas were measured in each section. Segmentation of the ventricles was controlled interactively using a data tablet. The mouse brain was reconstructed in three dimensions and shown as a surface display with different viewing angles and illumination positions. Different ventricular parts were shown separately.

INTRODUCTION

Several quantitative methods based on stereological principles have been developed for the analysis of histological serial sections. The basic aim is to obtain information on three dimensional morphological structure [21]. This type of analysis poses considerable problems, since the stereological prerequisite of random sectioning is not satisfied when serial tissue sections are analysed. An astronomical amount of information is potentially contained in each 3D image. The 3D reconstruction of objects is an interesting method for morphology since it is difficult to envisage a complete structure from serial section images only. Although the shape of anatomical structures can be seen in each section the structures may change from section to section. Various methods have been employed for physical 3D reconstruction but all have severe limitations allowing, for example, only surface views, selected interior views or limited direction viewing [11, 16]. The reconstruction can be done easily using a computer system. This has the considerable advantage that methods of display, viewing direction, interior views etc. can be selected more or less at will.

Several kinds of display technique have been developed for visualizing 3D images using 2D display monitors. The techniques can be classified in the following categories:

- Cross section display: An arbitrarily oriented cross section through the 3D image is reproduced [18],
- Contour display: After extraction of the boundary of the specified object only the contours are displayed [15],
- Shaded surface display: The surface of the object is generated from the contour lines. The display techniques provide depth cues by selected shading and removal of hidden surfaces [4,19].
- Volume display: A mixture of stereo display and semi - transparent viewing [23].

The aim of the study described here was to demonstrate morphological alterations in the brain ventricular system of NMRI mice following x-irradiation during late organogenesis (12 GT). Our research interests are concerned mainly with the volume of the brains, their different ventricles and the visual assessment of special ventricular shapes. We used shaded surface display on a raster graphics device to generate 3D images of the different brain parts.

MATERIAL AND METHODS

Preparation:

Brains were taken from one untreated NMRI mouse and one mouse x-irradiated during late organogenesis. The brains were fixed by perfusion with buffered glutaraldehyde, dehydrated, and embedded in paraffin. 6 µm serial sections were cut and stained with haematoxylin - eosin. On average 800 sections were taken from each brain. Every 8th section was used for the analysis. Sections were visualized with a Leitz Orthoplane microscope using a 1x objective and a 2x ocular magnification and a revolving stage. The macroscopic appearance of the two brains is shown in Fig. 1.

Data Aquisition:

Scanning was performed with a TV- chalnicon camera C1000 (Hamamatsu TV Co. Ltd, Japan). The sections were scanned with 512 x 512 spatial resolution. The scanned data were transferred to a VICOM system (VICOM Inc., San Jose, USA), interfaced with a VAX 11/750 computer (Digital Equipment Corp., Maynard, USA). A graphic tablet connected with the VICOM system was used for segmentation.

The layout of the hardware system for data aquisition, interactive manipulation and processing of serial section images is shown in Fig. 2.

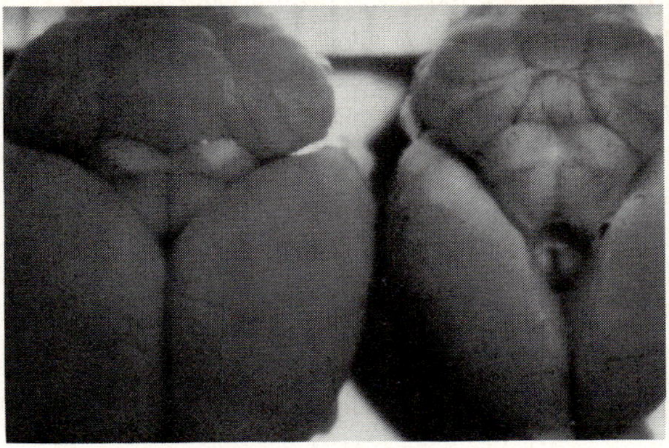

Figure 1
Macroscopic image of mice brains:
Control animal (left) and treated animal (right).

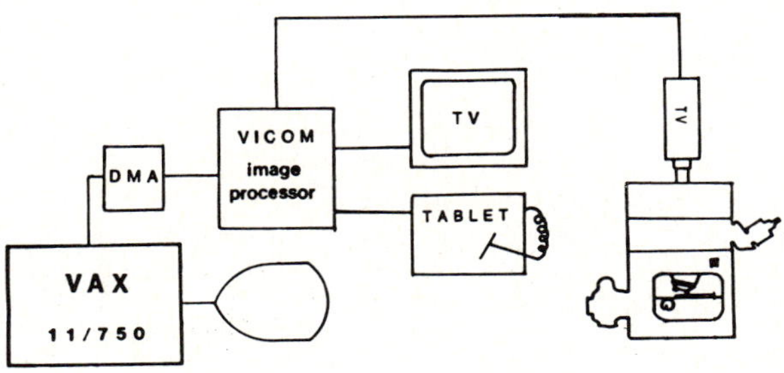

Figure 2
Hardware system for data aquisition and analysis.

Section Matching:

After sectioning the brain slices were deposited manually on a glass slide. The position of the section on the slide was arbitrary. Production of sections is also associated with unavoidable geometric distortions such as stretching, folding, curling and tearing. A high accuracy of local conformity of adjacent images is necessary for 3D reconstruction of serial section images. One of the main problems in the analysis of serial sections is that of accurate alignment. For this task two sections were inspected simultaneously using the VICOM system. The image from the section currently under the microscope was transferred to the red display buffer and the image from the previous section was stored in the blue display buffer. The images were displayed simultaneously using the VICOM system and matched manually, under visual control on the monitor, by moving the microscope revolving stage in the x - y direction for translational correction and in phi for rotational correction. The match was judged successful, when the red and blue colour vanished and a grey image appeared (Fig. 3).

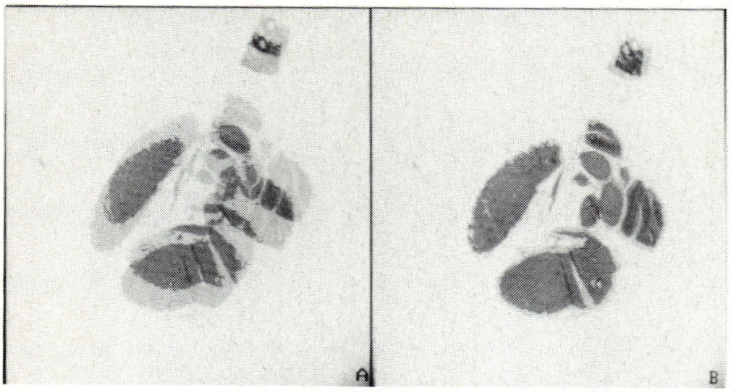

Figure 3
Matching of two images: lighter grey values show unmatched parts and darker grey values show matched parts.

Fig. 4A shows a series of 16 consecutive serial section images through a mouse brain. The distance between two sections is about 300 µm.

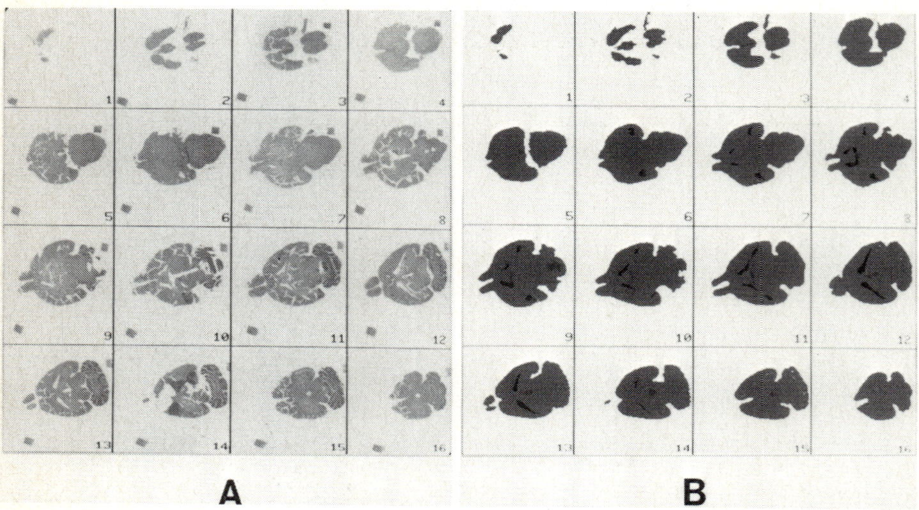

Figure 4
A) Serial sections through a mouse brain (every 6th section, control animal).
B) Serial sections after segmentation.

The success of matching is shown in fig 5. The whole brain was divided into two parts each consisting of 50 sections superposed by addition. The generated grey image took on the appearance of a radiographic image but with considerably better contrast and resolution.

Image processing:

Image processing was performed on a VAX/VMS 750 using the interactive command oriented image processing system for biomedical images - BIP [10]. The MOVIE.BYU program, developed at the Brigham Young University, Utah, USA [4] was used for 3D representation of the serial section images.

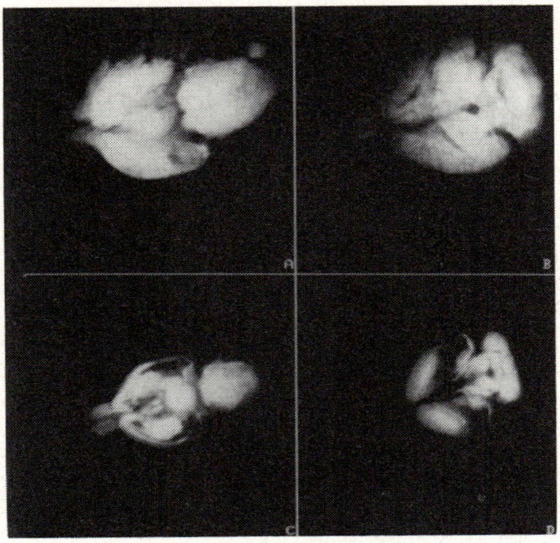

Figure 5
Superposition of serial section images by addition:
Control animal: section 1 - 50 (upper left), and section 51 - 112 (upper right).
Treated animal: section 1 - 50 (lower left), and section 51 - 101 (lower right).

PREPROCESSING OF SERIAL SECTIONS

Preprocessing of the original data for enhancement of certain features of interest is necessary. The kind of processing chosen depends on the input data and the features that are of interest to the observer. Useful steps include:

- scaling of the image (histogram modification),
- 3D filtering (smoothing and sharpening),
- segmentation,
- contour tracing.

The scaling of images is a point transformation in which a pixel with a given grey value is transformed into another grey-level. After scaling image details are visible with more contrast because regions of interest are spread over a wide range of grey values. Point spread operations for 3D images can be applied sequentially to the x-y image series ordered along the z coordinate.

Smoothing and sharpening of 3D images uses a local neighbourhood of, for example, 3 x 3 x 3 pixels in the x, y and z directions. In this case images from 3 adjacent serial sections have to be used in order to perform the operation.

Image segmentation is a very important step but not easy to perform even in 2D images. Many investigations have been made in this field [7,2Ø]. Problems with automatic segmentation arise from the tremendous computing time and judgment of the results. Segmentation in 3D images is a field of research. It remains to be proved that methods of 2D processing can be transferred to 3D images [12].

In the processing of serial section images of the mice brains the elements of segmentation are anatomical structures:

- whole brain morphology
- ventricular system (right, left 3rd, 4th ventricle)
- white and grey brain substance,
- blood vessels and commissure system
- pathological alterations.

Segmentation in the series of serial sections in order to get 3D surfaces was performed in our case using a combination of automatic and interactive steps applied to the segmentation of 2D section images. First the section images were smoothed. Three adjacent images along the z coordinate and an area of 3 x 3 pixels in the x and y directions were used. All pixels in this neighbourhood of 3 x 3 x 3 were added and the mean value calculated. In a second step the image was scaled to black values of Ø.Ø and white values of 1.Ø. A threshold of Ø.5 was selected and a black and white image generated. Borders corresponding to a cross-section of the object surface were extracted from each slice automatically by computer processing and displayed on the screen. The 'wrong' borders were corrected manually using a graphic tablet. The borders of the brains were generally extracted without human interaction whereas the ventricles were not easy to detect because of their complex shape and therefore required more interactive control (fig 4B).

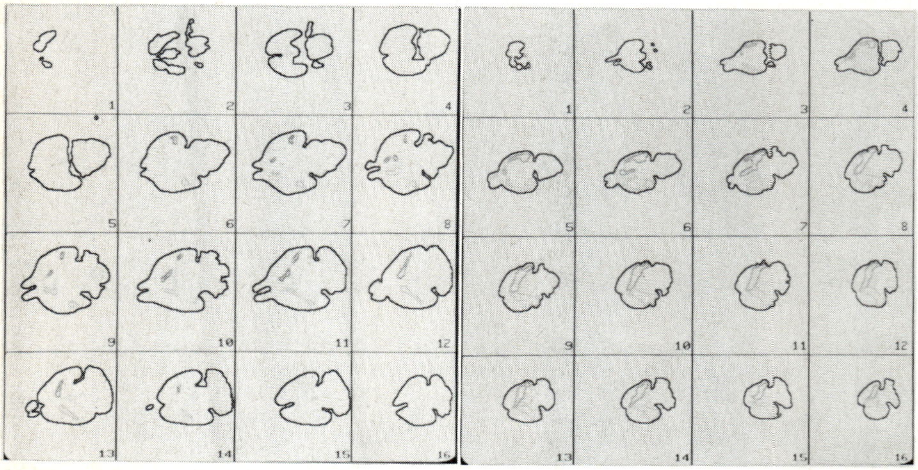

Figure 6
Contour lines from mice brain sections:
Left: Control animal (same sections as in fig 4A und 4B).
Right: Treated animal.

Binary image processing [17] was applied to smooth the edge of each object, fill the detected areas, and prepare the binary image for the subsequent contour tracing algorithm described by Pavlidis [13].

A numerical description of a contour line is approximated as a string of straight line segments. This digitized contour line offers two pieces of information: nodal coordinates and connectivity of nodes. Open ended lines and touching loops must be avoided. A closed contour line is a prerequisite for transforming a series of contour line images into a 3D surface model using the MOVIE program MOSAIC [4,5]. Fig. 6 shows contour lines from the mouse brain sections.

TRIANGULATION

There is a disparity between the conventional method of describing topographical surfaces using contour lines and the method of surface description used in continuous tone computer graphics. The conversion is not a trivial problem [5]. The 3D surface of the object is ordinarily described by a polyhedral approximation [8]. Points on the object's surface form the vertices of the polygonal face of the polyhedron. Triangular elements are commonly used for the face, since it is always possible to pass a plane through three points. Planar quadrilateral elements cannot always connect four points on a surface.

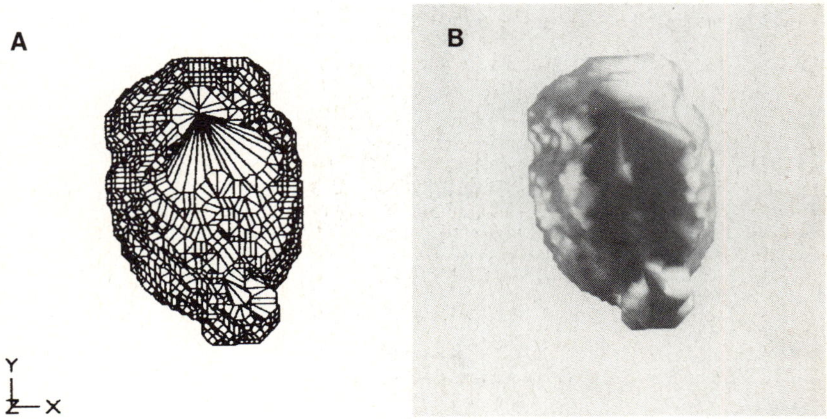

Figure 7
Mouse brain after polyhedral approximation of the surface:
A) Output after quadrilation on a vector graphics device.
B) Shaded surface display on a raster graphics device.

Starting with a series of contour line images in which the z-axis goes along the serial image number, a surface was calculated by triangulation between two adjacent contour lines. Problems are caused by the rough surface of biological material which results in a high number of nodes for each contour image. Many triangles are calculated and a large computing power is needed to handle the information. In order to reduce the number of nodes our images were zoomed to a size of 64 x 64 pixels. The number of surface elements were reduced by transforming the triangular elements into quadrilateral elements. Fig. 7A shows the plot of a mouse brain generated using a polyhedral approximation of quadrilateral elements presented on a vector graphics device.

SHADED SURFACE DISPLAY

Since we limited ourselves to a TV monitor as the display device we had to compute 2D projections of 3D data. The basic idea of shaded surface display is to generate an image of a 3D object that exists only as a mathematical description. This cannot be performed on conventional computer vector graphics systems, it requires the raster graphic devices used in digital image processing [3]. The object of interest is given by a mathematical description of its opaque outer surface in a 3D coordinate system. The user specifies the location of all light sources and of the imaginary camera where the image has to be generated. The latter position is called the viewpoint. The display algorithm then computes the image that the imaginary camera would make of the object (Fig. 7B).

Figure 8
Left and right ventricle in a rectangular glass.

Surface display requires modelling of three things: spacial surface description, light-reflecting phenomenon at the surface, and geometry of the light source and the imaging projection. With the MOVIE Program interesting features are available for surface display of continuous tone images on a 2D raster graphics display. The user has complete control over the location of up to four light sources. With the glass option it is possible to demonstrate different parts in one image and make the surface transparent. Fig. 8 demonstrates an example of hidden line surface removal using 3 parts (left ventricle, right ventricle and a rectangular glass with the dimension of the hull of the brain).

RESULTS

1. Quantitative measurements of serial section images:

The sequence of 2D serial section images was analysed. The area of different parts (whole brain, 1st lateral ventricle, 2nd lateral ventricle, 3rd ventricle) of each section image were measured after segmentation. The volumes of the different parts were determined as the sum of all section areas multiplied by the section thickness. The measured volumes are shown in Table 1. Whereas the volume of the whole brain was reduced by about 50% in the treated animal as compared with the control, the volume of the ventricular system was increased 4x. The ventricular volume was about 1 % of the whole brain volume in the control animal and about 8% in the treated animal.

Table 1

	control	treated
	*	*
brain volume	261.0	131.0
1st l.ventricle	2.4 (1%)	10.7 (8,2%)
2nd l.ventricle	2.9 (1%)	10.7 (8.2%)
3rd ventricle	1.6 (0.6%)	2.9 (2.2%)

* in cubic millimetre

2. Demonstration of anatomical structures by surface display:

The whole brains of both the control animal and the treated animal were shown as a shaded surface display under different viewpoints (Fig. 9). A comparison of both lateral ventricles for the control animal and the treated animal is shown in Fig. 10. The morphological differences in both size and shape are clearly visible.

DISCUSSION

The 2D presentation of anatomical and morphological structures using serial section images visualized with a microscope is an important task because mental reconstruction of serial images is difficult even for experienced anatomists and pathologists. False interpretation of 2D section images can lead to a variety of structural misunderstandings [6]. In the investigation described here matching of serial section images was performed under visual control. The accuracy of the matching method which we developed enabled a 3D reconstruction of the serial section brain images, after triangulation of contour line images, using the MOVIE.BYU software package. Using this method we were able to demonstrate clearly differences in the morphology of brains from untreated and x-irradiated mice. The quality of the 3D images can be increased by increasing the resolution of the contour line images.

The 3D presentation of microscopic serial section images in a computer is a powerful tool for the anatomical and morphological analysis of 3D structures. It opens up new possibilities for embryological and histopathological work.

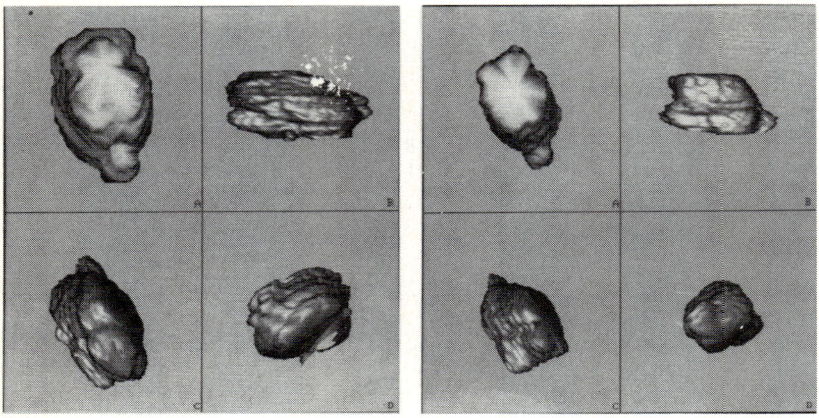

Figure 9
Different projections of whole brain surface:
Left: Normal animal (A,B,C,D)
Right: Treated animal (A,B,C,D)

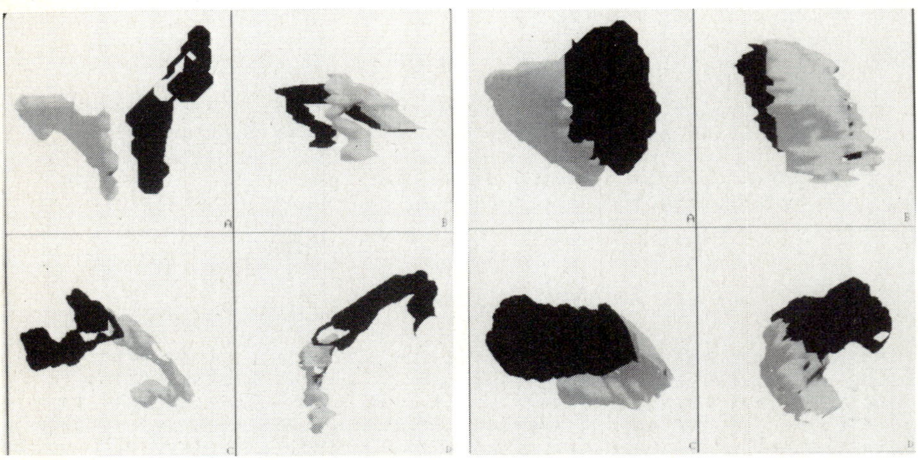

Figure 10
Both lateral ventricles: Control animal (left), treated animal (right).

ACKNOWLEDGEMENTS

The authors are grateful to Dr. A. B. Murray for discussion and correction of the manuscript and to E. Mannweiler for support in programming.

REFERENCES

[1] Aggarwal JK, Davis LS, Martin WN, Roach JW: Survey:Representation Methods for Three-Dimensional Objects. in Progress in Pattern Recognition, Vol. 1. Edited by Kanal LN and Rosenfeld A. 1981

[2] Bartels PH, Wied GL: Computer analysis and biomedical interpretation of microscopic images: current problems and future directions. Proceedings of the IEEE 65: 252 - 261, 1977.

[3] Castleman K.R.: Digital Image Processing. Prentice-Hall INC., Englewood Cliffs, New Jersey 1979.

[4] Christiansen HN, Stephenson MB: Movie.byu - a general purpose computer graphics display system. Proceedings of the Symposium on Application of Computer Methods in Engineering, University of Southern California, Los Angeles, 759 - 769, 1977

[5] Christiansen HN, Sederberg TW: Conversion of complex contour line definitions into polygonal element mosaics. Computer Graphics, Vol, 12(3), 187-192, 1978

[6] Elias H: Three-dimensional structure identified from single sections. Science 174, 993 - 1000, 1971

[7] Fu KS, Mui JK: A survey on image segmentation. Pattern Recognition 13: 3 - 16, 1981

[8] Fuchs H, Kedem Z, Uselton S: Optimal surface reconstruction from planar contours. Comm. ACM, 20, 693-702, 1977

[9] Lenz R: Processing and presentation of 3D- images. IEEE 1984 International Symposium on Medical Images and Icons-ISMII'84, 298-303, 1984

[10] Mannweiler E. Rappl W. Abmayr W: Software for interactive biomedical image processing - BIP. Proceedings 6th International Conference on Pattern Recognition, IEEE Computer Society Press: 1213, 1982.

[11] Murray AB, Davies HG: Three- dimensional reconstruction of the chromatin bodies in the nuclei of mature erythrocytes from the newt triturus cristatus: The number of nuclear envelope- attachment sites. J. Cell Sci. 35, 59 - 66, 1979

[12] Oswald H, Leberl F, Gell G, Sager WD: Digitale Bearbeitung

und Auswertung Computertomographischer Bilder. Institut fuer Digitale Bildverarbeitung und Graphik, Forschungszentrum Graz A-8010 DIBAG - Bericht Nr. 15, Februar 1984

[13] Pavlidis T: Algorithms for Graphics and Image Processing. Springer Verlag Berlin - Heidelberg, 1982

[14] Preston K: Tissue section analysis: Feature selection and image processing. Pattern Recognition vol. 13: 17 - 36, 1981

[15] Rager G, Zimmermann CW, Teckhaus L: Zur Entwicklung des Gehirns: Dreidimensionale Rekonstruction mit dem Leitz T.A.S. Leitz Mitt. Wiss. u. Techn. Bd VIII (7), 202 - 207, 1984

[16] Rieder CL: Thick and thin serial sectioning for the three-dimensonal reconstruction of biological ultrastructure. Methods in Cell Biology 22, 215 - 249, 1981

[17] Serra J: Image analysis and mathematical morphology. Academic Press, London: 1982

[18] Tamura et al.: Tomogram reconstruction in desired plane based on serial Tomograms. Computer in Biology and Medicine 9(4), 245 - 355, 1979

[19] Upuda JK: Display of 3D information in discrete 3D scenes produced by computerized tomography. Proc IEEE, Vol 17 (3), 420 - 421, 1983

[20] Weszka JS: A survey of threshold selection techniques. Computer Graphics and Image Processing 7: 259 - 265, 1978

[21] Williams MA: Quantitative methods in biology. Practical methods in electron microscopy ed. A. M. Glauert, North-Holland Publishing Company 6: 5 - 80, 1977

[22] Yasuda T, Toriwaki J, Yokoi S, Katada K: A three-dimensional display system of CT images for surgical planning. IEEE 1984 International Symposium on Medical Images and Icons-ISMII'84, 322-328, 1984

[23] Yokoya N, Tamura H, Funakubo N: 3D view of serial section images by binocular stereo. IEEE International Symposium on Medical Images and Icons-ISMII'84, 318 - 321, 1984

PATTERN RECOGNITION IN PRACTICE II
E.S. Gelsema and L.N. Kanal (Editors)

DIRECT 3D RECONSTRUCTION FROM PROJECTIONS WITH INITIALLY UNKNOWN ANGLES

George Harauz and Marin van Heel

Fritz-Haber-Institut der Max-Planck-Gesellschaft,
Faradayweg 4-6, D-1000 Berlin 33, West Germany.

1. Introduction

The problem of reconstructing an object from its projections arises in many diverse fields, such as radio astronomy, medical imaging, and electron microscopy (1). Normally, the reconstruction geometry, i.e., the angular relations between the various projections, is known *a priori*. In medical computerised tomography, for example, one knows the positions of the X-ray source and detectors exactly for each of the measured line projections. This knowledge, however, is not always available. In particular, we consider as an example the application of macromolecular structure determination by electron microscopy (3,4,5). In an electron micrograph made of a preparation of biological macromolecules, one may find hundreds of macromolecular images, each representing a projection through the 3D electron density distribution of the macromolecule. Since the macromolecules may lie in random orientation on the support, each image represents a projection in a different direction of the structure. Moreover, three Eulerian angles are needed to describe the orientational relations of any two molecular projections, making the problem a "true" or direct 3D reconstruction problem (3,7). One cannot define an axis of rotation which would reduce the problem to tomography, i.e., the reconstruction of 2D slices. Before a reconstruction can be performed, however, these angular relationships between projections must somehow be determined.

The most straightforward way to determine the orientation of our electron microscopical projections is to compare each image with projections in many different directions of some sort of model of the object's structure (4,5). Either subjective (visual) or more objective (cross-correlation) criteria can be used to choose the best match between projections of the object and projections of its model. Thus, directions can be assigned to the projection images to within a certain accuracy. This approach, however, requires *a priori* information about the object's structure and thus is not generally applicable. In this paper, we shall describe the use of pattern recognition techniques to assist in solving this problem.

2. Multivariate statistical analysis and classification of images

As described in the companion paper in these proceedings (13), electron images of single macromolecules are extremely noisy and not easily interpretable by themselves. For this reason, we have developed computer algorithms to sort and classify these images according to particle orientation (9-11,14). Molecular images falling into the same orientational class are averaged to give an image in which reproducible structural details are enhanced with respect to the random background noise.

Initially the image information is compressed using a eigenvector eigenvalue technique called correspondence analysis. The original images are expressed as linear combinations of the main 2 to 8 "eigenimages". The main (orthogonal!) eigenimages are the eigenvectors corresponding to the largest eigenvalues. Since each image is now expressed by merely 2 to 8 numbers as opposed to the original 64x64 = 4096 pixels, an extreme reduction of the dimensionality of the noisy data is achieved.

The classification step then uses the distance measures in hyperspace determined by the correspondence analysis to group together those images that are most similar. The hierachical classification process can be stopped when either a specified total number of classes is obtained, or when classes containing a specified number of members are obtained. The initial partition into classes is further refined iteratively as described in (9) until the partition is stabilised.

When the set of images represents different projections of the molecular structure, and with a viewpoint towards 3D reconstruction, we wish the classes to contain small groups of images corresponding to narrow angular ranges of projection, i.e., we wish the classification to be consistent with the logical angular relationships between images. In addition, we wish the classification to distinguish between mirror views of the same object, which may occur simultaneously in an experimental situation.

In the following two sections, we demonstrate the performance of the classification algorithms in this respect with model data for both 2D tomography and direct 3D reconstruction.

3. Classification of 1D projections for 2D tomography

A two dimensional image comprising 3 Gaussian functions, centered at different positions within the image, was used as a test object for model experiments. All image analyses were performed within the framework of the IMAGIC image processing system (15). One dimensional projections of the (digital) test image were computed using bilinear interpolation and weighting as described elsewhere (12). A total of 360 projections were generated, at angles of 0, 1, 2, 3,..., 357, 358, 359 degrees, i.e., 180 projections and their mirror views. This 1D projection data set was used as direct input to the correspondence analysis program, and the eigenvalue - eigenvector decomposition of the data set resulted in the following:

factorial coordinate	% variance	cumulative % variance	histogram of variance (one * represents 1.5%)
1	48.454	48.454	!*********************************
2	30.011	78.465	!********************
3	11.470	89.935	!********
4	4.289	94.224	!**
5	1.953	96.177	!*
6	1.454	97.631	!*
7	0.773	98.404	!
8	0.563	98.967	!
9	0.372	99.339	!
10	0.221	99.561	!

The first 3 factorial coordinates describe already 90% of the total inter-image variance. The remaining factorial coordinates describe smaller and smaller amounts of inter-image variance, and eventually describe only noise. Here, we have noise due to factors such as interpolation errors (2). Thus, a decision must be made as to how many factorial coordinates to use for the classification. Such a decision depends on the experimental situation at hand and remains

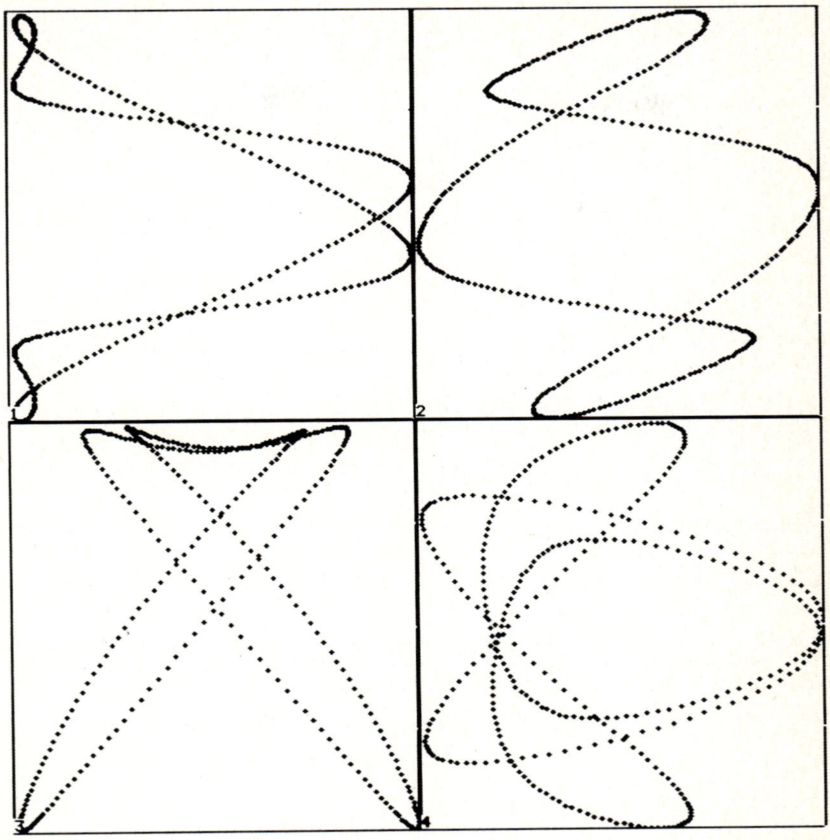

FIGURE 1
This figure shows plots of various combinations of the factorial coordinates of 360 one dimensional projection images. These are TOP LEFT: 2 versus 1, TOP RIGHT: 3 versus 1, BOTTOM LEFT: 3 versus 2, and BOTTOM RIGHT: 4 versus 3.

subjective. Figure 1 show two dimensional plots of various combinations of the first four factorial coordinates of the 360 projection images. Although the logical relationships between factorial coordinates are themselves fairly complex, they clearly reflect the symmetries inherent in the input data set.

In the classification step, the chosen factorial coordinates of the images can be weighted in a number of different ways:
(a) All factorial coordinates can be weighted equally by unity, so that the classification takes place strictly according to the variance relations present in the data set. The first few factors are most influential in determining the partition as they account for most of the total variance.
(b) The factorial coordinates of each image can be weighted by the inverse square root of the corresponding eigenvalue. This "standard" weighting leads to an equal appreciation of all significant eigenvectors, irrespective of the total power that they describe.
(c) The first few factorial coordinates may be weighted in the standard manner, and the remainder are unweighted.

Finally, a third degree of freedom that we have is how to partition the classification tree. In a situation where we are reasonably certain of a uniform angular distribution of projections, then the data set should be divided into classes of approximately equal size. In this model experiment of 360 1D projections, we have chosen a maximum class size of 25 members. (Note that the iterative refinement of the initial partition may change the maximum class size slightly). Moreover, we weight all factorial coordinates equally by unity, and demonstrate only the effect of the number of coordinates used for the classification.

The results of the classification using unit weighting of the first two factorial coordinates, and a maximum specified class size of 25 members prior to refinement of the first partition, are shown below:

CLASS	# OF MEMBERS	ANGLES OF PROJECTIONS (ranges in degrees)
1	14	175 : 181 and 284 : 290
2	16	161 : 168 and 298 : 305
3	15	119 : 126 and 340 : 346
4	13	169 : 174 and 291 : 297
5	16	182 : 189 and 276 : 283
6	14	4 : 11 and 96 : 101
7	22	318 : 339
8	22	139 : 160
9	11	108 : 113 and 353 : 357
10	11	114 : 118 and 347 : 352
11	12	-2 : 3 and 102 : 107
12	21	12 : 32
13	19	190 : 208
14	24	127 : 138 and 306 : 317
15	18	209 : 220 and 270 : 275
16	19	221 : 231 and 262 : 269
17	18	43 : 53 and 82 : 88
18	17	33 : 42 and 89 : 95
19	28	54 : 81
20	30	232 : 261

The classification thus obtained is unsuitable for further use by reconstruction programs. The classes do not represent "pure" projection classes, in which the members of one class are all related to one another by a small angle of rotation. Instead, the classes here represent mixtures of pure projection classes.

In contrast, the use of four factorial coordinates for the classification instead of just two improved the classification significantly (results not shown). All of the classes excepting two now represented pure projection classes.

Finally, the results of the classification using unit weighting of the first eight factorial coordinates, and a maximum specified class size of 25 members prior to refinement of the first partition, are shown below:

CLASS	# OF MEMBERS	ANGLES OF PROJECTIONS (ranges in degrees)
1	11	173 : 183
2	10	-5 : 4
3	13	342 : 354
4	21	184 : 204
5	23	5 : 27
6	13	160 : 172
7	14	117 : 130
8	12	278 : 289
9	11	106 : 116
10	11	290 : 300
11	27	315 : 341
12	17	28 : 44
13	29	131 : 159
14	14	205 : 218
15	16	262 : 277
16	22	71 : 92
17	23	239 : 261
18	13	93 : 105
19	26	45 : 70
20	20	219 : 238
21	14	301 : 314

All of the projection classes now represent pure projection classes. Moreover, mirror views (those differing by a 180 degree rotation) fall into different classes. Indeed, it is possible to distinguish rough "mirror class" pairs, namely (1,2), (3,6), (4,5), (7,21), (11,13), (12,14), (15,16), with a slightly less clear distinction between (8,9,10,18) and (17,19,20).

It can be appreciated that the use of as many factorial coordinates as possible, but not those representing mere noise, is required for the hierarchical ascendant classification scheme to partition a set of projection images into pure projection classes. The best partition, however, also depends on other factors such as the class size chosen and the weighting of the factorial coordinates. We have found, in experiments using the data set described here, that too large a specified class size tends to give mixed projection classes, and that standard instead of unit weighting of the factorial coordinates tends to give slightly "purer" projection classes, but this does not cause a dramatic difference. These simulation experiments serve to indicate the important factors that one should consider before applying correspondence analysis and hierarchical ascendant classification to real data; however, the exact choice of parameters depends on the experimental situation at hand, and the results obtained must be evaluated using criteria such as experimental data from other sources.

4. Classification of 2D projections for direct 3D reconstruction

A much more difficult problem than that of 2D tomography is direct 3D reconstruction. In this situation, the 2D projection images are 2D projections of density of a 3D object viewed at an orientation which can be described by the familiar Euler angles (α , β , γ). Angle α is radial and β is azimuthal; γ describes a rotation in the projection plane and will be considered to be zero here, i.e., we will assume that the projection images are aligned.

As a 3D test image for the model experiments described here, we generated a 3D digital (48x48x48) image comprising random noise with a Gaussian distribution about a zero mean and with a standard deviation of 10.0. Voxels outside a spherical mask of diameter 34 voxels were set to zero. The 3D volume was then Fourier filtered using a Lorentzian mask with a full width at half maximum of 0.46 times the Nyquist frequency. Finally, all voxels with negative density values were set to zero. Such a phantom has the disadvantage that it does not represent familiar objects such as spheres. However, for objective evaluation of image analysis algorithms, this phantom is most flexible in that its power spectrum can be easily designed by the user. A total of 200 2D projections of this (digital) phantom were generated using bicubic spline interpolation (2) in directions uniformly distributed over the unit hemisphere (3). A further 200 mirror views of these projections (covering the other "bottom" half of the unit sphere) were also generated. Figure 2 shows some of the forward projections thus generated.

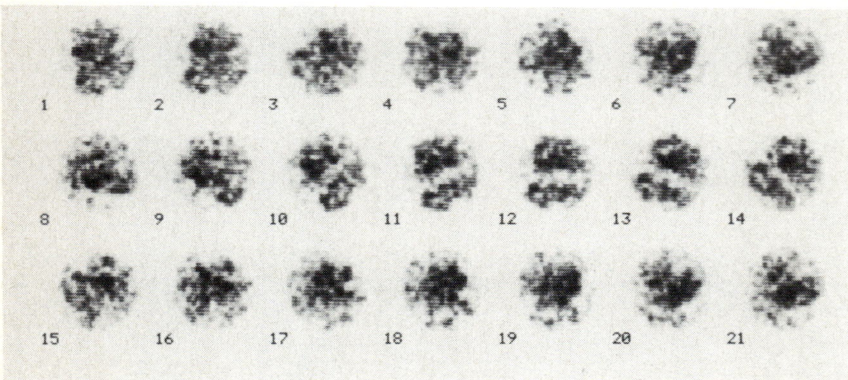

FIGURE 2

The distribution of Euler angles is shown in Figure 3 below.

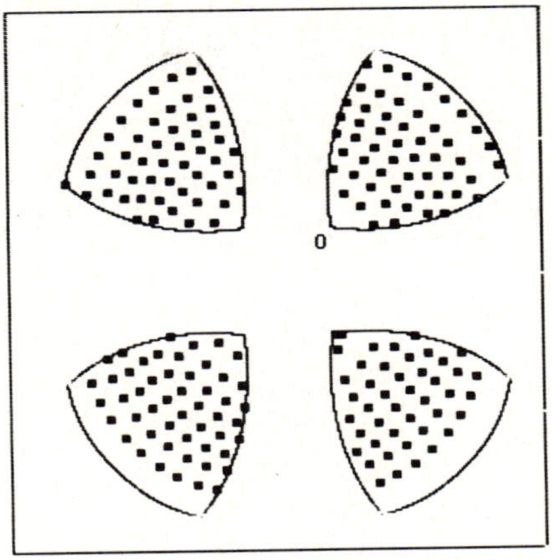

FIGURE 3

In this figure, the 4 quadrants of the "top" hemisphere have been separated and "lifted" to give a less distorted two dimensional rendition. The top pole of this hemisphere, marked by an "0", is the point (α , β) = (0,0). The direction vectors of the projections are marked by squares. The direction vectors of the mirror projections fall on the bottom half of the unit sphere, but are coincident with those of the original projections except for a change in sign. The value of β increases from point 0 along lines of longitude. Along lines of latitude, β is constant, but α varies radially.

This 2D projection data set was used as direct input to the correspondence analysis program, and the eigenvalue - eigenvector decomposition of the data set resulted in the following:

factorial coordinate	% variance	cumulative % variance	histogram of variance (one * represents 1%)
1	9.875	9.875	!**********
2	9.249	19.124	!*********
3	5.772	24.896	!******
4	5.093	29.998	!*****
5	4.273	34.262	!****
6	2.837	37.099	!***
7	2.737	39.835	!***
8	2.223	42.059	!**
9	2.021	44.080	!**
10	1.911	45.990	!**
15	1.420	53.987	!*
20	1.128	60.127	!*
30	0.643	68.544	!*
40	0.459	73.937	!

The increased complexity of the reconstruction geometry (as compared with tomography) is evident in that many more factorial coordinates are required to describe inter-image variance. Nonetheless, we performed a classification with unit weighting of just 8 factorial coordinates, and a maximum specified class size of 20 members. The results are shown in Figure 4 below.

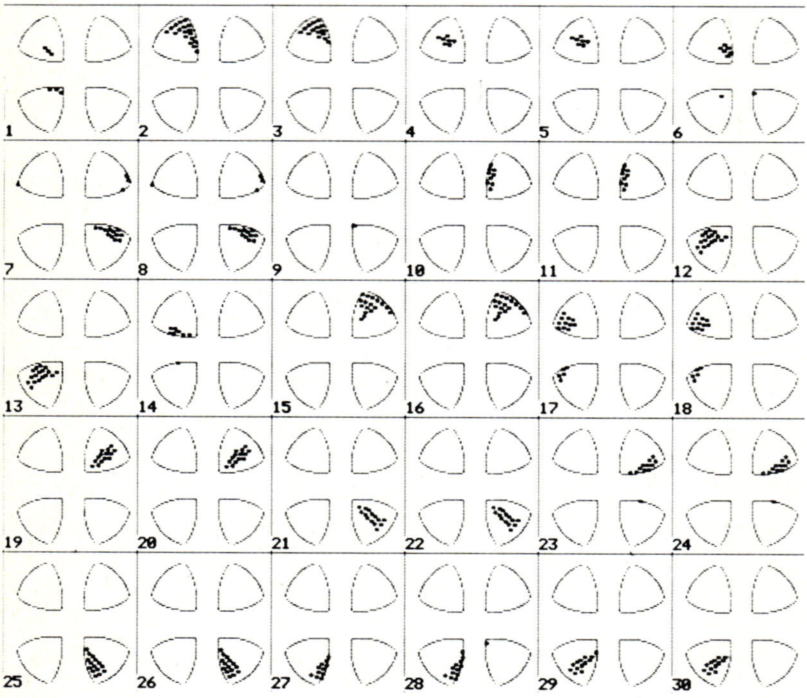

FIGURE 4

Even using only 8 factorial coordinates, the classes obtained are pure projection classes with 4 exceptions, viz., classes 1, 6, 9, and 14. In these classes, projections and their corresponding mirror views have been grouped together. In the remaining classes, the projections have direction vectors falling either on the top or on the bottom half of the unit sphere, with no mixing. Moreover, "mirror class" pairs are found, viz., (2,3), (4,5), (7,8), (10,11), (12,13), (15,16), (17,18), (19,20), (21,22), (23,24), (25,26), (27,28), and (29,30).

Some interesting points arise out of this analysis. Class 9 contains 4 members: the 2 most polar (β about 0°) projections and their mirror views. The other classes have a tendency to follow polar grand circles (along which varies from 0 to 90 degrees), except near the equator (β = 90°) where the classes follow the equatorial grand circle as well. The reason for this behaviour is that for small β , the rotation by angle α results in a noticeable rotation in the projection plane (see figure 3). In this experiment, we have set γ to zero, and γ affects <u>only</u> rotation in the projection plane. Thus, although projection images may appear similar and are related only by a small change in α and β, the in-plane rotation will cause the correspondence analysis to find great differences between these images. Experiments are currently in progress to generate projections using angle γ to compensate for this effect.

5. Reconstruction from projections with initially unknown angles

We have demonstrated by simulation experiments that a data set consisting of different projection images of an object can be analysed using correspondence analysis and hierarchical ascendant classification algorithms, giving classes which reflect the various projection directions and symmetries. The absolute angular relationships between classes are NOT thus obtained. However, the algorithm provides us with proximity relations between the classes, and we are currently investigating nonlinear mapping of the distances in the classification space onto the unit semicircle, in order to give better initial estimates to the orientation angles of the projections.

At present, we have developed a scheme to obtain reconstructions of an object without knowing the absolute angular relations between the projection classes. Initially, we simply assign a random orientation angle to each of the projections. An initial reconstruction is performed using these random angular assignments, with the filtered back-projection algorithm, which we favour because of its speed and accuracy (1,3). The 3D data volume is then reprojected in many equidistant directions, and the original projections are cross-correlated against all the reprojections. From the cross-correlation curves obtained, new, refined angles are calculated which are used for a new, refined, 3D reconstruction. After about 3 to 5 iterations of this process, individual angular assignments are usually not changed much further, indicating that a self-consistency has been reached between the projections and the reconstruction. At this stage, also, no further improvement in the reconstruction is possible without further information about the structure of the object.

It is worthwhile to note two elegant reconstruction algorithms that do not require absolute angular relations for the projections (6,8). These algorithms are based on decomposing the input projections into linear combinations of spherical harmonic functions, and combining these by means of correlation or least squares techniques to give the reconstruction. Both require as input many (of the order of a few hundred) projection images. However, the method of Kam (6) requires a perfect distribution of projection directions over the full angular range, and is greatly influenced by possible inconsistencies in the experimental data. The method of Provencher (8) is currently being evaluated using real experimental data, although promising results were obtained using simulations. The approach that we have outlined here, though, allows one to deal better with a practical problem inherent in electron microscopy: in the correspondence analysis and classification stages, "bad" projection images representing distorted or damaged macromolecules can be removed from the data set, and do not influence the final reconstruction.

References

(1) Gordon, R. and Herman, G.T., Three-dimensional reconstruction from projections: A review of algorithms, International Review of Cytology 38 (1974) 111-151.

(2) Harauz, G. and Ottensmeyer, F.P., Interpolation in computing forward projections in direct three-dimensional reconstruction, Physics in Medicine and Biology 28 (1983) 1419-1427.

(3) Harauz, G. and Ottensmeyer, F.P., Direct three-dimensional reconstruction for macromolecular complexes from electron micrographs, Ultramicroscopy 12 (1984) 309-320.

(4) Harauz, G., Nucleosome reconstruction via phosphorus mapping, Ph.D. Thesis, Department of Medical Biophysics, University of Toronto (May, 1984).

(5) Harauz, G. and Ottensmeyer, F.P., Nucleosome reconstruction via phosphorus mapping, Science 226 (1984) 936-940.

(6) Kam, Z., The reconstruction of structure from electron micrographs of randomly oriented particles, Journal of Theoretical Biology 82 (1980) 15-39.

(7) Pelc, N.J. and Chesler, D.A., Utilization of cross-plane rays for three-dimensional reconstruction by filtered back-projection, Journal of Computer Assisted Tomography 3 (1979) 385-395.

(8) Provencher, S.W. and Vogel, R.H., Regularization techniques for inverse problems in molecular biology, in: Abarbanel, S., Glowinski, R., Golub, G. and Kreiss, H.-O. (eds.), Progress in Scientific Computing (Birkhauser, Boston, Basel, Stuttgart, 1983).

(9) van Heel, M., Multivariate statistical classification of noisy images (randomly oriented biological macromolecules), Ultramicroscopy 13 (1984) 165-184.

(10) van Heel, M., Multivariate statistical analysis of biological macromolecules: Powerful new methods, Proceedings of the 8th European Congress on Electron Microscopy, Budapest, (1984) 1317-1325.

(11) van Heel, M., Three-dimensional reconstruction from projections with unknown angular relationships, Proceedings of the 8th European Congress on Electron Microscopy, Budapest, (1984) 1347-1348.

(12) van Heel, M., Stereographic representation of three dimensional density distributions, Ultramicroscopy 11 (1983) 307-314.

(13) van Heel, M., Finding the characteristic views of molecules in extremely noisy electron micrographs, in: these Proceedings.

(14) van Heel, M. and Frank, J., Use of multivariate statistics in analysing the images of biological macromolecules, Ultramicroscopy, 6 (1981) 187-194.

(15) van Heel, M. and Keegstra, W., IMAGIC: A fast, flexible and friendly image analysis software system, Utramicroscopy 7 (1981) 113-130.

SECTION IV

APPLICATIONS

PATTERN RECOGNITION IN PRACTICE II
E.S. Gelsema and L.N. Kanal (Editors)

FINDING THE CHARACTERISTIC VIEWS OF MACROMOLECULES IN EXTREMELY NOISY ELECTRON MICROGRAPHS.

Marin van Heel

Fritz Haber Institute of the Max Planck Society,
Faradayweg 4-6, D-1000 Berlin-Dahlem, West Germany.

INTRODUCTION

Noise is the major problem in the interpretation of structure in electron microscopical images of biological macromolecules. The instrumental resolution of modern electron microscopes lies well under 0.2 nm, which is in principle high enough not only to visualise directly the polypeptide chains of proteins, but also to recognise the individual amino acid residues and thereby solve the protein structure. However, biological macromolecules rapidly disintegrate in the electron beam, and so one seldom manages to directly register significant structural information on details smaller than 10 nm! This very high radiation sensitivity forces us to use low electron exposures in recording the micrographs. This implies that the average noise levels (quantum noise: Poisson statistics) in the images are high and hence the corresponding signal-to-noise ratios (SNR) are low. Embedding the molecules in heavy-metal staining salts (typically uranyl acetate) boosts the contrast in the image and protects the molecules somewhat by building a supporting film around them. Staining thus allows for better images at lower electron exposure. However, staining also introduces another source of noise in the images: the statistical nature of the distribution of the heavy metal stain around the individual macromolecules. Even in the presence of stain it is therefore very difficult to obtain significant details smaller than 5 nm in the micrographs. In short: electron microscopical images of biological macromolecules are noise limited and any attempt to increase the interpretable resolution of the images must be aimed at increasing the SNR.

AVERAGING

Averaging of a large number of individual images of identical molecules is now a well established technique to increase the SNR. Averaging boosts the signal common to the images and strongly suppresses the (random) noise. Averaging methods were originally developed for molecules arranged in two-dimensional crystals sometimes giving spectacular increases in SNR of about four orders of magnitude (20). Since each individual molecule receives only a very small share of the total electron exposure needed to obtain a high SNR image, the structure remains undamaged and the resulting average may be interpreted to high resolution. Although two-dimensional crystals do occur in vivo, they often have to be crystallized specifically for the experiment. This crystallization is a time consuming and rather unpredictable procedure, very much like the 3D crystallisation needed for X-ray diffraction experiments (cf. 4). Furthermore, many, if not most, of the key proteins in life are active as individual molecules either in solution or in membranes and they are best studied in their natural environment.

Averaging techniques for individual molecules (6,7) were developed later than the crystallographic ones. In contrast to molecules arranged in crystals, single molecules are not kept in a fixed position by their neighbours and exhibit a large orientational freedom. This freedom of orientation has, in the past, limited the application of the single particle averaging technique to molecules with just one clear preferential view relative to the plane of the supporting film, such as the very flat glutamine synthetase molecule (6,7).

For the more usual case in which the molecules assume more than one stable position on the grid, the orientational freedom has to be accounted for before averaging of the aligned molecules; it is only permitted to average molecular views if these views are indeed very similar.

ALIGNMENT

A prerequisite for any averaging procedure is that the images of the individual molecules be aligned relative to each other. In a two-dimensional crystal, this alignment is given a priori (the unit vectors of the crystal lattice can readily be determined) and one only needs to extract the unit cells and add them together to obtain the average. In the case of single molecules, on the other hand, the individual molecular images have to be aligned by more complex means. Two molecules that are in the same orientation relative to the plane of the support film have to be aligned translationally ($\Delta x, \Delta y$) and rotationally ($\Delta\varphi$) prior to averaging.

Translational alignment between a molecular image and a reference image is achieved by searching for the position of the maximum in the crosscorrelation function (CCF) of the two images (18). The image to be aligned is then shifted over minus the peak coordinates, i.e., shifted to the position of maximum translational overlap. The CCF is calculated by multiplying the Fourier transform (FT) of the image with the complex conjugate of the FT of the reference; the CCF is obtained from this result by an inverse FT operation. Rotational alignment is then obtained similarly by searching for a maximum in the rotational correlation function (RCF). The image and reference are both converted to cylindrical coordinates, and the cylindrical images are then Fourier transformed in the tangential direction. The resulting one-dimensional FT's are (conjugate) multiplied with each other; the RCF is the inverse FT of this product, integrated over the radial coordinate. The sequence of translational and rotational alignments is normally repeated iteratively until an optimum is obtained (19,7). This method of aligning images is very sensitive and its theoretical noise limit has been calculated (18). Since, however, we use correlation functions to align an image relative to a reference, the image and the reference must be similar (must correlate!). In a mixed population of images this is not always guaranteed; this complication will be discussed later. As an instrument to help sorting mixed populations of images, eigenvector eigenvalue analysis methods in the form of correspondence analysis (2,16) were introduced to this field of research recently (11,5,8,9,14).

MULTIVARIATE STATISTICAL DATA COMPRESSION

Given a set of aligned images, it is possible to express each of the images as a linear combination of predominant, independent "eigenimages" extracted from the set. The prdominant eigenimages are the eigenvectors, of the eigenvector eigenvalue problem to be described below, corresponding to the largest eigenvalues.

A full set of n images, each containing p pixels, can be represented by a single n x p matrix X. The matrix X has as its general element the measured density values x(i,j) at row number i and column j. Row number i contains the densities of all p pixels of image number i. The data set may be seen as a "cloud" of n points in a p-dimensional "image-space" (p-space) or as a cloud of p points in a n-dimensional "pixel-space" (n-space). We can extract the most characteristic properties of the data set X by solving the eigenvector equation:

$$X' \,.\, N \,.\, X \,.\, M \,.\, U \;=\; U \,.\, \Lambda \qquad (1),$$

under the orthonormalization constraint:

$$U' \,.\, M \,.\, U \;=\; I \qquad (2).$$

In these formulae X' is the transposed matrix of X ; M is a p x p diagonal matrix containing weights ("metric" of the image-space); N is a n x n diagonal weight matrix for assigning different weights to different images (metric of pixel-space (14,16)), Λ is the diagonal eigenvalue matrix and I is the unit matrix. The eigenvectors u, the columns of the eigenvector matrix U, are sorted according to the size of the corresponding eigenvalue.

If the metric matrices are taken to be unit matrices (which may be left out) we obtain the eigenvector equation for principal component analysis (cf. (16)), also known as the Karhunen-Loève transform in the field of image processing (cf. 17). In correspondence analysis (2,16), the diagonal elements of the metric matrices N and M contain as their diagonal elements:

$$n_i = \left(\sum_{j=1}^{p} x_{i,j}\right)^{-1} \qquad m_j = \left(\sum_{i=1}^{n} x_{i,j}\right)^{-1} \qquad (3)$$

With these metrics, the first eigenvector will necessarily point to the centre of mass of the data cloud; this eigenvector is predictable and may be ignored. In any subspace excluding the first eigenvector, the analysis is automatically relative to the centre of mass of the cloud which, in turn, allows for a straightforward simultaneous representation of "cases" and "variates" (2,16), or images and pixels in our nomenclature. This simultaneous representation in the "same" subspace, is one of the powerful properties of correspondence analysis, since it facilitates the study of interrelations between the behaviour of the cases (in p-space) and the behaviour of the variates (in n-space) in the subspace. With our generalized metrics M and N , the square distance in p-space between two images is given by:

$$d^2_{i,i'} = \sum_{j=1}^{p} m_j \,.\, (n_i \,.\, x_{i,j} - n_{i'} \,.\, x_{i',j})^2 \qquad (4),$$

which is the Chi-square distance for the metrics given by equation (3) (16,2). The cross-correlation between image i and i' associated with this distance measure is:

$$vc_{i,i'} = \sum_{j=1}^{p} m_j \,.\, n_i \,.\, x_{i,j} \,.\, n_{i'} \,.\, x_{i',j} \qquad (5),$$

which is the general term of the symmetric variance-covariance matrix:

$$VC = N \,.\, X \,.\, M \,.\, X' \,.\, N \qquad (6)$$

The eigenvectors U obtained from equation (1) under the constraint (eq. 2), form a new basis of the image space which now is adapted to the shape of the cloud. The first eigenvector describes the largest variance of the cloud; the second, perpendicular to the first, describes the direction of the largest remaining variance etc. The matrix C containing the coordinates ("factorial coordinates" (2,16)) of all images relative to the unit vectors U of the new basis of the image hyper-space, is calculated by the weighted projection:

$$C = N . X . M . U \qquad (7).$$

It is interesting to note that:

$$C . C' = N . X . M . U . U' . M . X' . N \qquad (8)$$

$$= N . X . M . X' . N = VC .$$

This implies that the Euclidean cross-correlation as well as the corresponding Euclidean distance between image i and image i' in the coordinate space (factorial coordinate space or factor space) is identical to the generalised cross-correlation (eq. 5) and the corresponding generalised square distance (eq. 4) between images in our original data space.

Up to this point in the calculations, no actual reduction of the amount of data has taken place; we still have n eigenimages of dimension p and the number of coordinates per image is n. The data reduction occurs when we restrict ourselves to the eigenimages corresponding to the largest eigenvalues, thereby disregarding the higher ones which describe less and less of the variance in the data set and in our case contain merely noise. We typically use the first four to eight eigenvectors which means that the images are now described by four to eight numbers instead of the original 64x64 = 4096 density values. The data reduction considerably facilitates the understanding of the information present in the set of molecular images in terms of classes or general trends. However, most of the (artificial) intelligence of the procedure lies in the next phase of the procedure: the decision making or classification phase. A didactically oriented paper on eigenvector analysis with generalized metrics is in preparation.

CLASSIFICATION

Since we want to group similar images together in spite of the high noise present in the original data, we exploit the noise reduction and data compression achieved with the eigenvector analysis, and group the images in the compact factor space. In this space we apply a hierarchical ascendant classification (HAC) scheme (3) which means that images (or classes) are merged two-by-two to form larger classes until, for example, a predetermined number of classes has been reached. The merging of images and/or classes into larger classes is based on a variance oriented proximity measure.

This criterion is based on an interesting theorem that can be traced back to Huyghens (cf. ref. 1). The theorem states that for every possible partitioning of a collection of points in an Euclidean space into classes, the total variance of the set equals the sum of the inter-class variance and the total intra-class variance of the classes. The inter-class variance is defined as the variance ("second central moment" or "inertia") of the centers of mass of all classes relative to the center of mass of the total data set. The total intra-class variance is the sum of the internal variances of each of the classes, that is, the variance of each class relative to its center of mass. An optimal partition, for a given number of classes, can now be defined as that partition in which the inter-class variance is maximal and the total intra-class variance is (therefore) minimal. These classes are then as compact as possible in terms of their internal variance, while being at the same time as far apart as possible. To find this optimal partition, however, we have to check out an n! "infinity" of possibilities! The best solution for larger data sets is therefore a local minimum which need not necessarily be the optimal partition defined above.

One of the best schemes to attain such a local minimum is the HAC, using the "minimum added intra-class variance" as merging criterion. We merge two classes if the increase of the total intra-class variance associated with this merging is the minimum possible increase at that level of the classification. The added intra-class variance (AIV) of the partition when merging two classes (or images) i and i' , having the masses w(i) and w(i'):

$$\text{Add.Var.}_{i,i'} = \frac{w_i \,.\, w_{i'}}{w_i + w_{i'}} \,.\, d^2_{i,i'} \qquad (9),$$

where d(i,i') is the Euclidean distance in factor space, which was shown to correspond to the generalised distance in the original data space. At the starting point of the HAC procedure, each image has a mass w(i) equal to 1/n(i).

As was mentioned before, the partitions obtained through the HAC procedure are necessarily suboptimal. The fact that we take two classes (or images) together at a certain level of the HAC procedure binds the members of the two classes together forever. After an initial partitioning with the HAC scheme we therefore enhance the partition obtained by an iterative migration post-processor. Each original image is taken out of the class to which it is allocated and the AIV-proximity relative to all other classes is calculated. If the image is found to fit better in a different class after all, the image is placed into that other class and the intra-class variance of its original class and of its new class are recalculated; the process is then repeated with the next original image. Once all images have been checked and possibly reclassified, the whole partition has normally been changed so much that we have to restart the process. After a few such iterations, no further migrations of images between classes occur, meaning that the process is stabilized. The reclassification refinement was found to decrease the total intra-class variance of the partition by values between 10% and 40% : a considerable enhancement of the quality of the partition.

Furthermore, a number of original images are notoriously bad in the sense that they are not typical within the data set. They may be misaligned particles (see below) or impurities in biochemical preparation etc., and we would like to exclude then from the data set. Since untypical images are not well represented by the first few eigenvectors, these images will all lie relatively close to the origin in the compact factorial coordinate space and thus also lie close to each other. In the subsequent classification procedure, they may end in the same class due to their proximity, although these images have very little in common! To avoid this effect, we may sort the images according to how much of their variance is described by the first few eigenimages, and exclude the poorly represented ones from the classification. Alternatively we may handicap the poorly represented images by giving them a larger initial mass (eq. 9) in the classification procedure.

Another reason for (automatically) ignoring original images is that some images, although they are well represented by the first few eigenimages, have a very large AIV at the time they are merged into a class. In other words, these images do not resemble other images or classes very much. By ignoring the last images to be merged into a class (a predetermined number) in the HAC procedure, this type of "bad" image may be excluded from the classification procedure. The percentage of images to be ignored in this manner may be determined from a histogram of the AIV's of the images at the time they are being merged into a class. We also found it useful to sort the classes obtained by their compactness measured in terms of intra-class variance per class member.

Both the eigenvector analysis and the classification scheme are aimed at reaching an optimal extraction of the information in the data set in a variance oriented (or least-squares) sense. However, the "logical" information and relations that we seek to extract from the data set need not necessarily be directly related to the variance relations! For example, in the model experiments reported in the companion paper (10), what we want to obtain from the classification are small groups containing images corresponding to a narrow angular range of projection. The logical relations that we want to reveal are of angular nature in that case. Weighting of the factorial coordinates may help to obtain "logical" classes (14). However, what logical relations are, or what a satisfactory partioning of the data set is, are determined by the user and thus by "outside intelligence" (14). This may be seen as a fundamental limit of any classication scheme: a partition is "satisfactory" because it fits with some sort of a priori information that the user has. If the program were capable of providing us with an absolute partition into classes, plus their justification, it would no longer be merely a classification program but would rather represent artificial intelligence! For further details on the classification algorithm and its efficient implementation see reference (14).

MULTI-REFERENCE ALIGNMENT PROCEDURE

The need to align the images prior to the multivariate statistical analysis is a unique and interesting problem. In the statistical analysis of questionnaires, for example, question j for individual i is at the same position as question j for individual i' and we can readily compare the various answers to that question. In our type of image processing, however, we first have to bring corresponding image areas in the different images in register prior to the statistical analysis. To align the data set we start aligning the images relative to a first reference image, chosen at random from the data set, using the techniques described above. For a good alignment, however, the reference image must be as noise-free as possible (18). We therefore add those images together from the data set, aligned with respect to the first reference, that have a high correlation coefficient relative to that first reference and we then repeat the alignment using this relatively noise-free sum as a second reference.

Moreover, we can only align an image relative to a reference if that image looks like the reference. In a mixed population of images, this implies that we have to use the various class-averages as references, which are not available in the early stages of the analysis! The alignments are therefore alternated by classifications to find new references and the whole procedure is of an iterative nature. In aligning the set of images relative to a number of references, we proceed with that aligned version of each image which has the highest correlation coefficient relative to one of the references. The references themselves are also subjected to this "multi reference alignment" procedure so as to assure a good total alignment of the data set. The approach leads to a minimization of the total variance of the data set relative to the centre of mass (13). The variance represented by the centre of mass is thereby maximized. The spectrum of eigenvalues shows characteristic changes during the various iterations of the multi-reference alignment procedure: the first few eigenvalues represent an increasing percentage of the total variance of the data set. It is therefore not only the first eigenvector which points to the centre of mass (correspondence analysis metrics) that is maximized, but the lower eigenimages in general.

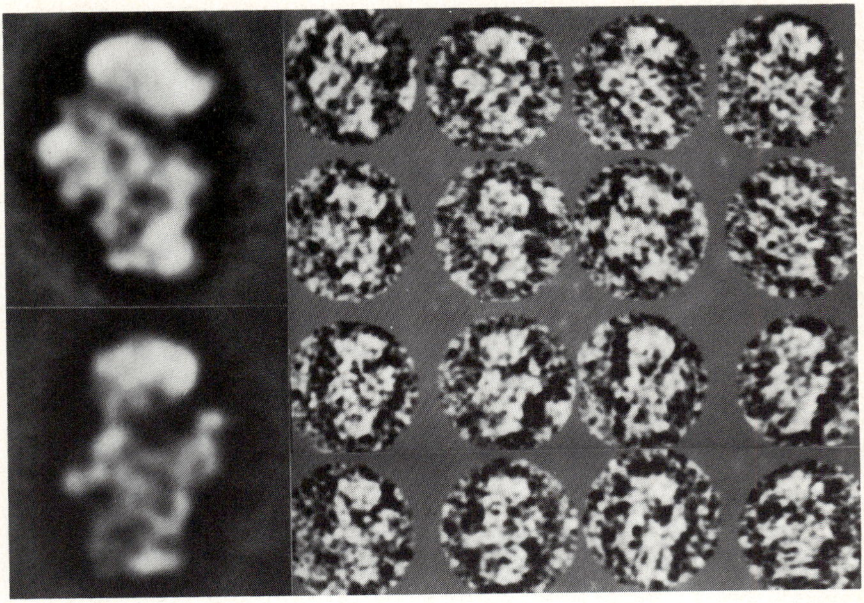

DISCUSSION

As an example of the results obtained with the technique, results are presented of our recent research on the 30S Ribosomal subunits of Bacillus stearothermophilus (15). The data set consisted of 914 individual images that were aligned and classified as described above. This resulted in 30 good classes, of which two characteristic classes, each containing around 60 images, are shown in the figure above. Together with the two classes are some of the (aligned!) original images that were added into these class-averages. Since these images were all intermixed in the original micrographs (15), this example serves as a demonstration of the sorting power of the technique!

The whole iterative procedure of multi-reference alignments, eigenvector analysis and subsequent classifications is rather complex in its organization, and an efficient and easy to use image processing system such as IMAGIC (12) is indispensable. As an example of the calculation times involved, a double alignment (two iterations) of n=914 30S Ribosomal subunits of 64x64 density values relative to one reference takes about 4 hours of CPU on a VAX-780. We can thus align more than 400 molecules per hour. Since we aligned the set relative to ten different references and then repeated the alignment with new references, the full alignment took more than 80 hours of CPU of the VAX computer. The determination of the eigenvectors took about 15 hours of CPU. Human interaction (selection of new references, for example), is still required at different points in the analysis. In practice, the procedure takes around two full weeks to be completed on a dedicated computer. The main problem in extending the analysis to, for example, 5000 molecular images simultaneously is our current eigenvector analysis program of which the CPU requirements are roughly proportional to n**3. A new algorithm is being developed of which the CPU requirements are roughly proportional to n.

Once the various characteristic views of the molecule have been found, we want to fit these projections into a three-dimensional reconstruction of the object to get to the final goal of the study: the determination of the 3D structure of the macromolecule under investigation. This is the subject of a different paper in these proceedings (10).

ACKNOWLEDGEMENTS

I would like to thank Dr. George Harauz and Vesna Fijala for help with the programming effort and the image processing work. I would also like to thank Dr. Marina Stöffler-Meilicke for providing the images of the 30S Ribosomal subunit used in the example.

REFERENCES

(1) J.-P. Benzécri, M. Danech Pejouh, T. Moussa and J.-P. Romeder, Analyse descriminante et Analyse Factorielle, Les Cahiers de l'Analyse des Données 4 (1977) 369-406.

(2) J.-P. Benzécri, L'Analyse des Données, Vol 2: L'Analyse des Correspodances, (1980) Dunod, Paris.

(3) F. Benzécri, Introduction a la Classification Automatique d'Après un Example de Données Médicales, Les Cahiers de l'Analyse des Données 5 (1980) 311.

(4) T.L. Blundell and L.N. Johnson, Protein Crystallography, (1976) Academic Press, New York.

(5) M.M.C. Bijlholt, M.G. van Heel and E.F.J. van Bruggen, Comparison of 4x6-meric Hemocyanins from Three Different Arthropods using Computer Alignment and Correspondence Analysis, J. Mol. Biol. (1982) 161, 139-153.

(6) J.Frank., W. Goldfarb, D. Eisenberg, and T.S. Baker, Reconstruction of Glutamine Synthetase using Computer Averaging, Ultramicroscopy 3 (1978) 283-290.

(7) J. Frank, A. Verschoor and M. Boublik, Computer Averaging of Electron Micrographs of 40S Ribosomal Subunits, Science 214 (1981) 1353-1355.

(8) J. Frank, A. Verschoor and M. Boublik, Multivariate Statistical Analysis of Ribosome Electron Micrographs (L and R. Lateral Views of the 40S Subunit from HeLa Cells), J. Mol. Biol. (1982) 161, 107-137.

(9) J. Frank and M. van Heel, Correspondence analysis of Aligned Images of Biological Particles, appendix to: J. Frank, A. Verschoor and M. Boublik, J. Mol. Biol. (1982) 161, 107-137.

(10) G. Harauz and M. van Heel, Direct 3D Reconstruction from Projections with Initially Unknown Angles, these proceedings.

(11) M. van Heel and J. Frank, Use of Multivariate Statistics in Analysing

the Images of Biological Macromolecules, Ultramicroscopy 6 (1981) 187-194.

(12) M. van Heel and W. Keegstra, IMAGIC : a Fast, Flexible and Friendly Image Analysis Software System, Ultramicroscopy 7 (1981) 113-130.

(13) M. van Heel, J.P. Bretaudière and J. Frank, Classification and Multi-Reference Alignment of images of macromolecules, Proc. of 10th Int. Congr. on Elec. Mic., Hamburg 1982, Vol. 1, 563-564.

(14) M. van Heel, Multivariate Statistical Classification of Noisy Images (Randomly Oriented Biological Macromolecules), Ultramicroscopy 13 (1984) 165-184.

(15) M. van Heel and M. Stöffler-Meilicke, Characteristic Views of E.coli and B.stearothermophilus 30S Ribosomal Subunits in the Electron Microscope, EMBO Journal, in press.

(16) L. Lebart, A. Morineau and N. Tabard, Techniques de la Description Statistique (Dunod, Paris, 1977).

(17) A. Rosenfeld and A.C. Kak, Digital Picture Processing, Vol 1, 2nd ed., Academic press (1982): Chap. 5-10.

(18) W.O. Saxton and J. Frank, Motif Detection in Quantum Noise Limited Electron Micrographs by Cross-correlation, Ultramicroscopy 2 (1977) 219-227.

(19) M. Steinkilberg und H.J. Schramm, Eine verbesserte Drehkorrelationsmethode für die Strukturbestimmung, Hoppe-Seyler's Z. Physiol. Chem. 361 (1980) 1363-1369.

(20) P.N.T. Unwin and R. Henderson, Molecular Structure Determination by Electron Microscopy of Unstained Crystalline Specimens, J. Mol. Biol. 94 (1975) 425-440.

PATTERN RECOGNITION IN PRACTICE II
E.S. Gelsema and L.N. Kanal (Editors)
Elsevier Science Publishers B.V. (North-Holland), 1986

AUTOMATED ANALYSIS OF DIGITAL IMAGES GENERATED BY TWO-DIMENSIONAL GEL ELECTROPHORESIS

Reinhold C. Mann, Betty K. Mansfield, James K. Selkirk

Biology Division, Oak Ridge National Laboratory
Oak Ridge, Tennessee 37831

Two-dimensional gel electrophoresis is a method to separate proteins according to their molecular weights and mobilities in an electric field at a certain pH value. The presence of a radioactively or fluorescently labeled protein in a preparation is indicated by a spot that is produced on a film with the intensity of the spot indicative of the amount of protein. This article presents algorithms that accomplish automated quantitative analysis of digitized gel images. The limits of currently available analysis systems are discussed. The methods are implemented by software on a commercially available digital image processor that uses a minicomputer host.

INTRODUCTION

Mammalian cells contain thousands of proteins each representing a specific function for maintaining the cell's biochemical, genetic, or structural homeostasis. When a physical process or a chemical insult occurs, enzymatic systems are stimulated to repair the damage and/or metabolize xenobiotics to less toxic forms for excretion. Two-dimensional gel electrophoresis is uniquely sensitive in its ability to separate these proteins in the first dimension by isoelectric focusing as a function of net charge, and in the second dimension as a function of molecular weight. In order to fully comprehend transformation of a normal cell to a diseased cell (e.g., cancer, mutation) it is critical to determine the cascade of events that accompany this transformation process. Analysis of the voluminous information inherent in a two-dimensional gel requires localization, identification and quantitation of each protein. It is also necessary to make facile comparisons between multiple gels that reflect protein patterns from various disease states or after carcinogen or mutagen treatment, in order to demonstrate subtle changes that occur in the progression to the diseased state.

Throughout this article we will refer to images generated on X-ray film by radiolabeled proteins in the electrophoresis gels as gel images. We are dealing with one spectral band, i.e., images with gray values between 0 (black) and 255 (white), which correspond to optical densities (0 - 3 OD). The tasks that must be accomplished by an automated system can be summarized into three main problem areas as follows: (1) the reliable detection of protein spots, (2) quantification of spots, i.e., intensity distribution and possibly spot shape, and (3) the statistical comparison of several images in order to assess changes in the protein patterns.

Since the introduction of high resolution, two-dimensional gel electrophoresis [7], many approaches have been described to automate the quantitative analysis of gel images ([1], [2], [3], [4], [5], [11], [13]). With the exception of Lemkin et al. [4] who use a Vidicon camera, rotating drum scanners were used for image digitization in these reports. The spatial resolution varied from 100 μ to 200 μ between pixels. Although the question of sampling frequency appears to have not been studied rigorously for gel images, a value between 1 and 2 pixels per 200 μ is generally agreed upon as adequate.

All systems described so far in the literature reduce the pictorial data to a list of protein spots, each spot being defined by a triplet, quintuplet or a different but usually small amount of numbers, e.g., location (x,y), spread in x and y, integrated density, and sometimes boundary coordinates. Generally, the data set for each spot also contains verbal information to further characterize the spot. The original images are filtered to eliminate high and very low frequencies. The latter filter is necessary because of a locally varying image background that makes simple thresholding inappropriate for image segmentation. Some systems use a local thresholding technique for background elimination ([2], [4]), others a non-linear min/max filter to be described below ([1], [11]), and in one system [3] this processing step is incorporated into the spot detection and quantification.

For spot detection and quantification there are two different sets of methods: parametric methods that operate on the basis of some model for the spots ([1], [3], [5]), and non-parametric methods that do not rely on any assumptions as to the shape of the spots ([4], [11], [13]). Parametric methods usually assume Gaussian spots. In view of the diffusion processes involved in electrophoresis this appears to be reasonable for most gels that have been carefully prepared. Parametric methods have the advantage over non-parametric methods that considerable data reduction is achieved. Each spot is characterized by five numbers - location, spread in x and y, maximum intensity - and the synthetic image produced by the superposition of all Gaussians can be made to fit optimally in some sense to the original image from which the background has been removed. Further analyses are made on the basis of the optimally adjusted Gaussians, thus considerably reducing computer memory and time requirements. One obvious advantage of non-parametric methods is that non-Gaussian spots can be analyzed with accuracy. Complicated, time-consuming fitting of surfaces is not necessary. Data reduction to the degree accomplished by parametric methods, however, is impossible.

During the past two years computer based systems for gel image analysis have become commercially available. Some of these implement algorithms described in the literature. No attempt has been made so far to compare the accuracy and performance of different systems when applied to the same image data. This makes it difficult for new groups entering the field to decide which approach to follow. This article describes the choices and new developments that have been made in our group where a gel image analysis system has been implemented on a general purpose image processing system using a minicomputer host. We report on simulations performed with our system that allow us to specify the limits of sensitivity and accuracy of our method.

THE COMPUTER SYSTEM

The algorithms to be described below are implemented on one of the Biology Division's minicomputer systems, a PDP 11/70 (Digital Equipment Corp., Maynard, MA). The 11/70 has 1.5 Mbyte main memory, a 68 Mbyte RM03, and a 475 Mbyte RA81 disk, as well as a TE16 magnetic tape drive, and is operating under RSX-11M-PLUS. Images are digitized with an Optronics P-1000 scanning densitometer (Optronics International Inc., Chelmsford, MA). Some image processing functions, as well as image storage during analysis, and image display are performed by a specialized pipelined processor, the IIS Model 75 (International Imaging Systems, Milpitas, CA), with the PDP 11/70 as host computer. The IIS Model 75 is currently equipped with 12 512×512×8 bit refresh memory channels. Images are displayed on a Mitsubishi color TV monitor (Mitsubishi Electronics America Inc.,Compton, CA), and can be copied on film by a Color Graphic Recorder Model 3000 (Matrix Instruments Inc., Orangeburg, NY). All software is written in FORTRAN 77. It consists of a series of programs that have been added to the IIS System 575. A typical gel image is shown in Figure 1. The calibration area C1 is used to set up a look-up table for the conversion of grayvalues, i.e., optical densities, to dpm (disintegrations per minute). This look-up table is generated from each gel image and stored in the corresponding spotlist file. We will not elaborate on calibration, as it does not affect the methods described here. The gel images are approximately 15 cm × 15 cm, and are digitized at a resolution of 100 μ, leading to digital images of 1536 × 1536 pixels. We refer to the dimension of isoelectric focussing as x, the molecular weight dimension will be referred to as y. Although all the examples presented in this article involve either subsampled images or 512 × 512 sections of the original large gel images, all algorithms also operate on the full size images, and the programs can be executed using command files without any user interaction. The IIS image processor is capable of performing convolutions and non-linear point transformations in real time. Since many of the operations for spot detection and quantification are non-linear neighborhood transformations they are performed by the host CPU. Thus, execution times become a very important factor in the choice and/or development of algorithms. Whenever possible, the images are therefore processed line by line or column by column.

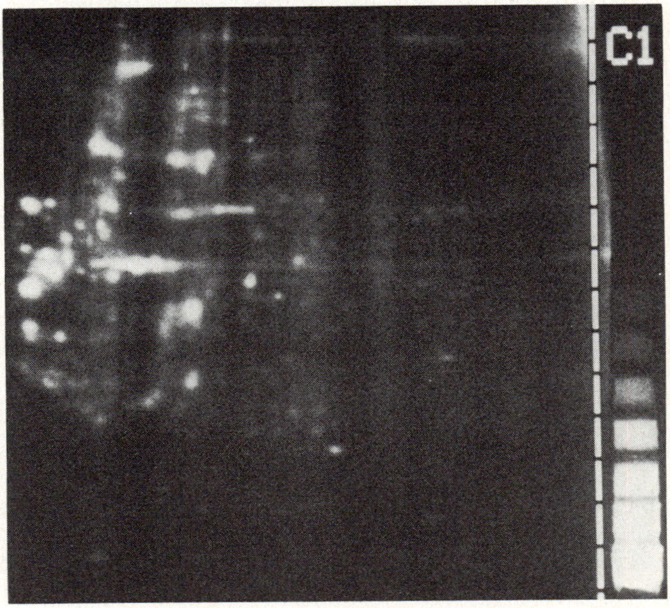

Figure 1: Typical gel image obtained with cytoplasmic proteins of mouse fibroblasts (10T1/2).

BACKGROUND SUBTRACTION

After smoothing the image with a Gaussian low pass filter (window size 7 × 7 pixels), locally varying background including streaks must be removed from the image. Although streaks contain protein too, they are usually not attributable to a well defined spot. The background is calculated using a min/max filter introduced for this application by Anderson [1], explained in more detail by Skolnick [11], and extensively described by Serra [10]. The filtering process consists of first substituting the center pixel of a region with the minimum pixel in that region. In a second pass, using the result of the first pass, the center pixel of the region is replaced by the maximum of all pixels in that region. Regions for the minimum and maximum operations have the same size. This filter can be seen as a three-dimensional analogon to the two-dimensional region shrinking and growing operation. The filter window is chosen to be larger than the largest spot in the image. In our system the window is one-dimensional and the filter is applied to compute the vertical and horizontal background separately. In that case the result of the min/max filter can be thought of as the surface that a pencil would follow if it were rolled across the surface that the image generates when seen from below. If the length of the pencil (i.e., the size of the filter window) is larger than the largest spot diameter, the pencil will not follow the curvature of the spots. Part of a typical gel image along with the vertical and horizontal background computed by the min/max filter, as well as the result of background subtraction are depicted in Figure 2.

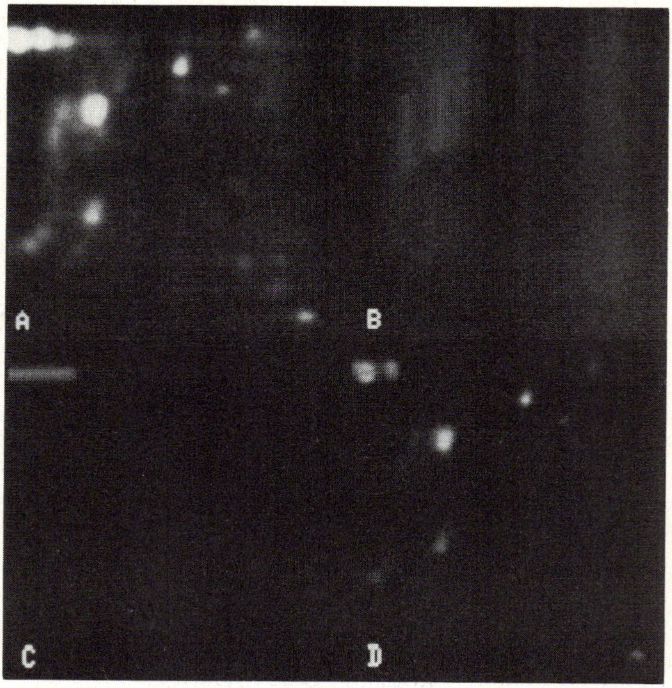

Figure 2: (A) original image, (B) vertical background, (C) horizontal background, (D) background removed.

SPOT DETECTION AND QUANTIFICATION

Once the background is removed, spot detection could be achieved by a simple threshold operation. For quantification, however, it is necessary to be able to address the different regions containing pixels above threshold. In order to accomplish quantitation we assume that the spots can be approximated by separable Gaussians with sufficient accuracy. This assumption allows us to perform the analysis for the two dimensions separately thereby considerably reducing computing time. Thus, we assume that the image is of the form

$$h(x,y) = \sum_{i=1}^{N} \alpha_i \exp\{-1/2(x-\mu_{x_i})^2/s_{x_i}^2\}\exp\{-1/2(y-\mu_{y_i})^2/s_{y_i}^2\}$$

The parameters N, α_i, μ_{x_i}, μ_{y_i}, s_{x_i}, s_{y_i} i=1...N are to be estimated. The information is extracted from the image in two passes. First, all peaks in every line of the image are found and their positions marked in an image that is temporarily stored in refresh memory. Optimal standard deviations (in the least squares sense) for the peaks are determined, and also stored in the temporary image. At this point, overlaps in the x-dimension are handled. This can be done by least squares curve fitting allowing all parameters involved to vary. A quicker, sub-optimal method relies on the assumption that the μ_{x_i} and s_{x_i} are already sufficiently well estimated. Then the α_i for the overlapping spots can be obtained by solving a system of linear equations. Figure 3A shows the result of the first pass for the gel image depicted in Figure 2A. The start of a peak is defined through three consecutive pixels with increasing slope and slope above a selected threshold ρ. The location of a peak maximum is determined by the first three consecutive pixels with negative slope following the start of a peak. ρ controls the sensitivity of the peak finder. The second pass consists of determining which peak can be traced through the second dimension to form a spot. The parameter controlling the sensitivity of this part of the analysis is the window within which a corresponding peak is searched in subsequent lines. It should be noted that this procedure minimizes time-consuming disk i/o, because the images are stored line by line on disk, and the intermediate result from the first pass is stored in the Model 75 refresh memory which can be accessed in both dimensions at the same speed. The pixel values that result form tracing the peaks found in the first pass in the y-direction are now analyzed using the same peak finding subroutine that was used for the analysis in x-direction. Overlapping spots are analyzed correspondingly. Spots that are smaller than an adjustable size threshold (usually 0.5 mm in either dimension) are rejected. The parameters for each spot are stored in a spotlist file. Currently 256 bytes are allocated to hold information on each spot. Figure 3B shows the synthetic image generated from the spotlist file that corresponds to the image shown in Figure 2A. Our method differs from Garrells' [3] in the set of rules that is used to define a spot. This is due to the fact that in our system the background is already removed when spot detection and quantification are performed. Moreover, our system is programmed such that it can easily be used without any spot model, although it is described here as a parametric system.

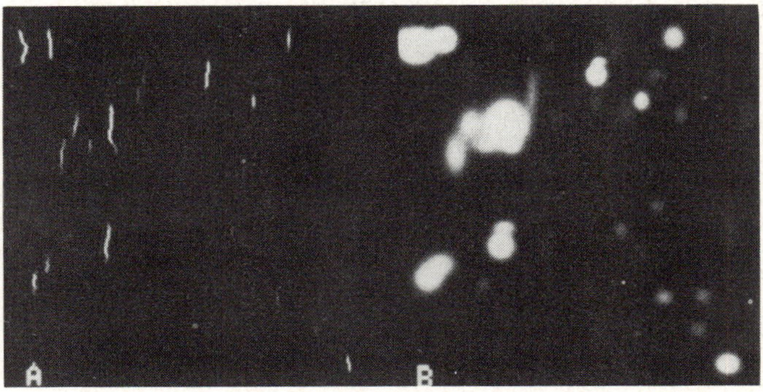

Figure 3: (A) result of analysis in x-dimension, (B) final result of analysis. Contrast enhanced for clearer photographic reproduction.

VALIDATION OF THE ANALYSIS METHOD

The problem with specifying the performance of the method described so far is that the patterns to be recognized, i.e., the protein spots, are not always well defined, especially at low optical densities. Scientists with experience in the reading of two-dimensional gels assert that anything that is reproducible within multiple gels from the same sample is potentially valuable information. There are two questions that must be addressed: (1) how reliably does the algorithm detect protein spots, and (2) how precise is the spot quantification? We performed several experiments to answer these questions.

In order to assess the reliability of spot detection 4 gel images were chosen at random, and the result of the automated analysis was compared to the analyses by two independent experienced technicians. Five non-overlapping 256 × 256 areas were selected at random from each image, and the technicians were asked to flag all spots that could be identified clearly. The results are summarized in Table I which shows false negative (i.e., spot missed by the computer) and false positive (i.e., spot falsely detected by the computer) detection rates. Between 100% and 67.57% of the spots detected by the technicians were also found by the algorithm. The spots that were missed were extremely faint, of non-Gaussian shape or located in crowded regions of gel images where many spots overlapped. 0 to 30% of the spots could clearly be identified as artifacts introduced by the algorithm. These were mostly located in the "tails" of big and bright spots, i.e., in areas that cannot be clearly identified as either background or spot, or in crowded image areas. The maximum false negative detection rate can be reduced substantially by lowering the thresholds of the spot finding algorithm. However, this also leads to an increase in the false positive errors. Detection error rates have not been reported for other systems in the literature making comparisons impossible. Table I shows that there can be quite a difference in the visual analysis of gels between two independent technicians. In view of this variability the results on false negative and positive error rates of our system should be regarded as an indication of the possible range of rates and not as an absolute measure of performance. Nevertheless, these observations indicate some of the serious difficulties encountered in automating gel image analysis.

Simulation experiments were performed in order to test the accuracy of spot quantitation. A test image with 17 Gaussian spots of different sizes, and degrees of overlap was generated. All spots had the same intensity which was varied from 50 to 200 during the experiment. Gaussian noise with varying mean value and standard deviation produced by a random number generator was added to the test image. The noise parameters were chosen to simulate realistic conditions (Kodak SB X-ray film, preflashed to 0.5 OD), i.e. the mean value was allowed to vary from 10 to 30, and the standard deviation from 1 to 5. For each set of parameters 3 independent analyses were performed. It is beyond the scope of this article to give a complete account of the outcome of these simulations. Instead, we present the results for one typical isolated spot as well as for four typical overlapping spots in Tables II and III. ANOVA revealed that the results obtained with different standard deviations were not significantly different. Neither was there a significant difference between the results obtained with different noise mean values. Therefore, the data obtained with different noise parameters were pooled. It should be pointed out that there was an increase in the number of erroneously detected spots with increasing noise standard deviation. None of the 17 test spots was ever missed. It can be seen from Table II that the algorithm approximates an isolated spot with positional error of less than 1 scanning interval. The error in the size estimate is in the same order of magnitude, which translates for the particular spot in this table ($s_x = 6$, $s_y = 15$) to relative average errors between 0 and 2.5%. The relative average errors in the intensity estimates vary from 9.95 to 11.74%, with no error when the image was not disturbed by noise.

Table I:
Reliability of spot detection by computer as compared to visual inspection by two independent human observers H1 and H2.

Gel	Image	N[a] H1	N[a] H2	% false negative H1	% false negative H2	% false positive H1	% false positive H2
AA9	A	47	40	10.64	0.00	4.26	10.00
	B	33	25	30.30	8.00	0.00	0.00
	C	35	36	20.00	22.22	5.71	5.56
	D	53	48	7.54	2.08	1.89	6.25
	E	17	15	23.53	0.00	23.53	13.33
TX3D	A	27	31	32.43	22.58	0.00	3.23
	B	10	9	10.00	0.00	0.00	0.00
	C	17	13	29.41	15.38	0.00	7.69
	D	37	36	2.70	2.77	5.40	8.33
	E	13	10	23.08	0.00	0.00	0.00
Y2101	A	9	7	0.00	0.00	11.11	30.00
	B	4	4	0.00	0.00	0.00	0.00
	C	10	11	20.00	27.27	0.00	0.00
	D	13	7	30.77	0.00	15.38	36.36
	E	14	13	14.29	15.38	0.00	7.69
Y2107	A	24	23	0.00	0.00	4.17	8.69
	B	25	24	4.35	4.17	8.70	4.17
	C	11	10	27.27	20.00	0.00	0.00
	D	21	17	14.29	11.76	0.00	17.65
	E	26	26	15.38	11.53	7.69	3.85

[a] Total number of spots scored.

Table II:
Application of algorithm to simulated image and additive noise: absolute errors obtained for isolated spot (mean values/std. deviations) in 45 independent simulations.

	position Δx	position Δy	size Δs_x	size Δs_y	intensity $\Delta\alpha$
$\alpha = 50$					
no noise:	0.00	0.00	0.00	0.00	0.00
noise:	0.16/0.37	0.22/0.42	0.02/0.15	0.31/0.47	5.87/0.97
$\alpha = 100$					
no noise:	0.00	0.00	0.00	0.00	2.00
noise:	0.33/0.48	0.18/0.39	0.00/0.00	0.18/0.39	10.53/0.59
$\alpha = 150$					
no noise:	0.00	0.00	0.00	0.00	1.00
noise:	0.27/0.45	0.20/0.41	0.00/0.00	0.20/0.41	15.31/0.60
$\alpha = 200$					
no noise:	0.00	0.00	0.00	0.00	1.00
noise:	0.36/0.48	0.38/0.49	0.02/0.15	0.38/0.49	19.89/0.96

Table III:
Application of algorithm to simulated image and additive noise: absolute errors obtained for selected pairwise overlapping spots (mean values/std. deviations) in 45 independent simulations. The case alpha=200 is not considered because of greyvalue overflow (> 255). Parameters for spot pair #1 : $\mu_{x\,1/2}$ = 50/70, $\mu_{y\,1/2}$ = 50/50, $s_{x\,1/2}$ = 10/5, $s_{y\,1/2}$ = 10/10; pair #2 : $\mu_{x\,1/2}$ = 270/270, $\mu_{y\,1/2}$ = 270/250, $s_{x\,1/2}$ = 10/7, $s_{y\,1/2}$ = 14/6

	position Δx	position Δy	size Δs_x	size Δs_y	intensity $\Delta\alpha$
pair #1 :					
$\alpha = 50$					
no noise:	0.00	0.00	0.00	0.00	0.00
	0.00	0.00	1.00	0.00	3.00
noise:	0.27/0.46	0.40/0.51	0.00/0.00	0.40/0.51	4.33/1.18
	0.80/0.41	0.20/0.41	2.20/0.41	0.20/0.41	2.73/4.88
$\alpha = 100$					
no noise:	0.00	0.00	0.00	0.00	0.00
	0.00	0.00	3.00	0.00	12.00
noise:	0.33/0.49	0.13/0.35	0.07/0.26	0.13/0.35	11.73/5.62
	0.87/0.35	0.07/0.26	2.87/0.35	0.07/0.26	10.47/9.16
$\alpha = 150$					
no noise:	0.00	0.00	0.00	0.00	0.00
	0.00	0.00	3.00	0.00	19.00
noise:	0.33/0.49	0.20/0.41	0.07/0.26	0.20/0.41	21.33/5.50
	1.00/0.00	0.13/0.35	3.07/0.46	0.13/0.35	20.40/9.31
pair #2 :					
$\alpha = 50$					
no noise:	0.00	4.00	0.00	2.00	2.00
	0.00	2.00	1.00	1.00	8.00
noise:	0.40/0.51	4.47/0.74	0.07/0.26	3.73/0.96	5.73/0.96
	0.33/0.49	2.40/0.51	1.13/0.35	1.60/0.63	11.47/0.74
$\alpha = 100$					
no noise:	0.00	3.00	0.00	3.00	2.00
	1.00	2.00	1.00	1.00	17.00
noise:	0.33/0.49	2.86/0.35	0.00/0.00	3.20/0.77	8.33/1.99
	0.86/0.35	2.20/0.41	1.47/0.52	2.00/0.00	21.33/7.88
$\alpha = 150$					
no noise:	0.00	0.00	0.00	3.00	1.00
	1.00	2.00	1.00	1.00	26.00
noise:	0.07/0.26	2.86/0.38	0.00/0.00	2.86/0.38	11.43/2.94
	1.00/0.00	2.47/0.52	1.87/0.35	2.00/0.00	37.80/0.77

Table III shows that the accuracy of spot estimation decreases for overlapping spots. The average positional error is between 0.33 and 4.47, the average errors in the size estimates are between 0 and 3.73 scanning intervals, which amounts to relative errors between 0 and 37.3% for the spots in this table. The relative average errors in the intensity estimates are between 8.66% and 25.2% with values between 0% and 17.33% in the absence of noise. A simple geometrical argument shows that if the major or minor axes of a spot form an angle γ of less than 10° with the vertical or horizontal then the error in the spot size estimate is less than 3%. The volume V of a Gaussian spot, i.e., the amount of radioactivity if a greyvalue - dpm calibration is performed, is given by

$$V = 2\,\pi\,\alpha\,s_x\,s_y$$

Thus the relative errors in the spot size and intensity estimates must be added to obtain the relative error for the radioactivity estimate. If we allow an angle γ of less than 10° (an assumption that is always fulfilled for gel images obtained in our lab) then we can conclude from the simulation experiments that we can expect relative errors in the radioactivity estimates of isolated spots between approximately 10% and 20%. For overlapping spots this range would be expected to increase to about 10% to 60% depending on the degree of overlap. This information is not available for many of the systems that have been described in the literature. Ridder et al. [9] report briefly on simulations performed with their system which performs non-parametric quantitation. The authors do not specify the kind of noise that was added or its level. Their result, an error around 10% for the radioactivity estimate, although similar to ours, should therefore be viewed with caution. Bossinger et al. [2] also describe a non-parametric quantitation method and report relative differences in the radioactivity estimates of up to 30% between analyses of two images obtained from the same gel. These authors did not perform any simulations. We shall elaborate on the significance of these error margins when we discuss the comparison of gel images in the next section.

COMPARISON OF GEL IMAGES

The goal in automating gel image analysis is to quantify a large number of protein spots on a gel, and to compare an eventually large number of gel images in order to detect the emergence of new proteins and/or a change in the amount of existing proteins. Comparison of two gel images becomes non-trivial because minute changes in the conditions under which gel electrophoresis is performed, result in considerable spatial distortions of the gel image. Registration errors due to small inconsistencies in the process of mounting the x-ray film on the scanner for digitization, add to the problem.

Several methods have been described to compare gel images ([1], [3], [4], [6], [8], [12], [13]). The common procedure is to start with a number of interactively defined matching spots, so-called "landmarks", and to apply heuristics in order to find more matching spots starting in the neighborhood of landmarks. Prior to the matching procedure, images are usually brought into close registration by spatial warping, generally consisting of globally or locally polynomial coordinate transformations. The only algorithm published so far that differs completely from this approach is the one by Skolnick et al. [12]. These authors completely avoid image warping by using graphs to describe the information extracted from gel images and comparing the graphs for the presence or absence of nodes. This method attempts to follow the apparent human approach to spot pattern comparison in that it looks for matches in characteristic spot constellations rather than individual spots. Their method, however, is not quantitative, i.e., only the presence or absence of protein spots is detected.

We are currently exploring both approaches, and report here on a method based on polynomial warping. This spatial transformation is applied to the spot location coordinates extracted from the original gel images and stored in the spotlist files. Crosses are displayed at spot locations in a 512 × 512 image that is obtained from the 1536 × 1536 original by subsampling (cp. Figure 4), and the user defines a series of landmarks, i.e., well-defined and clearly recognized matches. This is done interactively using the flicker function of the IIS System 575. This software package also contains a fast warp function that implements the following transformation:

$$u = a_0 + a_1\,x + a_2\,y + a_3\,x^2 + a_4\,xy + a_5\,y^2 + a_6\,x^3 + a_7\,x^2y + a_8\,xy^2 + a_9\,y^3$$

$$v = b_0 + b_1\,x + b_2\,y + b_3\,x^2 + b_4\,xy + b_5\,y^2 + b_6\,x^3 + b_7\,x^2y + b_8\,xy^2 + b_9\,y^3$$

The coefficients a and b are obtained by least squares estimation from the landmark coordinates. Figure 4C shows the result of warping the image in Figure 4B onto the image in Figure 4A. The effect of this transformation on a rectangular grid is depicted in Figure 4D. With the gels produced in our laboratory so far this transformation appears to be appropriate. It requires, however, that between 20 and 40 landmark spots be defined by the user.

Following the spatial adjustment of images such that the protein spots they have in common are in adequate registration, a search through the spotlist data base is performed that retrieves the desired pieces of information on selected or all spots in a series of images. This search can be controlled interactively by moving a cursor on the image display screen into the desired spot, or it can be carried out automatically as a batch operation. Two spots match if a weighted Euclidean distance between them is smaller than a specified threshold. Prior to comparison a grayvalue to dpm conversion is of course required.

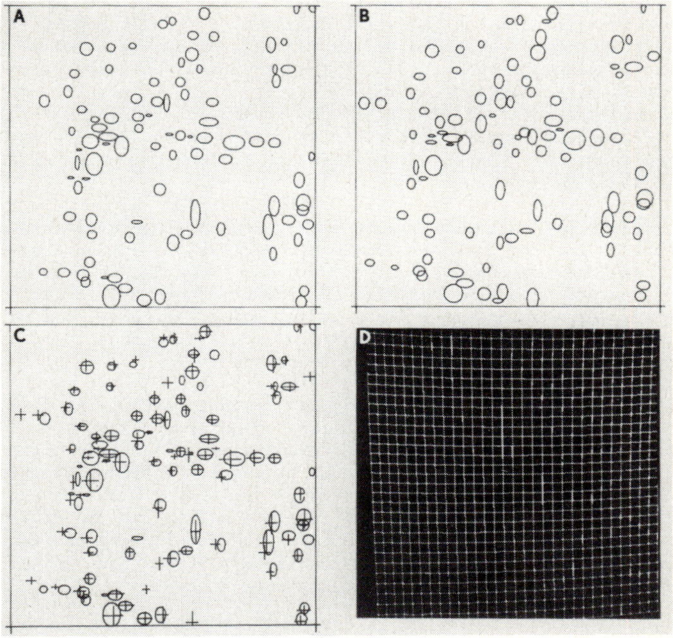

Figure 4: (A, B) two images of the same gel, (C) image in (A) (ellipses) and spatially transformed image in (B) (crosses), (D) effect of transformation on a rectangular grid.

It should be pointed out that due to statistical fluctuations in the results of spot detection and quantitation a comparison of two single spotlists cannot provide statistically significant statements as to the change in a spot pattern. Multiple gels from the same sample and multiple images from the same gel are required in order to characterize any possible differences between gel images. The simulations showed that the radioactivity estimate for an isolated spot can be in error by as much as 20%. This signifies that spots need to differ by at least that amount in order to be labeled significantly different from each other. In order to specify the probabilities of errors when making such a statement it is necessary to analyze several images.

DISCUSSION

To date some seven systems for automated analysis of images generated by two-dimensional electrophoresis have been described in the literature ([1], [2], [3], [4], [5], [12], [13]). Common to all methods is the division of the analysis into three steps: (1) smoothing and film background removal, (2) protein spot detection and quantitation, (3) comparison of spots in different gel images. These steps are performed sequentially and independently on each other. It is, however, quite obvious that the three tasks are not mutually independent. The choice of filter parameters in (1) influences the results of (2). Conversely, the size of the spots and their arrangement affect the results of (1). Naturally, all of this affects the outcome of (3) significantly.

In the course of our studies we have been examining the false negative and false positive detection errors committed by our analysis system as compared to independent experienced human observers. One of the results is that the error rates could probably be reduced significantly by guiding analysis step (2) with the help of a priori knowledge obtained from other gel images, i.e., by combining steps (2) and (3). Corresponding results with other systems have not been published, but can be assumed to be not substantially different from ours because of the similarity in the approaches.

Such a system would become more reliable with increasing number of images analyzed. This is not the case with currently available systems because every new gel image is analyzed independently of any already known images. It is being suggested to consider expert systems for the comparison of gel images and handling of the resulting large data bases. This is not going to improve the performance of any method measured in a pattern recognition context because the interdependence of steps (1), (2), and (3) is still being ignored.

The complexity and size of the problem suggest to apply methods of Artificial Intelligence, i.e., to study the applicability of an expert system that would combine steps (1), (2), and (3). We are currently exploring this approach. Such a system would implement to a certain degree procedures followed by people experienced in the reading and interpretation of gels. It would be able to learn and modify its rules if necessary as more and more gel images are analyzed. It appears that this system should be developed if the sensitivity and usefulness of two-dimensional gel electrophoresis as a technique for the study of mechanisms in carcinogenesis and mutagenesis is to be fully established.

ACKNOWLEDGEMENT

We thank Dan L. Million for support with system software, and Connie E. Schmid for help with application programs. This research was sponsored by the Office of Health and Environmental Research, U.S. Department of Energy, under contract DE-AC05-84OR21400 with the Martin Marietta Energy Systems, Inc.

REFERENCES

[1] Anderson, N.L., J. Taylor, A.E. Scandora, B.P. Coulter, N.G. Anderson, The TYCHO system for computer analysis of two-dimensional gel electrophoresis patterns. Clin. Chem. 27, 1807-1820 (1981).

[2] Bossinger, J., M.J. Miller, K.P. Vo, E.P. Geiduschek, N.H. Xuong, Quantitative analysis of two-dimensional electrophoretograms. J. Biol. Chem. 254, 7986-7998 (1979).

[3] Garrels, J.I., Two-dimensional gel electrophoresis and computer analysis of protein synthesized by clonal cell lines. J. Biol. Chem. 7961-7979 (1979).

[4] Lemkin, P.F., L.E. Lipkin, GELLAB: A computer system for 2d gel electrophoresis analysis. Parts I, II, III. Comp. Biomed. Res. 14, 272-297, 335-380, 407-446 (1981).

[5] Lutin, W.A., C.F. Kyle, J.A. Freeman, Quantitation of brain proteins by computer analyzed two-dimensional electrophoresis. in: Electrophoresis '78, N. Catsimpoolas, ed., Elsevier/North Holland, Amsterdam-New York, 1979.

[6] Miller, M.J. P.K. Vo, C. Nielsen, E.P. Geiduschek, N.H. Xuong, Computer analysis of two-dimensional gels: Semi-automatic matching. Clin. Chem. 28, 867-875 (1982).

[7] O'Farrell, P.H., High resolution two-dimensional electrophoresis of proteins. J. Biol. Chem. 250, 4007-4021 (1975).

[8] Pardowitz, I., H.G. Zimmer, V. Neuhoff, Spot identification in two-dimensional patterns by a least-squares template matching. Clin. Chem. 30, 1985-1988 (1984).

[9] Ridder, G., E. VonBargen, D. Burgard, H. Pickrum, E. Williams, Quantitative analysis and pattern recognition of two-dimensional electrophoresis gels. Clin. Chem. 30, 1919-1924 (1984).

[10] Serra, J., Image analysis and mathematical morphology. Academic Press, London-New York, 1982.

[11] Skolnick, M.M. S.R. Sternberg, J.V. Neel, Computer programs for adapting two-dimensional gels to the study of mutation. Clin. Chem. 28, 969-978 (1982).

[12] Skolnick, M.M., J.V. Neel, An algorithm for comparing 2-d electrophoretic gels, with particular reference to the study of mutation. in Advances in Human Genetics, Vol. 16, H. Harris, K. Hirschhorn, eds., Plenum Press, New York, in press (1984).

[13] Vo, K.P., M.J. Miller, E.P. Geiduschek, C. Nielsen, A. Olson, N. H. Xuong, Computer analysis of two-dimensional gels. Anal. Biochem. 112, 258-271 (1981).

DISCUSSION

Abmayr:

What is the resolution of your imaging system?

Mann:

The optical density range is three optical densities and it is digitized with a resolution of 8 bits. We feel that a spatial resolution of 100 micron in both directions is sufficient. We really did not do any definite studies on that. One hundred micron seems to be generally agreed upon for this application. We did a few images with 50 micron resolution which produced a huge amount of data. We analyzed subsections of the image and compared the results with those for the 100 micron resolution images. We didn't really find major differences. I wouldn't say significant because we did only a few images. When you go up to 200 micron in spatial resolution, the separation of overlapping spots becomes more difficult and you might identify a number of them as single spots.

Aus:

How much error is introduced by the film and its processing?

Mann:

I have no figures on that. It is known that considerable errors may occur. I know that there are some efforts to by-pass the film and to measure the intensity of the spots directly.

Perkins:

The assumption is made that the electrophoresis image signal has a Gaussian distribution and further processing is based on this fact. However, there are variations in the electrophoresis measurement which are independent upon the procedure for separation. Would not a model distribution based upon separation and labelling parameters be more accurate?

Mann:

In view of the diffusion processes involved in electrophoresis it appears appropriate to assume Gaussian spot profiles, and visual inspection of a great many profiles can confirm that. Our assumption of separable Gaussians was made solely to reduce computational effort, and does indeed constitute a source of error in the analysis of some spots, as pointed out before. In my opinion, however, the possible inadequacy of the Gaussian spot model does not represent the main source of error in quantitative two-dimensional gel electrophoresis. It would be interesting to compare the results of a parametric gel image analysis system like ours with the results obtained with a non-parametric system like the one by Lemkin and Lipkin. It appears advisable to apply current systems to a common set of gel images and compare the results.

PATTERN RECOGNITION IN PRACTICE II
E.S. Gelsema and L.N. Kanal (Editors)

USE OF MODELS IN THE RECOGNITION OF PATTERNS OF CELLULAR MOVEMENT

M. M. Jordan, W. J. Perkins

National Institute for Medical Research
The Ridgeway
Mill Hill
London. NW7

In recent years, there has been an increasing interest in the mechanisms controlling cellular movement, both complete cell movement and the movement of intracellular features. One group of cells being studied are macrophages and their action in destroying foreign organisms and debris. To try to understand more of the mechanisms controlling this action, a study of the intracellular movement of the macrophages was undertaken. This has been linked to a descriptive model which can be used in a deductive manner to obtain a better understanding of the biological process and to test possible hyphotheses.

INTRODUCTION

In recent years, there has been an increased interest in the mechanisms of cellular function and one area of particular interest is cellular movement, both of the whole cell and of the intracellular structures. Different types of cell are of interest but this study involved the action of macrophages. These are large phagocytic cells which engulf foreign organisms, surrounding them with a membrane from the cell wall. Once inside the cell, an organism is known as a phagosome. The study began with an investigation of the role of lysosomes, which are small enzymes containing spherical structures within the macrophage, in the destruction of phagosomes (phagocytosis). The lysosomes in this study measured approximately 0.5 μm in diameter. In normal cells they move to surround a phagosome and fuse with it. Their movement is described as saltatory i.e. consisting of discrete jumps. Little is known about the control of this movement but it enables the lysosome to contact a phagosome containing an ingested foreign object, fuse with it and, in many instances, digest it.

In earlier studies,(Hart et al 1983, Jordan et al 1985) the action of different drugs on the process of phagosome/lysosome fusion, and on corresponding lysosome movement, was investigated using computer graphics and statistical techniques. It was found that certain drugs stopped lysosome movement and with it the fusion process. This gave some clues to what was happening in the fusion process but also raised more questions. This study was therefore combined with a modelling procedure to check possible hypotheses of lysosome behaviour and as a guide to further experimentation. It consisted of providing descriptive models of the cellular data already obtained which could then be used in a deductive manner to test ideas of possible types of movement.

Such an approach is often necessary in basic biomedical research where the objective is often to obtain a better understanding of the mechanisms under investigation. Using a combination of experiments and modelling of possible hypotheses, clues to the real nature of the subject being studied can be gained.

MOVEMENT OF LYSOSOMES - GRAPHICAL & STATISTICAL TECHNIQUES

Methods

It was noted that certain drugs viz. ammonium chloride (NH_4Cl) and Polyglutamic Acid (PGA), reduced or even stopped lysosome/phagosome fusion when yeast cells were introduced into macrophages. These drugs also seemed to slow or stop the movement of the lysosome. Whilst it was possible to measure fusion on a semi-quantatitive basis by examining the ingestion of yeast cells, it was very difficult to measure related changes in lysosome movement since the individual trajectories of moving lysosomes were impossible to follow. The movement was therefore assessed by using computer graphics displays of the lysosomes over different time periods to obtain a subjective measurement of relative movement and statistical techniques to obtain an objective analysis.

Two series of cells were studied. There were several groups of cells in each series and, in each group, one cell was treated with NH_4Cl, one with PGA and one left untreated as a control. In Series 1, the cells were selected by the microscopist as typical and in Series 2 they were randomly selected.

The cells were photographed using phase-contrast microscopy and serial photographs of each cell were taken over appropriate intervals (2, 10 or 30 seconds). Each enlarged print of the photomicrographs (final magnification x 2200) was covered with a transparent plastic sheet which was marked by the microscopist with the position of the cell boundaries and lysosomes. In addition, fixed reference points, which remained stationary during the recording time and could be easily recognised, were marked in each picture. Biological reference points were used, usually prominent fat globules inside or near the cell being studied. All the transparent sheets were marked by one very experienced microscopist to ensure consistent results.

The marked transparent sheets were used to produce the data for input. The co-ordinates of the cell wall, lysosomes and reference points were entered manually into a PDP-11/34 computer using a graphics tablet with a probe (Perkins & Green 1982). At this stage the images of each cell at the two times to be compared were aligned as closely as possible using the reference points. As each component of a cell was entered, it was categorised to allow separate display or analysis of that component. This meant that different categories could be displayed as different symbols and/or colours. Separate categories were used for the cell wall, reference markers and lysosomes at each time so that, not only could these three components be discriminated from each other, they could also be distinguished from the same components taken at a later time. Only one operator digitised this data to ensure consistency. However, the process was subjected to repeated tests and the results were found to vary by up to 0.2 mm (1 mm is equivalent to 0.5 μm). This error in digitisation was considered acceptable.

Two methods were used to study the time-dependent changes in lysosome positions. The first was a graphical assessment using a three-dimensional reconstruction package (Perkins & Green 1982), which allowed the pattern of the same cell at two (or more) successive times to be superimposed to provide a visual appreciation of movement over that period. Also, the alignment of reference markers could be checked and the cells realigned if necessary.

The computer system is based on a PDP-11/34 with 128 Kbytes, two 5 Mbyte disks and a display system which uses Matrox colour graphics boards. The graphics memory was 512 x 512 x 8 bits giving a choice of 256 colours through a colour look-up table. The display monitor is a 50 cm Barco monitor. The cell walls, reference points and lysosomes were displayed in different symbols and/or colours. Initially the system was based on a monochrome display, with different symbols and patterns used to highlight the various features, but the colour display provided a far superior method of discrimination. By using green and red to represent the lysosomes at the two times, overlap caused the green and red to be superimposed and to appear as yellow. If lysosomes were moving, those at time 0 would tend not to overlap with those at time 1, producing a display with red and green as the predominant colours: on the other hand, lack of movement should lead to more overlap of red and green to produce a display with a significant amount of yellow. All the graphical analysis was done using this method.

The second method consisted of a quantitative numerical analysis using a nearest-neighbour technique to assess how well lysosomes could be paired over a time period. Since individual lysosomes at the two times being compared could not be identified and related with each other on a one-to-one basis, it was assumed that the lysosomes from each time that were closest to each other could be treated as corresponding pairs. For this approach, the analysis was based on all the lysosomes in the cell in order to obtain sufficient numbers for reliable results. Since manual methods would have been complex, inaccurate and sometimes impossible with the numbers of lysosomes involved, a computer algorithm was devised to obtain the results. The lysosome positions at an initial time were compared with those at a later time (2, 10 or 30 seconds later). The user was allowed to input a recognition distance which was taken as the distance within which two lysosomes at different times must lie for them to be considered as a possible pair.

In the analysis, a selection of recognition distances were used and, as one might expect, the larger the recognition distance, the higher the number of pairs obtained. At large recognition distances it became possible to pair lysosomes which could not be considered as corresponding since the recognition distance was approaching the normal inter-lysosomal distance.

Results

Figure 1 shows an example of the results of the graphical analysis. This is a monochrome representation of sections of two cells, one treated with NH_4Cl and one untreated. The lysosomes at different times are represented by different symbols. In the actual analysis the whole cell was used and the symbols were represented by different colours which was a better way of distinguishing lack of movement. It can be seen that the symbols are closely paired in the NH_4Cl treated cell (Fig. 1(a))but more widely dispersed in the normal cell (Fig. 1(b)). This corroborates lack of movement in the NH_4Cl treated cell compared to the normal cell.

The nearest neighbour analysis showed a statistically significant pattern between the NH_4Cl or PGA treated cells and the normal cells. In the former, the pairing of lysosomes over the time interval was large, even at small recognition distances, and significantly greater than that found in normal cells. This again corroborated the lack of movement in the treated cells.

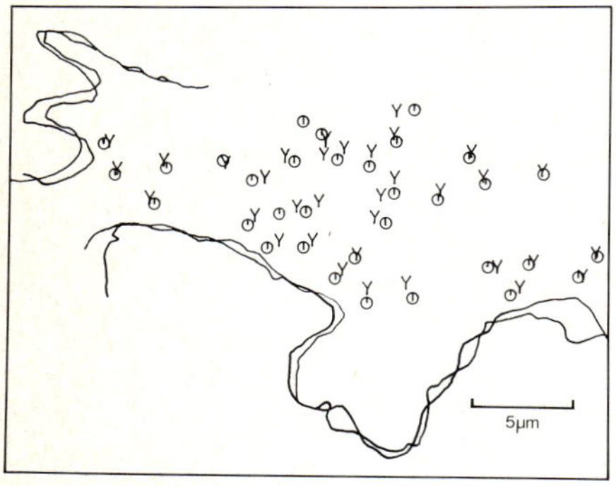

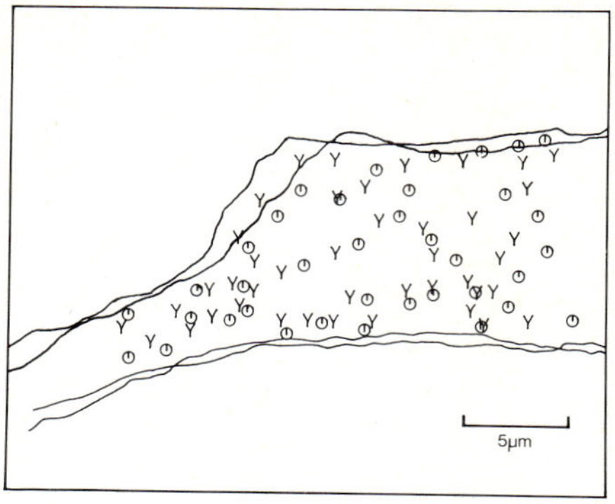

Figure 1 Computer plot of lysosomes at time 0 seconds (O) and time 30 seconds (Y) in (a) a cell treated with NH_4Cl and (b) an untreated cell. It is possible to pair the lysosomes in (a) but not in (b).

MODEL OF LYSOSOME MOVEMENT

Parameters

In order to obtain a better appreciation of the patterns of movement of lysosomes, a simple model was constructed to assess the effect of different assumptions about movement. The parameters of this model were based, in the first instance, on data obtained by visual observation. One of the most important features is the way in which the lysosomes move. When they are removed from the cell, they exhibit Brownian movement so it is believed that, inside the cell, they are attached to and controlled by the cytoskeleton. In this state, they are observed to move in discrete jumps (saltatory motion). Visual observation suggested that the path length of these jumps was of the order of 1-2 μm and occurred several times per second for each lysosome. The lysosomes also seemed to move independently of each other.

The previous studies shared a definite link between movement and phagosome/lysosome fusion but the cause is not obvious. A direct casual effect would be that the lack of movement, caused by the changes, stops the lysosomes clustering around the phagosome so that there is an insufficient number to cause fusion. An indirect effect would occur if the changes cause chemical changes in the cytoskeleton which stop fusion. Either of these theories could be true but in this study, the former possibility was being examined.

The parameters considered in the first model were chosen so that movement over a time period could be examined. The saltatory movement pattern was simplified by assuming that each lysosome moved a fixed number of times per second and that all the lysosomes moved together. It was thought that this assumption would make the patterns easier to generate in programming terms but would still allow satisfactory results. The parameters used in the model were as follows:-

d = path length of each movement - this can be specified as a fixed distance or as a random number in the range d_1 to d_2 where d_1 and d_2 are input variables.

ø = direction - this is a random number in the range 0° to 360°

n = number of movements of each lysosome/second (taken as 2 for all tests appearing in this paper)

T = total elapsed time in seconds

In each run, the number of steps moved by each lysosome = nT

The values of T used were the same as thos associated with the previous graphics studies. The graphic display of the results of the model were identical to those used in the graphic analysis of the original data.

Results

One of the main problems with the data obtained experimentally was that it was impossible to follow individual lysosomes. To test the model therefore, a simple set of test data was used and is shown in figure 2(a). This consists of a cell wall outline with nine points. The modelling routine was used to move these nine points in fixed and random path lengths over periods of up to 30 seconds.

Figure 2(b) shows the amount of movement in a random direction for a fixed path length of 1 um over 20 seconds. This movement is greater than that seen over the same period in the experimental data. The modelling routine was then run using the parameters suggested by visual observations i.e. a random path length of 1 - 2 μm, 2 movements per second, in a random direction, over a period of 30 seconds. The resultant movement obtained was much more than that seen in the experimental data. The figures which best matched the real data are shown in Figure 2 (c) and (d) which were the results of random path lengths for ranges of 0 - 1 μm (c), and 0.25 - 0.5 μm (d). Both were run over 30 seconds and the movement was in a random direction.

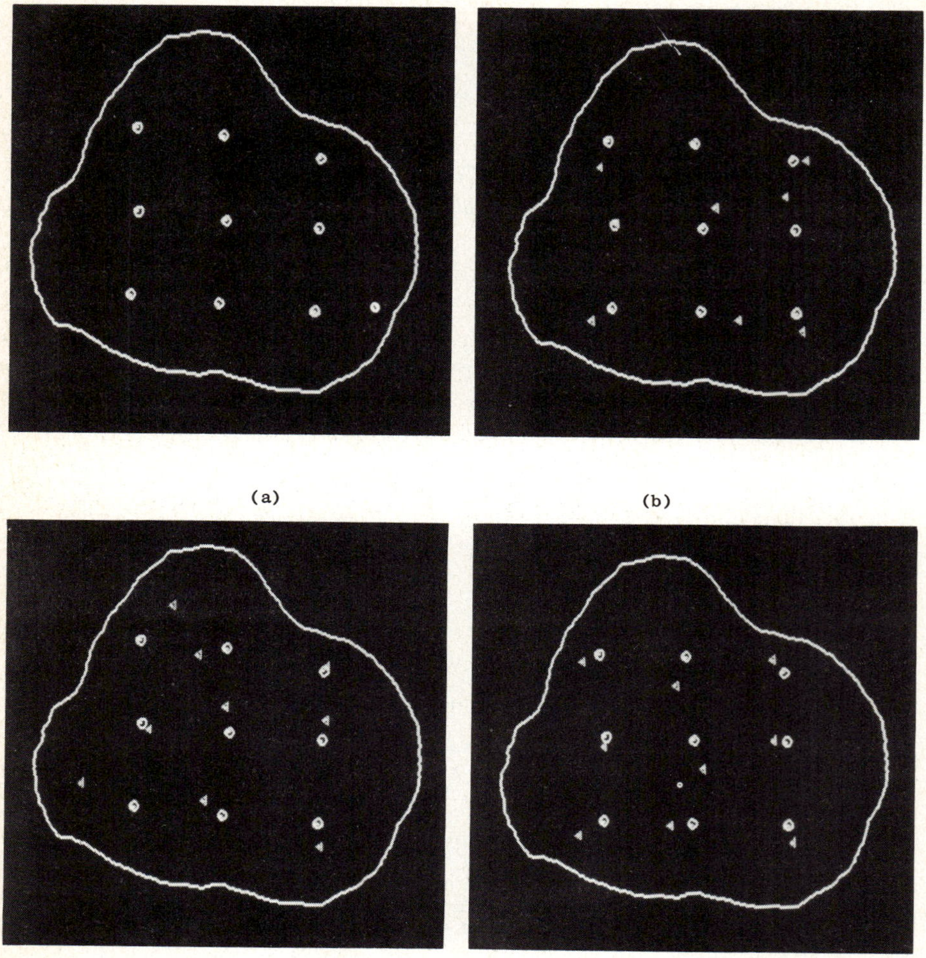

(a) (b) (c) (d)

Figure 2 (a) Test data shown as 0 symbols. Results of the model (shown as Δ symbols)

(b) Fixed path length = 1 μm (two points have moved out of range)

(c) Random path length in range 0 - 1 μm

(d) Random path length in range 0.25 - 0.5 μm

In all cases the direction of movement was random at 2 movements per second over 30 seconds.

Figure 3 shows a section of a real cell obtained experimentally. The lysosomes are shown over a 30 second interval. The results of the model over the same period for a random path length of 0–1 μm are also shown.

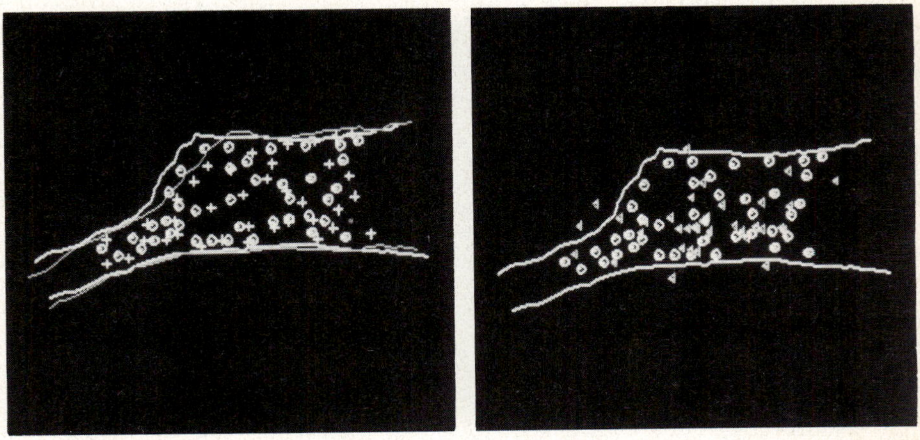

(a) (b)

Figure 3 Results of the model on real data over a time period of 30 seconds with movements 2 times per second and a path length of 0–1 μm.

(a) Real data over 30 seconds, **o** marks the position at time 0 and **+** after 30 seconds

(b) **o** marks the position of the real data at time 0 and **Δ** shows the results of the model after 30 seconds.

The model was also used to test the effect of shorter intervals on the pattern of movement. Surprisingly, an interval of 10 seconds did not produce less overall movement than an interval of 30 seconds. Of all the parameters used, path length was the most sensitive in producing changes in the results of the model.

CONCLUSIONS

The first results of the use of the model led to questions about the visual assessment of movement. The parameters given from visual observation seem unlikely to be correct under the present assumption about movement. The model, although very simple at this stage, has already helped in investigating the mechanism controlling lysosome movement and has raised questions about the visual interpretation. The next step is to confirm or reject these findings in the experimental situation.

This approach of a mixture of modelling and experiments takes the understanding of a process ahead much faster than the use of either one of them alone. The recognition of the power of the computer in terms of memory and processing capabilities, and of the human brain in terms of reasoning and deduction is very important. The best use of both can be made by using the computer to help in the deductive process, by using it in an interactive way which allows users to test their ideas and to change their hypotheses depending on the results. This is a very simple example in that the model is in its initial stages. As our understanding grows, so will the model. Eventually, it should take account of the 3-dimensional structure of the cell, the action of the cytoskeleton and the role of overall cell movement for example. It is important to realise, however, that the aim is not to produce a complex model which deals with all possible structures and variations, but simply to build in as much as is necessary to guide us to the next step in the process of understanding the problem. In this approach, the experts ideas are not built into the computer software, they are an essential part in the study of a changing system.

REFERENCES

1. Hart, P. D'Arcy, Young M. R., Jordan M. M. Perkins W. J. and Geisow M. J. Chemical inhibitors of phagosome-lysosome fusion in cultured macrophages also inhibit saltatory lysosomal movements - a combined microscopic and computer study. Journal of Experimental Medicine 1983, 158, 477.

2. Jordan M. M., Perkins W. J., Young M. R. and Hart, P. D'Arcy Computer graphics and numerical techniques in the measurement of movements within cells. Medical and Biological Engineering and Computing 1985, 23, 48-54.

3. Perkins W. J., Green R. J. Three-Dimensional reconstruction of biological sections. Journal of Biomedical Engineering 1982, Vol. 4. 37 - 43.

DISCUSSION

Choudry:

If you had enough contrast you could have made a time exposure and then got streaks instead of dots. That would have been easier to analyse.

Jordan:

No, you cannot really get streaks instead of dots because these particles are quite faint. I find it difficult to recognize them; an experienced microscopist can recognize them. I was relying on a microscopist to actually mark them.

Van Heel:

Are there mathematical models available for the movements of the cyto-skeleton which might be of help for your analysis?

Jordan:

No, not that I know of.

Young:

That suggestion of Choudry for looking at streaks rather than for dots is actually quite elegant. You could perhaps also look at the fluorescent labelling of the lysosomes; then you have no background, only the image you are interested in.

Jordan:

We did two series. One using phase contrast and another one using fluorescent labelling. It was extremely difficult to pinpoint the lysosomes. They were very, very small. I know that you can use streaks like you do in astronomy when you look at the stars. But in my opinion this will be difficult to use in our problem.

Perkins:

Another point about modelling. One of the problems we have with large numbers of lysosomes is that you really want to label each lysosome and see what each one does. What we can do in the model is to determine the movements for specific items. So we can study the likely behaviour in our model by saying we now know where all these individual lysosomes go. This is another possibility we shall try.

Mulder:

Just a suggestion. Instead of streaks you should probably just store an image and then subtract the next one and so on.

Jordan:

That is true, we are planning this type of analysis right now.

Aus:

Why do you want to label all your lysosomes? What are the biological questions behind the project?

Jordan:

We don't want to label them. We just try to understand the function of the cell. We try to understand what the mechanism is behind the movement and how this mechanism affects the microphage in actually getting rid of the foreign organisms.

Persoon:

I have a question concerning your experiments. I have seen that you use DEC equipment. I have nothing against DEC but you should check your random generator. I know that the one from DEC has some regularities which may affect your results. A good way to inspect the random generator is to display the random numbers on the CRT screen and to look for regularities.

Jordan:

I am aware of the problems that can arise from using an improper random generator and the one being used is not ideal.

PATTERN RECOGNITION IN PRACTICE II
E.S. Gelsema and L.N. Kanal (Editors)
Elsevier Science Publishers B.V. (North-Holland), 1986

COMPUTER COLOUR VISION: AUTOMATED SEGMENTATION OF HISTOLOGICAL TISSUE SECTIONS

Harry Harms and Hans M. Aus

Biomedical Image Processing Laboraory
Institute of Virology and Immunobiology
The Bavarian Julius-Maximilians University
Würzburg, Federal Republic of Germany

Results from multifocus, true color scene segmentation algorithms are presented. The test data image base consists of digitized scenes from rat liver sections.The 3-D reconstructed cell masks correspond directly to the cells diagnosed by laboratory personnel.

INTRODUCTION

Segmentation, identification and classification of tissue sections remains a major unsolved challenge in computer aided cytophotometry. Common difficulties encountered include limited depth of focus, overlapping cells and incomplete structures. A histological tissue section is typically 1 - 10 microns thick, whereas the depth of focus is limited to 0.3 - 0.8 microns in our microscope TV system. Consequently, only parts of the nucleus and cytoplasm are visible at any single focus setting. Cellular material from the same cell usually spreads over several focus settings. Depending on the location of the microtome cut, some cellular material may have been removed in the preparation procedure. Also, considerable damage can result from the microtome cutting process itself. Perfect nuclei and cytoplasm images, with completely closed cellular membranes, are a rare event in histological tissue sections.

Laboratory personnel routinely diagnose many health related problems with such preparations. It is interesting to observe that one has to continuously focus up and down through the preparation in order to obtain a complete mental picture of the section. And, a value judgement about the quality of the cut has to be made before reaching a diagnosis.

Color image acquisition and color image processing are essential subtasks in this method. Reproducible color balancing, compensating for the usual staining variations, and color differencing composes major components of the analysis. The computer method presented here is an extension of those developed in our blood cell project (1). The three major differences in the tissue analysis techniques are: 1) the processing of color images at different focus levels; 2) the addition of a quality judgement step; and 3) a slightly modified cell model to match the specific application. This paper outlines the method and presents the first results on tissue sections.

THE METHOD

As in our segmentation of stained blood cell smears, the first step partitions all those subregions of the tissue which are most likely background or nuclei. A first estimate of the nuclear region mask is generated and subsequently refined, at 5 focus levels. Masks which occur at several levels are combined. An initial value judgement on the quality of the nuclear image eliminates the masks which are probably either not nuclei or too damaged to be further analyzed. Next, characteristic cytoplasm masks are calculated from the regions bordering the nuclei. Geometric and size factors, as well as color differences, further refine the final cytoplasm masks. Lastly, the computer programs reconstruct the cell masks from the nuclear and cytoplasm region masks, according to a cell model. A final quality judgement of the cell masks and regions completes the segmentation of the tissue section.

Only the differences and extentions of our blood smear segmentaion work to tissue sections are detailed below. An exact description of the subtasks envolved has already been published in (1).

Initial Background and Nuclear Subregion Partitioning

The first step in the algorithm locates all subregions in the tissue section which are most likely background or nucleus. Because the section is thicker than the microscopic depth of focus, the process has to be repeated, in this case, at five different focus settings. The initial image acquisition digitizes a three color image red (R), green (G), blue (B) at 5 focus levels. This image acquisition phase stores 15 scans with a maximum single scan size of 512 x 640 pixels with 256 grey levels.

At each focus level the green (T1) and the color difference image (R-G) plus (B-G) (T2) are successively thresholded to obtain the initial coarse background (T1) and nuclear (T2) partitioning, respectively. A simple green or intensity threshold T1 suffices for segmenting those subregions which are definately not part of any nuclei. The complex structure and color variations in the nuclei require the color difference thresholds T2 for the nuclear regions (1). This initial partitioning locates those regions which are most probably background (T1) or nuclear subregions (T2).

Locating the Centers of the Nuclear Subregions

The next step in the initial partitioning marks the approximate center of all the nuclear subregions at each focus setting. The Connectedness algorithms defined by Rosenfeld generate isograms of equal distances from the border of each subregion. Each isogram contains at least one maximum distance to the nearest border. These maxima represent the approximate center of each subregion (see fig 3 in 1). At this point several centers can represent one single nucleus and one center can represent two or more nuclei.

Estimating the Nuclear Mask.

Because the contours in the nuclei are only partially visible at any single focus setting, the common contour and edge following algorithms have limited application in analyzing tissue sections. Alternative methods which avoid contour following need to be developed.

One possible approach assumes a cell model of round nuclei with a maximum radius. The size of the radius depends upon the specific cell/tissue system being investigated. An ideal circular region is placed around each nuclear subregion center. These regions overlap considerably. Analogue to the blood cell segmentation, characteristic separate color difference thresholds are calculated in each circular region. With these new threshold and isograms of equidistances from the region's border, each individual nuclear mask is succesively refined. This processing results in an intermediate collection of nuclear region masks at all 5 focus levels.

Combining the Multifocus Nuclear Masks

Next, the algorithm compares each nuclear mask with any masks located directly above or below it. All corresponding masks are relabeled as belonging to the same nuclear region. Only those masks which occur in atleast 3 levels are marked for further processing. The remaining nuclear regions and their associated cytoplasm found later, are excluded from the final cell mask reconstruction. Such uninteresting regions are either artifacts or nuclei which have been cut during the preparation. At this stage in the processing, the nuclear masks do not necessarily correspond directly to the nuclei in the image. This is resolved during the cytoplasm segmentation.

First Quality Judgement of the Nucleus

Before proceeding with the cytoplasm partition it is essential to identify those nuclear masks which are most probably nuclei. This step is necessary in analyzing histological sections because not all nuclei are intact. Depending upon the location of the microtome cut, considerable nuclear material may have been cut away. In addition to the requirement that a nucleus occur at more than 2 focus levels, one possible measure of the nuclei's intactness is the nuclei shape factor. A high shape factor results when the nucleus has been damaged. Lower shape factors results imply that the nucleus conforms to the shapes expected in the model. This range of acceptable shape factors need to be determined experimentally for each application. This correlates closly to the visual quality judgement performed by laboratory personnel during the diagnosis of a tissue specimen.

Characteristic Cytoplasm Color Differences

Our cell model states that if cytoplasm occurs it usually surrounds a nucleus. Consequently, the algorithm assumes that the region near the nuclear mask's border contains, with high probability, cytoplasm. The first step in the cytoplasm segmentation extends the nuclear isogram 15 pixels beyond the border of the final nuclear masks. In this 15 pixel ring, the characteristic intensity (G) and color difference (R-G) thresholds are calculated at the three middle focus levels for each nuclear mask. These thresholds define the initial color and intensity characteristics of the cytoplasm surrounding the corresponding nuclei. The computer program then partitions the entire tissue section, at all 5 levels, with this cytoplasm learning set (1). At this point in the processing the masks can still contain regions which do not correspond directly to a cell in the tissue. The next step eliminates masks which are too small to fit our cell model. The more difficult task is to decide which masks correspond to single cells and which contain two ore more overlapping or touching cells. Some masks can be further segmented by refining the color difference thresholds in each mask. However, it is often the case that two or more fully identical cell cytoplasms appear next to each other. Such complex images can be solved with geometric shape factors and isograms. The essential assumption is that the cell model does not allow cytoplasm which first decreases and then increases again further away from the nuclei centers. The method assumes that all such masks, where a minimum occurs between two centers, are two overlapping or touching cells with identical cytoplasm. See figure 3 in (1). After locating the minimum between two centers the program simply cuts the cytoplasm image.

Reconstructing Cell Masks

The last step combines and labels the various nuclear and cytoplasm subregions to form the cell masks. One or more nuclear subregions belong to the same cell if surrounded by the same cytoplasm. Two different cytoplasms can not surround parts of the same nucleus. Two different types of nuclei do not occur in one cytoplasm. The algorithm eliminates all such inconsistences. These decisions are consistant with established clinical and biological knowledge. The final labeled image is a reconstruction of the cells occuring in the tissue section.

Final Quality Judgement

The nature of histological tissue sections necessitates one final value judgement of the quality of the reconstructed image. Any nuclear masks which occur at only one or two focus levels have most likely been severely damaged during the preparation and the cutting. All nuclei which touch the edge of the image are also eliminated from further consideration. Laboratory personnel usually avoid diagnosing such incomplete cells.

BIOLOGICAL MATERIAL AND HARDWARE

The biological specimen consists of 4 micron thick paraplast sections of rat liver stained with Mayer Iron Haematoxilin The sections were scanned with an Zeiss Axiomat- microscope Sony color camera system at a sampling rate of 12.5 pixels/micron. The objective is a planapochromat 100x, NA = 1.3. The sections were scanned at 5 different focus levels spaced 0.8 microns appart. The FORTRAN 77 image processing algorithms run on a DEC VAX 11/750. All images in this paper are photographed from a COMTAL Vision One/20.

AN EXAMPLE

Figures 1 and 2 show one TV image of a single tissue section scanned at two different focus levels. The visual quality and contrasts of the nuclei vary in in both this images. Cell "A" in figure 1 can not be identified or properly segmented. The cytoplasm of cell "B" touches that of "C". At the other focus setting, both cells "A" and "B" clearly visible and can be identified. The reconstructed cell masks are shown figure 3, with the appropriate label. Neither "A" nor "E" have passed the two quality judgements. Cell "A" is not labeled because it occurs only at two focus levels. The nucleus of cell "E" touches the edge of the image and has also been eliminated. The touching cytoplasm from cells "B" and "C" has been separated and the uncertain subregions have been removed.

Two focus settings from another area in the same specimen are documented in figures 4 and 5. Typical of all tissue sections, the image and contrast quality varies considerably. The reconstructed cell masks are shown in figures 6 and 7 with the nuclear regions and their most likely cytoplasm areas. The nuclei of the cells touching the image's edge ("F","I") and those detected in less than 3 levels ("G","H") have been removed from the mask. Uncertain cytoplasm regions between cells has also been eliminated.

DISCUSSION

The computer method presented here extends the power of the blood cell smear image processing subtasks to analyze histological tissue sections. The capability and reproducibility of these subtasks has been tested on over 20 000 blood cells. Contrary to most other biomedical image processing algorithms, our methods require neither standardized stains nor interactive scene segmentation. Our specimens consist solely of routine preparations from the clinical laboratory, with the usual variations in color and general quality. Color difference processing eliminates many artifacts.

The nature of histological specimens necessitates 3-D analysis and quality judgement as an integrate part of the scene segmentation. The cell model also plays a major role in this algorithm. Depending on the specific problem, the cell model can easily be changed to match the application.

Contours in histological tissue sections are seldom consistent, reliable or reproducible. Our method does not rely on contour following image processing techniques. This is a major reason for the success of the method reported here and in the blood cell study.

LITERATURE

1) Harms H., Aus H.M., and Haucke, M. High Resolution Digital Segmentation of Stained Cells. Computer Vision, Graphics and Image Processing, submitted.

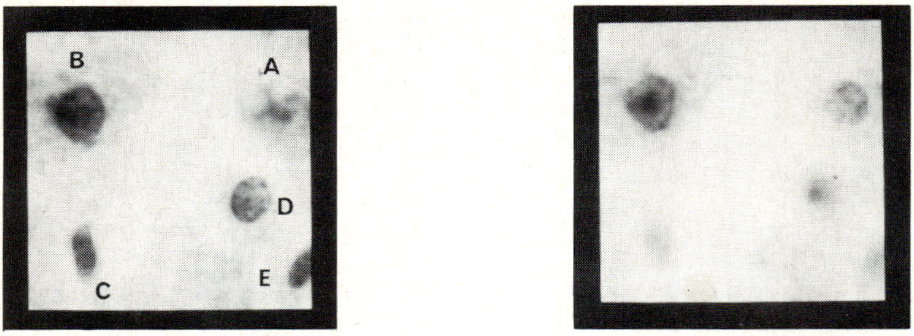

Figure 1 (left) and 2 (right).
Black and white images at two different focus levels, located 2.4 microns appart, from the stained rat liver tissue section.

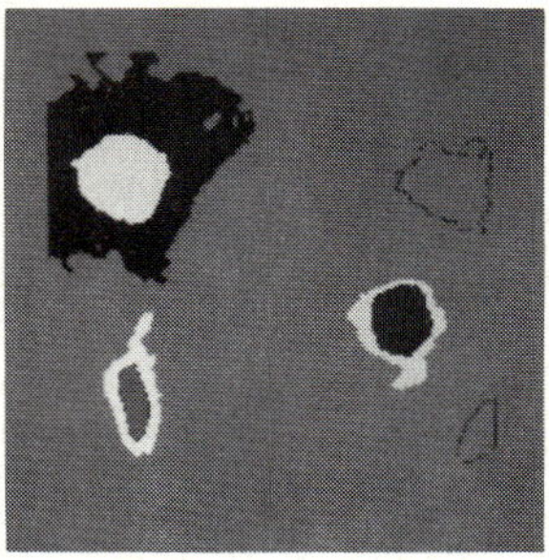

Figure 3.
Reconstructed cell masks from 5 focus levels corresponding to the images in figure 1 and 2.

ACKNOWLEDGEMENTS

Supported in part by the German Science Foundation and German Ministry for Research and Technology, Bonn, Federal Republic of Germany. The specimens were supplied by Prof. Dr. Schäffer, Institute of Pathology, University of Würzburg. The technical assistance of Ms. M. Haucke and J. Beritova is greatly appreciated.

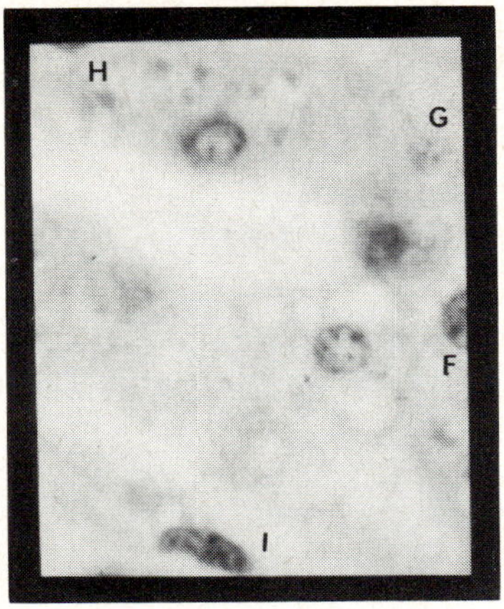

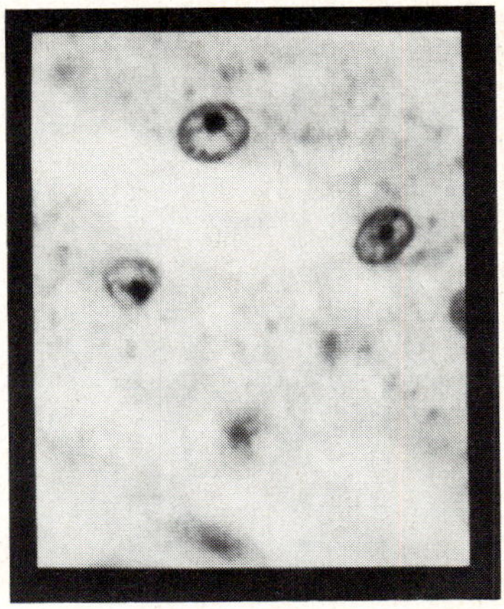

Figure 4 (left) and 5 (right).
Two additional black and white images at two different focus levels, spaced 2.4 microns appart, from the stained rat liver tissue section.

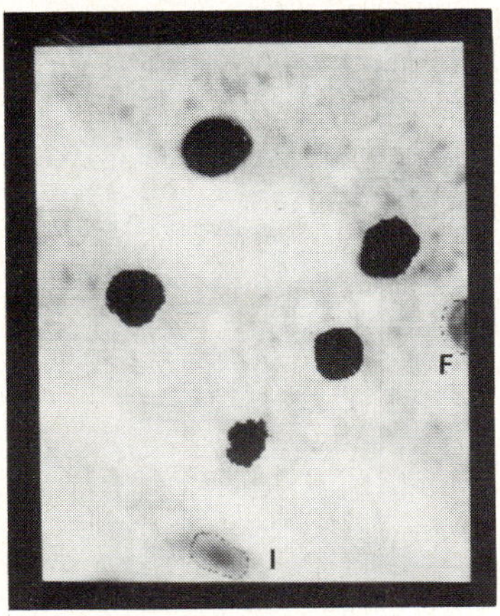

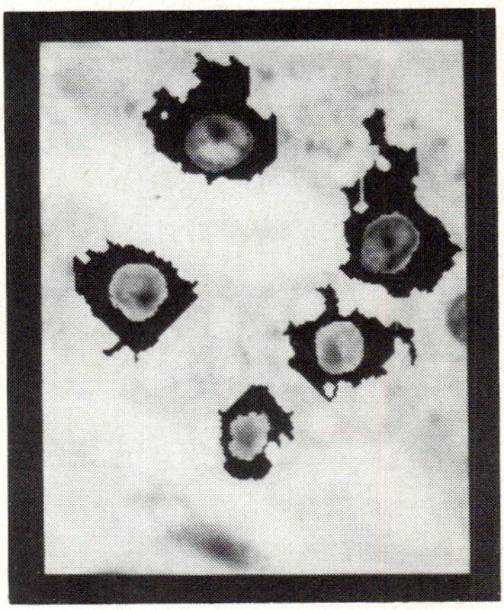

Figure 6 (left).
Reconstructed nuclear masks from 5 focus levels coressponding to the images in figure 4 and 5. The masks are superimposed on the scanned section image from the center of the focus levels.

Figure 7 (right).
Reconstructed cytoplasm masks from 5 focus levels coressponding to the images in figure 4 and 5. The masks are superimposed on the scanned section image from the center of the focus levels.

DISCUSSION

Verbeek:

The TV system and the stains you use are quite anthropomorphic because you want to be able to assess what is happening. On the other hand, I could imagine that in the future it would be interesting to have special stains which humans cannot analyze but which could be analyzed by special filtered TV systems.

Aus:

I tend to disagree with you because you are then entering a different world where no clinician will be able to follow what you are doing. We have stayed very close to clinically established facts, and made the computer talk about things the clinicians are used to talk about. If you come up with something new which makes it easier for the computer to function you will have to re-educate the clinicians. The danger is that you will end up with a system that nobody will use.

Nagy:

I have two related questions. A number of pixels are borderpixels between two colors. The first question is how much would your results be improved if you increased the resolution of your system by a factor of 2? If you cannot answer that question, how much would your results deteriorate if you made the resolution twice as bad, in other words, if you increased your pixel size by a factor of two?

Aus:

How these features change on the basis of the sampling rate is a very complex question which we did not investigate. However, there is an article by us published last year in Cytometry on the information content in the light-microscope image and its relationship to the sampling density. This work is indirectly related to the question you raised. If you undersample you are essentially using a low-pass mechanical filter which results in the elimination of some high frequency texture.

PATTERN RECOGNITION IN PRACTICE II
E.S. Gelsema and L.N. Kanal (Editors)

ARTERY DETECTION AND ANALYSIS IN CINE-ANGIOGRAMS

J. van Ommeren, C.J. Kooijman, R.J. van Meenen*, J.J. Gerbrands*, A.V.M.C.L. Schulte**, J.H.C. Reiber

Laboratory for Clinical and Experimental Image Processing, Erasmus University Rotterdam,
* Information Theory Group, Delft University of Technology,
and
** Eye Hospital, Erasmus University Rotterdam, The Netherlands

A coronary cine-angiogram is a sequence of roentgen absorption images, where each frame represents the two-dimensional projection of the coronary arterial system at a given instant in the cardiac cycle. New developments in our laboratory in the field of quantitative coronary angiography have been directed towards frame-to-frame analysis of the entire coronary tree. In the first frame of a series of cineframes to be analyzed, a tentative centerline of a major vessel is found with a controlled tracing routine, followed by minimum cost contour detection. In subsequent frames the segmentation process is guided by utilizing a priori information, represented in terms of a structured model of the arterial system. As a result of this guidance, user interaction may be reduced to a minimum. The controlled maxtracing procedure has been found to be useful in other applications as well, e.g. in retinal angiography, as illustrated in this paper.

INTRODUCTION

In coronary angiography, roentgen contrast agent is selectively injected into one of the main coronary arteries by means of a catheter. A cineangiogram is obtained with a cine-camera optically coupled to the output screen of the image intensifier. Each frame of the cinefilm represents the projection of the three-dimensional arterial tree on a two-dimensional plane at a given instant in time. The film speed is usually between 25 and 50 frames per second.
In our and other laboratories computer methods have been developed for the accurate analysis of the severity of coronary obstructions from optically magnified portions of 35 mm cineframes (1,2). An overview of these methods can be found in (3). These data are of great importance for the evaluation of the efficacy of modern therapeutic procedures in the catheterization laboratory (4-6), the effects of vasoactive drugs (7,8), as well as the effects of short and long term interventions on the regression or progression of coronary artery disease (9). However, little attention has been given to the possibilities of frame-to-frame analysis of the entire coronary tree from nonmagnified images for research or diagnostic purposes.
If one would be able to determine in a semi- or a fully-automated manner the centerlines and boundaries of all major-branches and side-branches of the coronary arterial system in each frame over a complete cardiac cycle, a number of clinically relevant questions could possibly be answered. Among these are:

1. Automated search for locations of coronary lesions exceeding a certain percentage diameter or area narrowing.
2. Computer-identification of the anatomy of the coronary tree and automated classification of the tree in one of a number of structure classes.
3. Research towards the possibly existing relation between the physical configuration of the coronary tree and the presence or development of coronary artery disease.

4. Assessment of epicardial contraction patterns by using the arterial bifurcations as landmarks.

In this paper our approaches towards the computer processing of the entire coronary tree implemented on our Coronary Angiography Analysis System (CAAS) will be described. Our software developments have been applied to nonmagnified cineframes digitized with a spatial resolution of 512x512 pixels and 256 grey levels. However, since the pictorial information at the output screen of the image intensifier can also be digitized on-line with progressive or interlaced scan video camera's with the same spatial and temporal resolution, the algorithms will in principle be applicable to such on-line acquisition procedures as well. A block diagram of the CAAS is given in figure 1.

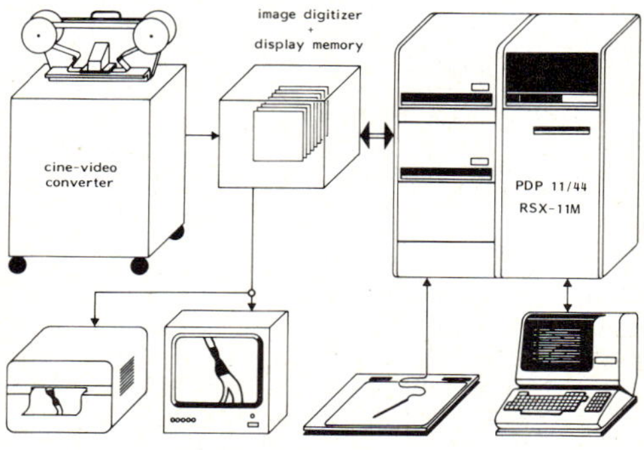

Fig. 1. Block diagram of the Coronary Angiography Analysis System (CAAS).

Our first goal, the automated detection and analysis of coronary obstructions from nonmagnified images requires the processing of only one single image, e.g. the end-diastolic image. Therefore, if one would be able to process selected arterial segments from on-line digitally acquired images with a clinically acceptable speed, then the arteriographist would be provided with immediate diagnostic information during the cardiac catheterization. This means that the procedure must be imbedded in a digital vascular imaging system (on-line CAAS) with the digitized video images obtained directly from the image intensifier. It will be clear that the accuracy of the on-line results will be lower than those from cinefilms, but most probably sufficient for diagnostic decision making. For research purposes requiring maximal accuracy, arterial dimensions must be assessed off-line from cinefilm, thereby allowing for optical magnification of the selected arterial segments (1,2).

The three other applications require analysis of all the images over one or more cardiac cycles. Because of the large amounts of data that need to be processed for these applications, only off-line analysis either from cineframes or from digitized video images acquired directly from the image intensifier seems feasible for the time being. Each of the four applications requires the accurate delineation of the projected arterial system in one or more frames. With the permissible exception of the very first frame, we want to apply a relatively simple and, if possible, fully automated segmentation procedure for the subsequent frames of a coronary angiogram.

At first, the segmentation of the coronary tree in the first of a series of frames will be discussed, followed by a description of the approaches towards the frame-to-frame segmentation. At the end of this paper it will be demonstrated that the techniques developed for the automated tracing of the centerlines of the coronary arteries, can also be applied successfully to retinal angiograms, providing information about arrival times of fluorescein in the arterial branches and about arterial blood flow velocities.

METHODOLOGY

Preprocessing

In each frame, the arterial system is represented by one connected component, which consists of a number of major branches and side branches. The actual brightness levels within the projected arteries depend a.o. on the absorption by the contrast agent and thus on artery size. Arterial segments which are separated in 3-D space may very well show partial overlap in the 2-D projection images. The background is rather nonuniform and may show a number of disturbing structures like the vertebral column, the diafragm, catheters and possibly even metal structures. Segmentation of a frame into arterial structures and background cannot be accomplished by global thresholding techniques or straightforward edge detection. The connectivity of the object justifies the use of sequential tracing procedures, which can easily be made locally-adaptive. In our approach, the disturbing background structures are removed to a large extent by applying a gated background subtraction method. Each frame is corrected by logarithmically subtracting a corresponding background image, which is recorded in the same phase of the cardiac cycle prior to the contrast injection (10,11). If necessary, spatial fluctuations due to quantum noise are decreased by smoothing the subtraction image with an unweighted 3x3 operator.

Segmentation in first frame

Under the assumption of complete and homogeneous filling with the contrast agent, the brightness values within a projected artery in the subtraction images are approximately proportional to irradiated object thicknesses (10). For a circle-cylindrical artery with main axis orthogonal to the X-ray beam, this means that the brightness values show maxima in the center of the projected artery. This approximation seems to be applicable in most practical cases, which leads to a segmentation procedure basically consisting of the following steps:

I) detection of the tentative centerline of an arterial branch by tracing local brightness maxima;
II) detection of the contours of the arterial branch using a minimum cost path search algorithm.
III) detection of possible side branches and
IV) repetition of steps I to III.

These various steps will be described in this section. More detailed descriptions of these procedures can be found in earlier publications (11-15).

For the detection of the tentative centerline of the first major artery, the user defines a starting point in the root of this artery as well as a global starting direction. The tracing procedure is applied to a low-resolution version of the subtracted image, which is obtained by first applying a 5x5 spatial low-pass filter to the image. As a result of this filter operation the spatial frequency band of the image is reduced by a factor of 3. Next, the filtered image is resampled with a sampling distance of three pixel positions in the original image.

For the tracing procedure 8 main search directions are defined (Fig. 2a). The direction of the last detected point with respect to its predecessor defines the current search direction. Three points are candidate for the next point of the tentative centerline. These candidate points are the point lying in the current search direction and the points lying in the two neighboring main directions which have angles of 45° with respect to the current search direction. The forthcoming point of the centerline is selected from among the three candidate points by searching for the maximum average brightness level over a number of pixels in the current search direction and in two other directions which differ by 22.5° from the current direction. The candidate point with the highest average brightness level computed in the corresponding search direction is defined as the next path position. The number of pixels used in the calculation of the average brightness value in a particular direction is dependent on the local diameter of the artery. The length of these search windows must be of the same order as the local arterial diameter. In figure 2b the search windows are shown for a look-ahead distance of 5 pixels.

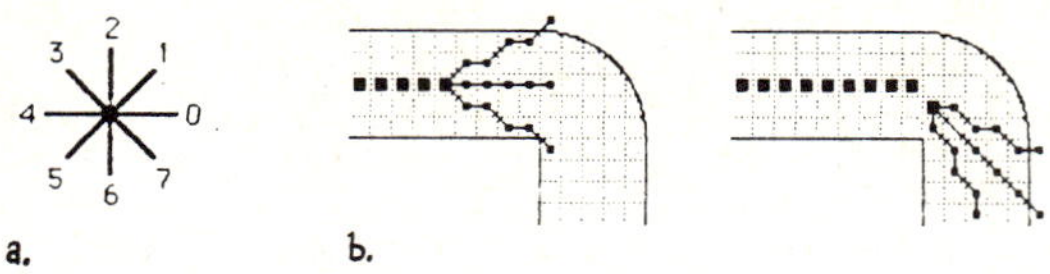

Fig. 2. a. Main search directions.
b. Search windows for a look-ahead distance of 5 pixels.

The detection of the tentative centerline is achieved piecewise, in subsegments. In each detected subsegment a number of parameters are calculated, such as the local arterial diameter, the mean brightness value within that subsegment and the background brightness value. These parameters are used as a priori information in the detection of the next subsegment. For example, the length of the next subsegment to be traced is set equal to the measured local diameter of the artery. Restrictions set on the change of mean brightness values in subsequent subsegments, on the contrast between object and background and on the minimum local arterial diameter yield criteria that make it possible to check whether the last detected subsegment of the centerline still lies within the artery.
If the centerline has left the artery and entered the background area, or if it has entered a severely obstructed region, the max-tracing procedure stops. A traceback procedure is then initiated towards the last point of the centerline that still belonged to the normal sized arterial segment. At this point, the user must decide whether the end of the artery has been reached. If this is not the case, a continuation point is searched for at a distance of two times the local diameter of the artery from the last defined point. This search procedure is illustrated in figure 3. Along the circumference of a circle with radius equal to two times the local diameter of the artery, the brightness profile in the image is determined. Each local maximum in this brightness profile is a potential position of an artery in the image. The position along the circular path for which the height and width of the brightness peak correspond best with these parameters from the reference position (being the intersection of the circle with the known centerline $\emptyset = 0°$) is defined as the continuation point for the tracing procedure.

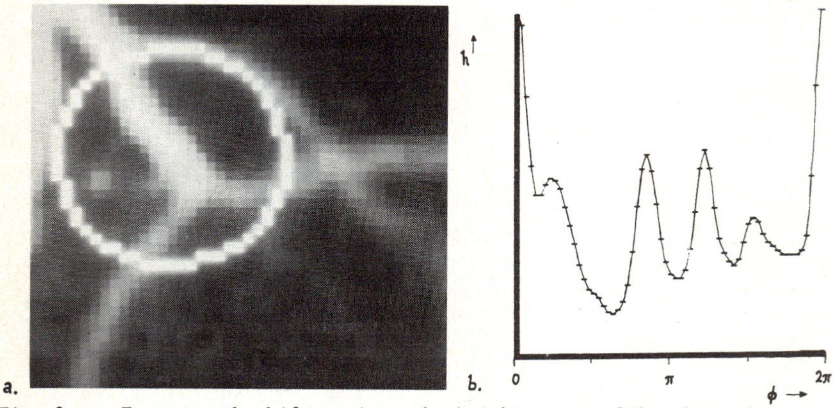

Fig. 3. To cross the bifurcation, the brightness profile along the circumference of a circle is determined (Fig. 3b). The image is scanned at a distance of two times the local diameter of the artery from the last defined point (Fig. 3a).

Between the last accepted centerline point and the continuation point a centerline path is defined on the basis of maximal cumulative grey values. Subsequently, the normal max-tracing procedure continues from the continuation point until another error occurs or the end of the artery is reached.

Following the max-tracing procedure the contours of the arterial branch are detected in the following way. First, the low-resolution max-tracer path is expanded to a high-resolution path and subsequently filtered to obtain a smooth, continuous curve. Next, the low-pass filtered full resolution image is locally resampled along straight lines perpendicular to the local centerline directions; these lines are denoted scanlines. To each point a cost coefficient is assigned, defined by the inverse of the weighted sum of first- and second-order derivatives. These derivatives are obtained by convolving each scanline with one-dimensional difference operators. The two contours of the arterial segment are obtained by searching in the resulting cost matrix for minimal cost paths, using dynamic programming methods (12).

Side branches are identified by searching for local maxima in background brightness profiles defined along the boundaries of the detected arterial segment. The complete procedure of max-tracing, edge detection and side-branch detection is then subsequently applied to each of the identified starting points of the side-branches. Results of the entire procedure will be presented in the section Applications in this paper.

Frame-to-frame segmentation

Following the segmentation of the first frame in which some user-interaction may be required, the subsequent frames should preferably be segmented without any user-interaction. The question arises to what extent information gathered from a given frame can be utilized to guide the segmentation of the next frame. Due to contraction, rotation, etc. of the coronary tree in 3-D space, substantial changes in the projection of the tree may occur in subsequent frames. However, in most practical cases the shape of the object is rather similar in two adjacent frames. This leads to the assumption that an object detected in a given frame may be used to construct a structural model which then guides the segmentation process for the next frame and so on.

Since the actual contour detection process has been shown to be sufficiently reliable, the model is only needed to guide the max-tracer. Furthermore, the model needs to contain just enough information to guide the max-tracer at those locations, where it tends to wander off the right track e.g. at high curvature sections where the max-tracer might proceed into the background and near bifurcations where the max-tracer may choose another branch than the one selected in the previous frame.

The model is constructed in the following way. The coronary tree is represented by a polygonal approximation of the various centerlines representing the coronary branches in the previous frame. In this way the centerline is decomposed into sections (straight line segments). Bifurcations are always identified as breakpoints between sections.

Each time the max-tracer has proceeded a little further in the new frame, the model and the actual path must be matched to detect local scale variations, thus synchronizing model and actual data. Matching of model and data is performed by employing a distance measure for polygonal curves to describe the differences between the model and a newly detected centerline section. The result of the matching is used to specify the expected direction and length of subsequent new centerline sections. Further details will be described in the following section (16).

Model/data synchronization

Contraction and relaxation, rotation and translation of the cardiac structures in 3-D space result in local shortening, lengthening, rotation and translation of arterial segments as observed in consecutive projection frames. The model-guided tracing procedure requires that we know at all times which part of the model is applicable. In other words, one must keep track of the position of the max-tracer with respect to the structural model. The simple approach of overlaying the model on the data and applying a minimum euclidean distance criterion between points of the model centerline and the max-tracer path cannot be used here. Even a slight shift results in serious misinterpretations, especially near high curvature sections.

The method that has been implemented is based on a measure for comparing linearly segmented curves that are geometrically distorted relative to one another. This method was introduced by Burr, who applied the technique to the problem of on-line recognition of handprinted characters (17). This comparitive procedure makes use of dynamic programming, a technique for finding minimal cost paths in certain weighted networks. When used to match linearly segmented curves, dynamic programming produces section pairs, which have been optimized in the sense that the sum of pairwise differences between curve-sections is minimal under the constraint of connectivity of subsequent sections of model and traced data.
In order to compute the costs for both model and data sections, a geometric distortion measure is introduced, that relies on positional and angular differences between sections of model and data. The angular distance measure D_{ang} is defined by the cross product of two vectors $\vec{A}$ and $\vec{B}$, normalized by the magnitude of vector $\vec{A}$; $\vec{A}$ is always the vector with the greatest magnitude (Fig. 4a). In formula (17):

$$D_{ang} = \frac{|\vec{B} \times \vec{A}|}{|\vec{A}|} + 3U.(-\vec{B}.\vec{A}) \,.\, \frac{|\vec{B}.\vec{A}|}{|\vec{A}|} \tag{1}$$

This angular distance measure is a good estimate of gross directional error. The second term in formula (1) is necessary to impose a greater distance measure for opposing vectors. When the projection of $\vec{B}$ onto $\vec{A}$ is negative, a value proportional to $|\vec{B}.\vec{A}| / |\vec{A}|$ is added by means of the unit step function U, defined by:

$$U(t) = 0 \quad (t < 0)$$
$$U(t) = 1 \quad (t \geqslant 0) \tag{2}$$

The positional distance measure is also based on a cross product; however, for this purpose a third vector $\vec{C}$ is introduced (Fig. 4b). Vector $\vec{C}$ connects the beginning point of vector $\vec{A}$ with the midpoint of vector $\vec{B}$. The cross term

$\dfrac{|\vec{C}\times\vec{A}|}{|\vec{A}|}$ is a measure for the perpendicular distance between the vectors $\vec{A}$ and $\vec{B}$.

The positional distance measure D_{pos} is defined by (17):

$$D_{pos} = \frac{|\vec{C}\times\vec{A}|}{|\vec{A}|} + U.\left\{\frac{\vec{C}.\vec{A}}{|\vec{A}|} - |\vec{A}|\right\} . \left|\frac{\vec{C}.\vec{A}}{|\vec{A}|} - |\vec{A}|\right| + U.\left\{-\frac{\vec{C}.\vec{A}}{|\vec{A}|} . \frac{|\vec{C}.\vec{A}|}{|\vec{A}|}\right\} \tag{3}$$

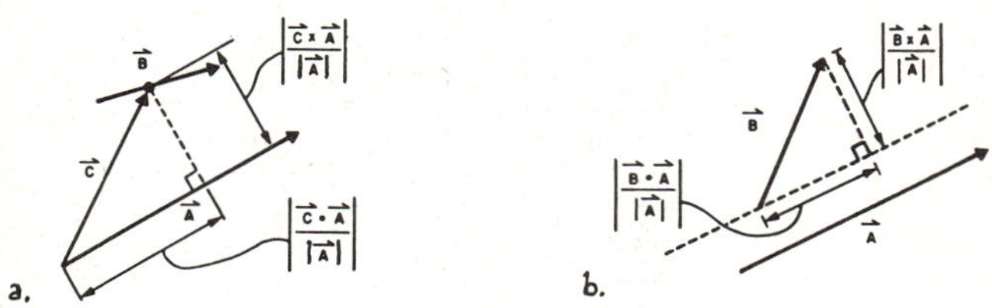

Fig. 4. a. Quantities relating to the positional distance measure D_{pos} between the vectors $\vec{A}$ and $\vec{B}$ ($|\vec{A}| \geqslant |\vec{B}|$).
b. Quantities relating to the angular distance measure D_{ang} between vectors $\vec{A}$ and $\vec{B}$ ($|\vec{A}| \geqslant |\vec{B}|$).

The two additional terms are added to increase the positional distance measure for two specific cases: 1) the projection of $\vec{C}$ onto $\vec{A}$ is greater than $|\vec{A}|$; and

2) the projection of $\vec{C}$ onto $\vec{A}$ is less than zero.
Finally, the total distance measure D(i,j) between a traced data section s(i) and model section m(j) is defined by:

$$D(i,j) = D_{pos}(i,j) + 2\, D_{ang}(i,j). \qquad (4)$$

The angular measure is weighted heavier than the positional measure, since angles are more meaningful than positions when distortions occur.
For the matching of the traced data with the model, the costs for the differences of the various section pairs are computed. The sum of costs for subsequent sections is then minimized by means of dynamic programming. In figure 5 the dynamic programming lattice is illustrated. The nodes represent the costs for the corresponding section pairs. Cost cumulation takes place from left to right along the traced data, and from bottom to top along the model sections. In practice, a number of section pairs (i,j) are exempted from the matching procedure; these pairs have been shaded in figure 5. It is not useful to try to match section pairs for which the difference in section numbers exceeds a certain value (a difference of 8 in figure 5). The arrows in the figure denote the section pairs, that may preceed the section pair (i,j) in order to satisfy the constraint for connectivity.

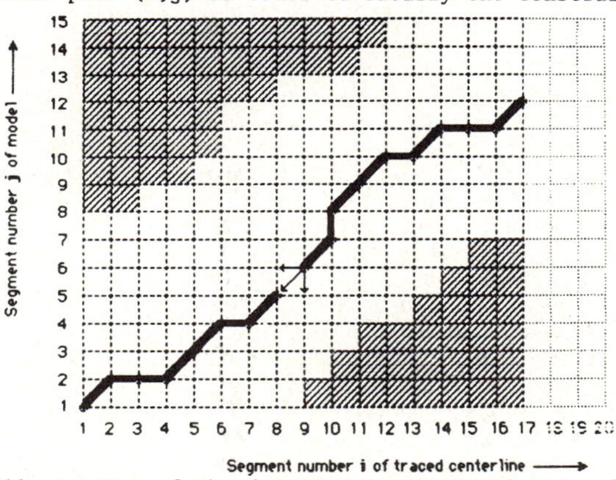

Fig. 5. Illustration of the dynamic programming lattice for data sections ($1 \leqslant i \leqslant 17$) and model sections ($1 \leqslant j \leqslant 15$).

The cumulated cost for section pair (i,j) is defined by:

$$S(i,j) = D(i,j) + \min\ S(i-1,j),\ S(i-1,j-1),\ S(i,j-1) \qquad (5)$$

under the following constraints:

$$\begin{aligned} S(1,1) &= D(1,1) \\ S(i,1) &= D(i,1) + S(i-1,1) \quad i \geqslant 2 \\ S(1,j) &= D(1,j) + S(1,j-1) \quad j \geqslant 2. \end{aligned} \qquad (6)$$

When the tracing proceeds into a new section, a new column is added to the dynamic programming lattice and filled with cumulative costs, as shown in figure 5 with the dotted part of the lattice (last three columns).
To find an optimal match between model and current tracer-data, the minimum cumulative costs are searched for in the last column. A backtrace through the dynamic programming lattice then yields the best match. In this way the best point on the model centerline, corresponding with the current tracer position can be determined.

APPLICATIONS

Some of the earlier mentioned applications, like the automated classification of the coronary tree and the automated labeling of arterial segments are still only at a very early stage of development. Others, like the computation of epicardial wall motion have been implemented in our laboratory (11), but clinical evaluation studies still need to be performed. The application first mentioned in the introduction, the automated selection of coronary obstructions in nonmagnified images and the determination of the severity in terms of percentage diameter- and densitometric area-stenosis, will be implemented in our catheterization laboratory as soon as an on-line digital vascular imaging system has been installed. An extensive performance evaluation will then be carried out, but preliminary results from routinely obtained cine-angiograms are certainly promising. An example of the proposed analysis procedure is presented in the following paragraphs.

Figure 6 shows a subtraction image of the right coronary arterial system. The tentative centerline of the right coronary artery as found by the max-tracing routine is displayed in figure 7. In the centerline the breakpoints between different sections which are used to guide the max-tracer in the next frame are indicated by the square markers. This centerline is input for the contour detection algorithm, which locates the contours of the artery by searching for minimal cost paths.

The detected contours of the right coronary tree are shown in figure 8. In addition, figure 9 shows the computed diameter and densitometric area functions for the mid-portion of this RCA and the patient-data block. The position of the obstruction is found by looking for a significant local minimum in the diameter function. The percentage diameter stenosis is determined following an interpolated stenosis measurement technique. This particular procedure has been described in earlier publications (1,2,18). It will be clear that such data will be extremely useful for the cardiologist if it can be provided during the cardiac catheterization.

The accuracy of these percentage diameter stenosis measurements has not been determined as yet, but worst case assumptions show an upper limit of approximately 8%, based on our experiences with the analysis of optically magnified coronary segments.

An example of the outcome of a frame-to-frame analysis of a right coronary tree is given in figure 10. This figure displays the centerlines of the coronary arteries for a number of consecutive frames during the systolic time-interval. These data may be used as input, together with similar data obtained from an orthogonal projection, to a procedure for computing epicardial wall motion. Studying the so obtained contraction patterns could result in a classification scheme of coronary tree structures, where each class is homogeneous with respect to the geometrical patterns. Such classification scheme may then be used to validate the hypothesis that there is diagnostic and prognostic value in the geometric configuration of the coronary tree.

In achieving this goal it is necessary to develop techniques for assessing the similarity between coronary trees. A useful utility in obtaining a similarity measure for coronary trees is a cardiovascular database. This database should have the ability to efficiently store, retrieve and display the three-dimensional structure of the coronary trees. In this way, it will be possible to look for pattern similarities by visual methods, to use the results from this classification and for obtaining a similarity measure (19).

ANALYSIS OF RETINAL ANGIOGRAMS

Experiences with the controlled tracing procedure have shown that it can be applied successfully in other areas as well, such as in retinal angiography. The retinal arteries are the only vessels that can be observed in a direct optical manner. Such an optical technique allows the physician to study the quality of the vessels and to quantitate the flow in the arterial and capillary retinal vessels, which is of great importance in certain types of patients, such as those with diabetes mellitus and hypertension (20).

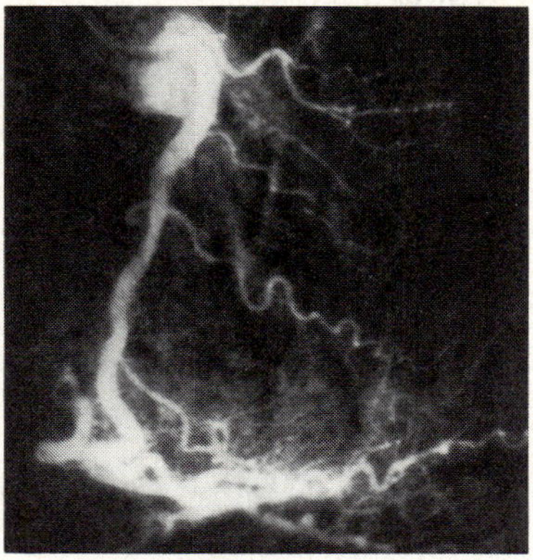

Fig. 6. Gated background subtracted image of right coronary arterial system.

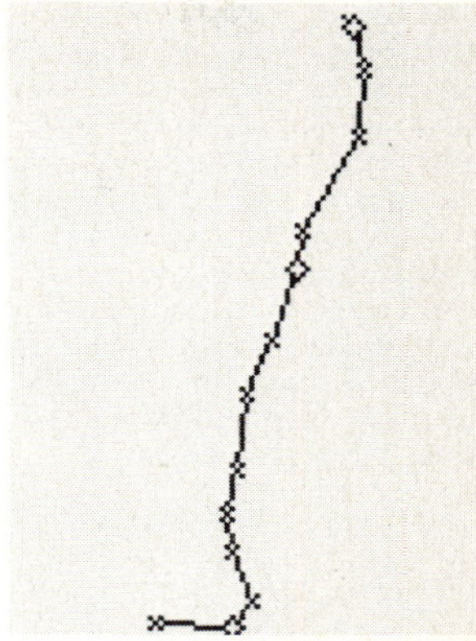

Fig. 7. Detected tentative centerline in right coronary artery together with section break-points.

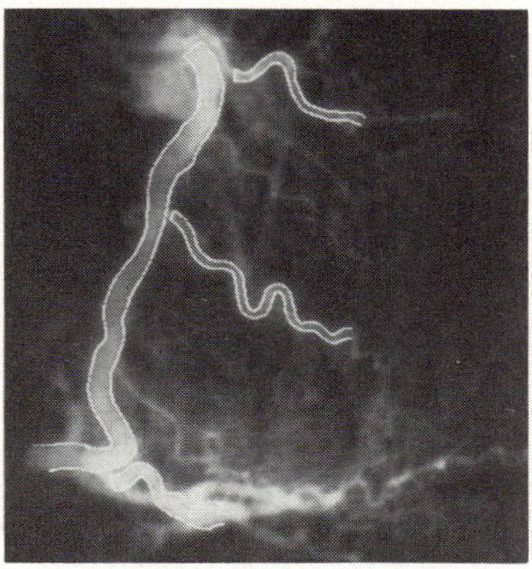

Fig. 8. Detected contours of right coronary tree.

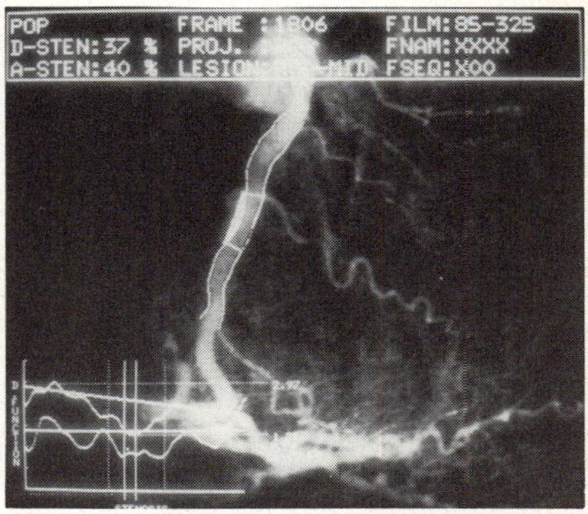

Fig. 9. Contour analysis provides percentage diameter- and densitometric area-stenoses.

Fig. 10. Coronary tree movement during the systolic time-interval.

To be able to measure retinal blood flow a fluorescein dye must be administered, usually through an arm-vein. The fluorescein mixes with the blood and is transported via the heart and lungs to all parts of the body, including the eyes. By means of a special technique, a bolus of the fluorescein mixed blood enters the retinal vessels. By illuminating the eye with a monochromatic light source, the fluorescein present in the vessels is excited and reacts by radiating luminescent light that can be registered with a 35 mm cinefilm at high frame speed (50 to 150 frames/s; cinematography). Visual analysis of such films may reveal abnormal flow patterns or distributions in the retinal arteries. Quantitative analysis of these films may provide the clinician with objective information about arrival times and changes in these measurements due to interventions. In an attempt to derive such quantitative data, we have applied our techniques for vessel tracing to these retinal images.

Detection of retinal arteries

During the acquisition of the retinal cineangiograms, the patient fixes one eye on a fixed light source, so that the other eye that is investigated does not move either. As a result, the positions of the retinal vessels do not change during the acquisition period. An example of four retinal images, acquired during the arterial filling phase is shown in Fig. 11; the time between successive images is approximately 80 msec. The last image of such a sequence shows the entire arterial structure. Therefore, if we could determine the centerlines of the vessels in this last image and superimpose these centerlines on the preceding images, the brightness distributions along these lines can be measured in the different images, providing information about arrival times.

For these purposes, an accurate definition of the centerlines is required. As a first approximation of a centerline, the maxtracer-algorithm described in this paper can be applied to a low resolution image. Additional possibilities for user-interaction have been implemented, allowing the maxtracer to trace side-branches at bifurcations, so that arrival times can be assessed for all arteries in the image. Following detection of a vessel in the low resolution image, the centerline is determined more accurately in the high resolution image based on this approximative information. Thereto, the maxtracer-path is projected onto the high resolution image. Subsequently, the high resolution image is resampled along scanlines, perpendicular to the local centerline directions of the maxtracer-path. The resampled data are stored in a matrix such that the (enlarged) maxtracer-path forms the straight center column of this matrix. A maximum brightness path is determined in this matrix on the basis of a minimum cost algorithm. This path is retransformed to the original high resolution image and filtered. Experiments have shown that this final path follows precisely the actual centerlines of the detected retinal arteries. Fig. 13 shows the centerlines detected in the last image of Fig. 11.

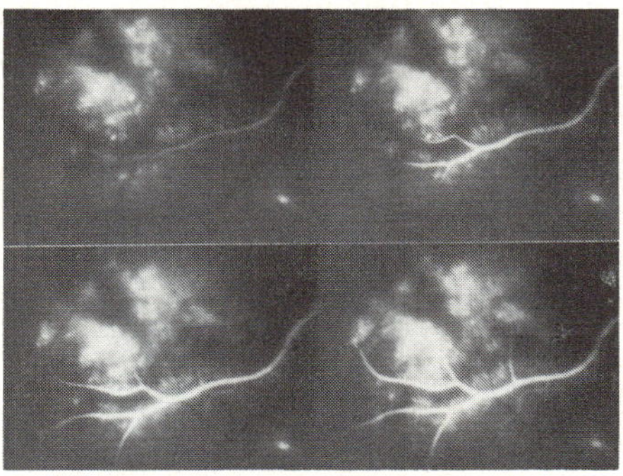

Fig. 11. Example of four retinal images acquired during arterial filling phase; time between successive images is approximately 80 msec.

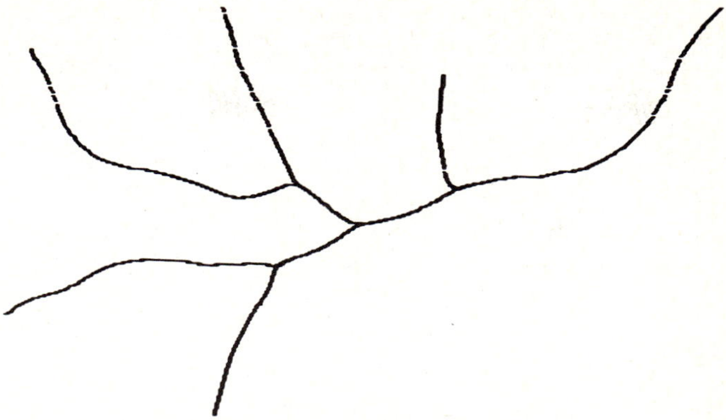

Fig. 12. Detected centerlines of retinal arteries.

Measurement flow velocities in retinal vessels

To measure the flow velocity of the fluorescein front in a given retinal artery, the front displacement must be determined as a function of time. The assessment of the front displacement is achieved by the analysis of the brightness curves measured along the centerline of the vessel in the successive images. An example of these brightness curves for one of the centerlines of Fig. 12 is given in Fig. 13. The increasing brightness levels in the successive images indicate an increasing fluorescein concentration in the blood. The front displacement can be appreciated from this figure.

The spatial position of the front along the centerline is based on an algorithm involving the brightness curve and its first- and second-derivates. From these front displacements, the flow velocity can be calculated as a function of time if the film speed and the ratio of pixel size and true distance between pixels are known. The filmspeed for the example of Fig. 11 was 60 frames/s, yielding a frame-period of 17 msec. This particular experiment was carried out with a monkey having a heart frequency of 130 to 180 beats per minute. As a result, a complete cardiac cycle covers about 20 frames. The relation between pixel size and true distance was not exactly known, but was estimated to be 300 pixel distances per centimeter. From these data, blood flow velocity can be readily assessed. If the

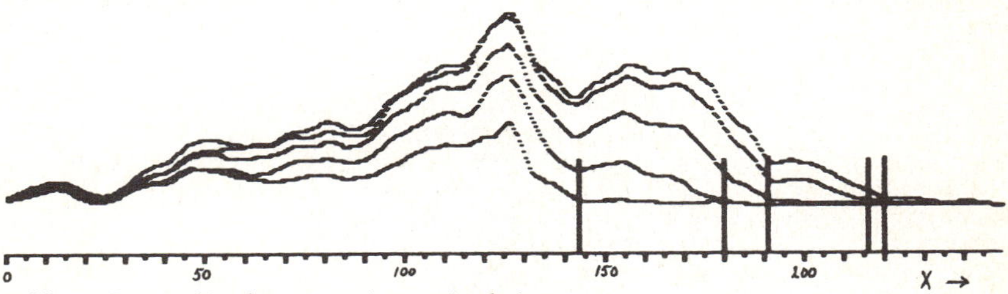

Fig. 13. Front displacement in retinal images.

front displacement between two successive images equals X pixel distances, the flow velocity V equals:

$$V = X \cdot \frac{60}{300} = 0.2\ X\ \text{cm/s} \qquad (7)$$

The results of flow velocity measurements for two different arteries in the same

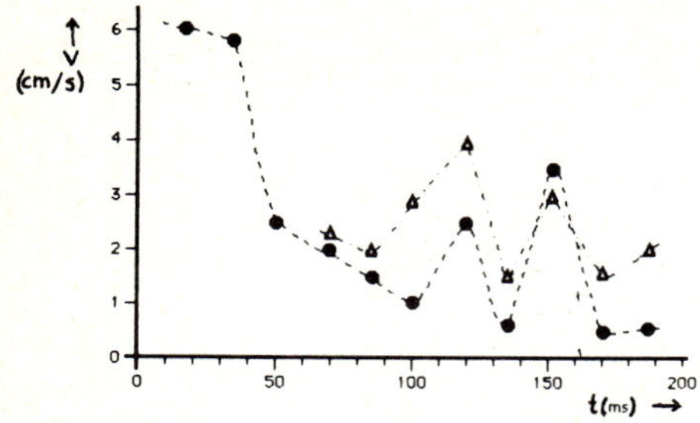

Fig. 14. Flow velocities as a function of time.

angiographic investigation are displayed in Fig. 14. There is a high degree of resemblance between these two curves. The flow velocity is dependent on the instantaneous blood pressure, which is dependent on the phase in the cardiac cycle. Further investigations are necessary to determine the precise relation between the blood flow velocity and instantaneous blood pressure.

Concluding remarks analysis retinal images

Our results in a limited validation study have shown that the arteries could be traced fully automatically without any operator interaction. The procedure for finding the maximal brightness path in the high resolution image resulted in all cases in an excellent approximation of the centerline of the retinal arteries. Extensive validation studies are planned for the near future; furthermore, the advantages and limitations of this technique in clinical practice need to be established.

Acknowledgements

The authors wish to thank Mrs. M.J. Kanters-Stam for her secretarial help in preparing this paper and J. Tuin for making the photographs. This work has been supported in part by the Dutch Heart Foundation under grant no. NHS 80.129.

References

1. Reiber JHC, Kooijman CJ, Slager CJ, Gerbrands JJ, Schuurbiers JCH, Boer A den, Wijns W, Serruys PW, Hugenholtz PG, Coronary artery dimensions from cineangiograms; methodology and validation of a computer-assisted analysis procedure, IEEE Trans. Med. Imaging MI-3 (1984) 131-141.
2. Reiber JHC, Serruys PW, Kooijman CJ, Wijns W, Slager CJ, Gerbrands JJ, Schuurbiers JCH, Boer A den, Hugenholtz PG, Assessment of short-, medium-, and long-term variations in arterial dimensions from computer assisted quantitation of coronary cineangiograms, Circulation 71 (1985) 280-288.
3. Reiber JHC, Kooijman CJ, Slager CJ, Gerbrands JJ, Schuurbiers JCH, Boer A den, Wijns W, Serruys PW, Computer assisted analysis of the severity of obstructions from coronary cineangiograms; a methodological review, Automedica 5 (1984) 219-238.
4. Serruys PW, Booman F, Troost GJ, Reiber JHC, Gerbrands JJ, Brand M van den, Cherrier F, Hugenholtz PG, Computerized quantitative coronary angiography applied to percutaneous transluminal coronary angioplasty; advantages and limitations, in: M. Kaltenbach, A. Grüntzig, K Rentrop, W.D. Bussmann (eds.), Transluminal coronary angioplasty and intracoronary thrombolysis (Springer Verlag, Berlin, 1982) 110-124.

5. Serruys PW, Wijns W, Brand M van den, Ribeiro V, Fioretti P, Simoons ML, Kooijman CJ, Reiber JHC, Hugenholtz PG, Is transluminal coronary angioplasty mandatory after successful thrombolysis? Br. Heart J. 50 (1983) 257-265.
6. Wijns W, Serruys PW, Brand M van den, Suryapranata H, Kooijman CJ, Reiber JHC, Hugenholtz PG, Progression to complete coronary obstruction without myocardial infarction in patients who are candidates for percutaneous transluminal angioplasty: a 90-day angiographic follow-up, in: H. Roskamm (ed.), Prognosis of coronary heart disease - progression of coronary arteriosclerosis (Springer Verlag, Berlin, 1983) 190-195.
7. Serruys PW, Hooghoudt TEH, Reiber JHC, Slager C, Brower RW, Hugenholtz PG, Influence of intracoronary nifedipine on left ventricular function, coronary vasomotility, and myocardial oxygen consumption, Br. Heart J. 49 (1983) 427-441.
8. Serruys PW, Lablanche JM, Reiber JHC, Bertrand ME, Hugenholtz PG, Contribution of dynamic vascular wall thickening to luminal narrowing during coronary arterial vasomotion, Z. Kardiol. 72 (1983) 116-123.
9. Arntzenius AC, Barth JD, Bruschke AVG, Buis B, Gent CM van, Houtsmuller UMT, Kempen-Voogd N, Kromhout D, Reiber JHC, Strikwerda S, Velde EA van der, Wezel LA van, Preliminary report on coronary lesions and serum lipids before and after 2 years dietary intervention in 22 patients, in: F.G. Schettler, A.M. Gotto, G. Middelhoff, A.J.R. Habenicht, K.R. Jurutka (eds.), Atherosclerosis VI (Springer-Verlag, Berlin, 1983) 187-196.
10. Reiber JHC, Slager CJ, Schuurbiers JCH, Boer A den, Gerbrands JJ, Troost GJ, Scholts B, Kooijman CJ, Serruys PW, Transfer functions of the X-ray-cine-video chain applied to digital processing of coronary cineangiograms, in: P.H. Heintzen, R. Brennecke (eds.), Digital imaging in cardiovascular radiology (Georg Thieme Verlag, Stuttgart, 1983) 89-104.
11. Gerbrands JJ, Reiber JHC, Scholts B, Langhout G, Kooijman CJ, Structural analysis of the coronary arterial tree. Int. Symp. Medical Imaging and Image Interpretation, ISMIII'82, IEEE Press, Cat.No. 82 CH1804-4 (1982) 54-58.
12. Gerbrands JJ, Reiber JHC, Kooijman CJ, Rademaker RT, Model-guided segmentation of coronary cine-angiograms, in: H.W. Schüssler (ed.), Signal processing II: theories and applications (Elsevier Science Publishers B.V., North-Holland, 1983) 601-604.
13. Kooijman CJ, Rademaker RT, Gerbrands JJ, Reiber JHC, Developments towards frame-to-frame computer processing of the entire coronary tree, Comp. Cardiol. (1983) 389-392.
14. Kooijman CJ, Gerbrands JJ, Reiber JHC, Rademaker RT, Ommeren J van, Developments towards frame-to-frame computer processing of coronary angiograms, Proc. Int. Symp. on Medical Images and Icons, ISMII '84, IEEE Press, Cat.No. CH2047-9/84 (1984) 356-362.
15. Ommeren J van, Coronary tree detection, M.Sc. Thesis, Information Theory Group, Delft University of Technology (1984).
16. Meenen RJ van, Detection of the coronary tree in series of digital subtraction images, M.Sc. Thesis, Information Theory Group, Delft University of Technology (1985).
17. Burr DJ, A technique for comparing curves, Proc. IEEE Comp. Soc. Conf. on Pattern Recogn. and Image Proc. (1979) 271-277.
18. Kooijman CJ, Reiber JHC, Gerbrands JJ, Schuurbiers JCH, Slager CJ, Boer A den, Serruys PW, Computer-aided quantitation of the severity of coronary obstructions from single view cine-angiograms, Symp. Med. Imaging and Image Interpr. ISMIII '82, IEEE Press, Cat. No. 82 CH1804-4 (1982) 59-64.
19. Smith WM, Starmer CF, Computer representation of coronary arterial trees, Comp. Biomed. Res. 9 (1976) 187-201.
20. Schulte AVM, Retinal fluorotachometry, Ph.D. Thesis, Erasmus University and Eye Hospital, Rotterdam (in press).

PATTERN RECOGNITION IN PRACTICE II
E.S. Gelsema and L.N. Kanal (Editors)

INDUSTRIAL PATTERN RECOGNITION

P. Suetens*, A. Oosterlinck

University of Leuven
Division E.S.A.T.
de Croylaan 52B
3030 Heverlee
Belgium

This paper focuses on industrial applications of pattern recognition, i.e. visual inspection and robot vision.
First, the algorithmic aspects of pattern recognition are briefly reviewed.
Second, the different elements of a visual inspection or robot vision system are discussed.
Finally, special attention is paid to image processing operations for visual inspection and robot vision which can be executed in real time or pseudo real time. They include run length encoding, the calculation of projections, windowing, edge detection, texture analysis and the calculation of spatial moments. A hardware implementation of each of those operations exists or is being developed at our laboratory.

I. INTRODUCTION

The algorithms to solve a visual inspection or robot vision problem, or, more generally, to solve an image analysis problem, can be classified into two categories, usually called pattern recognition and scene analysis respectively.
The pattern recognition approach assumes that a 2-D or 3-D scene or object can be represented as a set of numbers, each of these numbers being the value of one particular global feature of the object, such as area, perimeter, length, width, number of holes, and so on. Recognition or interpretation of an unknown object is then performed by calculating its characteristic features and assigning it to one of the known object classes with similar features.
In the scene analysis approach, a scene or object is considered as a number of primitives it consists of. These primitives may be small surface or volume elements. The object is then characterized by the features of its primitives and by the relations between its primitives. The method for scene analysis can be subdivided into grammatical and nongrammatical methods, as will further be discussed. We note, however, that the grammatical methods are also known as syntactic pattern recognition. Hence, in the literature, they may be classed among the pattern recognition methods, while scene analysis is then related to the nongrammatical approach only.

To a certain extent, pattern recognition and scene analysis are

---

*research associate of the Belgian National Fund for Scientific Research (N.F.W.O.).

related respectively to 2-D and 3-D image analysis. In 2-D image analysis, also called 2-D vision, the objects to be interpreted are two-dimensional, while in 3-D image analysis, also called 3-D vision, they are three-dimensional. The reason is that the scene analysis approach offers a more general way to describe and interpret objects. Especially 3-D objects, which are usually more complex than 2-D objects, cannot always be sufficiently defined by a number of global features only. Therefore, it can be expected that pattern recognition has more applications in the field of 2-D vision, while scene analysis is the obvious way to approach more complex scenes, abundantly available in 3-D vision.

Most applications of visual inspection and robot vision today can be classed among 2-D vision and can be solved with the pattern recognition approach. In section II, the principles of pattern recognition are discussed in more detail.

An efficient implementation of an algorithm for visual inspection or robot vision requires a computer system with special characteristics, such as an image memory bank, a camera interface, and special hardware. Computer systems that meet those requirements are called vision systems. They are particularly suited for visual inspection tasks that can be solved with a pattern recognition algorithm.
Although the vision system is the brain of a visual inspection system, its importance must be relativized. Today, industrial companies prefer complete solutions including the handling and the sorting of objects. The acquiring, manipulation and disposing of the parts to be inspected amount to a substantial part of the whole installation cost.
In section III, the different elements of an image processing system for visual inspection are therefore briefly reviewed.

Since visual inspection and robot vision often require gray level processing and the use of high resolution images, hardware processing may be the only means to perform the inspection task within an acceptable time.
Run length encoding, the calculation of projections and windowing are examples of hardware processing. They perform a strong data reduction. Other hardware processing operations include edge detection, texture analysis and the calculation of spatial moments. Edges and texture are the most important local image features, used to segment objects from their surroundings. Spatial moments are among the most useful global 2-D features.
At our laboratory, most of those operations have been implemented in hardware, the other are being developed. In section IV, we will therefore discuss each of them more in detail.

II. PATTERN RECOGNITION

In general, a pattern recognition algorithm can be subdivided into three steps: segmentation, feature extraction and classification.

In the first step, called segmentation, the objects in the image which are of interest for further processing are outlined.
In component measurement tasks, these objects can be complete workpieces, but they can also be part components, such as bore holes and the head or the tail of long strips. If defects have to be inspected, the objects to be segmented may be scratches, cracks, foreign material, and so on. Generally, objects are segmented from their surroundings on the basis of local image or intrinsic features, such as

local color or gray value, texture, the appearance of edges, relative position of the image, and for 3-D objects, local surface orientation and range data. The segmentation process then combines image elements (usually pixels) with similar local characteristics.
Different methods exist for segmenting an image. The easiest way is called global thresholding. In this method the objects are separated from the background by means of a fixed gray level or threshold value. This threshold divides the image pixels into two classes, the object pixels, which have a gray value at one side of the threshold, and the background pixels, which have a gray value at the other side of the threshold. It is clear that global thresholding can only be used if the contrast in the image between the objects and the background is high and if the gray levels of the objects and of the background respectively lie on different side of the threshold value (bimodal histogram). Global thresholding can either interactively or automatically be performed. For interactive thresholding, a light pen or cursor e.g. may be used to indicate the desired threshold value. In automatic thresholding, the threshold value that corresponds to the minimum histogram value may e.g. be chosen or the threshold value may e.g. be placed somewhere in the dip between the two peaks of the bimodal histogram.
Other possibilities are e.g. adaptive thresholding, gradient thresholding and region growing. In adaptive thresholding a floating threshold is chosen and its value depends partly on local image content. Gradient thresholding consists of an edge finding operation (gradient calculation), followed by a global thresholding. The output of an edge finding operation is a gray scale image in which gray values are proportional to the edge inclinations. When this image is thresholded, the significant pixels in the output binary image correspond to the sharpest edges in the original image. A region growing method starts by partitioning the image into many small areas. These areas may even be single pixels. Each area is then characterized by one or more features, such as average gray value, texture, or, for 3-D objects, range or surface orientation. Next, all boundaries between adjacent regions are examined. If the features of the regions on either side of a boundary do not differ significantly, that particular boundary is dissolved and the adjacent regions are merged. This progress is iterated for the enlarged areas until all boundaries are strong, i.e. until the features of all adjacent regions differ significantly.
Because of their simplicity, the previously described methods can be classified as low level processing techniques, as contrasted with feature extraction and classification, which, as we will see in next paragraphs, are clearly high level algorithms. Often, however, these simple methods are not adequate to complete the segmentation phase successfully. For instance, gradient thresholding may result in non-closed boundaries. While this is no limitation in the scene analysis approach, a pattern recognition algorithm requires the object contours to be closed in order to extract global features of the outlined objects. Therefore, higher level processing techniques such as edge tracking and thinning, may be needed after the gradient operation.

In a second step of the pattern recognition algorithm, called feature extraction, global features of the outlined objects are calculated. Hence, an object is represented as an n-dimensional vector, the vector elements being the different feature values. Examples of global 2-D features, which are commonly used in current commercial vision systems, are number of holes, area, area of holes, perimeter, centroid, i.e. the center of area, length of the minimum and maximum radius from the centroid to the perimeter, the angles of this minimum and maximum radius, orientation, length and width of the bounding box with the same orientation, peround, first and second invariant moments, color value (e.g. black or white), and so on.

In a third step, called classification, the objects are matched with the different model descriptions on the basis of their global features, and, according to a chosen classifier or decision rule, they are assigned to one of the object classes with similar properties. In visual inspection applications, there are two main classes, corresponding to good and bad parts respectively. However, the class of the defect parts is usually subdivided into a number of different subclasses, called error classes, each corresponding to a different defect. The subclasses are defined by the manufacturer and allow him to find the origin of the defect workpieces and, hence, to improve the production process and in this way to save money.
In the literature, close attention is paid to the choice of the classifier. Extensive theories have been developed to minimize the probability of misclassification. A classifier can be either deterministic or statistical. While a statistical classifier makes certain assumptions on the statistical properties of the different object classes, a deterministic classifier does not.

One of the easiest deterministic classifiers is the minimum-distance-classifier. According to this decision rule, an unknown object is assigned to the class of the closest known object. "Closest" means that the distance between the n-dimensional feature vector of the unknown and the particular known object respectively must be minimal. Obviously, a so-called learning or training phase must precede the classification of unknown objects. During this training phase, the feature vector of a set of representative samples of each class must be calculated.

The most popular statistical decision rule is the Bayes classifier. This decision rule states that the unknown object has to be assigned to the class which makes the expected loss resulting from this assignment, minimal. It is a statistical classifier because it assumes that the probability function of each object class is known. Besides, these probability functions must be known in their parametric form. Often, they can be assumed to be normal distributions. Hence, the mean value and the variance are the only unknown parameters, which can easily be estimated during a learning phase. Assuming that the loss by assigning an unknown object to a wrong class is a fixed value independant of the object class, the Bayes classifier has the important property that the probability of misclassification is minimal.

For the sake of completeness, we have to mention a classification method that is not based on object features, but that starts from the object itself. Hence, the feature extraction phase does not exist in this case. This direct classification method is known as template matching. It compares the image of the object to be classified with the images (masks) that are representative for each object class e.g. by means of cross correlation.

Until now, we have discussed the three main steps of a pattern recognition algorithm. Pattern recognition is commercially exploited in current industrial vision systems. These systems mainly find their applications in two domains. A first domain is robotics, where the vision system can be used as a robot sensor, which calculates position, orientation and identification when flexible automation is aimed at. A second domain is visual inspection, where it can be used to detect defects in parts during or after the production process.

However, complex 2-D and particularly 3-D scenes mostly cannot be classified or interpreted by means of global features only. For applications which cannot be solved by pattern recognition, scene analysis, which is discussed in [1] is the obvious approach. Nevertheless, we want to emphasize that a lot of applications which are at first sight unsolvable with present vision systems, may become much simpler by proper lighting and viewing techniques. The importance of good lighting cannot be over-emphasized. The range of illumination techniques which can be used, is very wide and is discussed in paragraph III.3.

III. SYSTEM ASPECTS

An automatic visual inspection or robot vision system consists of the following subsystems: the part handling system, the optics and the sensor, the illumination, and the vision system. Each of them will now be discussed subsequently.

1. The part handling system.
The part handling system consists of a feeding system for the transportation of the objects to the sensor, and a separation system for sorting the inspected objects according to the classification results. Both mechanical parts are necessary if the visual inspection process is required to be automatical.

The complexity of the inspection task strongly depends on the feeding procedure. Workpieces in a completely random spatial organization and unseparated, jumbled together in a container or bin, are difficult to inspect. The vision system has to cope with poor contrast, a partial view of the parts, an infinite number of stable states, variable incident and reflected lighting, shadows, etc.
Simpler machine vision techniques can be applied if the parts are separated and lying stably on a belt. Moreover, an exact positioning of the workpieces under the camera allows the use of relatively easy and very fast template matching techniques. For example, missing components may be detected by matching the gray levels in isolated windows that contain the particular components. Instead of windows, even isolated points, which correspond e.g. with the centroids of the different components, may be used.
A vision guided X-Y-θ table for accurate positioning has e.g. been described in [2].

2. Sensors and optics. In [3], the most important sensor devices for visual inspection today are briefly reviewed. They are vidicon cameras, solid state area and line array cameras, laser scanners, and image dissector tubes. We will shortly discuss them now. For more details on image sensors, we refer to [4].

Vidicon cameras are operating at broadcast television standards and are inexpensive. But for industrial applications, they may have some intolerable disadvantages. Tube life is short, they are fragile, constant readjustments for drift and aging are necessary and their (constant) resolution is sometimes too high and sometimes too low.

Solid state area cameras contain area arrays of photo-sensitive elements (CCD and CID technology) and have none of the mentioned problems of vidicon tubes. Metrological accuracy, important for inspection, can be attained by precisely selecting the geometry of the sensor array. The pitch can be manufactured with submicron accuracy.

Uniformity between the elements of the array is satisfactory, resolution varies from 128x128 to 512x480 and is therefore comparable with that of vidicons.

Solid state linear sensors consist of linear arrays of photo-sensitive elements. Sensors with 2048 elements and a pixel scan rate of up to 20 MHz are commercially available today, and higher resolutions are announced. It has to be noted that either the object or the sensor itself must continuously move in a direction perpendicular to the linear array in order to achieve 2-D images.

Laser scanners mostly use rotating mirrors to move the laser beam across the scene that must be inspected. Photodetectors measure the reflected, scattered or transmitted light. In [5] e.g. a laser scanner is used for the automatic inspection of PC boards.

Image dissector cameras permit to program circular, radial or other scans. As a result of this random access, storage and processing of an entire image is unnecessary if only a portion of the image is of interest. Therefore, those scanners are more suitable for certain applications than conventional cameras.

The previously described sensors may also be combined with special optics, such as an X-ray intensifier tube for X-ray inspection, fiber optics to collect the light or optical filters for color separation. Besides vidicon tubes, solid state cameras, laser scanners and image dissector tubes, a large number of other sensors can be used for particular applications. Examples of other sensors are infrared detectors, ultrasound sensors, X-ray sensitive CCD's, laser phase shift detectors, gamma cameras and holographic interferograms. A detailed discussion of these special purpose sensors, however, is beyond the scope of this paper.

3. Illumination.

A lot of applications which, at a first glance, require complex vision algorithms, may become much simpler by proper lighting and viewing conditions. The importance of good lighting cannot be over-emphasized. A great variety of lighting techniques is listed in [6]. They include back lighting, specular reflection, dye penetrant and magnetic particle indication techniques, ultraviolet, polarized and stroboscopic lighting and dark ground or dark field illumination. Their goal is to provide high contrast images, to allow of the objects or features of interest being separated from the background by simple thresholding.

Back lighting produces high contrast images of solid objects. These images can then easily be thresholded to get a binary image. Detecting particulate impurities or bubbles in a liquid held in a glass container is another example where back lighting is very helpful.

The appearance of scratches and cracks in a shiny surface e.g. can be enhanced by using specular reflection. In Fig. 1.a. the light source and the camera are directed perpendicular to the surface. The light is reflected to the camera except in cracks, which scatter the light in all directions and which, therefore, appear to be dark on a bright background. An alternative procedure for crack detection is shown in Fig. 1.b. In this case the light is projected onto the surface at 45 degrees to its normal and the surface is viewed normally. Since the shiny surface reflects the light in all directions, including in the direction of the camera, cracks appear to be bright on a dark background.

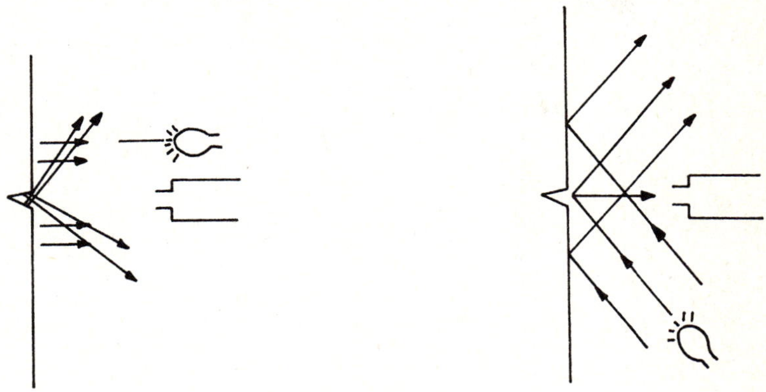

a. b.

Fig. 1.: Specular reflection for crack detection.

The appearance of cracks on rough surfaces can be emphasized by using dye penetrant and magnetic particle indication techniques in combination with ultraviolet radiation. Polarized light may be used to detect stress in glass or clear plastic and to detect sugars in foodstuffs. Stroboscopic lighting may be used to 'freeze' continuously moving objects on a conveyor. Dark ground or dark field illumination may be used to highlight the edges of a glass container.

Structured lighting and coherent lighting are more specialized illumination techniques.
With structured illumination a light pattern, e.g. a laser spot or one or more light stripes, is projected onto the scene. The light pattern reflected by the scene then provides information about the object surface structure (range), which can be reconstructed by triangulation. A narrow and intense line of light in combination with a linear array camera can also be used to obtain high contrast images. This principle is applied in the GM's CONSIGHT vision system and represented in Fig. 2. The light stripe is projected across the transport belt surface. The line camera is positioned so as to image the target line across the belt. When an object passes into the beam, the light is intercepted before it reaches the belt surface. When viewed from above, the line appears deflected from its target wherever a part is passing on the belt. Therefore, wherever the camera sees brightness, it is viewing the unobstructed belt surface. Wherever the camera sees darkness, it is viewing the passing part. Unfortunately, shadowing effect may cause the object to block the light before it actually reaches the imaged line, thus distorting the part image. Therefore, multiple light sources directed at the same strip across the belt, but with a different angle of incidence, should be used.
In coherent optical processing, coherent (in phase) light is produced by lasers. Powerful tools of this technique include coherent Fourier

transformation and filtering and the detection of small irregularities such as very small cracks, by means of interferometry. Coherent light is frequently used to measure vibration and the minute distortions caused in machine tools and air frame structures when they are stressed. More details on coherent optical processing can be found in [7].

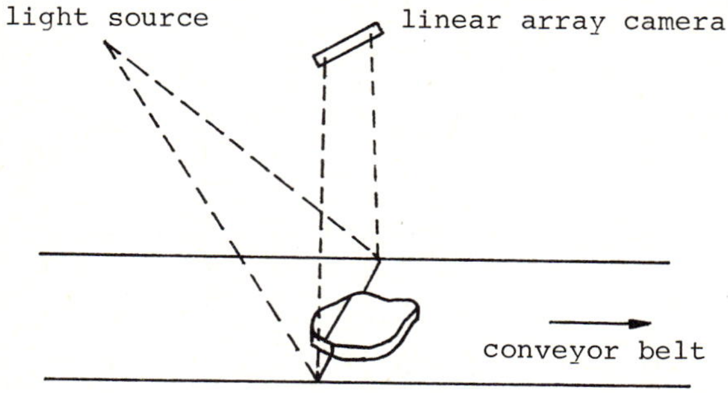

Fig. 2.: Principle of structured lighting for high contrast images.

For the sake of completeness, we have to mention that other energy sources, such as X-rays and ultrasound have also successfully been applied in visual inspection problems.

By now, it is clear that the great variety of sensor-illumination combinations offers a useful tool to simplify and reduce the further processing task. However, at present, no simple method exists to find the best configuration. In practice, experience and experimenting is the only recipe to find the optimal lighting and viewing conditions.

4. Vision systems.

An overview of commercial vision systems at the end of 1983 is given in [8]. Most of them are mentioned as 'general purpose' image computers. They consist of a microcomputer, an image memory bank, different from the microcomputer RAM and connected to the microcomputer bus, an interface that connects the camera with the image memory bank, and a sensor controller, which provides the camera with the necessary synchronisation signals.
General purpose vision systems have no application dependent hardware and all tasks are performed by the microcomputer. They are particularly suited for robot vision and visual inspection tasks that can be solved with a pattern recognition algorithm. Their application field can generally be subdivided into two classes [3].

A first class includes component measurement tasks, in which the parts must satisfy some general features concerning size and shape, such as area, number of holes, peround, and so on. Binary vision systems, which convert the input image into a binary one by simply thresholding, are usually capable of performing these measurement operations, provided that the objects to be inspected highly contrast with their background and provided that the background gray level is relatively constant throughout the image. Otherwise, the gray level image itself has to be processed.

A second class of inspection tasks includes the inspection of defects like scratches, cracks and foreign material. Here, the definition of

global features to describe the defects is not always simple. Instead of a systematic solution, an intuitive approach based on experience is usually required.
With proper lighting and viewing conditions, this kind of inspection problems may be solved with a general binary vision system. In most cases, however, gray level processing is unavoidable. Moreover, high resolution images (e.g. 2048x2048) may be necessary.

Obviously, gray level processing and the use of high resolution images strongly increase the amount of image data. Hardware processing is then the only means to perform the inspection task within an acceptable time. It has to be noted, however, that hardware processing is usually dedicated, and, as a result, limits the field of possible applications.

IV. HIGH SPEED PATTERN RECOGNITION USING HARDWARE PROCESSING

As previously mentioned, hardware processing may be the only means to perform the inspection task within an acceptable time. At our laboratory, we have built and are building several hardware processing units suited for visual inspection or robot vision.
It is not our intention in this paper to discuss their different algorithms at a hardware level, but rather to give an overview of our work in this context.
For more detailed descriptions, we will refer to the literature that we have published.

1. Run length encoding

Run length encoding is a data reduction technique which stores segmented objects as a data structure. It is particularly suited for binary images and has already been used in early vision systems, such as the VS-100 of Machine Intelligence Corporation. For each line in the image the line number and the position of each background-to-object transition together with the number of consecutive object pixels (run length) are stored. For gray level images, this number is followed by the corresponding gray level values of this sequence of adjacent object pixels. A random access memory is used to store this data structure. It must be as large as the largest number of data that can be expected in a given application.

A hardware run length encoding diagram for binary images, which has been realized at our laboratory, can be found in [9].

We note that, according to the previous definition of run length encoding, the encoded data do not contain explicit information about the object number they belong to. Object oriented run length encoding is more complex and requires an additional pass to link or rearrange the different runs belonging to one and the same object.

2. Calculation of projections

Projections are one-dimensional arrays in which the i-th element corresponds to a particular feature of the i-th row (or column) in the image. Possible features are the coordinate of the first object pixel along each line, the coordinate of the last object pixel, the number of object pixels, the sum of gray level values and the number of background-to-object transitions.

An early hardware processor for the calculation of profiles has been described in [10]. It has been built for the automatic inspection of reed switches and is still in use. More than 35 features are detected and controlled for each switch within 1 second.

Recently, a new prototype has been built at our laboratory. The system has a modular configuration and consists of:

- an 8 bit ADC card to convert the camera signal into digital format.
- 1 or more preprocessors directly connected to the VME bus (double Eurocard format). Each preprocessor transforms the camera image into a binary image by means of a programmable threshold (video look-up table) and extracts a number of features from the image (projections) in real time. These projections are stored in RAM on the preprocessor card.
- MC 68000 based microcomputer.
- Pascal written system and utility software.
- 3 RS-232 interfaces and 8 parallel input and 8 parallel output lines, high voltage or TTL compatible.

Different cameras can be connected to this system, such as a Fairchild 1500R linear array camera with 2048 pixels. The preprocessor operates at 12M pixels/sec. and is able to store projections of 4096 elements.

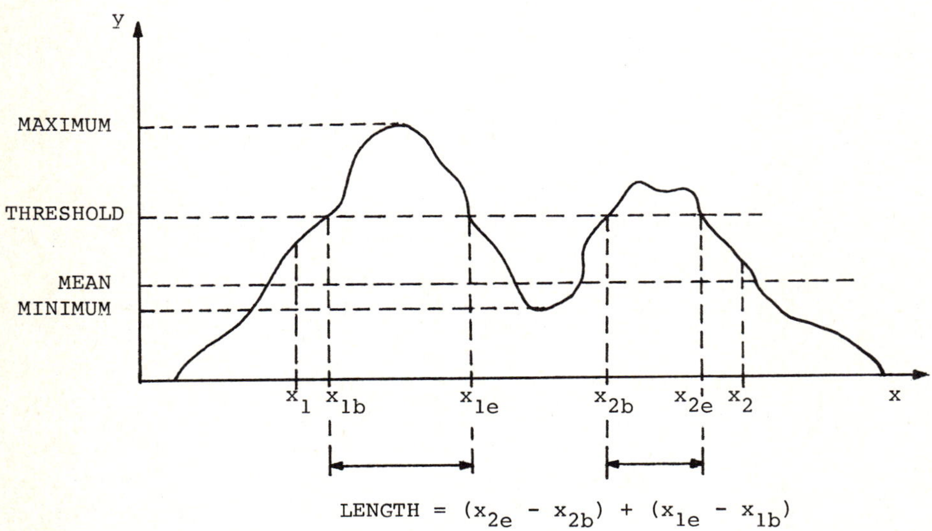

Fig. 3.: Projection y(x) and corresponding global features.

The system software includes procedures such as INITIALIZATION, THRESHOLD, TAKEPICTURE, READPROFILE, etc. and are available to the user. The utility software consists of the procedures MEAN, MAXIMUM, MINIMUM, LENGTH, LENGTHS and AREA, which calculate global features of the projections in an arbitrary interval $[x_1, x_2]$ (Fig. 3.). They are defined as follows:

$$\text{MEAN} = \frac{1}{x_2 - x_1} \cdot \int_{x_1}^{x_2} y(x)\, dx$$

$$\text{MAXIMUM} = \max_{x_1 \leqslant x \leqslant x_2} y(x)$$

$$\text{MINIMUM} = \min_{x_1 \leqslant x \leqslant x_2} y(x)$$

$$\text{LENGTH} = \sum_i (x_{ie} - x_{ib})$$

(in each interval $[x_{ie}, x_{ib}]$, $y(x) \geqslant$ THRESHOLD)

LENGTHS : LENGTHS [i,1] = x_{ib}

LENGTHS [i,2] = x_{ie}

$$\text{AREA} = \int_{x_1}^{x_2} y(x)\, dx$$

3. Windowing

Windowing extracts information by distributing a number of - possibly overlapping - rectangular frames over a scene and by analyzing the image in each window without regard to the rest of the image.
A separate set of conditions can be set for each window, including the threshold. Each window can then be tested for a variety of features such as area, width and location of specific edges. The information extracted from each window is usually simple and can be accomplished in hardware. Inspection of stamps for openings, cracks and dimensions is usually done using windowing. The individual features of each window may also be combined in a feature vector, which then provides the basis for a decision and allows for fairly complex inspections.

Windowing is available in the commercialized ICOS 20000 vision system [11].

4. Edge detection

Edge detection is a strong tool to extract the most interesting image features. Low contrast images or images with a nonuniform background, and the detection of defects such as scratches and cracks, are just a few cases where edge detection may be recommended. A lot of edge finding operations exist. Gradient operations, such as the Sobel and the Roberts operator, zero crossing operators and template matching are the most widespread because they are simple and are well suited for hardware implementation.

In [9] a specific block diagram for the Sobel operator and in [12] a block diagram for 3x3 convolutions in general have been described. The hardware implementation of this 3x3 convolver is part of a general purpose image computer system built at our laboratory and described in[13] . In[14] a single board hardware processor for adaptive filtering, developed at our laboratory, has been presented. The processor can perform point operations (sum, difference, product, logical operations and grayscale transformations all at 350 nsec. per pixel), adaptive and nonadaptive filters with a kernel of size up to 16x16 (at 200 nsec. times the kernel size per pixel), and erosion and dilation on binary and grayscale images with a structuring element of size up to 16x16. All arithmetic operations are performed on 8 bit values without any internal loss of accuracy except at the output since the result is converted back to an 8 bit value.

In spite of all those hardware implementations of edge detection operators, the resulting edge image cannot simply be used for visual inspection or robot vision. Object edges must be segmented and noise must be removed. Besides, the edges must be connected lines of single pixels and, often, they are required to be closed. Therefore, the question which edge detection operator yields the best results, is not of ultimate importance, as is stated by Ballard and Brown [15]:

> 'The efforts are usually best spent in developing methods that can use or improve the measurements from unreliable edges rather than in a search for the ideal edge detector.'

Gradient thresholding, edge thinning and edge tracking are extensively described in literature. All of those methods have in common that they are a compromise between speed and image complexity.

The result of a contour detection algorithm that has recently been developed at our laboratory, is shown in Fig. 4.
Fig. 4. upper left shows the original image of a part of a PC board. Fig. 4. upper right is the result of global thresholding, Fig. 4. lower left of a Sobel operator, followed by global thresholding and Fig. 4. lower right of our edge tracking algorithm. We are currently investigating the possibility of a high speed implementation of this algorithm for use in visual inspection or robot vision applications.

5. Texture analysis

Although edges are of critical importance in image analysis, they do not always fully describe the image content. Abrupt texture changes, for instance, do not always give rise to steep edges. Texture is therefore another important local image feature.

At our laboratory, we have succesfully applied a texture analysis algorithm to textile inspection. The results are shown in Fig. 5.a. and 5.b. The method is relatively simple and can be implemented in hardware. It works as follows.

During the calibration of the vision system, the periodicity vector of one or more representative samples of textile is calculated. Afterwards, during the inspection, the image is devided into a number of adjacent windows (see windowing). Each window is then shifted over the periodicity vector and for this particular shift, the gray level difference vector (GLDV) is calculated.
Next, the second order moment of this GLDV is calculated.
The second order moment will be small for windows that do not include textile defects, while it will be large for imperfect textile windows. We note that all of the operations during the inspection phase can be performed in hardware.

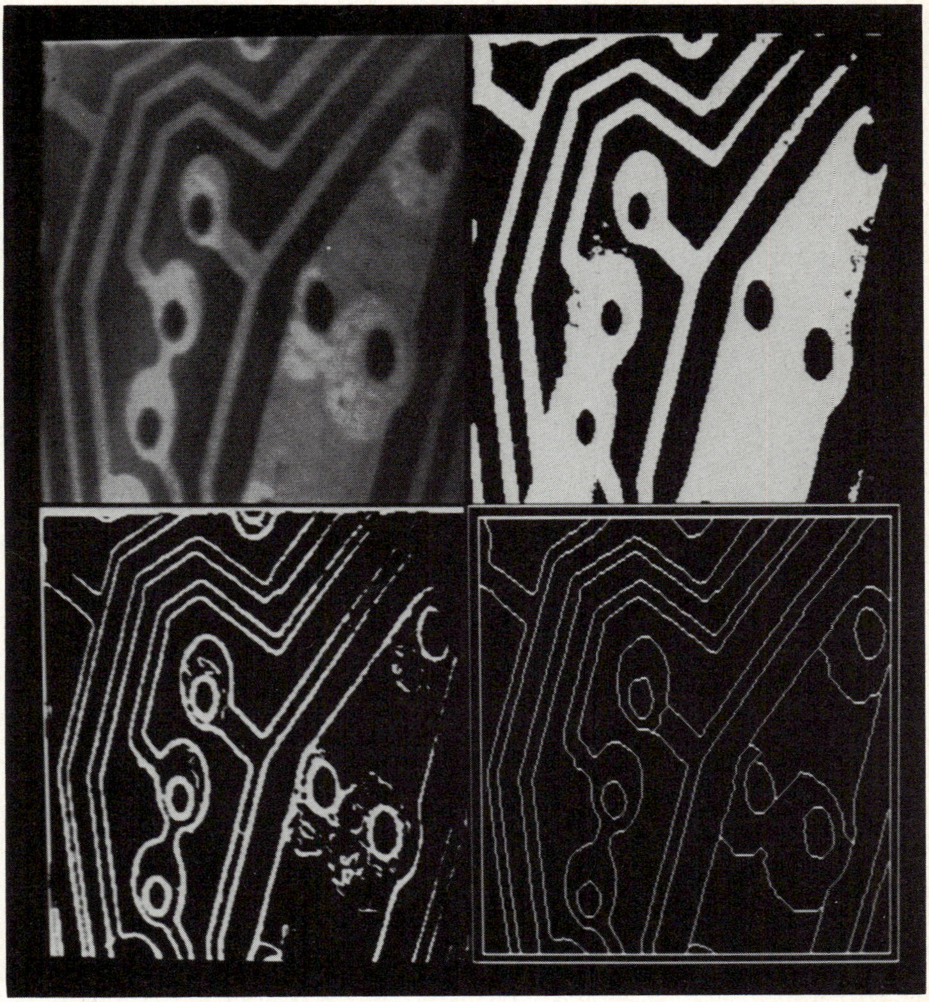

Fig. 4. upper left: original image of PCB
upper right: global thresholding
lower left: gradient thresholding
lower right: edge tracking algorithm

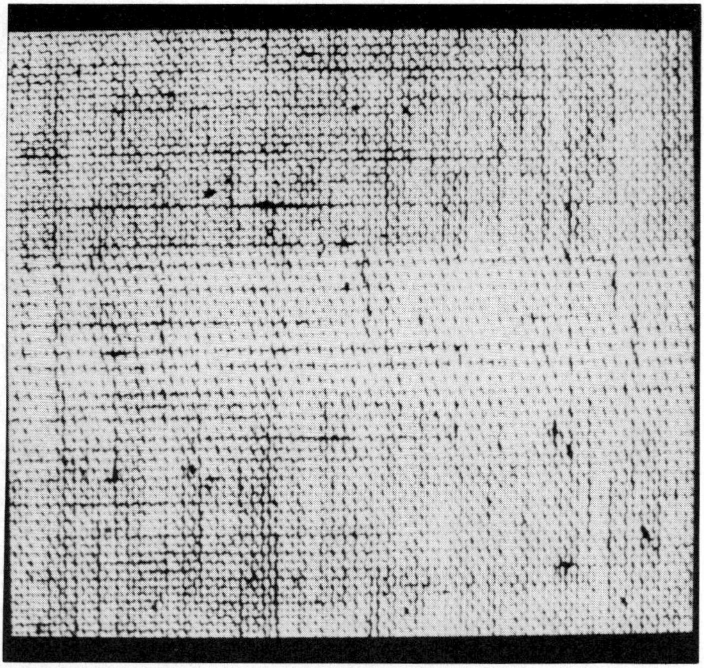

Fig. 5.a.:

Textile sample with defective horizontal band.

Fig. 5.b.:

Detection of abnormal tissue: brightness is proportional to defectiveness.

6. Spatial moments
Zero order, first order and second order spatial moments describe the object area, the object's centroid and a rough indication of the object shape respectively. More recently, a block diagram for the calculation of low order moments has been described in [9].
It is assumed that there is only one object in the binary image. If there are more objects, it is necessary to divide the image into a number of windows (see windowing).

V. CONCLUSION

Today, manufacturers of visual inspection or robot vision systems are particularly concerned about a reduction in processing time, a reduction in cost, and the development of vision systems as components of larger flexible manufacturing systems. Advances in hardware will increase the processing speed and allow higher resolution imaging, gray scale and color analysis, and the use of more complex calculations within acceptable processing times. At our laboratory we are therefore investigating pattern recognition methods which can be implemented in hardware.
A lot of promising methods have been discussed in this paper. They have all been converted into an optimal hardware architecture and prototypes have mostly been realized in cooperation with industrial companies.

VI. ACKNOWLEDGMENTS

The authors are thankful to all the personnel involved in visual inspection or robot vision. In particular, they are grateful to E. Hulsmans, G. Schreurs and R. Gielis who provided the photographs, and to P. Waege for typing the manuscript.

VII. REFERENCES

[1] Suetens, P. and Oosterlinck, A., Critical Review of Visual Inspection, Proc. S.P.I.E. Los Angeles, Vol. 528 - Digital Image Processing: Critical Review of Technology (Jan. 22-24, 1985).

[2] Chen, M.J., Vision Guided X-Y Table for Inspection, Proc. S.P.I.E., Vol. 360 (1982) 287-296.

[3] Winkler, G., Automatic Visual Inspection, in: Zimmerman, N.J. and Oosterlinck, A. (eds.), Proc. Industrial Applications of Image Analysis (Antwerp, Oct. 17-19, 1983, 13-30), (D.E.B. Publishers, 1983).

[4] Mundy, J.L., Image Input Systems, in: Zimmerman, N.J. and Oosterlinck, A. (eds.), Proc. Industrial Applications of Image Analysis (Antwerp, Oct. 17-19, 1983, 69-95), (D.E.B. Publishers, 1983).

[5] Danielsson, P.-E., Computer Architectures for Image Analysis, in: Zimmerman, N.J. and Oosterlinck, A. (eds.), Proc. Industrial Applications of Image Analysis (Antwerp, Oct. 17-19, 1983, 119-139), (D.E.B. Publishers, 1983).

[6] Batchelor, B.G., Illumination and Image Acquisition Techniques for Industrial Vision Systems, in: Zimmerman, N.J. and Oosterlinck, A. (eds.), Proc. Industrial Applications of Image Analysis (Antwerp, Oct. 17-19, 1983, 97-118), (D.E.B. Publishers, 1983).

[7] Bamler, R. and Lenz, R., Optical Processing, in: Zimmerman, N.J. and Oosterlinck, A. (eds.), Proc. Industrial Applications of Image Analysis (Antwerp, Oct. 17-19, 1983, 153-174), (D.E.B. Publishers, 1983).

[8] Zimmerman, N.J., Van Boven, G.J.R. and Oosterlinck, A., Overview of Industrial Vision Systems, in: Zimmerman, N.J. and Oosterlinck, A. (eds.), Proc. Industrial Applications of Image Analysis (Antwerp, Oct. 17-19, 1983, 193-231), (D.E.B. Publishers, 1983).

[9] Wambacq, P., Van Eycken, L., Oosterlinck, A. and Van den Berghe, H., High Speed Robot Vision Using Specialized Hardware, Proc. S.P.I.E. Cambridge, Massachusetts, Vol. 521 (1984).

[10] Van Daele, J., Oosterlinck, A. and Van den Berghe, H., Automatic Visual Inspection of Reed Switches, Optical Engineering Jrnl., Vol. 19(2) (1980) 240-244.

[11] De Roo, J. and Oosterlinck, A., Vision Automation with the ICOS 20000 Image Computer, Proc. S.P.I.E., Vol. 397 (1983) 374-378.

[12] Wambacq, P., Van Eycken, L., De Roo, J., Oosterlinck, A. and Van den Berghe, H., Description of Two Hardware Convolvers as a Part of a General Image Computer, Proc. P.R.I.P., I.E.E.E. Computer Society Conf. Dallas, Aug. 3-5, 1981 (1981) 294-296.

[13] Wambacq, P., De Roo, J., Van Eycken, L., Oosterlinck, A. and Van den Berghe, H., A Real Time Image Computer Configuration, Proc. S.P.I.E., Vol. 301 (1981) 38-42.

[14] Wambacq, P., Van Eycken, L., Oosterlinck, A. and Van den Berghe, H., A Simple Arithmetic Processor for Image Operations, Proc. S.P.I.E., Vol. 504 (1984) 122-126.

[15] Ballard, D. and Brown, C., Computer Vision (Prentice-Hall, Inc., Englewood Cliffs, New Jersey, 1982).

[16] Vuylsteke, P., Defraeye, P., Van Daele, J., Oosterlinck, A. and Van den Berghe, H., Video Rate Recognition of Plane Objects, Sensor Review Jrnl., Vol. 1(3) (1981) 132-135.

DISCUSSION

Suetens:

What is the opinion of the audience of the practical application of expert systems in industry?

Kanal:

It seems that people are developing expert systems for some areas of industrial inspection. Especially where there may be data bases available on the description of parts as well as CAD/CAM data bases, so that model based rules can be used along with image processing. I have heard people talk about it. I don't think any such system exists yet.

Jansen:

It is surprising to see that the first applications of expert systems were in the area of medicine and well-logging or oil exploration. That are exactly two areas where you have either a lack of experts or the experts do not agree or it is impossible to get confirmation afterwards. In industrial applications, specifically the part inspection, you have a very clear description of the part and there is no uncertainty whether there is a defect. So I am puzzled by the lack of applications in this field. It could also point in the direction that expert systems are completely useless. This may be supported by the fact that industry is very keen on not spending money as opposed to medicine where money is not an issue and oil exploration where money may not be an issue either.

Kanal:

One of my colleagues in my laboratory at the University of Maryland, Dr Dana Nau, has already demonstrated a very good expert system for process planning which is an area in manufacturing where people are feeling that those experts who do exist today are dying out. The old people who know how to do process planning are not being replaced. I think expert systems are going to come into manufacturing.

Persoon:

One important thing is that the specialist doesn't work fast enough. We have several applications where an expert could do it but he doesn't do it fast enough. Another point is that not enough specialists are available for certain problems. There is a general trend that factories are going to work 24 hours a day. That will be quite common in 5 years from now. Then, human inspectors can only work 6 hours a day, so we need 4 specialists for one task. This is impossible. This is also going to be a major driving force.

Choudry:

This question on the lack of industrial expert systems is basically related to the question of throughput and memory and this boils down to the computer architecture. This is a highly polarized opinion for whatever it is worth. Traditionally computer architecture has been dominated by number crunching. Both the software and hardware have been devoted to that. Logic programming or even the concept of how many LIPS somebody can execute has not been systematically addressed. The only large-scale attempt perhaps is the Japanese 5th-Generation project. In my opinion you will get the expert systems working only if you address the problem of throughput and memory in the context of logical processing architectures.

Suetens:
Thank you for answering my question.

PATTERN RECOGNITION IN PRACTICE II
E.S. Gelsema and L.N. Kanal (Editors)

COMPUTER AIDED ANALYSIS OF SCHEMATIC DIAGRAMS.

Frans C.A. Groen
Pattern Recognition Group
Applied Physics Dept
Delft University of Technology
Delft, The Netherlands

Ruud J. van Munster
Signal Processing Group
Institute of Applied Physics
P.O. Box 155
Delft, The Netherlands

This paper describes a method to interpret schematic diagrams. The objective is a system for (semi)-automatic input of drawings into the database of CAD systems, to facilitate maintenance of existing line-drawings. We propose a top-down approach in which first the global topology is investigated using cellular logic operations and component labeling. Next, the different objects found, are classified based upon probabilistic graph matching. Preprocessing using cellular logic operations has been made feasible by the development of special VME-bus oriented hardware for the fast execution of these operations.

1 INTRODUCTION

During the last years the introduction of computer aided design (CAD) systems has increased drasticly. One of the major problems with the use of CAD systems in industry is the large amount of drawings, which were produced before a CAD system was available. A majority of these drawings represents designs which are still active : they have to be maintained or modified. The maintenance of these existing drawings becomes more difficult. The experience to modify these drawings disappears with the introduction of the CAD system. However the life cycle of these existing drawings is estimated to be about several tens of years. A description of this difficulty can be found in [1].
This leads to a growing need for systems that provide (semi-) automatic input and analysis of manually produced diagrams. The output of such a system should be in the format of the CAD database.
In this paper we describe the first stage of a project to develop a system for the interpretation of manually produced schematic line-drawings.
These schematic diagrams consist of symbols and their interconnections, combined with character strings to specify the parameters of these symbols. Examples of these drawings include electrical circuit diagrams, flow charts, process diagrams and construction drawings. These all have in common that they are, in principle, two valued (binary) line images. The processing and analysis involve the following steps:

1. Scanning the drawing, resulting in a grey level image;
2. Noise removal, shading correction, and thresholding into a binary representation;
3. Separation of the binary image into a line-drawing part and a part containing the character strings;
4. Segmentation of the line-drawing part into symbolic objects and an interconnection structure;
5. Classification of the objects;
6. Coding of the interconnection structure;
7. Interpretation of the character strings;
8. User interaction for the identification of unidentified and ambiguous symbols;
9. Description of the drawings in the format of the CAD systems database;

The first stage of the project concentrates on the processing-steps 2 to 6, applied to the analysis of electronical circuit diagrams, which will be described in this paper.

2 OVERVIEW OF THE METHOD.

As stated in the introduction, the objective is to develop a system that describes the line-drawing in the format of the CAD database. Descriptions normally refer to parts of an image. Thus an important step in the analysis process is the segmentation : the distinction between the symbolic objects and interconnections.
We can cite some usual algorithms for the segmentation of line-drawings [1] :

- following algorithms, including line-following [2,3];
- line-synthesis algorithms;
- thinning algorithms [3];

The majority of these algorithms have in common that they operate directly on the vector representation of the image.
In this project we use a top-down approach, in which the segmentation is based upon the investigation of the global topology in the line-drawing. This technique is described in section 4.
Next, the different symbolic objects found during the segmentation, are represented by graphs. Now the objects are classified using probabilistic graph matching with model graphs of the different classes, as is described in section 6.
Both the separation of the drawing into a line-drawing part and the part representing the character strings, as the segmentation into (symbolic) objects are based upon cellular logic operations, such as erosions, dilations, skeletonization, propagation, and removal of singular points (Serra, [7]).
To use these techniques for the segmentation, we made the following assumptions on the electronical circuit diagrams :

1. the character symbols are relatively small with respect to the symbols in the line-drawing;
2. the line-drawing consists of large connected regions;
3. the symbolic objects in the line-drawing form locally closed loops, resulting in connected background components, except for a limited number of well known exceptions, such as capacitors;

The segmentation techniques were developed using the image processing system described by Duin et al [4]. Part of this system is the Delft Image Processor (DIP-1), developed by Gerritsen and Aardema [5]. Cellular logic operations are executed fast using the special cellular logic processor in the DIP-1.
Within the project a special board has been developed based on this cellular logic processor to perform these operations very fast on low cost micro-processor systems, such as the MC 68000. This hardware board will be described in section 5.
The probabilistic matching techniques for this project were developed at the Robotics Institute of Carnegie Mellon University, Pittsburgh, PA, using the POPEYE Image Processing System,developed by Bracho et al. [6]

3 IMAGE INPUT AND PREPROCESSING

Due to their age a number of drawings will be degraded ; both line- drawing and background will have non-uniform reflectivity (shading). To realize shading correction the drawings have to be scanned as grey valued images.
Figure 1a shows an original part of a heavily shaded line-drawing image.

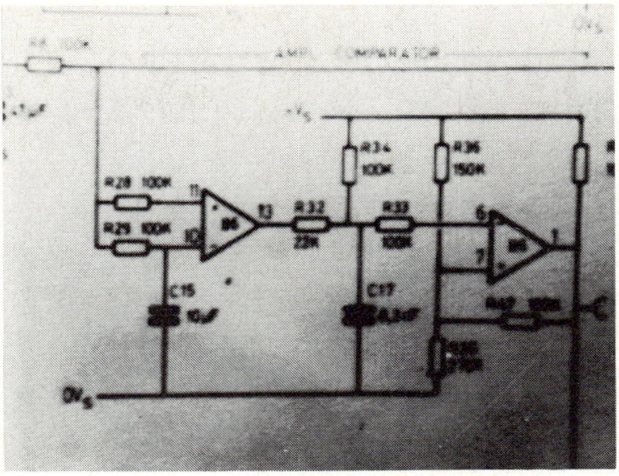

Figure 1a
Original part of a shaded line-drawing image.

Because the image consists of dark lines on a light background (or reverse), the majority of the pixels within a certain region will belong to the background and a minority of the pixels will belong to the foreground.
Thus an average background estimation can be obtained by a local high percentile filtering of the image and an average foreground estimation can be obtained from a local low percentile filtering.
Application of a x percentile filter means that for each pixel-neighbourhood a histogram is computed, and the grey-value below which x % of the values are present, is taken as the filter output. This local percentile filter can be seen as a generalisation of the well-known median filter.
Next, the binary representation is obtained by local thresholding, based upon the estimated intensities of foreground and background.
Figure 1b shows the result after the adaptive thresholding. The size of the percentile filters in this example is a 15 x 15 neighbourhood. The percentiles were respectively 2 % and 98 % .

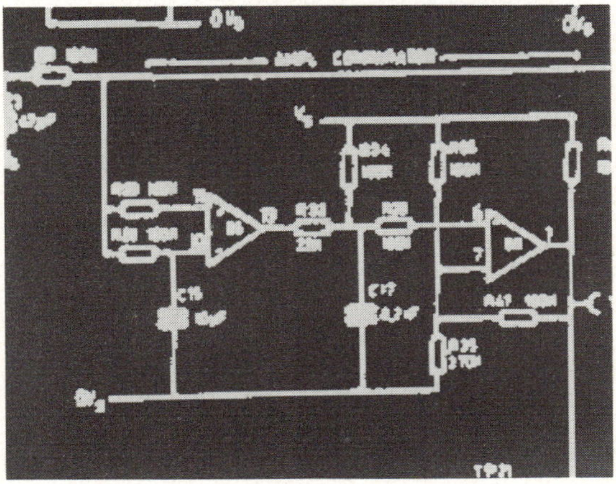

Figure 1b
Image of figure 1 after adaptive thresholding.

4 SEPARATION AND SEGMENTATION

The largest components in the image are assumed to be part of the line drawing, the smallest are assumed to be the text-strings. Thus, a separation between line-drawing and text-strings can be obtained based on the size of the different components.
This step consists of a detailed analysis of the drawing for small strokes and small closed contours indicating text both free and connected to the line-drawing.
First the small holes in the characters are filled. This is realized with the cellular logic operation closing (Serra, [7]). First the drawing is expanded (dilation) and then shrinked (erosion), resulting in a closing of small holes and gaps.
The next step is the complete skeletonization of the line-drawing, preserving the endpoints of the skeleton (Hilditch, [8]). Text-strings are now small strokes to the skeleton or isolated small lines. These small lines are found by a limited number of skeleton cycles without preserving the endpoints, resulting in singular points.
The branchpoints in the first skeleton are used to indicate the small strokes connected to the line-drawing part. Figure 2 shows the result of this text removal.

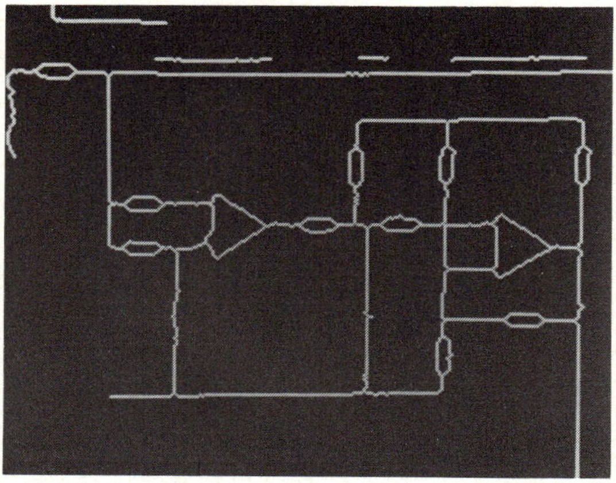

Figure 2
Result of the text removal.

In this step capacitors and diodes are also removed. So, these type of symbolic objects are found by another closing operation prior to this text removal.
When the line-drawing forms a locally closed contour resulting in a connected background component, we have a second type of symbolic objects. These candidate objects are selected on their size, using erosions and dilations applied to the background components.
The corresponding skeletons of the symbolic objects are the input for the classification process.

5 HARDWARE DEVELOPMENTS.

A special low-cost board for the very fast execution of the cellular logic operations on VME-bus oriented micro-computers has been developed. (Boekamp [9]) This board, called CLP is based on the design of the cellular logic processor in

the Delft Image Processor DIP-1.
The CLP consists of two double euroboards suitable for use as a slaveprocessor on a bus oriented system.
The processor is designed to work at 10 MHz pixel rate which brings the processing time for one image on 6.4 milliseconds per operation. Composite operations like skeletons are executed typically within .5 s. On the board there is space for four binary images, size 256 x 256.
The operators are implemented by the use of a table lookup, using the 9-bit binary data of every 3*3 neighbourhood as the address for the table. The skeletonization is realized with the recursive Hilditch algorithm. The control is done by a sequential circuit using a high speed Register-Rom combination.
A professionalized version is currently available on the VME-bus and will also be supported as a part of a general purpose image processing workstation.

6 CLASSIFICATION OF THE OBJECTS.

The recognition of the different objects found in the global analysis, is based on probabilistic graph matching. (Groen et al [10]) The graphs are constructed from the skeleton of the objects.
Starting from endpoints and nodes in the skeleton, the different skeleton parts are approximated by piece-wise linear and circular segments. During this approximation the segments and corresponding vertices (ends, corners and junctions) are represented in a graph.
A graph consists of a list of vertices and segments and attributes attached to each vertex and segment.
Among others, these attributes are for a vertex :

- a list of attached segments
- a list of segment angles
- the position
- type (end, corner or junction)

These attributes are for a segment :

- the length
- curvature
- the vertices it connects

The graphs are matched to the different class models. These class models are constructed during the training stage and contain also statistical attributes of the vertices and segments. These are the numbers of occurrences of a vertex or a segment, a histogram of the number of segments attached to a vertex, and the mean and variance in the vertex position. For a segment the mean and variance in length and curvature are calculated.
In the training procedure the statistical attributes of the model are updated. If a part of the observed training graph is not present in the model, the model may be updated by adding the not-matched part of the training graph.
The matching consists of the following steps :

- Find the position, orientation and scale of the observed graph with respect to the different model graphs. (pose matching)
- Match the vertices and segments of the model graphs to the observed graph and calculate the likelihood of the different matches.
- Assign the class with the maximum likelihood to the observed graph.

6.1 Pose Matching.

To find the pose (position, orientation and scale), 4 vertices of each class model are assigned as handle vertices. These handles are selected using a-priori information. Selection criteria are :

- The handles must have a high probability of occurence in the observed graphs.
- They must contain reliable information about the pose.

The pose matching of an observed graph versus a model graph consists of the following steps :

- For all pairs of vertices in the observed graph the likelihood is calculated to match a handle pair (based on the number of segments and distance).
- The pairs are sorted on likelihood, the best N are kept.
- For the N**2 combined pairs (4-tuples) the likelihood is calculated to match a handle 4-tuple (based on pair likelihood and angle between the pairs).
- These 4-tuples are sorted on likelihood, the best N are kept.
- The 4-tuple giving the minimum square error in the transform from observed graph into model graph is chosen.

6.2 Graph Matching

After finding the pose, the position of the vertices is known and for all vertices in the model graph a list of possible corresponding vertices in the observed graph is made. This primary matched list is based on the distance between the model vertices and the observed vertex.
When there are multiple matches, structural information is used to uniquely identify the multiple matches. First the vertex type is considered. When the vertex type is a corner, the angle of the corner is also taken into account. When there remains an ambiguity, the closest vertex is taken.
The segment matches are derived from the matched vertices.
For all vertices and segments the likelihood of the match is calculated.
The likelihood of the segments is determined by the probability of occurrence of the segment, the probability of the length, and the probability of the curvature.
The likelihood of the vertices is determined by the probability of occurence of the vertex, the probability of the number of segments attached to it, and the probability of the distance between the model and the observed vertex. When a vertex is not matched a minimum likelihood is assigned.

6.3 Results

In figure 3 an example of the processing of an invertor gate is given. In figure 3a the thresholded image is shown and in figure 3b the result after text removal.

The resulting graph from figure 3b is given in figure 3c.
In table 1 the unlikelihood is given for the matching of hand drawn symbols with templates. Six classes were considered : resistor (R), variable resistor (V), diode (D), capacitor (C), electrolytic capacitor (E) and amplifier (A).
The test set used for this table was different from the training set used to construct the model.
In each row of the table the unlikelihoods are given for the test samples of a certain class to the class-models. The standard deviation is given between brackets. When no pose-matching was possible, no likelihood is given.
No errors occurred in this small experiment (52 samples) when the symbol was assigned to the class of minimum unlikelihood. The table clearly reveals the strong resemblance between classes E and C. Some care must be taken with the interpretation of the mean and standard deviation. When there are additional vertices or segments present in a test-sample, there is a general increase in the

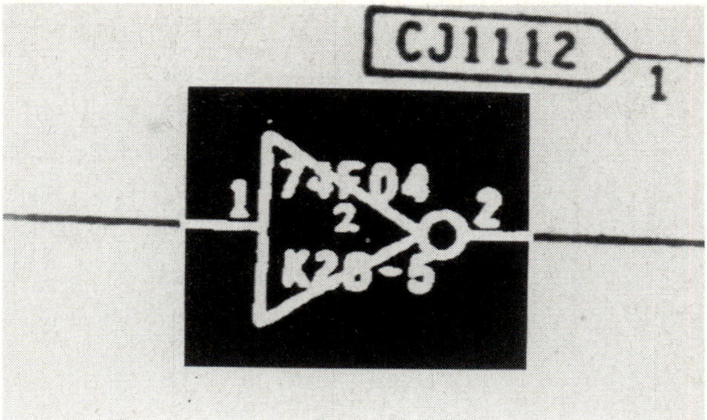

Figure 3a
Thresholded image of an invertor gate.

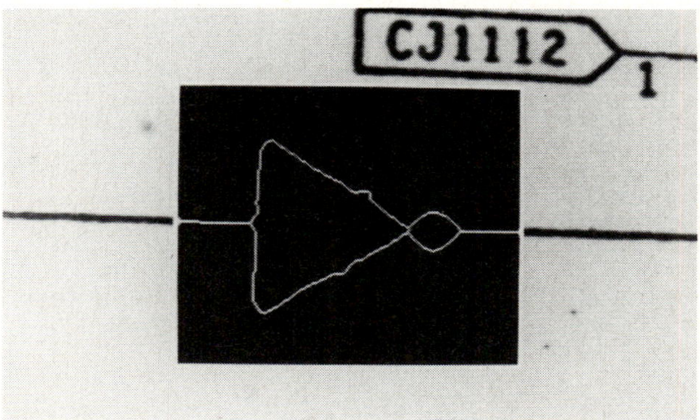

Figure 3b
Result of the text removal, applied to figure 3b.

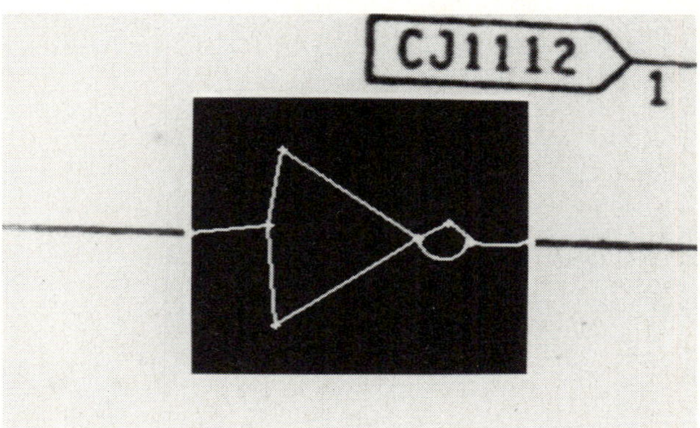

Figure 3c
Graph representation of the invertor gate.

unlikelihood to all classes. Secondly, outliers in the unlikelihood result always in high values of the unlikelihood as a result of an incorrect pose for strongly different classes.

H a n d   D r a w n   w i t h   T e m p l a t e

real class	n	Unlikelihood to the class models. R	V	D	C	E	A
R	10	109 (24)	159 (19)	215 (33)	324 (29)	296 (32)	506 (28)
V	6	283 (53)	147 (51)	259 (30)	484 (38)	450 (41)	706 (31)
D	7	428 (32)	363 (20)	94 (34)	240 (55)	182 (36)	420 (43)
C	9	-	-	-	50 (3)	73 (7)	-
E	9	384 (38)	306 (40)	189 (18)	143 (15)	79 (27)	445 (20)
A	11	273 (1)	177 (30)	123 (9)	232 (11)	236 (9)	67 (26)

Table 1. Average Unlikelihood (-L) for the matching of the test set of hand drawn symbols with a template to the class models.
Each row gives the unlikelihood for the test samples of a certain class. The standard deviation is given between brackets. The classes are R(esistor), V(ariable resistor), D(iode), C(apacitor), E(lectrolytic capacitor) and A(mplifier). No errors occurred in this experiment.

7 CONCLUSIONS

Cellular logic operations are potentially a very fast tool to analyse electronical circuit diagrams globally and to segment them into objects and interconnections.
Probabilistic graph matching looks a robust method to classify the symbols in the drawing. It incorporates also the possibility to adapt to different designers and drawing types in a training stage.

8 ACKNOWLEDGEMENT

The probabilistic graph matching of symbols was realized during a Fulbright Grant of Dr. Groen at The Robotics Institute of Carnegie Mellon University, Pittsburgh, PA, extending the work of John F. Schlag. The suggestions, discussion and cooperation with Prof. A.C. Sanderson were greatly appreciated.

9 REFERENCES

[1] Karima, M., Sadhal, K.S., and McNeil, T.O., From Paper Drawings to Computer-Aided Design,
IEEE Computer Graphics and Applications 2 (1985) 27-39.

[2] Rosenfeld, A., Image Pattern Recognition,
Proc. IEEE, Vol. 69, 5 (1981) 596-605.

[3] Harris, J.F., Kittler, J., Llewllyn, B., and Preston, G.,
A modular system for interpreting binary pixel representations of Line-Structured Data,
In : Pattern Recognition Theory and Applications, Proc. NATO Advanced Study Institute, Oxford, England, (March 1981) 311-351.

[4] Duin, R.P.W., Gerritsen, F.A., Groen, F.C.A., Verbeek, P.W., Verhagen, C.J.D.M .,
The Delft Image Processing System, design and use,
Proc 5th ICPR, Miami Beach, Florida, (1980) 768-774.

[5] Gerritsen, F.A, Aardema, L.G., Design and use of DIP-1:
A fast, flexible and dynamically microprogrammable pipelined image processor.
Pattern recognition 14, 319-330.

[6] Bracho, R., Schlag, J., Sanderson, A.C., POPEYE:
A Gray-Level Vison System for Robotics Applications.
Technical Report CMU-RI-TR-83-6, Robotics Institute
CMU, (1983 May)

[7] Serra, J., Image Analysis and Mathematical Morphology.
(Academic Press, London, New York, 1982).

[8] Hilditch, C.J., Linear Skeletons from Square Cupboards,
In : Meltzer, B., and Mitchie, D., (eds), Machine Intelligence, Vol. 4 (University Press, Edinburgh, 1969), 403-420.

[9] Boekamp, R., The CLP, a processing system for binary images.
Thesis, Dept. of Applied Physics, Delft University of Technology, The Netherlands, (1985) (in Dutch)

[10] Groen, F.C.A., Sanderson, A.C., Schlag, J.F., Symbol recognition in electrical diagrams, using probabilistic graph matching. Delft University of Technology, The Netherlands, & Carnegie-Mellon University Pittsburgh,PA, (1985, to be published)

DISCUSSION

Haralick:
How many operations did the matching use?

Van Munster:
Each symbol takes, I think, about one second to calculate on a 68000 system.

Groen:
That is right. The main part of the complexity is in the pose-matching of course. That was done by the bounded search, which has a complexity of N-squared. The rest is linear so that takes almost no time.

De Vogel:
After skeletonization all your characters had disappeared or were ruined. What do you do in cases when you have a bigger image, do you rescan or do you have the entire original image somewhere in solid state memory.

Van Munster:
We are not that close to a practical system. But the idea is that the text strings are processed with a much higher resolution. The objective is to scan at high resolution, then to use a low resolution image for classification of objects and process the textstring parts in high resolution.

Van Bemmel:
Will you use intelligence to interpret the entire drawing?

Van Munster:
I do not think so, I think that matching is in fact the intelligence. The coding of the interconnection structure will be a step but I think that will be relatively simple as compared to the matching. We have plans to evaluate different techniques of matching in September of this year. This, I think, is an important step.

PATTERN RECOGNITION IN PRACTICE II
E.S. Gelsema and L.N. Kanal (Editors)

AUTOMATIC TECHNIQUES FOR EXTRACTION OF GEOLOGICAL FRACTURE PATTERNS*

Jo Ann Parikh

Southern Connecticut State University
New Haven, Connecticut
U.S.A.

A major problem in automatic detection of geological fracture patterns is the integration of information from low level processes for linear feature extraction with geological expertise. This paper describes a knowledge-based approach which utilizes a set of decision rules developed by geologists to guide the interpretation of low level outputs. Low level operators extract low level features such as gradient, curvature, and line length from the image data. Selection, integration, and interpretation of low level outputs are performed by the high level decision processes which may, in certain instances, trigger additional low level processing. Global and contextual information collected by the high level decision processes is employed by the decision rules in addition to local information to determine which linear features are geologically significant. Experimental results of the approach are presented for Landsat TM data.

I. INTRODUCTION

Automatic generation of a regional map of geological fracture patterns entails delineation and categorization of straight or gently curving structures extracted or inferred from features in image and map data. Linear features observable in satellite imagery may represent cultural patterns or structures resulting from human activity such as clear-cut areas and section lines, structures which appear on the surface of the earth, and/or structures which extend into the Earth's crust. The desired geologic lines (which will be referred to as lineaments in this paper) result from fracturing (faulting and jointing) of the Earth's crust and, in the area under consideration for this study, the Canadian Shield, correspond in general to steeply-dipping fractures caused by brittle failure.

Fracture patterns form an important subclass of geologic lines. Statistical analyses of the location, density, and distribution of lineaments are used in tectonic studies and structural investigations. The location of fractures helps to pinpoint accumulations of petroleum, gas, and minerals and to determine susceptibility to ground water pollution. Detection of active faults is a key component in earthquake studies.

*The work reported in this paper was performed under a NASA-ASEE Summer Faculty Fellowship Program at NASA/GSFC.

A long-range goal at the National Aeronautics and Space Administration/Goddard Space Flight Center (NASA/GSFC) is the development of an interactive system for automatic extraction of lineaments. The system would permit the user to optionally select low level processing methods for specific tasks and modify any lineament maps produced by the system.

Tasks associated with generation of an automatic product include:

1) implementation of several low level operators for extraction of fracture patterns,

2) development of a methodology for combining image data with ancillary data such as geological and topographic maps and for integrating results from low level operators within a given frame and between frames

3) collection and codification of geological expertise in a form suitable for automatic processing

4) development of a systems framework with control mechanisms for dynamic selection of processing methods and a knowledge-based representation scheme that can be easily modified.

One of the major problems in implementing a system as described above is the computational effort and resources required for processing the image data.

This paper describes a modification of a systems architecture orginially proposed by H. K. Ramapriyan, P. D. Lowman, and H. W. Blodget (12) of NASA/GSFC for automatic extraction of lineaments and presents some preliminary results of experiments with low level operators on Landsat TM data. The proposed system (described in further detail in Section III) is designed for implementation on the Massively Parallel Processor (MPP) (described by Batcher (1)) at NASA/GSFC. The experiments described in Section IV and performed on a VAX-11/780 using the Land Analysis System (LAS) at NASA/GSFC illustrate one possible approach suitable for working with results from multiple sources of data -- construction of a cost array in which a low cost at a pixel denotes a high probability of the presence of a lineament followed by the application of a minimum-cost path algorithm.

II. BACKGROUND

Lineament extraction from Landsat imagery consists in general of a tedious and subjective process of manual interpretation of photographic products and/or computer-enhanced images by one or more analysts. Automatic procedures for lineament enhancement have been developed by several investigators. Many of the procedures involve multiple applications of filters. A lineament analysis technique developed by Takahashi (14) consists of applying two different filters designed specifically for lineament enhancement followed possibly by thinning and line tracking. Moore and Waltz (10) developed a five-step convolution procedure for lineament enhancement. The authors suggested that "because the decision rules for a line-connection algorithm are themselves subjective", the "best method (for construction of a final lineament map from extracted line segments) may consist of . . . manually connecting the segments that may have geologic significance". Coupland and Vincent (3) developed an automatic computer program LIRA (Linear Recognition and Analysis) that examines for each of M azimuth directions the MxN possible locations of linears in an NxN subframe whose size is selected to correspond to the length of linears to be mapped. A linear is identified if the magnitude of its correlation with a linear model (a two-dimensional step function with the same azimuth and orientation) exceeds a user-specified threshold which controls the strength of the linears to be mapped. The program was designed as an aid to human interpretation and the authors reported that it "remains for the human interpreter to discriminate the large scale patterns crossing many subframes . . . and to synthesize the linear information with available geologic maps or other data".

Fukue et al. (6) and Rochon and Roksandic (13) incorporated information from ancillary data in procedures developed for lineament enhancement. Fukue et al. (6) used information from the Land Numerical Information Data Base and ground truth data for land cover classification categories (in addition to a shadow-free Landsat image) to generate virtual Landsat images at any sun angle. This technique was particularly useful in aiding the human interpreter in detecting lineaments parallel to the sun direction in mountainous areas. Rochon and Roksandic (13) used topographic data in combination with Landsat imagery to produce images with different sun azimuthal positions and to enhance geologic lines. The authors reported that one of the major constraints on use of their technique was "the long computing time needed to process the data".

Xu et al. (15) developed an automated procedure for extracting and linking linear segments. The algorithm for extraction of linear segments consisted first of applying gradient operators in each of eight different directions to a variance thresholded image (since lineaments were characterized in their lineament model as having one side darker than the other with consequently a large local variance in intensity across the lineament). The number and distribution of pixels within overlapping windows of size 32x32 were then examined on each of the eight gradient maps and clusters of pixels were identified as linear segments. The principal eigenvector of a cluster center was accepted under certain conditions (notably in special cases involving large elongated clusters with gaps in the middle) as the representation of a linear segment. The linking algorithm consisted of linking appropriate linear segments in neighboring windows, resulting in piecewise linear approximations for lineaments. Problems mentioned by the authors included development of a "more global trend search . . . to identify the possible alignment of several linear segments which are separated far apart".

A survey of recent work relevant to the design and implementation of the system described in Section III would have to include at least some of the major developments in the fields of artificial intelligence, image understanding, and image processing which have influenced the system design. No attempt will be made in this paper to review advances in development of edge and line detectors, parallel search algorithms, procedures for building expert systems, and methods for knowledge representation. Specific algorithms under consideration for testing and inclusion in the system for lineament extraction, however, will be mentioned in the next section.

III. SYSTEM OVERVIEW

The major modules of the proposed system for lineament extraction are:

1) Image Processing and Image Understanding Component,
2) Expert Subsystems,
3) Geological Data Base,
4) Control Structure.

The input to the system consists of image data and user requests. Landsat and Shuttle Imaging Radar data will be the primary sources of image data. Output from the system will consist of regional lineament maps in a form adaptable to modification by human geologists.

The Image Processing and Image Understanding Component will contain a library of low level operators suitable for lineament extraction. Edge and line detection algorithms, algorithms for construction of connected components, classification algorithms (maximum likelihood and clustering), skeletonization algorithms, and algorithms for textural feature extraction will be included in the library of low level image processing methods. Algorithms for textural feature extraction will be used in feature extraction for classification algorithms and in lineament detection. Lineaments may correspond to texture edges and may occur in highly textured backgrounds. Classification algorithms are important in several aspects of processing -- for example, in separating cultural from natural patterns and determining land cover categories used in decision rules in expert subsystems. Since, typically, many such low level operations will be applied to a given image, they will require significant amounts of computation. Hence, they will be implemented on the MPP at NASA/GSFC.

Analyses of the multiple sources of data used by the system could be handled on an individual basis by expert subsystems. A global Geological Data Base containing various types of maps and geological models should be accessible from each expert subsystem. Each expert subsystem would have it own knowledge base and scheme for knowledge representation. Initially each expert subsystem could be implemented as a production-rules system.

One of the functions of the Control Structure would be to integrate information from the expert subsystems and interface with user requests. The approach currently under study is to construct a regional cost array (confidence image) in which a low cost at a given pixel denotes a high likelihood for a lineament. The final cost array would reflect information derived from cost arrays constructed by individual expert subsystems which, in turn, would integrate outputs from several low level operators. The synthesis of the information would be optionally under user control, perhaps in the form of specifying weights for individual outputs. The technique of using cost arrays to combine outputs from several sources has been used by Fischler et al. (4) for detection of roads and linear structures and by Mitchell and Keirsey (9) for planning strategic paths through terrain data.

The control strategies would ideally combine data-driven analysis with model-driven prediction. Initially, low level operators would be applied to the input image data. The establishment of regional trends and predictions about the occurrence of geological structures could then be formulated and tested. It may then be necessary to employ top-down strategies which would trigger low level operators in the Image Processing and Understanding Component.

After the final cost array is constructed, minimum-cost path algorithms could be used to outline lineaments. In this approach, a lineament or portion of a lineament would correspond to a minimum-cost path from one side of a mask to another. More than one lineament might be present within a given mask and masks could overlap neighboring frames or alternatively algorithms could be constructed to link together portions of lineaments located in different frames. Masks could be oriented along different directions and the possible positioning and size of masks could be constrained either directly by user intervention or by information from ancillary data. A direct but exhaustive approach would be first to center masks around points with a high likelihood for being on a lineament and then examine the distribution of points within the masked region, continually altering the size of the mask until certain constraints were not satisfied. The problem of identification of the beginning and ending points of a lineament is a major problem in automated lineament extraction and involves, even for the photoanalyst, a subjective decision process.

IV. EXPERIMENTS ON LANDSAT TM DATA USING LOW LEVEL OPERATORS

The Landsat frame of size 512x512 shown in figure 1 was selected from a Landsat TM image (size 6967x5965) of the Canadian Shield for a preliminary study of lineament detection methods. Lineaments within the frame or crossing through the frame (see figure 2) were outlined by Paul Lowman (Geophysics Branch, NASA/GSFC) as part of a study (Lowman et al. (7))to investigate regional fracture patterns and to test the theory that there is a regmatic fracture pattern in the Earth's crust. The scene in figure 1 illustrates many of the problems associated with automatic lineament detection. One lineament appears to run straight through the center of a lake, another lineament follows the edge of a lake, another resembles a curve more than a line, some are difficult to detect even visually for the untrained observer (narrowing his field of vision to a single frame), and several linear features within the frame bear no correspondence to lineaments. The lineaments outlined in figure 2 and in the sixty or more Landsat images used in the study by Lowman et al. (7) were mapped using entire Landsat images, not just single frames, by interpreters who supplemented their general geological expertise with knowledge acquired from familiarity with ancillary data and from, in some instances, personal on-site investigations of areas in the Canadian Shield.

The lineaments mapped from the Landsat images were generally associated with easily distinguishable surface structures such as elongate bodies of water or depressions rather than elevations -- features which could be embodied in lineament models and subsequently used in the selection process for low level edge and line detectors. For this particular set of data, sun-azimuth biasing was negligible and it was not necessary, therefore, to preprocess the data to enhance lineaments parallel to the sun direction. Since there were relatively few artificial linear features present in any of the images and none in the selected frame, no classification experiments were performed to separate cultural from natural linear features.

Since preprocessing was unnecessary, the initial processing step consisted of applying edge and line detectors to the image data. Several directional filters (implemented as convolution procedures) were applied either singly or in multi-step procedures. The edge magnitude image resulting from applying the 5x5 Kirsch templates (see figure 3) followed by thinning and thresholding at the 95 percent level is shown in figure 4. The thinning algorithm (also used by Nevatia and Babu (11) and Chittineni (2)) consisted simply of deleting from consideration as edge points the two neighboring pixels (in a direction normal to the direction of the edge) of a given pixel if their edge directions were within 45^{0} of the pixel and the edge magnitude of the pixel was larger than that of its neighbors. The thresholding step was performed primarily for display purposes as it is the intent in the proposed system to adhere as closely as possible to Marr's Principle of Least Commitment (8). Figure 5 illustrates the result of applying a "road operator" instead of an edge operator to the data. The "Duda Road Operator" (described in Fischler et al. (4))was designed to detect line-like structures of constant width and thus could be used in combination with other edge operators to detect line-like lineaments. The Kirsch template could be used to detect lineaments which, for example, coincide with the edge of a lake. All the operators tested produced many short linear segments -- most of which bore no relation to the desired fracture patterns.

It appeared that more knowledge had to embodied in the algorithms used for the next step than would typically be supplied to line-linking or line-connection operators. There were many wide gaps between the linear segments output from the first step -- some of which were to be bridged automatically to form lineaments while others, using the geologists' rule of no extrapolation, could not be connected. Linear segments that followed lines of foliation or flow structure in igneous rocks, even though they might appear to be connected, had to be discarded unless there was sufficient evidence to believe that they corresponded to fracture patterns.

The next step in processing the image data was to construct a cost array by remapping the edge magnitude image and run a minimum-cost path algorithm through masked regions in the array. Using one or more cost arrays (possibly a separate cost array for each edge direction) provides a framework that can be initially constructed from low level outputs and later modified by expert subsystems. The result of applying the minimum-cost path algorithm F^* (a variation of an algorithm by Ford (5) described by Fischer et al. (4)) through a masked region in a cost array derived from application of Roberts' gradient is shown in figure 6. The masked regions can be specified interactively or automatically using expert knowledge. The F^* algorithm locates a minimum-cost path between a start point and a goal point or alternatively (as used in the experiments) from one end of a masked region to the opposite end. Running the algorithm through several large-sized regions in several directions using the VAX-11/780 was computationally prohibitive.

V. FUTURE RESEARCH AND WORK

Our immediate objective is to add several of the low level operators to the library of image processing programs on the MPP. Also a parallel minimum-cost path algorithm needs to be developed and implemented on the MPP.

After all the relevant low level operators have been implemented, a new set of experiments should be designed and performed using the MPP to assess the limits of the Image Processing and Understanding Component. Building the Expert Subsystems will require extensive collaboration between geologists and system designers. Further research is needed to determine appropriate knowledge representation schemes for the Expert Subsystems and control structures for the Control Structure Component.

ACKNOWLEDGMENT

The author wishes to extend her sincere appreciation to H. K. Ramapriyan for his support, his review of this paper, and his valuable assistance in this study and to P. D. Lowman for sharing his geological expertise in many enlightening discussions and for photointerpretation of the Landsat TM data used in the experiments.

REFERENCES

(1) K. E. Batcher, "Design of a Massively Parallel Processor", IEEE Transactions on Computers, September, 1980.

(2) C. B. Chittineni, "Edge and Line Detection in Multidimensional Noisy Imagery Data", IEEE Transactions on Geoscience and Remote Sensing, Vol. GE-21, no. 2, pp. 163-174, 1983.

(3) D. H. Coupland and R. K. Vincent, "Automatic Linear Recognition and Analysis Using Computer Program LIRA," Fifteenth International Symposium on Remote Sensing of Environment, pp. 499-508, 1981.

(4) M. A. Fischler, J. M. Tenenbaum, and H. C. Wolf, "Detection of Roads and Linear Structures in Low-Resolution Aerial Imagery Using a Multisource Knowledge Integration Technique," Computer Graphics and Image Processing 15, pp. 201-223, 1981.

(5) L. R. Ford, Jr., Network Flow Theory, The Rand Corporation, P-923, 1956.

(6) K. Fukue, H. Shimoda, and T. Sakata, "Complete Lineament Extraction with the Aid of Shadow-Free Landsat Image," Machine Processing of Remotely Sensed Data Symposium, pp. 94-102, 1981.

(7) P. D. Lowman, N. M. Short, P. J. Whiting, A. M. Lohman, and G. Lee, "Fracture Patterns of the Canadian Shield; Implications for Plate Tectonics and the Regmatic Shear Theory,", 1985. (Under Review Publication).

(8) D. Marr, "Early Processing of Visual Information", Philosophical Transactions of Royal Society of London, Series B, Vol. 275, pp. 484-519, 1976.

(9) J. S. B. Mitchell, and D. M. Keirsey, "Planning Strategic Paths Through Variable Terrain Data," SPIE Applications of Artificial Intelligence, Vol. 485, pp. 172-179, 1984.

(10) G. K. Moore and F. A. Waltz, "Objective Procedures for Lineament Enhancement and Extraction", Photogrammetric Engineering and Remote Sensing, pp. 641-647, 1983.

(11) R. Nevatia and K. R. Babu, "Linear Feature Extraction and Description", Computer Graphics and Image Processing, 15, pp. 257-269, 1980.

(12) H. K. Ramapriyan, P. D. Lowman, and H. W. Blodget, "Development of Automatic Techniques for Detection of Geological Fracture Patterns", July 1984. (Personal Communication)

(13) G. Rochon and M. Roksandic, "Geologic Application of Landsat Imagery Enhanced by Topographic Data," Machine Processing of Remotely Sensed Data Symposium, pp. 124-131, 1981.

(14) H. Takahashi, "A Lineament Enhancement Technique for Active Fault Analysis," Machine Processing of Remotely Sensed Data Symposium, pp. 103-112, 1981.

(15) S. R. Xu, C. C. Li, and N. K. Flint, "Extraction of Geological Lineaments from Landsat Imagery by Using Local Variance and Gradient Trend," Machine Processing of Remotely Sensed Data Symposium, pp. 124-131, 1984.

Figure 1. Landsat TM Scene (512x512) of an Area of the Canadian Shield.

Figure 2. Lineament Map for the Scene Shown in Figure 1.

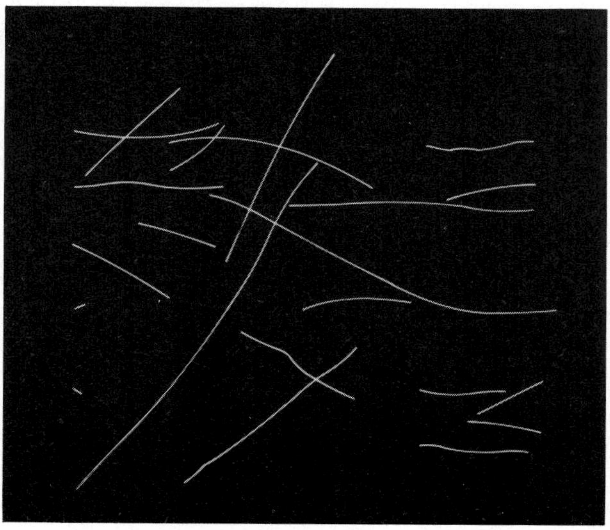

Figure 3. Kirsch Templates.

-1	-1	0	1	1
-1	-1	0	1	1
-1	-1	0	1	1
-1	-1	0	1	1
-1	-1	0	1	1

1	1	1	1	1
1	1	1	1	1
0	0	0	0	0
-1	-1	-1	-1	-1
-1	-1	-1	-1	-1

0	1	1	1	1
-1	0	1	1	1
-1	-1	0	1	1
-1	-1	-1	0	1
-1	-1	-1	-1	0

1	1	1	1	0
1	1	1	0	-1
1	1	0	-1	-1
1	0	-1	-1	-1
0	-1	-1	-1	-1

Figure 4. Thinned and Thresholded Edge Magnitude Image.

Figure 5. Thresholded Duda Road Operator Image for Horizontal, Dark Roads.

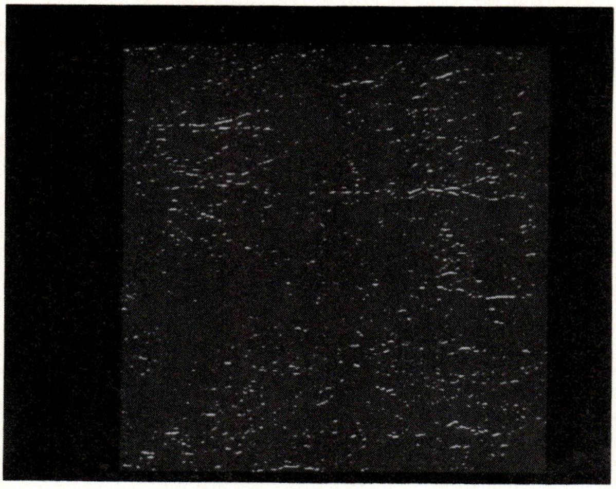

Figure 6. Minimum-Cost Path Through Masked Rectangular Region Using Cost Array Derived from Roberts' Gradient.

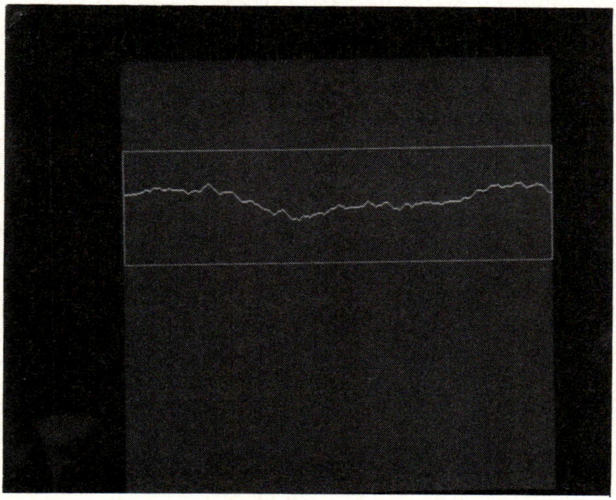

DISCUSSION

Choudry:

In the ordinary laboratory type of pattern recognition there is a nice feedback feature. You can write an algorithm and test whether it works or not. Suppose you find some fracture, is there then any independent check you run on it, to see if what you have found is really there.

Parikh:

We are trying to compare our results to what the geologists agreed upon beforehand which is, of course, a very subjective process.

Mulder:

How does the geologist know that there is a fracture through for example a lake?

Parikh:

From ground studies, geological maps and other geological sources of information. In this particular case we are looking at very well studied areas.

Persoon:

Is the MPP operational?

Parikh:

Yes, it was delivered in May 1983. In May 1984 it was operational for assembly language and system programmers, primarily. Now we are putting application programs on it which are written in parallel Pascal.

PART II

PATTERN RECOGNITION

SECTION V

FEATURE EXTRACTION
CLASSIFICATION
MAPPING

PATTERN RECOGNITION IN PRACTICE II
E.S. Gelsema and L.N. Kanal (Editors)

COMPUTATIONAL COMPLEXITY AND VLSI IMPLEMENTATION OF AN OPTIMAL FEATURE SELECTION STRATEGY†

Salvatore D. Morgera

Concordia University
Department of Electrical Engineering
1455 de Maisonneuve Blvd. W.
Montréal H3G 1M8 Québec, Canada

Certain algorithms and their computational complexity are examined for use in a VLSI implementation of a real-time pattern classifier. The most computationally intensive processing is found in the classifier training mode wherein subsets of the largest and smallest eigenvalues and associated eigenvectors of the input data covariance pair must be computed. It is shown that if the matrix of interest is centrosymmetric, the problem architecture assumes a parallel form. Such a matrix structure is found in a wide variety of speech and signal processing applications. Each of the parallel channels requires only two specialized matrix-arithmetic modules. These modules may be implemented as linear arrays of processing elements having at most $\mathcal{O}(N)$ elements, where N is the input data vector dimension. The computations may be done in $\mathcal{O}(N)$ time steps. This compares very favorably with the $\mathcal{O}(N^2)$ computing time required for the sequential approach. Some examples are provided on the convergence of the suggested iterative approach for eigensystem decomposition; it is felt that the factored method used may lead to sub-problems which are well-conditioned.

1. INTRODUCTION

This work deals with the computational complexity analysis of a VLSI-based real-time pattern classifier employing the feature selection scheme described in detail in [1,2]. The classifier discriminates, using a reduced dimensionality space, between two (or more) weakly stationary Gaussian stochastic processes having similar means and different covariance matrices. Since the dimensionality reduction or feature selection utilizes a very accurate approximation to the Bayesian error, the resulting set of features appears to be quite optimal for a given compression ratio. If one desires to maintain a fixed classification error, rather than a fixed compression ratio, it is possible to compute an estimate of the error in real-time and alter the compression ratio accordingly. In [1,2] errors as low as 10^{-8} are accurately computed from explicit relationships, indicating that the scheme may be useful for comparing competing classification schemes and computational approximations thereof, in lieu of exhaustive simulation studies.

General operation of the pattern classifier is described in [3] and is seen to have three modes of operation: training, processing, and decision-directed, as shown in Figure 1. Using training sequences for the various hypotheses, the rectangular transformation for data feature extraction is computed during the training mode. Actual classification of patterns is accomplished during the processing mode and, periodically, the decision-directed mode is used to update the feature extractor using training mode processing functions.

† Work supported by Canada NSERC Grant A0912.

The most computationally complex processing is found in the training mode, with the most complex step being the computation of subsets of the largest and smallest eigenvalues and associated eigenvectors of the data covariance matrices. Due to the intensive processing required in the training mode, in this work we concentrate on the partial eigensystem computations required. To minimize the computational complexity, the iterative scheme that we describe for principal component extraction utilizes the a priori information that the true covariances are Toeplitz. Since matrices of Toeplitz form occur frequently in speech and image processing, the described methods may also prove to be useful in other applications.

2. THE TRAINING MODE

Let $\underline{x}$ be an N-dimensional data vector with a multivariate normal (MVN) distribution, $N(\underline{0},R_i)$ under hypothesis H_i $i = 1,2$ for the binary hypothesis testing problem. We assume that the covariances R_i $i = 1,2$ are positive definite, symmetric Toeplitz matrices. Extension of the methods to more than two hypotheses and also to complex Hermitian Toeplitz covariances [4] is straightforward. Feature selection requires the application of an $(n \times N)$- dimensional transformation A to the data. This operation results in the n-dimensional feature vector $\underline{y}$, i.e.,

$$\underline{y} = A\underline{x} \tag{1}$$

The transformation matrix A is assumed to be of rank n. As shown in [1,5], the best choice for A, in the sense of Bayesian error minimization, is to choose the rows of A as the (right-hand) eigenvectors $\{\underline{e}_i\}$ of the matrix $R_1^{-1}R_2$ corresponding to an n-dimensional extremal set $\{\lambda_i\}$ of eigenvalues. Such a set contains a mix of the largest and smallest eigenvalues of $R_1^{-1}R_2$. Since the best set is not a priori known, we must extract the n smallest and n largest principal components of $R_1^{-1}R_2$ and then utilize estimates of the Bayesian error on (n+1) ordered extremal sets to determine the best choice. Normally, we have $n \ll N$.

In practice, we estimate R_1 and R_2 from training data as symmetric constrained Toeplitz matrices as described in [6]. The number of training vectors N_s used must be sufficiently large compared to N in order to insure a good approximation to the true covariances; this is particularly important if low classification error rates are required. In order to simplify notation, we assume R_1 and R_2 are the estimates so obtained. In the following, we describe the procedure for principal component extraction of $R = R_1^{-1}R_2$. The procedure uses the facts that the estimated covariances R_1 and R_2 are symmetric centrosymmetric matrices and that the product R is a centrosymmetric matrix.

2.1 PRINCIPAL COMPONENT EXTRACTION - FACTORS

For convenience, we assume N even. The symmetric centrosymmetric covariances R_i $i = 1,2$ may be partitioned into (N/2)-dimensional submatrices as,

$$R_i = \left[\begin{array}{c|c} A_i & B_iP \\ \hline PB_i & PA_iP \end{array}\right] \qquad i = 1,2 \tag{2}$$

where P is a reflection matrix having unity on the secondary diagonal and zeroes elsewhere ($P^{-1} = P$), $A_i^T = A_i$, $B_i^T = B_i$, and $A_i = PA_iP$. The covariances R_i may be put in block-diagonal form by the same orthogonal transformation L [7,8], i.e.,

$$R_i' = LR_iL^T = \left[\begin{array}{c|c} A_i+B_i & 0 \\ \hline 0 & A_i-B_i \end{array}\right] \qquad i = 1,2 \tag{3a}$$

where,

$$L = \frac{1}{\sqrt{2}} \left[\begin{array}{c|c} I & P \\ \hline I & -P \end{array}\right] \tag{3b}$$

From (2) and (3), we may write R in block diagonal form,

$$R = R_1^{-1} R_2 = L^T \left[\begin{array}{c|c} [A_1+B_1]^{-1}[A_2+B_2] & 0 \\ \hline 0 & [A_1-B_1]^{-1}[A_2-B_2] \end{array}\right] L \tag{4}$$

The matrix R is centrosymmetric, but not symmetric; the constituent submatrices A_i $i = 1,2$ are symmetric Toeplitz and the constituent submatrices B_i $i = 1,2$ are (symmetric) Hankel. It is noted that application of the orthogonality transformation L requires trivial operations only.

We define the diagonal blocks of (4) as,

$$M^{\pm} = [A_1 \pm B_1]^{-1}[A_2 \pm B_2] \tag{5}$$

The eigenproblem $[R - \lambda I]\underline{e} = \underline{0}$ may now be written from (4) and (5) in partitioned form as,

$$[M^+ - \mu I]\underline{f}_1 = \underline{0} \quad , \quad [M^- - \mu I]\underline{f}_2 = \underline{0} \tag{6}$$

where we use μ here in place of λ, $\underline{f}^T = [\underline{f}_1^T, \underline{f}_2^T]^T$, and $\underline{e} = L^T \underline{f}$. The eigenvalues of (6) are real and positive, but may not be distinct. The N-dimensional problem is thereby reduced to two (N/2)-dimensional problems. This reduction is advantageous for the purposes of parallel computation using finite word size. The following sequence of steps permits the calculation of a portion of the eigenspectrum of R in a manner similar to that of Andrew [9]. The factor of $1/\sqrt{2}$ from L multiplying all eigenvectors is omitted.

Algorithm Factors

1. Compute the matrices M^+, M^-.
2. Compute the eigenvalues $\mu_1, \ldots, \mu_\ell$, where $\ell \leq N/2$, and corresponding eigenvectors $\{\underline{f}_1\}$ of M^+, and the eigenvalues $\mu_{\ell+1}, \ldots, \mu_{2\ell}$ and corresponding eigenvectors $\{\underline{f}_2\}$ of M^-. (See Section 2.2 for details.) Then, 2ℓ eigenvalues $\{\lambda\}$ of R are given by $\mu_1, \mu_2, \ldots, \mu_{2\ell}$. Computation of the corresponding eigenvectors $\{\underline{e}\}$ of R requires steps 3-5.
3. If $i \leq \ell$ go to step 4. Otherwise, go to step 5.
4. If $\ell < j \leq 2\ell \Rightarrow \mu_i \neq \mu_j$, then $\underline{e}_i = [\underline{f}_{1i}^T, (P\underline{f}_{1i})^T]^T$. Otherwise, $\underline{e}_i = [\underline{f}_{1i}^T + \underline{f}_{2j}^T, (P\underline{f}_{1i})^T - (P\underline{f}_{2j}^T)^T]$. Exit.
5. If $j \leq \ell \Rightarrow \mu_i \neq \mu_j$; then $\underline{e}_i = [\underline{f}_{2i}^T, -(P\underline{f}_{2i})^T]^T$. Otherwise, $\underline{e}_i = [\underline{f}_{1j}^T + \underline{f}_{2i}^T, (P\underline{f}_{1j})^T - (P\underline{f}_{2i})^T]^T$.

From the algorithm we see that if the eigenvalues are distinct, the situation we shall assume in the sequel, the eigenvectors associated with M^+ are symmetric ($P\underline{e} = \underline{e}$) and those associated with M^- are skew-symmetric ($P\underline{e} = -\underline{e}$). In many problems of practical interest, the eigenvalues of the factors $M^{\pm}$ are <u>interleaved</u>, or approximately interleaved, with the largest eigenvalue of R being the largest eigenvalue of M^+. From [7,8], we know that interleaving occurs for the covariances R_i when B_i is of rank unity; the same holds for R, when, for example, the R_i are first order Markovian or of tridiagonal form. When the eigenvalues of the factors are approximately interleaved and we desire the n largest eigenvalues and associated eigenvectors of R, we set $\ell \cong n/2$ in the above algorithm. To find the n smallest eigenvalues and associated eigenvectors of R, we replace $M^{\pm}$ everywhere by $[M^{\pm}]^{-1}$, again set $\ell \cong n/2$, and take the inverse of the resulting set $\{\mu\}$. The computations for the two cases may be done in parallel. To do this efficiently requires that we select a method that locates eigenvalues in descending order, as described in the next section.

2.2 PRINCIPAL COMPONENT EXTRACTION - POWER METHOD

We assume that the eigenvalues of R are ordered as $\lambda_1 > \lambda_2 > \cdots > \lambda_N$ with corresponding eigenvectors $\underline{e}_1, \underline{e}_2, \ldots, \underline{e}_N$. Also, the eigenvalues of the factors $M^{\pm}$ are ordered, i.e., $\mu_1 > \mu_2 > \cdots > \mu_\ell$ and $\mu_{\ell+1} > \mu_{\ell+2} > \cdots > \mu_{2\ell}$, respectively. The power method with deflation is a simple and effective technique for finding the n largest (and n smallest) principal components of R using the factors $M^{\pm}$ (and $[M^{\pm}]^{-1}$) as required in Step 2 of the algorithm in Section 2.1.

Let $\underline{u}_o$ be an arbitrary vector and let the sequences $\underline{v}_s$ and $\underline{u}_s$ be defined by,

$$\underline{v}_{s+1} = M\underline{u}_s \qquad \underline{u}_{s+1} = \underline{v}_{s+1}/\|\underline{v}_{s+1}\| \tag{7}$$

where $\|\underline{x}\|$ denotes the norm at infinity of $\underline{x}$, i.e., the element of maximum modulus of $\underline{x}$ [10]. The matrix M of (7) is either M^+ or M^-. Provided that the coefficient of $\underline{e}_1$ in a general expansion of $\underline{u}_o$ is not zero, we have the following convergence results,

$$\underline{u}_s \to \begin{cases} \underline{f}_{11}/\|\underline{f}_{11}\| & M = M^+ \\ \underline{f}_{2,\ell+1}/\|\underline{f}_{2,\ell+1}\| & M = M^- \end{cases} \quad \text{and} \quad \|\underline{v}_s\| \to \begin{cases} \mu_1 & M = + \\ \mu_{\ell+1} & M = M^- \end{cases} \tag{8}$$

This procedure, implemented in parallel, simultaneously finds the largest eigenvalue and corresponding eigenvector of each factor; The eigenvectors of R are found using the trivial operations of steps 3-5 of the preceding algorithm. As previously discussed, in some cases, $\{\mu_1, \mu_{\ell+1}\} = \{\lambda_1, \lambda_2\}$ with the eigenvectors $\{\underline{e}_1, \underline{e}_2\}$. After each iteration of (7), $\underline{u}_s$ and $\underline{u}_{s+1}$ are compared and the process is terminated when they are within a specified tolerance.

Once $\{\underline{f}_{11}, \underline{f}_{2,\ell+1}\}$ and $\{\mu_1, u_{\ell+1}\}$ are computed, we deflate the factors $M^{\pm}$ in order to compute the next largest set of eigenvalues and corresponding eigenvectors [11]. Since the matrices $M^{\pm}$ are not symmetric, we must also compute the left-hand eigenvectors $\{\underline{g}_1\}$, $\{\underline{g}_2\}$ of M^+ and M^-, respectively, using a procedure similar to (7). The left-hand eigenvectors are the solutions of,

$$[M^+ - \mu I]^T \underline{g}_1 = \underline{0} \quad , \quad [M^- - \mu I]^T \underline{g}_2 = \underline{0} \tag{9}$$

For a given $\underline{f}_{1i}$ and $\underline{f}_{2i}$, we normalize $\underline{g}_{1i}$ and $\underline{g}_{2i}$ such that $\underline{g}_{1i}^T\underline{f}_{1i} = \underline{g}_{2i}^T\underline{f}_{2i} = 1$. Defining M_1^+ and M_1^- as,

$$M_1^+ = M^+ - \mu_1 \underline{f}_{11}\underline{g}_{11}^T \tag{10a}$$

$$M_1^- = M^- - \mu_{\ell+1}\underline{f}_{2,\ell+1}\underline{g}_{2,\ell+1}^T \tag{10b}$$

we have, from conditions of bi-orthogonality,

$$M_1^+\underline{f}_{1i} = M^+\underline{f}_{1i} - \mu_1\underline{f}_{11}\underline{g}_{11}^T\underline{f}_{1i} = \begin{cases} 0 & i = 1 \\ \mu_i \underline{f}_{1i} & 1 < i < \ell \end{cases} \tag{11a}$$

$$M_1^-\underline{f}_{2i} = M^-\underline{f}_{2i} - \mu_{\ell+1}\underline{f}_{2,\ell+1}\underline{g}_{2,\ell+1}^T\underline{f}_{2i} = \begin{cases} 0 & i = \ell+1 \\ \mu_i \underline{f}_{2i} & \ell+1 < i < 2\ell \end{cases} \tag{11b}$$

Thus, $M_1^{\pm}$ have eigenvalues zero corresponding to the eigenvectors $\underline{f}_{11}$ and $\underline{f}_{2,\ell+1}$, respectively. The matrix M_1 is now used in place of M in (7) to find $\{\underline{f}_{12}, \underline{f}_{2,\ell+2}\}$ and the (now) dominant eigenvalues $\{\mu_2, \mu_{\ell+2}\}$. The process of deflation and iteration proceeds by straightforward extension of the above.

As described earlier, the above procedure starting from (7), can be used to estimate the 2ℓ smallest eigenvalues of R by iterating on $[M^{\pm}]^{-1}$ in place of $M^{\pm}$. We then take the inverse of the eigenvalues so obtained. This is far more accurate than finding the entire eigensystem using $M^{\pm}$, due to the fact that successive deflations cause an increasing ill-conditioning of the problem. Furthermore, we have observed for a number of practical examples that the eigenvalues of R cluster in value around the value of $\lambda_{N/2}$. Since the described method works essentially from λ_1 down and λ_N up, the central region is avoided, especially if $n << N$. In the case of eigenvalues interleaved in the factors $M^{\pm}$, the factors are better conditioned than R itself, and we would expect more rapid convergence. A block diagram exposing the parallel processing structure of the method is shown in Figure 2.

3.0 SIMULATION OF THE METHOD

Two examples are examined, both having $N = 14$. The number of each of the smallest and largest eigenvalues and associated eigenvectors desired is four. Thus, ultimately, $n = 4$ and the data compression for feature selection is 71%.

Example 1

This example uses Toeplitz, non-Markovian covariances. The first rows of R_1 and R_2 are, respectively,

$$[R_1]_{1\cdot} = [11.56, 1.4, 1.3, 1.2, 1.1, 1.0, 0.94, 0.80, 0.81, 0.70, 0.60, 5.60, 0.40, 3.00]$$

$$[R_2]_{1\cdot} = [20.00, 1.94, 1.88, 1.70, 1.60, 1.56, 1.40, 1.30, 1.20, 1.10, 1.00, 9.40, 8.80, 0.70]$$

The matrix R has the eigenvalues,

$$\{\lambda\} = \{3.9526, 2.1785, 1.8039, 1.7894, 1.7734, 1.7727, 1.76557, 1.76556, 1.7649, 1.7394, 1.6897, 1.5966, 0.8848, 0.8470\}$$

In terms of the eigenvalues of the factors $M^{\pm}$, the eigenvalues are ordered as,

$$\mu_8 > \mu_1 > \mu_2 > \mu_9 > \mu_{10} > \mu_3 > \mu_4 > \mu_{11} > \mu_{12} > \mu_5 > \mu_{13} > \mu_6 > \mu_7 > \mu_{14}$$

where the μ_i $i = 1,2,\ldots, N/2$ correspond to M^+ and the μ_i $i = N/2+1, N/2+2, \ldots, N$ correspond to M^-. In this case, the eigenvalues are not evenly interleaved and the largest has a skew-symmetric eigenvector.

The procedure of (7) is terminated when $\|\underline{u}_{s+1} - \underline{u}_s\| < 10^{-5}$, this being consistent with approximately 16 bit accuracy. In all cases, the initial starting vector used is $\underline{u}_o^T = [1,0,\ldots, 0]^T$. Table 1 shows the number of iterations required for the four largest and four smallest eigenvalues and eigenvectors. Results are also shown for computing the left-hand eigenvectors required in the deflation process. Because procedures are in parallel, the maximum number of iterations for a parallel processor is 794 for λ_4 obtained using M^-. Since this is the last eigenvalue in the subset for $M^{\pm}$, we need not actually compute the associated left-hand eigenvector. The number of iterations is comparatively large due to the fact that $\lambda_4/\lambda_5 \cong 1$.

Example 2

In this example, the covariances R_1 and R_2 are first order Markovian with one-step correlation of 0.5 and 0.9, respectively. The matrix R has the eigenvalues,

EIGENVALUE	LEFT-HAND EIGENVECTOR	EIGENVECTOR
USING $M^{\pm}$:		
λ_1	12	15
λ_2	34	50
λ_3	421	424
λ_4	673	794
USING $[M^{\pm}]^{-1}$:		
λ_{11}	175	226
λ_{12}	109	119
λ_{13}	15	18
λ_{14}	16	16

TABLE 1. Number of iterations for Example 1; N = 14, n = 4.

$$\{\lambda\} = \{3.3738,\ 1.0900,\ 0.4963,\ 0.3147,\ 0.2422,\ 0.2074,\ 0.1884,\ 0.1771,\ 0.1700,\ 0.1654,\ 0.1623,\ 0.1602,\ 0.1589,\ 0.1581\}$$

In terms of the factors, the eigenvalues are ordered as,

$$\mu_1 > \mu_8 > \mu_2 > \mu_9 > \mu_3 > \mu_{10} > \mu_4 > \mu_{11} > \mu_5 > \mu_{12} > \mu_6 > \mu_{13} > \mu_7 > \mu_{14}$$

indicating an even interleaving, with the largest eigenvalue having a symmetric eigenvector.

Table 2 shows the number of iterations required for this example. The maximum number of iterations for a parallel processor in this case is 671 for λ_{14} obtained using $[M^-]^{-1}$. Again, we note that $\lambda_{13}/\lambda_{14} \cong 1$.

EIGENVALUE	LEFT-HAND EIGENVECTOR	EIGENVECTOR
USING $M^{\pm}$:		
λ_1	8	8
λ_2	11	10
λ_3	17	16
λ_4	26	26
USING $[M^{\pm}]^{-1}$:		
λ_{11}	205	205
λ_{12}	281	281
λ_{13}	401	401
λ_{14}	671	671

TABLE 2. Number of iterations for Example 2; N = 14, n = 4

4.0 COMPUTATIONAL COMPLEXITY AND VLSI IMPLEMENTATION

The (multiplicative) complexity of the procedure described in Section 2.0 for the training mode is described below for the right-hand (r.h.) portion of the $M^{\pm}$ parallel channels. Each channel has the same complexity per iteration. Successive iterations of the power method (7) are carried out by first forming $[A_2 \pm B_2]$ and computing,

$$[A_2 \pm B_2]\underline{u}_s^{\pm} = \underline{\ell}_{s+1}^{\pm} \tag{12}$$

and then solving the systems,

$$[A_1 \pm B_1]\underline{v}_{s+1}^{\pm} = \underline{\ell}_{s+1}^{\pm} \tag{13}$$

after which we set $\underline{u}_{s+1}^{\pm} = \underline{v}_{s+1}^{\pm}/\|\underline{v}_{s+1}^{\pm}\|$. The two-step approach of (12) and (13) avoids the direct inversion required in computing $M^{\pm}$.

As A_2 is Toeplitz and B_2 is Hankel, (12) requires $\mathcal{O}[N \log_2(N/2)]$ multiplications and (13), including normalization, requires $\mathcal{O}(N^2) + N/2$ multiplications, using a block-Levinson algorithm [12]. Precisely the same number of computations are required for computing the left-hand eigenvectors of $M^{\pm}$ needed for the deflation process. Extending (10), we see that iterating with the ith deflated factor requires an additional $(i-1)N$ multiplications, where $1 \leqslant i \leqslant \ell$. Re-normalizing an eigenvector set of order $n/2$ using the Euclidean norm requires $nN/2$ multiplications. Now, for $n << N$, the total complexity is $\mathcal{O}(N^2) + \mathcal{O}(N \log_2(N/2))$ multiplications/iteration/channel. As shown in Figure 1 and described in [3], other training mode computations, e.g., construction of the extremal distribution function (df) family $\mathcal{F}^*$, root computation, and optimum df determination are comparatively trivial. This is also true of the on-line probability of error calculation.

It is important to realize that only two specialized (or custom) matrix arithmetic modules are needed in the parallel channels: (1) a Toeplitz (Hankel) matrix-vector product module for (12) and (2) a Toeplitz-plus-Hankel linear system module for (13). The first module may be constructed as a linear convolution array of $\mathcal{O}[\log_2(N/2)]$ processors requiring $\mathcal{O}(N)$ time steps [13]. The second module may be constructed as a vector array of $\mathcal{O}(N)$ processing elements requiring $\mathcal{O}(N)$ time steps with a pipelined processor architecture using only localized interconnections [14]. Both modules exhibit maximum parallelism.

5.0 CONCLUSIONS

In this work we have attempted to expose the processing architecture required for a new feature selection and pattern classification technique. The most intensive computation is the partial eigensystem decomposition found in the training mode and periodically required in the decision-directed mode. To accomplish this principal component extraction, we have first broken the N-dimensional problem into two sub-problems of dimension N/2 operating in parallel. Within these subproblems, the requirements of an operator-based iterative method allow further parallel processing. The computational complexity, however, for each parallel channel is still $\mathcal{O}(N^2) + \mathcal{O}(N \log_2(N/2))$. When N is large, the problem may still be too intensive to be handled in real-time by a SISD uniprocessor; furthermore, it is not felt to be cost-effective to perform the many simple, repetitive operations using an SIMD array processor or pipelined vector processor.

Recent advances in VLSI technology and highly concurrent architectures, do, however, offer a cost-effective way of implementing the pattern classification system. For the system described, only two specialized matrix arithmetic modules are required: (1) a Toeplitz (Hankel) matrix-vector product module and (2) a Toeplitz-plus-Hankel linear system module. Implementing these as linear convolution arrays of $\mathcal{O}(\log_2(N/2))$ and $\mathcal{O}(N)$ processors, respectively, permits the computations for each module to be carried out in $\mathcal{O}(N)$ time steps per iteration. With multiplication speeds possible with a commercially available ALU, very high real-time rates are attainable. For example, when $N = 14$, the maximum total number of iterations required/parallel channel $I \cong 1.5 \times 10^3$ for Example 2; thus, we have approximately $4.2 \times 10^4 t_o \leqslant T$, where t_o is the time per arithmetic operation and T is the input vector sampling time period. For speech processing, we may have $T \cong 1.75 \times 10^{-3}$s, in which case $t_o \leqslant 42$ ns.

ACKNOWLEDGEMENT

The author wishes to thank H. Krishna of Concordia University, Department of Electrical Engineering, for the simulation results of Section 3.0. Also, Ms. Anita Claassen is to be acknowledged for doing a very professional job of typing the manuscript.

REFERENCES

[1] Morgera, S.D. and Datta, L., Toward a Fundamental Theory of Optimal Feature Selection: Part I, IEEE Trans. Pattern Anal. and Mach. Intell. PAMI-6, (Sept. 1984) 601-616.

[2] Morgera, S.D. and Datta, L., Optimal Feature Selection: Part I - Theory, in Proc. IEEE Seventh Intern. Conf. on Patt. Recog., Montréal (July-Aug. 1984) 134-137.

[3] Datta, L. and Morgera, S.D., Optimal Feature Selection: Part II - Implementation, in Proc. IEEE Seventh Intern. on Patt. Recog., Montréal (July-Aug. 1984) 138-141.

[4] Datta, L. and Morgera, S.D., Efficient Principal Component Extraction for a New Class of Matrices: Application to Feature Selection, in Proc. Intern. Conf. on Comp., Sys., and Sig. Proc., Bangalore (Dec. 1984) 81-84.

[5] Okamoto, M., Discrimination for Variance Matrices", Osaka Math. Journ. 13, (June 1961) 1-39.

[6] Morgera, S.D. and Cooper, D.B., Structured Estimation: Sample Size Reduction for Adaptive Pattern Classification, IEEE Trans. Inform. Theory. IT-23, (Nov. 1977) 728-741.

[7] Morgera, S.D., On the Reducibility of Finite Toeplitz Matrices - Applications in Speech Analysis and Pattern Recognition, Signal Processing. 4 (Oct. 1982) 425-443.

[8] Cantoni, A. and Butler, P., Eigenvalues and Eigenvectors of Symmetric Centrosymmetric Matrices, Lin. Alg. and App. 13 (1976) 275-288.

[9] Andrew, A.L., Eigenvectors of Certain Matrices, Lin. Alg. and App. 7 (1973) 151-162.

[10] Wilkinson, J.H., The Algebraic Eigenvalue Problem (Oxford University Press, London, 1965).

[11] Hotelling, H., Analysis of a Complex of Statistical Variates into Principal Components, Journ. Educ. Psychol. 24 (1933) 417-441, 498-520.

[12] Merchant, G.A. and Parks, T.W., Efficient Solution of a Toeplitz-Plus-Hankel Coefficient Matrix System of Equations, IEEE Trans. Acoust. Speech, and Sig. Proc. ASSP-30 (Feb. 1982) 40-44.

[13] Danielson, P.E., Serial/Parallel convolvers, IEEE Trans. Comp. C-33 (July 1984) 652-667.

[14] Kung, S-Y. and Hu, Y.H., A Highly Concurrent Algorithm and Pipelined Architecture for Solving Toeplitz Systems, IEEE Trans. Acoust., Speech, and Sig. Proc. ASSP-31 (Feb. 1983) 66-76.

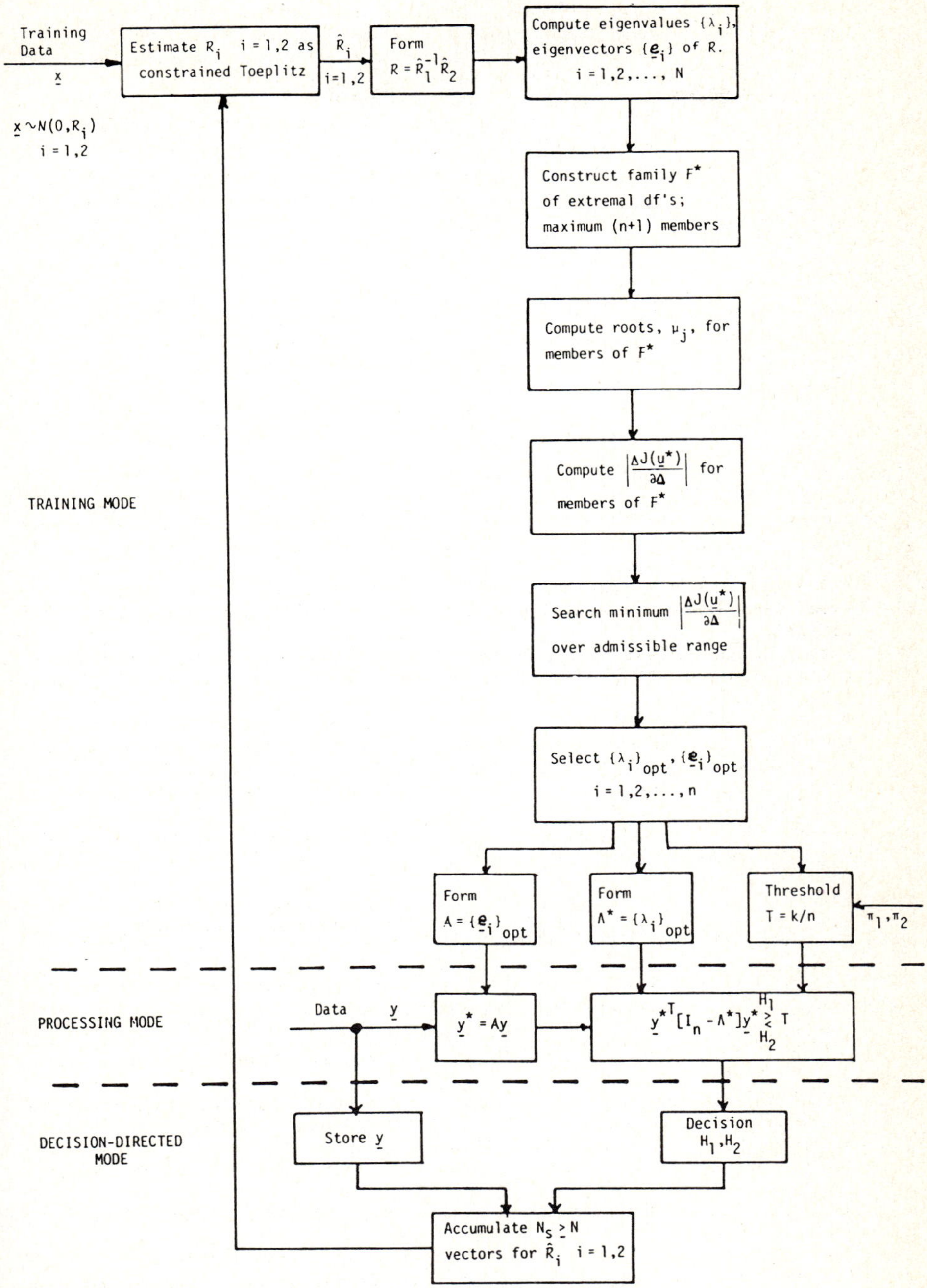

Fig. 1. The strategy for optimal feature selection.

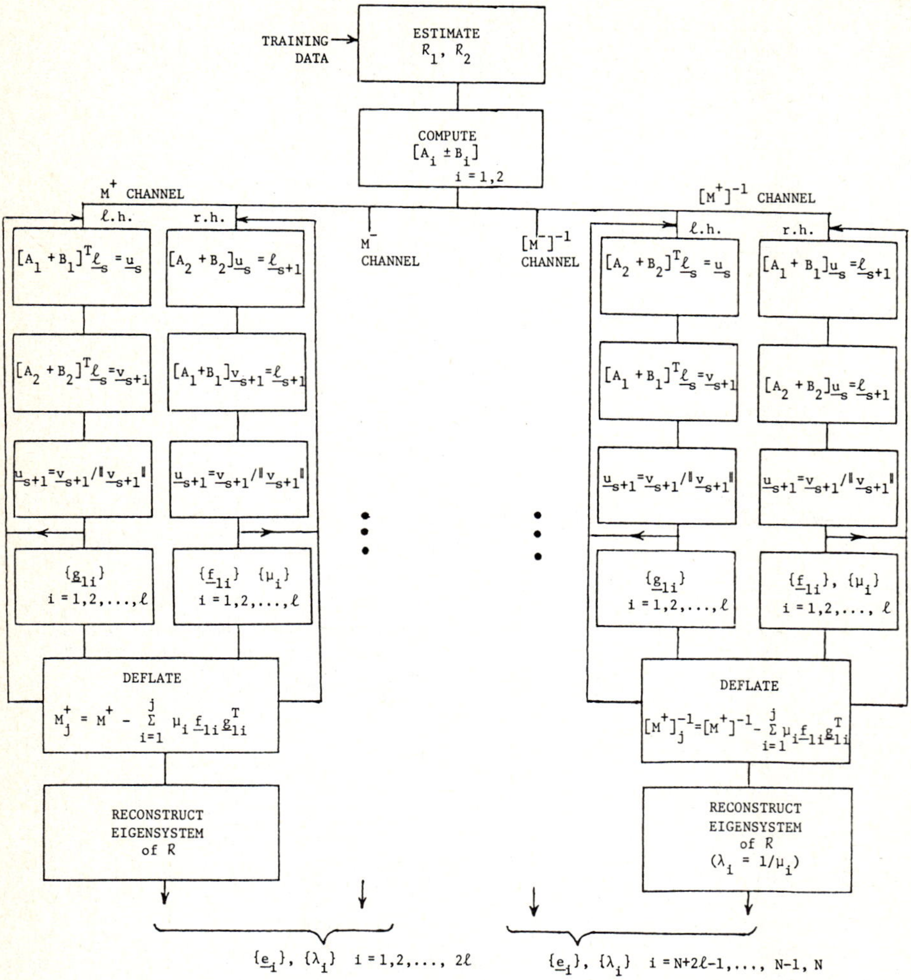

FIGURE 2. PARALLEL ARCHITECTURE OF EIGENSYSTEM DECOMPOSITION

DISCUSSION

Toussaint:

You said that the accuracy of the numerical computations was ten to the power minus five. How can you then estimate error rates of ten to the power minus seven?

Morgera:

The error rates were estimated with the exact implementation of the method. The accuracy of ten to the power minus five holds for the VLSI implementation and I agree that such an accuracy is not sufficient. When we want to estimate error rates of the order of like ten to the power minus seven or minus eight we need more accurate procedures.

However, it turned out that the eigenvalues are extremely accurate but the eigenvectors are not as accurate because we used the norm as a criterion.

We would like to introduce a little more accuracy in the eigenvector estimates by using something that looks at each individual element.

Persoon:

I'm curious about the applications. You are saying that you are working with speech signals and a 2-class problem. But what type of 2-class problems you are dealing with?

Morgera:

We are, more generally, working with signal detection problems. In these two hypothesis signal detection problems the means are equal and the covariances are different. You can think of this as the stochastic signal in noise detection problem.

Persoon:

But then I don't understand why you have to estimate the eigenvalues so accurately and so fast. You know the covariance matrices beforehand.

Morgera:

Our signals may not be weakly stationary. We are really thinking in terms of problems that are quasi-stationary in which you may know something on the average of the covariance matrices. The covariances, however, are time dependent in these cases and updating is required. Of course, you are right up to a point. The decomposition doesn't need to be as accurate as ten to the power minus seven in these cases. It will depend on the application.

The formula we have developed for predicting the Bayesian error is very accurate, even down to ten to the power minus seven and ten to the power minus eight. If one wants to use this method for predicting error rates and using the result as a guide for deciding how many eigenvalues, and hence eigenvectors, are to be used in the data reduction or feature selection, you need an accuracy for the computational method which is of the same order as the estimated error rate.

Stark:

Your method for feature selection is actually the Fukunaga-Koontz procedure, in which you use some of the largest and some of the smallest eigenvalues. The space you are spanning with these eigenvectors is the best one for separating two classes. I am just wondering why you used that method. It has been shown by Foley and Sammon that it can give you some weird results.

Morgera:

Our method is not exactly the Fukunaga-Koontz procedure. The only thing that is similar is that some of the large eigenvalues and some of the small eigenvalues are used. Fukunaga and Koontz never told us which to select in order to minimize the Bayesian error. One of the objectives of our work was to show which should be taken, but our results are certainly not the last word on this issue. Another aspect of our work was to compare several of the popular methods for feature selection with the results of our procedure.

PATTERN RECOGNITION IN PRACTICE II
E.S. Gelsema and L.N. Kanal (Editors)

ROTATION-INVARIANT PATTERN RECOGNITION USING OPTIMUM FEATURE EXTRACTION

R. Wu and H. Stark

Department of Electrical, Computer and Systems Engineering
Rensselaer Polytechnic Institute
Troy, New York 12180

We consider the problem of detecting a target regardless of its orientation when it is known that the target must be from one of two classes. We assume significant random intraclass variability, a complication which requires techniques from statistical pattern recognition for amelioration. The Foley-Sammon transformation for selecting optimum features from random training samples is used to solve the problem.

I. INTRODUCTION

Among the numerous capabilities one would expect from a flexible machine vision system are the abilities to: 1) recognize objects regardless of orientation; and 2) recognize objects from a given class even if there are significant intraclass variations within that class. Casasent and Psaltis[1] use the magnitude of the polar Fourier transform to achieve rotation-invariant recognition based on correlation[2]. However, correlation techniques are generally fine-tuned to the Fourier amplitude and phase of the object to be recognized and therefore such techniques are often defeated when significant intraclass variations are present.

Hsu and Arsenault and co-workers[3,4] recently showed how the method of circular harmonic function (CHF) expansion could be effectively used for achieving rotation-invariant pattern recognition by either optical or digital means. By a careful choice of the proper harmonic, Arsenault and Hsu[5] achieved rotation-invariant discrimination between almost-similar objects using the pseudo-object technique of Paek and Lee[6]. A subsequent modification by Wu[7], in which a scalar test statistic was replaced by a vector one, enabled the CHF expansion method to be used in poor signal-to-noise or low-contrast environments. Because Wu's test statistic involved the correlation of the unknown image function with a set of primitives, i.e., the first two non-DC components of the CHF expansion, it allowed for rotation-invariant detection in the presence of minor intraclass variation. However, in many pattern recognition problems one can expect to deal with major intraclass variations, e.g., distinguishing military from civilian aircraft; or cultivated from uncultivated regions in aerial photography. Problems of this type fall within the realm of statistical pattern recognition in which a central operation that deals with such variations is that of _feature selection_[8]. Feature selection achieves two things: 1) it reduces the dimensionality of the space (decision space) in which a decision is made; and 2) it finds the best subspaces for separating the classes.

In this paper we use a subspace projection method for finding the optimum features for two-class separability. The resulting transformation is called the Foley-Sammon[9] (F-S) transform and has given good results in other problems[10,11]. We show that using rotation-invariant vectors combined with optimum feature selection enables the (rotation-invariant) recognition of an object g from class, say, C_1, when it is imbedded in another object g+f from class, say, C_2 even when there are significant variations in the members of C_1 and C_2. Furthermore this is done without restoring to pseudo-object correlations.

In Section II we describe the full classification algorithm and in Section III we furnish experimental results for artificial and natural imagery.

II. CLASSIFICATION ALGORITHM

The overall algorithm consists of several parts. First, is the generation of rotation-invariant data; next is the extraction of features; and finally is the actual classification routine. We describe each in turn.

a) Generation of Rotation-invariant Data

Consider an object $\mathcal{O}$ with image function $\tilde{f}(r,\theta)$ in polar coordinates or $f(x,y)$ in Cartesian coordinates. We shall use the (~) to denote functions in polar coordinates. A CHF expansion of $\tilde{f}(r,\theta)$ is given by

$$\tilde{f}(r,\theta) = \sum_{n=-\infty}^{\infty} \tilde{f}_n(r)e^{jn\theta} \tag{1}$$

where

$$\tilde{f}_n(r) = \frac{1}{2\pi}\int_0^{2\pi} \tilde{f}(r,\theta)e^{-jn\theta}d\theta \ . \tag{2}$$

Let $\tilde{f}_n(r)e^{jn\theta}$ be denoted by $\tilde{f}_n(r,\theta)$ in polar coordinates or by $f_n(x,y)$ in Cartesian coordinates. Then a rotation-invariant vector for $\mathcal{O}$ is

$$\underline{Z} \triangleq (Z_1,\ldots,Z_N)^T, \tag{3}$$

where

$$Z_n \triangleq \left| \int_{-\infty}^{\infty}\int_{-\infty}^{\infty} f_n^*(x,y)\, f(x,y)\, dxdy \right| , \qquad n=1,2,\ldots,N. \tag{4}$$

Next, assume that there exists two well-defined object classes ω_1 and ω_2. Let $\tilde{a}(r,\theta) = \sum_{-\infty}^{\infty} \tilde{a}_n(r,\theta)$ be a reference image for ω_1 and $\tilde{b}(r,\theta) = \sum_{-\infty}^{\infty} \tilde{b}_n(r,\theta)$ a reference image for ω_2. Recall $\tilde{a}_n(r,\theta) \triangleq \tilde{a}_n(r)e^{jn\theta}$ etc. for $\tilde{b}_n(r,\theta)$. If $\tilde{f}(r,\theta)$ denotes the function of an object $\mathcal{U}$ to be classified then we wish to generate two rotation-invariant signature vectors suitable for the eventual classification of $\mathcal{U}$[or, equivalently, its function $\tilde{f}(r,\theta)$]. Two such vectors are

$$\underline{Z}_1 \triangleq (Z_{11},\ldots,Z_{1N})^T \tag{5a}$$

$$\underline{Z}_2 \triangleq (Z_{21},\ldots,Z_{2N})^T, \tag{5b}$$

where

$$Z_{1n} = \left| \int_{-\infty}^{\infty} \int_{-\infty}^{\infty} a_n^*(x,y)\ f(x,y)dxdy \right| \tag{6a}$$

$$n=1,\ldots,N$$

$$Z_{2n} = \left| \int_{-\infty}^{\infty} \int_{-\infty}^{\infty} b_n^*(x,y)\ f(x,y)dxdy \right| \tag{6b}$$

and N denotes the number of harmonics required to recognize a pattern. It is determined from tests. The next step is to extract from $\underline{Z}_j$, j=1,2, the <u>features</u> that will enable us to classify $\mathcal{U}$ in some optimum way.

b) <u>Feature Selection</u>

For extraction features from $\underline{Z}_j$, j=1,2, we use the Foley-Sammon transform. The F-S transform finds optimum subspaces for separation of two classes, when separability is defined by the Fisher ratio $R(\underline{\phi})$ given by

$$R(\underline{\phi}) = \frac{[\underline{\phi}^T(\underline{\mu}_1-\underline{\mu}_2)]^2}{\underline{\phi}^T(\underline{K}_1+\underline{K}_2)\underline{\phi}}. \tag{7}$$

In Eq. (7) $\underline{\mu}_j$, $\underline{K}_j$ are the mean vector and covariance matrix of class j, and $\underline{\phi}$ is a unit vector. The Fisher ratio is the ratio of projected difference in means <u>between</u> classes divided by the sum of the <u>within-class</u> scatter along direction $\underline{\phi}$. When $R(\underline{\phi})$ is large, then $\underline{\phi}$ is a good direction for class separation; conversely if $R(\underline{\phi})$ is small, $\underline{\phi}$ should be ignored as a projection direction. Now consider the M-dimensional subspace $\mathcal{S}_M$ spanned by $\underline{\phi},\ldots,\underline{\phi}_M$ such that $R(\underline{\phi}_1) \geq R(\underline{\phi}_1) \geq \ldots \geq R(\underline{\phi}_M) \geq R(\underline{\phi}_j)$, j=M+1,... . The set of vectors $\underline{\phi}_i$, i=1,...,M make up an optimum M-dimensional linear subspace for class separation. When we project a signature vector $\underline{Z}$ onto $\mathcal{S}_M$ we generate a feature vector $\underline{Y}$ according to

$$\underline{Y} = \underline{A}\ \underline{Z} \tag{8}$$

where $\underline{A}$ is the Foley-Sammon transformation matrix. Note that $\underline{Z}$ is Nx1, $\underline{Y}$ is Mx1 and $\underline{A}$ is MxN.

The parameters $\underline{\mu}_i$ and $\underline{K}_j$ are estimated from <u>training sets</u>. Let $\mathcal{R}_j$ be a training set for class ω_j. Then $\mathcal{R}_j = (\underline{Z}_1^{(j)},\ldots,\underline{Z}_\ell^{(j)},\ldots,\underline{Z}_L^{(j)})$ where $\underline{Z}_\ell^{(j)}$ is the ℓth training sample from class ω_j. We obtain

$$\underline{\mu}_j = \frac{1}{L}\sum_{\ell=1}^{L} \underline{Z}_\ell^{(j)} \qquad j=1,2 \tag{9}$$

$$\underline{K}_j \triangleq \frac{1}{L}\sum_{\ell=1}^{L} [\underline{Z}_\ell^{(j)}-\underline{\mu}^{(j)}][\underline{Z}_\ell^{(j)}-\underline{\mu}^{(j)}]^T. \tag{10}$$

Let us now anticipate what might happen in an actual test. Every pixel (x,y) in the test image is tested to see whether it is the CHF expansion center for an object in ω_1 or ω_2. There are five possible outcomes: 1) (x,y) could be the expansion center for an object f(x,y) in ω_1; 2) (x,y) could be the expansion center for an object f(x,y) in ω_2; 3) (x,y) could be <u>near</u> the expansion center for f(x,y) in ω_1 -- in which case it is subject to autocorrelation noise resulting from signatures with terms like

$$\left| \int_{-\infty}^{\infty} \int_{-\infty}^{\infty} a_n^*(x,y)\, f(x-u,y-v)dxdy \right| \tag{11}$$

for every u,v near the origin <u>except</u> u=v=0; 4) (x,y) could be near the expansion center for f(x,y) in ω_2 -- in which case it is subject to auto-correlation noise resulting from signatures with terms like

$$\left| \int_{-\infty}^{\infty} \int_{-\infty}^{\infty} b_n^*(x,y)\, f(x-u,y-v)dxdy \right| \tag{12}$$

for every u,v near the origin except u=v=0; and finally none of the above could happen in which case (x,y) is regarded as containing background noise of undetermined origin.

The pattern recognition problem, then, as structured in this paper consists not of two but actually five classes: the two original classes ω_1,ω_2; ω_3 -- the background noise affiliated with ω_1; ω_4 -- the background noise affiliated with ω_2; and ω_5 -- unaffiliated noise. Since the F-S feature extractor works only for pairs, we must determine a different F-S transform for each test. We shall denote by $\underline{A}_{jk}$ the F-S transformation matrix for projecting onto the optimum subspace for separating class ω_j from ω_k.

c) <u>Classification</u>

The structure of the classification algorithm is shown in Figure 1. For simplicity assume that the test pixel is located at the origin. Centered about the test pixel is the unknown object with image function f(x,y).

The first step is to generate the signatures $\underline{Z}_1$ and $\underline{Z}_2$ from Eqs. (5) and (6). Next we generate the feature vectors $\underline{Y}_1 = \underline{A}_{12}\underline{Z}_1$ and $\underline{Y}_2 = \underline{A}_{12}\underline{Z}_2$. From the training samples it is easy to determine in M-dimensional feature space where the members of class, say, ω_i cluster. The collection of ω_1-class-related noise vectors that comprise ω_3 will cluster much closer to ω_1 than to ω_2. Similarly the collection of ω_2-class-related noise vectors that comprise ω_4 will cluster much closer to ω_2 than ω_1. Hence in initially testing ω_1 versus ω_2 one is really testing (ω_1,ω_3) versus (ω_2,ω_4). After this first test one can proceed to test ω_1 versus ω_3 or ω_2 versus ω_4.

Refer now to Figure 1. If $\underline{Y}_1$ falls in the M-dimensional region $^{12}C_{13}$ where -- from training -- it has been determined that the (ω_1,ω_3) cluster exists we proceed to test ω_1 versus ω_3. This requires another F-S transform since the optimum subspace for ω_1 versus ω_3 is different from that of (ω_1,ω_3) versus

(ω_2,ω_4). Let C_1 denote the M-dimensional parallelopiped that frames the ω_1 training cluster in the ω_1 versus ω_3 feature space. If $\underline{Y}_1 \in C_1$ then f(x,y) centered at (0,0) gets assigned to ω_1. Otherwise the object gets assigned to ω_3. Note that this is really an assignment for the pixel at (0,0) since the entire test is repeated for the adjacent pixel, etc. until all pixels in the image are exhausted.

Continuing in this fashion, if $\underline{Y}_1 \notin C_{13}$ then we test whether $\underline{Y}_2 \in C_{24}$ (C_{24} represents the M-dimensional rectangular parallelopiped framing the (ω_2,ω_4) cluster in optimal M-dimensional (ω_1,ω_2) space). If $\underline{Y}_2 \in C_{24}$ then we proceed to test whether the image f(x,y) is ω_2-related noise or a bonafide member of ω_2. If $\underline{Y}_2 \notin C_{24}$ then f(x,y) is assigned to ω_5, i.e., unaffiliated noise.

The sequential logic in use in this classification scheme enables us to use an optimum two-class feature selection algorithm to discriminate between five classes.

III. EXPERIMENTAL RESULTS

Two experiments were performed: 1) The recognition of computer generated, arbitrarily rotated, letters P and B with strong font variations; and 2) the recognition of fish from the genera *Raja* and *Anchoa*. In both cases the recognition scheme was that of Figure 1.

a) Recognition of P's from B's

Figure 2 shows the extent of the font variations within a given class (in this case the B's). Figure 3a shows the test scene; Figure 3b shows the reference characters (the $\tilde{a}(r,\theta)$ and $\tilde{b}(r,\theta)$ of Section II). Figure 3c shows the location of the B's while Figure 3d shows the location of the P's. In this example, 100 percent correct recognition was achieved despite the added complication that the P is a "subset" of the B which would tend to defeat ordinary, i.e., unnormalized correlation type detection. Still there was no need to involve pseudo-object signatures as done by Paek and Lee[6].

b) Recognition of *Raja* from *Anchoa* Fish

Figure 4 shows typical examples and the resulting intra-class variations from the genus *Raja*. Figure 5 shows examples from the genus *Anchoa*. A test scene containing both classes of fish is shown in Figure 6a. Figure 6b shows the reference fish. The detected members of genus *Raja* are shown in Figure 6c; those of genus *Anchoa* are shown in Figure 6d.

The hard copy output furnished in this paper has a much lower resolution than the digitized images processed by computer. Each object was framed by a 64x64 window and the entire test scene was 192x192 pixels. The correlations done in Eqs. (6) and (11) and (12) were realized using fast Fourier transforms.

IV. CONCLUSION

By combining vector rotation-invariant signatures with sequential projection onto optimum subspaces for enhancing class-separability we have been able to achieve rotation-invariant recognition with a high-degree of accuracy. The use of vector signatures enables correct recognition in relatively poor signal-to-noise environments where other methods might fail.[7] Optimum feature extraction enables object-class recognition when strong statistical variations exist within the object classes. We have demonstrated this property even when one object is embedded in another (as P is embedded in B).

Some of these gains are brought about at the expense of greater computational complexity. The number of harmonics N needed to recognize an object depends on the complexity of the object and is determined from tests. Thus, to a first approximation, our algorithm requires N times as many computations as Hsu's. On the other hand, we do not need to search for a proper expansion center. The derivation of the optimum subspaces for feature selection is computationally intensive but is done only once, i.e., before the actual recognition problem begins. The projection of the signatures $\{\underline{Z}_j\}$ onto the optimum subspaces requires only a matrix multiplication. In the worst case, only three sequential tests need to be done for separating two classes. In situations where processing time must be kept low, a high-speed array processor of a microprocessor dedicated to the recognition problem can be used.

ACKNOWLEDGEMENTS

This work was supported by Rome Air Development Center under Contract F30602-82-K-0151.

REFERENCES

1. D. Casasent and D. Psaltis, Appl. Opt. 15, 1795 (1976).

2. In Ref. 1, the problem of scale invariance was also considered. We shall consider this issue in a subsequent paper.

3. Y-N. Hsu, H. H. Arsenault, and G. April, Appl. Opt. 21, 4012 (1982).

4. Y-N. Hsu and H. H. Arsenault, Appl. Opt. 21, 4016 (1982).

5. H. Arsenault and Y-N. Hsu, Appl. Opt. 22, 130 (1983).

6. E. G. Paek and S. S. Lee, Can. J. Phys. 57, 1335 (1979).

7. R. Wu and H. Stark, Appl. Opt. 23, 838 (1984).

8. K. Fukunaga, Introduction to Statistical Pattern Recognition (Academic, New York, 1972), p. 261.

9. D. H. Foley and J. W. Sammon, Jr., IEEE Trans. Comp. C-24, 281 (1975).

10. H. Stark and D. Lee, IEEE Trans. Syst. Man Cybern., SMC-6, 788 (1976).

11. R. K. O'Toole and H. Stark, Appl. Opt. 19, 2496 (1980).

12. The regions {C} are M-dimensional parallelopipeds whose dimensions along different coordinates are determined from the training samples. Typically each side of this hyper-box is centered at the projected center on that coordinate and has dimension 2σ where σ is the standard deviation of the projected sample along the same coordinate.

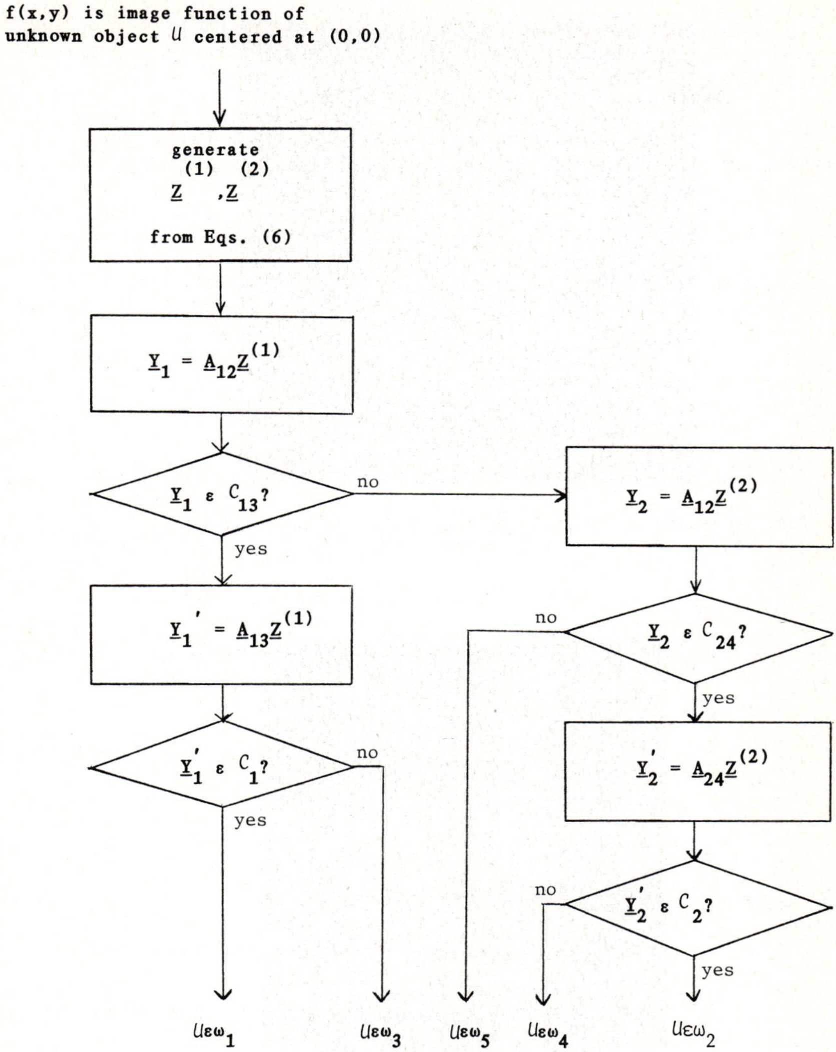

Fig. 1 Flow diagram showing sequential logic of classification algorithm.

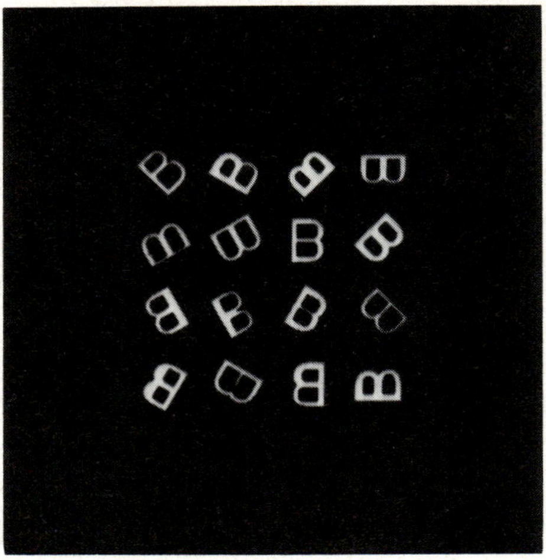

Fig. 2 Intraclass variations realized by randomly varying the font of letter B.

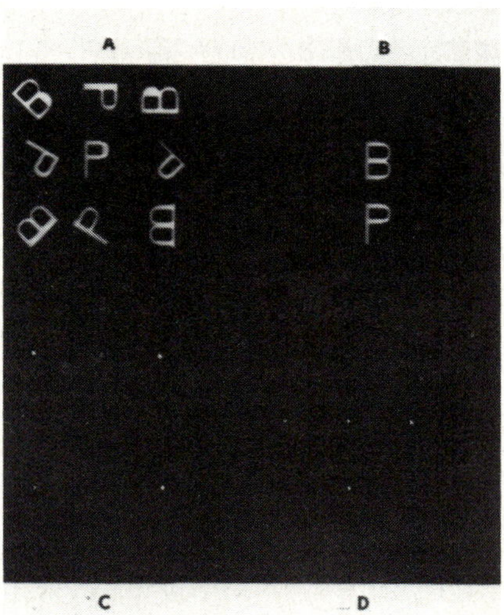

Fig. 3 Results of the first experiment: (A) the test scene; (B) the reference letters; (C) highlighted pixels showing detected location of centers of B's; (D) highlighted pixels showing location of centers of P's.

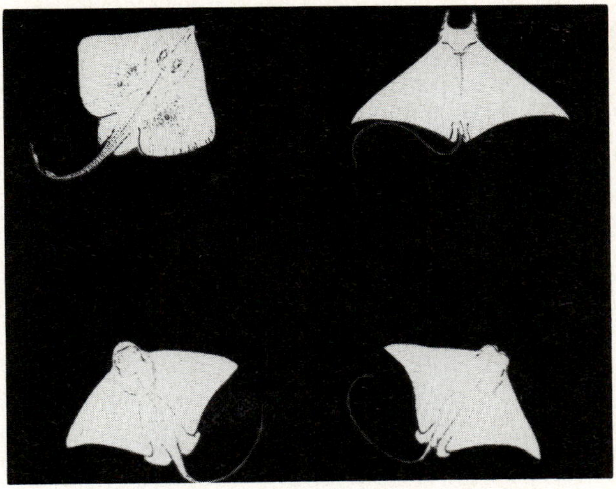

Fig. 4 Intraclass variability of genus *Raja*.

Fig. 5 Intraclass variability of genra *Anchoa*.

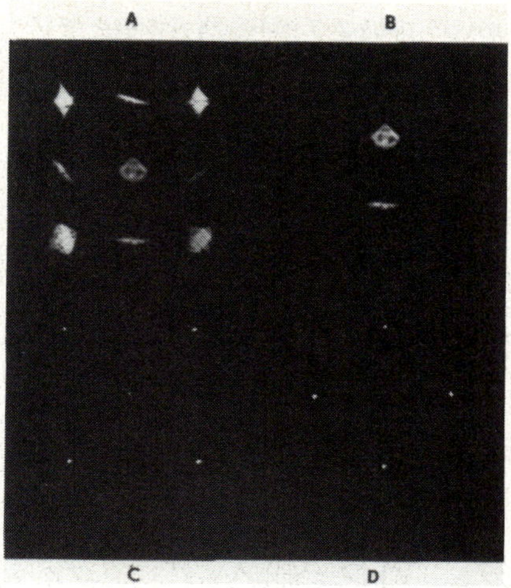

Fig. 6 Results of second experiment: (A) the test scene; (B) the reference fish; (C) highlighted pixels showing detected locations of members of *Raja*; (D) highlighted pixels showing detected locations of members of *Anchoa*.

PATTERN RECOGNITION IN PRACTICE II
E.S. Gelsema and L.N. Kanal (Editors)
Elsevier Science Publishers B.V. (North-Holland), 1986

AN EXTENSION OF HIERARCHICAL CLUSTERING : THE PYRAMIDAL PRESENTATION

E. DIDAY, P. BERTRAND

INRIA

Domaine de Voluceau - Rocquencourt
B.P. 105 - 78153 LE CHESNAY CEDEX (FRANCE)

INTRODUCTION

Confronted with a multidimensional reality, man has since the beginning of time sought visual representations to better understand this reality. Hierarchical representation is a visual mode of picturing which has been used through the ages from Aristotle and his tree of life to the recent work of Sokal and Sneath (1973), of Benzecri and his collaborators (1973), and includes that of Adanson (1957) on algorithm (of hierarchical construction) to group plants. Throughout history, hierarchy has been a useful tool for representing multidimensional data.

Due to the quantity and variety of practical applications created by the rapid development of computer science, many authors have devoted themselves in recent years to the research of overlapping clusters and four approaches have mainly been studied : 1) the use of graph theory by Hubert (1974) and B. Monjardet (1981) 2) a probability approach : the splitting up of a set of laws (Hartigan (1975 and 1977) and by Diday et al. (1979)). 3) the optimization of criteria by multidimensional scaling, by Shepard and Arabie (1978) and Arabie and Caroll (1980), the dynamic nucleus approach (Diday (1982) that uses overlapping nuclei or weak forms). 4) a hierarchical approach by Jardine and Sibson (1971) and improvements such as those of Rohlf (1975) (in fact, these are techniques leading to an improvement of the hierarchies obtained by means of the single link index which are subject to the chain effect).

Hierarchy is made up of a series of nesting partitions. We will show in this study that all hierarchies may be placed in a much greater scheme leading to representations (called pyramids), which give more information, are closer to the initial data and result in overlapping classes instead of partitions.

We know that there is a bijection between index hierarchies and ultrametrics (see 6). This result is interesting in that the search for a hierarchy with a good fit with the initial data can be replaced by the search for an ultrametric distance. This classical result was laid out in the following fashion : we showed that there is an order wich gives "Robinson", an ultrametric distance matrix. This matrix must take into account ultrametric inequality. By doing away with the constraints of this inequality we arrive at a specific set of dissimilarity indices called "pyramidal indices" which include all the ultrametrics (see 7). With these indices we can associate a new form of visual representation which includes the hierarchical representation and supplies enriched data to the user. The basic goal of this work is to study this new form of representation which is "pyramidal" (see figure 1).

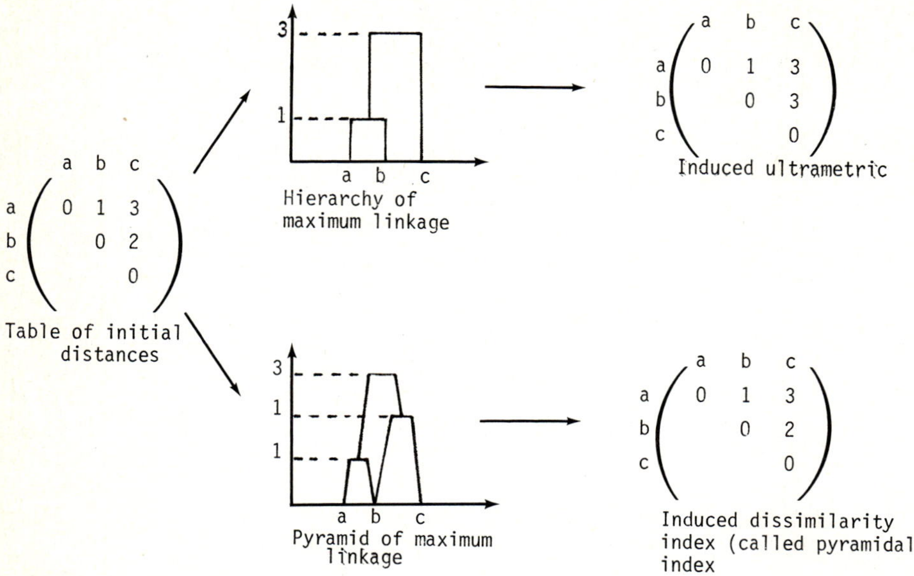

This example shows that :

1) - the hierarchy is included in the pyramid (each hierarchy plateau is a pyramid plateau),
2) - by its induced dissimilarity index the pyramidal representation pictures the initial distances more faithfully than the hierarchical representation.

Figure 1

In the first part, we present the essential theoretical characteristics of pyramids : definition by set properties, graphic representation, indices associated with a pyramid.

We will then give a construction algorithm, followed by the flowchart of the "PYRAMID" program written in Fortran 77. This program can be used with an arbitrary aggregation index.

Finally, we shall illustrate this theory with two examples. The results are shown graphically, by means of programs using the graphic standard GKS (Graphical Kernel System).

I. - DEFINITIONS AND THEORICAL PROPERTIES

Subsequently, let Ω be a finite set of objects.

Although there is a bijection between indexed pyramids and Robinson matrices (see [4]), we prefer, as with the hierarchies, to define pyramids by their own set properties.

Therefore we give several definitions (see [7]) :

Let us say that a part p of Ω is connex according to an order θ, if p is an interval of the order θ, i.e. :

$\{w$ is between the smallest and the largest element of $p\} \leftrightarrow \{w \in p\}$.

An order θ is compatible with a set P of parts of Ω if any element $\in P$ is connex according to θ.

a) Definition of a pyramid

Let Ω be a finite set, P a set of non-empty parts (called clusters) of Ω, P will be a pyramid if :

1) $\Omega \in P$ (the largest cluster contains all the objects)

2) $\forall w \in \Omega, \{w\} \in P$ (the terminal points)

3) $\forall (h,h') \in P^2$ we have $h \cap h' = \emptyset$ or $h \cap h' \in P$

4) An order θ exists compatible with P.

Example

Let $\Omega = \{w_1,w_2,w_3\}$ and $P_1 = \{\{w_1\},\{w_2\},\{w_3\},\{w_1,w_2\},\{w_2,w_3\},\Omega\}$
$P_2 = P_1 \cup \{w_1,w_3\}$.

We can easily check that P_1 is a pyramid while P_2 is not, since it does not satisfy the fourth condition.

Proposition 1

The set of hierarchies is included in the set of pyramids.

Proof : see [4]. □

b) Visualization of a pyramid

Concepts of successors, predecessors and levels

Given a pyramid P, we can say that $h \in P$ is a successor of $h' \subset P$ if

$h \subset h'$ (strictly)

and There is no h" different from h and h', such that :
$h \subset h" \subset h'$ (strictly) .

We also say that h' is a predecessor of h.

We know that Ω belongs to P; the set of the successors of Ω "overlaps" Ω, since P contains the one object sets. This overlapping is called the level of the pyramid. The successors of the overlapping elements constitute a new level which is also an overlapping of Ω. We can go from one level to the next, and stop when the level contains only the one object sets since the size of elements of P decreases, as we move down each level.

Graphic representation

The graphic representation of the pyramids that we have chosen, is possible because of the following properties :

1) one order θ exists compatible with P

2) each element of P has no more than two predecessors.

The first property is exactly the fourth condition (C4). Let us prove the second point.

Proposition 2

Each element of P has no more than two predecessors.

Proof

If h is an element of P and has more than one predecessor, then it is equal to their interaction. If not, it would be included in this intersection and could not be a successor (the intersection is a successor, because it belongs to P, and it does not belong to the preceding level. In effect, the intersection is strictly included in the predecessors that create it).

Supposing that h_1, h_2, h_3 are distinct predecessors of h, then we would have :

$$h = h_1 \cap h_2 = h_1 \cap h_2 \cap h_3 = (h_1 \cap h_2) \cap h_3$$

then

$$h_3 \subset (h_1 \cap h_2), \text{ and } h_3 \subset h_2 ,$$

which is a contradiction because h_3 and h_2 belong to the same level. □

We have chosen the following graphic representation : each cluster is represented by a horizontal segment. It is linked to its predecessors by an oblique line. Each oblique line links the middle of the segment associated with a cluster to the extremity of the segment associated with its predecessor or predecessors.

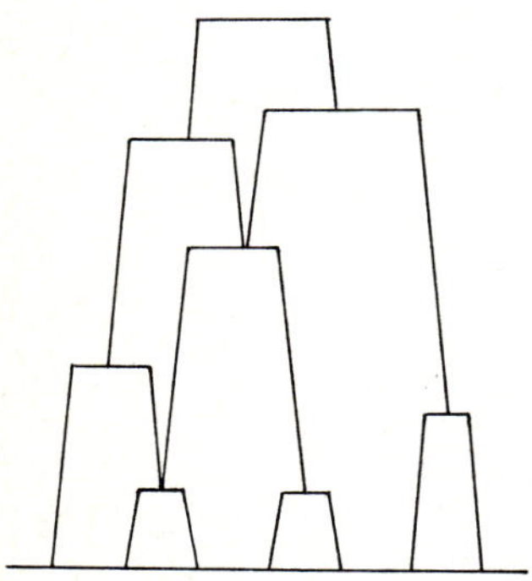

Pyramid

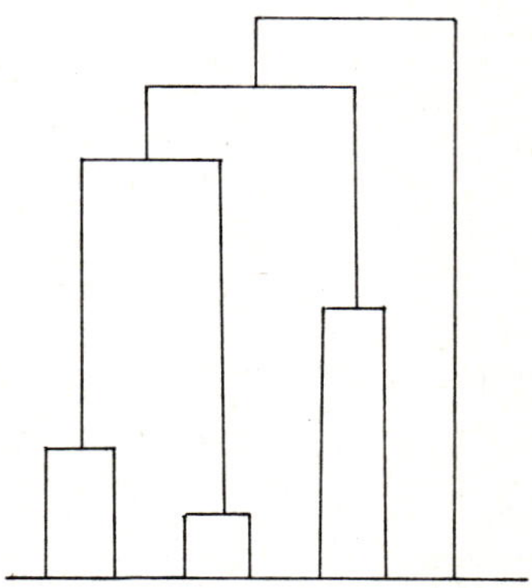

Hierarchy

c) Pyramid indexing

Definition of an indexed pyramid

An indexed pyramid is a pair (P,f) where P is a pyramid and f an application of P in $\mathbb{R}^+$ so that :

1) $f(h) = 0$ if and only if h contains only one element

2) for any h and h' in P, $h \subset h'$ (strict inclusion) implies $f(h) \leq f(h')$.

Definition of an indexed pyramid in the broad sense and strict sense

An indexed pyramid is indexed in the broad sense if $h \subset h'$ strictly and $f(h) = f(h')$ implies the existence of h_1 and h_2 in P different from h such that

$$h = h_1 \cap h_2 .$$

An indexed pyramid is indexed in the strict sense if :

$$h \subset h' \text{ (strictly) implies } f(h) < f(h') .$$

The quantity $f(h)$ is called the height of cluster h.

Definition of a pyramidal index

This is a dissimilarity index which further verifies the two following conditions :

1) $s(w,w') = 0 \leftrightarrow w = w'$

2) an order θ on Ω exists such that any triplet w,w',w'' with w' between w and w'' according to θ satisfies the following inequality :

$$s(w,w') \geq \mathrm{Max}\{s(w,w'),s(w',w'')\} \quad \text{(pyramidal inequality)} .$$

Definition of a Robinson matrix

A matrix is Robinson if and only if the terms of the rows and columns never decrease when moving away from the main diagonal in either direction.

Properties

Proposition 3

The ultrametric set is included in the set of pyramidal indices.

Proof

Since an ultrametric is a distance, the first condition is satisfied. We also know that as an ultrametric δ is given we can associate to it the order θ so that $M(\delta,\theta)$ is an ultrametric matrix (and therefore a Robinson matrix); the second condition is thus satisfied. (See [7]).

Proposition 4

If s is a pyramidal index, then the following conditions are equivalent :

1) θ is compatible with s

2) $M(s,\theta)$ is a Robinson matrix

3) All paired elements (w,w') included (in the broad sense) according to θ between two elements w_i and w_j is such that $s(w_i,w_j) \geq s(w,w')$.

Proof

1) → 2).
We know (see [7]) that if θ is compatible with a dissimilarity index then the matrix $M(s,\theta)$ is a Robinson matrix.

2) → 3).
We know (see [7]) that if $M(s,\theta)$ is a Robinson matrix then $M(s,\theta)$ is an SDR matrix which implies that s and θ are semi-compatible whereby the condition 3) is met.

3) → 1).
We only need to take $w_i = w$ or $w' = w_j$ to find condition 1).

Proposition 5

There exists a bijection between the set of pyramids indexed in the broad sense and the set of pyramidal indices.

Proof : see [1].

II. - CONSTRUCTION (algorithm and program)

a) Algorithm

We suppose that the given data are in the form of a dissimilarity index matrix. We call Ω the whole set of objects. By analogy with the ascending hierarchical clustering and after having chosen an aggregation index (this is a dissimilarity index between clusters, see [4] for a list of possible choices) we can construct an ascending clustering algorithm in the following manner :

Step 1 (initialization) : the set of clusters is composed of the one object clusters (or end points)

Step 2 (cluster formation) : we aggregate the two nearest clusters among the clusters which have not been aggregated twice and which verify the following two conditions :
(i) the cluster created (i.e. the union of the two aggregated clusters) must be connex according to the order created in step 3;
(ii) let i and j be extreme elements of cluster h; if a cluster is connected to another cluster included in h, then it must contain either i or j.

Step 3 (order choice) : we associate an order with the two groups that make it up.

Step 4 (test for stopping) : if the last cluster formed is equal to Ω, then we stop. If not, we return to step 1.

Note : step 3 induces an order θ on the element of Ω. Conditions (i) and (ii) are necessary if we do not want to obtain the forms indicated in figures 2 and 3 :

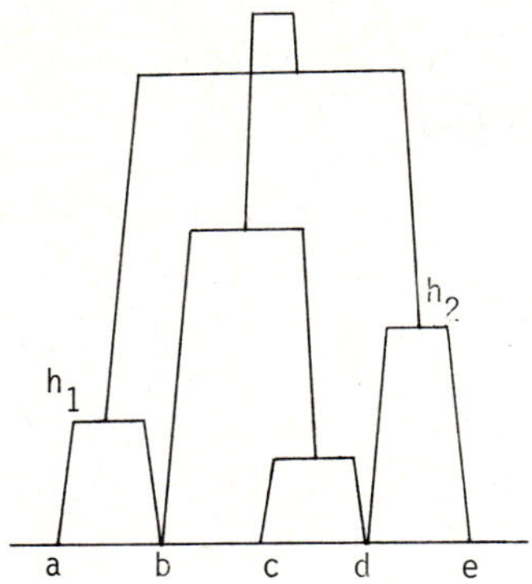

Figure 2

(ii) $\not\to$ (i)
Condition (i) is not met because h_1 and h_2 are not connected

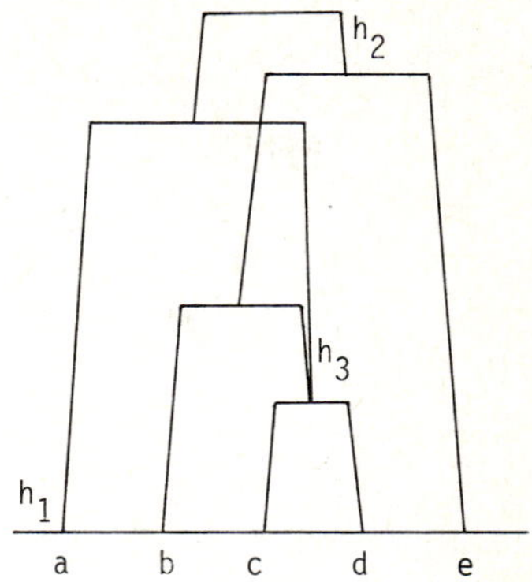

Figure 3

(i) $\not\to$ (ii)
(ii) is not satisfied (take $h = h_2$)

Proposition 6

The preceding algorithm, called PAC (pyramidal ascending construction), constructs a pyramid.

Proof : see [1].

b) Program

As we have just seen, the pyramidal construction algorithm has two goals :

1) to construct clusters according to the proximity criterium
2) to construct an order compatible with the set of created clusters (at the beginning, the order is partial).

We shall now present the principles of the program "PYRAMID". It is written in Fortran 77, and carries out the algorithm described in a). The program is principally based on the notion of "connex group". A connex group C is a set of clusters that satisfies the following property : if h and h' are clusters of C, then there exists a series $(h_1,\ldots,h_q)$ in C such that :

$$h_1 = h \quad , \quad h_q = h' \quad , \quad h_i \cap h_{i+1} = \emptyset \quad \text{for} \quad i=1,\ldots,q-1 \; .$$

Moreover, this set C must be a maximum. That is to say, no set included in C that has the same property as C, can exist. It is clear that at the beginning of the algorithm, there are as many connex groups as there are objects, and at the end, only one connex group exists. Inside the loop the number of connex groups decreases. The user may stop the program when the number of connex groups equals the value k that he has chosen : he then obtains a partitioning into k groups. Each (connex) group has a pyramidal structure.

The structure of a pyramid to be can be represented as follows :

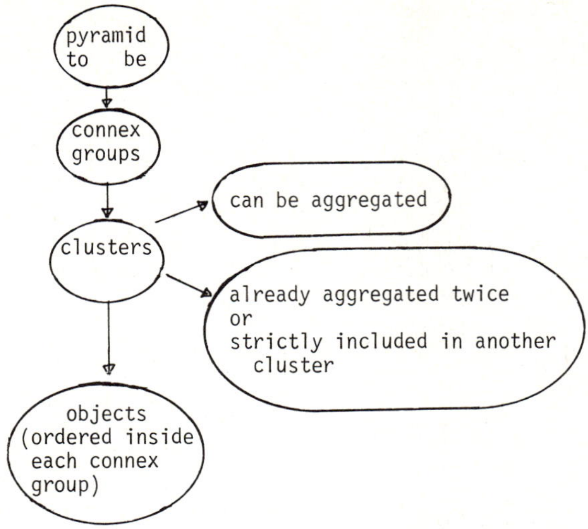

In this program, we describe this structure by referring, as often as possible, to the basic unit : objects. Thus, we reduce the number of arrays used. The notations used at each step are :

n : connected group
k : cluster
i : object

bmin(k) : the smallest element of cluster k
bmax(k) : the greatest element of cluster k
size(n) : number of elements in the connex group n
clus(i) : connex group that contains the cluster {i}.
rank(i) : position of the object i in its connex group
dist(indi(k_1,k_2)) : dissimilarity between the clusters k_1 and k_2
(indi determines the position of (k_1,k_2) in the vector dist)
nctot : total number of created clusters
nlife : number of clusters that we can aggregate
nta(k) : number of times that the cluster k has been aggregated.

The algorithm just described takes the following form in the program :

(A) Initialization

For each : n,k,i, we have :
size(n) = 1
bmin(k) = k , bmax(k) = k and nta(k) = 0
clus(i) = i and rank(i) = 1 .
The vector dist describes the dissimilarities between the objects.

(B) Choice of the clusters that are aggregated

They are the closest among the clusters, such that :
(i) if the clusters belong to the same group, they must not be separated by an object (rank(bmax(k1)) ≥ rank(bmin(k2))-1 or the opposite.
(ii) If they do not belong to the same group, they must be extreme (i.e. size (clus(bmin(k))) = rank(bmax(k)) or 1 = rank(bmin(k)))

(iii) We must check that the union of these two clusters has not already been created.

(C) Relative position of the clusters that have just been aggregated

If the clusters do not belong to the same group, we have to choose an order for them (this order is equivalent to the relative position of two clusters in the two groups). Therefore, we can reverse the order of the objects in one group. We can also move one group, keeping the order of the clusters in this group.

(D) Array update

bmin, bmax, dist, rank, size, clus, nta are updated.

(E) Storage of the clusters that we cannot aggregate

If nta(k) = 2 or k is strictly included in the last cluster created, then we store cluster k.

(F) Stop test

If the last cluster created is equal to the set of the objects, we stop the procedure. If the number of connex groups has reached a value k0 chosen by the user, we can also stop the program. Otherwise we go back to (B).

The program PYRAMID is completed first by a graphic output program (written with the standard GKS) and second, by a program that eliminates useless clusters of the pyramid (if there are too many clusters, some are unnecessary for the visualization and the interpretation of the pyramid).

III. - EXAMPLES

1. Example : classification of a set of points on the plane

We consider 10 points on the plane (see figure 4) : the representation of these points has a linear shape : more precisely there is a curve which represents the shape of this set of points. With this example, we show how a pyramidal classification enables us to find again the order of the points when they are projected on this curve.

The given data is an array describing the distances between the points. The aggregation index used is the complete link. This index allows us to avoid having too many inversions, which using our present way of visualizing a pyramid, are an inconvenience in the graphic representation. If the points are not too far from the curve and if the curve does not look like a loop, then we are sure to avoid inversions (i.e. $f(h) > f(h')$ with $h' \supset h$).

In these cases, there may be inversions.

2. Application : production automation (flexible workshops)

The given data are a set of machines $\{M_j\}_{j=1,p}$ and a set of tasks $\{T_i\}_{i=1,n}$. Each machine can do one or several tasks, and, each task can be carried out by one or several machines. We have coded this relation with a binary array $B(T_i,M_j)$, where $B(T_i,M_j)$ has a value of 1, if the machine M_j completes the task T_i, and a value of 0 if not.

In figure 5, we represent this initial binary array, indicating each machine-task association by filling in the corresponding square in the array.

Our goal is to group the machines which complete the same tasks and, to group the tasks which are accomplished by the same machines.

Thus we have to construct two classifications : one on the rows (tasks) and the other on the columns (machines). For the row and column classifications, we have a dissimilarity index between binary vectors (Rogers and Tanimoto's index (see [4])).

We could also have used the correlation index between binary vectors. After arranging the rows and columns according to the obtained orders, we are able to distinguish 4 blocks, for which, with some rare exceptions, each machine completes the same tasks, and each task is accomplished by the same machine (see figure 5).

For arrays of larger size (200×100), we must adopt new strategies in order to reduce the memory space and computing time. We can, for example, choose to refine the pyramid while creating it, or consider only the largest clusters of each connex group.

REFERENCES

[1] ADANSON M. (1757), "Histoire naturelle du Sénégal", Bauche, Paris.

[2] ARABIE P. and CAROLL J.D. (1980), "MAPCLUS : a mathematical programming approach to fitting the ADCLUS model".

[3] BENZECRI J.P. et coll. (1973), "L'analyse des Données. Tome I, La Taxonomie", Dunod.

[4] DIDAY E. (1984), "Une représentation visuelle des classes empiétantes : les pyramides", Rapport de recherche n° 291, INRIA Rocquencourt 78150 (France).

[5] DIDAY E. et coll. (1979, "Optimisation en classification automatique", INRIA, Roquencourt 78150 (France).

[6] DIDAY E., LEMAIRE J., POUGET J., TESTU F. (1982), "Eléménts d'analyse des Données", Dunod.

[7] DIDAY E. (1982), "Crossing order and ultrametrics", Compstat-Proceedings in Computer Statistics-Physica-Verlag, Vienna.

[8] HARTIGAN J.A. (1975), "Clustering Algorithm", Wiley.

[9] HARTIGAN J.A. (1977), "Clustering as modes", First International Symposium on data analysis and Informatics.

[10] HUBERT L. (1974),"Some applications on graph theory and related non-metrics techniques to problems of approximate seriation", The British Journal of Mathematical and Statistical Psychology.

[11] HUBERT L. (1974), "Some applications of graph theory to clustering", Psychometrica 1974, <u>39</u>, pp. 283-309.

[12] MONJARDET B. (1980), "Théorie des graphes et Taxonomie mathématique", in "Regards sur la théorie des graphes", Presses Polytechniques Romandes, Lausanne, pp. 111-125.

[13] ROLPH F. (1975), "A new approach to the computation of the Jardine-Sibson B_K clusters", Computer Journal, <u>18</u>, pp. 164-168.

[14] SHEPARD R., ARABIE P. (1979, "Additive clustering : representation of similaries as combinations of discrete overlapping properties", Psychological Review, <u>86</u>, n° 2, pp. 87-123.

[15] SNEATH P., SOKAL R. (1973), "Numerical Taxonomy", Freeman.

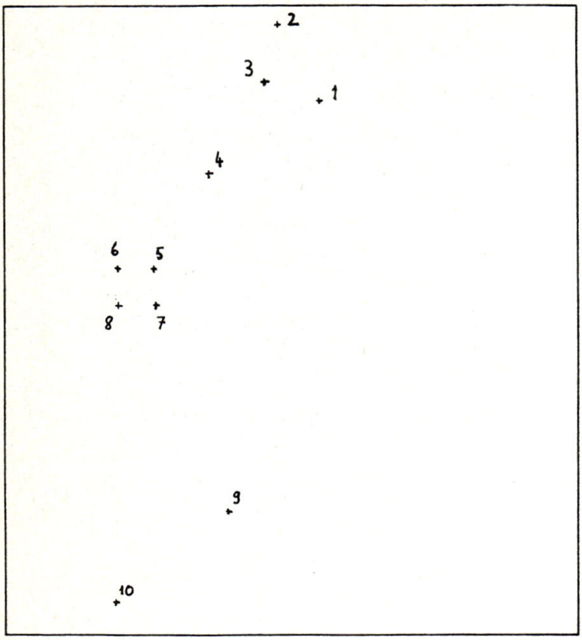

Figure 4

Pyramid obtained with the complete link index on the 10 points using the euclidian distance

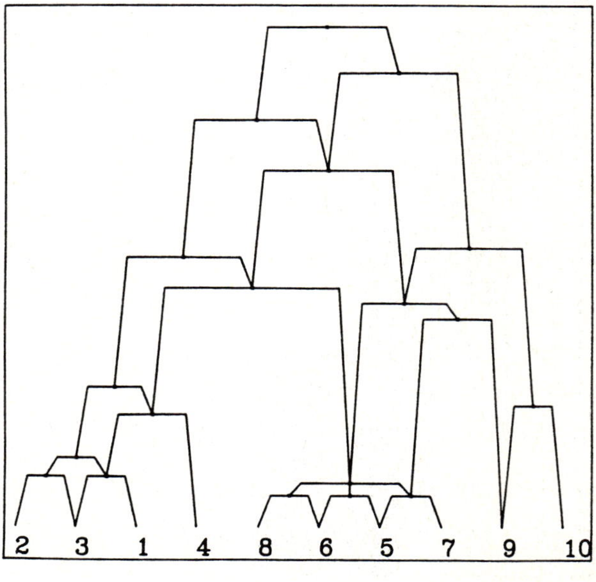

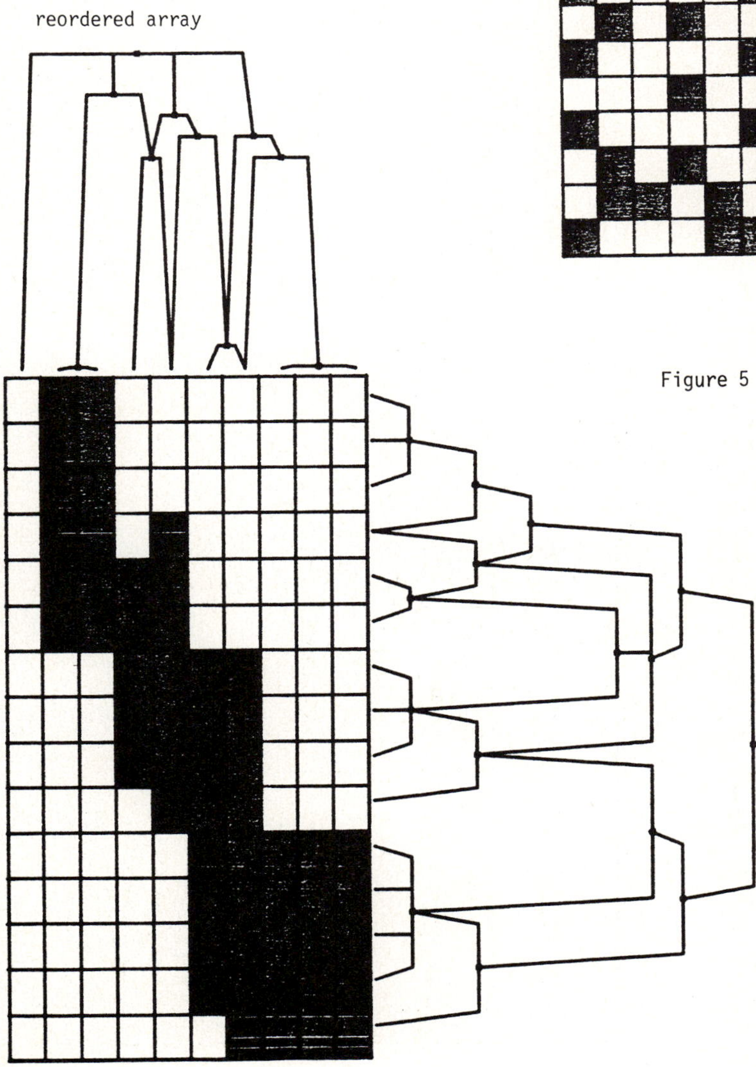

Figure 5

DISCUSSION

Backer:

It is common practice in cluster analysis to compare the different updating schemes of the dissimilarity matrices by calculating the cophenetic correlation coefficient in order to see whether you are representing your original information rather than artefacts resulting from the algorithm.

For example, if you apply single, complete or average linkage to your data it depends on your data whether the cophenetic correlation coefficient will be the highest for average linkage or for complete linkage and consequently which model best fits to the properties of the data.

PATTERN RECOGNITION IN PRACTICE II
E.S. Gelsema and L.N. Kanal (Editors)

CLUSTERING LARGE DATA SETS

Leonard Kaufman

Department of Pharmaceutical and Biomedical Analysis
University of Brussels
Laarbeeklaan 103
1190 Brussels, Belgium

Peter J. Rousseeuw

Department of Mathematics
Delft University of Technology
Julianalaan 132
2628 BL Delft, The Netherlands

In this paper a method is proposed for partitioning very large data sets. The number of calculations and memory requirements are of the order O(n), where n is the number of objects. The computer program CLARA is described, and some possible extensions are mentioned.

HISTORY

Few authors of clustering algorithms have paid much attention to the specific problems encountered when clustering large data sets. The reason for this might be that these problems mainly concern the implementation of the methods, which strongly depends upon the computer hardware and software being used.

A first obstacle to solving problems with large sets of objects concerns the necessity to store and frequently retrieve the $n(n-1)/2$ dissimilarities between the n objects of the data set. Some authors have suggested either using an external storage device for this purpose or calculating the dissimilarities each time they are needed. Both methods usually result in considerable increases in computation time. This leads us to the second obstacle to solving large problems, namely the considerable computation time necessary for the algorithms, particularly those of nonhierarchical clustering. In this context Steinhausen and Langer (1977) have made a suggestion for solving problems with large sets of objects, based on any algorithm of the improvement type (for example a variance minimization technique). It consists of the following general steps :

1. draw a sample from the set of objects and cluster the objects of this sample
2. assign the objects not belonging to the sample to the closest of the clusters found during the first step
3. use the inflated clusters as starting point of an iterative procedure

An important drawback of this suggestion is that most iterative procedures which can be used in step 3 are of order n^2, becoming very expensive for large n.

Particularly suited for large data sets are the single pass methods, such as the leader algorithm proposed by Hartigan (1975). In this method the objects are considered one by one and assigned to one of the previously generated clusters. If the "distances" of the object to all previous clusters exceed a given threshold value, a new cluster is initiated. Deichsel (1980) also gives a technique of determining a threshold value for which the expected number of clusters (in a statistical sense) is a given value k. Single pass sequential algorithms involve very few calculations and are therefore well adapted to large sets of objects.However they suffer from several shortcomings :

- the results are strongly dependent on the order of the objects in the input file
- one is not sure of finding exactly k clusters
- as observed by Hartigan (1975), the first clusters are usually much larger than the later ones, since they get first chance at each object as it is allocated
- an inherent clustering philosophy (like optimization of a goal function) appears to be lacking, making it difficult to interpret the results.

In his book Hartigan (1975) also proposes a more refined approach for solving large clustering problems, based upon the same method. The set of objects is first clustered into about 100 clusters using a single pass sequential algorithm (here a guess must be made of the threshold value which will lead to 100 clusters). The centroids of the obtained clusters are determined and themselves clustered using the k-means algorithm (in this algorithm the centroids are given weights equal to the numbers of objects in the corresponding clusters produced by the sequential algorithm). The clusters of centroids are then used to obtain a partition of the entire data set into k clusters. This method clearly suffers from the same problems as the original single pass algorithm.

Diday (1975) proposes a family of so-called sequential dynamic clusters algorithms which are closely related to his original dynamic clusters methods. Starting with an initial set of kernels (which can be centroids, medoids, or even a whole set of objects or points), each of the objects of the data set is assigned to the "closest" kernel, defining a first partition, which is used to yield a new set of kernels. This process is continued until a stable clustering is reached. The sequential version of this method is based upon the same principle but does not require the storing of all the data of the problem, while the computation times are not much longer. One starts with a first partition of the set of objects together with a set of kernels. One then considers one of the clusters of the current partition and assigns each of the objects to the nearest kernel. When all objects of the cluster have been assigned, a new set of kernels is determined. The next cluster is then considered, and each of the objects assigned to the nearest kernel. This process is continued until a complete pass through the clusters does not lead to a new assignment of any of the objects.

Also several hierarchical methods for clustering large data sets have been investigated. Most of these are adaptations of the single linkage algorithm and suffer from the same problems. Zupan (1980) proposed a method which proceeds by the construction of a binary tree using an update procedure. The most significant aspect of the procedure is that objects are inserted into the tree one at a time, and it can therefore be used effectively for classifying new objects once a first set of objects has been clustered. An analysis of the method shows that it suffers from several problems. The first is that the method only yields a binary tree and gives no information on the strength or cohesion of the clusters. Another is that the results obtained strongly depend upon the order of the objects in the input file. Moreover, our own experience indicates that the program is very slow.

THE CLARA ALGORITHM

In the k-medoid model (see Massart et al,1983), a data set of n objects is clustered by selecting k representative or centrally located objects and constructing the k clusters around these objects. These k representative objects are chosen so as to minimize

$$\frac{1}{n} \sum_{i=1}^{n} d(i, m_i) \tag{1}$$

where d is a measure of dissimilarity and m_i is the representative object closest to object i. The centrally located objects m_i are called median objects, medoids, or centrotypes. The main computational effort made in this algorithm is a search among a large number of subsets of k objects (there are C_n^k such subsets but the algorithm only examines some of these). With increasing values of n the number of subsets increases dramatically: for fixed k its order of magnitude is like the kth power of n. As a consequence it is clear that the k-medoid method is only feasible for relatively small (to medium) numbers of objects, because the computation time becomes enormous otherwise. Another factor with the same effect is the storage requirement. The method requires the calculation and frequent retrieval of n(n-1)/2 dissimilarities between objects.

The clustering of a set of objects with the CLARA algorithm (Clustering LARge Applications) is carried out in two steps. First a sample of n* objects is drawn from the data set and clustered into k subsets using the k-medoid model, which also gives k representative objects. Then each object not belonging to the sample is assigned to the nearest of the k. This yields a clustering of the entire set of objects. A measure of the quality of this clustering is obtained by computing the average distance between all the objects of the data set and their representative objects. After m samples have been drawn and clustered, the one is selected for which the lowest average distance is obtained.

The size of the samples depends on the number of clusters k. For values of k between one and five, samples of 80 objects are taken, while for values between six and ten the samples consist of 120 objects. These choices are motivated by the probability of finding objects from all the "existing" clusters in at least one of the generated samples. The possibility of finding a large number of small clusters is related to the sampling technique used in the program. When clustering a set of 1000 objects, the probability of drawing at least one object from a cluster of 10 objects (in at least one of three samples of 120 objects) is 0.98. For a cluster of five objects this probability is reduced to 0.85, and for a singleton it is only 0.32 . For larger data sets, these probabilities are smaller. Therefore, it was made easy to change the number of samples.

The objects selected by the random number generator are stored in an array and ordered by increasing index. Each time an object is drawn, it is checked against already drawn objects. If it has not yet been selected, it is inserted in the correct place in the array. If the sample size is only slightly smaller than the number of objects, it happens very often that the same object is drawn several times. For this reason, the random number generator is used to select the objects <u>not</u> belonging to the sample, whenever the number of objects is smaller than twice the sample size.

After a sample of n^* objects has been drawn, it is partitioned into k clusters using the same algorithm as in the k-medoid model. This algorithm consists of two parts called BUILD and SWAP. In the BUILD part successive representative objects are selected, with the purpose of obtaining the smallest possible average distance between the objects (of the sample) and their most similar representative object. In SWAP it is attempted to decrease the average distance obtained, by shifting representative objects.

Once k representative objects of the sample have been selected, each of the objects of the entire data set (and not only the sample) is assigned to the nearest representative object. The average distance obtained for the assignment is taken as a measure of the quality of the clustering. After this calculation has been done for each of the m samples, the sample is withheld for which the average distance is as small as possible.

Note that we use the average dissimilarity in expression (1), instead of the more customary sum of dissimilarities. This makes the objective nearly independent of the number of objects. At the same time this makes (1) statistically consistent: indeed, if more and more objects are drawn from a multivariate probability distribution, this quantity will converge to its theoretical value.

A further analysis is then carried out on the optimal clustering. The list of objects of each of the clusters is given, together with the medoid and size of each cluster. Then for each cluster the average distance and maximum distance to the medoid are given. Finally the maximum distance is divided by the minimum distance of the medoid to another medoid. This value gives information on the tightness of a cluster. A small value (for example 0.2) indicates a very tight cluster, while a value exceeding 1 suggests a weak cluster. A graphical representation of the clustering is then given by means of so-called silhouettes (see Rousseeuw, 1984.) This is only done for the selected sample, because the silhouettes of the entire data set would become too large and consume too much computation time.

The main idea of algorithm CLARA is that both the number of calculations and storage requirements are of the order of magnitude O(n) which means that they increase in a roughly linear way with the size of the problem. This is the principal distinction between CLARA and other available algorithms.

THE CLARA PROGRAM

Structure of the program

Program CLARA consists of about 1000 statement lines. It is written in a portable subset of FORTRAN allowing it to run on most FORTRAN IV and FORTRAN 77 compilers. For example, it has successfully run on mainframe IBM, CDC, and VAX computers, as well as on the IBM PC. Also, the program was tested using the PFORT verifier (see Ryder, 1974), and gave error free results. The structure of the program is quite simple : there is one input unit containing the data set (which may be on punch cards, disc, floppy, magnetic tape,..., or entered with the keyboard) and one output unit (which may be a printer, video screen, floppy,...)

The program consists of a main unit, one function and seven subroutines. The main program unit consists of the following parts :

- dimensions of the arrays : upper bounds are given for the number of variables (p), the number of objects in the sample (n*), and the number of clusters (k).
- setting the maximum value of n x p :
  this maximum value is called MAXXX in the program: typically it is given the values ten or twenty thousand, depending on available storage. In the program the measurement values are stored in a one-dimensional array called X. The objects are stored in the order in which they are read, and the p measurements for each object are stored contiguously.
- setting m, the number of samples to be drawn, equal to three (the user can change this line if he wants more samples to be drawn)
- tests on the numbers of objects and clusters
- calculation of the number of objects n* of the samples (80 or 120)
- test on missing values :
  if provision is made for missing values,
  a. message indicating this
  b. test on the number of variables
  c. the user indicates which variables might have missing values
  d. input of the codes corresponding to missing measurements
- input of measurements
- section in which missing measurements are counted
- if this was requested the measurements are standardized
- output of the number of clusters, k
- loop over the samples to be drawn
  - draw a sample or its complement (if the complement is drawn, subsequently determine the actual sample) by means of subroutine RANDM
  - list of the objects of the sample
  - calculate the Euclidean or Manhattan distances between the n* objects in the sample (subroutine DYSTA) : if it is not possible to calculate all distances, a message is given and the next sample is drawn
  - calculate the maximum distance S (this value is used for initialization purposes in the algorithm)
  - carry out the algorithm on the sample (subroutine BSWAP)
  - output of the average distance, AZ
  - assignment of objects and calculation of ZB, the average distance for the entire data set (subroutine SELEC)

- if ZB is better (lower) than all previous values :
  a. replace the best value found so far by ZB
  b. store the sample number
  c. store the objects of the sample
  d. store the representative objects
  e. store the maximum distance
- test if for at least one sample it was possible to calculate all distances, if not the program stops
- for the best sample :
  - if k = 1 print the sample number, its medoid, and the average distance
  - if k > 1 :
    a. print the sample number and the average distance
    b. recalculate the distances in the sample
    c. carry out subroutine RESUL : calculation of the list of clusters
    d. graphical output showing the best sample, in subroutine BLACK.

Subroutine STAND : in this subroutine, which is only called if standardization is requested, standardized measurements are computed. Before the actual standardization, the average and standardized mean deviation of each variable are calculated and printed.

Subroutine DYSTA : computes Euclidean or Manhattan distances between all objects of a sample : these distances are used in the actual clustering algorithm. After their calculation, the distances are stored in a one-dimensional array called DYS. To save memory space only the lower triangular part of the distance matrix is stored. Also to save memory space, the same array is used to store the distances for all the samples. As the distances between objects of the optimal sample are needed for the silhouettes, these must be computed again when it has been determined which sample is the optimal one.

Function MEET : when the distance between two objects L and J is needed, function MEET(L,J) gives the index of array DYS where this distance is stored :

d(L,J) = DYS(MEET(L,J)).

Subroutine RANDM : generates a pseudo-random number RAN in the interval]0,1[each time it is called. An integer variable, NRUN (equal to 2^{16}.RAN) is used as initial value. It is set equal to zero in the main program before the first call of subroutine RANDM, and ensures that a new pseudo-random number is generated at each call. The structure of the subroutine implies that if the program is run more than once on the same data set (with a number of clusters remaining within the same interval, one to five or six to ten) the same objects are selected in the samples.

Subroutine BSWAP performes the clustering of the sample. It consists of two parts in which the BUILD and SWAP techniques are used.

Subroutine SELEC consists of the following parts :
- assignment of the objects of the entire data set to their clusters ; an object is assigned to a cluster if its distance to the representative object is smaller than to all other representative objects (in case of ties, the smallest

numbered cluster is taken). If there are missing values when calculating the distance, only those variables are considered which have been measured for both the object and the representative object. The result is then multiplied by the number of variables considered, and divided by the total number of variables (in case of Euclidean distances the multiplication and division are done before taking the square root). If an object is found for which it is not possible to calculate the distance to any of the representative objects in the optimal sample, the program stops (after giving a message)

- during the process of assigning objects the following statistics are calculated :
  a. average distance to each medoid
  b. maximum distance to each medoid
  c. number of objects in each cluster
- output of total and average distance for the entire data set
- output for each cluster :
  a. size (number of objects)
  b. medoid
  c. coordinates of the medoid (if standardization is requested only the standardized coordinates are given)
  d. average distance to the medoid
  e. maximum distance to the medoid
- if the number of clusters (k) exceeds one : computation and output of the maximum distance to a medoid divided by the minimum distance of the medoid to another medoid.

Subroutine RESUL : the purpose of this subroutine is to provide a description of the clustering obtained using the optimal sample. It starts with the determination of the clustering vector : this vector gives the number of the cluster to which each object belongs. In order to save memory space the number of the cluster to which an object belongs is stored in the place of the first measurement value for this object, in array X. This is done for all objects except the representative ones of the optimal sample (the information lost in this way is not important, because once a non-representative object has been assigned, its coordinates are no longer needed in the program). The clustering vector is then output, 30 elements per line. If rather large output was requested, another representation is given of the optimal clustering. In this case a list of clusters is provided with for each cluster :

- the number of objects (size)
- the medoid
- a list of objects

Subroutine BLACK : this subroutine gives the graphical output for the optimal sample. It produces the silhouettes of the clusters.

Modifications of the program

During the process of clustering a set of data using a particular computer system, it can happen that program CLARA must be slightly adapted. The necessity for adaptation has been kept to a strict minimum by making the program as portable as possible. For example the random number generator used in the program was constructed by us in order to make it machine independent.

A first requirement for implementing the program concerns the availability of sufficient storage. The compiled version of the program, when stored in central memory of a CDC Cyber 170/750, uses approximately 22,500 words. This consists of a fixed part of 12,500 words and 10,000 words necessary for array X which is used for storing the measurement values. If more than 10,000 measurements are to be processed, the value of MAXXX must be increased (this can be done by adapting the statement located right after the dimension statements), and also the dimension of array X in the main program unit. (In the subroutines the variable MAXXX is used for this purpose). However, as will be seen in the next subsection, the number of objects must be more than 120 ; and if there are missing values, the number of variables must not exceed 100.

A limitation of the program which one sometimes wishes to avoid is that at most ten clusters can be determined. Indeed, in many large data sets there are outliers which should first be removed before looking for the actual clusters, and even if this is not the case it is possible that there are more than ten groups in the set of objects. A possible solution to this problem is to first cluster into ten clusters and then to eliminate outliers or small clusters, before running the program again on a reduced data set. Alternatively, the program could be adapted to accomodate more than ten clusters, in which case some small changes must be made.

Finally it is easy to change the number of samples by altering the statement which assigns a value to m.

Limitations and special messages

Program CLARA is intended for the clustering of large sets of objects. For this reason it was necessary to build into the program a number of limitations and restrictions. The first such restriction is that the program only admits input of measurement values and not of dissimilarity coefficients. Indeed, a major problem of clustering large data sets concerns the memory requirements, and in many situations it impossible to store the n(n-1)/2 dissimilarities which result from n objects. Two restrictions which are consequences of the sampling method concern the minimum number of objects and the maximum number of clusters. As it appeared that a reasonable maximum size of the sample to be drawn is 120 objects (for reasons of both processing time and memory requirements), it was decided that program CLARA could only be used with sets of more than 120 objects. In order to have a reasonable probability of drawing objects of the different groups, the number of clusters is limited to ten. The program only performs one clustering at a time (because the data matrix X is overwritten during execution), and therefore a single value of k must be specified. Another feature designed to limit the memory requirements concerns the method used for storing the measurement values. Instead of a two-dimensional array used in the other programs, a one-dimensional vector is used. This feature imposes a maximum total number of measurements instead of maxima on both the numbers of objects and variables. For example, if the maximum number of measurements is set equal to 10,000 one may consider 10,000 objects characterized by a single variable, or 1000 objects defined on ten variables.

In the program the following tests are carried out on the number of objects (m), the number of clusters (k), the number of variables (P), and the number of measurements (n x p).

condition	action
n < 120	STOP
k > 10	k = 10
k < 1	k = 1
n x p > MAXXX	STOP

If the missing value option is chosen, both objects and variables are examined for missing values. If an object or variable is encountered for which all values are missing it is printed, and after all objects and variables have been examined the program stops. (Actually, all objects are examined, but only those variables for which missing values have been foreseen and given a code). If an object causes the program to stop it should be removed by changing the input file. In order to delete a variable, a simple remedy is to adapt the input format and change the number of variables.

During the standardization (subroutine STAND) the standardized mean deviation of each variable is calculated. A special message is given for each variable with zero standardized mean deviation. If there are any such variables the program stops after all variables have been examined. Also here, the problem can be solved by removing such variables.

Subroutine DYSTA is used to calculate the distances between all pairs of objects in a sample. During its execution all pairs of objects are printed which do not have common measurements (because there are too many missing data). If there are any such pairs, the sample is disregarded and the next sample is drawn. If such pairs of objects are found for all three samples, the program stops.

In subroutine SELEC each of the objects is assigned to one of the representative objects in the sample. If there is an object which does not have common measurements with any of the representative objects (and therefore cannot be assigned) it is printed and the program stops.

Performance of the program

Program CLARA was conceived to deal with large data sets. This was achieved by making both the number of calculations and the necessary storage, linear in the number of objects. (That is for a given number of variables and a given number of clusters.) On our computer (a CDC Cyber 170/750) , we could easily process ten to fifteen thousand objects. As an indication of the speed of the program, the times (in seconds on CDC Cyber 170/750) for solving a set of randomly generated problems are given in Table 1. These problems were solved without standardization, used Euclidean distances, and provided the output of silhouettes. The measurements were two-dimensional, and are divided in two or five clusters.

Number of objects	Number of clusters	
	k = 2	k = 5
200	4.004	14.343
400	4.320	14.773
600	4.447	16.009
800	4.771	21.071
1000	4.906	18.790

Table 1
Computation times in seconds on CDC Cyber 170/750 for five randomly generated problems

Note that the times in the second column are not always increasing in n. It turns out that most of the computation time is needed for applying the partitioning algorithm BSWAP to the three samples, and this time has an important random component because the number of iterations can vary strongly. Only the assignment part of the method is linear in n.

POSSIBLE EXTENSIONS

Several extensions of the algorithm are possible. For example, H. Van Oorschot (personal communication) suggested to enrich subsequent samples by always including the medoids of the previous sample. In this way, the next sample is likely to yield at least as good results as the previous one.

In general, when the number of samples (m) becomes large, the objective will have a tendency to approach its optimal value. In such a case there are many resamplings from the same data set, which clearly reminds us of the bootstrap. It might prove useful to keep a record of the average distances resulting from these samplings, and even to study the distribution of this quantity. Indeed, when the optimal value is quite separated from the bulk of the average distances, this might have been caused by the occurence of one or several very small clusters or outliers, which only intersect with some of the samples.

The program itself could also be extended. For one thing, it could be made easier for the user to increase the number of clusters (at the cost of increased computation times, to be sure). B. Van Zomeren (personal communication) suggested a variant of the program making use of external memory on disk for storing the array X of measurements. This slight restructuring would make it possible to go through the external memory only once at each assignment (of the objects of the entire data set), and allows the clustering of really enormous data sets, say a million objects. Such a variant may be called CELIA (Clustering Extremely Large Industrial Applications).

Some additional options are possible for the treatment of missing values, such as case-wise deletion. The present version of CLARA simply stops when one of the objects of the entire data set does not have common measurements with all representative objects of that particular sample. An alternative would be to go to the next sample. Moreover, one could assign the object whenever it has common measurements with at least one of the representative objects, by selecting the smallest of the existing distances.

REFERENCES

[1] Deichsel, G., Random walk clustering in large data sets, COMPSTAT 4 (1980) 454-459.

[2] Diday, E., Classification automatique sequentielle pour grands tableaux, Revue Francaise d'Automatique, d'Informatique et de Recherche Operationnelle B1 (1975) 29-61.

[3] Hartigan, J.A., Clustering Algorithms (Wiley, New York, 1975).

[4] Massart, D.L., Kaufman, L. and Plastria, F., Non-Hierarchical Clustering with MASLOC, Pattern Recognition 16(5) (1983) 507-516.

[5] Rousseeuw, P.J., Silhouettes: a Graphical Aid to the Interpretation and Validation of Cluster Analysis, Reports of the Dept. of Mathematics and Informatics No. 84-41, Delft University of Technology (1984).

[6] Ryder, B.G., The PFORT Verifier, Software Practice and Experience 4(4) (1974) 359-377.

[7] Steinhausen, D. and Langer, K., Clusteranalyse : Einfuehrung in Methoden und Verfahren der automatischen Klassifikation (W. De Gruyter, Berlin, 1977).

[8] Zupan, J., Clustering of Large Data Sets (Research Studies Press, Chichester, 1982).

DISCUSSION

Smeulders:

There are two reasons why you might use large data sets. Firstly, small data sets do not permit you to draw conclusions, which are accurate enough. Secondly, you may draw other conclusions because you have, for instance, a very small cluster to be detected in a very large space. Is your method suitable for both reasons or only for one of the two.

Kaufman:

It's probably more suited for more accurate conclusions than for different conclusions.

Mayall:

I very much like your approach of sampling large sets to get a manageable estimate as a starting point. There is, however, the danger that your sample may not include the relevant points which may be rarely occuring events in such a large data set. Of course, you might put some constraints on the algorithm in the sense that you do not force outliers into the clusters but allow them to form their own clusters as the analysis proceeds.

Kaufman:

That is an interesting possibility. We have not looked into that, but I will follow up your suggestion and try to find something in that area. I would like to remind you that once we have found an outlier during the sampling process we keep it aside and look at its effect on subsequent samples.

Aus:

May I state the same question in another way? If you have two classes and one class has say 6000 members and the other less than 50, say 12, how does your method handle that?

Kaufman:

The method doesn't have a specific provision to handle that but if the number of samples is large enough we will find one of the elements. When one of the elements is in a small cluster, you will keep it since it will represent in essence a part of the structure of your data. So you need to be a little bit lucky in selecting one of the elements of the small class. But with this little bit of luck you have found everything of interest in your data set.

Mulder:

I've got a sample set of 8,000,000 with 4 features. Do you expect that distance is a better measure for clustering than density or just the reverse.

Kaufman:

I have no experience with using density. I used different distance measures and correlation functions. So if distance, based on density , could be incorporated, I anticipate that your data set could be handled, even with 8,000,000 points in it.

Mulder:

The density can easily be achieved by multi-dimensional convolution. So if you take in two dimensions a cone function it would be equivalent to distance.

Aus:

What bothers me a little bit is that I failed, as a user of statistical methods, to appreciate the advantages that I can have from the methods presented this morning which are not available to me in standard packages like BMDP, SAS, IMSL etc.

Kaufman:

Well, I can't give you a general answer but in the area of cluster analysis, most of the packages contain very few methods for cluster analysis and basically only the hierarchical ones. In most applications where hierarchies do not fit the structure of the data I would advise you to go into nonhierarchical methods. Unfortunately only a very few algorithms are suited for this task and they are not found in the standard packages. Furthermore, most packages can handle only a limited number of cases while the algorithm I presented was specifically designed for handling large data sets.

Backer:

Just a small remark. It is not difficult to make a cluster generating program. The difficult part is the validation of the results obtained. Normally, that part is not included in the standard packages.

Aus:

There is another problem with the standard packages. In my experience it often happens that when you change your input data a little bit, for example leaving out misclassified cases, the selected features are seldom the same when you rerun the program. Consequently it is difficult to understand the classification process.

Kaufman:

You are perfectly right. The same problem occurs in multiple regression analysis, maybe in discriminant analysis but certainly in most of the multivariate statistical techniques.

PATTERN RECOGNITION IN PRACTICE II
E.S. Gelsema and L.N. Kanal (Editors)

TECHNIQUES OF SUPERVISED AND UNSUPERVISED PATTERN RECOGNITION WITH THE AID OF FUZZY SET THEORY

Witold Pedrycz

Research and Development Center of Electronic Medical Instrumentation, 41 800 Zabrze, Poland
and
Department of Automatic Control and Computer Science
Silesian Technical University, 44-100 Gliwice

Fuzzy sets as a mathematical formalism for copying with imprecision have been studied as a tool for supervised and unsupervised pattern recognition. An algorithm for supervised pattern recognition in presence of the linguistic form of data is derived in a general setting of fuzzy relation equations. Moreover a certain problem of feature selection ordering is solved. We deal also with various modifications of clustering methods enabling us to process additional information coming from a subset of the labelled patterns (clustering with partial supervision).

INTRODUCTION

Recently a significant amount of research has been devoted to studies on the role of fuzzy sets in pattern recognition. This led to a more penetrating treatment this theory viewed as a tool for modelling cognitive processes of a human being and, in turn, to construction the algorithms that are able to cope with a factor of uncertainty (fuzziness). Some conceptual background has been proposed by Zadeh (1967), (1977). A potential power of the fuzzy sets lies in fact they allow us to express some uncertain notions in a plausible way, mainly by means of linguistic categories and relationships between them and the classes of the patterns. Such a linguistic, fuzzy notions are quite natural while describing variety of patterns put into studies. This also makes it possible to underline some links existing between pattern recognition and expert systems. To make the fuzzy sets a well-known and widely accepted tool for practitioners in the field of pattern recognition, beside fundamental concepts, we need to establish a reasonable methodological framework, the same as exists in statistical pattern recognition. A lot of work has been already done in unsupervised pattern recognition with the aid of fuzzy sets (cf. Backer (1978), Bezdek (1981), Roubens (1978), Ruspini (1969)). Despite different algorithms proposed, their merit lies in fact the patterns clustered are characterized by a partial membership to the group (cluster). This enriched vision of the detected structure is much more convenient than the crisp clustering methods. One can easily establish some "core" structure and "outliers" (patterns forming the bridges between the clusters). There are some studies in a global evaluation of the results of fuzzy clustering, see e.g. Hirota and Pedrycz (1984) that are of value while interpreting the results. Another stream of studies deals with situations of supervised pattern recognition. Contrary to the unsupervised recognition, we cannot enumerate such a long list of contributions; here we suffer from classification algorithms that are able to establish a proper learning mechanisms. Contributions in this field are mainly conceptual ones (Zadeh (1977)). Moreover we are unable to speak about the classifier for the fuzzy data standing in any loose analogy to Bayesian, deterministic (linear, nonlinear) classifiers known in literature.

The aim of this paper is to propose algorithms of supervised pattern recognition (classifiers) working in presence of the patterns specified by numerical or linguistic features. In opposition to statistical classifiers, this construction is based on a coarse specification of the objects, whose description is formulated in a global sense. The classifier is designed by the use of the results of fuzzy relation equations: the dependence between the feature vector and the membership grade to the classes is specified by a fuzzy relation (discriminant relation). We will present the method of the determination the fuzzy relation of the classifier with the aid of any learning set (training set). A special attention will be paid to a problem of feature selection. The second topic studied carefully in the paper is concerned with fuzzy clustering with additional information, viz. clustering with partial supervision. It deals with a situation that is intermediate between supervised and unsupervised learning. A small subset of "anchor" patterns that are initially labelled permits us to discover the structure of the entire data set. We will study various ways in which this extra information can modify the clustering methods available nowadays. Several numerical examples using real-life data sets illustrate the methods studied.

A CLASSIFICATION ALGORITHM IN PRESENCE OF FUZZINESS

In practice of pattern recognition we are faced with objects described in a linguistic fashion. It means their features are specified in terms of some labels corresponding to the linguistic description rather than precise numerical quantities. Due to properties of the process of human cognition and perception, the linguistic description of the patterns is much more flexible and general. And, the classification results may be also fuzzy, viz. the patterns are allowed to belong to several classes with various grades of membership, see examples of learning with imperfect teacher (Shanmugan and Breipohl (1971)). Usually classification is thought as a statistical decision-making problem (Fukunaga (1972)), where uncertainty is of a probabilistic character. This mature approach provides by an ornamentarium of methods of (i) constructing or at least estimation relevant parameters of the classifier, (ii) calculation a misclassification error, and (iii) feature ordering. Due to quite different form of uncertainty handled by the fuzzy sets, we need to employ novel techniques to cope with fuzziness in an efficient way.

A general problem statement is the following. Each object pattern is characterized by a set of features $X_1, X_2, \ldots X_n$. Each coordinate of the feature space $\mathfrak{X} = \mathfrak{X}_1 \times \mathfrak{X}_2 \times \ldots \times \mathfrak{X}_n$ consists of several linguistic labels modelled by reference fuzzy sets specified by their membership functions $\mathcal{X}_{i1}, \mathcal{X}_{i2}, \ldots, \mathcal{X}_{im(i)} : \mathfrak{X}_i (\subset \mathbb{R}) \rightarrow [0,1]$. They reflect basic notions that make sense in the process of pattern classification. Each pattern is assigned to a fixed family of classes $\Omega = \{\omega_1, \omega_2, \ldots, \omega_c\}$, where we suppose it may belong to several of them with the grades of membership varying in [0,1] interval; the higher the value of $\Omega(\omega_j)$, the higher grade of belongingness of the pattern to the j-th class. A clue of the task of the designing the classifier deals with establishment the relationships existing bwteeen the linguistic categories (fuzzy sets) and the classes observed. To make this construction as general as possible, we will look for the structure of the classifier represented by the fuzzy relation R defined in $\mathfrak{X}$ and the set of the membership grades to the classes Ω. More formally, we get $R: \mathfrak{X} \times \Omega \rightarrow [0,1]$. The fuzzy relation admits to perform classification of any pattern given by feature vector. Let the pattern is specified by the values of their features collected in the vector $\underline{X} = [X_1\ X_2\ \ldots\ X_n]^T$ which coordinates are fuzzy or nonfuzzy. Each X_i is matched against all the labels defined in the respective feature space $\mathfrak{X}_i$, namely

$$M(X_i|\mathcal{X}_{i1}),\ M(X_i|\mathcal{X}_{i2}), \ldots,\ M(X_i|\mathcal{X}_{im(i)}) .$$

The matching operator may be treated as possibility (Zadeh (1978)) of X_i with respect to $\mathcal{X}_{ij}$, $j=1,2,\ldots,m(i)$,

$$M(X_i|\mathcal{X}_{ij}) = \mathrm{Poss}(X_i|\mathcal{X}_{ij}) = \sup_{z \in \mathbb{R}} [\min(X_i(z), \mathcal{X}_{ij}(z))] \qquad (1)$$

It measures to which degree X_i is contained in $\mathcal{X}_{ij}$; for total containment (in sense of fuzzy set theory) the above value attains 1.0. By such a transformation $\underline{X}$ converts into a fuzzy relation $\underline{x}$ which membership function constitues a matrix with the entries $\xi_{i_1 i_2 \ldots i_n}$, $i_1=1,2,\ldots,m(1)$, $i_2=1,2,\ldots,m(2)$, $\ldots$, $i_n=1,2,\ldots,m(n)$, where

$$\xi_{i_1 i_2 \ldots i_n} = \mathrm{Min}[\mathrm{Poss}(X_1|x_{1i_1}), \mathrm{Poss}(X_2|x_{2i_2}), \ldots, \mathrm{Poss}(X_n|x_{ni_n})]$$

The general form of the classifier can be put down as $\underline{x}R\,\Omega$, where $\Omega=[\Omega(\omega_1)\ \Omega(\omega_2)\ldots(\omega)]$ forms the vector of grades of membership to the classes of Ω. In analogy to linear or nonlinear discriminant functions, R will be called the discriminant relation of the classifier. Usually it is convenient to rewrite this formula of the classifier in the form of a fuzzy relation equation (Miyakoshi and Shimbo, (1985), Pedrycz, (1985), Pedrycz, (1982))

$$\Omega = \underline{x} \circledast R \tag{2}$$

viz.

$$\Omega(\omega_j) = \min[\xi_{i_1 i_2 \ldots i_1 \ldots i_n} \varphi R(i_1, i_2, \ldots, i_1, \ldots, i_n, \omega_j)] \tag{3}$$

where minimum is taken over all the indices, $i_1=1,2,\ldots,m(1)$, $i_2=1,2,\ldots,m(2)$, $\ldots$ $i_n=1,2,\ldots,m(n)$, and $j=1,2,\ldots,c$.

"t" stands for t-norm (viz, two-placed function that is symmetrical, monotonic, and associative), while "φ" denotes a pseudocomplement associated with the t-norm (if exists) as $a\varphi b=\sup[c\in[0,1]|\ atc\leq b]$, $a,b\in[0,1]$. It has been shown (Pedrycz (1985b)) the classifier given by (2)-(3) possesses interesting discriminant capabilities: it discriminates the patterns even they are nonseparable by any linear classifier (Duda and Hart (1973)).

Let us discuss now a step of a primordial significance dealt with the determination the fuzzy relation of the classifier. As usually in pattern recognition the classifier is learnt on the basis of the training set of data, say $(\underline{x}_I, \Omega_I)$ $I=1,2,\ldots,N$. Recalling some fundamental results in the theory of fuzzy relation equation (Pedrycz, (1985a)) we have the following expression for the relation of the classifier,

$$R = \bigcup_{I=1}^{N} (\underline{x}_I \times \Omega_I) \tag{4}$$

which in terms of the membership function reads accordingly,

$$R(i_1, i_2, \ldots, i_n, \omega_j) = \max[\xi^I_{i_1 i_2 \ldots i_n}\ t\ \Omega^I(\omega_j)] \tag{5}$$

The above formula is valid if all the elements of the training set fulfils the equation of the classifier (2). Otherwise one should look for approximate relation and determine its accuracy, as introduced for instance by Gottwald and Pedrycz (1985).

The relational form of the classifier allows us to study a problem of feature selection. This important problem arises while we are interested to diminish the size of the classification problem. In sequel we explain how the features may be ordered with respect to their discriminant abilities. Consider the equation of the classifier (2) and the learning set used in (4). If the j-th feature is neglected then we can expect a certain error of misclassification. It reveals by some deviation between the results of classification performed with the aid of the entire set of features and those for which the j-th feature is not taken for the classification purposes. The higher the deviation, the more significant the j-th feature. The lack of the j-th feature will be modelled as the term "unknown" which in fuzzy sets is viewed as the fuzzy set with the membership function equal identically to 1.0 (Wenstøp (1976)). In virtue of the limit condition of the t-norm $at1=a$, for all $a\in[0,1]$, the fuzzy relation of the classifier reduces to the form,

$$R(i_1, i_2, \ldots, i_n, \omega_k) = \max[\xi^I_{i_1 i_2 \ldots i_{j-1} i_{j+1} \ldots i_n}\ t\ \Omega^I(\omega_k)] \tag{6}$$

The fuzzy set concerning the grades of membership will be denoted now by $\Omega_i^{(j)}$, namely

$$\Omega_i^{(j)} = \underline{x}_i^{(j)} \circledast R \tag{7}$$

Afterwards an averaged sum of distances "d" between the fuzzy sets $\Omega_i^{(j)}$ and Ω_i $D=\sum_{i=1}^{N} d(\Omega_i^{(j)}, \Omega_i)/N$ forms an index reflecting the discriminant power of the j-th feature. The distance function "d" may be defined in a different manner as indicated in Kaufmann (1977). By such a procedure all the features can be easily ordered: we speak the j-th feature dominates the l-th one if the respective distances satisfy relationship $D(j) \gg D(l)$.

The structure of the proposed classifier and the mechanism of classification is closely related to a broad class of expert systems, in which a knowledge base consists of production rules (If-then statements). To make this statement more transparent, let us rewrite the equation of the classifier in the form,

-<u>If</u> (x_{1i_1} and x_{2i_2} and ... and x_{ni_n}) <u>then</u> the pattern belongs to the class ω_j with the grade μ,

where μ is the respective entry of the discriminant relation, i.e. $\mu=R(i_1, i_2, \ldots, i_n, \omega_j)$. The production rules are represented in a compact form as

$$x_{1i_1} \,\&\, x_{2i_2} \,\&\, \ldots \,\&\, x_{ni_n} \xrightarrow{\mu} \omega_j$$

Loosely speaking μ plays a similar role as a certainty factor introduced in MYCIN (Shortliffe (1976)), where, as usually, the left-hand side denotes a condition part while the right-hand one forms a relevant hypothesis.

FUZZY CLUSTERING WITH PARTIAL SUPERVISION

Fuzzy clustering is meant as a tool for interpreting the data sets by putting them into some categories (clusters) such that a cluster is thought to be a subset of data points which are highly similar associated and relatively unassociated with the points lying outside the subset. Fuzziness appears as a grade of membership to the clusters (classes) lying in [0,1] interval. Because in many cases one deals with ill-defined categories, this approach is more plausible. One can easily detect the patterns that are outliers, viz. their membership grades to all the classes are equal to 1/c, where "c" stands for the number of the clusters. The problem we are interested in is concerned with the analysis of intermediate situation between a supervised and unsupervised learning (fuzzy clustering with partial supervision). This situation arises in cases when we have to analyze a data set containing some labelled elements. Due to a time-consuming process of the labelling only a small portion of them has been classified. This may happen in the process of learning with an imperfect teacher. Take for instance ECG signals: only a small portion of them has been analyzed manually, and the rest is left for the analysis by the clustering method. We will study how the information coming from the labelled patterns can control the structure of the clusters detected. Among a broad variety of the clustering methods Fuzzy C-Means will be chosen as one being well-known.

An original performance index (Bezdek (1981)) is equal to a sum of distances of the patterns $\underline{x}_k$, $k=1,2,\ldots,n$, $\underline{x}_k \in \mathbb{R}^p$ from the prototypes (fuzzy means) $\underline{v}_i \in \mathbb{R}^p$ of the clusters

$$Q_1 = \sum_{i=1}^{c} \sum_{k=1}^{n} u_{ik}^2 \, \|\underline{x}_k - \underline{v}_i\|^2 \tag{8}$$

where $U=[u_{ik}]$ stands for partition matrix; u_{ik} denotes the grade of membership of the k-th pattern to the i-th cluster. The partition matrix U satisfies two important conditions (cf. Bezdek (1981)),

$$\sum_{i=1}^{c} u_{ik} = 1 \,, \qquad \sum_{k=1}^{n} u_{ik} > 0 \tag{9}$$

The set of all matrices U satisfying the above conditions will be denoted by $\mathcal{U}$. Now the performance index is minimized over the elements of $\mathcal{U}$ and the prototypes.

Let $X_1 \subset X$ denote a subset of the labelled patterns. The elements of X_1 are indicated by the Boolean vector $\underline{g}=[g_1\ g_2\ \dots\ g_n]^T$ such that

$$g_k = \begin{cases} 1, \text{if } \underline{x}_k \in X_1 \\ 0, \text{otherwise} \end{cases} \tag{10}$$

An additional partition matrix F conveys information on the labelled patterns. The values of F are assigned accordingly,

-if $\underline{x}_k \in X_1$, the values of the k-th column of F, f_{ik}, i=1,2,...,c are given by the data analyst,

-if $\underline{x}_k \notin X_1$, the values of the corresponding column of F are irrelevant.

Three possible ways of modification the performance index are given below (Pedrycz (1985c)).

The original performance index (8) is extended to include a weighted sum of differences between u_{ik} and f_{ik} with weights equal to distances between $\underline{x}_i$ and $\underline{x}_k$, $d_{ik}=\|\underline{x}_k-\underline{v}_i\|^2$. Thus we get,

$$Q_2 = \sum_{i=1}^{c}\sum_{k=1}^{n} u_{ik}^2 d_{ik}^2 + \sum_{i=1}^{c}\sum_{k=1}^{n} (u_{ik}-f_{ik}g_k)^2 d_{ik}^2 \tag{11}$$

The labelled patterns specify, at least partially, the internal structure of the data set, that is feasible by an inner product induced in $\mathbb{R}^p$. This may be represented by the fuzzy covariance matrix equal to

$$C_i = \sum_{k=1}^{n} f_{ik}^2 g_k (\underline{x}_k-\underline{w}_i)(\underline{x}_k-\underline{w}_i)^T \Big/ \sum_{k=1}^{n} f_{ik}^2 g_k \tag{12}$$

where

$$\underline{w}_i = \sum_{k=1}^{n} f_{ik}^2 g_k \underline{x}_k \Big/ \sum_{k=1}^{n} f_{ik}^2 g_k$$

Now the minimized performance index similar to Q_1 takes a form,

$$Q_3 = \sum_{i=1}^{c}\sum_{k=1}^{n} u_{ik}^2 d'^2_{ik} \tag{13}$$

with d'_{ik} being the Mahalanobis distance equal to

$$d'^2_{ik} = (\underline{x}_k-\underline{v}_i)^T C_i^{-1} (\underline{x}_k-\underline{v}_i) = \|\underline{x}_k-\underline{v}_i\|^2_{C_i^{-1}} \tag{14}$$

The following performance index makes use of the labelled patterns in two ways: firstly they imply the inner product generated by C_i, i=1,2,...,c, and secondly their partition matrix is considered,

$$Q_4 = \sum_{i=1}^{c}\sum_{k=1}^{n} u_{ik}^2 d'^2_{ik} + \sum_{i=1}^{c}\sum_{k=1}^{n} (u_{ik}-f_{ik}g_k)^2 d'^2_{ik} \tag{15}$$

Despite the fact the attention has been focused on the Fuzzy C-Means clustering method, this additional information can be introduced in non-metric clustering algorithms as well.

NUMERICAL STUDIES

Our studies will be illustrated by three numerical examples. Two of them come from the problems of ECG signal recognition. ECG signals are representative examples where the set of features is qualitatively expressed by a human being. In this area one is faced with fuzziness resulting from imprecision of determination the ECG features, especially QRS complexes and linguistic knowledge about the classification process performed by the clinician. It is not suprising that fuzzy sets have been studied here (cf. Degani and Pacini (1978), Bortolan and Degani (1983)).

Example 1.

The data set training set (see Fig.1) consists of QRS complexes coming from the second lead and containing the patterns forming four classes, i.e. N(1), SVPB(2) VPB(3), VB(4). The QRS complexes are described by two features: (i) a duration rate of succesive RR intervals, $\delta_{RR}=RR_i/RR_{i-1}$, (ii) a width of the QRS complexes, W_{QRS}. The features are specified by attaching to them the following linguistic labels,

-for δ_{RR} $\quad x_{11}(x)=1-x$, for $x\in[0,1]$

$$x_{12}(x)=\begin{cases}(x-0.7)/0.4, & \text{for } x\in[0.7,1.1]\\ 1, & \text{for } x\geq 1.1\end{cases}$$

-for W_{QRS}

$$x_{21}(x)=\begin{cases}0, & \text{for } x<85\\ (x-85)/35, & \text{for } x\in[85,120]\end{cases}$$

$$x_{22}(x)=\begin{cases}1-(x-110)/30, & \text{for } x\in[110,140]\\ 1, & \text{for } x\in[90,110]\end{cases}$$

$$x_{23}(x)=\begin{cases}(x-100)/20, & \text{for } x\in[100,120]\\ 1, & \text{for } x\geq 120\end{cases}$$

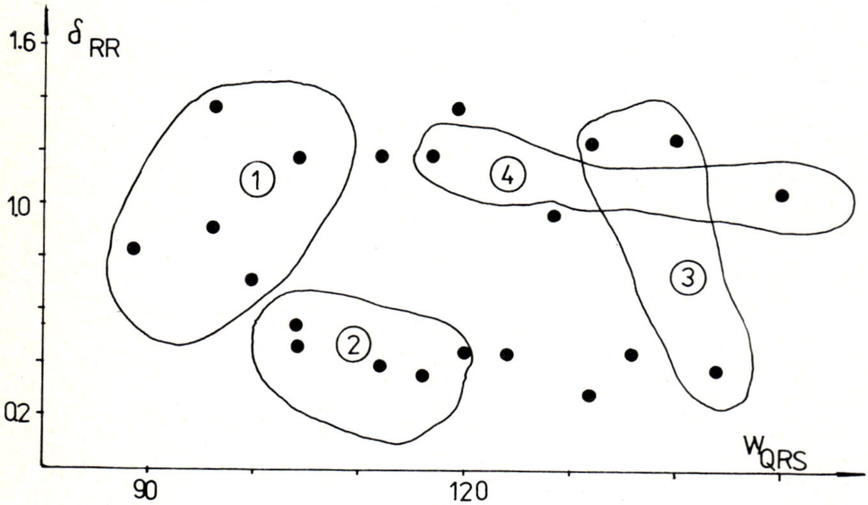

Figure 1
The data set of the QRS complexes

Evaluation of the grades of membership of the patterns to the respective classes has been realized by a group of testees and intermediate values of membership have been obtained i.e. lying in [0,1] interval, Hence the clusters indicated in Fig.1 can be viewed as approximate only.

The discriminant relation of the classifier calculated as presented in Section 2 (the t-norm is specified as minimum) is equal to

	x_{11}	x_{12}						
x_{21}	0.33	0.66	0.46	0.33	0.33	0.46	0.33	0.33
x_{22}	0.53	0.93	0.65	0.67	0.33	0.67	0.33	0.67
x_{23}	0.33	0.60	0.65	0.33	0.33	0.67	0.33	0.67
	ω_1		ω_2		ω_3		ω_4	

An averaged classification error is the sum of the Hamming distances of the fuzzy sets,

$$e_{av}=\sum_{k=1}^{N}\sum_{l=1}^{c}|\Omega_k(\omega_l)-\Omega_k^*(\omega_l)|/4N$$

Ω'_k results from the equation of the classifier with the fuzzy relation given above. This index indicates to which extent the results of the fuzzy classification and the clinicians differ for the individual patterns. For the data set put into discussion e_{av} achieved the value 0.44.

The fuzzy relation of the classifier can be immediately encoded into a set of 6x4=24 production rules; some of them for the first and the fourth class are listed below,

$x_{22} \,\&\, x_{12} \longrightarrow \omega_1 (\mu=0.93)$, $x_{22} \,\&\, x_{11} \longrightarrow \omega_2 (\mu=0.53)$, $x_{23} \,\&\, x_{12} \longrightarrow \omega_4 (\mu=0.67)$, $x_{23} \,\&\, x_{12} \longrightarrow \omega_4 (\mu=0.67)$.

Example 2.

We deal with a collection of the ECG patterns shown in two-dimensional space (Fig. 2), where the first coordinate is an area of the QRS complex (A), while the second is a duration time between R waves in succesive complexes (RR). As before the same four classes have been recognized. Some of the patterns have been labelled by three testees are marked in the Figure 2. The clusters are of elongated shapes with a significant overlap between the first and the second class. Four methods described in the previous section have been tested. The results are listed below,

method (formula)	performance index q
Q_1	3.13
Q_2	2.61
Q_3	2.25
Q_4	1.88

where q is the averaged Hamming distance between the membership functions derived by the algorithms and those specified by the testees,

$$q=\sum_{i=1}^{c} \sum_{\underline{x}_k \in X_1} |u_{ik}-f_{ik}| \,/c$$

It is remarkable the fourth method enabled us to diminish the value of this performance index two times in comparison to the first one, which has not used any information about the structure of the data set.

Example 3.

This example makes use of the data set discussed by L. de Mantaras and Aguilar Martin (1983) that deals with an analysis of characteristics of the working situations in a lumber factory. The features describing each worker pattern form 14-dimensional feature vector $\underline{x}=[x_1\ x_2 \ldots\ x_{14}]$. Each coordinate of $\underline{x}$ describes a given property of the worker e.g. x_1-professional training, x_{11}-supervision of tasks, etc. Its value lies in [0,1] interval and indicates to which extent the listed property is satisfied by the specified pattern. The workers are divided into four nonfuzzy classes (categories) for instance ω_1-the workers having relatively high academic standard and intelectual activity. The fuzzy classifier built on the basis of 18 training patterns gives the classification error q equal to 0.123. Calculating the discriminant power of the features we obtain the following ordering: physical effort, supervision of tasks, incidence the production process, and adverse environmental conditions.

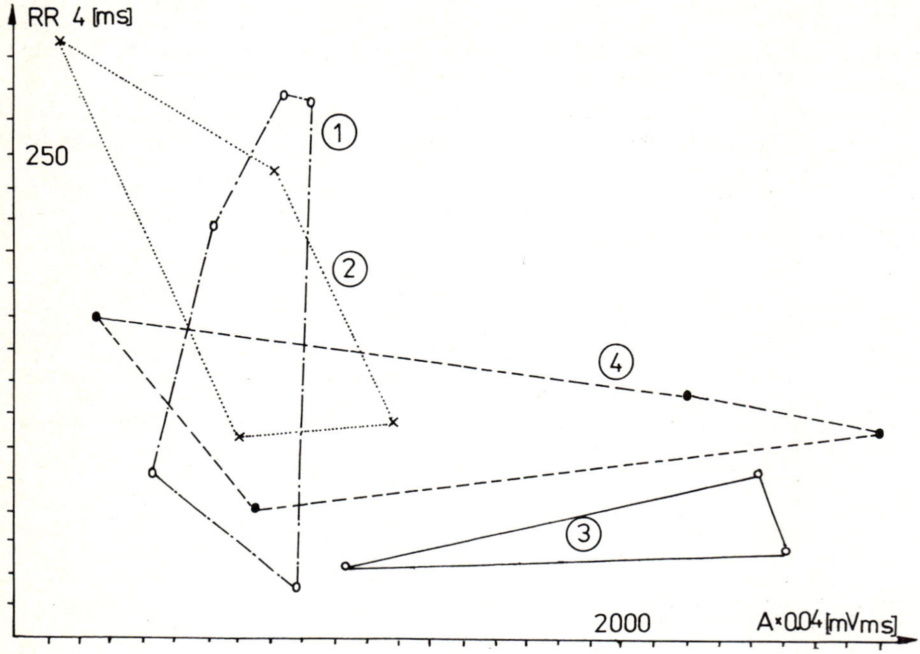

Figure 2
The structure of the data set

CONCLUSIONS

We have presented the efficient way of handling linguistic form of information for supervised and unsupervised pattern recognition.This creates much more flexible tool (in comparison to deterministic or probabilistic techniques) which benefits are obvious when arranging a computer-aided dialogue.The input information could not be necessarily a numerical one,and,therefore the user is not forced to formulate his judgements in language of numerical quantities. The method applied for the fuzzy classifier is valuable because it requires only a small portion of elements of the training set to establish the discriminant relation and the basic mechanism of human inference can be implemented as well.The fuzzy classifier may be reformulated in the form of the production rules the same as studied in expert systems.The discussion on clustering procedures with partial supervision indicated the additional information can be introduced in the performance index and efficiently used for searching the structure of the entire data set.

REFERENCES

1 Backer,E.,Cluster analysis by optimal decomposition of induced fuzzy sets (Delft Univ.Press,Delft,1978).

2 Bellman,R.E.,R.Kalaba and Zadeh,L.A.,Abstraction and pattern recognition, J.of Math.Anal.and Appl. 13(1967) 1-7.

3 Bezdek,J.C.,Pattern Recognition with fuzzy objective function algorithms (Plenum Press,New York,1981).

4 Bortolan,G.and Degani,R.,Ranking of fuzzy alternatives in electrocardiography,Conf.Fuzzy Information,Knowledge Representation and Decision Analysis,Marseille,1983,397-402.

5 Degani,R. and Pacini,G.,Linguistic pattern recognition algorithms for computer analysis of ECG.Conf."Biosigma",Paris,1978,18-26.

6 Duda,R.O.and Hart,P.E.,Pattern classification and scene analysis(J.Wiley, New York,1973).

7 Fukunaga,K.,Introduction to statistical pattern recognition(Academic Press, New York,1972).

8 Gottwald,S.and Pedrycz,W.,Solvability of fuzzy relational equations and manipulation of fuzzy data,Fuzzy Sets and Systems,(1985) to appear .

9 Hirota,K.and Pedrycz,W.,Characterization of fuzzy clustering algorithms in terms of entropy of probabilistic sets,Pattern Recognition Letters 2(1984) 213-216.

10 Kaufmann,A.,Introduction a la theorie des sous-ensembles flous(Masson Paris,1977).

11 Lopez de Mantaras,R.and Aguilar Martin,J.,Classification and linguistic characterization of non-deterministic data,Pattern Recognition Letters 2(1983) 33-41.

12 Miyakoshi,M.and Shimbo,M.,Solutions of fuzzy relational equations with triangular norms.Fuzzy Sets and Systems(1985) to appear .

13 Pedrycz,W.,Fuzzy relational equations with triangular norms,BUSEFAL 11 (1982) 24-32.

14 Pedrycz,W.,Applications of fuzzy relational equations for methods of reasoning in presence of fuzzy data,Fuzzy Sets and Systems(1985a) to appear .

15 Pedrycz,W.,A method of classifier design for fuzzy data,BUSEFAL 21(1985b) 113-116.

16 Pedrycz,W.,Algorithms of fuzzy clustering with partial supervision,Pattern Recognition Letters 3(1985c) 13-20 .

17 Roubens,M.,Pattern classification problems and fuzzy sets,Fuzzy Sets and Systems 1(1978) 239-253.

18 Ruspini,E.R.,A new approach for clustering,Information and Control 15 (1969) 22-32.

19 Shanmugam,K.and Breipohl,A.M.,An error correcting procedure for learning with an imperfect teacher,IEEE Trans.Systems Man and Cybernetics 3(1971) 223-229.

20 Shortliffe,E,H.,MYCIN:Computer based medical consultations(American Elsevier,New York,1976).

21 Wenstøp,F.,Deductive verbal models of organizations.Int.J.Man-Machine Stud. 8(1976) 293-311.

22 Winston,P., Artificial intelligence(Reading,Mass:Addison Wesley,1975).

23 Zadeh,L.A.,Fuzzy sets and their applications to pattern classification and clustering analysis,in:van Ryzin,J.(ed). ,Classification and clustering (Academic Press,New York,1977) 251-299.

24 Zadeh,L.A.,Fuzzy sets as a basis for a theory of possibility,Fuzzy Sets and Systems 1(1978) 3-28.

DISCUSSION

Persoon:

Can you tell something about your experience with assigning fuzzy labels to practical data?

Pedrycz:

One possible solution is that you ask the expert several questions in order to assess the values of the membership function. This solution is quite empirical and sometimes not satisfactory. A second possibility is based on cluster analysis. Suppose you have a data set. Then this set is clustered using fuzzy clustering algorithms by trying to split it in a given number of categories. For instance, consider the width of the QRS-complex. The clinician uses about four categories. This means that the number of clusters is, in a certain sense, specified by the user. This implies that the resulting fuzzy model fits well the needs of the user. However, one should not try to construct many linguistic levels because it is nonsense. We do not try to describe very detailed information but we try to describe concepts that are useful.

PATTERN RECOGNITION IN PRACTICE II
E.S. Gelsema and L.N. Kanal (Editors)

A MULTICLASS NONPARAMETRIC PARTITIONING ALGORITHM

Jan L. Talmon
Dept. of Medical Informatics, Free University
Amsterdam, The Netherlands

ABSTRACT

In many classification problems parametric procedures cannot be used because the probability distributions of the data are not in agreement with the assumptions made by these procedures.
Several nonparametric procedures designed to overcome these difficulties are described in the literature. Some of these algorithms try to divide the high dimensional feature space into a number of regions in such a way that each region contains (almost) only cases of one single a priori class.
We describe a nonparametric partitioning procedure for multiclass classification problems which generates a binary decision tree. The feature selection procedure at each node is based on the reduction in the uncertainty on the classmembership of the objects which is obtained by dividing the set of objects at that node into two groups, one with the objects that have a feature value less than the threshold and one with the objects with feature values greater than the threshold. For each feature an optimal threshold is determined and the feature that reduces the uncertainty most is selected.
The implementation of the algorithm will be discussed and several examples of the performance of the algorithm will be presented.

INTRODUCTION

In many real-life classification problems, one is faced with the fact that the probability distributions of the features violate the assumptions made in parametric classification procedures. There may be a mixure of continuous and discrete features, the probability distributions of the features may not be normal and even have a multimodal shape. The application of parametric procedures will, in general, yield nonoptimal classification results.
With the aid of interactive systems like ISPAHAN, one can try to improve the results of the classification procedures by adapting threshold values and by the definition of, for example, piecewise linear discriminants. However, procedures for feature selection and object mapping are still based on parametric procedures and there is no guarantee that the optimal features are selected and hence optimal discriminants are defined.
In order to cope with these difficulties nonparametric classification procedures have been suggested.
The essential feature of a class of such nonparametric procedures is that one tries to partition the feature space into regions that contain (almost) only cases of one a priori class. This region generation procedure is mostly used in a sequential way. This means that at each step a certain region is subdivided into two or more subregions by selecting a (combination) of features and one or more threshold values in such a way that some criterion describing the performance of the classifier (for example the number of misclassifications) is

optimized.
The final partitioning of the feature space can equally well be described by a decision tree. Each decision node defines one or more hyperplanes perpendicular to the axis of the selected feature. These planes are the boundaries between the regions in the feature space.
Several of such procedures have been suggested in the literature. A number of them will be described in the next section.
Thereafter, we will present the nonparametric classification procedure that we developed. Details on the actual implementation of the procedure will be given.
The utility of the procedure will be demonstrated with a number of examples, using both artificial data and data from practical classification problems.

LITERATURE

Henrichon and Fu (1) have described a nonparametric partitioning algorithm in which each feature axis is divided in a number of regions, each of them containing the same number of objects (K). A class label is assigned to each region based on the number of objects from each a priori class in that region. The cost of misclassification is used to assign this class label. Also a 'indecision' label is possible because the cost of indecision is also considered. The next step is to merge adjacent regions which have been assigned the same class label. Now, region boundaries are shifted over at most K/2 objects in both directions. The final region boundary is set at the point where optimal classification accuracy is obtained.
Regions with less than K/2 objects are dissolved in such a way that the classification error is minimally increased and a SCORE is computed for this partitioning based on the cost of misclassification and indecision. This procedure is repeated for each feature and the optimal partitioning will be that one for which the SCORE (as an estimate of the cost of misclassification) is minimal.
The partitioning procedure is continued for each region where no definite decision has been made until the complete space has been partitioned into regions which each have an a priori class label.
Henrichon and Fu remark that the transgeneration of features is possible at each node and that the partitioning can take place for these transgenerated features.

Gleser and Collen (2) have proposed a method for the computerized generation of decision trees for medical diagnosis. The process of generating such decision trees can be viewed as a partitioning of the feature space and since they do not use any parametric description of the density functions of the features this procedure can also be viewed as a nonparametric partitioning algorithm.
In their approach it is assumed that the features have discrete values. Continuous features are transformed into discrete ones by means of a prepartitioning of the feature axis. This prepartitioning has to be defined beforehand and is not related to the feature values taken by the objects in a specific region that has to be partitioned. This poses, in our opinion, a limitation on the flexibility of the proposed algorithm. One point, which is of interest to mention, is their criterion for the selection of the feature that provides the optimal partitioning. They describe the diagnostic process as the reduction in the uncertainty of making the diagnosis for a specific problem. By using the information provided by a feature the uncertainty is reduced. For the construction of the decision tree that feature is selected at each node which reduces the uncertainty most. This approach of feature selection has been adopted by us and will be described in the next section.

The procedures described by Henrichon and Fu and by Gleser and Collen both have the disadvantage that the number of regions in the high-dimensional feature space can grow rapidly and that there is a tendency that the number of objects in each region rapidly decreases at lower levels of the decision tree.
The algorithm of Henrichon and Fu is more robust in this respect since it starts with equally sized regions. On the other hand, this property makes it more difficult to also include coded or discrete features. In the algorithm of Gleser and Collen there is hardly any control mechanism for the number of objects at each node that is generated except that some statistic is used to merge adjacent intervals of the feature axis when no significant difference in the distribution of the a priori classes in both regions exist.

Friedman (3), and later also Rounds (4), has proposed an algorithm that better controls the number of regions generated since it produces a binary decision tree. Unfortunately, the algorithm is only suitable for a two-class problem since the feature selection criterion is based on the difference between the cumulative probability density of the features for the two classes. Friedman has suggested to solve the multiclass problem by generating several decision trees, one for each a priori class versus all others. At each terminal node, a likelihood can be defined that an object belongs to the class the decision tree is designed for. When a new object has to be classified it is passed through all decision trees and that class is selected for which the highest likelihood is obtained.

Concurrently with our research (5) Sethi and Sarvarayudu (6) developed a nonparametric partitioning algorithm based on the idea of entropy reduction similar to that described in 2. The major difference between both procedures is the termination criterion. Sethi and Sarvarayudu use a criterion based on the relation between the maximally obtainable entropy reduction at a node and the error rate of the classifier. In our approach we followed the strategy proposed by Gleser and Collen. Also implementation differences exist.

Recently, Wang and Suen (7) have proposed a nonparametric procedure that is also based on the idea of entropy reduction. In contrast with our approach and that of Sethi and Sarvarayudu, they considered a more general decision tree that can have more than two branches at each node where a partitioning occurs. They claim that especially in problems where the number of classes is large such an approach is most advantageous. However, it is well known that each general decision tree can be rewritten as a binary decision tree.

A MULTICLASS NONPARAMETRIC PARTITIONING ALGORITHM

Based on the above mentioned algorithms we designed a nonparametric partitioning algorithm that

- can solve N-class problems
- results in a binary decision tree
- searches for optimal threshold values

Let us assume that the N classes in a certain region of the feature space have a probability of occurrence given by P(i), i=1,....,N.
The degree of uncertainty on the class membership of an object, i.e. the classification C, in that region is given by Shannon's entropy:

$$H(C) = -\sum_{i=1}^{N} P(i)\ln P(i)$$

Suppose that we partition such a region by means of feature f with threshold value t(f). Let us denote the conditional probability of occurrence of a class i in the region with feature values less than t(f) by P(i,1) and in the region corresponding with greater feature values by P(i,2). The Shannon entropy for the region given the partitioning, is now given by:

$$H(C|t(f)) = -\sum_{j=1}^{2} P(.,j) \sum_{i=1}^{N} \frac{P(i,j)}{P(.,j)} \ln \frac{P(i,j)}{P(.,j)}$$

P(.,1) is the probability that an object in the region has a feature value less than t(f) and P(.,2) = 1 - P(.,1). Since the probabilities are unknown, they are estimated from the training set by means of

$$P(i,j) = m(i,j)/M$$

in which m(i,j) is the number of objects of class i that have a feature value less than or greater than t(f) for j=1,2 resp. and M is the total number of objects in the region. An estimate of the reduction in uncertainty is now given by

$$I(t(f)) = \hat{H}(C) - \hat{H}(C|t(f))$$

with $\hat{H}(C)$ and $\hat{H}(C|t(f))$ similar to H(C) and H(C|t(f)) but with the probabilities P(i,j) replaced by their estimates.
It is easy to show that

$$I(t(f)) = \frac{1}{M} \sum_{i=1}^{N} \sum_{j=1}^{2} m(i,j) \ln \frac{m(i,j)M}{m(.,j)m(i,.)}$$

The problem of the partitioning is now reduced to the selection of a feature F and a threshold T such that I(T(F)) is maximal. This means that the uncertainty is maximally reduced by the selection of the feature and the associated threshold.
Let us assume that we have K ordered sets of $\{x_k i\}$, k=1,...,K with K the number of features. These ordered sets are from the M objects in a region. Associated with each element of each ordered set is the a priori class membership of the corresponding object: c(i).
A candidate threshold value is defined by

$$t(f) = (x_k i+1 - x_k i)/2$$

under the condition that c(i)≠c(i+1). In order to handle discrete features smoothly we required as an additional condition that the two feature values of the ordered set had to be different. Or formulated more precisely, when c(i)≠c(i+1) for an element in one of the ordered sets, a candidate threshold value is defined as being the average of the feature value $x_k i$ and the first feature value in the ordered list following i that differs from $x_k i$. For each possible threshold value I(t(f)) can be computed. The optimal threshold T(f) for feature f is that one for which I(t(f)) is maximal. The optimal partitioning of the region under consideration is obtained with feature F for which I(T(f)) is maximal.
Wilks (8) has shown that

- I(T(F)) is an unbiased estimate of H(C)-H(C|T(F)) and that
- if $M \to \infty$, 2MI(T(F)) has a χ^2 distribution with M-1 degrees of freedom.

This last point offers the possibility to estimate the probability that a certain reduction in entropy occurred by chance alone.
We decided not to partition a region

- when only objects of one a priori class are present - a trivial situation

- when the probability that the entropy reduction occurred by chance alone -P(I(T(F)))- was more than 2.5% or
- when the cumulative probability of having a real reduction in entropy $-\Pi(1-P(I(T(F))))$- became less than 95% with the product taken over the path from the root to the current node.

When it is decided that a region will not be further partitioned, a class name has to be assigned to such a region. When only objects of one class are present, this class assignment is easy. However, when objects of two or more classes are present, one has to decide which class label has to be provided. An automatic procedure would be to give that region the label of the most prominent class, but this might not be an optimal assignment when there is a (large) difference in the number of objects per a priori class that were initially present in the input data. Of course, this can be accounted for but for sake of flexibility we selected another approach (see next section).

IMPLEMENTATION OF THE ALGORITHM

In order to be able to apply the nonparametric partitioning algorithm to data sets which might also be analyzed with other pattern recognition techniques it was decided that our program should be able to read ISPAHAN input files (9). The implementation of the nonparametric partitioning algorithm in ISPAHAN itself is rather difficult because the structure of the decision trees which are built by the algorithm poorly fit with those of ISPAHAN.

Because of this limitation a separate program was developed for the nonparametric partitioning algorithm. The input part of the program facilitates the deletion of objects based on some simple decision functions which can be entered interactively. It is also possible to delete the objects of certain a priori classes from the input to the algorithm or to merge two or more classes into a new one.

In the algorithm described in the previous paragraph, the estimated reduction in entropy is derived from estimates of the class probabilities. It is therefore necessary that at each node to be partitioned a sufficiently large number of objects of each class is present. This number of objects can be defined by the user (Magic Number - MN) and will depend on the total number of objects in the input file and/or the number of objects in the smallest a priori class considered. Experience has shown that MN values between 5 and 10 perform best in most practical applications.

In order to test the validity of the decision tree that is generated with the algorithm, the user has the possibility to have a training and a test set be defined by the program. As of yet, this generation of a training and test set is based on the sequence in which the objects occur rather than on a randomization process.

Instead of generating the ordered set of feature values for each node, the sorting process is done only once. For each node in the decision tree a bitmap defines which objects belong to it.

In order to have some influence on the partitionings given by the algorithm, the user is asked after completion of the partitioning to provide the class labels for the regions that do not contain objects of one single class. In the current implementation the user can assign one of the a priori class labels to such a region or delete that region.

After the class assignment procedure, the binary decision tree will be 'polished' in the following way.

When two descendants of a node are both terminal with the same class label, they are removed and the father node becomes a terminal node with the same class label as the descendants (figure 1a).

When two descendants of a node are terminal ones and one of them is marked to be deleted, both are removed from the tree and the user is asked to provide a label for the father node (figure 1b).
The most complicated situation arises when a node is marked to be deleted but its brother node is a nonterminal node and hence the root of a subtree. In this case, all objects of the node to be deleted are passed through the subtree attached to the brother node. All terminal nodes that have a label different from the label of at least one of the objects reaching such a node are marked to be relabelled by the user. The father node of the node to be deleted is also removed from the tree and the brother node (the root of the subtree) takes the place of the father (see figure 1c).

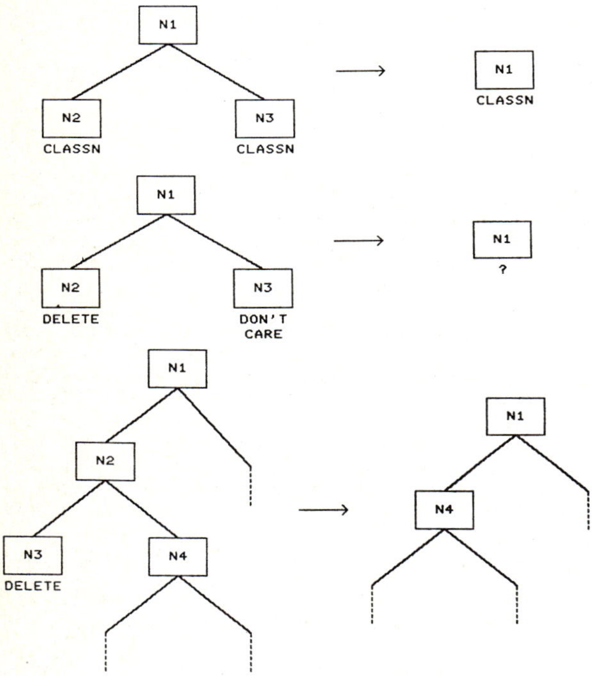

Figure 1.

This figure shows how the binary decision tree is reduced by removing two terminal nodes which have the same father and which obtained the same class label and by removing a node that was labelled to be deleted.

ILLUSTRATIVE EXAMPLES

Example 1.

This experiment is similar to that described by Friedman (3). A decision tree has to be designed for a 7-class problem. The class centers are located at the vertices of a regular simplex in a 6-dimensional feature space. The classes have an identity variance-covariance matrix and all distances between the class centers are equal to 4. Twenty data sets were generated with in each set 500 objects in each class. 250 cases per class were used as training set; the other 250 as test samples. For each set three decision trees were generated with MN = 2, 5 and 10.
A terminal node was given a certain class label when

- The number of objects of that class was at least equal to MN and
- The number of objects of that class was at least twice as large as the number of objects of the second largest class at the terminal node.

Otherwise the node was deleted even when objects of only one a priori

class were present but with a prevalence less than MN.
With the aid of ISPAHAN Fisher discriminants were computed for the same data sets. Table 1 compares the results of the different classification schemes that were computed and the results published by Friedman. It is clear that the Fisher discriminants perform better than the nonparametric procedures. The results obtained with our nonparametric partitioning algorithm are about the same as the results of Friedman. One should note that in our procedure only original features were used and no transgenerated ones.

	ERROR RATE		# TERM. NODES	
	AVER.	SD.	AVER.	SD.
FISHER	9.67	0.72		
FRIEDMAN	13.30	1.30		
NPPA 2	14.91	0.81	54.25	6.98
NPPA 5	15.36	1.05	22.90	3.62
NPPA 10	15.97	1.13	13.80	2.97

Table 1. Averaged error rates and standard deviations for the experiment described by Friedman (3). A comparison is made between the results of Friedman, the results with the Fisher discriminant option of ISPAHAN (9) and the algorithm described in this paper.

As was to be expected the averaged size of the decision trees obtained with our algorithm decreases when MN is increased. The error rate, however, is hardly related to the value of MN.

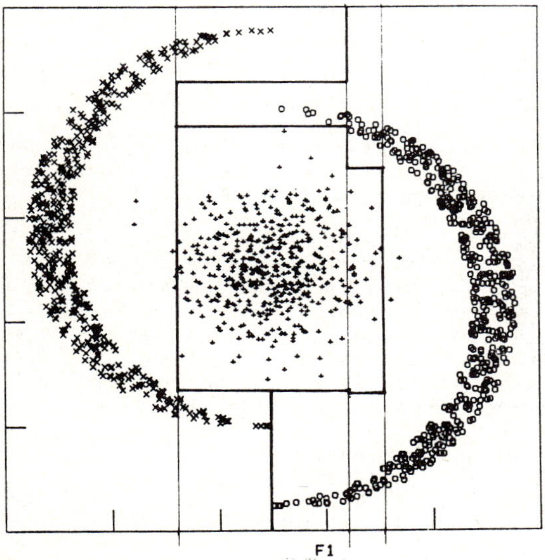

Figure 2.

Decision boundaries obtained with the described algorithm in the experiment with 3 nonlinearly separable classes.

Example 2.

The advantage of the nonparametric approach is demonstrated by the following 3-class classification problem. The scatter plot of the objects in the 2-dimensional feature space is given in figure 2. Class 1 has an identity variance-covariance matrix and the class mean is (Ø,Ø). Class 2 has a uniform distribution along the F2 axis between -4 and 6. For each object in this group the value of feature F1 follows from

$$F1 = -(25 - (F2 - 1)^2)^{\frac{1}{2}} + \nu$$

with F2 from a uniform distribution between -4 and 6 and ν drawn from a uniform distribution between -Ø.5 and Ø.5. Class 3 was generated as the mirror image of class 2 with respect to the origin in the F1-F2 plane.

		FISHER			NPPA		
		CLASS1	CLASS2	CLASS3	CLASS1	CLASS2	CLASS3
A PRIORI LABELS	CLASS1	462	15	23	483	12	5
	CLASS2	30	470	0	0	500	0
	CLASS3	42	0	458	0	0	500

Table 2. Classification results for the experiment with three non-linearly separable classes. Data are given for a test set with the same distribution as the data given in figure 2.

Table 2 compares the results for the Fisher discriminants and the results with the nonparametric procedure for a test set of 5ØØ cases for each class. It is clear that the nonparametric procedures performs much better in this example.

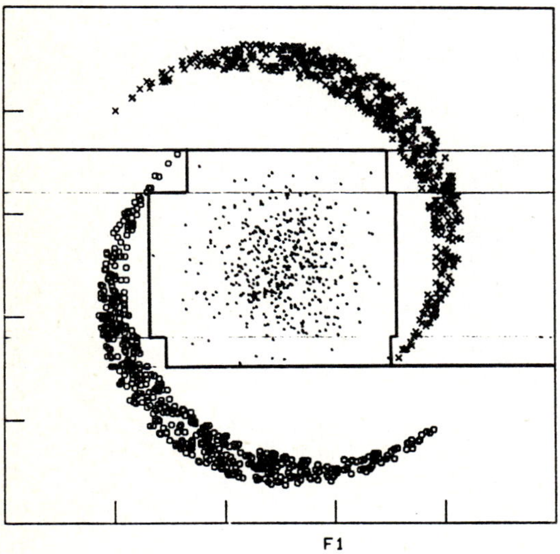

Figure 3.

The same data set as in figure 2 but now rotated over 45 degrees.

Example 3.
Since only primary features are used, both the generated decision tree and the classification results depend on the orientation of the classes with respect to the feature axis (see figure 3 and table 3).

A PRIORI LABELS	CLASS1	CLASS2	CLASS3
CLASS1	496	1	3
CLASS2	0	500	0
CLASS3	5	0	495

Table 3.

Classification results obtained with the nonparametric partitioning algorithm for the rotated test set. Note the reduced error rate.

Example 4.
In this example a decision tree for detection of needle-like distortions (spikes) in electrocardiograms is considered. Features derived from both the original data and filtered signals are used to decide whether or not a spike occurs at a certain time instant. Since also QRS complexes might evoke the spike detector we are dealing with a 4-class problem. Class 1 consists of large spikes. These signal segments should be discarded for further analysis. Class 2 consists of small spikes which should be detected but the effect of missing them on the final analysis is minimal. Class 3 consists of signal segments from the QRS complex. These cases should certainly not be considered as large spikes. The last class consists of signal segments which contain neither spikes nor QRS complexes. A more detailed description of this example can be found in 5.
Table 4 gives the evaluation results for a test set. Also a cost matrix is provided. With the aid of the cost matrix we were able to perform the labelling of the terminal nodes of the decision tree with objects of more than one a priori class.

		NPPA				COST			
		L	S	Q	N	L	S	Q	N
REFERENCE	L	26	2	1	0	0	3	5	5
	S	1	48	0	4	0	0	3	3
	Q	0	8	106	4	5	1	0	0
	N	0	0	7	9	5	3	0	0

Table 4. Classification results for the spike detection algorithm as designed with the nonparametric partitioning algorithm. A cost matrix is also defined to assist the labelling of terminal nodes which have objects of more than one a priori class.

SUMMARY AND CONCLUSIONS

A nonparametric partitioning algorithm was presented that combines the features of some of the algorithms published in the literature. It is able to solve multiclass problems; it generates a binary decision tree. The feature and threshold selection is based on the concept of the reduction in uncertainty on the class membership of objects due to the partitioning of the feature space. The most important aspects of the implementation of the algorithm were discussed. With the aid of some examples, we have shown that the procedure works well in situations where parametric procedures fail. However, when the problem is well formed in the sense that the conditions for the application of parametric procedures are fulfilled, the parametric procedures perform better.

There are a few points which have to be considered as limitations of our procedure. First of all, as of yet it is not possible to define an 'undecided' class. In some studies the need for such a category was present. Secondly, the limitation to a binary tree can result in a large number of nodes in the decision tree. Furthermore, the decision tree may become unbalanced. In our experiments, however, we did not feel this as a serious limitation of our procedure. Only in problems where the separation between many classes is poor and where a large number of features is used, the decision tree cannot be stored. Even the built-in garbage collection procedure might in these cases not yield sufficient space for further partitionings.

In contrast to others (1, 3) our procedure is not able to transgenerate features at a specific node on the bases of the objects present at that node. We restricted ourselves to the use of pure features which are present in the input file. Since the nonparametric partitioning algorithm was especially designed for those studies where parametric procedures could not be used, the use of transgenerated features is also questionable since the feature selection proces prior to the transgeneration will mainly be based on parametric methods. The experiments have shown that our algorithm can be a valuable tool for solving pattern recognition problems in addition to parametric procedures.

REFERENCES

1 Henrichon jr, E.G. and K-S Fu:
A nonparametric partitioning procedure for pattern classification. IEEE trans. on Comp., C-18, 614-624, 1969.

2 Gleser, M.A. and M.F. Collen:
Towards automated medical decisions. Comp. and Biomed. Res., 5, 180-189, 1972.

3 Friedman, J.H.:
A recursive partitioning decision rule for nonparametric classification. IEEE trans. on Comp., C-26, 404-408, 1977.

4 Rounds, E.M.:
A combined nonparametric approach to feature selection and binary decision tree design. Pattern Recognition, 12, 313-317, 1980.

5 Talmon, J.L.:
Pattern recognition of the ECG. A structured analysis. Ph.D. thesis. Free University, Amsterdam, 1983.

6 Sethi, I.K. and G.P.R. Sarvarayudu:
Hierarchical classifier design using mutual information. IEEE trans. on Pattern analysis and machine intelligence, PAMI-4, 441-445, 1982.

7 Wang, Q.R. and C.Y. Suen:
Analysis and design of a decision tree based on entropy reduction and its application to large character set recognition. IEEE trans. on Pattern analysis and machine intelligence, PAMI-6, 406-417, 1984.

8 Wilks, S.:
Mathematical statistics. John Wiley, New York, USA, 1962.

9 Gelsema, E.S.:
ISPAHAN, users manual. 4th edition, Dept. of Med. Inform., Free University, Amsterdam, 1981.

DISCUSSION

Haralick:

Could you relate the information criterion that you are using at a node to the following? At each node you make a decision, you split your data into two mutually exclusive groups of classes. Now take for example, the left branch of the node. There is a distribution of classes in such a branch. You can measure the uncertainty or entropy if you like for that mixture. How does that entropy relate to the criterion you are using?

Talmon:

The entropies of the lefthand and righthand branches are weighted with the probabilites for the test outcome to be less than or greater than the threshold value. This forms the criterion and is essentially the same as the entropy referred to by you. The splitting of the training set at a given node is based on only one feature. Both the threshold and feature are selected in such a way that the uncertainty is maximally reduced and hence that both mixtures are maximally different.

Morgera:

Do you actually use the percentage points of the chi-square distribution to do the sorting of the features? The formula you showed only holds for the asymptotical case.

Talmon:

No. As a matter of fact we look at the estimated reduction in uncertainty and then we select the feature that reduces the uncertainty most.

PATTERN RECOGNITION IN PRACTICE II
E.S. Gelsema and L.N. Kanal (Editors)

PLS DISCRIMINANT PLOTS

Michael Sjöström and Svante Wold

Research Group for Chemometrics
Department of Chemistry
Umeå University
S-901 87 Umeå
Sweden

Bengt Söderström

Department of Microbiological Ecology
University of Lund
S-223 62 Lund
Sweden

A projection method for multivariate classification problems is presented, which is based on partial least squares in latent variables (PLS). PLS models the dependency between two multivariate blocks X and Y. For a pattern recognition problem we use a dummy matrix Y which describes the class-membership of the training-set objects. The multivariate characterization of the objects forms the X block. The PLS model describes the X-block with a principal component (PC) like model, where class separation is enhanced. The significance of the class separation is tested by cross-validation. Plotting the score vectors of the PLS model gives a PLS discriminant plot.

INTRODUCTION

Projections of multivariate data sets down to two or three dimensions are important in classification or pattern recognition (PaRC) problems. Projections give information which is difficult to reach in other ways, e.g. the detection of outliers, inhomogeneities in classes and asymmetric class structures.

A projection often used to illustrate the relationship between a set of multivariately described objects is the principal components (PC) score plot (eigenvector plot). Two or three dimensional PC score plots are constructed by plotting the scores for two or three PC against each other along orthogonal axis.

In PC projections for a pattern recognition problem with a set of objects with known class-belonging (a training-set), the knowledge of the class of the objects is not used to find the PC axes. The PC model is just calculated to approximate the unlabeled data as well as possible. Here, we want to present the method of partial least squares in latent variables (PLS) as a projection method where the class memberships of the objects are taken into account in the data modelling.

In the PLS model the X block, which consists of the multivariate description of the objects, is described by a PC like model. However, the latent variables (object scores) are simultaneously related to a Y block (the dependent variables) through a regression step. For a classification problem with a training-set with class assigned objects, we use this framework with a dummy matrix Y, which describes the class belonging of the objects. Thus, with the PLS method fewdimensional projections of the X block are constructed in which the new dimensions well describes X and simultaneously they correlate with the class labels of the objects. In the following these projections will be referred to as PLS discriminant plots. The loading plot of the PLS projection gives direct information about the discrimination power of each variable. The number of significant dimensions is determined by investigating the predictive abilities of the model with a cross-validation technique.

PLS can be shown to converge towards multiple regression (MR) in the case with a single y-variable and $n > p$ (1) (n, number of objects and p number of variables in X). Here PLS is a regularized version of MR. Since linear discriminant analysis for a two class problem is equivalent to MR, the PLS discriminant plot is then a regularized linear discriminant plot. The advantage with PLS is that collinearities in X are handled by a projection which makes the method applicable even when $p > n$.

Use of PLS discriminant plots is illustrated with a multiclass problem in which the number of variables describing the samples is large compared to the number samples in each class. The PLS discriminant plots are compared with PC plots of the same problem.

CLASSIFICATION EXAMPLE

The twenty amino acids used in the genetic code can be divided into classes depending on how they are coded in the genetic synthesis. Four classes can be formed, depending on which one of the four bases, adenosine (A), uracil (U), cytosine (C) and guanine (G) is the coding base, in say, the second codon position. The "dummy matrix" in Table 1, in the following denoted Y, gives this class belonging of the amino acid.

A question of interest in molecular biology is if the physical and chemical properties of the amino acids are related to which base is used in a specific codon position in the genetic code. For a more comprehensive presentation of the data analytical problem, see ref. (2).

A matrix X with 20 chemical and physical variables (see (2)) was compiled for the amino acids. It was necessary to include many variables to at least partly describe as many aspects of the amino acids as possible. We note that from chemical point of view many variables should be included. In contrast, the number of objects (amino acids) in each class can not be increased due to the fact that only the twenty listed amino acids are coded in the genetic code. A listing of the data-set is published elsewhere (3).

PLS DISCRIMINANT PLOTS

The PLS model has been developed by H. Wold and co-workers (1), (4)-(6). The PLS algorithm is presented below.

We have a (n x p) matrix X and a (n x q) matrix Y. Here p and q are the number of variables in Y and X and n the number of objects. Notice that p and q also are used as model parameters below. X and Y are assumed to be appropriately scaled. When no prior information is available about the importance of the variables, this scaling is usually done by dividing each column by its standard deviation giving the standardized data with unit column variances. With the PLS method the X and Y are described by PC like models. First the mean values $\bar{x}$ and $\bar{y}$ of the variable columns are subtracted from X and Y. Then the first pair (a=1) of latent variables is estimated as in eqn. (1) and (2) and where the latent variables are related to each other in the regression step in eqn. (3). Notice that in the regression step, u is the dependent variable and t the independent variable.

$$X = \bar{x} + tp + E \qquad \text{eqn. (1)}$$

$$Y = \bar{y} + uq + F \qquad \text{eqn. (2)}$$

$$u = tb + d \qquad \text{eqn. (3)}$$

In the model the elements in E, F and d are the residuals after the first pairs of latent variables has been extracted from the data. Additional pairs (a=2, 3 ... A) of latent variables can then be estimated sequentially from E, which forms the new X block. The new Y block is formed from $Y - \bar{y} - tbq$. Thus the model parameters t (object scores) and p (the loadings) from the PLS model will be different from those of PC analysis. This is due to that in PLS the latent variables are determined to describe X as well as possible and simultaneously to correlate with the latent variables from the Y block. This is in contrast to the PC model where just the variance of E is minimized.

The significance of the a:th component is determined with a cross-validation technique. Some objects in X are deleted. From the remaining data set a new PLS model is calculated. The row vectors for the deleted objects are then fitted to the new model parameters $\bar{x}$ and p. This will give calculated t values for the deleted object and u values can be estimated as tb. From u and q predictions of y are obtained. The prediction errors of the deleted objects are then calculated and summed in square. The deleted objects are put back in the data and another part of the data is excluded, a new PLS model is calculated etc. This is repeated until the objects have been excluded once. In the present study one third of the data is deleted at a time. The squared sum of the prediction errors is then compared with the squared sum of the residuals in a model with a-1 components. For the details of the cross validation in PLS see ref. (1).

Once the number of significant components has been determined, the significant t vectors are plotted against each other as well as the p vectors. The t plot gives information of the relationships between the objects and the p plot gives information of the discriminating variables. New objects which form a test-set can be projected down on the new space by fitting the test-set objects to the model parameters $\bar{x}$ and p.

PLS algorithm

Scale and center X and Y.

1. Start t = first column in X.

2. q = t'Y/t't — q is a row vector of coefficients relating X to Y. t' is the transpose of t.

3. u = Yq'/qq'

4. w = Xu'/u'u — w is a row vector.

5. normalize $\|w\| = 1$

6. t = Xw' — Check or convergence. If convergence not is not reached return to 2. and use t from 6. This makes t be a eigenvector to XX'YY'.

7. p = t'X/t't — Loadings p.

8. E = X - tp
   F = Y - tbq — In the next dimension a+1 use E as X and F as Y. The column vectors t(a) are orthogonal to each other however not the row vectors p(a).

LEGENDS TO FIGURES

FIGURE 1.

PLS discriminant plot of the two first latent variables and based on all object. The same numbering of the objects is used as in Table 1 and the class-symbols are the following: class A, pentagons; class C, triangles; class G, hexagons and class U, diamonds. The U, C and A classes are encircled so the class structures can be found.

FIGURES 2(a)-(c).

PC object score plots for the three first PCs (denoted z(1), z(2) and z(3)) against each other. For notation see figure 1.

FIGURE 3.

PLS discriminant plot base on all objects except the (G) class (deleted objects 7, 10, 12 and 15). For notation see figure 1.

FIGURE 4.

Loading plot for the variables for the PLS model with the G class deleted. The most discriminating variables (1, 5, 13-17, 19 and 20) are on the periphery and the nonparticipating variables (4, 7, 8 and 11) are in the center of the plot.

FIGURE 1. PLS discriminant plot

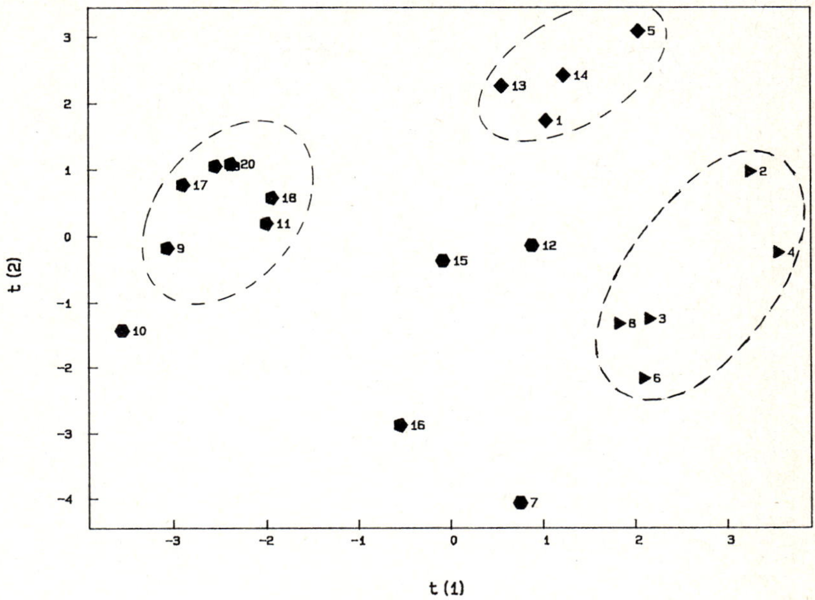

FIGURE 2 (a) . PC plot

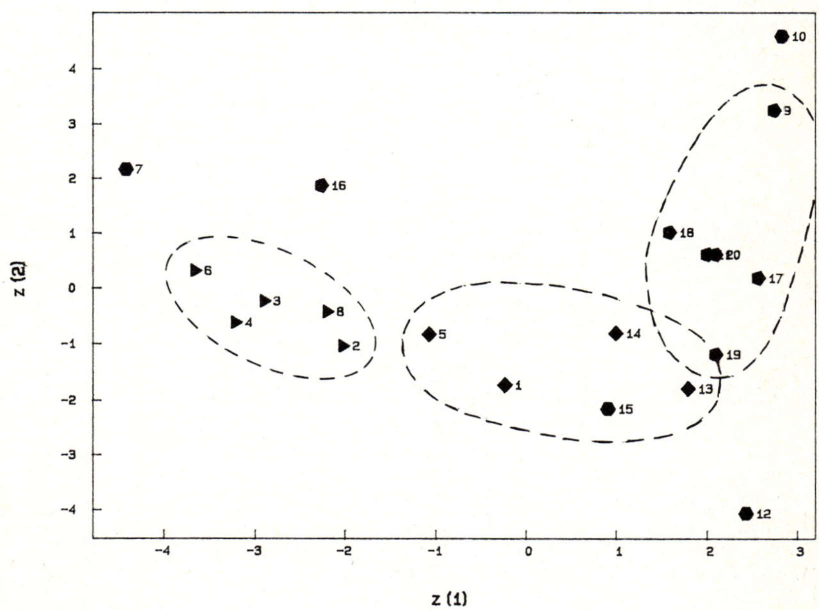

FIGURE 2(b). PC plot

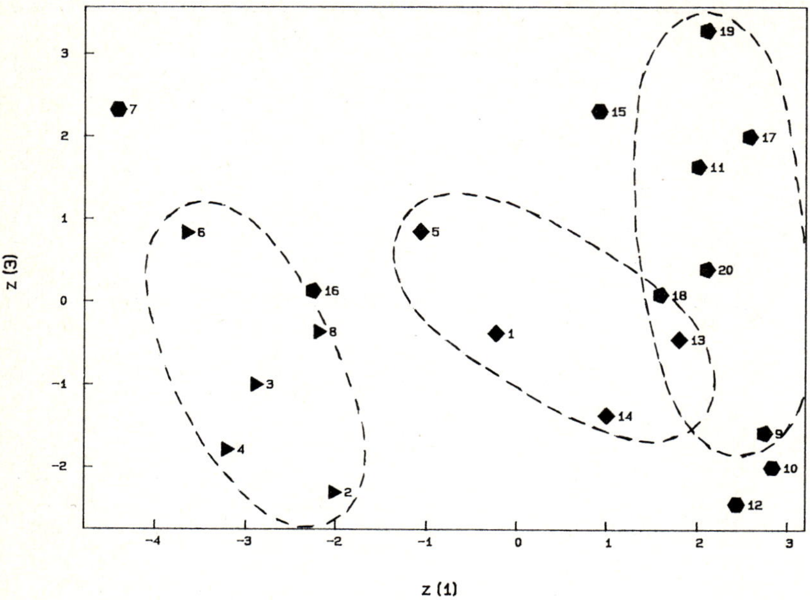

FIGURE 2(c). PC plot

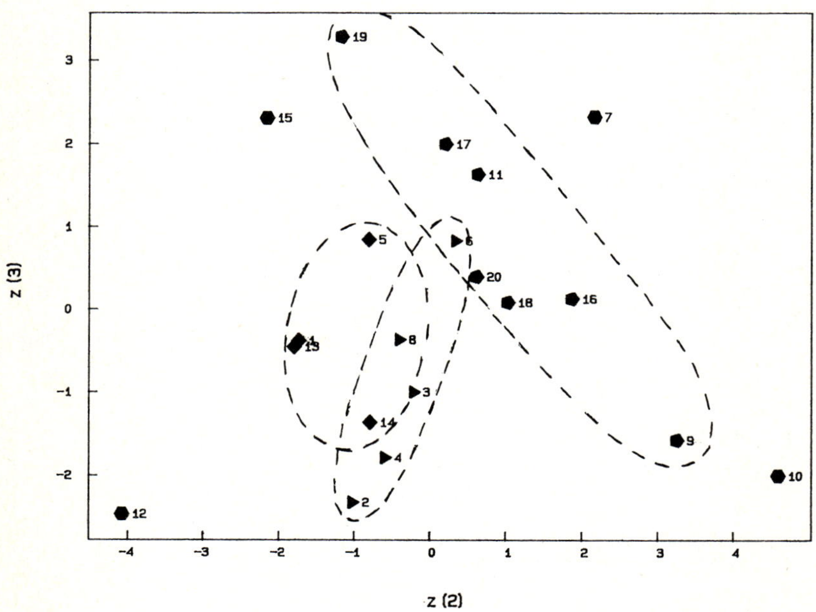

FIGURE 3. PLS discriminant plot

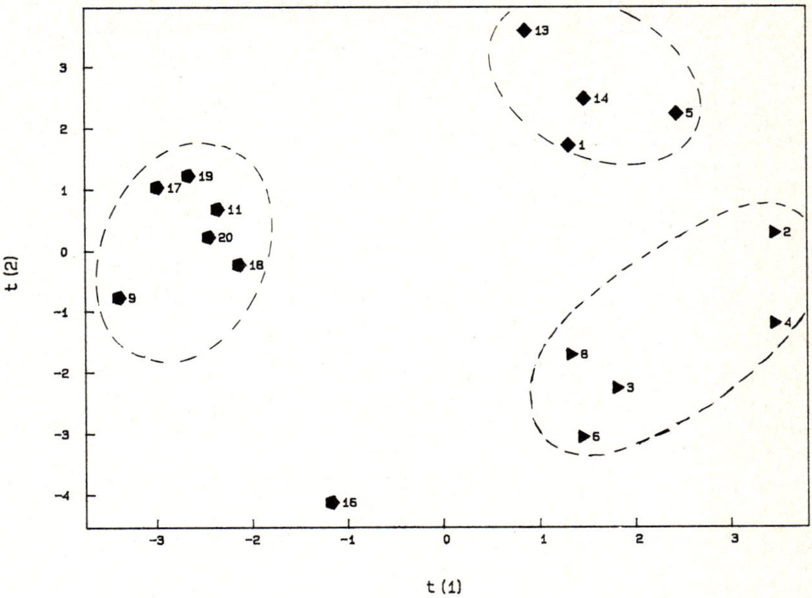

FIGURE 4. PLS loading plot

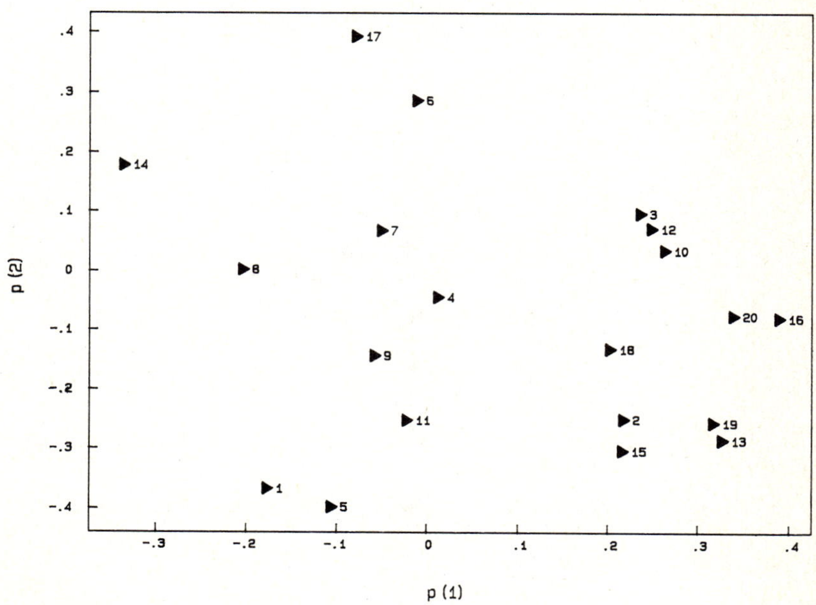

Table 1. Dummy matrix for the twenty coded amino acids and the object scores for the new dimensions estimated with PLS and PCA. The classes are described for the second codon position in the following way: 0,0,0 = uracil (U): 1,0,0 = cytosine (C): 0,1,0 = adenosine (A) and 0,0,1 = guanidine (G).

		Y	PLS		PCA				
i	amino-acids	class	t(i1)	t(i2)	z(i1)	z(i2)	z(i3)	z(i4)	z(i5)
1	Ala	1 0 0	1.03	1.73	-.23	-1.73	-.39	2.89	-1.84
2	Val	0 0 0	3.24	0.96	-2.03	-1.04	-2.33	-1.21	-.95
3	Leu	0 0 0	2.14	-1.24	-2.90	-.22	-1.00	1.79	-.53
4	Ile	0 0 0	3.54	-.25	-3.22	-.60	-1.79	-1.01	-.55
5	Pro	1 0 0	2.04	3.08	-1.07	-.82	.83	-1.68	-2.72
6	Phe	0 0 0	2.08	-2.18	-3.66	.33	.83	.19	.84
7	Trp	0 0 1	.75	-4.07	-4.42	2.16	2.32	.45	1.22
8	Met	0 0 0	1.81	-1.32	-2.20	-.41	-.38	.32	.55
9	Lys	0 1 0	-3.06	-.18	2.74	3.26	-1.58	.21	-.06
10	Arg	0 0 1	-3.55	-1.41	2.82	4.59	-2.00	-.16	.56
11	His	0 1 0	-2.00	.19	2.00	.62	1.63	-1.06	.74
12	Gly	0 0 1	.88	-.15	2.43	-4.07	-2.47	2.07	2.54
13	Ser$	1 0 0	.56	2.25	1.79	-1.80	-.45	-1.90	.49
14	Thr	1 0 0	1.23	2.41	1.00	-.79	-1.38	-2.64	-.52
15	Cys	0 0 1	-0.09	-.38	.91	-2.16	2.30	-1.89	1.91
16	Tyr	0 1 0	-.55	-2.88	-2.26	1.87	.12	.29	1.53
17	Asn	0 1 0	-2.89	.76	2.57	.20	2.00	1.05	-.21
18	Gln	0 1 0	-1.94	.58	1.58	1.03	.08	.67	-.71
19	Asp	0 1 0	-2.55	1.05	2.10	-1.18	3.27	.87	-1.07
20	Glu	0 1 0	-2.38	1.08	2.10	.61	.39	.72	-1.27

$ Serine can be coded with two different combinations in the second codon position: either the (U) class or the (G) class. In the PLS study serine is assigned to the (U) class.

Table 2. Loadings p(1k) and p(2k) from the PLS analysis with all objects and the variable residual variance ss(k) from X with A=2.

k$	p(1k)	p(2k)	ss(k)	k	p(1k)	p(2k)	ss(k)
1	-.13	-.40	.41	11	-.04	-.18	.99
2	.21	-.22	.70	12	.17	.10	.92
3	.21	.18	.75	13	.36	-.28	.05
4	-.10	-.11	1.02	14	-.35	.18	.32
5	-.12	-.38	.50	15	.23	-.32	.46
6	-.02	.18	1.0	16	.40	.05	.23
7	.05	.03	1.1	17	-.12	.43	.36
8	-.13	-.13	.95	18	.25	-.13	.70
9	-.05	-.07	1.09	19	.35	-.27	.16
10	.15	.08	.96	20	.36	-.07	.37

$ Variable index. For a listing of the variables see (2).

RESULTS AND DISCUSSION

Table 1 gives the scores (t(i1) and t(i2) for the two first latent variables and Table 2 the corresponding loadings. The variables that participate most to the model are 1, 5, 13 - 18 and 20 as seen from the size of the loadings and the variable residual variances. The object scores 1 (z(i1)-z(i5) for five first PCs are listed in Table 1.

In figures 2(a) - (c) pairwise plots are shown of the three first PCs. The plots reveal that three classes are grouped and have typical class-structures. However the classes are not perfectly separated from each other in the two dimensional PC plots. An outlier seems to be present in class A (object 16). The fourth class (G) shows no grouping of the amino acids. If the two dimensional plots are merged to a three dimensional plot three separated classes are seen ((U), (C) and (A)) and the fourth class shows no class structure. Tyrosine (no. 16) is an outlier to the (A) class in this projection.

Figure 1 is the PLS discriminant plot of the two first latent variables from the X-block. In the cross-validation none of the latent variables were significant. In the plot three of the classes are grouped and separated, but not the fourth class (G). The insignificance of the latent variables was probably due to the asymmetric structure of the G class. The analysis was repeated without the G class and now two highly significant latent variables were obtained. The plot of these two latent variables are shown in figure 3. In this plot the three classes are well separated from each other. Object 16 is still an outlier to the A class as in the PC plots (figure 2(a)-(c)).

Figure 4 is the variable loading plot for the PLS model based on 16 objects. In the plot the most discriminating variables are found on the periphery and the variables that make a small or no contribution to the discrimination are close to the center of the plot.

The information content in the PC and PLS scores was also compared by regressing the three and five first PC upon the PLS latent variables. The three first PC left 25% of the variance in t(1) and t(2) unexplained. The main contributing variables were z(1) and z(2). If the five first PC (z(1)-z(5) were regressed upon t(1) and t(2) only 2% the variance in t(1) and t(2) was unexplained and the main contributing variables were z(1), z(2) and z(5). This shows that with PLS, information of importance for the classification can be extracted from the X block and where this information is modelled by the two first PLS latent variables; information that not necessarily is modelled by the major PCs.

PLS discriminant plots have the advantage over PC plots in that they give a better illustration of the separation of the classes with low dimensional plots. PLS has the same properties as PCA analysis and thus PLS can be applied with confidence also on data sets with few samples compared to the number of variables. This as long as cross-validation is used to determine the number of significant components.

As demonstrated in the present case PLS discriminant plots can be informative even if cross-validation gives no significant latent variables. The insignificance of the components can be due to an asymmetric class structure of one of the classes. This can be confirmed by deleting the class as in the present case and repeating the projection.

The PLS algorithm is simple to implement on microcomputers. In the case of a two class problem the algorithm is noniterative and for multiclass problems the algorithm converge fast compared to iterative PC algorithms.

ACKNOWLEDGEMENTS

We are grateful for financial support from the Swedish Natural Science Research Council (NFR).

REFERENCES

1. Wold, S., Ruhe, A., Wold, H. and Dunn III, W. J., SIAM J. Sci. Stat. Comput. 5 (1984) 735 - 743.

2. Sjöström, M. and Wold, S., J. Molec. Evol. in press.

3. Hellberg, S., Sjöström, M. and Wold, S., Acta Chem. Scand. B, in press.

4. Wold, H. in System under Indirect Observation Vol I and II (eds Jöreskog, K. G. and Wold, H.) (North Holland, Amsterdam, 1982).

5. Wold, S. et al., Multivariate analysis in chemistry, in: Kowalski, B. R. (ed.), Chemometrics, Mathematics and Statistics in Chemistry, NATO ASI series, Series C: Mathematical and Physical Sciences, Vol 138 (Reidel Publishing Company, Dordrecht 1984)

6. Wold, S., Martens, H. and Wold, H., The Multivariate Calibration Problem in Chemistry solved by the PLS Method, in: Ruhe, A and Kågström B. (eds.), Proc. Conf. Matrix Pencils, Lecture Notes in Mathematics (Springer Verlag, Heidelberg 1983). 286-293.

DISCUSSION

Toussaint:
How does your algorithm compare with discriminant analysis techniques for the multiple class problem?

Sjostrom:
The relationship to multiclass LDA has not been thouroughly investigated.

Verbeek:
What role plays the scaling of the y-variables in this problem?

Sjostrom:
This doesn't play a role since you normalize your data including the class labelling information.

PATTERN RECOGNITION IN PRACTICE II
E.S. Gelsema and L.N. Kanal (Editors)

THE USE OF PATTERN RECOGNITION IN ORDER TO IMPROVE FAST NUCLEAR REACTOR MONITORING

B. Dubuisson*, P. Malvache**, D. Grenier*

* University of Compiegne, U.A. 817, G.I., B.P. 233, 60206 COMPIEGNE CEDEX, FRANCE

** CEA Cadarache, DRNR/SPCI/LMIN B.P. 4, 13108 ST PAUL LEZ DURANCE Cédex, France

Use of Pattern Recognition methodology has improved the monitoring system of a fast nuclear reactor. Decisions can become more sharp and so knowledge of the phenomena more complete. This paper presents the modifications introduced in pattern recognition methodologies in order to solve this real problem.

1. CHRONOLOGICAL ACCOUNT OF STUDIES

The problem of introducing Pattern Recognition methodologies in a computer-aided monitoring system for nuclear reactors has been studied for more than 10 years. At the beginning, men in charge of this problem simply wondered if these methodologies could increment the accuracy of existing systems. Of course nuclear reactors were well monitored by classical approaches such as signal processing, thresholding, ..., but it seems to men in charge of studies that more information can be extracted from observed signals. So as an experiment some research was initialized in 1975 (B. Dubuisson (1980)) between our University and the French Atomic Agency (Commissariat à l'Energie Atomique, CEA) on this problem.

At this time only classical situations or simulated ones were studied. We tried to use recorded signals corresponding to different situations or states of the reactor heart. This simple demand gave birth to some important problems. In fact a nuclear reactor is always working in a normal state or very near to it. So nobody has recorded data corresponding to an unclassical state or abnormal one. So first work was done on data recorded during simulated experiments or experiments done on an experimental reactor. The aim of these studies was to prove that a pattern recognition approach can improve the information extracted from the signals (as first study, at our knowledge, of R.C. Gonzalez (1974)).
First experiments were successful in sense that detection of an abnormal simulated state was done with a small value of estimated error probability.

1.1. Representation problem

The first problem to solve was a representation one : how to define a vector from a sampled signal ? Many solutions are possible and according to our knowledge no general solution exists : the kept solution is often the result of an arbitrary choice. The only proposed solution is the following. Suppose that recorded signals were issued from two different classes corresponding to two different states of the observed system. Choose a vector representation in R^d and apply a clustering algorithm on your data set. If the solution is a compound of two classes, whatever algorithm is used,(the chosen parameter and initial partition), one can say that the representation you used is a realistic one because the most important information (class information) is kept in memory. This solution is unrealistic because nobody can try all the existing clustering algorithms. A possible solution is to look at the stability of the solution when using a competitive clustering algorithm (E. Diday (1979)): one can think a representation is adapted if the class information a priori known about the learning set is kept in the solution proposed by a clustering algorithm. This problem of representation is an important one and our experience has convinced us that the best one can only be found after analysis of the problem with an expert man, that is a man who is in charge of the problem.

1.2. First results

In this first step of our study, after a choice of a vector representation we used classical pattern recognition methodologies (K. Fukunaga (1972)) such as linear discrimination or k nearest neighbor rules. As indicated before results were so good that it was decided to continue this study and to consider the possibility of a real time system working on the reactor heart.

The same questions as at the beginning of this study arise : how is it possible to detect system states (classes) for which no learning set exists. Because simulated experiments cannot be sufficient, we proposed to do experiments on a real reactor. This solution was not accepted because of security reasons. All the classical pattern recognition approach is based on either a knowledge of classes statistical properties or the existence of a learning set (each class being described by some representative samples). So developments have be done on the problems of :

1) discrimination when knowledge is not complete

2) increase of knowledge when new information from classes is obtained

These two developments have been done using on the one hand a classification based on a membership function or the method proposed by Chow (1969) and on the other hand a clustering algorithm updating the learning set.

2. DETECTION WITH INCOMPLETE KNOWLEDGE

We do not develop a method based on the Chow approach and the gaussian hypothesis on the probability law of classes : it is indicated in A. Smolarz (1984). We simply give in this paper a recall of a distance method based on the fuzzy approach (Bedzek (1981)). Using the fuzzy concept of classification, the criterion for a given vector to be put into a class is no longer 1 or 0 but a value in the range $[0,1]$ and called the membership factor. It is computed from the distance between vector $\underline{x}$ to be classified into M known classes and a present reference in the space as :

$$\mu(\underline{x}) = \frac{1}{1+d(\underline{x},\underline{R})}$$

Other membership factors have been studied, we do not develop them in this paper. In our case the references are M pre-defined classes C_i, the ith class being represented by a kernel of n_i vectors ; and the calculation of $\mu_i(\underline{x})$, membership factor of $\underline{x}$ for the ith class is :

$$\mu_i(\underline{x}) = \frac{1}{1+D(\underline{x},C_i)} \qquad i=1,M$$

with

$$D(\underline{x},C_i) = \frac{1}{n_i}\Big[\sum_{j=i}^{n_i} \frac{(\underline{x}-\underline{R}_{ij})^t(\underline{x}-\underline{R}_{ij})}{\sigma_i}\Big]^{1/2}$$

when using normalized Euclidian distance

or

$$D(\underline{x},C_i) = \frac{1}{n_i}\Big[\sum_{j=1}^{n_i} [(\underline{x}-\underline{R}_{ij})^t\, \Sigma_i^{-1}\, (\underline{x}-\underline{R}_{ij})]\Big]^{1/2}$$

when using the Mahalanobis distance.

R_{ij} is the jth vector of the kernel C_i

σ_i is the standard deviation for class C

Σ_i is the covariance matrix of class i

The set of vectors R_{ij} for each class can be a predefined set (kernel for example obtained by applying a dynamic clustering algorithm) or a variable one (it can be built with the n_i nearest neighbors of $\underline{x}$ in class C_i). In this way any new vector may be provided with as many membership factors as there exist preidentified classes in the reference set.

In our case this self training procedure initiates by itself in the case where the number of preidentified classes is one. This class corresponds to the normal state of the system, generally all the knowledge one has. Then any current vector is completely defined by only one membership factor.

A preliminary analysis is done on the learning set, that is on the only class one knows. It enables to provide a threshold for this factor leading to a twofold decision :

If $\mu(\underline{x}) > A$ the vector is said to be an element of the known class
$\mu(\underline{x}) < A$ the vector is said to be from a new class, not known at this time, and is stored in a memory

When a sufficient number of such unclassified vectors is available, they are added to the initial reference set and a clustering algorithm is applied. At this time one or more new classes can appear meaning that the initial description was not sufficient. A new computation at the learning step gives threshold for the new identified classes. This procedure is more completely described in A. Smolarz (1984) so we do not give here more details.

A full sketch of the procedure can be described as follows :

Stage 1 (analysis of recorded signals)
1) signals recording
2) vector representation
3) decision and storage of rejected vectors
4) go to step 1

Stage 2 (learning of rejected vectors)
1) clustering rejected vectors
2) updating learning sets (classes and threshold classes)

A sophisticated procedure has also be used introducing two thresholds A_1, A_2 for each class :

if $\mu(\underline{x}) > A_1$ the vector is associated to the class and a membership factor is computed
if $\mu(\underline{x}) < A_2$ the vector is said to be of an abnormal state (class of abnormalities)
if $A_2 < \mu(\underline{x}) < A_1$ the vector is rejected.

An application of the aboves principles has been built around a small HP 85 desk computer on Phenix reactor (M. Brunet (1984)). For tests of the method only one set of 12 signals recorded is processed by this system. The vector representation used the Power Spectral Density computed on the signal.

It is obvious that sophisticated algorithms such as that of the learning phase or the clustering one are not available on such a small computer. Actually the very first samples are only stored on a floppy disk and this information is transferred on a VAX computer and processed in on off-line mode. The 50 first samples are taken as the initial reference set and the learning step sets the parameter for the decision procedure.

Four types of membership factors are computed :

- two of them using the normalized Euclidian distance, the reference being either the complete learning set, or its centre of gravity
- two others based on the Mahalanobis distance using the same choice of references. The calculation taking into account the full set of reference vectors represents about 80% of the total computing time.

We can now give some information about the first results. A comparison between the computed membership (on line) and the known (a posteriori) physical situation shows that the distance computed from the "mean" vector using the Euclidian distance leads to a ratio of 10% misclassification while the others three remain in the range of less than 2%. In fact the shape of the multivariate distribution function is taken into account by the two last procedures.

A statistical study of the membership values (for 4000 vectors) has shown that if a limit of 0.1 is taken to reject vectors from a given reference class, the number of missclassifications is less than 3%, this ratio falling to 0.1% when the limit is lowered to 0.05.

A clustering calculation performed on the rejected vectors exhibits the existence of a second normal class which was taken into account via a further learning calculation. Since then and up to now the rejection rate has fallen to 0.5%, the rejected vectors (from both normal classes) being in fact in the alarm state.

This instrument of Phenix is considered as a test bench for further applications, one of which being the surveillance of Super Phenix.

3. DETECTION OF EVOLVING STATES

Another problem of concern was about the detection of evolving classes. In fact in physical systems the observation vector does not proceed suddenly from one state (class) to another one, except where an incident happens. Often one observes an evolution from one class to another and it is interesting for the man who is in charge of the system because an alert can be given if the evolution is turned to an abnormal state. A solution is given in M. Usaī (1984) but with experience this solution has not been a source of great satisfaction to operators. So we propose a new solution which has been tried out on a water reactor during a study for E.D.F. (France Electricity Agency).

This method is based on the potential function defined by Mizoguchi-Shimura (1980). We define the potential induced by a class on any point of the space. Two steps are needed

1) in a first step one calculates a weighting function at every point
2) in a second step one analyses the different potential functions induced by the different known classes.

Let x_i (i=1,n) be the set of points of one class (we consider at this time only one class). Let $\underline{X}_i(1)$ (1=1,k) be the k nearest neighbors of the observed vector $\underline{x}_i$. The weighting function of $\underline{x}$ is defined by a vector $\underline{w}$

$$\underline{w}^t = (w_1 \dots w_n)$$

$$w_i = \frac{1}{k} \sum_{1=1}^{k} d(\underline{x}_i, x_{i1})$$

d(.,.) is a distance function defined in the observation space.

Parameter k is an average factor related to the sensitivity of the weighting functions. We define also the mean variation of the weighting function of a point x_i by

$$D_i = D(x_i) = \frac{1}{k} \sum_{1=1}^{k} (w(\underline{x}_i) - w(\underline{x}_{i1}))$$

The value D_i represents the variation of the "density" (not in the sense of probability density) on an area adjusted around the point x_i.
With these two functions we can define what we call the potential P(Y) at any point Y in the observation space by

$$P(Y) = \underset{i=1,n}{\mathrm{Min}} \left(W(\underline{X}_i) + D(\underline{X}_i) \frac{d^2(\underline{X}_i, \underline{Y})}{W^2(\underline{X}_i)} \right)$$

This function has been introduced after mathematical consideration on local continuity. This property is checked in the majority of cases. This function is similar to a membership function introduced in the beginning of this paper. With this definition we accurately determine geometrical areas corresponding to the known classes : each cluster can be surrounded by an equipotential surface corresponding to a fixed value of potential (the potential function is minimum near the gravity center of the class).

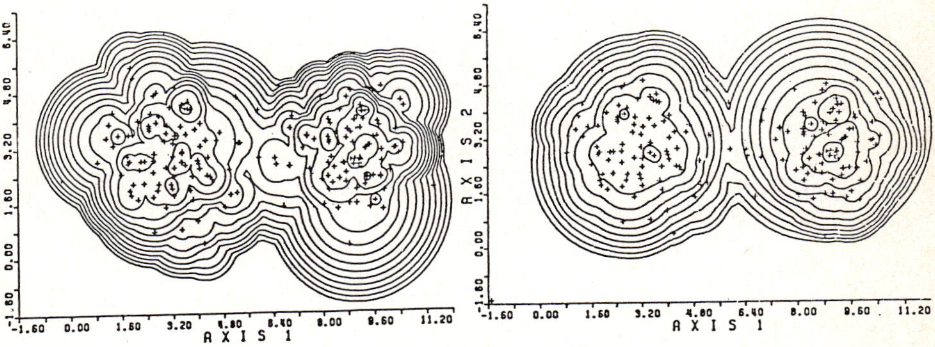

Fig 1 : Equipotential curves obtained for k=4 (left figure) k=10 (right figure) on a simulated 2-dimension set.

The results given in Fig 1 are obtained with a simulated data set with 180 points issued from two gaussian populations. In this simulation k takes the values 4 and 10.

This function can be used in order to cluster data points. As indicated by the solution given in Fig 1, two modes are exhibited. By a threshold on P(Y) one can determine clusters ; we do not develop this possibility in this paper and suppose we have classes being determined by the potential function or by another algorithm.

Now we determine the kernel points of each class: the kernel of a class is made up of points lying inside the curves corresponding to the threshold potential. This threshold is chosen so the number of equipotential curves is equal to the chosen number of modes. These points are representative for each class. Then we can build new equipotential curves related to each cluster (Fig 2).

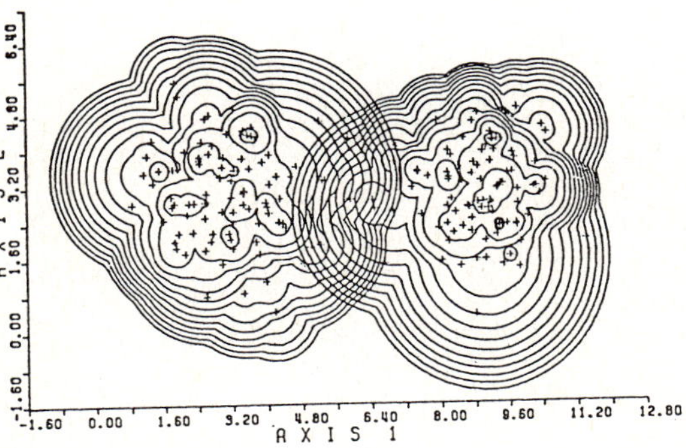

Fig 2 : Equipotential curves considering 2 classes in the previous simulated data set.

So when a new point Y is to be analysed we compute the value of its potential regarding each class. So with each point is associated a potential vector $\underline{P}(Y)^t = (P_1(Y \ldots P_M(Y))$. $P_i(Y)$ is the value of its potential considering the ith class (computed with kernel points of this class). So this function can also be used to classify a point : a point is associated to the class corresponding to the smallest component of $\underline{P}$-Y).

More interesting is the case where we can use it for detecting evolutions. let $P_e(\underline{Y})$ the minimum of $P_i(\underline{Y})$ (i=1,M, number of known classes). If $P_e(Y) > P_o$ $\underline{Y}$ belongs to the set of evolving points from class 1 which is the reference class for $\underline{Y}$. P_o is a threshold previously fixed for each class set. Labelling of such points can be obtained after a set of new points has been considered. Evolving points can correspond to different geometrical situations. Fig 3 gives the different cases.

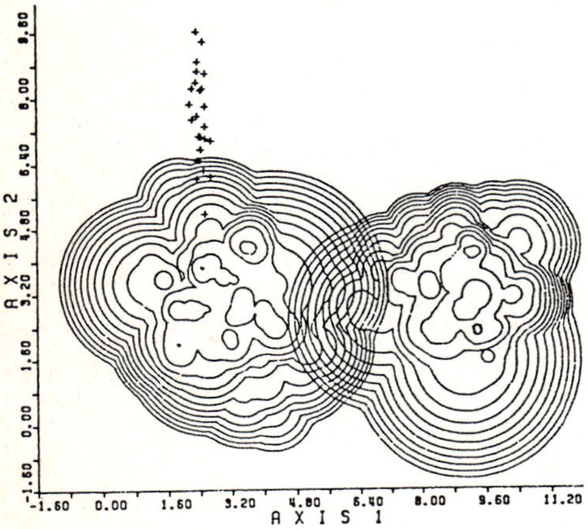

Fig 3.a : Points go from a class to another new one.

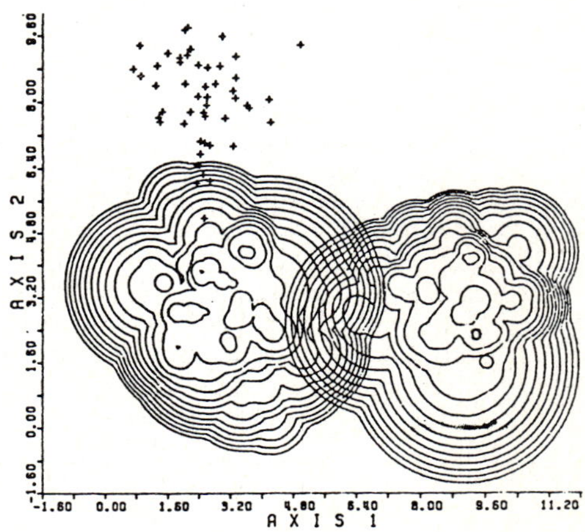

Fig 3.b : A new class is generated.

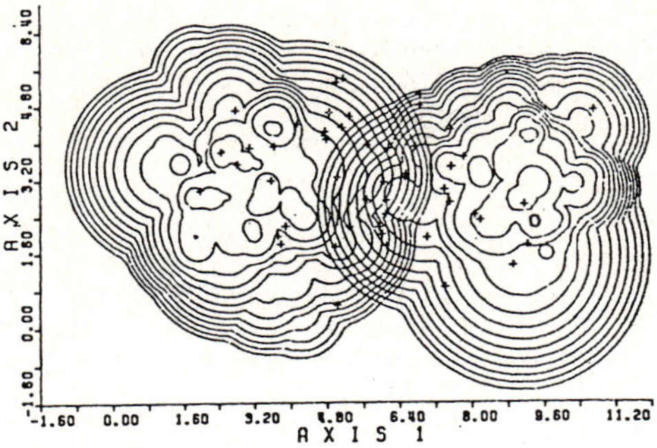

Fig 3.c : Two classes have to be merged

We have simulated different situations : a point can go from a class to another, a new class can be generated or two classes can merge . The analysis of evolution is done using the potential function. For each group of l observed points we compute the potential function regarding each class. So we have a matrix P

$$P = \{P_{ij}\} \qquad i=1,l \qquad j=1,n$$

For analysis we study the potential variations represented by the matrix DP

$$DP = \{DP_{ij}\} = P_{i-1,j} - P_{ij} \qquad i=2,l \qquad j=1,m$$

With these two sets of parameters we can fix rules for the analysis of evolution. This set of decision rules has been represented by an automaton. As an example all the cases of figure 3 are detected and explained (l=7 and M=2 are fixed in this example). The paper (D. Grenier (1986)) will give more details on these rules.

This method has also been tested on real examples.

CONCLUSION

The work we have done on this complex problem has given some interesting results. A pattern recognition method is now implemented on line on a nuclear reactor and gives excellent results. In fact two methods are implemented, one is based on a gaussian hypothesis and a second one based on a non-parametric approach. After studying the results we have been convinced of the fact that class membership is not sufficient, one needs detection of evolving states. So we proposed another complementary method . A first test seems very interesting.

At this time everything considered, only quantitative information has been analysed. Complementary information is also furnished by the men who are in charge of the reactor along day and night, the operators. Their knowledge is very important and has to be considered. So we are now working on a complete system, schema of which is given in Figure 4.

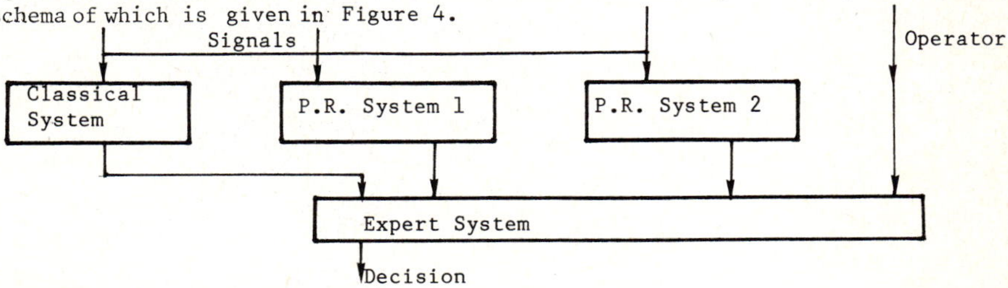

Fig 4 : General Schema of the Future System

This system is now studied : the problem lies in getting the exact knowledge operators have. After this system will have been constructed the possible information could be used for monitoring a nuclear reactor system.

REFERENCES

[1] Bezdek, Pattern Recognition with Fuzzy Objective Function Algorithms (Plenum Press, 1981).
[2] Brunet, M., Usaï, M., Malvache, P., and Buravand , Y., The Pattern Recognition Instrument as an Efficient Tool in the Field of the Permanent Surveillance of a Fast Reacor Core, SMORN IV Congress, Dijon (1984).
[3] Chow, C.L., An Optimum Recognition Error and Reject Trade-Off, IEEE Trans. On Information Theory, 1, IT 16, (1967).
[4] Diday, E., and al., Optimisation en Classification Automatique, INRIA (1979).
[5] Dubuisson B., and Lavison P., Surveillance of a Nuclear Reactor by Use of a Pattern Recognition Methodology, IEEE Trans. on Systems, Man & Cybernetics, SMC 10, (1980), 603-609
[6] Fukunaga K., Introduction to Statistical Pattern Recognition, (Academic Press, 1972).
[7] Gonzalez, R.C., Fry, D.N. and Kryter, R.C., Results in the Application of Pattern Recognition Methods to Nuclear Component Surveillance, IEEE Trans. on Nuclear Science, NS 21, 1, 750-756.
[8] Grenier D., Dubuisson, B., and Jacquot, M., Une Approche par Apprentissage et Reconnaissance des Formes du Suivi de Fonctionnement de Systèmes Technologiques, accepted for AFCET Congrès Automatique (1986)
[9] Mizoguchi, R. and Shimura, M., A non Parametric Algorithm for Detecting Clusters Using Hierarchical Structures, IEEE trans. on Pattern Analysis and Machine Intelligence, 2, July (1980).
[10] Smolarz, A., Usaï, M., and Dubuisson, B., A Distance Based Classification Method Using an Incomplete Training Set, Pattern Recognition Letters, 2, (1984), 355-364.
[11] Usaï, M., and Dubuisson, B., An Adaptative Non Parametric Classification Algorithm Whichan Incomplete Learning Set, 7th Int. Conf. on Patt. Recogn., Montréal, (1984).

DISCUSSION

Nagy:

How sensitive are the states that you have observed to the order in which you obtain the points and how explicitly do you take the sequence into account in your algorithm? There is surely some time correlation here.

Dubuisson:

The detection of an evolution is done after the last five measured points and, of course, correlation between these points is implicitly used.

Persoon:

How long have the operational systems been running?

Dubuisson:

Two and a half years.

Persoon:

And how many new classes have been detected in the course of time?

Dubuisson:

Ten classes, spread over this 2 years period.

Mayall:

Can you relate the 10 "normal" states of the reactor to the physical conditions of the reactor or are they just PR classes.

Dubuisson:

Finding a relation between the states and the conditions of the reactor can only be done when the reactor is stopped. When the reactor is "opened" we can physically inspect the situation.

Mayall:

And the interpretations agree with your classification?

Dubuisson:

At this time, yes.

Van Bemmel:

I see many parallels with an area I am working in which is patient care, the monitoring of patients and patient screening. It is my experience that unless you know something about the disease states you cannot say whether a patient is normal or not. I think this must be your major problem. Could you solve that by looking at some minor changes you might superimpose on the behaviour of the reactor to test it? I think when you look closer at those trends you assume to be present they all will appear to be stationary or gradually evolving. When I look at many technical systems and patients, and maybe reactors too, when something goes wrong it all happens all of a sudden. A valve breaks down, a wire breaks or a reactor explodes or things like that.

Dubuisson:

The states we did detect are not accident states, they are, for instance, induced by evaluation of mechanical or other physical parameters. When there is a big accident such as you think of, you have security and the reactor stops immediately. We are only interested in monitoring.

PATTERN RECOGNITION IN PRACTICE II
E.S. Gelsema and L.N. Kanal (Editors)

PRESENT STATUS OF ISPAHAN APPLICATIONS AT THE UNIVERSITY OF ROME (ITALY).

A. Bietti(+) (++), A. Burani(+++), L. Zanello(++)

(+) - Dept. of Animal and Human Biology, Sect. of Anthropology, University of Rome I.
(++)- Dept. of Physics, University of Rome I.
(+++)- S.O.G.E.I., V. Carucci 99, Rome.

In this paper we will describe the applications of the interactive Pattern Recognition system ISPAHAN obtained since 1982 on the D.E.C. VAX 11/780 computer of the National Institute of Nuclear Physics (INFN) at the University of Rome. The main field of investigation was in prehistoric Archaeology. ISPAHAN was used for typological studies of Paleolithic flint artifacts, for the chronological and cultural classification of the Italian upper Paleolithic assemblages, for the study of the chemical composition of prehistoric bronzes in the Middle-East region, and for the possible detection of "patterns" of social structures for an early Iron age cemetery in Latium. We will present in addition some results in Physics: the application of ISPAHAN to a series of events coming from gravitational antennae, and to the study of recognition of nuclear tracks in solid state detectors for dosimetry.

I - INTRODUCTION

The interactive Pattern recognition system ISPAHAN, created by E.S. Gelsema at the department of Medical Informatics at the University of Amsterdam on a D.E.C. PDP 11 - 34, was quickly implemented on a large series of computers in various Universities and Istitutions all over Europe.

In particular, during the spring of 1982, a version of it was installed on the D.E.C. VAX 11/780 computer of the National Institute of Nuclear Physics by one of us (L.Z.) and by E.S. Gelsema.

At that time we were mainly interested in the system for potential applications in prehistoric archaeology (Bietti, and Zanello, 1980): its structure and capabilities (see fig.1) largely illustrated for biomedical research (Gelsema, 1980, 1981) seemed particularly suited for the type of problems which actually arise in Archaeology, and especially in Prehistory: classificatory patterns, both unsupervised and supervised, univariate and multivariate statistical procedures, etc.

The first application was in fact, a study of two assemblages of end-scrapers coming from two sites of the late Italian upper Paleolithic, in order to obtain a reasonable typological classification of these artifacts (Bietti et al., 1983).

The range of archaeological applications has been widened in the last two years, as we will see in the next section, where some examples shown are also dealing with more recent phases of Prehistory: Bronze age and early Iron age. At the same time, some interest on the characteristics and the possibilities of ISPAHAN aroused also amongst some groups of physicists.

A first example, part of the thesis of one of us (A.Bu.) on the ISPAHAN System was provided by the analysis of a series of events coming from gravitational antennae. As a second example, quite recently, we have tried to analyze tracks in a plastic detector caused by α-rays coming from indoor radon radioactivity in order to separate properly the events from the spurious background.

As we shall see, the ISPAHAN options employed are essentially the same used

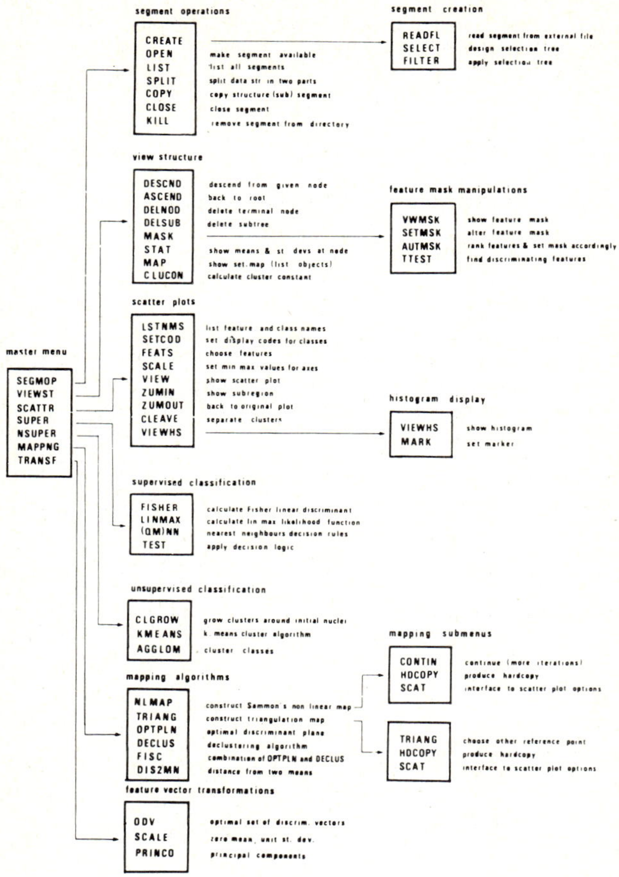

Fig. 1 - ISPAHAN Structure and options (from Gelsema(1980)).

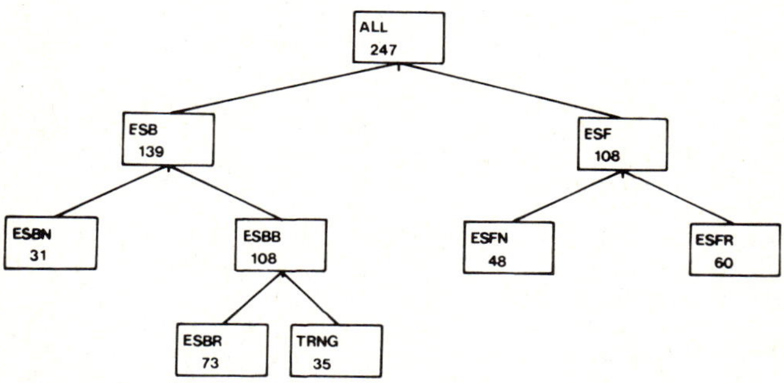

Fig. 2 - Tentative tree-structure for the end-scrapers of Grotta Polesini.

for the archaeological applications, but with different expectations and outcomes.

The archaeological applications, as we said before, will be described in the next section, while the third section will be devoted to a short outline of the applications in physics.

II - APPLICATIONS IN PREHISTORIC ARCHAEOLOGY.

II - 1. Typological classification of some upper Paleolithic end-scrapers.

This was the first application of ISPAHAN done at the University of Rome, (Bietti et al., 1983), so that we will only briefly summarize of the results of the analysis. Two assemblages of end-scrapers were considered: one coming from Grotta Romanelli in Southern Apulia (dated to about 11.000 years B.P.) and the other from Grotta Polesini in Latium (dated to about 10.000 years B.P.). Taking for example, Grotta Polesini we have considered a sample of 247 end-scrapers (layer A1) and a tentative tree-structure is given in fig.2. The two intermediate nodes ESF and ESB represent two classes distinguished by the type of "piece support": flakes (ESF) and blades (ESB), i.e. elongated flakes regularly chipped with almost parallel sides.

The presence or absence of complementary retouches for the end-scrapers on flake has been taken into account at the terminal nodes ESFR and ESFN respectively, and for the blades and the node ESBN (without complementary retouch) and ESBB (with complementary retouch). This last node has been further subdivided in end-scrapers with parallel sides (ESBR) and with convergent sides (TRNG, the so-called triangular end-scrapers).

Every end-scraper is characterized by six features: length, width, thickness, curvature of the front contour of the end-scraper, asymmetry of the front contour, and triangularity of the end-scraper. For the proper definition of these features see Bietti and Zanello, 1980, fig.5.

The tree structure in fig.2 corresponds more or less to a traditional qualitative subdivision of types, as is customarily used by the archaeologists (for one of these subdivisions see, for instance, Bietti and Zanello, 1980, fig.2).

The aim of our analysis was then to perform some statistical test in order to check the validity of this tree-structure.

First a t-test was done, at 99% confidence level, using the appropriate option in the MASK submenu of fig.1. The result (Bietti et al., 1983, Table 1, p.185) is that at the node ESB the triangular end-scrapers (TRNG) are separated from the ones with (ESBR) and without (ESBN) complementary retouch by the same three diagnostic features: length, thickness and triangularity, where <u>only</u> the width is diagnostic between the two classes ESBN and ESBR.

On the other hand, concerning the end-scrapers on flake (node ESF) only the curvature is diagnostic. Another interesting result is that the asymmetry of the front contour is never a diagnostic feature.

A principal component analysis did not reveal significant separation between the various classes, while the mapping algorithms (Gelsema and Eden, 1980) provided a better distinction. In particular, as compared to other classes, the triangular end-scrapers seem to be well separated from the ones on retouched blade, both using the FISC algorithm (Bietti et al., 1983, fig.6) and the DIS2MN (fig.3).

The same algorithm (fig.4) used for the two classes ESFN and ESFR, does not show any clear separation between the two classes, also in agreement with the results of the t-test.

It is then clear that the traditional typological classification may be seriously questioned by those results (the triangular end-scrapers seem to be the only ones distinguishable from a quantitative point of view).

Further work on these tools of Grotta Polesini is in progress, and, taking for instance the end-scrapers of the layer A1 as a learning set, we will try an application of the algorithms of supervised classification (see fig.1) on the end-scrapers of other layers of this site.

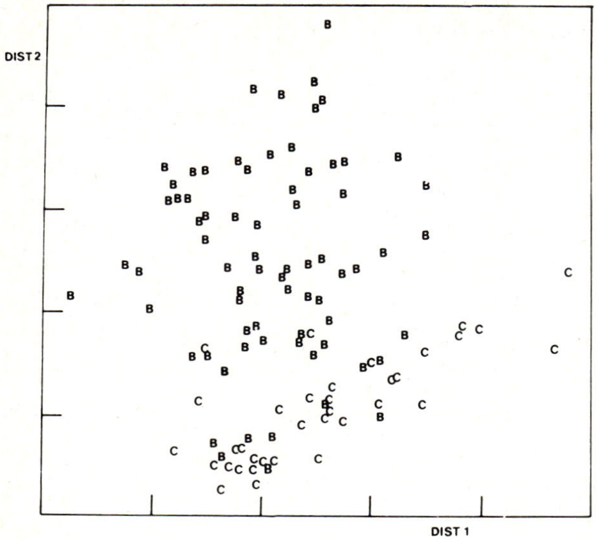

Fig. 3 - Scatterplot for the classes ESBR (B) and TRNG) (C) of the tree-structure given in fig.2, according to the mapping algorithm DIS2MN.

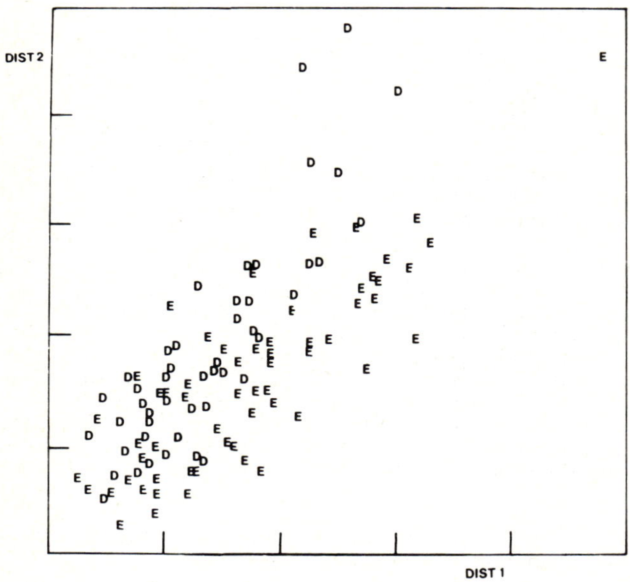

Fig. 4 - Same as in fig.3 for the classes ESFN (D) and ESFR (E).

II - 2 - Chronological and/or cultural classification of Continental Italian upper Paleolithic industrial assemblages.

This example deals with a tentative quantitative check of the traditional classification of the late Italian upper Paleolithic, the so-called Epigravettian, conventionally dated from about 20.000 to 10.000 years B.P.

From a qualitative point of view, it has been divided in three chronological phases (Laplace, 1964): "ancient", "evolved" and "final". This subdivision is maintained still by most Italian researchers, as it has been shown in a recent colloquium held at Siena (Palma di Cesnola, 1983), and it is essentially based on some "diagnostic" tools or groups of tools (percentages of end-scrapers, burins, etc.) which should provide not only the aforementioned chronological distinction, but also, for the "evolved" and "final" phases, regional differences: Northern Tyrrhenian, Middle and Southern Tyrrhenian, Northern and Middle Adriatic, Southern Adriatic zones.

On the basis of 124 sites (or layers of the same sites), traditionally classified, we have tried (Bietti and Burani, 1985) to verify quantitatively the "diagnostic" value (assigned "a priori" on qualitative grounds) of the tools (or groups of tools, or ratios between groups of tools) determined from the traditional classifications.

In fig.5 it is shown the "a priori" tree structure built on the latest results of the traditional classification (Palma di Cesnola, 1985): the node EPA represents the ancient Epigravettian which conventionally covers the period from about 20.000 B.P. to about 16.000 B.P., with the two terminal nodes EPGF (ancient Epigravettian "à foliacés") and EPGC (ancient Epigravettian "à crans"). The node EPEF represents the sites attributed to the evolved and final Epigravettian, divided in four geographical zones: Northern Tyrrhenian (EPNT), Northern Adriatic (EPNA), Southern Adriatic (EPSA) and Middle and Southern Tyrrhenian (EPS). For reasons of statistical consistency, only for the node EPS, it was possible to subdivide further the sites of the evolved (EPSE) and final (EPSF) Epigravettian ranging respectively (always by a conventional definition) from 16.000 to 14.000 B.P. and from 14.000 to 10.000 B.P. The features were 17, i.e. the percentages of tools (end-scrapers, burins, truncations, etc.) or the ratios between some tools (burins/ end-scrapers etc.) considered in the traditional classification presented at Siena (Palma di Cesnola, 1983).

We then applied the t-test and the stepwise discriminant analysis (the option AUTMSK in fig.1), and we found serious discrepancies between our quantitative results and the traditional qualitative ones (Bietti and Burani, 1985, Table 2-1, p. 19). As an example the circular end-scrapers are not diagnostic at the node ALL, even if they have always been considered characteristic of the final Epigravettian.

At the node EPA, the tanged ("à cran") tools are not diagnostic, even if one of the two terminal nodes (EPGC) has been named ancient Epigravettian "à crans"! The results of a principal component analysis (option PRINCO in fig.1) (the first six components account for about 92% of the total variance) are also in agreement with the ones obtained by the t-test and the stepwise discriminant analysis: in fig.6 one sees the plot of the sites along the two first principal axes. The three sites on the bottom, for instance, represent two layers of a site in Southern Apulia and a layer of a site in Liguria!

From these results, it is obvious that the traditional classification of the Late Italian Upper Paleolithic is highly questionable, and needs a serious rethinking.

II - 3 - Provenance studies on Middle-East bronzes.

A sample of 867 bronze objects from the Middle-East region has been given to us by M. Frangipane of the Institute of Palethnology of the University of Rome.

The aim of the research is to detect diagnostic features in the composition of the alloy, in order to ascertain clusters of chemical elements for a regional and/ or chronological distinction between various zones.

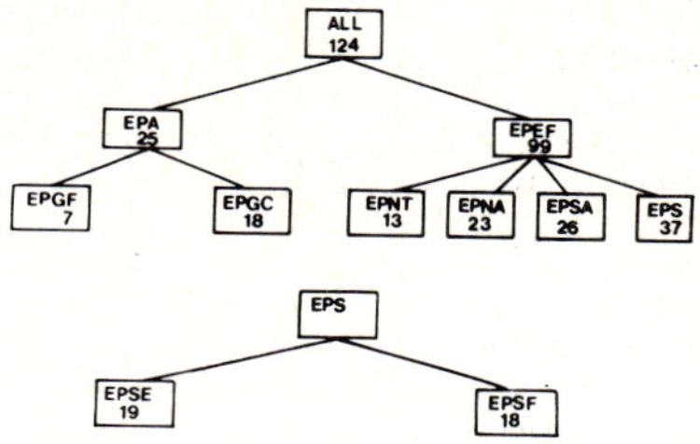

Fig. 5 - Tree-structure for the late upper Paleolithic sites of continental Italy.

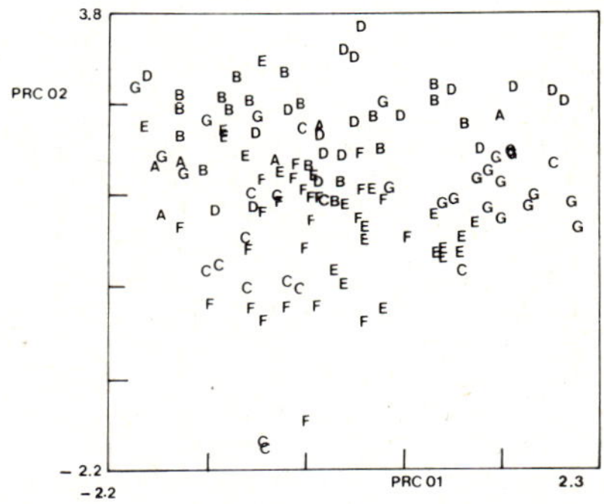

Fig. 6 - Scatterplot along the two first principal axes of the data given in fig. 5.

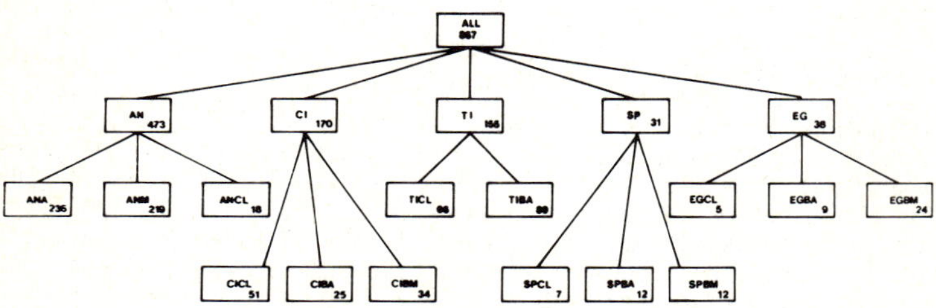

Fig. 7 - Tree-structure for a sample of Middle-East bronzes.

In fig.7 the tentative tree structure is given: the five geographical zones are represented by Anatolia (AN), Cilicia and Eastern Anatolia (CI), Iran and Transcaucasian region (TI), Syria and Palestina (SP) and Egypt (EG). Each zone has been further subdivided according to a general chronological classification, as it is shown at the terminal nodes of fig.7: Calcolithic, Ancient Bronze and Middle Bronze Period (e.g. at the node CI, the terminal nodes CICL, CIBA, and CIBM), with the exception of TI, where not enough data for the Middle Bronze period were available.

For every bronze object six features were considered: the percentages of tin, lead, arsenic, antimony, silver and nickel.

The options of ISPAHAN used are essentially the same of the previous upper Paleolithic example: t-test, AUTMSK and PRINCO.

The work is still at a preliminary stage, but we can say that lead, for instance does not discriminate between the geographical zones, while all others elements do. Tin, arsenic and silver, e.g., discriminate between Cilicia and Iran-Transcaucasia. Natural copper with arsenic content according to M. Frangipane, was commonly used in Anatolia and Cilicia in the early periods.

Another interesting result is that both the t-test and the stepwise discriminant analysis did not show any significant difference between the two periods (Calcolithic TICL and Ancient Bronze Age TIBA) in the Transcaucasian zone.

According to M. Frangipane, this circumstance may be due to the isolated geographic position of this region, resulting in a rather static bronze techology through time.

II - 4 - Social patterns in an early Iron age Cemetery in Latium.

The data presented here have been given to us by A.M. Bietti Sestieri, who is still digging the large Iron age Cemetery of Osteria dell'Osa about 18 Km NE of Rome.

The burials (about 80) are of the 9th century B.C., with adult males cremated, where females, young males and infants were inhumated. (Bietti-Sestieri, 1984).

The spatial distribution of these burials is shown in fig.8: according to the author, two clear "family groups" can be identified on the basis of their location and of the stylistic differences of the pottery and of the bronzes of the funerary outfit. In addition to these two groups (labelled North and South, see fig.8) some other "uncertain" burials were found. A first tentative hypothesis, drawn by A.M. Bietti Sestieri, is that these burials may represent a continuation in time of both the N. (in majority) and the S. groups.

For the capabilities of ISPAHAN, this problem represented in our opinion, an interesting example of supervised classification logic, even if the sample is rather limited (40 burials in the learning set and 22 in the "uncertain" set).

The funerary outfits have been chosen as primary features for every burial: the urn, ovoid jars, the jug, the bowl, concerning the pottery, and the spear, razor, male or fermale fibulae concerning the bronzes, for instance. All these features were considered as discrete: in general two-valued (presence or absence), with a few exceptions (the number of large liquid containers, the pottery style, e.g.) which are multiple-valued. Only two continuous features have been considered, i.e. the x and y coordinates of the burials.

In fig.9 we can see a tentative tree structure of the "learning set": the intermediate nodes are the spatial position of the burials (N or S) and the terminal ones the division by sex.

Appling the t-test and the stepwise discriminant analysis (AUTMSK in fig.1) at the node ALL only the pottery style and the y coordinate were diagnostic. If one applies the same tests to the nodes N and S of fig.9 the diagnostic features between the males and females of the N group are the urn and the male fibulae (characteristic of male graves). Those features also discriminate between the male and female burials of the S group, with the addition of the miniaturization of the funerary outfits, the ovoid jars and the spear (again typical features of the male graves and in particular of the cremations).

A principal component analysis showed that the first four components account

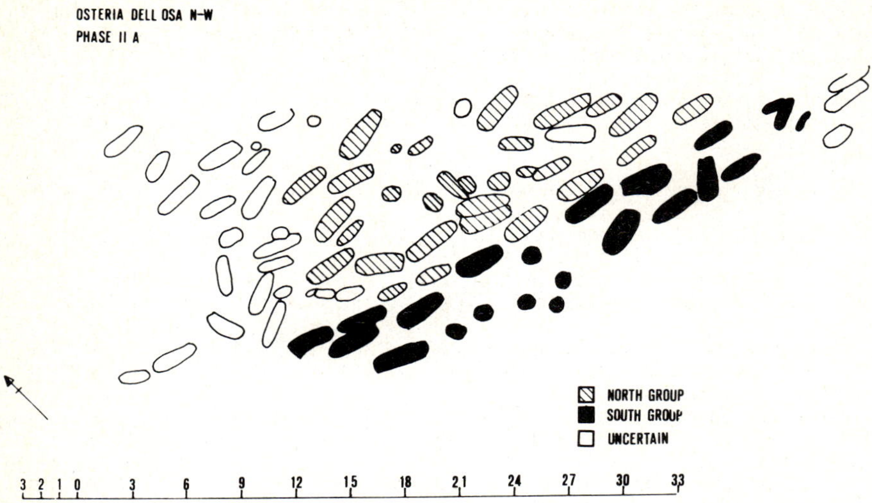

Fig. 8 - Spatial distribution of a sample of burials from the Osteria dell'Osa cemetery (adapted from Bietti-Sestieri (1985)).

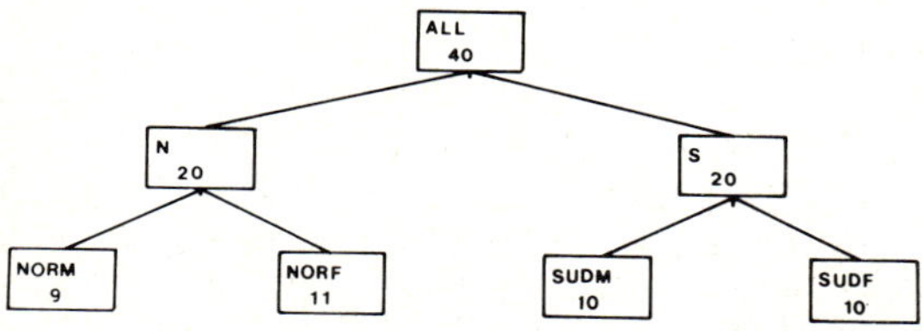

Fig. 9 - Tentative tree-structure for the North and South groups of burials from fig.8.

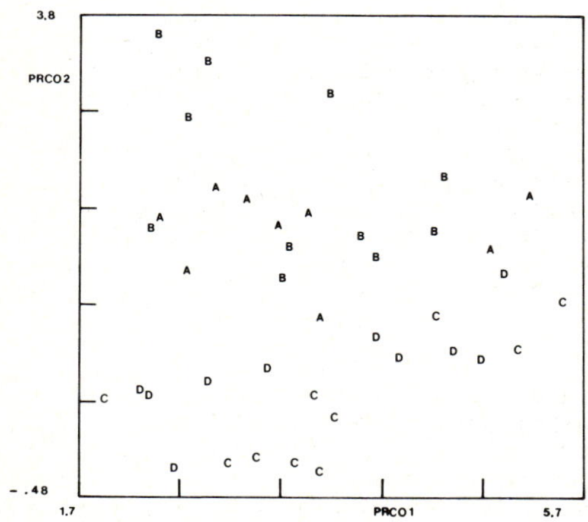

Fig. 10- Scatterplot along the two first principal axes of the data shown in fig. 9.

for about 95% of the total variance, and the relevant factor loadings are given by the x and y coordinates for the first principal component, where the pottery style and the male fibulae have relevant factor loadings also for the second and third principal component.

In any case, the N and S groups seem to by well separated as can be seen from fig.10 and 11, which show the scatterplots for the first and second, and for the second and third principal components.

We tried to perform also an "autotest" using the supervised decision logic of ISPAHAN, and more precisely the options LINMAX and FISHER to the three principal nodes of fig.9 (ALL, N, S): the misclassification, as can be seen from the confusion matrix in fig.12, is only of two objects over 40.

Even if this result seems to be encouraging, we are certainly aware of the small size of the sample: the burials considered are not enough in order to divide them in a "learning" and in a "test" set, according to a proper supervised classification.

The sampling bias is even more evident when we analyze the new "uncertain" set (fig.13) which consists of only 22 burials, tentatively classified according to the N - S frame of fig.9.

The TEST option, with a FISHER choice (fig.1) at all three non terminal nodes (ALL, N, S) agrees with the "a priori" classification of fig.9 only up to 60%. It seems, however, that this "uncertain" group of burials is closer to the old N group, in agreement with qualitative analysis drawn by A.M. Bietti Sestieri (private comunication). New diggings which are in progress, will give us a larger body of data and we hope to present in a next future, more reliable and accurate results and estimates on such an interesting pattern recognition problem.

III - APPLICATIONS IN PHYSIC

III - 1 - Gravitational Antennae.

This application deals with a preliminary analysis of a sample (which has been given to us by S. Frasca of the Dept. of Physics of the University of Rome) of 323 events recorded by two resonant gravitational-wave antennae. The first is a cryogenic detector (M=389 Kg) and is located at the Istituto di Fisica dello Spazio Interplanetario (ISFI) of the CNR in Frascati, near Rome; the second one is operated at environmental temperature (M=2500 Kg) and is installed at CERN laboratories in Geneva.

These resonant detectors have been designed and built in order to detect gravitational waves, whose existence is expected as a consequence of Einstein's General Theory of Relativity; gravitational waves are produced by sharp variations of spatial distribution of large quantities of matter, such as in the event of the gravitational collapse of a star.

Several considerations lead to exclude that the events analyzed in this application are due to gravitational waves of extraterrestrial origin; they are much likely to be noisy events probably caused by local disturbances.

The sample is characterized by a low dimensionality of the feature space; in fact each event is described by five features:

- the minute, relative to the 1st of January 1980, when the event began (MIN);
- event energy (AMPL);
- solar time (TSOL);
- sideral time (TSID);
- period phase of the tide due to the Moon (MTWO).

The feature vectors are splitted in two classes, named FRA and GEN, which contain respectively the events recorded in Frascati and in Geneva; the simple one-stage a priori tree structure imposed to the data (fig.14) reflects this choice. First of all we transformed the feature vectors into a new set of features with zero mean and unitary variance through option SCALE of sub-menu TRANSF; subsequently, as a first approach, we tried a t-test at 99% confidence level between the two classes, and we found only three diagnostic features: MIN, AMPL, and TSID.

Particularly interesting is the result of the option CLUCON at node ALL: the

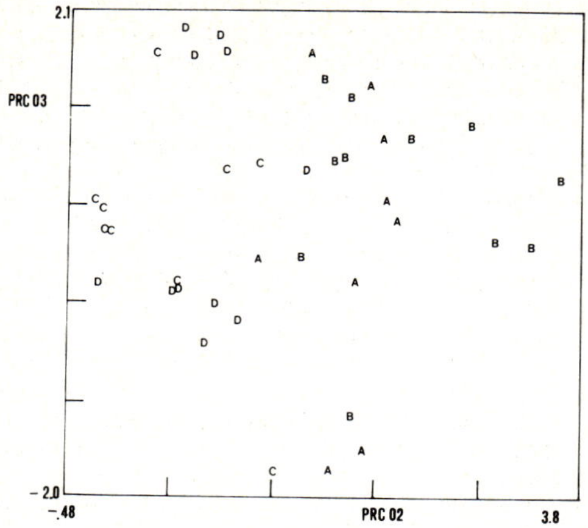

Fig. 11- Same as in fig.10 for the second and third principal components.

CLASSIFYING AT NODE ALL
CLASSIFYING AT NODE N
CLASSIFYING AT NODE S
CONFUSION MATRIX W.R.T. A PRIORI CLASSIFICATION
(HOR: POST VERT: PRIOR)

	N	S	NORM	NORF	SUDM	SUDF
NORM	9	0	9	0	0	0
NORF	10	1	0	10	1	0
SUDM	1	9	1	0	9	0
SUDF	0	10	0	0	0	10

Fig. 12- Confusion matrix from the TEST option of the supervised classification menu in fig.1.

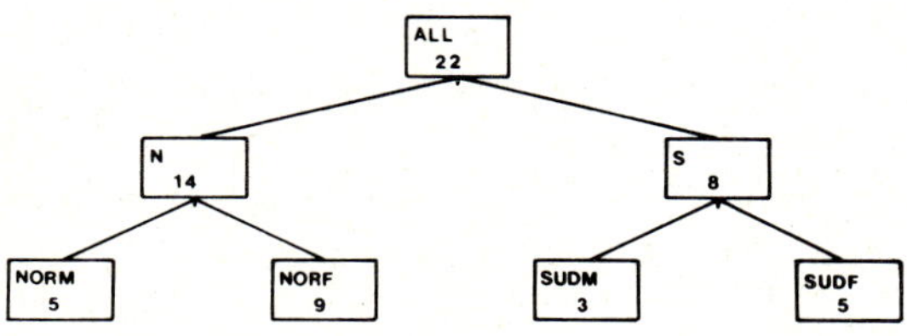

Fig. 13- Tree-structure for the "uncertain" burials of fig.8.

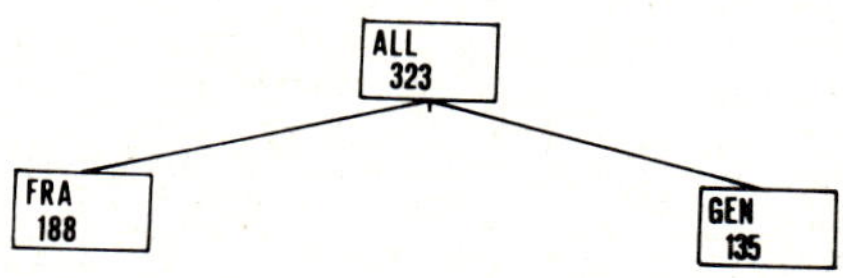

Fig. 14- Simple tree-structure for the Frascati-Geneva gravitational antennae events.

188 events of FRA node occupy 98.3% of the total volume, while the 135 events of GEN class take just 1.7% of total volume. This means that the events recorded in Geneva are well clustered, while the others are quite scattered in the feature space. The spatial distribution of the feature vectors, inspected in a lower dimensionality space by means of mapping algorithms, confirms this indication, as can be seen in the scatter plot in fig.15 obtained through the option DIS2MN (A= = FRA, B=GEN): the events labelled GEN are clustered and separated from the ones of FRA class; furthermore, some isolated Frascati events scatter in the upper right corner of the plot.

The next step was the principal component analysis in a transformed space of the same dimensionality as the original one. The eigenvalues obtained are:

$$\lambda_1 = 1.3539, \quad \lambda_2 = 1.0615, \quad \lambda_3 = 0.9661, \quad \lambda_4 = 0.8734, \quad \lambda_5 = 0.7451$$

This result is strongly different from the ones obtained in previously described applications: now all the five principal components show values of same order of magnitude and this implies an absence of redundancy of the features selected in order to describe the data. This result is not surprising, essentially because of the different nature of archaeological and physical applications. The analysis on archaeological samples were carried out from a classificatory point of view and, in that context, the existence of correlated features may give important indications to the researcher. In this application instead the goal is not so much classification, but rather a good representation of the data which might allow to reveal, on a background of "standard" and well-known events, the presence of "non-standard" events whose existence might be due to particular measurement conditions or might be diagnostic of a different nature.

According to these considerations, we decided to switch off the feature MIN because of its highly discriminant contribution; in fact Frascati signals were measured over a time range (1978-1980) considerably far from that of Geneva events (1981-1982). All scatter plots produced subsequently using the "mapping algorithms" submenu show in a common way a same situation in which GEN class events and a cluster of Frascati events overlap, while few objects belonging to FRA class appear separated in the plot.

III - 2 - Indoor radioactivity measurements in solid state detectors.

We have recently attacked a new line of ISPAHAN applications, concerning the problem of automatic measurement of track images in SSNTD (Solide State Nuclear Track Detectors).

The purpose of these studies, according to the researchers of the Istituto Superiore di Sanità in Rome (G. Campos-Venuti), is the quantitative analysis of indoor natural radioactivity caused by the decay products of ^{222}Rn; some of these, like for instance ^{218}Po, ^{214}Pb, ^{218}Bi and ^{214}Po are particularly dangerous for the human organism, due to their chemical characteristics and short decay times (3.05, 26.8, 19.7 and 2.7 minutes respectively).

The detection material, an organic polymer known as CR39 is permanently damaged by the passage of the ionizing α-particles. This damage is put into evidence by chemical etching (using NaOH) of its surface.

The plastic detector is then photographed and the track images which appear as dark circles or ellipses on a light background are measured on a Cathod Ray Tube automatic scanning and measuring machine (the PEPR of the Laboratori Nazionali di Frascati). The interesting parameters which the measurement tries to evaluate are the total number of tracks, the distribution of their geometrical features (minor axis and eccentricity of the ellipse, e.g.), the darkness and the presence and size of a spot in the track's image center. All these parameters are connected, in a rather complex way, to the particle mass, energy and impact angle with respect to the detector's surface (I. Laakso, priv. communication).

The background is mainly due to two sources: defects in the material which are enhanced by the chemical etching and the "old" tracks, i.e. real particles which have hit the detector during its life before the start of the real exposure.

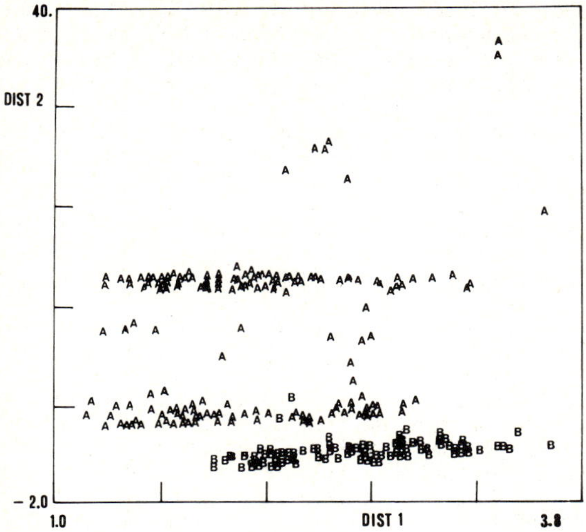

Fig. 15- Scatterplot of the two classes given in fig.14 according the DIS2MN mapping algorithm.

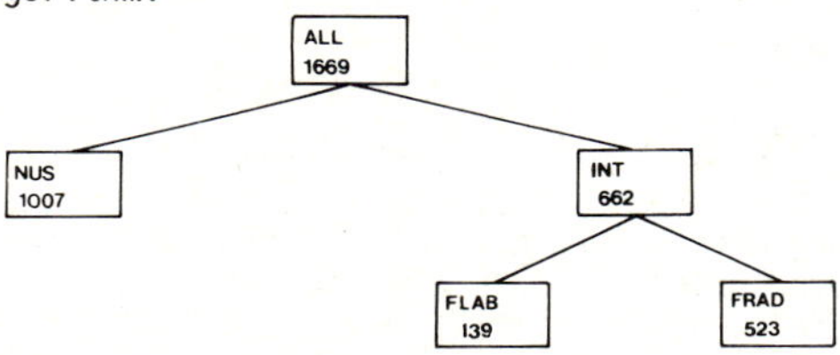

Fig. 16- Tentative tree-structure for the indoor radioactive measurements in solid state detectors.

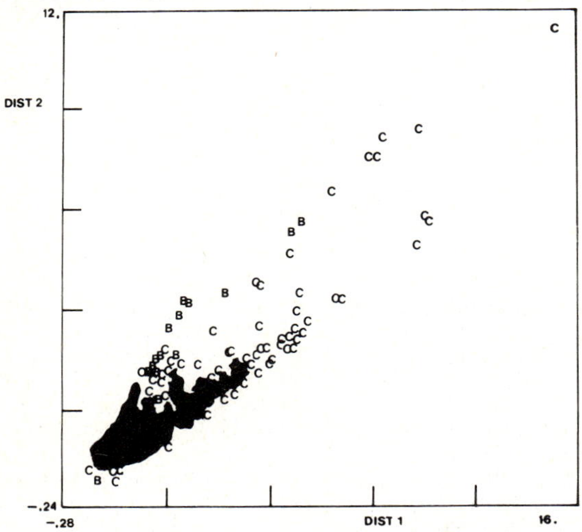

Fig. 17- Scatterplot of the classes FLAB (B) and FRAD (C) of the tree-structure shown in fig.16, according to the DIS2MN mapping algorithm.

We have at our disposal several groups of data obtained in different conditions: for instance a) measurements on plastic detectors taken immediately after its construction; b) after a variable time of exposure to the natural environment; c) after a selective exposure to some decay products only, through the use of some filters.

The purpose of our analysis with ISPAHAN was to try to disentangle the problem of background rejection, providing the intelligent automatic measuring machines with meaningful diagnostic features and thresholds for measurement guidance.

A tentative tree-structure is shown in fig.16: the NUS node represents the events described in the aforementioned class b), where the nodes FLAB and FRAD represent the events of the aforementioned classes a) and d) respectively. The features considered were, at a first instance, five: 1) a background estimate; 2) the minor axis of the ellipse formed by the track; 3) the signal amplitude measured in terms of the integrated photographic density; 4) the presence and intensity of a spot at the center of the ellipse; 5) the eccentricity of the ellipse.

The t-test was used first, and the result was that the feature n.4 is never diagnostic, while the features n.1 and 5 are always diagnostic for the three classes, and the feature n.2, the minor axis of the ellipse, is diagnostic between the classes NUS and FRAD. On the other hand, a principal component analysis did not give any clear separation between the three classes (with the exception of only a few events of the class FRAD), and the first principal component, accounting for more than 99% of the total variance, is mainly mastered by the feature n.4, which was never diagnostic in the t-test!

We tried also a classification with a new set of four variables, where the background effect (the previous feature n.1) has been eliminated, and we analyzed in particular the two nodes FLAB and FRAD. Now only the eccentricity of the ellipse is diagnostic, by t-test, between the two classes, but the principal component analysis shows always a strong dominance of the first one (now mainly dominated by the signal amplitude). Again, as can be seen in fig.17, which shows the result of the DIS2MN mapping algorithm of ISPAHAN, the two classes FLAB and FRAD are not at all separated, with the exception of some few events of both classes.

Our preliminary conclusion is therefore that a serious rethinking on the choice of the relevant features should be made by the researchers. In fact, a strong and cumbersome correlation between the features has been revealed by our analysis with ISPAHAN, in striking contrast, for instance, with the results previously seen for the events of the gravitational antennae.

REFERENCES

Bietti A. and Zanello L., A project of pattern recognition with an interactive system (ISPAHAN) in prehistoric archaeology: "quantitative" typology of the end-scrapers of an Italian upper Paleolithic assemblage, in: E.S. Gelsema and L.N. Kanal eds. Pattern Recognition in Practice, North-Holland, Amsterdam (1980), 517-526.

Bietti A., Burani A. and Zanello L., An application of ISPAHAN to the typological classification of some Italian upper Paleolithic end-scrapers, Pattern Recognition Letters 1 (1983), 181-186.

Bietti A. and Burani A., The late upper Paleolithic in Continental Italy: old classifications, new data and new perspectives. Papers in Italian Archaeology IV, II, B.A.R. International series n.244, (1985), 7-27.

Bietti-Sestieri A.M., The iron age cemetery of Osteria dell'Osa, Rome; Evidence of social change in Lazio in the 8th Century B.C., Papers in Italian Archaeology IV, III, B.A.R. International series n.245 (1985), 111-144.

Gelsema E.S., ISPAHAN; an interactive system for pattern analysis: structure and capabilities, in E.S. Gelsema and L.N. Kanal eds. Pattern Recognition in Practice, North-Holland, Amsterdam (1980), 481-491.

Gelsema E.S., ISPAHAN users manual (4th edition). Dept. of Medical Informatics, Free University of Amsterdam (1981).

Gelsema E.S. and Eden G., Mapping algorithms in ISPAHAN, Pattern Recognition 12 (1980), 127-136.

Laplace G., Les Subdivisions du Leptolithique Italien, Bull. Paletn. Ital. 73 (1964), 25-63.

Palma di Cesnola A. (Ed.), La position taxonomique et chronologique des industries à pointes à dos autour de la Méditerranée Européenne. Proc. of the Int. Colloquium held in Siena (1983).

SECTION VI

POPULATION CLASSIFICATION

PATTERN RECOGNITION IN PRACTICE II
E.S. Gelsema and L.N. Kanal (Editors)
Elsevier Science Publishers B.V. (North-Holland), 1986

NON PARAMETRIC POPULATION CLASSIFICATION

A.W.M. Smeulders

Pathological Institute
Free University Hospital
De Boelelaan 1117
1081 HV Amsterdam
The Netherlands

Population classification is a set of statistical techniques to classify populations on basis of observations of their constituing members. This decision making involves a cascade of classifiers: one for objects, and, based on the resulting classifications, one for populations. Also a rule is to be given how many objects should be analysed before the population is decidable. In search for a more integral view of the problem the population function is introduced. Consideration of the population function implies that rather then fixing the object classifier a priori, it is more efficient and more accurate to extend the classifier to a distinct range of the feature vector. The concept of sequential classification is defined as well. Population classification performance is favourably compared to [1,2,3,5,6].

1. INTRODUCTION

Population classification is the classification of a population on basis of observations on its members. Population classification deviates from usual decision making procedures in the two step classification procedure that is employed. In the first step, members of a population each are classified into one of the member classes. After the analysis of a certain number of members, in the second step the population itself is classified into one of the population classes. Population classification is a statistical technique with applications in many different fields such as industrial inspection, quality control and quality assessment of lots. For conceptual convenience, we will adopt here the terminology from the cytology field, where a specimen may be conceived as a population of cells.

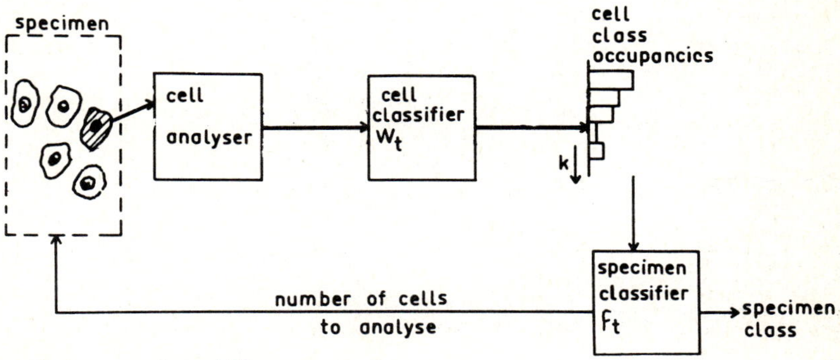

Fig. 1. The two classifier cascade.

In figure 1, the two step classification procedure is depicted. It is crucial in this cascade of classifiers that the accumulated outcome of the cell classification is the input of the specimen classification. So, an alteration in the cell classifier may influence the specimen classification result. In the analysis of specimens, the prime interest is not in the performance of the cell classifier on its own, but in its performance in respect to the specimen classification.

Let the cell of the I-th specimen be numbered by index i with $i=1,\ldots,n_I$. A feature vector $\overline{w}_i$ is computed per cell, giving a list of n_I observations. The cascade of classifiers is composed of three tunable entities:

1. The cell classifier ($\overline{w}_t$) provides a set of rules to classify a cell characterized by $\overline{w}_i$. The cell is classified into one or more cell classes k with $k=1,\ldots,m$.
   The cell classifications are accumulated in the cell class occupancy vector $\overline{f}$. It should be noted, that the results of this paper will suggest that it may be profitably not to use a cell classifier.
2. The number rule (n_t) controls the minimum number of cells to be classified before classifying the specimen.
3. The specimen classifier ($\overline{f}_t$) provides a set of rules to classify a specimen based on $\overline{f}$ after the analysis of n_t cells. The specimen is classified in specimen class K with $K=1,\ldots,M$.

The objective of statistical population analysis is to design a procedure such that the specimen classification error is acceptable and the number of cells to classify is minimized by controlling these three entities. It is important to note that a specimen may either be erroneously classified by the fact that only a limited number of cells are analysed or by the fact that the occupancy vector $\overline{f}$ of a specimen, when compared to $\overline{f}_t$, leads to erroneous classification. The first error, the sample error, is related to the system efficiency and may be avoided by analysing more cells. The second error is related to accuracy of the system and is intrinsic to the nature of the problem. For a fixed $\overline{w}_t$ and $\overline{f}_t$, it cannot be cured by analysing more cells.

Castleman and White were the first to design a procedure for cascaded classification. In a series of papers, using a simplified model, they have given guidelines how to address the cell classifier [1], how to address the specimen classifier [2], and how the proportionality of different classes of cells influences the performance of the specimen classifier [3], once the cell classifier has been fixed. All references are restricted to M=2 with K=1 : 'normal specimens' and K=2 : 'abnormal specimens'. In [1] and [3], the number of cell classes is restricted to m=2. In that case, we will call cells classified into class k=1 'non-events', and cells into class k=2, 'events'. In [2] there is no restriction to the number of cell classes.

The procedure of Castleman and White is discussed here, without loss of generality, for m=2. They consider a previously settled cell classifier such that a fraction (ε_1) of normal cells (k=1) is erroneously classified into class k=2, and fraction (ε_2) of abnormal cells erroneously into k=1. Secondly, the presumption is made that specimens of the normal specimen class (K=1) entirely consists of k=1-cells. Also, it is presumed that abnormal specimens (K=2) all have the same, fixed, fraction p of k=2-cells, and a fraction 1-p of k=1-cells. Let q_K for K = 1,2 be the proportion of events from a specimen of class K, then we have $q_1=\varepsilon_1$ and $q_2=\varepsilon_1+p(1-\varepsilon_1-\varepsilon_2)$. Both q_1 and q_2 are thus constants for all specimens of class K.

It should be noted that the discrimination of ε_1 and ε_2 from p is not necessary. The same result would have been obtained by the presumption that the cell classifier produces a proportion of q_1 events for normal specimens and q_2 events for abnormal ones.

Under these presumptions, the classification procedure reduces to the recognition whether an observed proportion $\hat{q}$ of an unknown specimen originates from a specimen with q_1 or q_2 events. As $\hat{q}$ is based on n cells, $\hat{q}$ is distributed binomially around q_K. The binomial distribution is, with a very good approximation, replaced by a Gaussian distribution with mean q_K and standard deviation $s_K = \sqrt{q_K(1-q_K)/n}$. Let $f_e(x)$ be the error function

$$f_e(x) = \frac{1}{\sqrt{2\pi}} \int_x^\infty e^{-\frac{1}{2}t^2} dt \qquad \text{with inverse } f_e^{-1}(x), \tag{1}$$

and E_K^S, K=1,2, be the tolerated fractions of specimens classified wrong. The minimum number of cells to be analysed (n_t) and the specimen classification threshold (q_t) may be solved now as follows:

$$n_t = \left(\frac{f_e^{-1}(E_2^S)\sqrt{q_2(1-q_2)} + f_e^{-1}(E_1^S)\sqrt{q_1(1-q_1)}}{q_2 - q_1} \right)^2 \tag{2}$$

$$q_t = \frac{f_e^{-1}(E_1^S) q_2 \sqrt{q_1(1-q_1)} + f_e^{-1}(E_2^S) q_1 \sqrt{q_2(1-q_2)}}{f_e^{-1}(E_1^S)\sqrt{q_1(1-q_1)} + f_e^{-1}(E_2^S)\sqrt{q_2(1-q_2)}} \tag{3}$$

In summary, the proposed procedure is:

1. Select cell features $\overline{w}$ and a cell classifier $\overline{w}_t$, see [1].
2. Select a value for q_1 representative for normal specimens on basis of experience with this cell classifier. Similarly, choose a q_2. Compute n_t and q_t.
3. In the operational phase, analyse n_t cells for each specimen and find $\hat{q}$. If $\hat{q}<q_t$ then decide "normal specimen" else $\hat{q}\geq q_t$ and decide "abnormal specimen".

Although the procedure is attractive in the sense that it provided a relationship between the cell clasifier and the specimen classifier, the presumptions tend to oversimplify reality. As a consequence all information in $\overline{w}_i$ is reduced two parts above and below $\overline{w}_t$. All other information in $\overline{w}$ is lost. Secondly, in many practical cases, it is in conflict with reality to presume that a class of specimens can be represented by a fixed proportion of events. Thirdly, it is not necessary to select n a priori. Wald [4] has demonstrated that n_t is most efficiently computed during the analysis of the specimen, as was also recognised in [2]. Finally, chosing a cell classifier prior to and separately from the establishment of the specimen classifier is not optimal, as will be demonstrated later on.

An alternative approach was followed by Tanaka [5], acquiring the values of one cell feature in a cumulative histogram $\hat{q}(v)$. The procedure that was used, was as follows:

1. One cell feature, v, is selected.
2. In the learning phase, derive histograms $q_K(v)$ representing the K-th specimen class.
3. In the operational phase, establish after the analysis of n cells, the specimen histogram $\hat{q}_n(v)$, and apply the non-parametric Kolmogorov Smirnov test for the difference of two histograms. For K=1,2:

$$v_t = v \text{ where } \max \left| \hat{q}_n(v) - q_K(v) \right| \tag{4a}$$

$$n_t = \frac{(f_{KS}(E_K^S))^2}{(\hat{q}_n(v_t) - q_K(v_t))^2} \tag{4b}$$

$$\text{if } n > n_t \text{ assign I to class K} \tag{4c}$$

else assign I not to a class.

In this decision rule $f_{KS}(E_K^S)$ is a factor based on the confidence level E_K^S of the Kolmogorov Smirnov test. The values of f_{KS} may be found in standard statistical tables [11].

The analysis with a non-parametric test, only permits the use of a one dimensional cell feature. Non-parametric tests on the difference of two distributions, do not exist for more than one dimension, as the more dimensional space cannot be uniquely ordered.

More dimensional cell features ($\bar{w}$) can be used still, by using non-linear mapping (M) of the cell features onto what is called the axis of cell atypia. The index (v)

$$v = M \circ \bar{w} \tag{5}$$

winds through the feature space, e.g. according to [6] or [7]. In reference [6], the axis is a result of a curve fitting procedure through a number of ordered cell classes represented by their covariance matrices, derived from a learning phase. The ordering of the cell classes permits the definition of a scale, called index of atypia, on the axis. De facto, this axis can be regarded as a way to order the cell feature space and classes, giving a meaning to the feature values in the context of the classification problem. The index of atypicality is an ordinal scale, and can on its own be regarded as a one dimensional cell feature. In [6], no hint is given how to use the index in a specimen classification procedure.

A conceptually different way to reduce the more dimensional cell feature space into a one dimensional cell scale, is making use of a posteriori probability of a cell classifier. Let M now denote a (set of) cell classifier(s), and let v now denote the resulting a posteriori probability of a cell to belong to cell class k=1, then v also is specified by equation 5. The feature v is an ordinal scale cell feature. For some problems, for M the Mahalanobis distance to the class of normal cells may be taken as a measure for the deviation of the cell from the normal [9]. In this concept and the previous one, a cell feature v is the residue from the more dimensional feature $\bar{w}$ by an operation M.

Ott [8] also applies a mapping from the more dimensional cell space onto a triangulated cell class space. Specimen features are defined on this cell class space as input to the specimen classifier. No hints are, however, given how to generally define specimen features or how to relate the number of cells to be analysed on a specimen to the classification error.

In the present paper, it is pointed out how the distribution of v relates to the specimen classification error by the introduction of the population function, see also [10].

2. THE POPULATION FUNCTION

Consider an arbitrary specimen I of specimen class K. For a one dimensional cell feature v, which may be the result of a mapping ($v = M \circ \bar{w}$), call the probability density function p(v). A convenient form to consider is the cumulative density function

$$q(v) = \int_{v}^{\infty} p(x)dx. \tag{6}$$

It is interesting to relate q(v) to a cell classifier v' of the following type, see figure 2.

$$\text{if } v_i < v' \text{ assign cell i to class k=1, else } v_i \geq v' \text{ and assign cell i to class k=2.} \tag{7}$$

In this context, q(v') denotes the fraction of cells that will be classified into class k=2 (events), when v' would have been used as the cell classifier. The fraction non-events accordingly is 1-q(v'). When v' is varied over the feature scale, q(v) denotes the performance for any cell classifier v on the given specimen.

For one cell classifier v', the fraction of events may vary from specimen to specimen, even within one class of specimen. This fraction q(v') thus is a variable itself, for which within one class of specimens K, a pdf may be formed: $P_K(q(v'))$. This function indicates the probability to observe a fraction q(v') of events when analysing a specimen of class K with cell classifier v'. Obviously the shape of $P_K(q(v'))$ is completely dependent on the nature of problem and is independent of q(v). Variation of v' over the feature

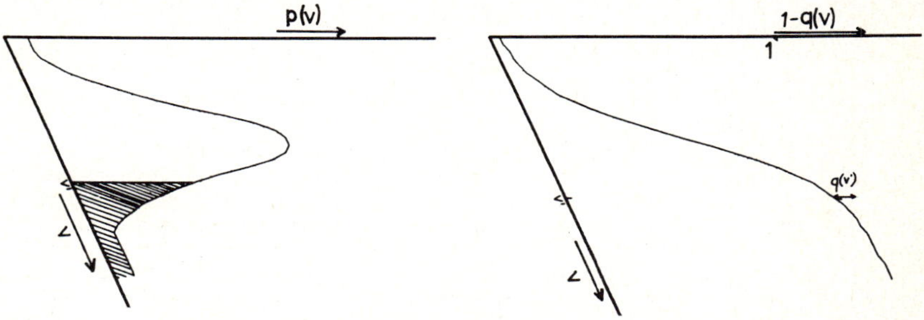

Figure 2: The proportion of events (cells classified into k=2) resulting from a cell classifier v' indicated by shading in the graph of p(v) and the cumulative function q(v).

scale yields the result for any feature: $P_K(v,q(v))$. This is the population function, giving a relationship between v and q(v) for population K. The integral form of P_K over q:

$$Q_K(v,q(v)) = \int_0^q P_K(v,x(v))dx \tag{8}$$

relates an arbitrary cell classifier to the obtainable specimen classification error as follows. Consider a specimen classifier q' such that:

$$\text{if } q_I < q' \text{ assign specimen I to specimen class K=1, else } q_I > q' \text{ and assign specimen I to class K=2.} \tag{9}$$

For a given cell classifier v' and a given specimen classifier q', $Q_K(v',q'(v'))$ denotes the probability of a specimen to be classified into class K=1. The function $1-Q_1(v,q(v))$ thus is the specimen classification error function for K=1-specimens, and the function $Q_2(v,q(v))$ is the specimen error-function for K=2-specimens.

The population function can be used in specimen classification procedures by considering for specimen class K=1,2, the population functions $P_K(v,q(v))$ as illustrated in figure 3a,b. For each value v' of v, the Bayes-rule implies that the specimen classifier with smallest total error is $q_B(v')$ at the point where $P_1(v',q(v')) = P_2(v',q(v'))$. Varying v' again over the feature scale gives a curve $q_B(v)$, indicating for each v the associated best specimen classifier. The cumulative population function is displayed in figure 3b. For each v', $q_B(v')$ now is positioned at the location of maximum vertical distance between $Q_1(v',q(v'))$ and $Q_2(v',q(v'))$. In figure 3c, the intersection of $q_B(v)$ with $Q_K(v,q(v))$ is indicated. The remaining specimen classification error, is indicated by $1-Q_1(v,q\ (v))$ and $Q_2(v,q\ (v))$. In the example of figure 3c, for the larger part of the feature v the population 1 is indistinguishable from population 2, and consequently on that part both errorfunctions have a value .5.

Several conclusions may be drawn from figure 3c. Firstly, there may be a part of the feature scale v where no or little discrimination is possible between class-K=1 and class-K=2 specimens. Secondly, for the part of the scale where discrimation is possible, in figure 3c denoted by the region v_{test}, the specimen classifiction error is $1-Q_1(v,q\ (v))$ for K=1 and $Q_2(v,q\ (v))$ for K=2. This error is due to the nature of the problem as expressed in the shapes of $Q_K(v,q(v))$ and can for this feature not be avoided. Thirdly, if desired, the single best cell classifier v_o can be selected by taking

$$v_o = \max_{v,q} \mid Q_1(v,q_B(v))-Q_2(v,q_B(v)) \mid . \qquad (10)$$

As we will see later on, it may still be advantageous not to select a cell classifier a priori.

3. LEARNING PHASE

Until thus far, we have considered cell classifiers and specimen classifiers for the true population functions. In principle, we cannot dispose of the true $P_K(v,q(v))$. Instead we have to rely on estimations or simplifications, based on a limited series of observations $\hat{q}_I(v)$, $I=1,\ldots,N_K$ for K=1,2. These observations constitute the learning set of specimens.

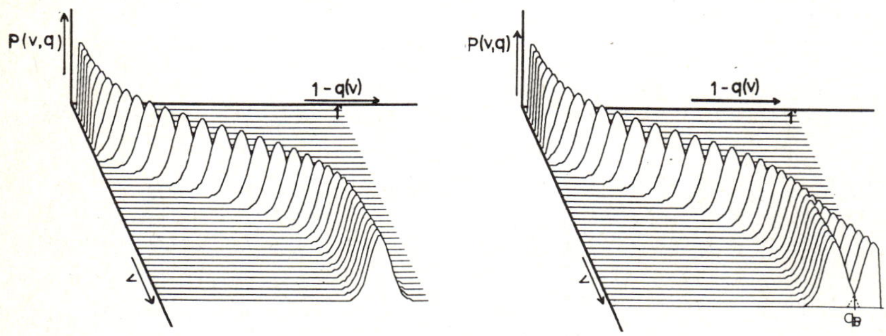

Figure 3a,b: The population function $P_K(v,q(v))$ shown left for one specimen class. For the ease of display P(v,q(v)) has been chosen here unimodal, Gaussian shaped for all cross-sections over v. Note that, in general, not all cross-sections of P(v,q(v)) are necessarily Gaussian shaped or even unimodal, nor have a similar shape. On the right side a pair of joint probability functions $P_K(v,q(v))$ is given. In the cross-section at the front, the Bayes specimen classifier for that cross-section is indicated by $q_B(v)$.

A rigorous simplification of the population function as used in [1-3] has already been discussed in the introduction. They use two independent simplifications. First, one cell classifier is selected, reducing $P_K(v,q(v))$ to a one dimensional function. Secondly, as $q(v)$ is assumed to be equal for all specimens of the same class, $P_K(v,q(v))$ then further reduces to a delta-pulse. Especially the second simplification is in conflict with common classification problems. Note, that in the context of this model no overlap occurs between the approximations for the population functions. As a consequence, there is no preference for a specimen classifier qt on basis of the assumed properties of the two populations at hand other than $q_1<q_t<q_2$. The expression for q_t given in eq.(3) is derived on basis of the finite number of cells only; a subject we will come to discuss in the next section.

Another, much better estimation, $\hat{P}_K(v,q(v))$ for the population function is the following Parzen-estimation procedure [10]:

$$\hat{P}_K(v,q(v)) = \frac{1}{N_K} \sum_{I\in K} \frac{1}{S_I\sqrt{2\pi}}\, e^{-\frac{1}{2}\left(\frac{q(v)-\hat{q}_I(v)}{S_I}\right)^2} \quad \text{with} \tag{11}$$

$$S_I = \sqrt{\frac{q_I(v)(1-q_I(v))}{N_I}} \tag{12}$$

Having established $\hat{P}_K(v,q(v))$ at the end of the learning phase, $q_t(v)$ can be determined as an estimate for $q_B(v)$. $q_t(v)$ is implicitly defined by $\hat{P}_1(v,q_t(v))=\hat{P}_2(v,q_t(v))$. Analogously to the cumulative population function, $Q(v,q(v))$ gives error estimates for this specimen classifier. If E_K^B is the tolerated specimen classifier error fraction for class K due to overlap of $\hat{P}_1(v,q(v))$ and $\hat{P}_2(v,q(v))$, then a region v_{test} of v may be selected as follows:

$$v_{test} = v \text{ where } 1-Q_1(v,q_t(v))<E_1^B \text{ .and. } Q_2(v,q_t(v))<E_2^B \tag{13}$$

If we could dispose of the cumulative probability density function $q_I(v)$ of an unknown specimen I, we could classify the specimen by comparing $q_t(v)$ to $q_I(v)$ for the region v_{test}. In that case, the error may be expected to be bounded by E_K^B. In reality, this specimen classification error is not the only source of error as shall be discussed in the next section.

4. SEQUENTIAL CLASSIFICATION

In the analysis of an unknown specimen I, a finite number n of cells

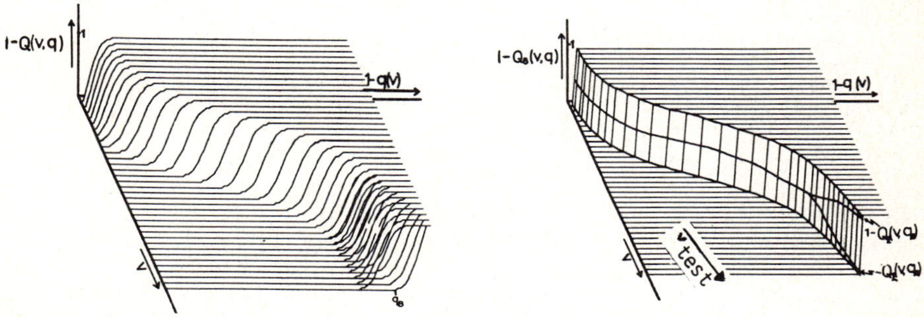

Figure 3c,d: The cumulative population fucntions $Q_K(v,q(v))$ on the left. The specimen classifier error as the intersection of $Q_K(v,q(v))$ with $q_B(v)$ on the right.

is analysed, resulting in a cumulative histogram of feature values $\hat{q}_n(v)$. The histogram is a sample of an unknown distribution $q_I(v)$. A specimen is said to be undecidable when $\hat{q}_n(v)$ may be a sample of $q_t(v)$ over the region v_{test}. In order to test the decidability a null hypothesis is formed stating that $\hat{q}_n(v)$ is a sample of $q_t(v)$. A hypothesis test on the difference of the two distributions is used. Two non-parametric tests are considered here.

The first to consider is the Kolmogorov Smirnov test. Let E^S_K be the tolerated specimen fraction to be classified wrong due to finite cell sample size. This factor then serves as the level of confidence in the test, see eq.(4). The specimen decision rule based on the KS-test is:

$$v_t = v \text{ where } \max_{v_{test}} |\hat{q}_n(v) - q_t(v)| \tag{14a}$$

$$n_t = \frac{(f_{KS}(E^S_K))^2}{(\hat{q}_n(v_t) - q_t(v_t))^2} \tag{14b}$$

if $\hat{q}_n(v) < q_t(v_t)$ .and. $n > n_t$ assign I to class K=1

if $\hat{q}_n(v) \geq q_t(v_t)$ .and. $n > n_t$ assign I to class K=2 (14c)

else specimen I is undecidable.

Note the difference between eq.(4) and eq.(14). The null hypothesis used in [5] was that $\hat{q}_n(v)$ originated from $q_1(v)$ or $q_2(v)$ which are example histograms of specimen class K=1 and K=2. In many problems, a class of specimens cannot reliably be represented by one example histogram. Doing so may lead to large classification errors. Alternatively, in eq. (14), $\hat{q}_n(v)$ is tested against $q_t(v)$, the critical function. When $\hat{q}_n(v)$ deviates significantly from $q_t(v)$, a decision can be taken with a known, bounded error probability.

A drawback of the KS-test is its aspecificity. Many samples are needed to demonstrate a significant difference. As a solution, the following test is proposed.

Consider one specimen class v'. Let the tolerated fraction of specimen to be classified wrong again be E^S_K. As $q_t(v')$ is a fraction, samples of $q_t(v')$ based on n observations (cells) are distributed binomially with mean $q_t(v')$ and standard deviation similar to eq.(12). With good approximation, the binomial distribution may be replaced by the Gaussian one with same mean and standard deviation. A relation now may be found between the value of $\hat{q}_n(v')$ needed to reject the hypothesis given $q_t(v')$, n and $f_e^{-1}(E^S_K)$, see eq.(15).

The same test holds, varying v' over v. In that case $q_I(v)$ is said to be decidable if one value v' is found for which $\hat{q}_n(v')$ significantly differs from $q_t(v')$.
The proposed test becomes:
For K=1,2

$$v_t = v \text{ where } \min_{v_{test}} n_t(v), \text{ with} \tag{15a}$$

$$n_t(v) = \frac{q_t(v)\,(1-q_t(v))\,(f_e^{-1}(E^S_K))^2}{(q_t(v) - \hat{q}_n(v))^2} \tag{15b}$$

if $n > n_t(v_t)$ assign specimen I to class K=1 if $\hat{q}_n(v_t) < q_t(v_t)$

if $n > n_t(v_t)$ assign specimen I to class K=2 if $\hat{q}_n(v_t) > q_t(v_t)$
else $n \leq n_t(v_t)$ and specimen I is undecidable.

The comparison of eq.(4) with eq.(14), can also be made for this test, comparing eq.(2) and (3) with eq.(15). Again, rather than comparing $\hat{q}_n(v)$ with one particular value $q_1(v)$ or $q_2(v)$ as was done in [1-3], $\hat{q}_n(v)$ here is compared with $q_t(v)$. In practice, it is likely to lead to smaller classification errors.

It should be noted that the above tests could be used to compute a value for n to analyze on all unknown specimens. It is more profitable, however, to apply eq.(14) or eq.(15) sequentially. In that case, the entire population classification becomes:

1. Define an operation M reducing the more dimensional cell feature space $\overline{w}$ to a one dimensional feature [6,9].
2. In the learning phase, estimate the population functions by eq.(11) and compute $q_t(v)$. Specify the tolerated error fractions due to specimen overlap and find v_{test}, eq.(13).
3. In the test phase, specify the tolerated error fractions due to the finite cell sample size. Update $\hat{q}_n(v)$ after the analysis of each cell and apply the following decision rule:

   Evaluate eq.(14) or eq.(15)
   If the specimen is decidable, stop the analysis,
   else proceed with the next cell.

It has been made plausible [10], that the procedure based on eq.(15) is both more efficient, in the sense that it needs fewer cells to arrive at a conclusion, and more accurate in the sense that it makes fewer errors in the classification, than the method of eq.(14). Also, this procedure is likely to be more efficient and accurate than the method based on eq.(2) and (3) [1-3], and more accurate than the method of eq.(4) [5]. Model studies are currently being done to investigate these conjectures.

5. CONCLUSION

In the foregoing, the population function $P_K(v,q(v))$ was introduced as a theoretical framework to describe the performance of cascade classifiers. Three items are important here, the cell (primary) classifier, the specimen (secondary) classifier and a rule prescribing how many cells need to be analysed before a specimen is decidable. The performance of a cascade classifier is established by its accuracy (specimen classification error) and its efficiency (number of cells to be analysed).

The population function is the equivalent of the probability density function for one-classifier problems. The equivalent of the Bayes-rule, optimizing overall accuracy, is for population classification given by eq.(10). Equation 10 will give the theoretical most accurate cell classifier selected prior to the analysis and the associated specimen classifier. This gives a theoretical solution to the problem raised in [1] and [2]. From eq.(10) it is also clear that the cell and specimen classifier are best optimized in combination, not separately, as was done in [1,2].

In practice, eq.(10) can only be approximated by a learning phase for which we propose the computation of the Parzen-estimation given in eq.(11), and the selection of a part of the cell feature as specified in eq.(13). The selection of this part of the feature implies that the specimen classification error is restricted to a bound.

In spite of eq.(10), it is not necessary (even unprofitable) to select a cell classifier prior to the analysis, as was done in [1,2,3]. Bounding the tolerated specimen classification error to a specified fraction as proposed in eq.(13), fewer cells need to be analysed when using sequential classification techniques. The technique differs from previous ones in that the difference is demonstrated with the threshold function $q_t(v)$ between the two populations rather then the concordance with the examplatory population functions [3,6,5]. This is expected to lead to a higher accuracy. Presently, model studies are carried out to investigate the accuracy and effiency of the proposed models in comparison to the existing ones.

ACKNOWLEDGEMENT

Prof. A.R. Bakker is gratefully acknowledged for raising an intriguing question, and L. Dorst and G. Bosveld for critically reviewing the paper. The manuscript was carefully typed by D.I.M. de Jong.

REFERENCES

1. Castleman KR, White BS: The tradeoff of cell classifier error rates. Cytometry 1, 601-613, 1980.
2. Castleman KR, White BS: Optimizing cervical specimen classifiers. IEEE trans. PAMI 2, 451-457, 1980.
3. Castleman KR, White BS: The effect of abnormal cell proportion on specimen classifier performance. Cytometry 2, 155-158, 1981.
4. Wald A: Sequential analysis. Dover Publications, New York, 1947.
5. Tanaka N, Ikeda H, Ueno T, Mukawa A, Kamitsuma K: Field test and experimental use of CYBEST model 2 for practical gynecologic mass screening. J. Anal. Quant. Cytol. 1, 122-126, 1979.
6. Bartels P, Bibbo M, Richards DL, Sychra JJ, Wied GL: Patient classification based on cytologic sample profiles. I Basic measures for profile contructions. Acta Cytol. 22, 253-260, 1978.
7. Gelsema ES, Hunink M, Queiros CE, Timmers T: The use of correspondence analysis in the assessment of morphological changes during carcinogenesis. Cytometry 5, 463-468, 1984.
   Submitted for publication in J. Anal. Quant. Cytol. 1985.
8. Ott R, Schurman J, Reinhardt ER, Bloss WH: Automated classification of cytological specimens based on features extracted from nuclei images. Pattern Recognition 13, 83-87, 1981.
9. Mayall B, Burger G: Personal communications.
10. Smeulders AWM: Pattern analysis of cervical specimens. Ph.D.-thesis, University of Leyden, The Netherlands, 1983.
11. Beyer WH et al: Handbook of probability and statistics. The Chemical Rubber co. Cleveland, 1968.

DISCUSSION

Timmers:

Do you see a way of going around the restriction that you work with only one feature?

Smeulders:

It should be noted that there is no possible way to define a Kolgomorov-Smirnov test in more than one dimension because you cannot order uniquely a two-dimensional space. This holds not only for this test but for any parameter-free distribution statistic. So basically the answer is no.

Kanal:

There was some work by Tukey on multivariant tolerance regions for nonparametric rank ordering.

Smeulders:

Basically you cannot order a two-dimensional space uniquely but I indicated that you use a multidimensional cell classifier to reduce the N-dimensional cell feature space to one dimension. This gives order in space and this is what you need. So you may either take an a posteriori probability of an arbitrary cell classifier or you may look at a (non)linear mapping of the multidimensional space. These are the ways to escape from this dilemma but essentially it cannot be solved.

Timmers:

Yes, but then you don't know whether it is optimal at the specimen level, isn't it?

Smeulders:

I believe it is optimal at least for the one-dimensional cell feature case. For the N-dimensional case it depends on the quality of the non-linear mapping.

Burger:

The reason why we think there is no escape in practice of single cell classifiers which precede the specimen classifier is that we would like to define the region of interest in the feature space. In many cases in cytometry a vast amount of the population is identical and is not worthwhile to be looked at with the same accuracy. So we apply an economic multivariate cell classifier in order to get rid of that part of the population with cheap features and then concentrate on that region in the feature space where we expect differences.

Smeulders:

I agree with you. In my terms this is the region where the two P-functions are different.

PATTERN RECOGNITION IN PRACTICE II
E.S. Gelsema and L.N. Kanal (Editors)

SPECIMEN CLASSIFICATION IN CYTOMETRY: AN INTERCOMPARISON OF VARIOUS MEANS OF DECISION MAKING

G. Burger and U. Jütting

Gesellschaft für Strahlen- und Umweltforschung mbH München
Institut für Strahlenschutz
Labor für Biomedizinische Bildanalyse
8042 Neuherberg - FR GERMANY

Automated specimen diagnosis in image cytometry is based on single cell recognition followed by population analysis of selected cells. In both steps of decision making the application of parametric stepwise discriminant analysis is possible. Some interesting features of linear discriminant analysis (LDA) are demonstrated for a synthetic three class example with respect to their impact on the performance of decision tree classifiers. Quadratic discriminant analysis is shown to be superior to LDA in all cases.
Finally clinical examples of specimen diagnosis are shown for two class, three class and multiclass problems. In the latter case the advantages of a decision tree classifier in comparison with multiclass single step LDA is demonstrated.

Introduction:

Important goals in diagnostic and clinical cytology are cancer screening, dignity diagnosis, cancer typing, prognostic grading etc. All these tasks are patient oriented and final decision making refers to specimens and not to cells. The connection between cellular and specimen classification depends on the task. In the case of cancer screening the task may be to search for cancer cells in a specimen. If the cell recognition is perfect, a specimen could be described by the binary feature 'cancer cells existent' or 'not existent'. In the case of limited validity of single cell recognition one may have to take the relative frequency of positive signals for specimen classification [1]. If in addition there is a grading amongst 'positive' cells, one may have to analyse the multivariate feature distribution of the interesting cell population in a specimen. This may be done by transforming the multidimensional feature space into a probability space, the dimensions of which correspond to the number of classes. This transformation can be achieved by LDA, using the a-posteriori probabilities for each object belonging to a pooled learning class.

Unknown specimen classification is then performed by comparing the relevant subspace-signal distribution with distributions from positive and negative training set specimens. This is again a classification problem, identical to that of single cell classification, if the interesting cell population and hence the specimen is described by a suitable feature vector. Univariate transformations of this feature vector may even lead to a single number, being called the atypicality or malignancy index of a specimen e.g. in the case of cancer screening.

Methods:

Multivariate supervised object classification may be performed by applying non-parametric or parametric classifiers. Non-parametric classifiers are not widely used in practice and are generally rather uneconomic in problems with high object, class and feature numbers.

We therefore prefer the application of parametric stepwise discriminant algorithms, which have the main advantage of selecting suitable subsets of features, the application of which minimizes the classification error rate. Both the linear discriminant analysis (LDA) and the quadratic discriminant analysis (QDA) are used. For multiclass discrimination they may be applied in one step or via a hierarchical decision tree. For reasons of simplicity we concentrate on LDA and trees with binary decision nodes only.

Linear discriminant analysis (LDA):

The easiest approach is the linear dicriminant analysis, which is thus called, because the discriminant function used is ilnear with respect to the variables x_i. It is based on the a-posteriori probability for the vector x belonging to the class A_i

$$P(A_i|x) = \frac{p(x|A_i) \cdot P(A_i)}{\sum_{m=1}^{k} p(x|A_m) \cdot P(A_m)} \qquad (1)$$

$p(x|A_i)$ is the probability for x belonging to class A_i and $P(A_i)$ is the a-priori probability of class A_i.

Without going into mathematical details which are well known and presented in textbooks, it should be recalled that the discriminant functions $d_i(x)$ become especially simple if one takes the logarithm of the a-posteriori probability and assumes normal feature distributions and the same (pooled) covariance matrix for all classes. In this case the function becomes:

$$\begin{aligned} d_i(x) &= \ln P(A_i|x) \\ &= (x-\mu_i)^t \, \Sigma^{-1} \, (x-\mu_i) + \ln P(A_i) + \text{const.} \end{aligned} \qquad (2)$$

μ_i is the mean vector of class A_i, Σ is the pooled covariance matrix and the whole first term in the second line is the square of the Mahalanobis-distance. Feature selection is then based on maximizing the Mahalanobis-distances among classes which can be shown to result in minimizing the classification error. This is realized in the widely used BMDP-7M programme package [2]. It performs the above mentioned stepwise discriminant analysis with feature selection (based on F-statistics where $F = s^2\text{interclass}/s^2\text{intraclass}$), evaluates all desired single group classifications in one step and computes a classification table based on the a-posteriori probabilities, by minimizing the total classification error. The programme is sensitive both to deviations of the feature distributions from normality as to their lack of homogeneity. The latter effect is demonstrated in fig. 1 for a univariate two-class case. The dashed curves are those of the pooled distributions with equal variance, the full curves represent the real distributions for equal a-priori probabilites. The computed a-posteriori probabilities for x of belonging to either class A_1 or A_2 are given by $p'(x|A_1)$ and $p'(x|A_2)$. They differ obviously from the true values $p(x|A_1)$ and $p(x|A_2)$. The same holds for the decision threshold x_t, minimizing the error, which is determined by the crossover of the probability distributions. In two-class cases the truly optimal or otherwise desirable classification rate can be found by setting arbitrary a-priori weights to any of the two distributions and calculating the ROC-characteristic. This approach is also very valuable for optimizing decision trees [3]. In multiclass cases such a procedure would imply multiple permutations of a-priori weights, which is practically not possible.

Decision tree classifiers (DTC)

The easiest way of escaping the above mentioned multiclass problems is the application of hierarchical classifiers with binary decision nodes only. For these decisions any classifier can be used. Again we concentrate on LDA. In constructing the tree one can either pool classes at certain nodes and separate them at nodes further down (pooling of classes-POC), or one can select at certain nodes and separate the nonselected classes later on (selection of classes-SOC).

It is obvious that the pooling of classes leads to separating hyperplanes which are not identical with those in the single step multiclass LDA. Hence the final results will depend on the architecture of the tree. They also depend on the set of hyperplanes based on ROC's at the different nodes. And, finally, different features may be selected at each node, after possible economic weighting of the features.

An interesting aspect is that multiclass discrimination may often be performed and leads to improved results even when the final number of relevant classes is much lower than that of the training set, and results are pooled after classification.

Quadratic discriminant analysis (QDA)

The main problems of LDA are caused by the homogeneity constraint, or in other words by the pooled covariance matrix. These problems can be overcome by nonlinear parametric approaches as e.g. by the quadratic discriminant analysis. No established programme package was, however, available until recently. The program now at our disposal was developed by W. Höbel and S.J. Pöppl [4] and combines all advantages of a parametric approach, including stepwise feature selection and error estimation with the acceptance of distribution nonhomogeneity. It uses the Bhattacharyya-distance as a measure of distance instead of the Mahalanobis-distance. In contrast to LDA there is no functional relationship between the Bhattacharyya-distance and the classification error. It is, however, possible to define upper and lower error bounds, depending on the distance. It can, in fact, be demonstrated experimentally that maximization of the Bh-distance leads to features which minimize the classification error [5].

All results of QDA applied to the cases discussed in the following sections demonstrate the excellent performance of the programme, delivering in all cases better results than the LDA (see e.g. table 1). The disadvantage of higher computer times and obviously much greater sensitivity to the constraint of normality of distributions is to some extent compensated for by steeper increase of classification validity with number of features and hence the possible application far fewer features than in the LDA.

Materials and results

For demonstration of performance of the above mentioned methods, with emphasis on LDA, a synthetic data set of three classes with 100 objects in each, described by two variables was generated.

In the following figs. 2 - 6, the scatter plots for the 3 class discriminant analysis and some possible permutations of the binary decision case at the first node of the tree classifier and the corresponding results are shown. In the plots equal a-priori probabilities are assumed for all pairs of classes. In this case the separating lines go through the crossing points of the ellipses of equal a-posteriori probabilities for the pooled distributions. The 2σ-ellipses are shown as well as those for the initial distributions of each class. Modifying the a-priori probabilities, as it is done in the numerical computations, where in case of pooling, the a-priori probability is doubled according to the double number of objects, causes a parallel shift of the separating line, as shown. Also shown is the separating line of the final second node.

The figures together with the numerical classification results are self-explanatory. Of interest is the comparison of the results at the first node and the final ones in case of initial class pooling (POC-strategy), with the results of the single step three class (LDA). This is relevant for decision tree optimizing, when one might argue that first node results being worse than the corresponding pooled ones of the three class LDA, can hardly justify the node or the manner of pooling, respectively. This can especially be seen when pooling classes 1 and 2 at the first node. As expected the final results of the three class problems are in all cases worse than for single step LDA. The best results are achieved with decision tree based on SOC-strategy.

Specimen classification in clinical cytometry

The following three examples demonstrate the steps for classification of cellular smear specimens from 26 mamma and 98 thyroidal fine needle aspirates and from 35 gynecological smears. The classifications are based upon the multivariate feature distribution of interactively selected cells in each smear. For this purpose all cells of specimens belonging to a certain training set subgroup are first pooled. Secondly, a LDA is performed and the a-posteriori probabilities are derived for all cells of each specimen to belong either to the corresponding pooled cell class or to the other pooled classes of the training set. In the corresponding class the specimen tested is generally not included (jackknife test). Thirdly the probability distributions are analysed for classification. This may be done by means of appropriate tests of hypothesis on mean values or variances. It may also be performed by an additional LDA based upon more features e.g. the moments of the distributions. For three classes an especially didactic way of estimating the results is a scatter plot in a triangular probability scheme [6].

Mamma (two class problem)

In case of the mamma, where only a correlation of cellular morphology and texture with measured hormon receptor status should be demonstrated [7], the patients above a certain combined estrogen and progesteron level were grouped as being receptor positive; all others were negative. For the two cell pools variance tests and single cell LDA demonstrate the significant difference of both groups. Fig. 7 is showing the a-posteriori probability distributions for the 26 mamma specimens with about 100 cells each. In the second step LDA only the mean value of the distributions was selected. The results are also shown.

Cervix (three class problems)

The problem analysed is that of classifying cervical smears, according to the grading scheme for cancer screening (PAP-grading), by means of selected intermediate cells only [8]. About 60 cells were selected from PAP I, PAP II and PAP IV_a specimens. The single cell three class LDA resulted in either classification rates [9] or again in probability distributions with mean values per specimen.

To both data sets simply a maximum decision rule may be applied for classification. Whenever the overall results are nearly identical, it should be stressed that the use of frequency distributions in subgroups after single cell classification may simulate a much clearer decision than the true distribution of cells in the feature space displays. This is demonstrated in fig. 8, where the mean classification probabilities for the specimens as well as the primary LDA-classification results are plotted in triangular scatter plots. In fig. 8b it is also demonstrated that additional decision spaces can be defined, equivalent to a modification of a-priori probabilities for the three classes.

Thyroid (multiclass problem)

About 100 cells were selected from about 100 specimens grouped cytopathologically into 5 relevant classes [10]. In this case again a multiclass single cell LDA was performed and secondly a multiclass specimen LDA (offering as features the moments of the probability distributions) as well as a decision tree analysis based upon a SOC-strategy. Both set of results as well as the tree are shown in fig. 9 and table 2.

For this problem a new aspect was introduced, namely the introduction of a probability channel (equivalent to a region in the specimen feature space), whenever a clear classification cannot be performed. The width of the channel depends on intraclass variances of the specimen probability distributions. The same could and should have been done in all other examples, when it was only abandoned for demonstration purposes.

Summary:

Specimen classification in automated cytometry may be based on a multiivariate single cell classification with subsequent transformation of the feature space into a probability space of much lower dimension and application of a second step discriminant analysis in this space. From the probability distributions for cells within a specimen the specimen classification can easily be derived. Stepwise parametric discriminant analysis is superior to any other for easy control of constraints, appropriate selection of features and availability of tested and well structured programs. In multiclass cases, decision tree strategies are superior to single step multiclass solutions. The quadratic discriminant analysis is in most cases superior to the linear discriminant analysis, however, it is less easy to handle and requires more computer time.

Acknowledgement:

We greatly acknowledge the inestimable contributions of our colleagues in the image laboratory P. Gais and K. Rodenacker and of our clinical partners H.-J. Soost and U. Schenck from the Institute for Clinical Cytology at the Technical University of Munich. We are also indebted to S. Pöppl for having made the program for stepwise quadratic discriminant analysis available to us.

REFERENCES:

[1] Castleman, K.R., White, B.S., Optimizing Cervical Cell Classifiers, Analyt. Quant. Cytol. 2: 117-122, (1980)

[2] BMDP Statistical Software, Department of Biomathematics, University of California Press, Berkeley-Los Angeles-London, (1981)

[3] Jütting, U. and Burger, G., Lineare Diskriminanzanalyse und Entscheidungsbaumstrategien zur Lösung von Klassifikationsproblemen in der Zytometrie, Workshop Morphometrie und Stereologie in der Pathologie, Neuherberg, 25.-27.6.1984, to be published by Thiemig-Verlag, Heidelberg, (eds. G. Burger, W. Gössner, M. Oberholzer) (1985).

[4] Höbel, W., Pöppl, S.J., Schrittweise Diskriminanzanalyse, Hannover'sche Arbeitstage für Med. Informatik, 29.-30.3.1982

[5] Höbel, W., Abmayr, W., Pöppl, S.J., Giaretti, W., Dörmer, W., Linear and Nonlinear Feature Extraction Methods Applied to Automatic Classification of Proliferating Cells, IEEE (1982)

[6] Ott, R., Schürmann, J. Reinhardt, E.R. and Bloss W.H., Automated Classification of Cytological Specimens Based on Features Extracted from Nuclei Images, Pattern Recognition, Vol. B, pp. 83-87 (1981).

[7] Schenck, U., Burger, G., Jütting, U., Peters-Welte, C., Eiermann, W., Punktionszytologie der Mamma: Korrelation visueller und bildanalytischer Untersuchungen mit dem Hormonrezeptorstatus, Geburtsh. u. Frauenheilk. 45 (1985) 17-21

[8] Burger, G., Jütting, U., Rodenacker, K., Changes in Benign Cell Populations in Case of Cervical Cancer and its Precursors, Analyt. and Quant. Cytology, Vol. 3, No. 4, 261-271 (1981).

[9] Timmers, T. and Gelsema E.S., Analysis of Two Data Sets of Papanicolaou-Stained Cervical Cells, Ph.D. Thesis of T. Timmers, Amsterdam, (1984), private communication.

[10] Burger, G., Gais, P., Jütting, U., Rodenacker, W., Anwendung bildanalytischer Verfahren und Ergebnisse in der Zytopathologie, Workshop Morphometrie und Stereologie in der Pathologie, Neuherberg, 25.-27.6.1984, to be published by Thiemig-Verlag, Heidelberg, (eds. G. Burger, W. Gössner, M. Oberholzer) (1985).

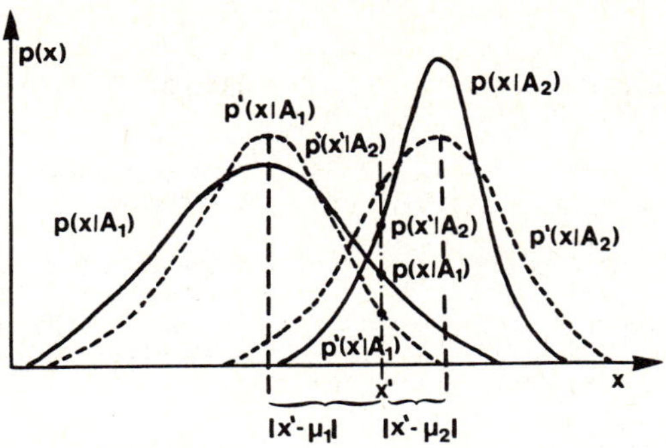

Fig. 1 Schematic univariate 2-class case with real and pooled distributions.

CLASSIFICATION RESULTS

3-CLASS CASE

LDA

	①	②	③	
①	86	12	2	86%
②	4	72	24	72%
③	1	1	98	98%
				85.3%

QDA

	①	②	③	
①	90	9	1	90%
②	2	91	7	91%
③	0	1	99	99%
				93.3%

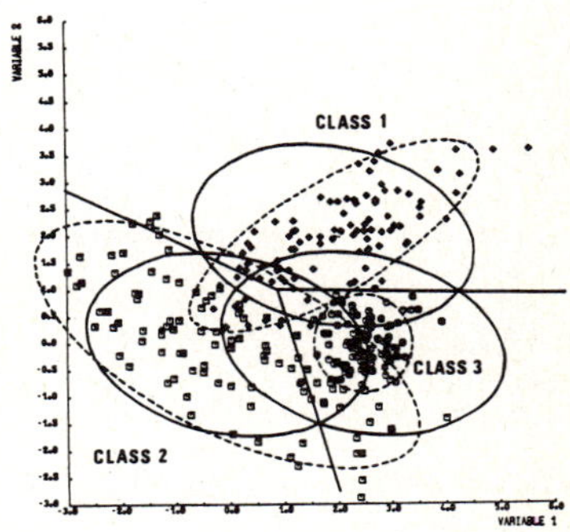

Fig. 2 Scatter plot and classification results of the 3-class case for linear discriminant analysis (LDA) and quadratic discriminant analysis (QDA).

CLASSES 1 + 2 POOLED VERSUS CLASS 3:

LDA

2-CLASS CASE

	1 + 2	3	
CLASS 1 + 2	170	30	85%
CLASS 3	20	80	80%
			83.7%

3-CLASS CASE

	1 + 2	3	
CLASS 1 + 2	174	26	87%
CLASS 3	2	98	98%
			91%

QDA

2-CLASS-CASE

	1 + 2	3	
CLASS 1 + 2	192	8	96%
CLASS 3	10	90	90%
			94%

3-CLASS-CASE

	1 + 2	3	
CLASS 1 + 2	181	11	90.5%
CLASS 3	1	99	99%
			93.3%

CLASSES 1 + 3 POOLED VERSUS CLASS 2:

LDA

2-CLASS CASE

	1 + 3	2	
CLASS 1 + 3	190	10	95%
CLASS 2	19	81	81%
			90%

3-CLASS CASE

	1 + 3	2	
CLASS 1 + 3	187	13	93.5%
CLASS 2	28	72	72.0%
			86.3%

QDA

2-CLASS-CASE

	1 + 3	2	
CLASS 1 + 3	200	0	100%
CLASS 2	14	86	86%
			95.3%

3-CLASS-CASE

	1 + 3	2	
CLASS 1 + 3	190	10	95%
CLASS 2	9	91	91%
			93.7%

Tab. 1 Classification results for final two classes pooled before classification (left columns) and after classification (right columns).

Decision trees

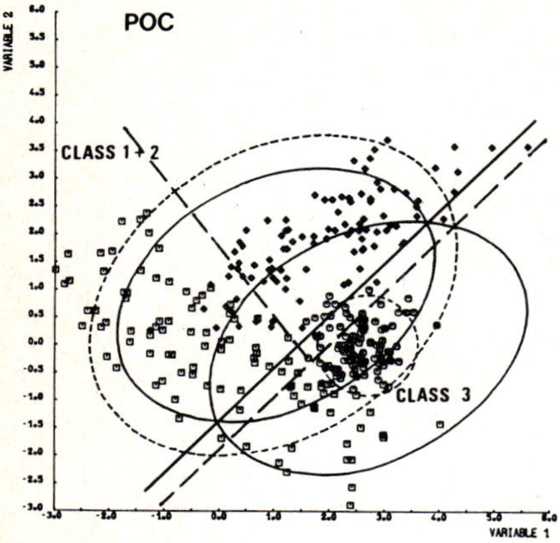

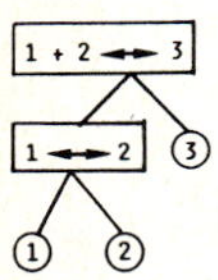

CLASSIFICATION RESULT:

	①	②	③	
①	85	14	1	85%
②	-	71	29	71%
③	18	2	80	80%
				78.7%

Fig. 3

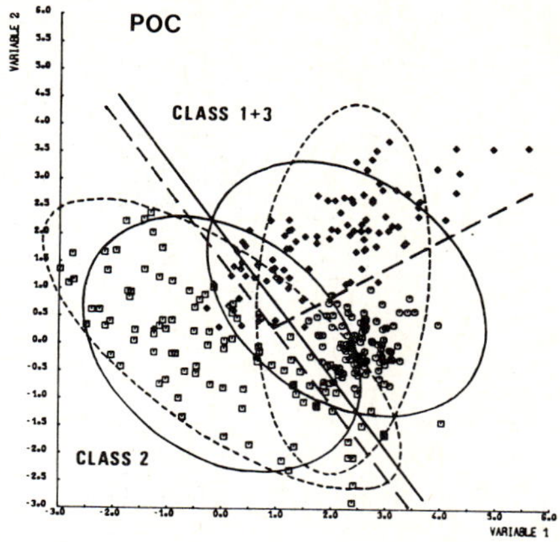

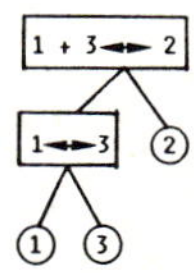

CLASSIFICATION RESULT:

	①	②	③	
①	87	9	4	87%
②	1	81	18	81%
③	1	1	98	98%
				88.7%

Fig. 4

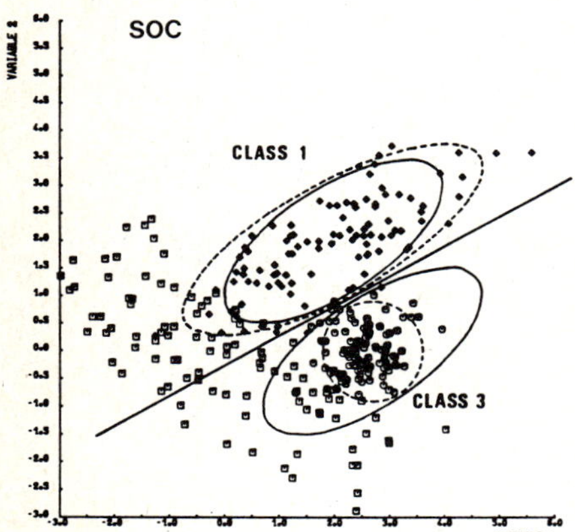

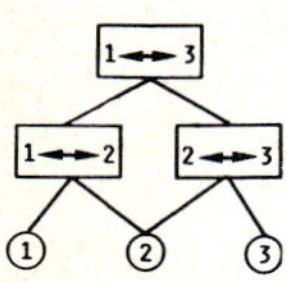

CLASSIFICATION RESULT:

	①	②	③	
①	94	4	2	94%
②	5	89	6	89%
③	1	4	95	95%
				92.7%

Fig. 5

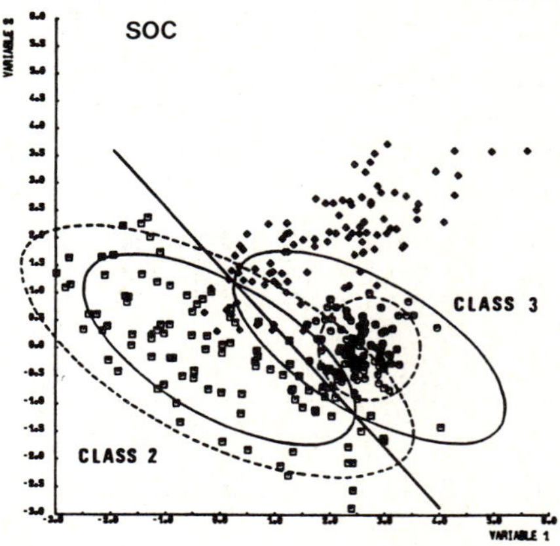

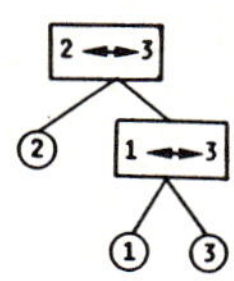

CLASSIFICATION RESULT:

	①	②	③	
①	90	9	1	90%
②	-	89	11	89%
③	2	2	96	96%
				91.7%

Fig. 6

Fig. 3-6 Classification results for selected decision trees (POC-figs. 3 and 4, SOC-figs. 5 and 6) for 3 classes.

Mamma

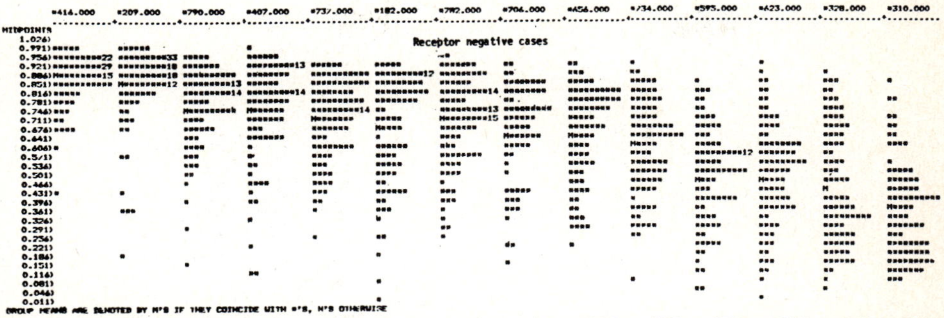

GROUP MEANS ARE DENOTED BY M'S IF THEY COINCIDE WITH *'S, N'S OTHERWISE

	*414.000	*209.000	*790.000	*407.000	*737.000	*182.000	*782.000	*706.000	*456.000	*734.000	*595.000	*423.000	*328.000	*310.000
MEAN	0.881	0.865	0.762	0.749	0.714	0.669	0.703	0.658	0.646	0.590	0.483	0.483	0.444	0.347
STD.DEV.	0.092	0.141	0.149	0.185	0.150	0.209	0.162	0.181	0.176	0.178	0.186	0.198	0.223	0.185
R.E.S.D.	0.085	0.115	0.144	0.177	0.153	0.220	0.161	0.181	0.185	0.186	0.189	0.200	0.242	0.190
S. E. M.	0.009	0.013	0.015	0.019	0.014	0.021	0.015	0.021	0.019	0.018	0.019	0.020	0.023	0.019
MAXIMUM	0.986	0.990	0.962	0.982	0.935	0.927	0.956	0.909	0.917	0.918	0.847	0.931	0.885	0.863
MINIMUM	0.437	0.192	0.159	0.122	0.251	0.011	0.247	0.165	0.230	0.095	0.062	0.017	0.030	0.066
SAMPLE SIZE	102	112	93	96	108	95	113	73	90	97	92	94	96	95

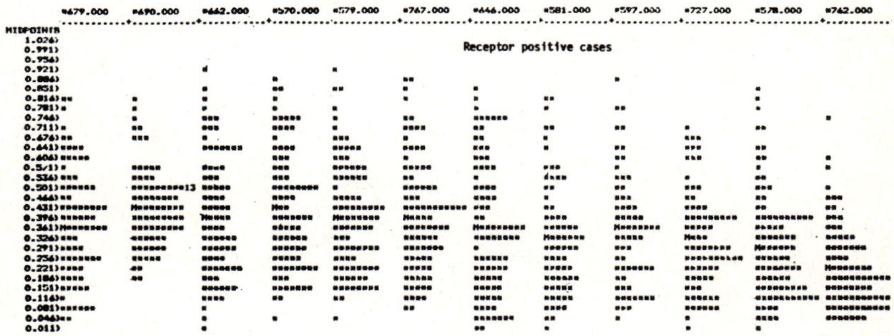

	*679.000	*690.000	*662.000	*570.000	*579.000	*767.000	*646.000	*581.000	*597.000	*727.000	*578.000	*762.000
MEAN	0.377	0.437	0.405	0.424	0.400	0.403	0.358	0.323	0.354	0.318	0.300	0.228
STD.DEV.	0.190	0.134	0.210	0.206	0.190	0.194	0.225	0.194	0.192	0.169	0.184	0.143
R.E.S.D.	0.176	0.130	0.220	0.218	0.195	0.195	0.235	0.193	0.191	0.170	0.183	0.141
S. E. M.	0.021	0.014	0.023	0.021	0.019	0.020	0.023	0.023	0.023	0.018	0.019	0.015
MAXIMUM	0.803	0.821	0.935	0.875	0.906	0.902	0.849	0.815	0.871	0.695	0.839	0.737
MINIMUM	0.053	0.169	0.020	0.040	0.037	0.078	0.018	0.022	0.038	0.027	0.014	0.038
SAMPLE SIZE	85	86	87	93	99	95	95	74	68	84	97	87

CLASSIFICATION RESULT:

	RECEPT. +	RECEPT. -	UNCLEAR
RECEPT. +	11	-	1
RECEPT. -	2	11	1

Fig. 7 Probability distributions of specimens and classification results for the two classes of hormon receptor positive and negative mamma cancer biopsies.

Cervix

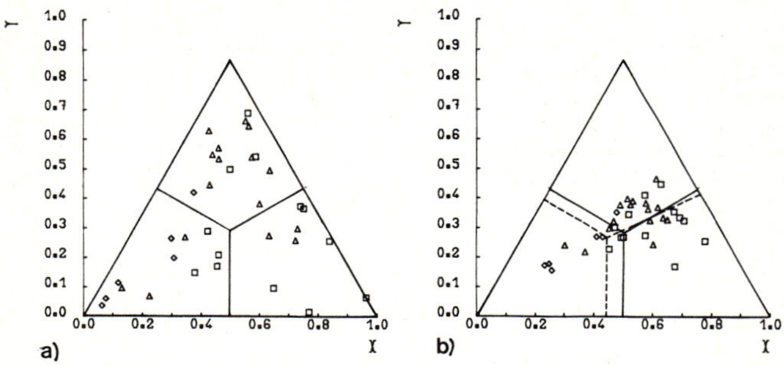

Fig.8a,b Scatter plot of atypia index for cervical specimens in a triangle probability diagramm. Fig. 8a is based on classified cell numbers per specimen, fig. 8b on average a-posteriori probabilities.

Thyroid

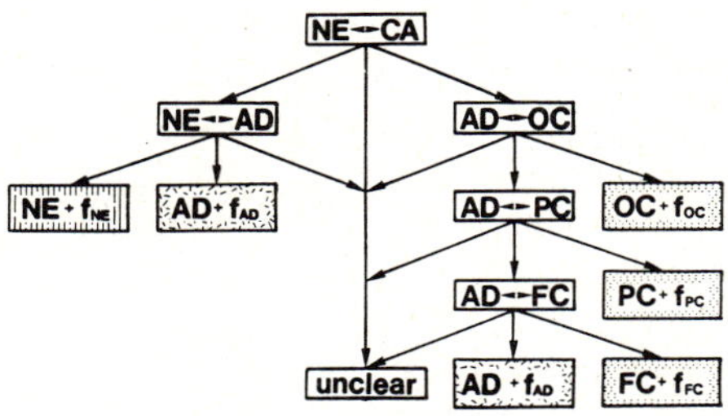

Fig. 9 Decision tree for classification of thyroid specimens (see legend table 2)

CLASSIFICATION RESULT OF THE DECISION TREE

	NEG/ FUNCT.	FOLLIC. AD	FOLLIC. CA	PAPILL. CA	ONKOCYT. CA	UNCL.	TOTAL
NEGATIVE	10	2	-	-	-	1	13
ADENOMA	-	18	3	2	-	10	33
FOLLIC. CA	2	3	6	6	2	9	28
PAPILL. CA	-	-	-	12	1	3	16
ONKOCYT. CA	-	-	-	-	8	-	8

RESULT AFTER POOLING ALL TYPES OF CARCINOMAS

	NEG	AD	CA	UNCL.	TOTAL
NEGATIVE	10	2	-	1	13
ADENOMA	-	18	5	10	33
CARCINOMA	2	3	35	12	52

CLASSIFICATION RESULT OF THE MULTICLASS CASE:

	NEG/ FUNCT.	FOLLIC. AD	FOLLIC. CA	PAPILL. CA	ONKOCYT. CA	UNCL.	TOTAL
NEGATIVE	5	4	1	-	-	3	13
ADENOMA	-	24	5	-	-	4	33
FOLLIC. CA	-	8	9	-	1	10	28
PAPILL. CA	-	9	3	2	-	2	16
ONKOCYT. CA	-	1	1	-	2	4	8

RESULT AFTER POOLING ALL TYPES OF CARCINOMAS

	NEG	AD	CA	UNCL.	TOTAL
NEGATIVE	5	4	1	3	13
ADENOMA	-	24	5	4	33
CARCINOMA	-	18	18	16	52

Tab. 2 Specimen classification results for 5 pathologically relevant classes of thyroid biopsies based upon the decision tree of fig. 9, and based upon single step multiclass LDA. (NE=negative, AD=Adenoma, FC=folliculary carcinoma, PC=papillary carcinoma, OC=oncocytary carcinoma).

DISCUSSION

Haralick:

In the example where you split classes one and three against class two, you never go back to the node that ideally should have only objects of class 2.

Due to misclassifications, that class will be impure. When the impurities come mostly from say class 3 you may well try to design a classifier to separate class 2 and class 3 objects for that node.

Burger:

Indeed that should be considered.

Timmers:

I have two remarks. Firstly, there are two different approaches to the problem of specimen classification. One is the cell classification approach which is the one you presented. In the other approach one goes directly from the feature distributions of the specimens to the diagnostic classes. One would expect that with the intermediate cells the latter approach would be better since you hardly expect clearly deviating cells in this kind of studies.

The second remark concerns the cell classification approach. When you optimize your procedure you should always keep in mind that it is a two-level classifier. Both levels should be combined in order to achieve optimal results. It is even perceivable that the best specimen classifier does not incorporate the best classifier at the cell level.

SECTION VII

PATTERN RECOGNITION AND ARTIFICIAL INTELLIGENCE

PATTERN RECOGNITION IN PRACTICE II
E.S. Gelsema and L.N. Kanal (Editors)

CONSENSUS AND EVIDENCE

by

Carlos Berenstein+*
Laveen N. Kanal+*
David Lavine*

University of Maryland+
and
L.N.K. Corporation*
P.O. Box 1619
College Park, Maryland 20742
U.S.A.

ABSTRACT

Combining the opinions of experts is a problem of broad interest and considerable difficulty. In one formulation of the problem, each expert estimates the probability of certain events, and the goal is to produce a single probability distribution which summarizes the various estimates. Consensus theory is the study of such combination procedures. This paper surveys consensus theory and describes possible directions for extensions of some of the techniques which may be useful in providing more flexible modeling. General results giving inherent limitations on the consensus process are described, as well as specific consensus rules. Extensions of consensus theory to the generalized probabilities developed in evidence theory are presented.

1. INTRODUCTION

The combination of opinions from several individuals is fundamental to the decision making process in many situations. One finds a variety of individuals assessing the likelihood of certain events and some procedure is required to form a single assessment of the likelihood of the events. In this paper, we examine work in this area of assessment combination, known as consensus theory. In a paper presented at the Army Conference on Application of Artificial Intelligence to Battlefield Information Management [Kanal et. al. 1983] we noted that consensus theory which had been of considerable interest in the social and management sciences, and had not hitherto been noticed by A.I. researchers, had potential applications in the combining of assessments in expert consulting systems. To understand more fully the potential applications of consensus theory in expert systems, we surveyed consensus theory and examined belief manipulation methods currently being proposed for use in expert systems. This paper summarizes some of this research. More extensive discussion and simulations of various approaches to consensus formation can be found in our report to the the U.S. Army Research Institute for the Behavioral and Social Sciences [Lambird et.al. 1984].

Although consensus theory has not been touched upon much in the literature on expert systems, several excellent surveys have recently appeared on techniques for

---

This paper is based on research supported in part by the U.S. Army Research Institute for the Behavioral and Social Sciences under a contract to L.N.K. Corporation, and in part by NSF grants to the University of Maryland.

dealing with uncertainty in artificial intelligence. Examples include [Prade 1985] which provides a unifying formalism for modelling of uncertainty in plausible reasoning schemes; and [Spiegelhalter 1985] which reviews a variety of qualitative and quantitative techniques for handling uncertainty in expert systems and presents arguments in favor of a subjectivist Bayesian view of uncertainty as being the most suitable technique.

Consensus theory is in the early stages of its development and no generally acceptable mathematical formulation exists. There exist a wide variety of tools which have been applied to the consensus problem. Some of the tools are probabilistic, others attempt to capture uncertainty while steering clear of the formal structure of probability theory. In the attempt to avoid the restrictions imposed by probability theory, some researchers have developed procedures generalizing probability theory, while others have used entirely different methods. Probabilistic interpretations of various existing ad hoc methods continue to appear: for example [Heckerman, 1985] and other papers presented at the AAAI/IEEE Workshop on Uncertainty and Probability in A.I., August 1985.

In this paper, we restrict our attention to techniques which are either probabilistic or closely related to probabilistic methods. The primary reason for this is that this permits a more systematic theoretical and experimental exploration of the possibilities for modifying consensus rules to take into account various factors we think are important in the consensus problem.

Among those consensus methods which have a strong relation to probability, we distinguish two types. First, we have those methods which use probabilities for the assessments, though the rules for combining assessments may not have a formal probabilistic basis. Second, we have those methods which use some generalized form of probability for the assessments. The use of generalized probabilities has the advantage of providing greater flexibility in modelling and the disadvantage of making the derivation of inference and decision procedures more difficult.

Before going into a mathematical description of the material, in Section 2 we present a more intuitive outline of the relevant ideas.

2. OVERVIEW

The first consensus approach we consider is called evidence theory [Shafer 1976]. Evidence theory is a generalization of probability theory in which belief in an event can be expressed without asserting how that belief is distributed over the subevents which form that event. Consider, for example, the problem of determining the presence of a major military unit such as a division without making any assertions about its subunits such as battalions and regiments. The evidence that is used to establish the presence of a division need not be derived from information about the presence of its battalions and regiments. On the other hand, any measure of confidence in the presence of these units could also be accommodated. In this formalism, there are two measures of certainty associated with an event. There is first, the degree of certainty which is associated with the entire event and is not derived from any estimate of certainty about its constituents. In our example, we may have received a message that a division is entering the battlefield. We may assign a degree of belief to this message, based on the source, and independent of sightings of individual units within the division. On the other hand, individual units likely to be in this division may have been sighted, each of which has an associated belief. The beliefs in these constituents can be combined with the belief in the division as a whole to get a total measure of belief in the presence of the division. This approach gives rise to a model in which the users information can be more accurately reflected than in a traditional probabilistic model in which all weights attached to an event are derived from the weights of its components.

One advantage of the evidence theory formulation is that it does not force evidence about an event to make strong implications in belief in the negation of the event. This feature is particularly useful in battlefield applications since weak evidence indicating the presence of a force element may be available, but we do not wish to treat this as being strong evidence for its absence. For example, a POW report of relatively low reliability may indicate the presence of a battalion. From this we do not want to conclude that there is a high likelihood of there not being a battalion, but only that there is little positive support for the presence of the battalion. In general, evidence theory provides a high degree of flexibility in modelling various facets of uncertainty in the data. The basic idea in evidence theory is that we set up a new space in which every event in the original space of situations becomes a point and the assessments of a given expert give a probability distribution, m, in this new space. The belief in any event, A, (even for those for which no assessment has been given) can be generated by the rule:

$$Bel(A) = \sum m(B),$$

where the sum is over all subsets B of A. The problem one faces now is how to combine these different probability distributions.

Evidence theory has a rule, known as the Dempster-Shafer rule, for combining the generalized probabilities known as beliefs. As has been mentioned by several authors and was confirmed in our numerical experiments, this rule will often not lead to realistic assessments, even under the assumption of independence of the experts. This is a limitation of the particular consensus rule and not of evidence theory in general. The Dempster-Shafer rule is, in no way, determined by the principles of evidence theory. To produce a better combination rule, we turned back to more probabilistic approaches for a hint of a suitable direction. Evidence theory appears to provide a generalization of probability theory which is useful for more realistic modelling of problems such as the battlefield situation; alternatives to the Dempster-Shafer rule of evidence theory should be sought. In our simulations we focused on alternative rules.

Several approaches to the consensus problem are briefly surveyed in subsequent sections. We consider linear and nonlinear combination rules; feedback, a linear combination rule [DeGroot 1974] provided one of the most reasonable starting points for consensus experimentation. The basic setting may be thought of as consisting of a set of experts, each of whom has assigned probabilities to various events. Each expert revises his probability assessment by replacing his probability of an event by a linear combination of the various expert opinions, including his own, for that event. The coefficients used in the linear combination do not vary from event to event. (This restriction is not essential to the feedback approach.) After one round of this, each expert has a new set of probabilities for the events, though the probabilities will generally vary from expert to expert. The whole process is repeated until the assessments of the various experts converge. Convergence can be shown under rather weak assumptions. Moreover, using a fundamental result encountered in the elementary theory of stochastic processes, it is possible to determine the limiting distribution directly from solving a system of linear equations rather than carrying out the limiting process. Details of this approach appear below. The feedback approach, is designed to provide a rough model of the process of experts sitting round a table listening to the opinions of others and revising their opinions when they feel it is appropriate.

The choice of coefficients in the feedback approach can be made in many ways. In our experiments we defined these coefficients to take into account several potentially important factors in the decision-making process. First, experts vary widely in their reliability. We attempted to take this into consideration by having the coefficients depend on a measure of each expert's reliability. This measure, which we refer to as the expert's self-confidence, could be estimated in various ways. The expert's knowledge and past performance would play a critical role in this estimation procedure. Each expert's coefficients, which determine the relative importance of all the experts including himself, sum to one. In addition, the self-confidence of each expert is between zero and one. If reliability is the only factor being incorporated, then each expert uses his self-confidence as his coefficient and divides the remaining weight among the other experts according to their relative self-confidences. Thus the most reliable experts tend to dominate the process.

A second factor, which we introduced was to modify the feedback approach in order to take into account the correlation between experts. Experts who tend to have the same conclusions may tend to dominate the consensus process, though the amount of independent information they represent is not great. Thus we introduced a measure of correlation between experts which is used in the definition of coefficients. Essentially, each expert decreases the weight he gives to experts who tend to produce conclusions similar to himself. While this may seem counterintuitive, consider the expert assessment values as being analogous to values of a random variable, and consider correlation in the expert sense as corresponding to positive correlation between random variables. Then as the correlation between experts goes to one, the expert assessments are deterministically related and all available information is contained in just one of the estimates. By giving high weights to several highly correlated assessments, we are giving considerable weight to redundant information. Alternate approaches to the use of correlation in assessments are possible and some suggested formulas are given below, but no experimental work has been done on these yet.

The number of variables which occur in most realistic situations is quite large and some means for structuring the problem to avoid a tremendous number of variable interactions is required. For example, observations on a given entity at different times may be treated as a set of distinct but related variables. Graphs provide a convenient approach to the structuring of variables. Each node in the graph corresponds to a collection of events. Dependency between nodes is only considered to be of importance if the nodes are joined by an arc. The consensus methods described above can then be used at each node to determine the probabilities or beliefs we attach to corresponding events. A new set of rules is then required to propagate these values throughout the graph. This propagation of beliefs should be studied in connection with the heuristic graph search procedures such as SSS* [Stockman and Kanal, 1983], [Leifker and Kanal, 1985]. Several formulations of the graph-based propagation of consensus appear promising. However, because of space limitations we defer our discussion of this topic to another occasion.

We conducted experiments to explore the feedback approach in detail. In these experiments, probabilities of several events were generated and each expert's assessments were generated by perturbing the true probabilities of the events. By varying the perturbation parameters, we were able to vary the reliability of the experts and the correlation between the experts. The feedback approach was compared against a simple averaging of assessment and a weighted averaging of assessments. In one experiment, we investigated the effect of making inaccuracies in the self-confidence value, where the self-confidence values did not reflect the reliability of the expert. In another experiment, we explored the effect of varying the correlation of the expert opinions. Several other experiments were conducted to determine if the coefficient matrix actually did mirror the underlying phenomena of expert reliability and noise. Except for a few anomalies at isolated parameter values, the procedure for incorporating self-confidence and correlation into the coefficients resulted in consensus values which were sensitive to expert reliability and correlation in the data. Since the procedures for incorporating these factors were ad hoc, there was no guarantee that they would perform well. The errors in the consensus estimates were reduced up to twenty percent of the maximum error possible given the noise generating mechanism. As the number of variations in coefficient definitions was small, it is quite possible that these results might be improved still further.

3. FOUNDATIONS OF CONSENSUS APPROACHES

We now give a more detailed description of some important theories and methods which have been used for consensus. With some of the methods described, we suggest modifications which we feel may make consensus techniques more practical. To aid in the discussion, we consider two primary classes of consensus problems, which we refer to as static and time-dependent. This characterization is not rigorous, but the basic notions are:

(i) In the "static" situation, we have several "events" $A_1, \ldots, A_N$ (i.e. subsets of a certain set Ω) and each expert j assigns a number p_{ij} to the i-th event A_i, $0 \le p_{ij} \le 1$. We want to assign numbers p_i to those events and also possibly to other related events, once and for all. There are situations in which we might "update" these numbers if we know that a certain event E has taken place by "conditioning on E" but this can be thought of as a new application of the same procedure. The several difficulties in this static situation, and methods available to work them out, will be discussed below.

(ii) In the time-dependent or "dynamic" case, a natural partial ordering of events arises for example, from the association of a time element with an event. This leads to the representation of the events as the nodes in an acyclic directed graph, with the edges indicating the partial order. Associated with each node is a vector whose components may represent assessments of the likelihood of that event. When the values associated with one of the nodes is changed, changes propagate to the other nodes. The problem of propagating such changes through the graph is more complex than that of case (i). It has been addressed by several authors including Marschak and Radner (1972), Lemmer (1976), and Pearl (1982). In this paper, we restrict attention to case (1)

This first difficulty one faces in (i) is that the experts might not be "consistent" in their assignments, i.e., the values p_{ij} do not arise out of a probability density function (p.d.f.), i.e., A_3 might be the disjoint version of A_1 and A_2 but $p_{1j}+p_{2j} \neq p_{3j}$. Similarly, $\sum_i p_{ij} \neq 1$. (In fact in practice we might not ever have probability assignments p_{ij} but "confidence intervals" $[l_{ij}, u_{ij}]$; we will come back to this point later). In case we do have underlying p.d.f.'s, we have several reasonable ways of combining them; in the other case, which one expects to occur fairly often in the battlefield situation or in medical applications, one could try to give up any pretense of structure but then what meaning do we give to the numbers one comes up with and how can we retain some of the advantages of having a p.d.f. This is the path taken by the Dempster-Shafer theory of belief functions which we now summarize.

3.1. Dempster-Shafer Theory

Belief theory ([Shafer, 1976], [Shafer, 1982], [Diaconis, 1978], [Garvey et. al., 1981], [Barnett, 1981]) is an attempt to deal with the limitations of probability theory in describing assessments. The key problem is that many people, when asked to indicate their confidence that an event has occurred give a number that is not readily interpretable as a probability. In particular one may specify one's confidence that an event has occurred based on observations. One's confidence that the event has not occurred may not be one minus one's confidence that it has occurred. As an example, one may assess the probability that a tank regiment is in the area. Several observations of opposing tanks may give a small amount of credence to the hypothesis that a tank regiment is in the area. This may result in a low level of confidence that a tank regiment is in the area. On the other hand, we may have little evidence that a tank regiment is not in the area. Weather conditions may reduce visibility, hilly terrain may severely limit viewing range, and few observers may be available to search the area. These conditions could all contribute to a reluctance in assigning a high probability that a tank regiment is not in the area. Consequently, the probability that a tank regiment is in the area and the probability that a tank regiment is not in the area may each be low. This is inconsistent with traditional probability theory.

A second shortcoming of traditional probability theory arises when we consider events which may be formed from other events. As an example, suppose we consider the event that a tank division is present in an area. A tank division consists of many smaller units, some of which may have been observed with varying degrees of certainty. Some of our confidence that a tank division is present may not be derived from our certainty of the presence of various parts of the division. For example, a message indicating the presence of a division in the area may have been intercepted. This message may or may not be correct so an assessment of the message reliability must be performed. Some measure of message reliability may be available solely based on the source of the information. This may be regarded as a measure of confidence that an event has occurred which is independent of one's confidence in the subevents forming that event. In traditional probability, if an event can be written as a disjoint union of other events, it's probability is the sum of the probabilities of the other events. Our tank division example necessitates an extension of probability theory to allow some of the confidence in an event to exist independent of the confidence in subevents.

The Dempster-Shafer theory of evidence provides a generalized theory of probability which overcomes the limitations of traditional probability theory described above. A price must be paid for the generality of the theory. Many of the traditional procedures of classical statistical analysis such as parameter inference and hypothesis testing become difficult to define. As a result of these limitations and other problems with the theory, few practical applications of the theory have been attempted. The general framework of the theory is quite flexible and modifications of the theory could overcome some of the objections. In particular, a rule for combining generalized probabilities is singled out and developed in the theory of evidence. This rule, called the Dempster combination rule has strong drawbacks and it's replacement by rules similar to those indicated in other parts of this paper would partially alleviate these drawbacks.

A central idea in the theory of evidence is that to get around inconsistencies in the relationship of probability assignment to events and subevents, one should consider a probability density function (p.d.f.) m on the set 2^{Ω} of all subsets of the sample space Ω (in applications Ω is usually a finite set of n elements and hence the cardinality of 2^{Ω} defined by $\#(2^{\Omega})=2^n$). Events $A_1,\ldots,A_N$ are now points of 2^{Ω} and we can define $m(A_i)=$ previously assigned probability of A_i (i.e. in the case of several experts we have several p.d.f.'s m on 2^{Ω} and $m_j(A_i)=p_{ij}$). This selection automatically eliminates most of the original inconsistencies, except that we need that

$$\sum_{A\in 2^{\Omega}} m(A) = 1$$

It is clear that in this context we can always assume $m(\emptyset)=0$, but as we said above, it might happen that

$$k = \sum_{j=1}^{N} m(A_j) \neq 1$$

If $k>1$ then we normalize by dividing by k. But if $k<1$ (we clearly can assume $0<k$ otherwise we do not believe at all in any of the possible events $A_1,\ldots,A_N$) then we have two distinct possibilities (and a choice has to be made in each situation):

(a) We think that $A_1,\ldots,A_N$ is an exhaustive collection of events we want to consider. In this case, we normalize by dividing by k.

(b) In the other case we assign to Ω the value $m(\Omega)=1-k$. Note that Ω is just another point in 2^{Ω}. This process is akin to the notion of discounting; if we think that an expert is overly optimistic in his assessments, we can introduce a new p.d.f. in 2^{Ω}, m_{α}, as follows: let $0<\alpha<1$ be a fixed number (the discount factor), then

$$m_{\alpha}(A) = \begin{cases} \alpha m(A) & \text{if} A \neq \Omega \\ \alpha m(\Omega)+(1-\alpha) & \textit{otherwise.} \end{cases}$$

Associated to m, occasionally called the basic probability mass, we have two functions on events in Ω, the belief function *Bel* and the plausibility function *Pl* which can be considered as giving the lower and upper limits of the confidence interval corresponding to the event A.

$$Bel(A) = \sum_{B\subseteq A} m(B)$$

and

$$Pl(A) = 1 - Bel(\neg A),$$

where $\neg A$ is the complement of A relative to Ω. We note that *Bel* and *Pl* use the relations between events in Ω and do not consider them as separate entities; on the other hand they are not p.d.f.'s in Ω. We have

$$Bel(A)+Bel(\neg A) = \sum_{B\subseteq A} m(B) + \sum_{B\subseteq \neg A} m(B) \leq \sum_{B\subseteq \Omega} m(B) = 1$$

and hence

$$0 \leq Bel(A) \leq Pl(A) \leq 1$$

as expected.

Belief functions are characterized among all functions $2^{\Omega} \to [0,1]$ by (i) $Bel(\emptyset) = 0$, (ii) $Bel(\Omega) = 1$, and (iii) for every collection $A_1, \ldots, A_N$ of N subsets of Ω we have $Bel(A_1 \bigcup \cdots \bigcup A_N) \geq \sum_{\substack{I \subseteq \{1,\ldots,N\} \\ I \neq \emptyset}} (-1)^{\#(I)+1} Bel(\bigcap_{i \in j} A_i)$. In which case

$$m(A) = \sum_{B \subseteq A} (-1)^{\#(A/B)} Bel(B)$$

is the corresponding basic probability mass.

A probability density function, p, is a particular kind of belief function on the finite set Ω; then the corresponding basic probability mass m is supported by the singletons:

$$m(\{x\}) = p(x), \quad \text{for } all \ x \in \Omega$$

and there is no mass associated with sets with more than one element,

$$i.e \quad m(A) = 0 \quad \text{if} \quad \#(A) \neq 1.$$

In this case the belief function is called Bayesian.

We are interested in combining the opinions of different experts when we consider them as belief functions. Shafer explores only one way of doing this, namely the Dempster combination rule, but as it is easy to see there are in fact many other reasonable choices. Let us recall Dempster's rule:

Let $Bel_1, \ldots, Bel_n$ be belief functions on Ω. Then their combination $Bel_1 + \cdots + Bel_n$ is the belief function corresponding to the basic probability mass

$$m(A) = \frac{1}{k} \sum_A m_1(A_1) m_2(A_2) \cdots m_n(A_n), \quad A \neq \emptyset.$$

where the sum takes place over all n-tuples of subsets of Ω such that $A_1 \bigcap \cdots \bigcap A_n = A$. This notion only makes sense when

$$\sum_{\emptyset} = \sum m_1(A_1) \cdots m_n(A_n) < 1,$$

i.e. the sum is taken over the collections $A_1, \ldots, A_n$ such that $A_1 \bigcap \cdots \bigcap A_n = \emptyset$. Then the normalization constant takes the value

$$k = 1 - \sum_{\emptyset}.$$

On the other hand $Bel_1 + \cdots + Bel_n$ cannot be defined if there are sets $A_1, \ldots, A_n$, $A_1 \bigcap \cdots \bigcap A_n = \emptyset$ and $Bel_j(A_j) = 1$, which means the experts hold completely contradictory views. When $Bel_1 + \cdots + Bel_n$ can be defined, we say the belief functions are combinable.

One consequence of the Dempster rule is that it makes it very easy to condition belief functions. Suppose we have absolute certainty of an event E, then define the basic probability mass m_2 by $m_2(E) = 1$. The original belief function Bel_1 is combinable with Bel_2 if and only if $Bel_1(\neg E) < 1$; then

$$Bel_1(A \mid E) := (Bel_1 + Bel_2)(A)$$

It is very curious that the plausibility function one obtains this way obeys Bayes' rule

$$Pl_1(A \mid E)=Pl_1(A \cap E)/Pl_1(E).$$

Before continuing with our summary of the Dempster-Shafer theory let us point out that any combination of the basic probability masses $m_1, \ldots, m_N$ that produces a new basic probability mass m could be used. In particular a combination rule such as the following which reflects possible correlation between the different experts could be used:

$$(LC) \qquad m(A)=k\sum_j w_j(A, m_1, \ldots, m_N)m_j(A), \quad A \in 2^{\Omega},$$

where the weights w_j are such that $m(A) \geq 0$, e.g. $0 \leq w_j \leq 1$ and $\sum_j w_j(A, m_1, \ldots, m_N)=1$ for all A. We write the weights in this fashion to indicate that the weights depend not only on A, but also on the whole knowledge of $m_1, \ldots, m_n$. The condition $m(\emptyset)=0$ is evidently satisfied. We need the constant k to make certain that $\sum m(A)=1$. If the w_j are constants and $\sum_j w_j=1$, then

$$\sum_A m(A)=k\sum_A\sum_j w_j\, m_j(A)=k\sum_j w_j \sum_A m_j(A)=k\sum_j w_j=k$$

so k can be taken to be 1, otherwise k might be $\neq 1$. To appreciate the full range of possible combination rules it is enough to note the following: let $n=\#(\Omega)$ and $d=2^n-1$, then a basic probability mass can be identified with a point $\overline{m}$ in the standard simplex Δ of R^d defined by:

$$\Delta=\{\overline{m}=(m^1, \ldots, m^d): m^k \geq 0, m^1+\ldots+m^d=1\}.$$

Hence a combination rule for $m_1, \ldots, m_N$ is just any function $\Delta^N \rightarrow \Delta$ (and in fact it does not even need to be defined in the whole of Δ^N, as the Dempster rule shows). Regretfully, for the moment at least, it is hard to choose among the several possible ad-hoc rules of the type (LC) that incorporate the knowledge of the correlation between the experts, but we reiterate that any combination rule for general p.d.f.'s automatically gives us a combination rule for basic probability masses and hence for belief functions.

3.1.1. Belief Theory - Parametric Inference

There are also several generalizations to belief functions of the Bayesian theory of parametric inference. In fact, Shafer gives two, one in his book [Shafer, 1976], and another more recently in [Shafer, 1982] based on an idea of P. Smets. The situation is as follows. We have a number of independent empirical belief functions P_θ about data $x \in X$, where θ runs over a finite space of parameters Θ. One constructs a belief function *Bel* over $\Theta \times X$ as follows: first we associate to each P_θ a belief function Bel_θ on $\Theta \times X$ by conditional embedding and then *Bel* equals combination of Bel_θ according to the previously described combination rule. The conditional embedding of P_θ is defined by

$$m(\{(\theta,x)\} \bigcup (\Theta\ \{\theta\}) \times X)=P_\theta(x); \ m \textit{ is zero otherwise.}$$

Then we have $Bel(\cdot \mid \{\theta\} \times X)=P_\theta$ and if one observes $x \in X$, one can condition *Bel* on $\Theta \times \{x\}$ and obtain *a posteriori* values of belief for Θ.

There are some problems with this theory though, and alternatives have been proposed by Smets, Walley and Fine respectively in [Shafer, 1982]. Part of the difficulties stem from the Dempster rule. It seems worthwhile to point out here the very interesting paper [Wolfenson and Fine, 1982] where upper and lower probabilities together with some Bayesian ideas are used for parameter estimation.

Of course, we might want to use inference rules even if we are not estimating parameters, using the interval of confidence $[Bel(A), Pl(A)]$. A set of such rules is proposed in [Garvey et. al, 1981] and then combined repeatedly with the Dempster rule to search through graphs. The difficulty is that some of the obvious, and we should say natural, rules of inference do not seem to produce intervals of confidence where the lower and upper limits are related to a single basic probability mass; e.g. see [Garvey et. al, 1981 p.322]. If A and B have intervals $[Bel(A), Pl(A)]$ and $[Bel(B), Pl(B)]$ respectively, then they define the intervals for $A \vee B$ as $[s(A \vee B), p(A \vee B)]$, where

$$s(A \vee B) = \max\{Bel(A), Bel(B)\}$$

$$p(A \vee B) = \min\{1, Pl(A) + Pl(B)\}.$$

Now we associate, as usual, the proposition $A \vee B$ to the set $A \bigcup B$ but there is no reason why $Bel(A \bigcup B) = s(A \vee B)$ or $p(A \vee B) = Pl(A \bigcup B)$. The only way around this might be to assume that one is willing to consider assigning a basic probability to a few sets such that no smaller sets are assigned any mass and produce a new function on 2^{Ω} by the inference rules of [Garvey et. al, 1981]. This might have to be normalized, nevertheless it is not clear that their process is consistent, since for instance out of $A \vee B$ (as above) and A they infer B with interval $[s(B), p(B)]$, where

$$s(B) = \max\{0, s(A \vee B) - Pl(A)\}$$

$$p(B) = p(A \vee B)$$

and there is no reason to conclude that $s(B) = Bel(B)$ and $p(B) = Pl(B)$.

3.2. Bayesian Approach

There is another, more classical, approach to reconcile incoherent probability assignments, given in [McConway], [Lindley et. al, 1979] and [French, 1980]. It is based on the ideas of Bayes theorem but mainly applied to the log-odds for robustness. For simplicity of exposition we follow [French, 1980]; for more details see [Lindley et. al, 1979]. The model is that of a manager who has to make up his mind in the light of experts' opinions. They work out the case of a single expert. To deal with several experts one repeats the procedure.

We are interested in a particular event A, to which we have assigned probabilities $p(A)$, $p(\neg A) = 1 - p(A)$. The expert assigns probabilities $q(A)$, $q(\neg A)$ (if he is coherent then $q(\neg A) = 1 - q(A)$ but if not we will have to multiply his values by the value $(q(A) + q(\neg A))^{-1}$. That causes difficulty when we look at the log-odds as we will do below). In other words, we have two vectors $\vec{p}$, $\vec{q}$ and we would like to construct a new assessment of $p(A)$ using them and also any knowledge T of the expert. Then we are looking for a value $p(\vec{A} \mid q, T)$ which reflects both the expert assessment as well as our knowledge T of the expert (i.e. of his expertise to judge the event A). Our knowledge of the expert is reflected by any a-priori assignments

$$p(\vec{q} \mid A, T),\ p(\vec{q} \mid \neg A, T)$$

Then by Bayes' theorem

$$(B) \quad p(\vec{A} \mid q, T) = p(\vec{q} \mid A, T)\, p(A \mid \vec{T}) / p(q \mid T),$$

where

$$p(q \mid T)=p(q \mid A,T)\, p(A \mid T) + p(q \mid \neg A,T)\, p(\neg A \mid T).$$

If we do not have any reason to believe the contrary one takes $p(A \mid T)=p(A)$, $p(\neg A \mid T)=p(\neg A)$ but it might occur that $p(A \mid T)$, $p(\neg A \mid T)$ are updated in light of the information T. Introducing the log-odds

$$l(A)=\ln(p(A)/p(\neg A)), \lambda(A)=\ln(q(A)/q(\neg A))$$

we can talk of $l(A \mid \lambda, T)$ as the updated value, and using $ll(\lambda \mid A,T)=\ln(p(\lambda \mid A,T)/p(\lambda \mid \neg A,T))$ we get (B) transformed into

$$l(A \mid ,\lambda T)=ll(\lambda \mid A,T)+l(A \mid T).$$

Notice that this is a general model. In [Lindley et. al., 1981] and [French, 1980] they proceed to develop it under the fairly reasonable assumption that the log-odds are normally distributed. To follow up on [French, 1980] one really assumes that one knows the past prediction performances of the manager M himself and the expert S, so one has $p(\lambda,l \mid A)$,$p(\lambda,l \mid \neg A)$ and their log-odds follow the distribution

$$\lambda,l \mid A \quad \sim N\left[\begin{pmatrix} m_s \\ m_M \end{pmatrix}, \begin{pmatrix} \sigma_s^2 & r\sigma_s\sigma_M \\ r\sigma_s\sigma_M & \sigma_M^2 \end{pmatrix}\right]$$

$$\lambda,l \mid A \quad \sim N\left[\begin{pmatrix} \overline{m}_s \\ \overline{m}_M \end{pmatrix}, \begin{pmatrix} \sigma_s^2 & r\sigma_s\sigma_M \\ r\sigma_s\sigma_M & \sigma_M^2 \end{pmatrix}\right]$$

where m_s, m_M (respectively $\overline{m}_s, \overline{m}_M$) are the mean log-odds that the experts and the manager M state in favor of A (resp. $\neg A$), σ_s is the standard deviation the manager expects of S'statements, σ_M the s.d. for its own statements and r is the correlation between the statements of S and M. By following Bayes' theorem and conditioning , one has

$$\lambda \mid A,l \quad \sim \quad N(\mu(l),\Sigma^2), \quad \lambda \mid \neg A,l \quad \sim \quad N(\overline{\mu}(l),\Sigma^2)$$

where

$$\mu(l)=m_s + (r\sigma_s/\sigma_M)(l-m_s), \quad \overline{\mu}(l)=\overline{m}_s + (r\sigma_s/\sigma_M)(l-\overline{m}_M), \quad \Sigma^2=\sigma_s^2(1-r^2).$$

So the updated assessment is

$$l(A,T)=\{(\lambda-\overline{\mu}(l))^2-(\lambda-\mu(l))^2\}/(2\Sigma^2)+l(A \mid T)=(\mu(l)-\overline{\mu}(l))\,(\lambda-(\overline{\mu}(l)+\overline{\mu}(l)/2)/\Sigma^2+l(A,T)$$

A simple example is that in which M and S are of the same calibre then $m_s=m_M=m$, $\overline{m}_s=\overline{m}_M=\overline{m}$, $\sigma_s=\sigma_M=\sigma$. If A is more likely (in our opinion) than $\neg A$, i.e. $m \geq \overline{m}$, one has

$$l(A \mid \lambda,T)=(m-\overline{m})((\lambda-rl)(m+\overline{m})(1-r)/2)/(\sigma^2(1+r))+l(A \mid T).$$

Two particular cases are:
(i) S and M always agree. Then $\lambda=l$ and $r=1$ (since they are completely correlated) so $l(A \mid \lambda,T)=l(A \mid T)$, as expected; (ii) If S and M are equally ignorant about A, i.e. $m=\overline{m}$, then $l(A \mid \lambda,T)=l(A \mid T)$, and the assessment doesn't change. Other cases can also be easily analyzed from the above formula. Further developments along these lines have appeared recently in the area of parameter estimation [Lindley, 1983], [Winkler, 1981] and we will return to these papers when we discuss parameter estimation later on.

3.3. Some Consensus Rule Characteristics

We return now to the subject of combining p.d.f.'s without any assumption on their form, i.e. without assuming they are estimates of a numerical parameter. The work of McConway [McConway, 1980] shows that if one imposes too many reasonable-looking constraints on the combination rule then there are only a few possibilities for the rule and one loses the flexibility desired. In fact, he considers the requirements that the combination rules commute with marginalization, or commute with updating based on observing new data, or both. (There was previous work in this direction by Dalkey and others [Dalkey and Helmer, 1972],[Bordley and Wolff, 1981] but [McConway, 1980] is more complete). The situation is as follows: let Ω be a set such that $\#(\Omega)\geq 3$ (it could very well be infinite) and we have a collection of consensus rules for N experts that depend only on the σ-algebra of events considered, i.e. for each σ-algebra S of Ω we have a function $C_S:[P(\Omega,S)]^N \to P(\Omega,S)$, where $P(\Omega,S)$ is the space of all probability measures with σ-algebra S. In other words, this says that if the experts have probability measures $\Pi_1, \ldots, \Pi_N$ then $C_S(\Pi_1, \ldots, \Pi_N)$ is a new probability measure on the same σ-algebra of events. Now if T is another σ-algebra such that $T\subseteq S$ then we can restrict the $\Pi_1, \ldots, \Pi_N$ to T, namely,

$$(\Pi_j \mid T)(A)=\Pi_j(A) \quad A\in T.$$

The property of marginalization is as follows:

$$(MP) \quad C_S((\Pi_1, \ldots, \Pi_N)\mid T) = C_T(\Pi_1 \mid T, \ldots, \Pi_N \mid T),$$

in other words, for events in T the rules C_S and C_T coincide.

There is another seemingly reasonable property for a consensus rule that if an event is considered impossible by the experts then its assigned probability is still zero, i.e. the null set property

$$(NSP) \quad \Pi_1(A)= \cdots =\Pi_N(A)=0 \to C_S(\Pi_1, \ldots, \Pi_N)(A)=0$$

Two other properties one could consider are that the consensus depends just on the event and the values of the experts assessment (weak setwise function property) or only on those values (strong setwise function property), namely,

$$(WSFP) \quad C_S(\Pi_1, \ldots, \Pi_N)(A)=G(A,\Pi_1(A), \ldots, \Pi_N(A)), \text{ or}$$

$$(SSFP) \quad C_S(\Pi_1, \ldots, \Pi_N)(A)=F(\Pi_1(A), \ldots, \Pi_N(A))$$

where G, F satisfy some obvious properties like $G(\emptyset,\ldots)=0$, $G(\Omega,\ldots)=1$, $F(0,\ldots,0)=0, F(1,\ldots,1)=1$, etc. The following relations are proved in [McConway].

THEOREM: Suppose we have a family of consensus rules $\{C_S\}$ in Ω. Then

(a) $(MP) \Longleftrightarrow (WSFF)$

(b) (MP) & $(NSP) \Longleftrightarrow (SSFP)$

(c) $(SSFP) \Longleftrightarrow$ there exists nonnegative numbers $\alpha_1, \ldots, \alpha_N$, $\sum\alpha_j=1$ such that for all σ-algebras, S, $A \in S$, all $\Pi_j\in P(\Omega,S)$ we have

$$C_S(\Pi_1, \ldots, \Pi_N)(A)= \sum_{j=1}^{N} \alpha_j \Pi_j(A).$$

Of course, it is part (c) that shows the striking consequence of imposing too many "natural" conditions on the consensus rules. The main point to remark is that one uses not only the (MP) and the (NSP) but also that the rules are defined for all σ-algebras (or in fact it is enough for all σ-subalgebras of a certain fixed one) and we obtain probability measures again. Note that in the belief theory approach one only obtains a function in 2^{Ω} and the belief function is not in general a probability measure in Ω.

Furthermore, if one imposes not only the (*SSFP*) property but also the property that we can condition without changing the consensus rule, then we must have a "dictatorship", i.e. only one of the experts counts. Namely, we have
THEOREM: [Dalkey and Helmer, 1972] Let the consensus rule F satisfy

$$F(R_1S_1, \ldots, R_N S_N) = F(R_1, \ldots, R_N) \times F(S_1, \ldots, S_N),$$

where R_i is the probability assigned by expert i to event A, S_i is the probability assignment for another event B given A, and $R_i S_i$ is his probability for the event "A and B" (this is the property: consensus of A and B = (consensus of A) $\times$ (consensus of B given A)). Then there exists a j such that $F(R_1, \ldots, R_N)=R_j$, i.e. all experts other than j are ignored.

If one wants to get around the above theorem and be able nevertheless to apply some Bayesian updating one needs to limit the possible p.d.f. and consensus rules one considers. First, following McConway, we consider only denumerable sets $\Omega=\{\theta_j : j=1,2,\ldots\}$ and call $\Pi_i(\{\theta_j\})=\Pi_{ij}$ for $i=1,\ldots,N$. Let $f(x \mid \theta_j)$ be the likelihood of the data x when the parameter has the value θ_j; denote it by $f_j \in [0,1]$ and assume $\{j : \Pi_{ij} f_j > 0\} \neq \emptyset$ for all i (i.e. x is not considered impossible a priori by any of the experts). We restrict the sets of p.d.f.'s of the experts to agreeable sets, i.e. given any pair Π_i, Π_k, then one of the p.d.f.'s is absolutely continuous with respect to the other. Then using Bayes theorem, we can define the posterior p.d.f.'s $\Pi_1', \ldots, \Pi_N'$ by

$$\Pi_i'(\theta_j)=\pi_{ij}' := \pi_{ij} f_j / \sum_l \Pi_{il} f_l$$

and we might want to have the data independent property for the consensus function

$$(DIP)\begin{cases} (i) & \{l : C(\Pi_1, \ldots, \Pi_N)(\theta_l).f_l > 0\} \neq \emptyset \\ (ii) & \dfrac{C(\Pi_1, \ldots, \Pi_N)(\theta_j) f_j}{\sum_l C(\Pi_1, \ldots, \Pi_N)(\theta_l) f_l} = C(\Pi_1', \ldots, \Pi_N')(\theta_j) \end{cases}$$

In words (DIP) means: (i) any data to which all experts give positive probability will still have positive probability after the consensus value is computed and (ii) we get the same value if we apply Bayes' theorem to the consensus of the individual priors or we compute the consensus of the individual posteriors.

Now suppose further that the consensus rule C satisfies the following property: if for a given i we change the values π_{ij} arbitrarily, j in a finite set, without affecting the consensus value, then c is independent of Π_i, then the following theorem holds.
THEOREM: If the (DIP) property holds, (a) holds and Ω is infinite, then the consensus rule is of the form:

$$C(\Pi_1, \ldots, \Pi_N)(\theta_j)= \psi_j \prod_{i=1}^{N} \pi_{ij}^{\alpha_i} / \sum_l (\psi_l \prod_{i=1}^{N} \pi_{il}^{\alpha_i}),$$

for some numbers $\psi_j \in (0,1]$, and constants $\alpha_1, \ldots, \alpha_N \geq 0$ such that $\sum_{i=1}^{N} \alpha_i = 1$, i.e. C is proportional to the product of powers of the original probabilities. (Under a slightly technical condition it also holds for Ω finite, $\#(\Omega) \geq 3$)

THEOREM: Under the same conditions as above, assume further that if for a pair j,k we have $\pi_{ij}=\pi_{ik}$ i then $C((\Pi_1 \cdots \Pi_N)(\theta_j)=C(\Pi_1 \cdots \Pi_N)(\theta_k)$, then we have a dictatorship, i.e. $C(Pi_1,..Pi_N)=\pi_{i_o}$ for some index i_o.

THEOREM: If the consensus function satisfies (DIP) and it is also a function of the p.d.f.'s then we have a dictatorship. This last result says that unconditional updating plus marginalization only occurs in dictatorships.

3.4. Choice of Weights for Linear Pools - Updating

Given that one wants to use a linear pool, the problem arises on how to choose the weights assigned to each expert. It is clear that there is no clear cut method of doing this. One school of thought, which one finds expounded in detail in [McConway, Chapter 3] and expressed in the work of Winkler, and others, is the following. Whatever the original weights α_i are, we have

$$C(A)=\sum_{i=1}^{N}\alpha_i\,\pi_i(A)$$

They can be revised if we find out that an event B is true, assuming that C satisfies the rule

$$C(A\mid B)=C\frac{(A\cap B)}{C(B)}$$

and then the new weights β_i are proportional to $\alpha_i\Pi_i(B)$ (recall we always want $\sum\beta_i=1$). If we have a sequence of updatings, we can proceed in this manner or use a scoring method if that reflects the goodness of the fit of the expert (see [McConway] for the details) but nevertheless the final choice is always proportional to the initial choice. The initial score could be chosen by giving all the experts the same weight and then having a "trial run" and updating them by the above rules. A different approach consists of giving the weights using the expert's own opinion of each other as suggested in [De Groot, 1974]. For this purpose, let p_{ij} denote the weight that the expert i assigns to the opinion of the experts j. Then $p_{ij}\geq 0$ and we normalize by $\sum_{j=1}^{N}p_{ij}=1$ for for all $i=1,...,N$. Then if they were given the p.d.f.'s Π_j of the others and were to update their own p.d.f. using the weights p_{ij} they would have new p.d.f.'s $\Pi_j{}'$ which satisfy

$$P\Pi=\begin{bmatrix}p_{11} & p_{1N}\\ p_{N1} & p_{NN}\end{bmatrix}\begin{bmatrix}\Pi_1\\ \cdot\\ \cdot\\ \Pi_N\end{bmatrix}=\begin{bmatrix}\Pi_1{}'\\ \cdot\\ \cdot\\ \Pi_N{}'\end{bmatrix}=\Pi'$$

Iterating this process the matrix P^n plays a role since a consensus is reached if and only if the p.d.f.'s $\Pi^{(n)}$ have a limit when $n\to\infty$. This occurs if and only if $\alpha_j=\lim_{n\to\infty}P_{ij}^{(n)}$ exists for all i,j.

If these limits exist then they satisfy

$$(*)\quad \sum_{j=1}^{N}\alpha_j=1,\quad \alpha_j\geq 0 \text{ and } [\alpha_1\cdots\alpha_N]\,P=[\alpha_1,..\alpha_N].$$

If the consensus is reached, then α is the only eigenvector of P^t corresponding to the eigenvalue 1 and satisfying (*). A sufficient condition for the existence of a consensus is that for some n, one of the columns of P^n has all the elements strictly positive. On the

other hand there are situations in which no consensus can be reached with this method, e.g. the two experts don't trust each other and $P = \begin{bmatrix} 1 & 0 \\ 0 & 1 \end{bmatrix}$. A particular choice of P for which there is a consensus is one that occurs in the "Delphi-technique" proposed by Dalkey [Dalkey et. al., 1972] in which $1 > p_{ii} > 0$ for all i are given, and then the other weights are uniformly subdivided, i.e. $p_{ij} = (1-p_{ii})/(N-1)$ for $j \neq i$.
Of course, one can use the de Groot technique to find the initial values of the weights α_i and then update the weights by the McConway suggestion if one event becomes known to be true. If we do not update we have

$$C(A \mid B) = \sum_{1}^{N} \alpha_i \Pi_i (A \mid B)$$

while if we do update

$$C(A \mid B) = \frac{C(A \cap B)}{C(B)} = \frac{\sum \alpha_i \Pi_i (A \mid B) \Pi_i (B)}{\sum \alpha_j \Pi_j (B)} =$$

$$\sum_{i=1}^{N} \left\{ \frac{\alpha_i \Pi_i (B)}{\sum_{\alpha_j} \Pi_j (B)} \right\} \Pi_i (A \mid B) = \sum_{i=1}^{N} \beta_i \Pi_i (A \mid B).$$

Though the de Groot procedure allows some room for use of the correlation between the experts, it does so insofar as that is reflected in their own self-assessments p_{ij}. The use of correlation arises naturally when finding the consensus in the problem of estimating a parameter, but some of these rules could be adapted to general p.d.f.'s as we will see below. Before that we would like to mention another possible combination rule, the pari-mutuel method of Eisenberg and Gale [Eisenberg and Gale, 1979].

3.5. Pari - Mutuel Betting

According to the pari-mutuel method there are m possible events and N experts or bettors. Each bettor is assigned some "budget" (or portion of the total bet) b_i, $\sum_{1}^{N} b_i = 1$; besides that each one has a probability assignment Π_{ij} (where as before Π_{ij} is the probability assigned to the j-th event by the i-th expert). If the posterior probabilities p_j of the events were known, the experts would place their bets β_{ij} only on those events for which their expectations are maximized. That is, the following relations hold:

Budget relation: $\sum_{j=1}^{m} \beta_{ij} = b_i \quad i = 1,\ldots,N$

Pari-mutuel condition: $\sum_{i=1}^{N} \beta_{ij} = p_j \quad j = 1,\ldots,m$

Maximum expectation: *Let* $\mu_i = \max_k \dfrac{\Pi_{ik}}{p_k};$

then the only $\beta_{ij} > 0$ *are those* for *which* $\mu_i = \dfrac{\Pi_{ij}}{p_j}$.

It turns out one can find the values p_j and β_{ij} by introducing an auxiliary function ψ of mN variables ξ_{ij} defined the formula

$$\psi(\xi) = \sum_{i=1}^{N} b_i \log \sum_{j=1}^{m} \pi_{ij}\, \xi_{ij}\,, \quad \xi_{ij} \geq 0, \quad \sum_{i=1}^{N} \xi_{ij} = 1$$

Then one has the following theorem

THEOREM: The probabilities p_j and a corresponding system of bets β_{ij} can be found as follows: Let $\bar{\xi}$ be a maximum point for ψ (this always exists) then

$$p_j = \max_i \frac{\partial \psi}{\partial \xi_{ij}}(\bar{\xi}) = \max_i \frac{b_i\, \pi_{ij}}{\sum_k \pi_{ik}\, \bar{\xi}_{ik}} \quad \text{and} \quad \beta_{ij} = \bar{\xi}_{ij}\, p_j\,.$$

Furthermore, the values $p_1,\ldots,p_m$ are independent of the choice of maximum $\bar{\xi}$. From the theorem one notes also that the best strategy of placing the bets is to maximize the weighted sum of the logarithms of expectations, since with the above choices $\psi = \sum_{i=1}^{N} b_i \log \sum_{j=1}^{m} \beta_{ij} \left(\frac{\pi_{ij}}{p_j}\right)$.

3.6. Parameter Estimation

There is a large literature on combining estimates of parameters either via some kind of Bayesian updating or minimizing the variance of the new p.d.f., generally making some assumption on the form of the p.d.f.'s [Halperin,1961], [Geisser, 1965], [Newbold and Granger, 1974]], [Hampton et. al., 1973], [Winkler, 1968], [Winkler and Makridakis, 1983], [Stone, 1961]). Most of these do not seem to be particularly useful for us except for the paper of Lindley [Lindley, 1983] and a method of Dickinson [Dickinson, 1973] [Dickinson, 1978] that accepts a natural modification in our context.

The paper [Lindley, 1983] might be useful for us due to the simplicity of the non-technical hypotheses on the experts. One assumes that they assert that the expected value of a parameter θ is m_i with a variance s_i, and one assumes a correlation between the experts of the following form:

$p(m_1,\ldots,m_N \mid s_1,\ldots,s_N, \theta)$ is multivariate normal with means $\alpha_i + \beta_i\,\theta$, standard deviations $\gamma_i\, s_i$ and correlations p_{ij}.

Then, according to [Lindley, 1983] θ has a consensus distribution which is normal with mean

$$\sum_{i,j} \beta_i\, \sigma^{ij}\,(m_j - \alpha_j) / \sum_{i,j} \beta_i\, \beta_j\, \sigma^{ij}\,, \text{ and } \textit{variance} \quad \left(\sum_{i,j} \beta_i\, \beta_j\, \sigma^{ij}\right)^{-1},$$

where $\sigma_{ii} = (\gamma_i\, s_i)^2$, $\sigma_{ij} = \rho_{ij}\,(\sigma_{ii}\,\sigma_{jj})$ for $i \neq j$ and the matrix $[\sigma^{ij}]$ is the inverse to $[\sigma_{ij}]$.

3.7. Introducing Correlations

In the Dickinson papers [Dickinson, 1973], [Dickinson, 1978] it is proposed to assign weights to several expert's forecasts under assumptions of normality, etc. but the point is that if under those conditions one wants to minimize the variance then the weights have to be chosen by

$$(D) \quad \begin{bmatrix} \alpha_1 \\ \cdot \\ \cdot \\ \cdot \\ \alpha_N \end{bmatrix} = \textit{1st n components of the } N+1 \textit{ vector} \quad \begin{bmatrix} 1 \cdots 1 & 0 \\ & 1 \\ & \cdot \\ \Sigma & \cdot \\ & 1 \end{bmatrix}^{-1} \begin{bmatrix} 1 \\ 0 \\ \cdot \\ \cdot \\ 0 \end{bmatrix}$$

where $\sum$ is the symmetric $N \times N$ correlation matrix $[\sigma_{ij}]$, and the first term on the right hand side is the $(N+1)\times(N+1)$ inverse of the augmented correlation matrix. If one has performed m experiments and found that the error of the i-th expert in the k-th experiment is e_{ik} then the matrix $\sum$ can be estimated by the $N\times N$ matrix

$$\frac{1}{m}\begin{bmatrix} \sum_{k=1}^{m} e_{1k}^2 & \sum_{k=1}^{m} e_{ik}\, e_{Nk} \\ \sum_{k=1}^{m} e_{Nk}\, e_{1k} & \sum_{k=1}^{m} e_{Nk}^2 \end{bmatrix}$$

It turns out that (D) has the disadvantage that when some experts are very bad their weights could be negative (though still $\sum_{i=1}^{i=N} \alpha_i = 1$). We think that it would be reasonable, in case one has some estimate of the correlation matrix Σ of the different experts to use the following weights

($\hat{D}$) Let α_j be computed by (D), choose $\hat{\alpha}_j$ proportional to $\max(\alpha_j, 0)$ so that $\sum_{j=1}^{j=N} \hat{\alpha}_j = 1$.

In the same spirit of finding weights or combinations in a way that depends on the correlations between the experts we have a few other natural rules:

(NLR) If we have two experts with correlation coefficient ρ, which we take to be $\rho=1$ if they are totally dependent and $\rho=0$ if they are uncorrelated, then we take $\theta=(1+\rho)/2$ and the combination of π_1 and π_2 is given by

$$C = \left(\frac{\pi_1^{\theta}\pi_2^{(1-\theta)} + \pi_1^{(1-\theta)}\pi_2^{\theta}}{2}\right)^{\frac{1}{\theta}}$$

This rule has the nice property that if $\rho=1$ then $C=\frac{(\pi_1+\pi_2)}{2}$ and if $\rho=0$ then $C=\pi_1\pi_2$. Generalization to N experts and similar nonlinear formulas seem very reasonable.

Generally speaking (and this is easier to enforce using belief theory so that events are points and we do not have to worry about coherence), we would like to have formulas that reinforce the probability estimates for an event A for which a pair of uncorrelated experts each give values which are close to each other. For instance, if $[\sigma_{ij}]$ is the correlation matrix with $0 \le \sigma_{ij} \le 1, 1=\sigma_{ii}$ for all i, indicating total correlation and zero uncorrelation, then we could write the basic probability consensus mass as proportional to:

$$C(A) = \sum_{i=1}^{i=N} w_i(A)\pi_i(A)[1+(\pi_i(A)-1).\sum_{j=1}^{N}(1-\sigma_{ij})\exp\{-4(\pi_i(A)-\pi_j(A))^2\}]$$

or similar expressions.

4. CONCLUDING REMARKS

In this paper, we have presented only a small selection from the broad literature on consensus methodology, to which many contributions are being made. We have focused on some basic ideas of probabilistic methods and presented some general results and limitations developed in probabilistic consensus theory and evidence theory. We have considered two broad directions of work pursued in consensus theory. First consensus processes have been studied to determine desirable classes of combination procedures. We described work showing that various natural restrictions on the combination process can force the use of linear combination procedures or imply the non-existence of any acceptable rule. We also discussed a second direction of work, viz., the exploration of various specific combination rules.

One limitation of the consensus theory approach is the need to specify probabilities which may be difficult for some experts to estimate. The theory of evidence provides an extension of convential probability theory which attempts to address the problem of incompletely specified distributions. The evidence theory literature describes one approach to the combination problem. As we have noted, although this approach has not proven particularly fruitful, evidence theory supports a much broader class of consensus methods. In this paper, we have presented potential directions of research for the combination of probabilistic consensus and evidence theory.

In the overview in section 2, we briefly touched upon some results of our experiments on consensus which, owing to space limitations, we are unable to present in this paper. The feedback approach to consensus theory appears to be a reasonable way to incorporate measures of reliability and correlation between experts.

We have not discussed rank-order based consensus methods and consensus methods in time series. Also, as noted in the beginning of the paper, an item of significant current interest which we have not discussed here is the developing methodology for the propagation of evidence through networks. Graph search algorithms provide a promising approach for handling time dependent consensus problems and we hope to present these aspects in later work.

We have completely omitted any discussion of strictly non-probabilistic methods which go under such names as the theory of endorsements, and Reason or Truth Maintenance Systems. These are topics we are currently examining.

While achieving a consensus is a very important practical problem for both human and machine decision making, there is no consensus as yet among researchers on how the problem should be formulated and what directions of research are likely to prove most fruitful. This situation may always prevail for as Ursula K. LeGuin has said "Truth is a matter of imagination. Facts are about the outside. Truth is about the inside."

REFERENCES

J. A. Barnett, "Computational Methods for a Mathematical Theory of Evidence", Proc. Seventh International Conference on Artificial Intelligence, Vancouver, B.C. (1981).

R. F. Bordley and R. W. Wolff, "On the Aggregation of Individual Probability Estimates", Management Science (1981), 27, 959-964.

N. Dalkey and O. Helmer, "An Improbability Theorem for Group Probability Functions", Rand Paper P-5863, The Rand Corp., (1972).

N. Dalkey et. al., Studies in the Quality of Life, Lexington Books (1972).

M. H. DeGroot, "Reaching a Consensus", Journal of the American Statistical Society (1974), 69, pp. 118-121.

P. Diaconis, Book review, Journal of the American Statistical Assoc., Sept. 1978, pp. 677-678.

J.P. Dickinson, "Some Statistical Results in the Combination of Forecasts", Operational Research Quarterly (1973) 24, pp. 253-260.

J.P. Dickinson, "Some Comments on the Combination of Forecasts", Operational Research Quarterly (1975) 26, pp. 205- 210.

E. Eisenberg and D. Gale, "Consensus of Subjective Probabilities: the Pari-Mutuel Method", Annals of Mathematical Statistics (1979), 30, pp. 165-168.

S. French, "Updating of Belief in the Light of Someone Else's Opinion", Journal of the Royal Statistical Society A (1980), 143, pp. 43-48.

T. Garvey, J. D. Lawrence and M. Fischler, "An Inference Technique for Iterating Knowledge from Disparate Sources", Proc. Seventh International Joint Conference on Artificial Intelligence, Vancouver, B.C., (1981).

S. Geisser, "A Bayes Approach for Combining Correlated Estimates", Journal of the American Statistical Assoc. (1965) 60, pp. 602-607.

M. Halperin, "Almost Linearly-Optimum Combination of Unbiased Estimates", Journal of the American Statistical Association (1961) 56, pp. 36-43.

J.M. Hampton, P.G. Moore, and H. Thomas, "Subjective Probability and its Measurement", Journal of the Royal Statistical Society A (1973), 136, pp. 21-42.

D. Heckerman, "Probabilistic Interpretations for MYCIN's Certainty Factors" Rept. #KSL 85-23, Medical Computer Science Group, TC 135, Standford University Medical Center.

L.N. Kanal, B.A. Lambird, D. Lavine, "Expert Systems for Understanding Remotely Sensed Images", Proc. The Army Conference on Application of A.I. to Battlefield Information Management. Battelle Labs., Washington, D.C., pp. 17-36, April 1983.

K. Konolige, "A Bayesian Inference in PROSPECTOR: Some Problems and a New Approach", SRI, 1978.

V. Kumar and L. Kanal, "The Composite Decision Process: A Unifying Formulation for Heuristic Search, Dynamic Programming and Branch and Bound Procedures", Proc. of the National Conference on Artificial Intelligence, Washington D.C., pp. 220-224, August 1983.

V. Kumar and L. Kanal, "A Branch and Bound Formulation for Understanding and Synthesizing AND/OR Graph Search Algorithms", Special Issue on Search and Heuristics, Artificial Intelligence, March/April 1983.

B.A. Lambird, et.al., "Research on the Fusion of Intelligence in a Distributed Problem Solving Environment", Final Report, U.S. Army Research Institute Contract No. MDA903-84-C-0119, November 1984.

V. Lindley, A. Tversky, and R.V. Brown, "On Reconciliation of Probability Assessments", Journal of the Royal Statistical Society A (1979), 142, pp. 146-180.

J. Marschak and R. Radner, "Economic Theory of Teams", Cowles Foundation Monograph, 1972.

K.J. McConway, "The Combination of Experts' Opinions in Probability Assessment: Some Theoretical Considerations", Ph.D. Thesis , University College, London, 1980.

P. Newbold and C. Granger, "Experience with Forecasting Univariate Time Series and the Combination of Forecasts", Journal of the Royal Statistical Society A (1974) 137, pp. 131-165.

J. Pearl, "Reverend Bayes or Inference Engines: A Distributed Hierarchical Approach", AAAI National Conference on Artificial Intelligence, August 1982.

H. Prade, "A Computational Approach to Approximate and Plausible Reasoning with Applications to Expert Systems", IEEE Trans. PAMI, Vol PAMI-7, No. 3, pp. 260-283, May 1985.

G. Shafer, A Mathematical Theory of Evidence, Princeton University Press, 1976.

G. Shafer, "Belief Functions and Parametric Models", Journal of the Royal Statistical Society B (1982), 44, pp. 322-352.

D.J. Spieglehalter, "A Statistical View of Uncertainty in Expert Systems", to appear in W. Gale (Ed). A.I. and Statistics, Addison-Wesley 1985.

G. Stockman and L.N. Kanal, "Problem Reduction Representation for the Linguistic Analysis of Waveforms", IEEE Trans. on Pattern Analysis and Machine Intelligence, Vol. PAMI-5, No. 3, pp. 287-298, May 1983.

M. Stone, "The Opinion Pool", Annals of Mathematical Statistics, (1961) 32, pp. 1339-1342.

R. L. Winkler, "The Consensus of Subjective Probability Distributions", Management Science (1968) 15, pp. B61-B75.

R. L. Winkler, "Combining Probability Distributions from Dependent Information Sources", Management Sciences (1981), 27, pp. 479-488.

R. L. Winkler and S. Makridakis, "The Combination of Forecasts", Journal of the Royal Statistical Society A (1983) 146, pp. 150-157.

M. Wolfenson and T. L. Fine, "Bayes-like Decision Making with Upper and Lower Probabilities", Journal of the American Statistical Association, (1982) 77, pp. 80-88.

DISCUSSION

Jansen:

Isn't it so tnat the whole theory of consensus is impossible if truth is in the mind or in belief and not in fact? I can come up with quite a few application areas where consensus is probably impossible to obtain. The prime example is medicine. I still have to see two physicians who agree or who are capable of reaching a consensus about a particular problem.

Kanal:

It is certainly easy to see that in various situations consensus may be difficult to achieve; it is also not easy to say what one should do to obtain such a consensus. However it is a desirable goal to strive for if one is going to depend on computer consultants and automation in various situations. We know that politicians seek and sometimes obtain the consensus of a majority on certain issues. It is however unlikely that there are simple rules to obtain a consensus since people are complex.

Jansen:

I think that was the whole reason to develop systems that mimic one particular expert. Such a system is much easier to develop than one that comes up with some sort of consensus.

Kanal:

Consider that currently a lot of money is being spent in trying to automate decision making in situations which are really very badly defined. For example in a distributed battle field, decisions may have to be made on the basis of incomplete and erroneous information by various command levels. Exercises in Europe and elsewhere suggest that usually much confusion results. While the press and politicians focus on sophisticated missiles and weapons, the "ground truth" is often that people are unable to process the information they are innundated with and also that there are serious gaps in the communication of information. This is the state of the technology.

In such situations the reaction is to use "seat of the pants" decision making which can be quite ad-hoc.

Jansen:

Even there again the idea of consensus will not work. You will bring together generals and colonels and they will look at all the information. One of them is looking at one particular piece of information, the others are looking at other pieces of information. And naturally they will have different conclusions.

Kanal:

That is exactly the situation. There may not be a consensus. The point is that we come up with some rules of behaviour. What I am interested in is the type of "impotence principle" that Louis Fine stated a long time ago in the 1966 conference on pattern recognition in Puerto Rico (see Kanal, L.N.(Ed), Pattern Recognition, 1968, Thompson Book co/L.N.K. Corp). The impotence principles define what is or is not possible in group decision making with uncertain and fragmentary information. MacConway's "dictatorship" theorem is an example of such a principle.

Young:

You cannot escape the problem of what to do with the advice of different experts. Choosing one expert from many is simply the solution that says that you have assigned a weight of one to one person and zero weight to all the rest. That is the decision you have made on how to deal with multiple experts. If the problem one has in battle field situations is unpalatable to people, consider the problem the governments have in deciding how to run their economies. Some people say that deficit spending is terrific; it is a real shot in the arm for the economy; that is the real Keynesian strategy; and there are other people who say: no, you should never have an unbalanced budget. And they are all experts. And yet you have to run the economy. How do you deal with twenty different voices that are telling you how to do this?

Kanal:

I am told that one of the reasons to introduce more automated information processing and computer consultancy in hospitals is that there is utter chaos because there are hordes of overburdened people running around and nobod- has time to think. We keep hearing of these wild cases such as recently in the Washington area in which somebody got injected in the spinal cord with something which was supposed to be for his eye.

Young:

A few remarks about that theorem of MacConway. It is a mathematical theorem which has implications far outside the domain of mathematics. I can think of two instances where a consensus is the modus operandi. One of them is the meeting of the Helsinki accords review committee, which just last week disbanded in Canada. This committee was designed to review the Helsinki accords of ten years ago. The only way in which that group, which was an international body, could come to any decision was by consensus. Therefore you understand the kind of decisions they came up with.

The second one is the EEC which also functions that way. We see the results in the way these bodies are functioning. The question then becomes whether or not the consensus agreement is compatible with the concept of a democratic system of government or decision making.

Kanal:

You should understand that his theorem resulted from specific restrictions on the consensus function. In the usual delphi method we go round robin. We have no idea of what the people actually use as a consensus function and they don't necessarily tell you about what evidence they use. Eventually one comes up with some weighting of everyones opinion. But in the weighting process they may use new information that is not revealed. The theory doesn't worry about that. I am not aware that a precise mathematical formulation of the process has been, or can be stated.

Stockman:

As we are penetrating the foundations of our field, I have a question about the existence of events. "You are being attacked on the eastern front". Is that an event that deserves evaluation in numerical terms?

"A person has cancer". I'm not sure that we even know what cancer is and I don't think anyone else is sure so there are very few events that are worthy of quantitative value assignment in the real world. In OCR this may be true but in the kind of decisions you brought up I am not so sure that there are many events that are worth having a number put on them.

Kanal:
The problem is that people are putting numbers on them. They are making decisions and taking actions and it is our job to understand what is going on. You can say: stop the world, I want to get off; I don't want to think about these things because they are not events. But people are thinking this way, they are acting this way, they are combining opinions, they do use computers to massage lots of data and the data is coming in larger and larger quantities.

Stockman:
But maybe it pays to spend some time on thinking about what events are.

Smeulders:
Imagine that two famous chess players start their play and that halfway in the game one of them is leaving and replaced by another famous chess player. Who would you guess would win the game? I would guess that the man or woman who remained seated would have the biggest chance to win, simply because in certain complex evaluation situations, I believe, the consistency of policy can be of much more importance than the quality of the incremental decisions. Take for instance the issue of economy or of medical care.

Kanal:
One might answer that the people who were building horse carriages when the automobile era started and continued to build them were very consistent. There are many areas where expertise based upon prior experience is important but there are also situations where that very prior experience makes you unable to see what is really going on. I generally bet on somebody new who comes into the field from outside that field, because I figure that persoon will look at the problems in a different way than those working in the field and will come up with something novel.

Smeulders:
That's true because you are a scientist and, by definition, always after something novel. But most situations are not for play but for real. So consistency in complex decision situations is of much more importance than incremental decisions.

Nagy:
I hate to think what we would be talking about if this were not the Pattern Recognition in Practice conference but something like the philosophy of Pattern Recognition.

PATTERN RECOGNITION IN PRACTICE II
E.S. Gelsema and L.N. Kanal (Editors)
© Elsevier Science Publishers B.V. (North-Holland), 1986

FROM NUMBERS TO SYMBOLS TO KNOWLEDGE STRUCTURES: PATTERN RECOGNITION AND ARTIFICIAL INTELLIGENCE PERSPECTIVES ON THE CLASSIFICATION TASK

B. Chandrasekaran

Laboratory for Artificial Intelligence Research
Department of Computer & Information Science
The Ohio State University
Columbus, OH 43210, USA

In this paper we consider a very general information processing task: *classification*, and review the perspectives of the classical pattern recognition approaches and the more recent artificial intelligence/ knowledge-based systems point of view. As the complexity of the problem increases, we trace the evolution of the algorithms from numerical parameter setting schemes through those using symbolic abstractions and then relations between symbolic entities, and finally to complex symbolic descriptions which incorporate explicit domain knowledge.

1. INTRODUCTION

In this paper we consider a very general information processing task: *classification*, and review the perspectives of the classical pattern recognition approaches and the more recent artificial intelligence/ knowledge-based systems point of view. As the complexity of the problem increases, we trace the evolution of the algorithms from numerical parameter setting schemes through those using symbolic abstractions and then relations between symbolic entities, and finally to complex symbolic descriptions which incorporate explicit domain knowledge. The paper can be viewed two perspectives: as a bridge-building activity, describing the approaches of two different research communities to the same general task; it can also be viewed as an attempt, by using the classification task as a concrete example, to give an intuitive account of how the information processing activity underlying thought necessarily needed to evolve into complex symbolic processes in order to handle increasing complexity of problems and requirements for flexibility.

2. THE CLASSIFICATION TASK

2.1. Expert Systems and the Classification Task

The area of expert systems, though of recent origin, is already a well-established subarea of Artificial Intelligence. The essential idea of the field is an attempt to capture in computer programs, explicitly and in symbolic form, the ***knowledge and problem solving methods*** of human experts in selected domains and tasks; in fact, because of the central role of explicit domain knowledge, the field itself is often called ***knowledge-based systems.*** This is not an appropriate place to discuss the knowledge representation and problem solving issues in the field of expert systems, many of which are thriving and open research issues. There are many expert tasks that have been successfully emulated by these systems, while there are an even larger number of things that human experts do that are beyond the current state of the expert system technology. If one were to examine the intrinsic nature of the tasks of the current generation of expert systems, a surprising fact emerges: most of them solve variants of problems which are intrinsically *classificatory* in nature. It is important to note that we are not claiming that the authors of these programs *recognized* them as classification problems and used methods appropriate to that task, but that, independent of *how they were solved*, the problems solved by them have an intrinsically classificatory character.

Let us take some examples:

1. MYCIN [23], in its diagnostic phase, has the task of classifying patient data in an *infectious agent hierarchy*. I.e., the diagnostic task is identification of the infectious agent class as specifically as possible.

2. PROSPECTOR [10] classifies a geological description as corresponding to one or more mineral formation classes.

3. MDX [4, 5] explicitly views a significant portion of the diagnostic task as classifying a complex description (the patient data) as an element in a disease classification hierarchy (e.g., liver disease, in particular hepatitis).

4. SACON [2] classifies structural analysis problems into classes for each of which a particular family of analysis methods will be appropriate.

The above is by no means to imply that all problems are classification problems or that can be usefully converted into such problems. R1 [17], e.g., performs a relatively simple version of an *object synthesis* problem, i.e., a version of the design problem. RED [13] Internist [21] and Dendral [3] are different systems all performing various versions of *assembly of composite hypothesis* for *abductive reasoning*. In [6, 7, 8] we have given taxonomies of such *generic tasks* for which expert systems can be designed and we identified classification as one of the generic tasks. Recently Clancey [9] has made a similar assessment of how several expert systems perform classificatory problem solving. Sticklen, et al [25] discuss the control issues inherent in the task.

What is important to note from the above list is that classification seems to be a rather ubiquitous problem solving process, and a number of real world problems including medical diagnosis can be thought of as having a large classification component. Further, classification has been one of the more *tractable* problems for the knowledge-based system technology to handle at this point in its development.

2.2. Classification in Pattern Recognition

There is another area of inquiry, which is now more than 20 years old, viz., *pattern recognition*, which has also been intimately connected with problems of classification. In fact, in the early days of the field the problem of recognition was *formulated* as a problem of classification, in particular one of *statistical classification* of multidimensional *pattern vectors* into one of a finite number of classes, each class characterized by some kind of probability distribution. In fact what started out as a useful formulation practically got to be so dominant that there was a need for a paper such as that by Kanal and Chandrasekaran [14] pointing out that classification is only one of the formulations for the more general recognition problem. Even when newer techniques such as *syntactic techniques* came into the field, the problem was still often formulated as a classification problem, this time into *grammatical categories*.

2.3. Classification in Biology

Taxonomic classification has long been a significant methodology in biology. Linnaeus's classification scheme is very famous, and more recently, mathematical taxonomy has been pressed into service for providing better classification in this area [24] The more recent controversies regarding evolutionary biology (the claddists vs traditional evolutionary theorists) revolve around implications of various theories for classification.

2.4. Why this Ubiquity? The Computational Power of Classification

Classification seems to be a powerful human method of organization for comprehension and action. This tendency is so strong that people often feel they have accomplished something by merely naming something as a class, even if they cannot do much about it. Why is classification so powerful?

A simple computational explanation can be given for the importance of classification as an *information processing strategy.* One can think of the task of an intelligent agent as performing actions on the world for certain goals. But often the correct action knowledge is a function of the state of the world. E.g., one can think of the general problem facing the physician as having the following formal character: For each subset of possible symptoms (the *state of the patient*), find an appropriate therapeutic action. But in general the cardinality of the relevant states of the world is too large: e.g., the total number of states of a patient is the cartesian product of the distinct states of each of the state variables (symptoms, laboratory values, manifestations of all kinds). A table relating the subset of state variables to action is bound to be too large for construction, looking up, and modification. This problem is made more tractable, however, if action knowledge can be *indexed*, not by the states of the world, but *by equivalence classes of states of the world.* Thus a physician's therapeutic knowledge is not indexed directly by the detailed values of the patient state variables, but by diseases each of which can be thought of as defining an equivalence class of patient state variables. The medical problem solving can then be organized first as mapping from symptoms to disease classes (diagnosis as classification), and then from disease classes to therapeutic actions. Since the number of equivalence classes is much smaller than the number of states, the complexity of the mapping is now considerably reduced.

Thus: classification into categories provides a great computational advantage. Much of human thinking is organized around classification, both in terms of creating useful classifications (concept learning) and using existing categories to perform classifications.

However, the process of creating useful classifications (concept learning) is a much harder process than using a classification structure to do the actual classification. Thus in medicine discovery of a disease (creation of a new class) is a relatively major event while diagnosis is much more routine. In this paper we only deal with the process of assigning an object to a class in a classification structure.

3. THE STATISTICAL CLASSIFICATION PARADIGM

The typical model in this paradigm is one where the aim is to arrive at a classification of a multidimensional vector (where each dimension is typically a numerical variable, even though ordinals are some times used) representing an object of unknown classification into one of a finite number of classes. Each dimension typically represents an *attribute* of the object that the system designer has had reason to believe carries useful information about class membership. Intuitively, one would try to choose attributes such that they have the potential to *distinguish* between classes. When the number of dimensions is small, it is possible to design classification systems that outperform human expert performance in that task domain. E.g., if it is desired to distinguish between diseases D1 and D2, and statistical evidence indicates that symptoms s1, s2, ..sN carry useful information for this discrimination, careful statistical data gathering is often possible such that a discriminant function of the variables s1,.. sN can often be a very accurate classifier. Human reasoning with the same variables may be less efficient in information extraction, and thus automatic procedures using the statistical model can be very powerful.

In this model, in spite of the enormous intrinsic interest of the mathematical problem of designing and improving classification algorithms -- virtually thousands of papers have been written in the pattern classification literature on solutions to this problem -- Kanal and Chandrasekaran [14] pointed out years ago that the real power often comes from the careful choice of the variables themselves based on a good knowledge of the domain rather than from the complexity of the separation algorithm.

What happens when the dimensionality of the vector gets to be very large, or the number of classes gets to be large? When the number of classes increases, in general, in order to make more and more distinctions the number of measurements on the object, i.e., the dimensionality of the pattern vector, also will need to grow rapidly. When the numbers of classes increases, the complexity of the algorithm to make the discrimination grows much more rapidly, and correspondingly the average performance, i.e., correct classification rate, deteriorates quite rapidly. Sensitivity problems begin to become quite severe: i.e., the required precision of the parameters in the classification algorithm becomes impractically high. Opacity problems result: it becomes increasingly hard to make any kind of statement about what attributes are playing what role in the recognition process. These problems exist whether statistical classification algorithms are used, or perceptron-like linear threshold devices are used. Szolovits and Pauker [26] discuss some of the problems with the Bayesian approaches, and Minsky and Papert [18] the problems with the latter.

4. ABSTRACTION BY INTERMEDIATE CONCEPTS

What is to be done when the number of classes is very large? Consider the following pedagogically useful example: the design of recognition devices for automatic reading of texts. Assume for the sake of discussion that the number of words in the language is 20,000, and we would like the words to be recognized. Consider solving the problem by designing a discriminant function which directly maps a multidimensional vector into one of 20,000 classes. One can sense that this is a pretty unworkable solution: the number of measurements that would need to be made on the words and the complexity of the decision algorithm will be too large to permit this solution in practice. Intuitively one would think that recognizing characters first, and then based on this recognition recognizing words would be computationally more attractive. Why is this a much more reasonable solution?

What is going on here is a two-fold strategy of *symbolization* and *hierarchicalization*. Instead of doing the classification by a direct discriminant function-like mapping, intermediate symbols are constructed, which are then used as attributes to a higher-level classification process. (Note that this is not the same as *hierarchical classification*, which if it were to be applied to this problem, will first involve classification of the words into groups of similar-looking words, each class will be further subclassified, and so on, until each word receives a classificatory status.) Symbols at each level are produced by a classificatory process using the symbols from the previous level as attributes. Each such computational process is much more tractable.

4.1. Signature Tables

Consider another example: evaluation functions in chess. These functions usually yield a number which is a measure of the "goodness" of the board. For most purposes, effective use of this information can be made if the goodness is classified into one of a small number of categories. One of the first forms for the evaluation functions was a linear polynomial of attributes of the board: both the attributes and their weights were chosen in consultation with domain experts. Then in order to take into account interactions between the variables in the evaluation function, higher order polynomials were later proposed. This of course resulted in a fairly rapid increase in the complexity of the function: if r-the order interactions were to be included and the number of attributes is n, then the number of terms was of the order of n**r. Samuel's *signature tables* [22] provided a solution which exemplifies the symbolization and hierarchicalization ideas mentioned earlier. For the purposes of our discussion, Samuel's method can be described as follows.

1. Identify groups of attributes such that on the basis of domain knowledge there is reason to believe that they contribute to an intermediate abstraction that can be used to construct the final abstraction, in this case, a measure of the "goodness" of the board. (Typically the attributes in a group may have some dependencies and interactions, in order to capture which, in the more traditional evaluation functions, polynomial term were included.) In chess, "defensibility of king" and "material advantage" may be such intermediate concepts, each of which can be estimated by a subset of board attributes, while the final decision about the goodness of a board configuration may be made in terms these intermediate abstractions.

2. Find a method of *classifying* the desirability of these intermediate concepts into a small number of categories from the values of the attributes in each group. (For the purpose of our discussion, the exact method is not important-- Samuel proposed a specific mechanism for this. The essence of his mechanism is a mapping from a multidimensional vector, each component of which can only be in one of a small number of distinct values, to a symbolic abstraction, which can also be in only one of a small number of distinct values. The mapping turns out to be a fairly simple one.)

3. The outputs of the classifiers for each group can themselves be thought of as qualitative attributes at the next level of abstraction. These can be grouped and abstracted into higher level concepts as necessary until the top-level concept is a classification of the "goodness" of the board in a qualitative way.

To repeat a point made earlier, by trading off the precision of numbers for the simplicity and robustness of a small number of symbolic states, and combining it with hierarchical abstractions, significant computational advantage is being gained. It also points to the fact that often numbers are too precise for the task at hand. Robust symbolic abstractions of the appropriate kind can capture almost all of the relevant information.

5. SYNTACTIC OR STRUCTURAL APPROACHES

After about a decade of work within the statistical classification paradigm (the work on the perceptron paradigm was going on in parallel in certain sections of the AI community), Narasimhan [20] proposed what he called a *syntactic approach* to pattern recognition. The idea was to describe classes of patterns, not in terms of probability distributions in multidimensional spaces, nor in terms of hierarchic symbolic abstractions, but in terms of *relations between symbols*, much as grammatical categories are described in linguistic analysis. Most of the readership of this book will be familiar with the principles behind and examples of syntactic methods for pattern recognition, so we forego a description here. (By now there is a vast literature on the subject.) The following point, however, can be noted: *The ability to describe a class in terms of relations is a move towards descriptions as the basis for class characterization.*

Note that the idea of syntactic pattern recognition is really a special case of the more general notion of *structural relations* as the basis of class characterization. (In [15] we discuss the relationship of the structural paradigm to the statistical one.) Thus, even when the idea of *syntax* is not appropriate -- it is very doubtful that the notion of a picture grammar is as general for the domain of visual objects as seems from a purely formal perspective -- the notion of structural relations as the basis for characterizing concepts and classes is a somewhat more general one.

With the introduction of *syntactic/structural models* for pattern recognition), the progression becomes:

numbers --> symbols --> relations.

The major research directions in pattern recognition for capturing structural relations in general were *formal*, i.e., some sort of a mathematical system within which theorems about relationships may be provable regarding the classification performance. In fact, this was the major reason for the original emphasis on syntactic methods, since there was a well-developed theory of formal grammars already available. In any case, the emphasis on formalisms led to two constraints: one, often an attempt was made to force-fit available formalisms to the pattern recognition problem, generally with unsatisfactory results; and two, because human classification performance was more heuristic in nature, restricted formalisms could only capture the quality of human performance only fleetingly.

If one is to use relations between symbolic attributes as the basis of class characterization, why restrict oneself to *syntactic* relations? Why not bring to bear the full power, to the extent possible or necessary, the *semantics* of the classes in forming class descriptions? Asking this question prepares the way for the next step in the progression, the AI/Knowledge-based paradigm:

numbers --> symbols --> relations --> complex symbolic descriptions.

These complex descriptions characterizing the classes are the relevant aspects of the domain knowledge for the task.

6. AI/KNOWLEDGE-BASED REASONING: A NEW PARADIGM

It is not an exaggeration to say that the knowledge-based approach in general, and to classification in particular, is a *new paradigm* in the sense that it emphasizes different issues, and poses them in a different language. E.g., instead of issues such as "optimality" and "error rate," which figure in the classical pattern recognition approach, the AI paradigm emphasizes the issues of "knowledge representation" and "control of problem solving". These relate to how the domain knowledge in explicit symbolic form is *represented* (i.e, what language is used to encode the knowledge), *organized* and *accessed*, and how the knowledge is *used* to arrive at classificatory conclusions.

We have already used medical diagnosis as an example to illustrate some of the ideas in this paper. In discussing the AI approach, the medical diagnosis example is particularly useful, since a number of AI systems have been built in this domain, and also the computational advantages of such an approach can be well motivated. We will briefly describe a system called MDX [5] [12] which has been developed in our Laboratory over the past several years. Our description will necessarily be brief, since our aim is to point to the role of knowledge structures and to give a feeling for what characterizes the AI approach.

6.1. The MDX System: Example of Knowledge-Based Approach to Classification

The MDX system performs medical diagnosis by essentially viewing the task as one of classifying a complex case description as a node in a disease classification hierarchy. A number of caveats need to be kept in mind:

1. Not all classification problems are necessarily solved as *hierarchical classification problems.* There are other AI systems that perform classification, but without using the hierarchical point of view: e.g., [1].

2. In general multiple classification hierarchies may exist in domain. (E.g., in medicine, "viral hepatitis" is a classificatory concept in the "infectious disease" hierarchy as well as in the "liver disease" portion of the hierarchy.) The general problem involves coordinating among the classifications by the different classification systems.

3. A particular case may not have a single classification, but instead have several classifications simultaneously applicable. (E.g., a patient may have both "cirrhosis" and "portal hypertension," and in addition, the two diseases may be causally related. This sort of situation may also arise in other domains: in character recognition, the image may really be two characters touching each other, e.g., rather than one character.) The MDX framework can deal with many of these complexities more or less well, but for the purpose of this paper we will concentrate on the single classification situation.

The *control problem* here can be stated as one that deals with what classificatory hypothesis to consider at what point in problem solving. In general we would like to use domain knowledge to consider only a subset of all the hypotheses for problem solving efficiency, or we would like to consider some hypotheses which are more promising ahead of others.

The MDX system is organized as a hierarchical collection of or "diagnostic concepts," each of which has diagnostic knowledge that helps it make a determination about the relevance of that hypothesis (at that level of abstraction) to the case at hand. This hierarchy of specialists mirrors the diagnostic classification hierarchy. The total diagnostic knowledge is then distributed through the conceptual nodes of the hierarchy in a specific manner to be discussed shortly. The problem-solving for this task will be performed top down, i.e., the top-most concept will first get control of the case, then control will pass to an appropriate successor concept, and so on. In the medical example,

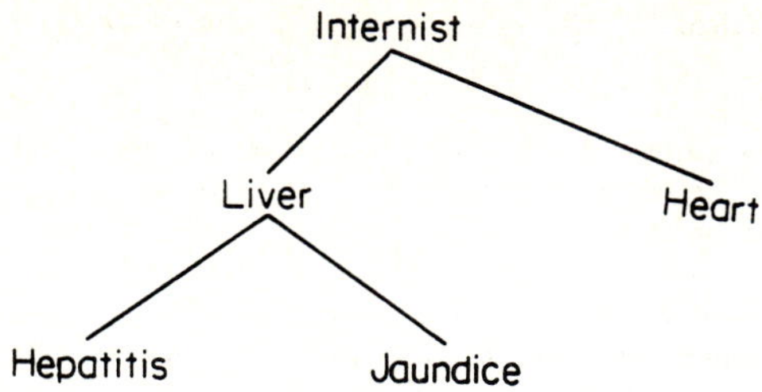

Figure 1: Fragment of a hierarchy

a fragment of such a hierarchy might be as shown in Fig. 1. More general classificatory concepts are higher in the structure, while more particular ones are lower in the hierarchy. It is as if INTERNIST first establishes that there is in fact a disease, then LIVER establishes that the case at hand is a liver disease, while say HEART etc. reject the case as being not in their domain. After this level, JAUNDICE may establish itself and so on.

Each of the concepts in the classification hierarchy has "how-to" knowledge in it in the form of a collection of *diagnostic rules* (This is only one possible method by which the specialists can make the determination about their fit with the data. In simple cases, statistical classification algorithms can be used. In DART [11] the decision about the fit of hypothesis to data is done by using theorem-proving techniques. In [19], we show how the concepts can make their decisions based on a causal knowledge of the domain. The point is that *how* the hypotheses are evaluated is somewhat independent of the flow of control for the classificatory task as such, even though for complex problems, a rich knowledge structure will be called for to make the decision about how well the hypothesis matches the case at hand). These rules are of the form: <symptoms> -----> <concept in hierarchy>, e.g., "If high SGOT, add n units of evidence in favor of cholestasis." Because of the fact that when a concept rules itself out from relevance to a case, all its successors also get ruled out, large portions of the diagnostic knowledge structure never get exercised. On the other hand, when a concept is properly invoked, a small, highly relevant body of knowledge comes into play.

The problem-solving that goes on in such a structure is *distributed.* The problem-solving regime that is implicit in the structure can be characterized as an *establish-refine* type. That is, each concept first tries to establish or reject itself. If it succeeds in establishing itself, the refinement process consists of seeing which of *its* successors can establish itself. Each concept has several clusters of rules: confirmatory rules, exclusionary rules, and perhaps some recommendation rules. The evidence for confirmation and exclusion can be suitably weighted and combined to arrive at a conclusion to establish, reject or suspend it. The last mentioned situation may arise if there is not sufficient data to make a decision. Recommendation rules are further optimization devices to reduce the work of the subconcepts. Further discussion of this type of rules is not necessary for our current purpose.

The concepts in the hierarchy are clearly not a static collection of knowledge. They are active in problem-solving. They also have knowledge only about establishing or rejecting the relevance of that conceptual entity. Thus they may be termed "specialists," in particular, "diagnostic specialists." The entire collection of specialists engages in distributed problem-solving.

The MDX system is a complex system that has been tested on a number of real-world cases with a high match between its conclusions and that of specialists. The number of symptoms, signs, and laboratory values that it can handle is in the hundreds, and the number of distinct hypotheses it has in its diagnostic hierarchy is also close to hundred. Some of the laboratory results about images is in complex descriptive form. Hard probability numbers are nowhere used; what the specialists compute can be thought of as qualitative probability values: "definitely present," "likely present,"... "definitely absent." This is the sort of problem for which a purely numerical mapping approach such as a Bayesian one will have considerable computational problems, in addition to posing difficulties of knowledge acquisition. It is often quite difficult to acquire probability distributions of the type needed for the classification algorithms from physicians, at least for problems of this degree of complexity, while the sort of knowledge MDX uses is directly available from domain experts.

7. CONCLUDING REMARKS

It is by now a truism that significant aspects of thinking can be modeled as symbolic information processing: creation and manipulation of complex symbolic structures bearing knowledge of various of types. Artificial intelligence deals with such models couched in explicitly computational terms. We have noted that classification seems to be an ubiquitous method used by human thought processes, and pointed out that the reason for that is the significant computational advantages that arise from storing knowledge useful for action by indexing it over *equivalence classes of the states of the world* rather than over the states of the world themselves.

We have taken the reader through a progression of approaches for classification: numerical measures and formulae of various types, symbolic abstractions, hierarchical symbol structures, structural relations between symbols, and finally to rich symbolic knowledge structures. Each stage in the progression gave more power in controlling the computational complexity by matching the structure of the classifier to the complex structure of the task. At the level of knowledge, the power comes from *task-specific control regimes* controlling access to *appropriate chunks of knowledge.* We motivated the discussion by using medical diagnosis as an example in various places, but the ideas are more generally applicable.

The discussion in this paper can be viewed as a bridge-building activity between two research paradigms: pattern recognition and artificial intelligence. Classification has been a major concern in the former, and an important task performed by many systems in the latter and thus the task provides a good place to understand the distinctions between the two research paradigms. For well-constrained classification problems with relatively small number of categories, the statistical and other numerical algorithms considered in the field of pattern recognition can provide powerful classifiers which often outperform human experts by extracting the last trace of information that the more discrete human symbolic processes can only approximate. On the other hand for complex problems involving many variables and classes the knowledge-based approach trades off the optimality of the best algorithms in pattern recognition for greater computational tractability and better matching with human knowledge in the domain.

Many of the points made in this paper transcend the particular task of classification. In that sense, this paper can be thought of as an attempt to point to the emergence of the need and power of symbolic structures for control and prediction. Cybernetics showed the power and usefulness of the concepts of feedback and stability in understanding many control and communication problems. But in classical control theory, numbers and functions hold sway. Learning and control in this framework involves parameter modification and signal propagation. The space over which parametric changes and numerical signals can provide control is limited. Symbolic models of the world provide greater leverage for change and control and still keep computational costs within manageable bounds. Thus in biological information processing, symbolization seems to have occurred very early in evolution: see [16] for an account of how early visual processing of the frog is symbolic in nature. Once symbols were available as the language in which to perform information processing, thought eventually evolved into more and more complex symbol structures. Thus the points in this paper can be viewed as an intuitive account of the emergence and power of symbolic structures for complex information processing activities.

Our approach within artificial intelligence has been to identify other *generic tasks* similar to classification, but with similar characteristic of being a building block for complex information processing activities. In [8] we give an account of the latest repertoire of such generic tasks we have identified.

Acknowledgment

Research supported by grants AFOSR 82-0255 and NSF MCS-8305032 for developing these ideas is gratefully acknowledged.

References

[1] Aikins, J.S.
Prototypical Knowledge for Expert Systems.
Artificial Intelligence 20(2):163-210, 1983.

[2] Bennett, J., Creary, L., Englemore, R., and Melosh, R.
SACON: A Knowledge-Based Consultant for Structural Analysis.
Sept 1978
STAN-CS-78-699 and HPP Memo 78-23, Stanford University.

[3] Buchanan, B.G. and Feigenbaum, E.A.
Dendral and Meta-Dendral: Their Applications Dimension.
Artificial Intelligence 11(1-2):5-24, 1978.

[4] Chandrasekaran, B., Mittal, S., Gomez, F., and Smith M.D., J.
An Approach to Medical Diagnosis Based on Conceptual Structures.
Proceedings of the 6th International Joint Conference on Artificial Intelligence :134-142, August, 1979.
IJCAI79.

[5] Chandrasekaran, B. and Mittal, S.
Conceptual Representation of Medical Knowledge for Diagnosis by Computer: MDX and Related Systems.
In M. Yovits (editor), *Advances in Computers*, pages 217-293. Academic Press, 1983.

[6] Chandrasekaran, B.
Towards a Taxonomy of Problem-Solving Types.
AI Magazine 4(1):9-17, Winter/Spring, 1983.

[7] Chandrasekaran, B.
Expert Systems: Matching Techniques to Tasks.
1983
Paper presented at NYU symposium on Applications of AI in Business. Appears in *Artificial Intelligence Applications for Business*, edited by W. Reitman, Ablex Corp., publishers.

[8] Chandrasekaran, B.
Generic Tasks in Expert System Design and Their Role in Explanation of Problem Solving.
May 1985
Invited presentation at the National Academy of Sciences Office of Naval Research Workshop on AI and Distributed Problem Solving, May 16-17, 1985. To appear in the Proceedings of the Workshop. .

[9] Clancey, William J.
Classification Problem Solving.
In *Proceedings of the National Conference on Artificial Intelligence*, pages 49-55. AAAI, University of Texas at Austin, August 6-10, 1984.

[10] Duda, R.O., Hart, P.E., Nilsson, N.J., Reboh, R., Slocum, J., and Sutherland, G.L.
Development of a Computer-Based Consultant for Mineral Exploration.
October 1977
Annual Report, SRI Projects 5821 and 6415, SRI International, Menlo Park, California.

[11] Genesereth, M.R.
Diagnosis Using Hierarchial Design Models.
Proc. National Conf. on AI, American Association for Artificial Intelligence , 1982.

[12] Gomez, F.
Understanding Programming Problems Stated in Natural Language.
OSU CISR Tech Report.
February, 1981

[13] Josephson, John R., Chandrasekaran, B. and Smith, J.W.
Assembling the Best Explanation.
In *Proceedings of the IEEE Workshop on Principles of Knowledge-Based Systems.* IEEE Computer Society, Denver, Colorado, December 3-4, 1984.

[14] Kanal, Laveen and Chandrasekaran, B.
Recognition, Machine 'Recognition' and Statistical Approaches.
Methodologies of Pattern Recognition.
Academic Press, 1969, pages 317-332.

[15] Kanal, Laveen and Chandrasekaran, B.
On Linguistic, Statistical and Mixed Models for Pattern Recognition.
Frontiers of Pattern Recognition.
Academic Press, 1972, pages 163-192.

[16] Lettvin, Jerome, Maturana, H., McCulloch, W.S., and Pitts, W.
What the Frog's Eye Tells the Frog's Brain.
In *Proceedings of the IRE*, pages 1940-1951. 1959.

[17] McDermott, J.
R1: A Rule-Based Configurer of Computer Systems.
Artificial Intelligence 19, 1:39-88, 1982.

[18] Minsky, Marvin, and Papert, Seymour.
Perceptrons.
The MIT Press, 1969.

[19] Sembugamoorthy, V. and Chandrasekaran, B.
Functional Representation of Devices and Compilation of Diagnostic Problem Solving Systems.
August, 1984
To appear in *Cognitive Science.*

[20] Narasimhan, R.
Labeling Schemata and Syntactic Description of Pictures.
Information and Control 7:151-179, June, 1964.

[21] Pople, H. W.
Heuristic Methods for Imposing Structure on Ill-Structured Problem.
Artificial Intelligence in Medicine.
Westview Press, 1982.

[22] Samuel, Arthur L.
Some Studies in Machine Learning Using the Game of Checkers II. Recent Progress.
IBM Journal of Research and Development 11(6), 1967.

[23] Shortliffe, E.H.
Computer-based Medical Consultations: MYCIN.
Elsevier/North-Holland Inc., 1976.

[24] Sokal, R.R. and Sneath, P.H.A.
Principles of Numerical Taxonomy.
Freeman, W.M., San Francisco, 1963.

[25] Sticklen, Jon, Chandrasekaran, B. and Josephson, John R.
Control Issues in Classificatory Diagnosis.
In *Ninth International Joint Conference on Artificial Intelligence.* 1985.

[26] Szolovits, P. and Pauker, S. G.
Categorical and Probabilistic Reasoning in Medical Diagnosis.
Artificial Intelligence :115-144, 1978.

AUTHOR INDEX

SUBJECT INDEX

The page numbers in this index refer to the first page of the papers which mention the subject.

LIST OF PARTICIPANTS

Abmayr, W.
Institut für Strahlen- und Umwelt-Forschung
Ingoldstädter Landstrasse 1
8042 München-Neuherberg
WEST GERMANY

Aus, H.M.
Biomedical Image Processing Lab.
Institute of Virology
Versbacher Strasse 7
8700 Würzburg
WEST GERMANY

Backer, E.
Delft University of Technology
Dept. of Electrical Engineering
Mekelweg 4
2628 CD Delft
THE NETHERLANDS

Bertrand, P.
INRIA
Domaine de Voluceau
B.P. 105
78150 Roquencourt
FRANCE

Biemond, J.
Delft University of Technology
Dept. of Electrical Engineering
Mekelweg 4
2628 CD Delft
THE NETHERLANDS

Bietti, A.
Università di Roma
Istituto di Fisica
Piazza Aldo Moro 2
00185 Roma
ITALY

Böhmer, L.G.
Holland Signaal
Afdeling SEAT
P.O. Box 42
7550 GD Hengelo
THE NETHERLANDS

Bolle, R.M.
IBM T.J. Watson Research Center
P.O. Box 218
Yorktown Heights, NY 10598
U. S. A.

Bosman, D.
Twente University of Technology
Dept. of Electrical Engineering
P.O. Box 217
Enschede
THE NETHERLANDS

Burger, G.
Institut für Strahlen- und Umwelt-Forschung
Ingoldstädter Landstrasse 1
8042 München-Neuherberg
WEST GERMANY

Choudry, A.
NIKHEF - H
H.E. Physics/Informatics
Kruislaan 409
1098 SJ Amsterdam
THE NETHERLANDS

Damen, J.T.W.
Dr. Neherlaboratorium PTT
St. Paulusstraat 4
2264 XZ Leidschendam
THE NETHERLANDS

Den Harink, H.C.
Dept. of Medical Informatics
Acad. Hospital Free University
P.O. Box 7057
1007 MB Amsterdam
THE NETHERLANDS

Devijver, P.A.
Philips Research Laboratory
Avenue van Becelaere 2
P.O. Box 8
1170 Brussels
BELGIUM

De Vogel, R.
Prins Hendrikstraat 11
5611 HH Eindhoven
THE NETHERLANDS

Dubuisson, B.
U.T.C.
Dept. Genie Informatique
B.P. 233
60206 Compiegne Cedex
FRANCE

Duin, R.P.W.
Delft University of Technology
Dept. of Applied Physics
Lorentzweg 1
2628 CJ Delft
THE NETHERLANDS

Förstner, W.
Institut für Photogrammetrie
Universität Stuttgart
Keplerstrasse 11
7 Stuttgart 1
WEST GERMANY

Franke, J.
AEG TELEFUNKEN
Research Institute Ulm
Sedanstrasse 10
7900 Ulm
WEST GERMANY

Gelsema, E.S.
Dept. of Medical Informatics
Acad. Hospital Free University
P.O. Box 7057
1007 MB Amsterdam
THE NETHERLANDS

Gerbrands, J.J.
Delft University of Technology
Dept. of Electrical Engineering
Mekelweg 4
2628 CD Delft
THE NETHERLANDS

Good, W.
Federal Institute for Snow- and
Avalanche Research
7260 Weissfluhjoch-Davos
SWITZERLAND

Groen, F.C.A.
Delft University of Technology
Dept. of Applied Physics
Lorentzweg 1
2628 CJ Delft
THE NETHERLANDS

Han-Fei, B.
Dept. of Medical Informatics
Acad. Hospital Free University
P.O Box 7057
1007 MB Amsterdam
THE NETHERLANDS

Haralick, R.M.
Viginia Polytechnic Institute
Dept. of Electrical Engineering
Blacksburg, VA 24061
U. S. A.

Harauz, G.
Fritz Haber Institut der Max Planck
Gesellschaft
Faradayweg 4-6
1000 Berlin 33
WEST GERMANY

Heinrich, K.
Ernst Leitz Wetzlar GmbH
P.O. Box 2020
633 Wetzlar
WEST GERMANY

Jansen, B.H.
University of Houston
Dept. of Electrical Engineering
Houston, TX 77004
U. S. A.

Janssen, J.G.A.
Stuksbeemden 47
5961 LJ Horst
THE NETHERLANDS

Jordan, M.M.
National Inst. for Medical Research
The Ridgeway, Mill Hill
London NW7 1AA
UNITED KINGDOM

Kalberg, R.J.N.
Erasmus University
Dr. Molenwaterplein 40
Room EE 2314
Rotterdam
THE NETHERLANDS

Kanal, L.N.
University of Maryland
Dept. of Computer Science
College Park, MD 20742
U. S. A.

Katzko, M.W.
St. Radboud Ziekenhuis
Afd. Quantitatieve Microscopie
Pathologie-Anatomie
Geert Grooteplein Zuid 24
6525 GA Nijmegen
THE NETHERLANDS

Kaufman, L.
Vrije Universiteit Brussel
Farmaceutisch Instituut
Laarbeeklaan 103
1090 Brussels
BELGIUM

Kors, J.A.
Dept. of Medical Informatics
Acad. Hospital Free University
P.O. Box 7057
1007 MB Amsterdam
THE NETHERLANDS

Kuijpers, E.A.
Rodekruislaan 1037
1111 ZZ Diemen
THE NETHERLANDS

Ledley, R.S.
Natl. Biomedical Research Found.
Georgetown University Medical Center
Div. of Medical Comp. and Biophysics
3900, Reservoir Road N.W.
Washington, DC 20007
U. S. A.

Lie, S.P.
Dr. Neherlaboratorium PTT
St. Paulusstraat 4
2264 XZ Leidschendam
THE NETHERLANDS

Luymes, B.J.
De Nederlandsche Bank N.V.
P.O. Box 98
1000 AB Amsterdam
THE NETHERLANDS

Manicke, R.L.
U.S. Naval Academy
Annapolis, MD 21402
U. S. A.

Mann, R.C.
Oak Ridge National Laboratory
Biology Division
P.O. Box Y
Oak Ridge, TE 37831
U. S. A.

Mansouri, M.
McGill University
School of Computer Science
805, Sherbrooke Street West
Montreal PQ H3A 2K6
CANADA

Mayall, B.H.
Lawrence Livermoore Laboratory
Biomedical Sciences L 452
P.O. Box 5507
Livermoore, CA 94550
U. S. A.

Minamikawa, R.
TIMS
18-22 Honkomagome 3-chome
Bunkyo-Ku
Tokyo 113
JAPAN

Morgera, S.D.
Concordia University
Dept. of Electrical Engineering
1455 de Maisonneuve Blvd. W.
Montreal PQ H3G 1M8
CANADA

Mulder, N.
ITC
P.O. Box 6
7500 AA Enschede
THE NETHERLANDS

Nagy, G.
University of Nebraska
Dept. of Computer Science
Ferguson Hall, 110 Ferguson
Lincoln, NE 68588
U. S. A.

Newell, J.
Queen Elizabeth Hospital
Dept. of Medical Physics
Birmingham 15
UNITED KINGDOM

Oscarsson, E.
Royal Institute of Technology
Instrumentation Laboratory
10044 Stockholm
SWEDEN

Pahlplatz, M.
St. Radboud Ziekenhuis
Afd. Quantitatieve Microscopie
Pathologie-Anatomie
Geert Grooteplein Zuid 24
6525 GA Nijmegen
THE NETHERLANDS

Parikh, J.A.
Southern Connecticut State University
877 Mount Carmel Avenue
North Haven, CT 06473
U. S. A.

Pedrycz, W.
Silesian Technical University
Dept. of Automatic Control
Pstrowskiego 16
44-100 Gliwice
POLAND

Perkins, W.J.
National Inst. for Medical Research
The Ridgeway, Mill Hill
London NW7 1AA
UNITED KINDOM

Persoon, E.H.J.
Philips Research Laboratories
Eindhoven
THE NETHERLANDS

Peters, M.
Dept. of Medical Informatics
Acad. Hospital Free University
P.O. Box 7057
1007 MB Amsterdam
THE NETHERLANDS

Peterson, P.L.
Institute of Electronic Systems
Aalborg University Center
Strandvejen 19
9000 Aalborg
DENMARK

Queiros, C.E.
Dept. of Medical Informatics
Acad. Hospital Free University
P.O. Box 7057
1007 MB Amsterdam
THE NETHERLANDS

Reiber, J.H.C.
Erasmus University
Thorax Center Image Processing Lab.
P.O. Box 1738
3000 DR Rotterdam
THE NETHERLANDS

Richetin, M.
University of Clermont II
Dept. of Electronics
B.P. 45
63170 Aubiere
FRANCE

Sagerer, G.
University of Erlangen-Nürnberg
Dept. of Informatics
Martensstrasse 3
8520 Erlangen
WEST GERMANY

Seixas, M.
University of Porto
Radioisotope Laboratory
St. Joao Hospital
Porto
PORTUGAL

Shapiro, L.G.
Machine Vision International
325 E. Eisenhower Pkwy
Ann Arbor, MI 48104
U. S. A.

Sjöström, M.
University of Umeå
Department of Chemistry
Research Group for Chemometrics
90187 Umeå
SWEDEN

Smeulders, A.W.M.
Dept. of Medical Informatics
Acad. Hospital Free University
P.O. Box 7057
1007 MB Amsterdam
THE NETHERLANDS

Stark, H.
Rensselaer Polytechnic Institute
Dept. of Electrical and Systems Eng.
Troy, NY 12181
U. S. A.

Stockman, G.C.
Michigan State University
Dept. of Computer Science
East Lansing, MI 48824
U. S. A.

Suetens, P.
University of Leuven
C.M.E./E.S.A.T.
Image Processing Section
De Croylaan 52
3030 Heverlee
BELGIUM

Tajima, J.
NEC Corporation
Peripheral Equipment Research Lab.
C & C Systems Research
1-1 Miyazaki 4-chome
Miyamae-Ku, Kawasaki
Kanagawa 213
JAPAN

Takagi, M.
University of Tokyo
Institute of Industrial Sciences
7-22-1 Rappongi, Minato-Ku
Tokyo 106
JAPAN

Talmon, J.L.
Dept. of Medical Informatics
Acad. Hospital Free University
P.O. Box 7057
1007 MB Amsterdam
THE NETHERLANDS

Tan, H.S.
Dr. Neherlaboratorium PTT
St. Paulusstraat 4
2264 XZ Leidschendam
THE NETHERLANDS

Timmers, T.
Free University
Dept. of Medical Physics
Van der Boechorststraat 7
1081 BT Amsterdam
THE NETHERLANDS

Toussaint, G.T.
McGill University
School of Computer Science
805, Sherbrooke Street West
Montreal PQ H3A 2K6
CANADA

Tropf, H.
Fraunhofer Institut für Informations
und Datenverarbeitung
Sebastian Kneipp Strasse 12-14
7500 Karsruhe 1
WEST GERMANY

Valeton, M.
TNO Instituut voor Zintuigfysiologie
Kampweg 5
Soesterberg
THE NETHERLANDS

Van Bemmel, J.H.
Dept. of Medical Informatics
Acad. Hospital Free University
P.O. Box 7057
1007 MB Amsterdam
THE NETHERLANDS

Van der Heijden, F.
Twente University of Technology
Dept. of Electrical Engineering
P.O. Box 217
Enschede
THE NETHERLANDS

Van der Lei, J.
Dept. of Medical Informatics
Acad. Hospital Free University
P.O. Box 7057
1007 MB Amsterdam
THE NETHERLANDS

Van Heel, M.
Fritz Haber Institut der Max Planck
Gesellschaft
Faradayweg 4-6
1000 Berlin
WEST GERMANY

Van Leeuwen, P.J.
Erasmus University
Dr. Molenwaterplein 40
Room EE 2314
Rotterdam
THE NETHERLANDS

Van Munster, R.J.
Technisch Physische Dienst TNO-TH
Afdeling Instrumentatie
P.O. Box 155
2600 AD Delft
THE NETHERLANDS

Van Ommeren, J.
Erasmus University
Dr. Molenwaterplein 40
Room EE 2314
Rotterdam
THE NETHERLANDS

Van Otterloo, P.J.
Philips Research Laboratories
P.O. Box 80000
5600 MD Eindhoven
THE NETHERLANDS

Verbeek, P.W.
Delft University of Technology
Dept. of Applied Physics
Lorentzweg 1
2628 CJ Delft
THE NETHERLANDS

Vollmerhaus, D.
KONTRON Bildanalyse GmbH
Breslauer Strasse 2
8057 Eching
WEST GERMANY

Young, I.T.
Delft University of Technology
Dept. of Applied Physics
Lorentzweg 1
2628 CJ Delft
THE NETHERLANDS